# Small and Medium-Sized Enterprises in International Economic Law

# INTERNATIONAL ECONOMIC LAW SERIES

International Economic Law series, established by the late Professor John H Jackson, addresses a range of issues in international economic law, which includes international trade law, international investment law, and the global financial order. The series aims to encourage interest in the broad contours of international economic law, heightening awareness of its significance across the globe as well as its continuous interactions with other areas. The series editors encourage quality submissions from a wide range of perspectives, including doctrinal, theoretical, empirical, and interdisciplinary viewpoints. Novel and cutting edge research is particularly welcome, as are contributions from both emerging and established scholars from around the world.

*Series Editors*



RECENT TITLES IN THE SERIES

**Domestic Law in International Arbitration**
Jarrod Hepburn

**Treaty Shopping in International Law**
Jorun Baumgartner

**Good Faith and International Economic Law**
Edited by Andrew D. Mitchel, M Sornarajah, and Tania Voon

**Development at the WTO**
Sonia E. Rolland

**The BRIC States and Outward Foreign Direct Investment**
David Collins

# Small and Medium-Sized Enterprises in International Economic Law

Edited by
THILO RENSMANN

OXFORD
UNIVERSITY PRESS

OXFORD
UNIVERSITY PRESS

Great Clarendon Street, Oxford, OX2 6DP,
United Kingdom

Oxford University Press is a department of the University of Oxford.
It furthers the University's objective of excellence in research, scholarship,
and education by publishing worldwide. Oxford is a registered trade mark of
Oxford University Press in the UK and in certain other countries



First Edition published in 2017



Published in the United States of America by Oxford University Press
198 Madison Avenue, New York, NY 10016, United States of America

British Library Cataloguing in Publication Data
Data available

Library of Congress Control Number: 2017934723

ISBN 978–0–19–879565–0

# *Series Editors' Preface*

This impressive collection edited by Thilo Rensmann represents a long overdue comprehensive analysis of the implications of international economic law for small and medium-sized enterprises (SMEs). The focus is on international trade law and international investment law, at the bilateral, plurilateral, and multilateral levels. Despite the significant proportion and role of SMEs in the international economy, they are largely ignored in the scholarly literature of international economic law. Against that background, this volume offers crucial insights into how international economic law does and should accommodate SMEs, given their special characteristics, as well as how SMEs can best manage the current international economic law framework as it affects their day-to-day business.

The volume investigates SMEs in the light of traditional institutions in international economic law such as the World Trade Organization, the United Nations Conference on Trade and Development, the United Nations Commission on International Trade Law, and the International Centre for Settlement of Investment Disputes (part of the World Bank), and core areas of international economic law, including trade in services, anti-dumping law, government procurement, and dispute settlement. At the same time, it covers related areas of domestic and international law, including human rights law, competition law, and sustainable development. As Rensmann explains in the Introduction, SMEs may play a role in 'generating more inclusive growth in a social sense', including through 'higher levels of employment, as well as improving wages and working conditions', especially in developing countries.

Most of the authors in this volume are based in Europe, reflecting the hubs of international trade law and international investment law in Brussels, Geneva, and London. However, the analysis, discussion, and expertise extend beyond Europe to countries such as the United States, South Africa, Brazil, Barbados, Malaysia, and Australia, including through coverage of negotiations such as the Transatlantic Trade and Investment Partnership (TTIP) between the European Union and the United States, and the Trans-Pacific Partnership (TPP) signed by twelve Pacific Rim countries, including jurisdictions as diverse as Canada, Chile, Japan, and Viet Nam.

Even as uncertainty abounds regarding the entry into force of mega-regional agreements such as the TTIP and TPP, the significance of SMEs to the global economy is only likely to increase. Dedicated discussions of the impact of international economic law on SMEs in the context of such negotiations provide a valuable basis for re-evaluating the role of international economic law in the life of an SME. Developments such as the WTO's Trade Facilitation Agreement can also improve the integration of SMEs into global value chains, enhancing their potential contributions to the international economy. By bringing together scholars, practitioners, and policymakers, this volume offers wide-ranging insights on all of these issues, beginning from the absence of even a universal definition of SME, and balancing theory with pragmatism, the ideal with the feasible, to provide thoughtful recommendations for the future.

Andrew D Mitchell and Tania Voon
November 2016

# *Acknowledgements*

This project was conceived and planned within the framework of the research group Global TranSAXion at the University of Dresden, which was funded by a research grant from the European Union and the Free State of Saxony. I would like to thank all members of the Global TranSAXion team who, under the leadership of Dr Heidrun Gross, made an invaluable contribution to formulating the research agenda and laying the foundations for this publication.

I am most grateful to all authors for sharing our belief in the timeliness and topicality of our project, for their effort, care, and attention in preparing their contributions, and their loyalty and patience throughout the entire genesis of this volume. Special thanks are due to Rudolf Adlung, Alexander Gebert, and Joachim Karl, who presented initial versions of their chapters as part of a lecture series at the University of Dresden, which was generously supported by Hogan Lovells.

During the editorial process I received valuable and indefatigable support from the entire Global TranSAXion team, as well as the staff at my former and current chairs in Dresden and Augsburg. I am very grateful to Johannes Baier, Paul Huber, Moritz Krause, Anne Lorenzat, Luise Seifert, Thomas Strehler, Natasha Thomson, and Marie-Theres Überlein, as well as my secretary Eleonora Hummel, for their assistance in preparing the manuscript for submission.

My assistants Johanna Stahlmann and Ulrike Will played a key role in bringing the project to a successful conclusion by managing and supervising the decisive stages of the editorial process. I am deeply indebted to them for their unfailing enthusiasm and dedication.

I would also like to express my thanks to our publisher Oxford University Press. We are particularly grateful to Merel Alstein, John Louth, and the series editors Tania Voon and Andrew Mitchell, as well as Emma Endean-Mills and Natasha Flemming for their encouragement, advice, and support.

Thilo Rensmann
January 2017

# *Table of Contents*

# *Detailed Table of Contents*

## PART III INTERNATIONAL INVESTMENT LAW

# *List of Figures*

# *List of Tables*

# *List of Boxes*

# *Table of Cases*

## PERMANENT COURT OF INTERNATIONAL JUSTICE



## INTERNATIONAL ARBITRAL TRIBUNALS

## GATT PANELS



## WTO DISPUTE SETTLEMENT BODY

## EUROPEAN COURT OF JUSTICE AND GENERAL COURT

## NATIONAL COURTS

### Germany



### South Africa



### United States of America

# *Table of Legislation*

# Table of Treaties

# *List of Abbreviations*

| | |
|---|---|
| AAAA | Addis Ababa Action Agenda |
| AB | Appellate Body |
| ACCA | Association of Chartered Certified Accountants |
| ACP | African, Caribbean, and Pacific |
| AD | anti-dumping |
| ADA | Anti-Dumping Agreement |
| ADR | alternative means of dispute resolution |
| AEI | Alliance for Entrepreneurship and Innovation |
| AFAS | Association of Southeast Asian Nations Framework Agreement on Services |
| AfDB | African Development Bank |
| AMPYME | Panamanian Ministry of Micro, Small and Medium-sized Enterprises (Spanish: Autoridad de la Micro Pequeña y Mediana Empresa) |
| APEC | Asia-Pacific Economic Cooperation |
| Art/Arts | Article/Articles |
| ASEAN | Association of Southeast Asian Nations |
| ASIL | American Society of International Law |
| AWU | annual work units |
| B2B | business to business |
| BB$ | Barbadian dollar |
| BC | before Christ |
| BEE | Black Economic Empowerment |
| BIPA | Bilateral Investment Promotion and Protection Agreement |
| BIT | bilateral investment treaty |
| BJP | Bharatiya Janata Party |
| BMW | Bayerische Motoren Werke |
| BRICS | Brazil, Russia, India, China and South Africa |
| CAF | Development Bank of Latin America |
| CCBF | Committee on Competitiveness and Business Facilitation |
| CECA | Comprehensive Economic Cooperation Agreement |
| CEPA | Comprehensive Economic Partnership Agreement |
| CEPR | Centre of Economic Policy Research |
| CETA | Comprehensive Economic and Trade Agreement |
| cf | compare (Latin: confer) |
| COM | European Commission |
| COMESA | Common Market for Eastern and Southern Africa |
| COSATU | Congress of South African Trade Unions |
| CPV | Common Procurement Vocabulary |
| CSIS | Centre for Strategic and International Studies |
| CSR | corporate social responsibility |
| DC | District of Columbia |
| DG | Directorate General |

| | |
|---|---|
| DG COMP | Directorate General Competition |
| Doc | Document |
| DOI | digital objective identifier |
| DOS | US Department of State |
| DRC | Democratic Republic of Congo |
| DR-CAFTA/CAFTA-DR | Dominican Republic–Central America Free Trade Agreement |
| DSU | Dispute Settlement Understanding |
| E15 | E15 Initiative launched jointly by the International Centre for Trade and Sustainable Development and the World Economic Forum |
| EBRD | European Bank for Reconstruction and Development |
| EC | European Commission |
| EC-CARIFORUM | EU–Caribbean Economic Partnership Agreement |
| ECD | Eastern Caribbean Dollars |
| ECJ | European Court of Justice |
| ECOWAS | Economic Community of West African States |
| ed/eds | editor/editors |
| edn | edition |
| eg | example given |
| EIU | Economist Intelligence Unit |
| EJIL | European Journal of International Law |
| EMDG | Export Market Development Grants |
| ENT | economic needs test |
| EPA | Economic Partnership Agreement |
| EPF | Entrepreneurship Policy Framework |
| ERSD | Economic Research and Statistics Division |
| ESA | Eastern and Southern Africa |
| etc | and so on (Latin: etcetera) |
| EU | European Union |
| FAO | Food and Agriculture Organization of the United Nations |
| FAPA | Fund for African Private Sector Assistance |
| FDI | foreign direct investment |
| FIW | Research Centre International Economics (German: Forschungsschwerpunkt Internationale Wirtschaft) |
| FTA | free trade agreement |
| G20 | Group of 20 |
| GA | General Assembly of the United Nations |
| GATS | General Agreement on Trade in Services |
| GATT | General Agreement on Tariffs and Trade |
| GBER | General Block Exception Regulation |
| GDP | gross domestic product |
| GEM | Global Entrepreneurship Monitor |
| GEN | Global Entrepreneurship Network |
| GER | Global Enterprise Registration |
| GI | geographical indication |
| GmbH | company with limited liability (German: Gesellschaft mit beschränkter Haftung) |
| GPA | Agreement on Government Procurement |
| GVC | global value chain |

| | |
|---|---|
| GWU | George Washington University |
| HFCS | High-Fructose Corn Syrup |
| HLWG | EU–US High Level Working Group on Jobs and Growth |
| IA | Investment Arbitration |
| ibid | in the same place (Latin: ibidem) |
| ICC | International Chamber of Commerce |
| ICCA | International Council for Commercial Arbitration |
| ICSID | International Centre for Settlement of Investment Disputes |
| ID | identification |
| ie | that is |
| IFAD | International Fund for Agricultural Development |
| IFC | International Finance Corporation |
| IfM | Institute for Small Business Research (German: Institut für Mittelstandsforschung) |
| IIA | International Investment Agreements |
| IIED | International Institute for Environment and Development |
| IISD | International Institute for Sustainable Development |
| ILM | International Legal Materials |
| ILSA | International Law Students Association |
| IP | intellectual property |
| IPCEI | Important Projects of Common European Interest |
| IPR | intellectual property rights |
| ISDS | Investor-state dispute settlement |
| ISSER | Institute of Statistical, Social and Economic Research |
| IT | information technology |
| ITC | International Trade Centre |
| KfW | Kreditanstalt für Wiederaufbau |
| KLRI | Korean Legislation Research Institute |
| KMU | SME (German: Kleine und mittelständische Unternehmen) |
| KPI | key performance indicator |
| LDC | least developed country |
| LLC | limited liability company |
| LLP | limited liability partnership |
| Ltd | Limited |
| MA | market access |
| MDIC | Brazilian Minister of Development, Industry and Foreign Trade |
| MERCOSUR | Mercado Común del Sur |
| MFN | most favoured nation |
| MIC | Dominican Ministry of Industry, Commerce and SMEs |
| MIGA | Multilateral Investment Guarantee Agency |
| MITI | Ministry of International Trade & Industry (Malaysia) |
| MNC | multinational company |
| MNE | multinational enterprise |
| MPA | Master of Public Administration |
| MRT | Ministers responsible for Trade |
| MSMEs | micro, small, and medium-sized enterprises |
| MTN | Multilateral Trade Negotiations |
| n/nn | footnote/footnotes |

| | |
|---|---|
| NAFTA | North American Free Trade Agreement |
| NDP | National Development Policy |
| NEM | Non-Equity Mode |
| NEP | New Economic Policy |
| NGO | non-governmental organization |
| NME | non-market economy |
| No | number |
| NT | national treatment |
| NTB | non-tariff barriers |
| NUMAS | National Union of Metal Workers in South Africa |
| NY | New York |
| OECD | Organisation for Economic Co-operation and Development |
| OHCHR | Office of the High Commissioner for Human Rights |
| para/paras | paragraph/paragraphs |
| PCA | Permanent Court of Arbitration |
| PCG | Professional Contractors Group |
| PCIJ | Permanent Court of International Justice |
| PDR | Peoples Democratic Republic |
| PLLC | professional limited liability company |
| PM | Prime Minister |
| pmbl | preamble |
| PPP | public–private partnership |
| PSDS | Private Sector Development Strategy |
| PSEG | Public Service Enterprise Group |
| Pty | Party |
| Q&As | questions and answers |
| R | South African rand |
| R&D | research and development |
| R&D&I | research, development, and innovation |
| RAG | Regional Aid Guidelines |
| Res | Resolution |
| RIA | Regulatory impact assessments |
| Rs | Rupee |
| RSCAS | Robert Schuman Centre for Advanced Studies |
| S&D | special and differential treatment |
| SpA | società per azioni (Italian joint-stock company) |
| SACCAWU | South African Commercial Catering and Allied Workers Union |
| SADC | South African Development Community |
| SAM | State Aid Modernization |
| SBA | Small Business Administration |
| SBDC | Small Business Development Center |
| SCM | Subsidies and Countervailing Measures |
| SDG | Sustainable Development Goal |
| SDR | Special Drawing Right |
| SEAF | Small Enterprise Assistance Fund |
| SEBRAE | Brazilian Micro-Enterprise and Small Business Support Service |
| SGEI | Services of General Economic Interest |

| | |
|---|---|
| sic | this (Latin: sic erat scriptum) |
| SME | small and medium-sized enterprise |
| SMEWG | Small and Medium Enterprises Working Group |
| SMMEF | South African Medium and Micro Enterprise Forum |
| SOE | state-owned enterprises |
| SPS | (Agreement on the Application of) Sanitary and Phytosanitary (Measures) |
| TBT | technical barriers to trade |
| TDI | trade defence instrument |
| TEC | trade by enterprise characteristics |
| TFA | Trade Facilitation Agreement |
| TFEU | Treaty on the Functioning of the European Union |
| TNC | transnational corporation |
| TPF | third-party funding |
| TPP | Trans-Pacific Partnership |
| TPR | Trade Policy Reviews |
| tralac | trade law centre |
| TRIMS | trade related investment measures |
| TRQ | tariff rate quota |
| TTIP | Transatlantic Trade and Investment Partnership |
| UAE | United Arab Emirates |
| UK | United Kingdom |
| UKTS | United Kingdom Treaty Series |
| UN | United Nations |
| UNCITRAL | UN Commission on International Trade Law |
| UNCLOS | UN Convention on the Law of the Sea |
| UNCTAD | UN Conference on Trade and Development |
| UNESCAP | UN Economic and Social Commission for Asia and the Pacific |
| UNFCCC | UN Framework Convention on Climate Change |
| UNIDO | UN Industrial Development Organization |
| UNIDROIT | International Institute for the Unification of Private Law |
| UNTS | UN Treaty Series |
| US/USA | United States of America |
| USAID | US Agency for International Development |
| USC | US Congress |
| USITC | US International Trade Commission |
| UST | US Treaties |
| v | versus |
| VAT | value added tax |
| vol | volume |
| wiwi | The Vienna Institute for International Economic Studies (German: Wiener Institut für Internationale Wirtschaftsvergleiche) |
| WTO | World Trade Organization |
| ZAR | South African rand |

# *List of Contributors*

**Michael K Addo** is Professor at the School of Law, University of Exeter and member of the UN Working Group on Business and Human Rights.

**Rudolf Adlung** is an independent trade policy analyst. Formerly he worked at the WTO Secretariat (Trade in Services Division).

**Perry S Bechky** is Partner at Berliner Corcoran & Rowe LLP and a Visiting Scholar at Seattle University School of Law.

**Lucian Cernat** is Chief Trade Economist of the European Commission.

**Tilman Michael Dralle** is a Doctoral Candidate in International Economic Law at the University of Dresden.

**Fulvia Farinelli** is Senior Economic Officer in the Entrepreneurship Section, Division on Investment and Enterprise, UNCTAD.

**Rebecca Fawcett-Feuillette** is Legal Counsel, Legal Compliance, LEGO Group, London.

**Alexander Gebert** is a solicitor (Rechtsanwalt) in Munich.

**Arancha González** serves as Executive Director of the International Trade Centre (ITC).

**Joachim Karl** is Chief of the Policy Research Section, Division on Investment and Enterprise, UNCTAD.

**Martina Lodrant** is a Policy Officer in the European Commission.

**Katrien Miclotte** is an Associate at the Brussels office of DLA Piper and research assistant at the Institute for European Law of the Catholic University of Leuven.

**Fiorina Mugione** has served as Chief of the Entrepreneurship Section, Division on Investment and Enterprise, UNCTAD.

**Anna Caroline Müller** is Legal Affairs Officer in the Intellectual Property, Government Procurement, and Competition Policy Division of the WTO.

**Caroline Nicholas** is Senior Legal Officer at the UNCITRAL Secretariat (International Trade Law Division, UN Office of Legal Affairs).

**Karsten Pötschke** is Head of Division Personnel & Organisation at KEM Kommunalberatung Mitteldeutschland GmbH.

**Thilo Rensmann** holds the Chair of Public, International, and European at the University of Augsburg. Formerly he was Director of the School of International Studies at the University of Dresden, where he led the Research Centre for International Economic Law.

**Ilan Sherr** is a Senior Associate at DLA Piper in their EU and Competition practice in London and a member of the Steering Committee of the UK State Aid Law Association.

**Marta Soprana** is an independent trade policy advisor.

**Heng Wang** is Associate Professor at the Faculty of Law of the University of New South Wales, Australia and Adjunct Professor at Southwest University of Political Science and Law, China.

# Introduction

*Thilo Rensmann*

## A. The Internationalization of SMEs as a Challenge to International Economic Law

It has become an almost proverbial truism that small and medium-sized enterprises (SMEs) form the backbone of practically every domestic economy.[1] Yet at the global level, international trade and investment remain primarily the domain of larger multinational enterprises (MNEs) or transnational corporations (TNCs).[2]

It is therefore hardly surprising that international economic law, which mainly regulates the transboundary movement of goods, services, and capital, has until recently largely ignored SMEs. To the extent to which corporate size and structure are addressed at all, the focus of international economic law has traditionally been almost exclusively on MNEs.[3] And even in the more frequent instances in which international economic law seems to be prima facie indifferent to corporate size, it becomes evident on closer inspection that its rules and principles were invariably created with the 'ideal type' of MNEs and their particular interests in mind.

While it remains true that MNEs still dominate transboundary trade and investment, SMEs are increasingly reaching out beyond their traditional domestic habitat.[4] This development has to some extent been masked by the fact that many SMEs enter the global economy indirectly via regional or global value chains (GVCs), for example as domestic suppliers to exporting MNEs.[5] Today, however, a significant number of SMEs are also directly engaged in transboundary trade and investment,[6]

[1] See WTO, *World Trade Report 2016: Levelling the Trading Field for SMEs* (WTO Publications 2016) 14–20.

[2] As to international trade, see ibid 31–55; as to investment, see Joachim Karl, Chapter 9 of this volume, 241.

[3] See, for example, Matthias Herdegen, *Principles of International Economic Law* (2nd edn, Oxford University Press 2016) 41–44.

[4] See references in n 2.

[5] Ana Paula Cusolito, Raed Safadi, and Daria Taglioni, *Inclusive Global Value Chains: Policy Options for Small and Medium Enterprises and Low-Income Countries* (World Bank and OECD 2016) 23–38; International Trade Centre, *Connect, Compete and Change for Inclusive Growth: SME Competitiveness Outlook 2015* (2015) 24–33 <http://www.intracen.org/uploadedFiles/intracenorg/2015SMEComp.pdf> accessed 20 January 2017; WTO (n 1) 39–46.

[6] WTO (n 1) 31–38.

and in the wake of the digital revolution the phenomenon of 'born global' SMEs can increasingly be observed.[7]

The growing internationalization of SMEs leads to an erosion of the established dichotomies underpinning the traditional focus of international economic law on MNEs. Small corporate size ceases to support a presumption against the transnational reach of economic activity. An increasing number of SMEs are 'going global' and thus joining forces with MNEs as 'actors of international economic law'.[8] GVCs, in particular, call for a holistic approach to the interplay between the domestic and the global economies. By linking up to GVCs, 'domestic' SMEs become inextricably involved in international economic transactions and are, therefore, in a substantive sense, gradually transformed into 'trans-' or 'multinational' enterprises ('micro-multinationals'[9]).

## B. Sustainable Development and the Internationalization of SMEs

International economic law, with its traditional focus on MNEs and their interests, is only slowly waking up to this new reality. At the same time, global economic policy is currently pressing for an even greater internationalization of SMEs. Since the global financial and economic crisis in 2008, there is a growing realization that opening up international trade and investment to SMEs provides one of the keys to creating more sustained and sustainable economic growth.[10]

Access to global markets—be it directly or indirectly via GVCs—is considered as providing SMEs with the opportunity to increase their productivity and thus develop their true potential as engines of economic growth and employment.[11] The internationalization of SMEs is also perceived as a means of generating more inclusive growth in a social sense. Since SMEs account for the largest share of global employment, the rise in productivity commonly attributed to the internationalization of SMEs holds out the prospect of creating higher levels of employment, as well as improving wages and working conditions, in particular in developing countries.[12] Given that SMEs are typically locally owned and controlled, their promotion also contributes to the strengthening of local entrepreneurship and employment, which in turn reinforces local community and civil society structures.[13] At the same time, SMEs have a transformative potential in offering women, young people, and disadvantaged groups significant opportunities for employment and entrepreneurship.[14]

[7] ITC (n 5) 6; WTO (n 1) 46–51, 59.

[8] Herdegen (n 3) 27.

[9] As to this notion, see OECD, *Interconnected Economies: Benefiting from Global Value Chains* (2013) 14.

[10] ITC (n 5) 12–23.

[11] ibid; WTO (n 1) 21–24.

[12] WTO (n 1) 17–18.

[13] Michael K Addo, Chapter 12 of this volume, 331.

[14] ITC (n 5) 14–19; WTO (n 1) 18, 24; Fiorina Mugione and Fulvia Farinelli, Chapter 13 of this volume, 340, 350–52.

The new focus of global economic policy on SMEs and their internationalization has found its most visible expression in the United Nations '2030 Agenda for Sustainable Development'.[15] In pronouncing the Sustainable Development Goals (SDGs) of '[p]romoting sustained, inclusive and sustainable economic growth'[16] and 'industrialization',[17] the importance of 'policies that … encourage the … growth of micro, small- and medium-sized enterprises',[18] as well as 'their integration into value chains', are explicitly highlighted.[19] The link between sustainable economic growth and the internationalization of SMEs is spelled out in more detail in the Addis Ababa Action Agenda (AAAA),[20] which forms an integral part of the 2030 Agenda for Sustainable Development.[21] The AAAA recognizes international trade as 'an engine for inclusive economic growth and poverty reduction'[22] and emphasizes the important role played by SMEs in realizing a country's full trading potential. Equally, the linkages between international trade and investment are underscored by pointing to the importance of foreign direct investment as a catalyst for integrating domestic SMEs into GVCs.[23]

The G20 Strategy for Global Trade Growth,[24] recently endorsed at the 2016 Hangzhou Summit,[25] echoes the United Nations' policy objective of promoting more inclusive economic growth by integrating SMEs into GVCs and opening up other avenues to allow SMEs more access to global economic markets. Particular emphasis is placed on the potential of e-commerce to boost the participation of SMEs in global trade.[26]

## C. Recalibrating International Economic Law in Response to the Internationalization of SMEs

### I. Regulatory developments at the multilateral and regional levels

At the multilateral and regional levels, international trade and investment law is currently being reassessed and gradually recalibrated in response to the emergence

[15] UN General Assembly, 'Transforming our World: The 2030 Agenda for Sustainable Development', UNGA Resolution 70/1 (25 September 2015) UN Doc A/RES/70/1.

[16] ibid 19, Goal 8. [17] ibid 20, Goal 9. [18] ibid 19, Target 8.3.

[19] ibid Target 9.3, 20.

[20] Addis Ababa Action Agenda of the Third International Conference on Financing for Development, UNGA Resolution 69/313 (27 July 2015) UN Doc A/RES/69/313, Annex.

[21] See UNGA Resolution 70/1 (25 September 2015) UN Doc A/RES/70/1, para 62.

[22] Addis Ababa Action Agenda (n 20) para 79. [23] ibid paras 16, 45, 81, 87–88.

[24] G20 Trade Ministers Meeting Statement, 'G20 Strategy for Global Trade Growth' (9–10 July 2016) <http://g20.org/English/Documents/Current/201607/t20160715_3057_2.html> accessed 20 January 2017.

[25] G20 Leaders' Communique Hangzhou Summit (4–5 September 2016) para 29 <http://g20.org/English/Documents/Current/201609/t20160906_3395.html> accessed 20 January 2017. On previous policy initiatives of the G20 relating to SMEs, see ITC (n 5) 98–100.

[26] G20 Trade Ministers (n 24) para 6.

of SMEs as 'transnational' economic actors and political calls for making the global economic system 'more inclusive' by levelling the playing field for SMEs.

Within the WTO, SMEs are not an entirely new issue. Certain WTO agreements, work programmes[27] and policy initiatives,[28] in fact, explicitly address SMEs.[29] Examples of treaty provisions directly touching upon capacity constraints of SMEs can be found with regard to procedures regulated by the Anti-Dumping Agreement (ADA)[30] and the Subsidies and Countervailing Measures (SCM) Agreement,[31] as well as in the more recently adopted Trade Facilitation Agreement (TFA).[32] The SCM Agreement also contains an express exemption for subsidies in support of SMEs.[33] Other agreements, such as the General Agreement on Trade in Services (GATS) and the (plurilateral) Agreement on Government Procurement (GPA), while not explicitly referring to SMEs, carve out regulatory space allowing contracting states to extend preferential and promotional treatment to SMEs.[34]

As further elaborated in the present volume, the general liberalization, transparency, and facilitation disciplines of WTO law are of particular benefit to SMEs wishing to trade across borders since trade barriers, border procedures, and difficulties encountered in obtaining relevant information are—due to their specific capacity constraints—more burdensome for SMEs than for their larger counterparts.[35] In this sense, the TFA (upon reaching the required quorum of ratifications), although applying across the board to transactions by both SMEs and larger enterprises, will mark an especially important step towards further opening up international trade and GVCs to SMEs.[36]

Despite thus having engaged with the topic of SMEs, the WTO has not yet, however, systematically embraced the challenges posed by the increasingly important role of SMEs in the international trading system.[37] The regulatory approach to

[27] For the work programmes on electronic commerce and on small economies, see WTO (n 1) 139–41, 144; for the work programme on SMEs by the Committee on Government Procurement, see Caroline Nicholas and Anna Caroline Müller, Chapter 5 of this volume, 128, 132–33.

[28] As to initiatives relating to trade finance for SMEs, see WTO (n 1) 141–42.

[29] For a comprehensive overview, see WTO (n 1) 130–46.

[30] Art 6.13 of the Agreement on Implementation of Article VI of the General Agreement on Tariffs and Trade 1994 (adopted 15 April 1994, entered into force 1 January 1995), 1868 UNTS 201; for a detailed analysis of this provision, see Karsten Pötschke, Chapter 3 of this volume.

[31] Art 12.11 of the Agreement on Subsidies and Countervailing Measures (adopted 15 April 1994, entered into force 1 January 1995) 1867 UNTS 14.

[32] Arts 3.9(d) and 7.2(b) of the Agreement on Trade Facilitation (adopted 15 July 2014) WT/L/931 <https://www.wto.org/english/thewto_e/minist_e/mc9_e/desci36_e.htm> accessed 20 January 2017. See also Arancha González, Chapter 2 of this volume, 49–50.

[33] Art 2.1 SCM Agreement in conjunction with n 2 of the Agreement.

[34] As to the GATS, see Rudolf Adlung and Marta Soprana, Chapter 1 of this volume; as to the GPA, see Nicholas and Müller (n 27).

[35] See Adlung and Soprana (n 34) 17; González (n 32) 39; Martina Lodrant and Lucian Cernat, Chapter 6 of this volume, 166–68.

[36] González (n 32).

[37] Adlung and Soprana (n 34) 18; European Commission, *Trade for All: Towards a More Responsible Trade and Investment Policy* (European Union 2015) 27–28.

date has been piecemeal and has focused selectively on exemptions for the protection of domestic SMEs rather than their integration into the international trading system.[38]

While even within the WTO it is openly acknowledged that 'in the broader trade debate over the years … the interests of … SMEs have sometimes been overlooked',[39] there does not seem to be a sufficient consensus among WTO members to readjust the focus of the current Doha Development Round to the changing configuration of global trade. Whereas certain members, such as the United States and the European Union, believe that the post-Nairobi trade agenda needs to be extended to GVCs and the internationalization of SMEs,[40] developing countries are concerned that such 'new issues' will amount rather to a Trojan Horse further undermining the 'domestic regulatory space' necessary to define their own economic and industrial development policies.[41]

Given the lack of resolve to tackle the issue resolutely and systematically within the WTO, regulatory initiatives aimed at improving access by SMEs to international trade and investment are currently primarily being developed in bilateral, regional, and transregional free trade agreements.[42] In particular, the recently signed Trans-Pacific Partnership (TPP) and the ongoing Transatlantic Trade and Investment Partnership (TTIP) negotiations point the way towards a comprehensive and integrated approach to 'support[ing] the growth and development of … [SMEs] by enhancing their ability to participate in and benefit from the opportunities created by [these] agreements' (TPP, Preamble). Regardless of whether the TPP and the TTIP eventually enter into force, they will certainly represent an important benchmark and reference point for future regulatory strategies aimed at further opening up international trade and investment to SMEs. Fragmented regional, and even mega- or transregional regulation will, however, be unable to provide an adequate response to the stated aim of creating a truly inclusive global economic system. In particular, the integration of SMEs into GVCs calls for a global regulatory approach. If the world community is serious about its '2030 Agenda for Sustainable Development', SMEs and inclusive GVCs will therefore inevitably remain firmly inscribed on the agenda of multilateral trade negotiations.

[38] European Commission (n 37) 27–28.

[39] Roberto Azevêdo, 'Foreword' in WTO (n 1) 3, 4.

[40] Statement by the United States at the Informal Meeting of WTO Heads of Delegation (9 May 2016) <https://ustr.gov/about-us/policy-offices/press-office/speechestranscripts/2016/may/US-Statement-Informal-Meeting-WTO-Heads-of-Delegationl> accessed 20 January 2017; European Commission (n 37) 27–28.

[41] South Centre, 'Key Substantive and Process Issues Arising from the WTO's Nairobi Ministerial Conference (MC10)', Analytical Note SC/AN/TDP/2016/1 (May 2016) 8–10 <https://www.southcentre.int/category/issues/trade-and-investment/wto/> accessed 20 January 2017.

[42] For an overview, see WTO (n 1) 116–26.

## II. SMEs as a new cross-cutting issue on the research agenda of international economic law

Against this backdrop, the present volume undertakes a first attempt at systematically analysing the interaction between SMEs and international economic law. SMEs have not only been long neglected in international trade policy and rule-making, they have also to date received relatively scant attention in scholarship on international economic law. Given that the internationalization of SMEs is gradually evolving as one of the key cross-cutting issues of current international trade and investment policy, academic research must follow suit and devote more attention to the role of SMEs in international economic law.

In order to chart this largely unexplored territory, the present volume brings together a team of distinguished authors who offer a broad range of perspectives on the mutual relationship between SMEs and international economic law. Academic scholars are joined by legal practitioners and experts working in international organizations and think-tanks in order to analyse the salient problems from different vantage points. This multifaceted approach is intended to ensure that in this first stocktaking exercise the views and perspectives of all relevant actors and stakeholders are duly considered.

The analysis covers a wide spectrum of international trade and investment law focusing on issues of particular relevance for SMEs, such as trade in services,[43] trade facilitation,[44] anti-dumping and competition law,[45] government procurement,[46] and access to investor-state dispute settlement.[47] Salient regional and transregional developments are also taken into account, including the treatment of support measures for SMEs under EU State aid law[48] and the implications of the recently signed TPP and the TTIP negotiations for SMEs.[49] Finally, the link between development, human rights, and the promotion of SMEs and entrepreneurship are further explored in the larger context of the 2030 Agenda for Sustainable Development.[50]

Despite the different substantive angles and functional perspectives from which the interaction of SMEs and international economic law is approached in this volume, a number of common threads emerge which at the same time delineate some key issues for the future research agenda on this topic.

### 1. *Identification and definition of SMEs*

Despite being an established economic and legal category, SMEs remain an extremely elusive concept. There is no commonly accepted definition applying across the

[43] Adlung and Soprana (n 34). [44] González (n 32).
[45] Pötschke (n 30); Tilman Michael Dralle, Chapter 4 of this volume.
[46] Nicholas and Müller (n 27).
[47] Alexander Gebert, Chapter 11 of this volume; Perry S Bechky, Chapter 10 of this volume; see also Karl (n 2) 261–63.
[48] Ilan Sherr, Katrien Miclotte, and Rebecca Fawcett-Feuillette, Chapter 8 of this volume.
[49] Lodrant and Cernat (n 35); Heng Wang, Chapter 7 of this volume.
[50] Addo (n 13); Mugione and Farinelli (n 14).

board at national, regional, and international levels.[51] While there is agreement in principle as to the relevant criteria for measuring the 'size' of an enterprise, namely in terms of the number of employees, the turnover volume, and the balance sheet total, there are considerable variations in relation to both the minimum and the maximum size.[52] In particular, at the lower end there is a definitional divide with regard to the question as to whether a separate category of micro-enterprises needs to be established and whether such a new category would be encompassed by the general notion of SMEs. This has led to the introduction of the competing notion of 'micro, small, and medium (-sized) enterprises (MSMEs)'.[53] Throughout this volume, however, the notion of SMEs is, unless otherwise indicated, used as the overarching category and is understood to encompass micro-enterprises.

These definitional issues should, however, not be overrated. From a legal perspective, it is a common phenomenon that definitions vary depending on the normative context in which they are used. In most of the areas of international economic law discussed in this volume, the number of staff and the economic performance are indeed the decisive factors for the identification of the particular capacity constraints of SMEs which need to be addressed and accommodated by international trade and investment law. However, it also needs to be borne in mind that the notion of SMEs covers an extremely wide and diverse spectrum of businesses, ranging from small-scale farmers or artisanal miners in developing countries to producers of high-tech goods and providers of sophisticated services in developed countries. In certain regulatory contexts, such as the interface between business and human rights, it will therefore be necessary to supplement the traditional quantitative criteria by qualitative criteria in order to target the relevant SMEs more precisely.[54]

## 2. *International economic law as cause and remedy for the underrepresentation of SMEs in international trade and investment*

The main focus of the present volume is to establish the extent to which international economic law can contribute to making the global economic system more inclusive by levelling the playing field for SMEs. This requires an initial enquiry into the specific obstacles which prevent SMEs from engaging in transboundary trade and investment. As is further elaborated in this volume, 'internal' capacity constraints relating to human, financial, and informational resources need to be distinguished from 'external' barriers which include the regulatory environment at the domestic and international levels.[55]

[51] See Rudolf Adlung and Marta Soprana, Annex to this volume; WTO (n 1) 15–16.
[52] ibid.
[53] See Adlung and Soprana (n 51) 357; Addo (n 13) 317; APEC Small and Medium Enterprises Ministerial Meeting, 'Mainstreaming Micro, Small and Medium Enterprises in the Global Economy' (25 September 2015) para 3 <http://www.apec.org/Meeting-Papers/Sectoral-Ministerial-Meetings/Small-and-Medium-Enterprise/2015_sme.aspx> accessed 20 January 2017.
[54] Addo (n 13) 317–18.
[55] See, in particular, Lodrant and Cernat (n 35) 166–68.

International economic law may thus be both cause and remedy for the difficulties with which SMEs are confronted when trading or investing across borders. Consequently, a systematic 'SME impact assessment' of international trade and investment law must first be undertaken with a view to identifying the critical issues which then need to be addressed in order to accommodate SMEs in the global economic system. Such 'SME mainstreaming'[56] of international economic law will in some cases require legal reform, but, as demonstrated in this volume, in other instances there is room for an SME-friendly 'capacity-based' interpretation[57] and application of the *lex lata*.

International economic law and international economic institutions also play an important role in helping to ease internal barriers to the internationalization of SMEs. Given that such capacity constraints are mostly addressed at the domestic level, the primary task of international economic law is to allow states sufficient regulatory space for such promotional measures.[58] However, particularly in the development context, international organizations and institutions are also substantively involved in capacity-building, such as the provision of trade finance and technical assistance in entrepreneurship.[59] In this field, the main challenge for international economic governance lies in the coordination of the different national and international actors involved.[60]

### 3. *The difficulty of SMEs being on both sides of the liberalization equation*

Current regulatory and policy initiatives aimed at leveraging international economic law to promote the internationalization of SMEs should not obscure the fact that the liberalization of international trade and investment is perceived by many as an existential threat to domestic SMEs rather than a gateway to new economic opportunities. The resistance of developing countries in the post-Nairobi process to opening up the Doha Development Agenda to SMEs as a new policy area,[61] together with the protests organized by a considerable number of Austrian, German, and Dutch SMEs against TTIP and the Comprehensive Economic and Trade Agreement between the European Union and Canada (CETA),[62] are clear expressions of the currency of such concerns. Many domestic SMEs fear that the further removal of barriers to transboundary trade and investment will make them

[56] As to this notion, see APEC Small and Medium Enterprises Ministerial Meeting (n 53).

[57] The concept of a 'capacity-based' interpretation is further developed in Pötschke (n 30) 75–77; for a different approach to a purposive interpretation in favour of SMEs, see Bechky (n 47) 287–88.

[58] See Lodrant and Cernat (n 35) 169–70; as to EU law, see Sherr and others (n 48) 218–19.

[59] As to entrepreneurship, see Mugione and Farinelli (n 14) 341–54; as to trade finance, see WTO (n 1) 129, 141–42.

[60] WTO (n 1) 130, 147, 151.

[61] See n 41.

[62] KMU gegen TTIP (Germany), KMU gegen TTIP (Austria), and Ondernemers van Nu (Netherlands), 'Small and Medium-Sized Enterprise from across Europe Call on European Governments to Reject the CETA Agreement', Joint Press Release (23 September 2016) <http://kmu-gegen-ttip.de/content/download/1643/41033/file/2016%2009%2023%20SME%20against%20CETA_TTIP%20press%20release.pdf> accessed 20 January 2017.

vulnerable to being crowded out by foreign MNEs.[63] Developing countries in particular appear to be concerned that international measures aimed at fostering the internationalization of SMEs will unduly restrict the regulatory space necessary to define their own economic strategy in promoting and protecting domestic SMEs.

Consequently, any regulatory initiative to internationalize SMEs will need to take into account both sides of the liberalization equation carefully. While opening up the global economy to SMEs will require an ambitious push for a further reduction of barriers to transboundary trade and investment, sufficient regulatory room for manoeuvre will need to be carved out for domestic SME policies.[64]

New economic phenomena such as GVCs or e-commerce render this balancing exercise increasingly complex, since they blur the dividing lines between global, regional, and national economies and therefore transcend simple dichotomies of transnational liberalization and domestic regulation. The real challenge accordingly lies in devising a holistic approach which carefully delineates and coordinates regulation at the domestic, regional, and international levels and which balances the necessary liberalization, harmonization, facilitation, and promotion measures needed to unlock the full economic potential of SMEs with a view to creating more inclusive and sustainable economic growth.

## D. Conclusion

The liberalization agenda of international economic law is currently facing increasing popular resistance. Hundreds of thousands have taken to the streets in Europe to voice their discontent with ambitious mega-regional trade agreements. In the largest case to date before the Federal German Constitutional Court, 125,000 applicants filed a constitutional complaint against CETA.[65] The further liberalization of international trade and investment is perceived as favouring multinationals and unduly restricting domestic regulatory space.

International economic law has, however, long ceased to be an exclusive matter for 'big business', but increasingly matters to SMEs, even if they are not directly involved in international trade and investment. Being able to demonstrate therefore that the liberalization agenda of international economic law goes to the heart of almost every domestic economy has the potential to instil a new sense of legitimacy into the global economic system.[66] The present volume is a modest contribution to making this case.

[63] See also Karl (n 2) 255.

[64] See Adlung and Soprana (n 34) 14, 18–28; Dralle (n 45) 93, 99–107, 113–14; Nicholas and Müller (n 27) 127–28.

[65] See German Federal Constitutional Court, Judgment of 13 October 2016 (application for a preliminary injunction), 2 BvR 1368/16 <http://www.bverfg.de/e/rs20161013_2bvr136816.html> accessed 20 January 2017.

[66] See also Arancha González, 'Foreword' in ITC (n 5) XII.

## References


APEC Small and Medium Enterprises Ministerial Meeting, 'Mainstreaming Micro, Small and Medium Enterprises in the Global Economy' (25 September 2015) para 3 <http://www.apec.org/Meeting-Papers/Sectoral-Ministerial-Meetings/Small-and-Medium-Enterprise/2015_sme.aspx> accessed 20 January 2017

Azevêdo, R, 'Foreword' in WTO, *World Trade Report 2016: Levelling the Trading Field for SMEs* (WTO Publications 2016) 3–4

Cusolito, AP, Safadi, R, and Taglioni, D, *Inclusive Global Value Chains: Policy Options for Small and Medium Enterprises and Low-Income Countries* (World Bank and OECD 2016)

European Commission, *Trade for All: Towards a More Responsible Trade and Investment Policy* (European Union 2015)

G20 Leaders' Communique Hangzhou Summit (4–5 September 2016) <http://g20.org/English/Documents/Current/201609/t20160906_3395.html> accessed 20 January 2017

G20 Trade Ministers Meeting Statement, 'G20 Strategy for Global Trade Growth' (9–10 July 2016) <http://g20.org/English/Documents/Current/201607/t20160715_3057_2.html> accessed 20 January 2017

González, A, 'Foreword' in International Trade Centre, *Connect, Compete and Change for Inclusive Growth: SME Competitiveness Outlook 2015* (ITC 2015) XII–XIII

Herdegen, M, *Principles of International Economic Law* (2nd edn, Oxford University Press 2016)

International Trade Centre, *Connect, Compete and Change for Inclusive Growth: SME Competitiveness Outlook 2015* (ITC 2015)

KMU gegen TTIP (Germany), KMU gegen TTIP (Austria), and Ondernemers van Nu (Netherlands), 'Small and Medium-sized Enterprise from across Europe Call on European Governments to Reject the CETA Agreement', Joint Press Release (23 September 2016) <http://kmu-gegen-ttip.de/content/download/1643/41033/file/2016%2009%2023%20SME%20against%20CETA_TTIP%20press%20release.pdf> accessed 20 January 2017

OECD, *Interconnected Economies: Benefiting from Global Value Chains* (OECD 2013)

South Centre, 'Key Substantive and Process Issues Arising from the WTO's Nairobi Ministerial Conference (MC10)', Analytical Note SC/AN/TDP/2016/1 (May 2016) 8–10, <https://www.southcentre.int/wp-content/uploads/2016/06/AN_MC10_2016_1_NMD-and-Process-Issues_EN.pdf> accessed 20 January 2017

United Nations, Addis Ababa Action Agenda of the Third International Conference on Financing for Development, UNGA Resolution 69/313 (27 July 2015) UN Doc A/RES/69/313, Annex

United Nations, 'Transforming our World: The 2030 Agenda for Sustainable Development', UNGA Resolution 70/1 (25 September 2015) UN Doc A/RES/70/1

US Mission to the WTO, Statement by the United States at the Informal Meeting of WTO Heads of Delegation (9 May 2016) <https://ustr.gov/about-us/policy-offices/press-office/speechestranscripts/2016/may/US-Statement-Informal-Meeting-WTO-Heads-of-Delegation> accessed 20 January 2017

WTO, *World Trade Report 2016: Levelling the Trading Field for SMEs* (WTO Publications 2016)

# PART I

# INTERNATIONAL TRADE LAW

# 1

# Trade Policy for SMEs from a GATS Perspective

*Rudolf Adlung and Marta Soprana**

*'Small opportunities are often the beginning of great enterprises.'*

Demosthenes (384–322 BC)

## A. Introduction

Studies and policy statements concerning small and medium-sized enterprises (SMEs) tend to concentrate on manufacturing firms if they distinguish at all between firms operating in different sectors. Relatively little attention is given to SMEs engaged in services production and trade, and even less to the status of SME-related policies under the General Agreement on Trade in Services (GATS). This may appear surprising for two reasons. First, services SMEs are a major contributor to overall production and employment in virtually all economies. Second, unlike the General Agreement on Tariffs and Trade (GATT), governing trade in goods since the late 1940s, GATS disciplines apply not only to products (services), but to suppliers as well. And the definitional scope of the Agreement has been extended to include consumer movements and factor flows (investment and labour). Thus, measures affecting different categories of service suppliers and their investments, according to whatever criterion, including size, are covered in principle. However, the GATS is still relatively young—it entered into force in 1995 as part of the World Trade Organization (WTO) Agreement—which might explain why it has not yet been explored as profoundly as its precursor in merchandise trade.

What types of government intervention could affect SMEs in services? The European Commission has listed, by way of example, the following types of legal (policy-induced) barriers that services suppliers encounter when engaging in cross-border activities: nationality requirements, minimum capital requirements,

* A shorter version of this chapter was initially published by Rudolf Adlung and Marta Soprana, 'SMEs in Services Trade: A GATS Perspective' (2013) 48 Intereconomics: Review of European Economic Policy 41.

quantitative restrictions, and restrictions on multi-disciplinary activities.[1] In turn, a study conducted by the US International Trade Commission identifies, inter alia, a lack of mutual recognition of licensing, credentials, and standards, as well as government subsidies and intellectual property and piracy issues as barriers affecting SMEs exporting services.[2] However, while disadvantaging exporters, such barriers might actually benefit their domestic counterparts. Nationality and residency requirements or restrictions on small-scale transactions, for example barring construction projects below a specified size, may well serve, unintentionally or otherwise, to protect market outlets for small, domestically established firms in the sectors concerned.[3] A broader picture would also cover support initiatives specifically targeted at SMEs, such as the free provision of market intelligence, trade promotion programmes, and the like.

In contrast with some other studies, the following discussion pays no particular attention to genuinely size-related constraints, including productivity problems and business risks attributable to a small product and customer base, difficulties in mobilizing adequate funding, shortages of managerial skills, or higher logistics costs.[4] Nor will it address potential advantages, such as shorter decision-making channels, closer client relations, and other flexibility-enhancing factors. Rather, our main objective is to explore the scope for accommodating SME-related policy interests under the GATS and GATS-based Regional Trade Agreements (RTAs), and to trace such attempts as far as these are reflected in schedules of services commitments and relevant information sources.

The starting point relates to empirical observations concerning the involvement of services SMEs in international trade, followed by an overview of GATS disciplines of various types from an SME-related policy perspective. In turn, this leads to a discussion of potentially relevant limitations as reflected in current commitments under the GATS and RTAs. A summary assessment of the current situation, in and around the WTO, concludes this chapter.

[1] European Commission, 'Report from the Commission to the Council and the European Parliament on the State of the Internal Market for Services Presented Under the First Stage of the Internal Market Strategy for Services' (30 July 2002) COM/2002/0441 final; European Commission, 'Upgrading the Single Market: More Opportunities for People and Business' (28 October 2015) COM/2015/0550 final.

[2] The study was conducted in the context of the negotiations on a Transatlantic Trade and Investment Partnership (TTIP) and focused on access problems to the European Union. Sector-specific complaints in addition to those mentioned above concerned in particular audiovisual services (quotas, dubbing requirements, etc). Overall, however, the view was held that the impediments encountered were fewer in services than in manufacturing trade. See US International Trade Commission (USITC), 'Trade Barriers that U.S. Small and Medium-Sized Enterprises Perceive as Affecting Exports to the European Union' (Investigation No 332-541, USITC Publication 4455, March 2014) <http://www.usitc.gov/publications/332/pub4455.pdf> accessed 20 January 2017.

[3] By the same token, however, such impediments might have a disproportionate impact on other SMEs which rely strongly on imported inputs (including of services) and might find it more difficult to switch to domestic alternatives than larger enterprises.

[4] A discussion of such factors is contained, for example, in International Trade Centre, *Connect, Compete and Change for Inclusive Growth: SME Competitiveness Outlook 2015* (International Trade Centre 2015) <http://www.intracen.org/uploadedFiles/intracenorg/2015SMEComp.pdf> accessed 20 January 2017.

## B. SME Involvement in International Trade

The world economy is made up mostly of SMEs. They are estimated to account for some 95 per cent of all firms, over 50 per cent of GDP, and 60 to 70 per cent of employment (including the informal sector). Compared to their larger peers, however, the SMEs' economic performance is less impressive. They tend to lag in productivity, pay lower wages, and are less export-oriented.[5] And this is generally true across all sectors, manufacturing and services.

A report by the European Commission confirms that the level of international activity is directly linked to firm size and negatively correlated with the size of the home-country population.[6] The report distinguishes different forms of internationalization: direct exports, foreign direct investment to set up a commercial presence abroad, technological cooperation with enterprises abroad, acting as a subcontractor for a foreign main contractor, and having foreign subcontractors. Not all findings thus fit into what might be considered exports within the modal structure of the GATS as described below (Section C.I).

Services apparently provide a particularly fertile economic environment for SMEs.[7] In the European Union, for example, the following four services already represent close to 60 per cent of total SME employment in non-financial sectors: wholesale and retail trade and repair (26 per cent); construction (12 per cent);

[5] See also ibid; Organisation for Economic Co-operation and Development (OECD) and World Bank Group, 'Inclusive Global Value Chains' (Report prepared for submission to G20 Trade Ministers Meeting, 6 October 2015) <http://www.oecd.org/trade/OECD-WBG-g20-gvc-report-2015.pdf> accessed 20 January 2017, 25; and OECD and WTO, *Aid for Trade at a Glance 2015: Reducing Trade Costs for Inclusive, Sustainable Growth* (OECD Publishing 2015) 192 <https://www.wto.org/english/res_e/booksp_e/aid4trade15_e.pdf> accessed 20 January 2017.

[6] EIM Business & Policy Research, 'Internationalisation of European SMEs' (European Commission 2010) 5–6, 15. The positive relationship between firm size and participation in international trade has been documented for quite a number of other economies as well, including the United States, especially with regard to services trade. See, for example, Kevin Barefoot and Jennifer Koncz-Bruner, 'A Profile of U.S. Exporters and Importers of Services' (2012) 92 Survey of Current Business 66 <http://www.bea.gov/scb/pdf/2012/06%20June/0612_MNC.pdf> accessed 20 January 2017; Iza Lejárraga and Harald Oberhofer, 'Internationalization of Service SMEs: Evidence from France' (2013) <http://www19.iadb.org/intal/intalcdi/PE/2013/12982a07.pdf> accessed 20 January 2017.

[7] The following observations are based on European Commission, *Annual Report on European SMEs 2014/15* (European Union 2015) <http://ec.europa.eu/growth/smes/business-friendly-environment/performance-review/index_en.htm> accessed 20 January 2017; Heinz Hollenstein, 'Patterns and Determinants of International Activities: Are SMEs Different?' (2001) <http://e-collection.library.ethz.ch/eserv.php?pid=eth:24913&dsID=eth-24913-01.pdf> accessed 20 January 2017; Holger Breinlich and Chiara Criscuolo, 'International Trade in Services: A Portrait of Importers and Exporters' (2011) 84 Journal of International Economics 188; Adrian Gourlay, Jonathan Seaton, and Joy Suppakitjarak, 'The Determinants of Export Behaviour in UK Service Firms' (2005) 25 Service Industries Journal 879; Maria Jesus González Sanz and Antonio Rodríguez Caloca, 'Las Características de las Empresas Españolas Exportadoras de Servicios no Turísticos' (November 2010) 11 Banco de España, Boletín Económico 63 <http://www.bde.es/f/webbde/SES/Secciones/Publicaciones/InformesBoletinesRevistas/BoletinEconomico/10/Nov/Fich/art4.pdf> accessed 20 January 2017; USITC, 'Small and Medium-Sized Enterprises: Characteristics and Performance' (Investigation No 332-510, USITC Publication 4189, November 2010) <https://www.usitc.gov/publications/332/

business services (11 per cent); and accommodation and food (10 per cent). The share of manufacturing SMEs amounts to 20 per cent.

Several studies point out behavioural differences between services and manufacturing firms, and also among the former. As a general feature, services firms tend to engage less in international trade than their counterparts in manufacturing. However, there is significant variation both across sectors and types of firms. A study on UK service suppliers found, for example, that transport and communication were the most export-oriented sub-sectors, whereas distribution, hotels, and catering lagged far behind (1988–2001). This finding is partly corroborated by firm-level evidence from Italy that suggests that enterprises operating in the communication and professional services sectors are more likely to be both exporters and importers, whereas firms operating in construction and financial services tend to perform neither function.[8] It also appears, according to another study, that large enterprises have more export destinations and trade in more types of services than small firms.[9]

Services exporters reportedly differ from non-exporting services firms in various regards. Research by the US International Trade Commission corroborates that exporting SMEs are more productive in general and earn more revenue than SMEs serving only their home market.[10] Similarly, studies on Spanish service firms, Dutch architectural firms, and the German business service sector suggest that exporters are larger, pay higher wages, and are more productive than non-exporters.[11] Such observations are widely shared in principle, although the definitional demarcation of SMEs varies significantly between countries, reflecting differences in overall economic size as well as national peculiarities.[12]

pub4189.pdf> accessed 20 January 2017; Asier Minondo, 'Exporters of Services in Spain' (Orkestra Working Paper Series in Territorial Competitiveness, No 2011-R04(ENG), Orkestra 2011); Anders Henten and Torben Vad, 'Services Internationalization, Characteristics, Potentials and Barriers of Danish Services Firms' in Marcela Miozzo and Ian Miles (eds), *Internationalization, Technology, and Services* (Edward Elgar 2002) 187–89; Enno Masurel, 'Export Behaviour of Service Sector SMEs' (2001) 19(2) International Small Business Journal 80; Alexander Vogel, 'Exporter Performance in the German Business Services Sector' (2011) 31 *Service Industry Journal* 1015; European Commission, 'Report on Cross-Border E-Commerce in the EU' (Commission Staff Working Document) SEC(2009) 283 final; Sietske de Groot, 'Small Businesses and Online Trading' (UK Federation of Small Businesses 2011) <http://www.fsb.org.uk/LegacySitePath/policy/assets/fsb1144%20online%20trading%20report_web.pdf> accessed 20 January 2017; OECD, 'Realising the Potential of Electronic Commerce for SMEs in the Global Economy' (Conference on 'Enhancing the Competitiveness of SMEs in the Global Economy: Strategies and Policies', Workshop 3, OECD, Bologna 2000) <http://www.oecd.org/cfe/smes/2011580.pdf> accessed 20 January 2017; Stefano Federico and Enrico Tosti, 'Exporters and Importers of Services: Firm-Level Evidence on Italy' (Working Papers, No 877, Banca d'Italia 2012) <http://www.bancaditalia.it/pubblicazioni/temi-discussione/2012/2012-0877/en_tema_877.pdf> accessed 20 January 2017; Iza Lejárraga and others, 'Small and Medium-Sized Enterprises in Global Markets: A Differential Approach for Services?' (OECD Trade Policy Papers, No 165, OECD 2014) <http://dx.doi.org/10.1787/5jz17jtfkmzt-en> accessed 20 January 2017.

[8] Federico and Tosti (n 7) 11.

[9] Breinlich and Criscuolo (n 7) 201. It is not always clear, however, whether the definitions used in all these studies correspond to the modal structure of the GATS. For example, in the latter case, the nights spent by foreign tourists in holiday resorts would be counted as exports of hotel services under mode 2 (see following section).

[10] USITC (n 2).

[11] Minondo (n 7) 21; Masurel (n 7) 7; Vogel (n 7) 1019, 1024.

[12] For an overview of SME definitions, see the Annex of this volume.

Firm-level data indicate that a supplier's size influences its choice of export channel; smaller firms tend to trade higher shares through indirect channels (eg via subcontracting or distribution agreements), though apparently with variations across sectors. Indeed, a closer look at European firms suggests that SMEs in wholesale trade rely predominantly on direct exports, while those providing transport and communication services prefer subcontracting as their main form of internationalization. SMEs offering business services were found to focus primarily on foreign direct investment and technical cooperation. Concerning relevant modes of supply, as defined under the GATS (see Section C.I), little empirical evidence is available and, if so, the sectoral and geographical scope is limited. According to a study for Denmark, smaller service firms prefer delivering cross-border to establishing and supplying through a commercial presence abroad (mode 3 of the GATS). This finding seems to apply across all sub-sectors, except financial services, where SMEs rely almost equally strongly on establishing abroad.[13] Yet such studies need to be interpreted with caution, as they do not distinguish between EU-internal and -external trade, although the economic conditions may differ markedly.

The rapid evolution of e-commerce offers new opportunities for many service suppliers. There have been several initiatives in the WTO, including the moratorium on customs duties on electronic transmissions and the work programme on e-commerce, intended to facilitate e-trade.[14] Its potential contribution, from an SME perspective, to furthering international market integration has been emphasized in various contexts.[15] By the same token, empirical evidence, though relatively scarce, also points out certain adjustment problems and policy-induced impediments. According to the European Commission, EU stakeholders perceive the risk of fraud and non-payments, different fiscal regulations, as well as intellectual property rights issues as significant deterrents. Also, language barriers, logistics, and payment problems were mentioned as potential constraints.

Small services suppliers are generally considered to be disproportionately affected by trade barriers such as discriminatory and non-transparent regulatory frameworks, commercial presence requirements, restrictions on the movement of personnel, and burdensome licensing and authorization procedures. To our knowledge, however, there is no study that seeks to explore how WTO/GATS instruments could help to overcome such barriers. Potentially relevant government initiatives might consist of liberalizing commitments in relevant sectors and modes of supply, development of effective regulatory disciplines, or, more immediately applicable, stricter compliance with existing transparency provisions.

[13] Henten and Vad (n 7).

[14] For a recent overview, see WTO, 'Electronic Commerce' <http://www.wto.org/english/tratop_e/ecom_e/ecom_e.htm> accessed 20 January 2017.

[15] See, for example, WTO, Committee on Trade and Development, 'Electronic Commerce, Development and Small, Medium-Sized Enterprises, Background Note by the Secretariat' (14 February 2013) WT/COMTD/W/193.

## C. Policies Affecting SMEs—Their Status under the GATS

After some intensive discussions at the early stages of the Doha Round, in 2001, the SME–GATS nexus apparently ceased to attract attention in WTO fora. In September 2011, the Swiss delegation sought to reanimate the debate with a communication on the role of SMEs in the Swiss services economy, complemented in early 2012 by a submission discussing issues surrounding the electronic delivery of services from the perspective of exporting SMEs.[16] However, despite repeated requests from the WTO Secretariat, apart from some references to existing studies, no Member provided evidence of barriers actually encountered by service-trading SMEs or established links with potential remedies under the GATS.

### I. General framework

The disciplines governing merchandise trade under the GATT essentially focus on the treatment of products traded cross-border. In contrast, reflecting the GATS' extension to three additional modes of supply—consumption abroad (mode 2), commercial presence (mode 3), and presence of natural persons (mode 4)—the Agreement's key disciplines also extend to the treatment of service suppliers and their staff. Relevant measures may take the form of investment grants, equity ceilings, work permits, and the like, or they may seek to tilt consumer preferences, for example via tax benefits or subsidies, in favour of particular products and suppliers. For each sub-sector subjected to specific commitments, a Member must specify the levels of market access and national treatment accorded under the four modes. While market-access commitments relate to the absence of six types of restrictions listed in Article XVI:2 GATS, national-treatment commitments, governed by Article XVII GATS, essentially guarantee the absence of any measure that would modify the competitive conditions in favour of domestic services and suppliers vis-à-vis their foreign equivalents.

In addition, pursuant to Article XVIII GATS, Members may undertake additional commitments concerning 'positive' undertakings relating, for example, to the adoption of international standards or specified competition disciplines. Although the Article would allow Members to schedule such undertakings in pursuit of SME-related policies, it has played no particular role to date, in whatever sector, except telecommunications.[17]

[16] WTO, Council for Trade in Services, 'Communication from Switzerland: The Services Sector, Small and Medium-Sized Enterprises and Employment: The Case of Switzerland' (20 September 2011) S/C/W/340; WTO, Council for Trade in Services, 'Communication from Switzerland: The Services Sector, Small and Medium-Sized Enterprises and Their Activities Related to Electronic Commerce: The Case of Switzerland' (5 March 2012) S/C/W/345.

[17] The vast majority of the 100-odd Members that assumed additional commitments confined these to the competition safeguards, interconnection guarantees, and other obligations contained in a so-called reference paper on telecommunications. SME-related interests are covered insofar as they coincide with the underlying pro-competitive policy paradigm.

To protect the right to depart from unfettered market access and national treatment, governments must inscribe the measures they might want to use in their schedules of commitments. Article XVI:2 GATS provides that four of the six types of restrictions concerned—quotas on the number of suppliers, value of transactions, number of operations (eg establishments) or quantity of output, and number of natural persons involved—might also be maintained in the form of an economic needs test (ENT). In non-scheduled sectors, market access or national treatment may be completely denied. In any event, however, most favoured nation (MFN) treatment must be extended regardless of the existence of commitments, though departures are permissible in specified circumstances, including among participants in RTAs. Similarly, even in committed sectors, individual modes can be completely exempt from any market access or national treatment obligations. Like tariff bindings under the GATT, such scheduled limitations allow governments to maintain or introduce the specified measure(s), but do not necessarily reflect the prevailing trade regime which might be more open at any point in time.

To be able to accommodate SME-related policy interests, Members may exempt particular sector segments from commitments. However, such cases are significantly less frequent than limitations that, without directly targeting suppliers of different size, have size-specific effects. For example, restrictions on cross-border supply could disadvantage smaller firms against larger companies that may find it easier to mobilize the resources necessary to establish and operate a permanent presence abroad. Similar effects may arise from limitations requiring the parent company to have been established for a minimum number of years, thus effectively precluding younger firms, which are likely to be smaller, from moving into the market concerned. However, a variety of policy measures that may have size-specific effects are not subject to scheduling at all, including minimum capital and other minimum size requirements that are applied on a national treatment basis. Given the Agreement's basic definitional distinction between liberalization and (re-)regulation of services trade, such measures may continue to exist even in sectors and modes that do not carry any limitations.[18]

The status of certain measures such as local incorporation requirements may need to be assessed on a case-by-case basis in the light of potentially relevant provisions. For example, it could be argued that such requirements modify the conditions of competition between national and foreign suppliers in the sense of Article XVII GATS whenever (1) the services concerned could easily be provided cross-border and (2) relevant rules are more difficult and costly for foreigners to comply with than for domestic firms.

[18] The GATS' Preamble explicitly recognizes 'the right of Members to regulate, and to introduce new regulations, on the supply of services within their territories in order to meet national policy objectives …'. See also the discussion in Hamid Mamdouh, 'Services Liberalization, Negotiations and Regulation: Some Lessons from the GATS Experience' in Aik Hoe Lim and Bart De Meester (eds), *WTO Domestic Regulation and Services Trade: Putting Principles into Practice* (Cambridge University Press 2014) 325.

## II. SME-related policies as reflected in schedules of commitments

The vast majority of current schedules has been submitted towards the end of the Uruguay Round in 1993/94 and thus reflects the prevailing policy considerations at the time. They should have been renegotiated since. Article XIX:1 GATS explicitly commits Members to enter into successive rounds of services negotiations 'with a view to achieving a progressively higher level of liberalization'. The first such round commenced in January 2000, as mandated in the Agreement, to be subsequently integrated into the wider context of the Doha Round which was launched in December 2001. While seventy-one Members tabled services negotiating offers between March 2003 and August 2007, which were later upgraded in thirty-one cases,[19] there have been no new submissions since early 2008, reflecting the stalemate in the Round. In general, the content of these offers does not depart extensively from current schedules. Many participants might have wanted to keep negotiating coinage for the final stages of the Round or for the many RTAs that are currently on the drawing board.

### *1. Sector column*

Virtually all Members, with few exceptions, have scheduled their commitments in accordance with the Sectoral Classification List (MTN.GNS/W/120) developed by the then GATT Secretariat in 1991. The list distinguishes approximately 160 sub-sectors, allocated to twelve 'mega-sectors'. Since compliance is not mandatory, Members could exclude sector segments from commitments that are typically served by SMEs, thus retaining the right to operate whatever measures they feel are needed, including outright entry prohibitions. For example, some developing countries have confined their commitments on hotel services to the luxury category (three or four stars and above), thus protecting more modest, and usually smaller, facilities from foreign competition.[20]

### *2. Market access*

Most size-related limitations can be found in the market access column, either in the horizontal section, which applies across all scheduled sectors, or in individual areas.[21] Relevant entries exist almost exclusively in schedules submitted by developing countries. For example, under mode 3, several Caribbean countries maintained the right, on a horizontal basis, to reserve 'a number of small business opportunities

[19] The then twenty-five EU Member States were covered by one offer.

[20] A number of newly acceded WTO Members, such as Seychelles and Laos, explicitly excluded smaller facilities (eg guesthouses, rooming and boarding houses and cabins, as well as establishments with less than fifteen units) from commitments in the tourism sector.

[21] In certain cases, entries might have been misplaced: measures that seem to fall under market access show up in the national treatment column and vice versa. As far as possible, we have treated the measures concerned as if they had been inscribed in conformity with GATS provisions.

for nationals'. Accordingly, the governments remain free to adopt any of the restrictions falling under Article XVI GATS to protect domestically owned SMEs.[22] On the other hand, considering the vagueness of the terms used, the question arises as to what extent such commitments actually serve their basic purpose to guarantee, in a transparent and predictable manner, specified degrees of market access.

Several Members explicitly spelled out size-related criteria in the context of the ENTs they scheduled under market access for mode 3. Cases in point are references to floor space or number of rooms, geographical spread, distance between existing facilities, and the like. However, over one-third of existing ENTs does not contain any criteria, while many more provide only vague indications. Like a variety of other 'foggy' entries in schedules, these may also be used to pursue size-related policy intentions.[23] Non-specified ENTs have also been scheduled by OECD (Organisation for Economic Co-operation and Development) countries, including EU Member States such as Italy, Malta, and Sweden.

Concerning mode 4, the level of commitments, mostly inscribed in the horizontal section, is quite shallow in virtually all schedules. Only few entries allow for independent access, outside established company networks, which would be particularly relevant for employees of small foreign-based suppliers and independent professionals.[24] A somewhat higher incidence of such commitments can be found in the schedules of newly acceded WTO Members. For example, Samoa and Seychelles inscribed commitments on the entry of independent service suppliers and contractual service suppliers, respectively, across all sectors.

Relatively frequent non-bindings on cross-border trade may also disadvantage SMEs, which tend to prefer such transactions to commercial establishment abroad. While the emergence of e-based trade, overall, has created new market opportunities not least for small firms, existing commitments mostly reflect the technical and institutional conditions of some twenty years ago. However, without progress in the Doha Round, the prospects for change appear quite slim.

### 3. *National treatment*

Frequent national-treatment limitations that are explicitly size-specific relate to subsidies under mode 3, sometimes in combination with one or more other modes. For example, Mexico has reserved the right to extend research and development

[22] There are also limitations, though rare, that provide niches for foreign-based SMEs. Concerning architectural services, South Africa stipulates that the services of a local architect are required for building plans of 500 square metres and above. Accordingly, foreign architects involved in smaller projects, not normally served by large firms, could directly interact with their clients. In a similar vein, Bulgaria's schedule stipulates that architectural and engineering services can be supplied 'only in partnership with, or as subcontractors of, local service suppliers [if] the project is of national or regional significance'.

[23] See Rudolf Adlung and others, 'FOG in GATS Commitments: Why WTO Members Should Care' (2013) 12 World Trade Review 1.

[24] WTO, Council for Trade in Services, 'Presence of Natural Persons (Mode 4): Background Note by the Secretariat' (15 September 2009) S/C/W/301.

subsidies only to domestically owned 'small service enterprises'. As in many other cases, an element of uncertainty remains as no further definition of such enterprises is provided.

As indicated above, various Members have scheduled residency, local partnership, and local presence requirements as limitations, mostly under modes 1, 2, and 4. For example, Poland, Slovenia, and Sweden have done so for travel agencies, tour operators, and the like. While it might still be possible to access these markets on a cross-border basis, using local offices as a conduit, the cost of doing so is certainly higher than in the case of unfettered access.[25] And SMEs are relatively more affected than their larger peers.

Certain training requirements, typically scheduled under modes 3 and 4, may have similar effects: increasing the fixed cost of market entry and participation and, thus, tilting the playing field against small foreign providers. Such requirements are contained in the horizontal section of fifteen schedules, primarily developing countries and least developed countries (LDCs). Further examples can be found in a sectoral context, including in tourism services (Egypt and Niger).

A note of caution is warranted in this context, however. As mentioned above, the Member scheduling such limitations reserves the right to operate the measures concerned, nothing more. Like under a GATT-bound tariff regime, the actually applied policies may well be more liberal than the respective commitments. Various empirical studies confirm that there is indeed quite some 'water' in GATS schedules.[26]

## III. Scheduling patterns across countries and sectors

While there is significant variation between individual countries, LDCs have scheduled far fewer sectors on average, less than thirty, than other groups of Members. For example, developed countries have inscribed slightly more than 100 sectors on average, which compares relatively poorly, nevertheless, with a number of transition economies that have acceded to the WTO since the late 1990s. Their schedules comprise 130 and more sectors. On average across all Members, no more than one-third of the 'services universe', as defined by the generally used Sectoral Classification List, is currently covered.[27]

While it is for any Member to decide individually on the composition of its schedule, there are certain shared preferences. Overall, tourism is clearly in the lead,

[25] Of course, this is true only for services that could normally be supplied without local assistance and not for others that are typically provided via commercial presence (hospitals, hotels, restaurants, etc). Local presence requirements in the latter sectors have thus been ignored in the context of Table 1.1.

[26] See, for example, Batshur Gootiiz and Aaditya Mattoo, 'Services in Doha: What's on the Table?' (2009) 43 Journal of World Trade 1013; Sébastien Miroudot and Kätlin Pertel, 'Water in the GATS: Methodology and Results' (OECD Working Paper, 6 August 2015) TAD/TC/WP(2014)19/FINAL.

[27] Rudolf Adlung and Martin Roy, 'Turning Hills into Mountains? Current Commitments under the General Agreement on Trade in Services and Prospects for Change' (2005) 6 Journal of World Trade 1161, 1170.

represented in around 95 per cent of all schedules.[28] Financial services, a broad range of professional and other business services, as well as telecommunications follow, trailing by 15 to 25 per cent. In contrast, education and health have been committed by less than 40 per cent of Members.[29] Interestingly, many of the most frequently scheduled services, including banking, insurance, and telecommunication services, tend to be dominated by larger firms, while sectors such as health or distribution, which feature less prominently, are made up of smaller entities as well.[30] This could imply that size-related considerations form part of the sensitivities and constraints governing governments' sector selection for scheduling.

## IV. Policy discretion in liberalized sectors and modes

Pursuant to its Article 1, the GATS applies to 'measures by Members affecting trade in services' as covered by the four modes of supply. These provisions, and their later interpretation in dispute cases, ensure a wide scope of application.[31] They extend to a variety of regulatory and other interventions that would be compatible with full commitments on market access and national treatment, but are deemed nevertheless to 'affect' services trade. This does not imply, however, that all conceivable measures are effectively disciplined at present. It may well be argued, for example, that in areas such as subsidies or standards and regulations, the GATT imposes stricter constraints on Members than the GATS. Government procurement is a special case insofar as a specific carve-out under both Agreements ensures that governments essentially retain a free hand.

### *1. Market regulation and control*

Among the many types of government intervention that define the conditions of market entry and participation, the following tend to favour small-scale entities vis-à-vis larger competitors:

- strict zoning laws, including restrictions on maximum service areas, and opening hours;
- obligations on providers of infrastructural services, in particular financial services, to prioritize SMEs, for example via preferential lending;

[28] Ibid.

[29] Not even all EU Members have undertaken commitments in these services. Cyprus, Finland, Malta, Romania, and Sweden have not scheduled any education sector, while hospital services have been omitted by Bulgaria, the Czech Republic, Cyprus, Finland, Malta, Romania, the Slovak Republic, and Sweden.

[30] At first glance, the most frequently scheduled sector, tourism, seems to defy this pattern, given its relatively high share of small enterprises. However, hotels and restaurants, a sub-sector of tourism, account for a very significant number of SME-related limitations (Table 1.1).

[31] According to the Appellate Body, 'the use of the term "affecting" reflects the intent of the drafters to give a broad reach to the GATS'. It is deemed to be wider in scope than such terms as 'regulating' or 'governing'. See WTO, *European Communities—Regime for the Importation, Sale and Distribution of Bananas*, Appellate Body Report (9 September 1997) WT/DS27/AB/R, para 220.

- competition disciplines that seek to ensure continued market contestability and prevent abuse of dominant positions (merger controls, prohibition of collusive practices, etc); and
- prohibitions or restrictions on performing multi-product activities (eg prohibition of partnerships between lawyers and non-lawyers such as accountants and tax consultants).[32]

In contrast, SMEs tend to be adversely affected by:

- high licensing fees, administrative red tape, and similar regulatory requirements that tend to increase the fixed cost of market entry and participation;
- minimum capital and comparable minimum size requirements which, while possibly serving public policy purposes (reliability and stability of supplies), effectively exclude small or occasional suppliers from the markets concerned; and
- universal service obligations on suppliers of telecom, transport, health, and other public services with similar intentions and effects.

As noted above, such measures would not need to be scheduled as long as they cannot be associated with restrictions falling under Article XVI GATS or with competitive distortions within the meaning of Article XVII GATS. However, the borderline with restrictions that require scheduling could be blurred in some instances.

An additional aspect might need to be kept in mind: the still ongoing negotiations on domestic regulatory disciplines under Article VI:4 GATS. The mandate provides for the development of any necessary disciplines to ensure that licensing and qualification requirements and procedures, and technical standards 'do not constitute unnecessary barriers to trade in services'. Such disciplines shall aim to avoid, inter alia, that relevant requirements are 'more burdensome than necessary to ensure the quality of the service'. This mandate is certainly broad enough to address some of the barriers mentioned above (excessive licensing fees, capital requirements, etc). However, given the wider context of the Doha Round (non-) negotiations, no outcome is currently in sight.

## *2. Investment- and production-related support schemes*

WTO Trade Policy Reviews (TPRs) are a potential source of information on subsidies and similar incentives, including measures targeted at small businesses, which might be used by individual WTO Members.[33] While it is fair to assume that

[32] Small businesses might benefit from such measures if the resulting market segmentation deprives larger (potential) competitors of size-related economies.

[33] The TPR mechanism was established during the Uruguay Round. It provides for periodic reviews of individual Members' trade policies, in intervals of two, four, or six years, depending on the size of the respective economies. The WTO Secretariat is mandated to prepare country-specific reports which are then discussed in meetings of the Trade Policy Review Body. The most recent overview of

such initiatives generally favour national investors, it was explicitly clarified in some cases that they were applied on a non-discriminatory basis, thus complying with any existing national treatment obligations. Relevant measures include subsidized loans, tax incentives related to investment or training, and import duty exemptions for materials used.

### 3. *Export assistance*

Unlike the GATT, the GATS does not restrict Members' ability to promote exports. There is no services equivalent to the prohibition of export subsidies pursuant to Article 3(a) of the Agreement on Subsidies and Countervailing Measures. Nor would such subsidies be inconsistent with any of the provisions governing market access or national treatment. There is thus no possibility to infer from scheduled limitations on the existence of export-related policy schemes, such as direct financial support, export guarantees, or specific professional training programmes if these are implemented in a non-discriminatory manner.[34]

Australia's Export Market Development Grants programme is a typical example of an SME-related export promotion scheme; qualifying Australian residents may get up to 50 per cent of their expenses reimbursed.[35] Further information on SME-related export assistance, though not systemically collected, may also be contained in TPR reports. The question remains, of course, whether such support schemes are actually known to, and easy to apply for, potentially qualifying exporters.

### 4. *Recognition measures under Article VII GATS*

Recognition measures relating to foreign educational degrees, professional training, and the like may facilitate access of the beneficiary suppliers, not least independent professionals and employees of SMEs, and help level the playing field vis-à-vis the sector incumbents. However, little information on such measures is available, as Members apparently have ignored relevant notification requirements under the GATS.[36] Between January 2000 and December 2015, no more than twenty-six such

subsidy-related observations, covering all reports circulated between 2007 and 2009 and nine more recent reports (until 2012), is contained in WTO, Working Party on GATS Rules, 'Subsidies for Services Sectors: Information Contained in WTO Trade Policy Reviews, Background Note by the Secretariat, Revision' (13 January 2015) S/WPGR/W/25/Add. 7/Rev.1. However, given the broad coverage of these reports, and the need for the Secretariat to establish priorities, they do not constitute a consistently comprehensive source of information.

[34] Rudolf Adlung, 'Export Policies and the General Agreement on Trade in Services' (2015) 18 Journal of International Economic Law 487, 509.

[35] The programme was launched in 1974. A recent review is available via Australian Trade Commission, '2015 Review of the Export Market Development Grants (EMDG) Scheme' <http://www.austrade.gov.au/Australian/Export/Export-Grants/review> accessed 20 January 2017.

[36] Pursuant to Art VII:4 GATS, the Council for Trade in Services must be promptly informed of the opening of negotiations on recognition agreements, as well as the adoption of (autonomous) recognition measures.

notifications were made, ten of which came from one Member only, Switzerland. It is quite unlikely that this is a reasonably comprehensive picture.[37]

### 5. *Preferences in government procurement*

In a communication on its strategy for supporting SMEs in international markets, some years ago, the European Union pledged 'to make the interests of small businesses in access to international procurement markets a priority in the WTO negotiations'.[38] However, to what extent are other WTO Members prepared to respond? The only substantive obligations that exist in a WTO context have been exchanged among the forty-five parties of the recently renegotiated plurilateral Agreement on Government Procurement (GPA), which covers goods and services.[39] According to its Article II, the GPA applies only to purchases above or equal to the threshold values specified in the Parties' annexes to Appendix I, usually around SDR130,000 for central government entities. And this appears to be well beyond the reach of many SMEs.

The GATS itself does not impose any effective disciplines on a government's use of procurement for whatever policy purposes. Article XIII GATS provides that the MFN, market access, and national treatment obligations do not apply to the purchase of services by governmental agencies for governmental purposes. Thus, Members' commitments do not capture any discriminatory elements contained in, or arising from, national procurement laws. While Article XIII GATS also calls for multilateral negotiations on government procurement to be conducted, no tangible progress has been achieved to date. The European Union is one of the very few Members that have sought, through various submissions, to advance these negotiations.[40] Size-related aspects have played no role in this context, however.

Relevant information on SME-related procurement practices may be derived from a variety of sources, including information submitted under the GPA. Relevant exemptions from GPA coverage have been listed, among others, by the United States, Canada, and Korea. The United States provides a particularly wide

[37] The poor notification record under Art VII GATS might, in part, be due to a perception that recognition measures agreed in the context of RTAs do not need to be notified separately. However, there is nothing in Art V GATS (Economic Integration) to suggest that its scope would extend to, and obviate compliance with, Art VII GATS. See Rudolf Adlung and Antonia Carzaniga, 'MFN Exemptions under the General Agreement on Trade in Services: Grandfathers Striving for Immortality?' (2009) 12 Journal of International Economic Law 357, 361.

[38] European Commission, 'Small Business, Big World: A New Partnership to Help SMEs Seize Global Opportunities' (Press Release, 9 November 2011) <http://europa.eu/rapid/press-release_MEMO-11-765_en.htm?locale=en> accessed 20 January 2017.

[39] Situation in late 2015, counting the twenty-eight EU Member States as one.

[40] The European Union's most significant contribution in this context, the proposed creation of an Annex to the GATS, dates back to 2005: WTO, Working Party on GATS Rules, 'Communication from the European Communities: Government Procurement in Services' (15 June 2005) S/WPGR/W/52. It has gained little traction. In contrast, the European Union has included procurement-related disciplines in several of its RTAs: see European Commission, 'Public Procurement' (31 October 2014) <http://ec.europa.eu/trade/policy/accessing-markets/public-procurement> accessed 20 January 2017.

range of set-asides for small and minority businesses;[41] the respective share in covered federal procurement amounted to 12.5 per cent in 1992 and has now reached about 23 per cent.[42] The European Commission, in turn, has repeatedly confirmed its interest in achieving GPA-plus access commitments, including the elimination of buy-national provisions favouring domestic SMEs, in its RTA negotiations with other Members, most notably Canada and the United States.[43] In addition, the Commission intends to develop a new mechanism ('International Procurement Instrument') that the European Union could ultimately use to disadvantage bids from non-GPA and non-RTA participants if these discriminate against European companies in their procurement markets.[44]

## V. Policy discretion under ill-specified commitments?

In addition to unspecified ENTs (see Section C.II.2), quite a number of GATS schedules contain further entries which are difficult to interpret. Cases in point are 'foggy commitments' which cannot be clearly associated with provisions of the Agreement,[45] but might be intended, nevertheless, to provide space for the use of various types of trade restrictions, possibly including measures favouring domestic SMEs.

Overall, 'foggy entries' are contained in close to 100 schedules, accounting for about one-fifth of all commitments inscribed under market access for mode 3 (counting horizontal limitations as if they had been inscribed sector by sector). The most frequent categories are references to licensing and qualification requirements that are not further specified, and similarly vague references to the titles of laws and regulations rather than to the measures concerned. These two categories represent some 70 and 20 per cent, respectively, of all 'fog' in schedules.

In case of a legal challenge, it is well conceivable that the Panel ruling in *Mexico—Telecoms* proves relevant. According to the Panel, an entry referring to the

[41] For an overview, see US Small Business Administration, 'What is a Small Business Set Aside?' <http://www.sba.gov/content/small-business-set-asides> accessed 20 January 2017.

[42] An overview of the multi-pronged US regime is provided in ibid; see also Jean Heilman Grier, 'U.S. Procurement Preferences for Small and Minority Businesses', *Perspectives on Trade* (8 December 2014) <http://trade.djaghe.com/?p=1123> accessed 20 January 2017. Relevant information may also be found in the TPR reports prepared by the WTO Secretariat.

[43] See, for example, European Commission, 'EU–US Transatlantic Trade and Investment Partnership, Public Procurement, Initial EU Position Paper' (2013) <http://trade.ec.europa.eu/doclib/docs/2013/july/tradoc_151623.pdf> accessed 20 January 2017. The negotiations on a Comprehensive Economic and Trade Agreement (CETA) with Canada were completed in August 2014. According to the European Commission, European businesses will have better access opportunities to Canadian procurement markets than those provided under any other international agreement concluded by Canada to date. European Commission, 'Comprehensive Economic and Trade Agreement (CETA)' (3 August 2016) <http://ec.europa.eu/trade/policy/in-focus/ceta> accessed 20 January 2017.

[44] For more information, see European Commission, 'European Commission Takes Action to Open up International Procurement Markets' (Press Release, 29 January 2016) <http://trade.ec.europa.eu/doclib/press/index.cfm?id=1448> accessed 20 January 2017.

[45] Adlung and others (n 23).

requirement of a permit (concession) does not indicate the existence of a quantitative limitation and, thus, serves no legal purpose in the sense of Article XVI GATS. In other words, if challenged, such entries would not provide cover for measures restricting market access with a view to protecting outlets for whatever type of domestic suppliers.[46]

## VI. Transparency disciplines

Pursuant to Article III:3 GATS, any changes to laws, regulations, or guidelines that 'significantly affect' trade in committed sectors need to be notified to the Council for Trade in Services. This is regardless of whether such changes fall under the provisions of Articles XVI or XVII GATS or whether they consist of domestic regulatory adjustments that are not subject to scheduling. It might thus be expected that the notifications received over the years, at least in committed sectors, would indicate directions of policy reform, including in areas relevant to SMEs. However, Article III:3 GATS has been ignored by most Members, including not least the European Union.[47]

Of approximately 350 notifications, submitted over the past decade, more than one-half originated from three Members only (Albania, China, and Switzerland). With possibly the sole exception of Brazil, there is no indication in any of these notifications that SME-related policy objectives or concerns played a dominant role.[48]

The GATS also contains transparency provisions that might prove relevant to developing country SMEs seeking to explore access opportunities abroad. Pursuant to Article IV:2 GATS, developed country Members and, to the extent possible, other Members are required to operate contact points through which developing country suppliers can obtain potentially relevant commercial and technical information. According to the notifications received, such entities have been established by over 100 Members. There are doubts, however, about whether they really perform their tasks.[49]

[46] For details, see WTO, *Mexico—Measures Affecting Telecommunications Services*, Panel Report (1 June 2004), WT/DS204/R. In particular, the Panel refers to Art XX:1 GATS, which, in its view, 'provides useful context' for the interpretation of Art XVI:2 GATS (para 7.359). Article XX:1 GATS states that '[e]ach Member shall set out in a schedule the specific commitments it undertakes under Part III of the Agreement. With respect to sectors where such commitments are undertaken, each schedule shall specify: (a) terms, limitations and conditions on market access ...'.

[47] In the context of a Trade Policy Review, the European Commission argued, by way of explanation, that the scope of potentially relevant measures was extremely broad, no reliable statistics were available, and no clear standards allowed to determine which trade effects were 'significant'. WTO, Trade Policy Review Body, 'Trade Policy Review, Report by the Secretariat: European Union' (1 August 2011) WT/TPR/S/248/Rev.1.

[48] Brazil notified two measures governing 'small entrepreneur finance companies'. WTO, Council for Trade in Services, 'Notification Pursuant to Article III:3 of the General Agreement on Trade in Services' (4 May 2001) S/C/N/145.

[49] In the context of a study on recognition measures, Marchetti and Mavroidis approached repeatedly the contact points of eighteen WTO Members. However, they remained without reply. Juan

## D. Overview of Size-Related Commitments—GATS and RTAs

The following observations are based on the GATS schedules in force in late December 2015, covering 162 WTO Members. Apart from the full range of horizontal entries, the limitations inscribed for a pre-selected sample of sectors were taken into account. The sample focuses on services considered to be particularly relevant for SMEs: professional services, other business services, distribution, construction and related engineering, hospital services, other human health and social services, hotels and restaurants, other tourism and travel-related services, insurance, and banking.

In counting limitations, we distinguished between measures that are directly size-related and others that may have indirect effects. The former category comprises: (a) reservations for or exclusions of SMEs from commitments; (b) prescribed minimum amounts of foreign investment or capital; (c) size-related ENTs; and (d) subsidy-related preferences in favour of domestic SMEs. In turn, indirect effects might be ascribed to restrictions on cross-border trade or on the entry of independent professionals, residency requirements, training requirements, as well as poorly specified ENTs, and the like.

It is important to note that the positive effects on domestic SMEs expected to arise from these measures may come at the expense of small foreign suppliers that also seek to serve the markets concerned under relevant modes.

### I. GATS commitments

#### *1. Horizontal limitations*

In total, thirty-three Members have inscribed explicitly size-related limitations in the horizontal section of their schedules: eighteen under market access (MA), ten under national treatment (NT), and the remaining five in both columns.[50] The focus is on mode 3 (twenty-four limitations), followed by mode 4 (ten). The most frequently scheduled measures are reservations of business opportunities for small companies, with eighteen cases in the horizontal section (Table 1.1).[51]

In addition, there are many entries that may impinge indirectly on suppliers of different sizes. In particular, over ninety Members inscribed mode 4 limitations that provide no scope for access unrelated to commercial presence. Independent service suppliers or employees of foreign-based firms seeking to perform a contract could

Marchetti and Petros Mavroidis, 'I Now Recognize You (and Only You) as Equal: An Anatomy of (Mutual) Recognition Agreements in the GATS' in Ioannis Lianos and Okeoghene Odudu (eds), *Regulating Trade in Services in the EU and the WTO* (Cambridge University Press 2012) 428–29.

[50] Some of these numbers differ from those recorded in Table 1.1 since the same Member may have inscribed more than one variant of a particular measure in its schedule.

[51] For example, Bulgaria's schedule provides under market access, mode 4, that the number of intra-corporate transferees within an internationally active company must not exceed 10 per cent of the number of nationals employed, except for companies with fewer than 100 employees, where higher shares may be authorized.

**Table 1.1** Entries in GATS schedules potentially benefitting domestically owned SMEs, 2016

| Measure | Most relevant column/ mode | Number of Members/Schedules | | | |
|---|---|---|---|---|---|
| | | Total | Horizontal Section | Sector Section[i] (Three most frequent cases) | |
| **(1) Explicitly size-related limitations** | | | | | |
| Reservations/exclusions of SMEs from commitments | MA/3 | 48 | 18 | Banking<br>Hotels and restaurants<br>Professional services | (16)<br>(15)<br>(6) |
| NT-inconsistent minimum capital or investment requirements | NT/3 | 19 | 9 | Banking<br>Insurance<br>Hotels and rest.; constr.; other bus. | (8)<br>(7)<br>(1) |
| Economic needs test with size-related criteria | MA/3 | 10 | 1 | Distribution<br>Hotels and restaurants | (4)<br>(2) |
| NT-inconsistent taxes or subsidies | NT/3 | 6 | 6 | 0 | |
| **(2) Potentially relevant limitations** | | | | | |
| No bindings on cross-border trade | MA, NT/1, 2 | 129 | 0 | Other business services<br>Hotels and restaurants<br>Professional services | (76)<br>(70)<br>(63) |
| No mode 4 commitments unrelated to establishment | MA, NT/4 | 94 | 94 | 0 | |
| Residency and commercial presence requirements[ii] | MA, NT/1, 4 | 50 | 6 | Other business services<br>Insurance<br>Professional services | (20)<br>(20)<br>(17) |
| Economic Needs Test without precise criteria | MA/3 | 41 | 8 | Insurance<br>Hospitals<br>Banking | (13)<br>(12)<br>(10) |
| Local incorporation and joint venture requirement | MA/3 | 43 | 23 | Insurance<br>Banking<br>Other business services | (18)<br>(17)<br>(6) |
| NT-inconsistent training requirements | NT/3 | 18 | 15 | Hotel and restaurants<br>Distribution | (2)<br>(1) |
| No bindings for taxes, subsidies, etc | NT/1, 2, 3 | 18 | 17 | Other business services | (1) |

Notes:

[i] Numbers of the most frequently affected sectors in parenthesis.

[ii] Includes local-partnership requirements.

thus be denied entry. Local incorporation and/or joint venture requirements rank second in this regard; they show up in more than twenty schedules.

### 2. *Sector patterns*

From a sectoral perspective, explicitly size-related limitations are particularly frequent in banking (twenty-two schedules), hotels and restaurants (seventeen), insurance (eleven), and distribution (eight).[52] The most prominent entries are, predictably, size-specific reservations or exclusions in commitments, followed by discriminatory minimum capital or investment requirements and size-related ENTs.

The relatively high shares of size-related limitations in financial services, including NT-inconsistent minimum capital and investment requirements, may reflect concerns of a predominantly prudential nature. However, this is certainly not the case for sectors such as hotel and restaurant services, where several size-related limitations may be intended to provide niches for domestically owned SMEs. They mostly specify the number of hotel rooms or the hotel ratings (stars).

The terms used to express limitations, as well as their clarity and precision, differ between sectors and schedules. For example, entries concerning construction and related engineering services and architectural services refer to minimum contract values or, more vaguely, to the geographical significance of projects as a prerequisite for access. In banking, size-related entries are expressed, inter alia, in terms of total assets, deposits, lending value, or capital.

Concerning the wide range of entries that may potentially benefit domestically owned SMEs, it is problematic to provide a ranking since the actual trade effects may vary widely between sectors.[53] Nevertheless, according to a rough count, non-bindings on cross-border supplies constitute the most frequent category, contained in close to 130 schedules. Residency and commercial presence requirements rank next; they have been scheduled by fifty WTO Members, including EU Member States, primarily under other business services, insurance, and professional services.

### 3. *Prospects for change*

The likelihood of current GATS commitments being upgraded any time soon is quite remote. As noted before, the Doha Round negotiations have been running idle, if at all, since a failed (informal) ministerial meeting in 2008. This is at least the case for three key areas, namely, the negotiations on agriculture, non-agricultural market access, and services. While the Declaration emanating from the tenth Ministerial Conference in Nairobi (December 2015) points out the existence of a strong commitment among all Members to advance the negotiations on the

[52] The numbers do not always correspond to those given in Table 1.1 since a single schedule might contain several types of limitations in the same sector.

[53] For example, a residency requirement is possibly more burdensome for architects than for medical doctors, who generally provide their services on a permanent basis in one location.

'remaining Doha issues', it provides no guidance as to how this could or should be done. Rather, the Declaration acknowledges, for the first time, that there is a split among the Membership between those who insist that the Round be continued and concluded on the basis of existing Declarations and Decisions, and other Members (mostly the large OECD countries) who believe that new approaches are necessary to achieve meaningful results.[54]

## II. Regional Trade Agreements

Issues related to SMEs have also been addressed in RTAs. Out of a sample of sixty-six RTAs, forty-six contain SME-related elements of different scope and depth, twenty of which refer specifically to trade in services.[55] About half of these deal with SME-related issues in the main text, often in general terms (eg facilitating SMEs' use of e-commerce, promoting a favourable environment for the development of SMEs), in addition to the respective schedules of commitments. Also relatively frequent (in ten RTAs) are references, again mostly in general terms, to SMEs' participation in government procurement. While a few RTAs provide for joint initiatives in favour of SMEs, the content mostly remains vague. It appears, in some cases at least, that such entries are intended mainly to pay tribute to popular policy concerns.

Typically, the twelve signatories of the recently concluded Trans-Pacific Partnership (TPP) Agreement are resolved, according to the Preamble, to 'support the growth and development of micro, small and medium-sized enterprises by enhancing their ability to participate in and benefit from the opportunities created by the Agreement'.[56] A particular chapter is devoted to SMEs (Chapter 24). Its main content is a commitment by the parties to operate publicly accessible websites containing pertinent information and the creation of a Committee on SMEs to discuss, develop, and promote relevant policies. Like similar agreements, the TPP does not specify any size brackets for SMEs, which in any event might have proven difficult to establish, given the diversity of the participating economies.[57] Issues arising under the SME Chapter are excluded from the Agreement's dispute settlement provisions.

Concerning the services schedules contained in our RTA data set, explicitly size-related limitations are almost equally distributed between market access and national treatment commitments. In seventeen schedules, horizontal limitations have been used, mostly consisting of exclusions of SMEs from commitments

[54] WTO, Ministerial Conference Tenth Session, 'Nairobi Ministerial Declaration' (21 December 2015) WT/MIN(15)/DEC.

[55] The sample has been taken from among eighty-four RTAs notified to the WTO under the relevant GATS provision, Art V:7, by late August 2011 (excluding the EC Treaty and subsequent EC enlargements) and covers all agreements in which China, India, or an OECD country participate.

[56] The Agreement is the largest RTA signed to date, estimated to account for close to 40 per cent of world merchandise trade. At the time of writing, however, it was still to be ratified by its parties (Australia, Brunei, Canada, Chile, Japan, Malaysia, Mexico, New Zealand, Peru, Singapore, United States, and Vietnam), and the prospects appeared highly uncertain.

[57] cf the Annex of this volume.

(fourteen schedules). Not surprisingly, similarities with GATS-scheduled limitations are frequent. Regarding individual services, hotels and restaurants again account for the lion's share of the sector-related limitations, contained in eleven schedules of our RTA sample, followed by financial services (four) and distribution (two).

In addition, of course, it needs to be taken into account that at least some of the more ambitious RTAs improve on existing GATS commitments in areas or modes, including the movement of services professionals under mode 4 which are particularly relevant for SMEs.[58] In addition, insofar as these agreements are used as fora for regulatory harmonization or deeper regulatory coordination and cooperation among participants, they could also render such commitments more commercially relevant than comparable obligations under the GATS.

### III. Size-related effects of scheduling patterns—GATS vs RTAs

An ever-increasing number of publications deal, in a comparative way, with the obligations assumed by WTO Members under the GATS and under RTAs. One study stands out insofar as it focuses on SME-related implications to be expected from differences in scheduling patterns between the two sets of commitments.[59] Starting from the assumption that SMEs typically prefer 'soft' modes of supply, de-linked from commercial presence (eg cross-border supply and movements of contractual service suppliers), while large companies rely more strongly on foreign direct investment (mode 3) and, subsequently, movements of intra-corporate transferees, the study shows that the gap between the two approaches is significantly smaller in RTAs than in Doha Round offers.[60] RTAs thus tend to level the playing field between SMEs and larger enterprises insofar as they improve market access also in modes presumably preferred by SMEs.

The comparison between RTAs and GATS commitments/offers could have been influenced by a time factor, however. Most current RTAs were concluded after 2003/04, when the majority of Doha Round offers had been submitted. It is thus not implausible that the observed differences between RTA commitments and those contained in these offers are attributable, inter alia, to policy perceptions at the time, possibly implying that future scheduling patterns under GATS could come closer to their RTA counterparts. Other interpretations are conceivable as well, however. For example, RTA participants may be more inclined to rely on each other's regulatory frameworks and controls, leading, in turn, to a more liberal policy stance concerning cross-border supplies and movements of persons than under MFN conditions.

[58] See Section C.II.2 and n 24.

[59] Daniela Persin, 'Market Access for Small versus Large Service Enterprises: The Preferential and Multilateral Trade Liberalization Tracks Compared' (2011) 45 Journal of World Trade 785.

[60] As noted above, the latter are largely comparable to existing GATS commitments.

## E. Summary

Given its broad policy coverage, including the extension from product trade to the treatment of suppliers, the GATS offers more scope for addressing SME-related issues than any other multilateral agreement within the remit of the WTO. Pursuant to Article I:1 GATS, the Agreement applies to government measures affecting trade in services, and this includes measures that differentiate between suppliers of different size. Accordingly, WTO Members could not only accommodate, but actively pursue, SME-related objectives under the GATS. In addition, the Agreement contains particular transparency disciplines, including the requirement to establish contact points for developing country suppliers which, provided they work properly, may not least benefit small companies and independent professionals.

Nevertheless, SME-related concerns have not been addressed systemically in WTO fora to date. Relevant exchanges, more recently, have focused mainly on the contribution of SMEs to production, employment, and trade. A discussion of trade barriers perceived to impede such suppliers, and remedial measures that Members might take, would still have to be launched.

A common denominator that could, or should, inform such a discussion is the economic importance of a smoothly functioning regulatory and institutional framework for trade. The smaller a company, the greater the benefits it derives from low-cost market entry and participation. While technical progress has dramatically increased the potential for cross-border trade through electronic means, other (policy-induced) impediments have remained. They might now deserve even more attention than one or two decades ago. The European Union might be well placed to stimulate relevant discussions in Geneva, given its own internal experience with, and analyses of, SME-related policy issues.

Potentially relevant barriers range from size-related restrictions falling under the market access or national treatment provisions of the GATS (eg local presence requirements) to regulatory measures not subject to scheduling (eg minimum equity standards and high licensing fees). Obviously, this would argue for a two-pronged strategy: trade liberalizing negotiations as mandated in Article XIX GATS; and the development of regulatory disciplines pursuant to Article VI:4 GATS. In addition, compliance with existing transparency obligations under the Agreement might deserve further attention. While most Members, including the European Union, have largely ignored such obligations to date, the European Commission at least expressed support for (nascent) initiatives to improve the GATS' notification mechanism and clarify its scope.

Ideally, a focused discussion of SME-related interests would extend to the external effects of domestic support policies. To what extent are these undermined by similar efforts abroad? Is there scope for parallel reductions of discriminatory procurement restrictions, subsidy schemes, and the like? And are there alternatives to regulatory interventions for prudential and similar reasons (high minimum equity standards, residency requirements, etc) that would have a less deterrent impact on SMEs?

The prospects of such initiatives in the WTO may appear gloomy at present, given the uncertain fate of the Doha Round. Nevertheless, the recent proliferation of RTAs clearly indicates that trade policy making has not come to a halt; quite the contrary. Yet bilateral or regional agreements do not offer the forum necessary for a systemic exploration of the issues raised above. If the underlying concerns are widely shared, there is no substitute for them being addressed in the WTO.

## References

Adlung, R, 'Export Policies and the General Agreement on Trade in Services' (2015) 18 Journal of International Economic Law 487

Adlung, R and Carzaniga, A, 'MFN Exemptions under the General Agreement on Trade in Services: Grandfathers Striving for Immortality?' (2009) 12 Journal of International Economic Law 357

Adlung, R and Roy, M, 'Turning Hills into Mountains? Current Commitments under the General Agreement on Trade in Services and Prospects for Change' (2005) 6 Journal of World Trade 1161

Adlung, R and Soprana, M, 'SMEs in Services Trade—A GATS Perspective' (2013) 48 Intereconomics: Review of European Economic Policy 41

Adlung, R, Morrison, P, Roy, M, and Zhang, W, 'FOG in GATS Commitments: Why WTO Members Should Care' (2013) 12 World Trade Review 1

Australian Trade Commission, '2015 Review of the Export Market Development Grants (EMDG) Scheme' <http://www.austrade.gov.au/Australian/Export/Export-Grants/review> accessed 20 January 2017

Barefoot, K and Koncz-Bruner, J, 'A Profile of U.S. Exporters and Importers of Services' (2012) 92 Survey of Current Business 66 <http://www.bea.gov/scb/pdf/2012/06%20June/0612_MNC.pdf> accessed 20 January 2017

Breinlich, H and Criscuolo, C, 'International Trade in Services: A Portrait of Importers and Exporters' (2011) 84 Journal of International Economics 188

de Groot, S, 'Small Businesses and Online Trading' (UK Federation of Small Businesses 2011) <http://www.fsb.org.uk/LegacySitePath/policy/assets/fsb1144%20online%20trading%20report_web.pdf> accessed 20 January 2017

EIM Business & Policy Research, *Internationalisation of European SMEs* (European Commission 2010)

European Commission, 'Report from the Commission to the Council and the European Parliament on the State of the Internal Market for Services Presented under the First Stage of the Internal Market Strategy for Services' (2002) COM/2002/0441 final

European Commission, 'Report on Cross-Border E-Commerce in the EU' (Commission Staff Working Document) SEC(2009) 283 final

European Commission, 'Small Business, Big World: A New Partnership to Help SMEs Seize Global Opportunities' (9 November 2011) <http://europa.eu/rapid/press-release_MEMO-11-765_en.htm?locale=en> accessed 20 January 2017

European Commission, 'EU–US Transatlantic Trade and Investment Partnership, Public Procurement, Initial EU Position Paper' (2013) <http://trade.ec.europa.eu/doclib/docs/2013/july/tradoc_151623.pdf> accessed 20 January 2017

European Commission, 'Public Procurement' (31 October 2014) <http://ec.europa.eu/trade/policy/accessing-markets/public-procurement> accessed 20 January 2017

European Commission, 'Upgrading the Single Market: More Opportunities for People and Business' (28 October 2015) COM/2015/0550 final

European Commission, 'Annual Report on European SMEs 2014/15' (European Union 2015) <http://ec.europa.eu/growth/smes/business-friendly-environment/performance-review/index_en.htm> accessed 20 January 2017

European Commission, 'European Commission Takes Action to Open Up International Procurement Markets' (Press Release, 29 January 2016) <http://trade.ec.europa.eu/doclib/press/index.cfm?id=1448> accessed 20 January 2017

Federico, S and Tosti, E, 'Exporters and Importers of Services: Firm-Level Evidence on Italy' (Working Papers, No 877, Banca d'Italia 2012) <http://www.bancaditalia.it/pubblicazioni/temi-discussione/2012/2012-0877/en_tema_877.pdf> accessed 20 January 2017

González Sanz, MJ and Caloca, AR, 'Las Características de las Empresas Españolas Exportadoras de Servicios no Turísticos' (2010) 11 Banco de España, Boletín Económico 63 <http://www.bde.es/f/webbde/SES/Secciones/Publicaciones/InformesBoletinesRevistas/BoletinEconomico/10/Nov/Fich/art4.pdf> accessed 20 January 2017

Gootiiz, B and Mattoo, A, 'Services in Doha: What's on the Table?' (2009) 43 Journal of World Trade 1013

Gourlay, A, Seaton, J, and Suppakitjarak, J, 'The Determinants of Export Behaviour in UK Service Firms' (2005) 25 Service Industries Journal 879

Grier, JH, 'U.S. Procurement Preferences for Small and Minority Businesses', *Perspectives on Trade* (8 December 2014) <http://trade.djaghe.com/?p=1123> accessed 20 January 2017

Henten, A and Vad, T, 'Services Internationalization, Characteristics, Potentials and Barriers of Danish Services Firms' in Marcela Miozzo and Ian Miles (eds), *Internationalization, Technology, and Services* (Edward Elgar 2002)

Hollenstein, H, 'Patterns and Determinants of International Activities: Are SMEs Different?' (2001) <http://e-collection.library.ethz.ch/eserv.php?pid=eth:24913&dsID=eth-24913-01.pdf> accessed 20 January 2017

International Trade Centre, 'Connect, Compete and Change for Inclusive Growth—SME Competitiveness Outlook 2015' (International Trade Centre 2015) <http://www.intracen.org/uploadedFiles/intracenorg/2015SMEComp.pdf> accessed 20 January 2017

Lejárraga, I and Oberhofer, H, 'Internationalization of Service SMEs: Evidence from France' (2013) <http://www19.iadb.org/intal/intalcdi/PE/2013/12982a07.pdf> accessed 20 January 2017

Lejárraga, I, López Rizzo, H, Oberhofer, H, Stone, S, and Shepherd, B, 'Small and Medium-Sized Enterprises in Global Markets: A Differential Approach for Services?' (OECD Trade Policy Papers, No 165, OECD 2014) <http://dx.doi.org/10.1787/5jz17jtfkmzt-en> accessed 20 January 2017

Mamdouh, H, 'Services Liberalization, Negotiations and Regulation: Some Lessons from the GATS Experience' in Aik Hoe Lim and Bart De Meester (eds), *WTO Domestic Regulation and Services Trade: Putting Principles into Practice* (Cambridge University Press 2014)

Marchetti, J and Mavroidis, P, 'I Now Recognize You (and Only You) as Equal: An Anatomy of (Mutual) Recognition Agreements in the GATS' in Ioannis Lianos and Okeoghene Odudu (eds), *Regulating Trade in Services in the EU and the WTO* (Cambridge University Press 2012)

Masurel, E, 'Export Behaviour of Service Sector SMEs' (2001) 19(2) International Small Business Journal 80

Minondo, A, 'Exporters of Services in Spain' (Orkestra Working Paper Series in Territorial Competitiveness, No 2011-R04(ENG), Orkestra 2011)

Miroudot, S and Pertel, K, 'Water in the GATS: Methodology and Results' (OECD Working Paper, 6 August 2015) TAD/TC/WP(2014)19/FINAL

OECD, 'Realising the Potential of Electronic Commerce for SMEs in the Global Economy' (Conference on 'Enhancing the Competitiveness of SMEs in the Global Economy: Strategies and Policies', Workshop 3, OECD, Bologna 2000) <http://www.oecd.org/cfe/smes/2011580.pdf> accessed 20 January 2017

OECD and World Bank Group, 'Inclusive Global Value Chains' (Report prepared for submission to G20 Trade Ministers Meeting, 6 October 2015) <http://www.oecd.org/trade/OECD-WBG-g20-gvc-report-2015.pdf> accessed 20 January 2017

OECD and WTO, *Aid for Trade at a Glance 2015: Reducing Trade Costs for Inclusive, Sustainable Growth* (OECD Publishing 2015) <https://www.wto.org/english/res_e/booksp_e/aid4trade15_e.pdf> accessed 20 January 2017

Persin, D, 'Market Access for Small versus Large Service Enterprises: The Preferential and Multilateral Trade Liberalization Tracks Compared' (2011) 45 Journal of World Trade 785

USITC, 'Small and Medium-Sized Enterprises: Characteristics and Performance' (Investigation No 332-510, USITC Publication 4189, November 2010) <https://www.usitc.gov/publications/332/pub4189.pdf> accessed 20 January 2017

USITC, 'Trade Barriers that U.S. Small and Medium-Sized Enterprises Perceive as Affecting Exports to the European Union' (Investigation No 332-541, USITC Publication 4455, March 2014) <https://www.usitc.gov/publications/332/pub4455.pdf> accessed 20 January 2017

US Small Business Administration, 'What is a Small Business Set Aside?' (2016) <http://www.sba.gov/content/small-business-set-asides> accessed 20 January 2017

Vogel, A, 'Exporter Performance in the German Business Services Sector' (2011) 31 Service Industry Journal 1015

# 2

# Leveraging Trade Facilitation Reforms for Increased SME Competitiveness

*Arancha González*

## A. Introduction

At the World Trade Organization's (WTO) 2013 Ministerial Conference, held in Bali, Indonesia, the WTO Member States concluded negotiations on a comprehensive Trade Facilitation Agreement (TFA).[1] The Agreement entered into force on 22 February 2017 after two-thirds of the WTO Members (currently 164 in total) ratified it and deposited their instruments of acceptance with the WTO Secretariat.[2] The TFA will be implemented in the coming years and obliges WTO Members to undertake customs procedural reforms and to improve the movement of goods across borders. For developing countries that lack the capacity, donor countries will provide support through technical capacity building and economic assistance through the establishment of the Trade Facilitation Agreement Facility.[3]

In a competitive market, the final price of a good reflects the combination of two general sets of costs: production costs, which indicate the representative costs of materials, labour and capital associated with each good; and transaction costs, which are a result of the process of bringing the product to market, finding a buyer, and delivering it to the buyer. When the product is brought to market in a country different from where it was produced, transaction costs will include export-related

[1] Agreement on Trade Facilitation (signed 15 July 2014) WT/L/931 <http://www.wcoomd.org/en/topics/wco-implementing-the-wto-atf/~/media/WCO/Public/Global/PDF/Topics/Facilitation/Activities%20and%20Programmes/TF%20Negociations/WTO%20Docs/TNTF/2014/931%20EN.ashx> accessed 20 January 2017.

[2] See WTO, 'WTO's Trade Facilitation Agreement enters into force' (22 February 2017) <https://www.wto.org/english/news_e/news17_e/fac_31jan17_e.htm> accessed 27 February 2017.

[3] See WTO, 'Trade Facilitation Agreement: Easing the Flow of Goods across Borders' (2016) <https://www.wto.org/english/thewto_e/20y_e/wto_tradefacilitation_e.pdf> accessed 20 January 2017; see also Trade Facilitation Agreement Facility, 'Donors & Organizations' <http://www.tfafacility.org/implementation-support> accessed 20 January 2017.

costs, such as clearing customs, transporting the goods to the border, and logistics. It is these costs that the TFA addresses directly by reducing the time goods spend in transit (eg Article 11 TFA), minimizing customs and transit-related fees (eg Article 6 TFA), and providing transparency and predictability throughout (eg Articles 1 to 5 TFA). However, as this chapter explains, the TFA will also indirectly lower production costs by reducing transaction costs associated with the trade in raw materials and intermediate goods. Here, the TFA will provide for increased trade in intermediate goods and will thus allow the most efficient intermediate producers to emerge.

While the TFA marks a return to multilateralism at the WTO, some question whether it will provide tangible benefits for small and medium-sized enterprises (SMEs).[4] The argument is that the TFA will equally benefit larger multinational companies (MNCs), and thus do nothing to change the *relative* ability of SMEs to compete. The response to this concern is that MNCs are already more adept at navigating the webs of customs procedures, and are capable of internalizing trade logistics.[5] Thus, while the TFA will benefit all companies active in trade, it should provide a proportionately greater benefit to SMEs. The additional hope is that implementation of the TFA, accompanied by the prescribed capacity building, will also help developing country SMEs trade more efficiently with each other. Whether the TFA will provide a comparative advantage for SMEs should be closely observed over the coming years.

This chapter takes the position that proper implementation of the TFA will benefit SMEs overall; this not only includes SMEs already active in international trade, but also those that would internationalize if not held back by higher relative transaction costs as a result of geographical and administrative barriers. In order to gain a thorough understanding of how the TFA can accomplish this goal, this chapter will first explain how trade models have changed over time and how the emerging role of global value chains (GVCs) offers SMEs the opportunity to compete and become efficient producers in more narrow facets of the production process. Second, it will highlight provisions of the TFA that can affect the way in which SMEs export, and may encourage larger firms to incorporate developing country SMEs into their GVCs. Finally, it will outline additional factors that could help developing country SMEs to maximize the opportunities offered by the TFA.

[4] See Bernard M Hoekman and Ben Shepherd, 'Who Profits from Trade Facilitation Initiatives?' (RSCAS, European University Institute Working Papers 07/2015) 14.

[5] See Alan M Field, 'Smaller Shippers Likely Beneficiaries of WTO Trade Facilitation Agreement' Journal of Commerce Online (Newark, 28 April 2015) <http://www.joc.com/regulation-policy/trade-agreements/international-trade-agreements/smaller-shippers-likely-beneficiaries-wto-trade-facilitation-agreement_20150428.html> accessed 20 January 2017.

## B. New Opportunities for SMEs to Go Global

### I. SME characteristics

SMEs are everywhere. They bring you fresh fruit, shape your cricket bat, package your coffee pods, and sew the buttons on your shirt. You may not even realize that they are around, but in a healthy economy they make up 95 to 99 per cent of businesses, and participate in all levels of commerce.[6] As a group, SMEs are also massive employers, accounting for up to 78 per cent of the jobs in low-income countries, and 66 per cent in the developed world.[7] In countries where they have access to competitive financial and logistics sectors, they are also increasingly able to sell their goods in foreign markets.[8] For example, in the United States, 98 per cent of all exporters are SMEs, accounting for 33 per cent of exports by value.[9]

Yet there is no universally accepted definition of an SME, and different countries have differing ideas. In Tanzania, SMEs are businesses with more than four, but fewer than ninety-nine employees.[10] In South Africa, SME status is based on the industry and ranges from 10 to 200 employees with annual turnover from ZAR200,000 to ZAR64 million.[11] China also varies the definition by industry, and includes enterprises with as many as 3,000 employees.[12] The European Union caps SME status at 250 employees, but allows a turnover of up to €50 million (roughly ten times that of South Africa).[13] In some cases, grouping entities under the term SMEs, for policy purposes, can be misleading. For example, in Rwanda, SMEs make up 98 per cent of private sector businesses, but of that, only 0.22 per cent are

[6] See Viral Pandya, 'Comparative Analysis of Development of SMEs in Developed and Developing Countries' (2012 International Conference on Business and Management, 6–7 September 2012, Phuket, Thailand) <https://www.researchgate.net/publication/266594413_Comparative_analysis_of_development_of_SMEs_in_developed_and_developing_countries> accessed 20 January 2017.

[7] See Meghana Ayyagari, Asli Demirguc-Kunt, and Vojislav Maksimovic, 'Small vs. Young Firms across the World: Contribution to Job Creation, Employment, and Growth' (Policy Research Working Paper 5631, World Bank, April 2011) 2–3 <http://elibrary.worldbank.org/doi/pdf/10.1596/1813-9450-5631> accessed 20 January 2017.

[8] See eg World Bank, 'Small and Medium Enterprises (SMEs) Finance' (1 September 2015) <http://www.worldbank.org/en/topic/financialsector/brief/smes-finance> accessed 20 January 2017.

[9] Based on information from the US Department of Commerce, 'National Export Initiative Fact Sheet' (2014) <http://trade.gov/nei/nei-fact-sheet.asp> accessed 20 January 2017.

[10] See Tanzanian Ministry of Industry and Trade, 'Small and Medium Enterprise Development Policy 2003' (Dar es Salaam, April 2003) xi <http://www.mit.go.tz/uploads/documents/sw/1455890063-SME-Development-Policy.pdf> accessed 20 January 2017.

[11] See National Small Business Act, No 102 of 1996 (SA) Section 1 (definition of small business and the Schedule applicable) <https://www.thedti.gov.za/sme_development/docs/act.pdf> accessed 20 January 2017.

[12] See Art 2 of the 'Law of the Peoples Republic of China on Promotion of Small and Medium-Sized Enterprises' and accompanying regulation 'Standard for Determining Small and Medium-Sized Enterprises' (released in 2003 by State Development Planning Commission and Ministry of Finance) <http://www.npc.gov.cn/englishnpc/Law/2007-12/06/content_1382128.htm> accessed 20 January 2017.

[13] See European Commission, Commission Recommendation 2003/361/EC concerning the definition of micro, small and medium-sized enterprises [2003] OJ L124/36, Annex I, Art 2.1; see also Rudolf Adlung and Marta Soprana in the Annex of this volume.

'medium-sized' (defined as containing, among other things, 31 to 100 employees), and 97.8 per cent are small- or micro-sized enterprises.[14]

Although a universal definition is elusive, there are still certain characteristics inherent to SMEs in general. SMEs are usually privately owned and lack sophisticated corporate governance structures and they are usually thinly capitalized, making them less able to undertake larger expansions, and more sensitive to macroeconomic shocks. From an operational perspective, SMEs are more likely to be risk-averse, and dedicate fewer resources to strategic planning and market research.[15] However, the small size of SMEs also allows them to react quickly to changing market realities and to be flexible in pursuing opportunities that larger firms may not.

Traditionally, SMEs focused sales on domestic and sometimes regional markets. This reality was based in part on the fact that, while SMEs could be competitive in narrow areas of production, they generally lacked the economies of scale needed to be efficient producers on an international level.

This traditional model, however, is starting to change as more SMEs tap into GVCs and are able to access export markets. SMEs participate in GVCs both by exporting intermediate goods to buyers in a different country, and by supplying intermediate goods to MNCs located domestically. In either case, the SME contribution is eventually incorporated into a finished product and sold in regional and global markets. This is a positive development for SME competitiveness because companies (SME or larger enterprises) that export, or compete with exports, are generally more efficient and obtain higher levels of productivity than those that do not. As SMEs become integrated into larger international business models, they learn (international) best practices merely by association. Moreover, attracting and maintaining internationally oriented SMEs brings tangible benefits to host countries, specifically in the form of employment. Collectively, SMEs are already the main source of jobs in most economies, but there is an extra employment boost associated with internationalized SMEs. For existing SMEs, adding international sales will usually create additional jobs and provide insulation against domestic business cycles. When a multinational enterprise makes the decision to locate a component of its value chain in a developing country, it often directs investment to the domestic economy (either to build new facilities or to improve existing SMEs' operations). As SMEs become more export-focused and more efficient, they are more likely to be oriented towards higher growth industries.[16]

Still, SMEs continue to face daunting challenges. Because SMEs export in smaller volumes, they typically have higher per-unit export-related costs relative to

[14] See Rwanda Ministry of Trade and Industry, 'Small and Medium Enterprises (SMEs) Development Policy' (June 2010) 15 <http://fortuneofafrica.com/rwanda/micro-small-medium-enterprises-in-rwanda/> accessed 20 January 2017.

[15] See in more detail Paul Westhead and David Storey, 'Management Training and Small Firm Performance: Why Is the Link So Weak?' (1996) 14(4) International Small Business Journal 13.

[16] See Organisation for Economic Co-operation and Development (OECD), 'High-Growth Enterprises: What Governments Can Do to Make a Difference' (OECD Studies on Entrepreneurship, November 2010) <http://www.keepeek.com/Digital-Asset-Management/oecd/industry-and-services/high-growth-enterprises_9789264048782-en#page3> accessed 20 January 2017.

MNCs. This relativity means that SMEs are affected to a greater extent by trade barriers and volatility surrounding export-related costs. In addition, relative to MNCs, SMEs have more asymmetrical access to the information necessary to sell products in international markets. Thus, where the information needed to export varies from one market to another, or the costs associated with exporting are high, SME exports are increasingly disadvantaged when compared to exports from MNCs or similar products domestically produced in the import market.

It is important to note that although the problems facing SMEs in developing countries are similar to those encountered by SMEs in developed countries, they are often of a much greater scope and are exacerbated by uncertainty and macroeconomic variations. Given the prevailing low cost of labour, one would expect that developing country SMEs could focus on labour-intensive products and thus be competitive in global markets. The changing structure of trade towards GVCs and the implementation of the TFA may present developing country SMEs with their best opportunity yet.

## II. The globalization of SMEs hinges on trade in intermediate goods

While it is true that some SMEs sell finished products to retail customers in international markets,[17] the real opportunity for SMEs to globalize lies in supplying intermediate goods to a niche in a global supply chain. To better understand the potential opportunities for SMEs under the TFA, a brief digression into the evolution of trade theory is necessary.

Traditional Ricardian trade theory implies that countries should devote resources and efforts to producing those products for which they have a comparative advantage. The implication is that countries maximize their productive capacity around just a couple of product sectors and then use the excess output to trade for other things they need, but are less efficient in producing. For example, a country with abundant pastures should focus on grazing cows and make cheese. That country can then trade its excess cheese to get coffee from a country with mountains, cloud forest, and cheap labour to harvest the coffee berries. This model, although central to an introductory economics course, is becoming increasingly outdated.[18]

Instead, events in the modern trade era, including lower tariff rates, innovation in shipping and freight forwarding, increased globalization, and the emergence of GVCs, have significantly changed trade theory. Countries no longer trade only

[17] As a result of the growth in e-commerce, led by online retailers such as Amazon, eBay, and Alibaba, there are increasing opportunities for SMEs to sell finished products. As infrastructure (both internet and transportation-based) improves in developing countries, many SMEs will be increasingly able to reach international customers directly. Proper implementation of the TFA will help SMEs export through this method. However, the remainder of this chapter will focus on SME contributions to supply chains.

[18] See eg Avinash Dixit and Victor Norman, *Theory of International Trade: A Dual, General Equilibrium Approach* (Cambridge University Press 1980).

finished goods, but engage in a value-adding chain of activities that transforms raw materials into finished goods. For some products, the production process might still occur within one country, but increasingly it is spread between multiple countries and across different firms, each specializing in certain aspects of the value-adding process. Automobiles provide a good example: the iron ore is mined in Brazil; the steel is made in China; simple parts are assembled in Thailand; precision parts are machined in Japan or Germany (sometimes even passed back and forth between countries where not cost-prohibitive); and the final automobile is assembled in Mexico and distributed throughout the Americas. The resulting model of trading value-added intermediate goods en route to final assembly has become the most efficient way of producing complicated products (eg those with an 'on' switch or multiple moving parts).

In the modern era of GVCs, an automotive-sector SME does not have to compete with German car manufacturers like BMW or Mercedes to succeed internationally, nor does an information-technology SME need to be more efficient than Samsung. Instead, the respective SME only needs to specialize in a few value-additive processes to be incorporated into BMW's or Samsung's global chain of supply. That same SME might also find a spot in Ford's or Apple's supply chain, providing the same or similar value-added task, in the manner most efficient to that GVC.

SMEs that find their way into larger GVCs realize dynamic benefits. First of all, they become more efficient and more productive through specializing only in a narrow area of expertise. Top winemakers do not at the same time need to be top grape farmers (or grape farmers at all). Instead, expert winemakers can consistently purchase top grapes from expert growers. In fact, by sourcing from expert growers in different regions, winemakers can diversify their wine offerings and protect against a poor harvest in just one region. Moreover, there are informational gains to the value chain approach: SMEs learn organizational disciplines and have access to better market information simply through their association with larger MNCs. For example, if Starbucks has previously battled coffee fungus problems with its African producers, it will be more able to share prevention and mitigation methods with its South American sources.

Yet given that dividing production into a series of value-adding tasks provides the opportunity for SMEs to specialize and become more efficient and productive, and given that SMEs benefit from being a part of larger GVCs, why do SMEs from developing and least developed countries still fail to take part in export growth through greater participation in this model? The answer is partially explained by transaction costs associated with exporting products from those countries. According to the World Bank 'Trading Across Border' indicators,[19] the cost to export in developing countries is 48 per cent higher than in developed economies. Similarly, time to export in developing countries is two times higher than in

[19] World Bank, 'Doing Business 2015: Going Beyond Efficiency' (2015) <http://www.doingbusiness.org/~/media/WBG/DoingBusiness/Documents/Annual-Reports/English/DB15-Full-Report.pdf> accessed 20 January 2017.

developed countries, thus limiting business ability to comply with the just-in-time manufacturing requirements.

## C. Trade in Intermediate Goods Expands as Transaction Costs Shrink

Research suggests a strong correlation between a country's level of exports, and the ease of moving goods from domestic producers to foreign customers. Although it seems intuitive, it has profound implications. According to the World Bank, every day that exported goods spend in transit reduces overall exports by 1 per cent; for perishable and time-sensitive items, the reduction is 6 per cent.[20] This relationship can be especially punitive for SMEs in low-income countries as they often lack sufficient resources to foster logistical efficiencies on their own.

Much scholarly work supports the idea that the transaction costs imbued in certain developing country exports create sizable barriers to trade. One study found that equipping low-income countries with even the average logistical capacity of a middle-income country would boost exports by 15 per cent.[21] A separate study explains how improving the trade-enabling environment—for example, by supporting simplified dispute settlement, and facilitating effective public–private dialogue—brings forth disproportionately larger increases in trade flows.[22] These and other similar studies demonstrate an important economic realization of trade policy in the modern trade era: efforts to further increase the benefits of trade, particularly for developing and least developed countries, must build on lower tariff by stripping out unnecessary export-related transaction costs, ie not only focus on reducing tariffs, but also on including/eliminating protective domestic regulations, increasing the predictability of cross-border transaction, and providing greater transparency into customs operations stripping out the export-related transaction costs.

In fact, the benefits that flow from reducing export-related transaction costs are amplified in favour of developing countries under the new trade model of GVCs. As producers trade increasingly in value-added tasks, goods pass across borders a greater number of times during the production process.[23] When the transaction

[20] Simeon Djankov, Caroline Freund, and Cong S Pham, 'Trading on Time' (World Bank Policy Research Working Paper 3909, May 2006) 21 <https://openknowledge.worldbank.org/bitstream/handle/10986/8674/wps3909.pdf?sequence=1> accessed 20 January 2017.

[21] Bernard Hoekman and Allesandro Nicita, 'Trade Policy, Trade Costs, and Developing Country Trade' (Policy Research Working Paper 4797, December 2008) 18 <http://elibrary.worldbank.org/doi/pdf/10.1596/1813-9450-4797> accessed 20 January 2017.

[22] Robert Z Lawrence, Margareta Drzeniek Hanouz, and Sean Doherty (eds), 'The Global Enabling Trade Report 2012: Reducing Supply Chain Barriers' (2012) <http://www3.weforum.org/docs/GETR/2012/GlobalEnablingTrade_Report.pdf> accessed 20 January 2017 (using a metric that measures the extent to which countries have developed institutions, policies, and services facilitating the free flow of goods across borders, and arguing that a 10 per cent change in a country's trade-enabling environment corresponds to a 40 per cent change in the amount of two-way trade).

[23] Bernard Hoekman, 'Adding Value' (2013) 50(4) Finance & Development 22 <http://www.imf.org/external/pubs/ft/fandd/2013/12/hoekman.htm> accessed 20 January 2017.

costs associated with crossing a border are reduced, it becomes economically feasible to seek out ever-more efficient value-adders, even if located in a different country. The fourth Global Review of Aid for Trade identified customs procedures as well as transportation costs as key factors preventing developing countries' participation in global value chains.[24] The overall result is a more efficient production process and greater amounts of trade in intermediate goods. Competition is also enhanced as the costs of trading across borders fall because firms begin to compete wholly on productivity and efficiency throughout all fragments of the production process instead of relying on geographic endowments, market power in one area of production, and proximity to final consumers.

## D. Binding TFA Commitments Will Jumpstart a Virtuous Cycle for Long-Term SME Growth

The TFA realizes the key insight to trade opening in the modern era of GVCs: there is 'low-hanging fruit' in trade logistics and customs practices (tariffs, quotas, and domestic regulations). The actual increases in trade flows stemming from implementation of the TFA will be substantial. The Organisation for Economic Co-operation and Development (OECD) estimates that if the TFA is properly implemented, it will reduce export-related transaction costs by 13 to 15 per cent.[25] A separate, but intricate study conducted in part by Bain & Company and the World Bank argues that the impact on global gross domestic product (GDP) of reducing supply chain inefficiencies would be six times more than that of removing all tariffs.[26] Even historically, one can observe the importance of logistical efficiency as a component of export growth: the adoption of standardized shipping containers resulted in a greater increase in functional market access than multilateral trade liberalization under the GATT.[27]

For these reasons, the TFA addresses the issue most germane to developing country SMEs because it reduces the transaction costs and information asymmetries currently present in the global economy. The direct effects of TFA implementation will provide greater opportunities for developing country SMEs to access and take part in GVCs. However, this is only half the story.

[24] WTO, 'Fourth Global Review of Aid for Trade 2013 Connecting to Value Chains' (Summary Report, July 2013) 63, 67, 68, 80, 157.

[25] See OECD, 'The WTO Trade Facilitation Agreement – Potential Impact on Trade Costs' (February 2014) <http://www.oecd.org/trade/tradedev/OECD_TAD_WTO_trade_facilitation_agreement_potential_impact_trade_costs_february_2014.pdf> accessed 20 January 2017.

[26] See World Economic Forum, 'Enabling Trade: Valuing Growth Opportunities' (Report from the World Economic Forum in collaboration with Bain & Company and the World Bank, Geneva 2013) 13 <http://www3.weforum.org/docs/WEF_SCT_EnablingTrade_Report_2013.pdf> accessed 20 January 2017.

[27] Daniel M Bernhofen, Zouheir El-Sahli, and Richard Kneller, 'Estimating the Effects of the Container Revolution on World Trade' (CESifo Working Paper 4136, February 2013) <http://ssrn.com/abstract=2228625> accessed 20 January 2017 (estimating an increase of 790 per cent in bilateral trade over a twenty-year period compared to only 285 per cent for membership in the GATT).

The TFA will set off a cascade of secondary pro-growth effects in developing countries. As countries in terms of Article 24 of the TFA[28] make binding trade facilitation commitments, the international private sector will have greater incentives to invest additional resources in developing countries.[29] The need for efficient customs processing is so important for decisions on foreign direct investment (FDI) that large companies have in the past even resorted to direct negotiations with governments.[30] By making binding trade facilitation commitments to reduce export-related transaction costs,[31] developing countries will remove a major investment concern and can begin to profit from their comparative advantages. Moreover, because the TFA reforms are solidified in an international agreement, they will be seen as insulated from wavering domestic political regimes. Thus, private enterprises will direct longer-term FDI to developing countries with newly improved business environments and trade-facilitative customs practices.

The positive effects from the TFA will be especially relevant for landlocked countries where labour costs are low, but export costs have been high due to the need for goods to cross multiple borders and checkpoints—each one adding transaction costs—in order to reach foreign markets via the sea. In this way, the TFA will do more than just maximize current value chain efficiencies; it will jump-start the creation of value chains in those countries that need increased economic activity most.

It is not just a story of selling more of the same thing. Faster, more efficient, and predictable exporting will also allow SMEs to climb up the value chain into higher-margin products. For example, reducing the time exports spend in transit will allow an apparel-sector SME to supply products to more fashion-oriented brands (as opposed to commodity clothing). Because fashions change monthly, or even weekly, fashion-brand retailers cannot wait for inventory that must pass through a slow export process. SME suppliers that can meet the shorter deadlines can deliver clothing according to the 'just-in-time' inventory policies of the fashion industry, and can therefore increase their participation in different product markets.

Reducing export-related transaction costs in this manner will ignite a vicious circle in developing countries: as increased FDI comes into the country, private enterprises will also invest in improving the business and trade infrastructure. Yet, as the infrastructure and business environment improve, more FDI will follow.

Rwanda provides a great example of this virtuous cycle in progress. In the early 2000s, at the outset of private sector and customs reforms, Rwanda ranked in the bottom 20 per cent of countries in the World Bank 'Doing Business' Report, had

[28] See Art 24(2) TFA.

[29] See OECD, Working Party of the Trade Committee, 'The Economic Impact of Trade Facilitation' (Trade Policy Working Paper No 21, October 2005) 17 <http://www.oecd.org/officialdocuments/publicdisplaydocumentpdf/?doclanguage=en&cote=td/tc/wp(2005)12/FINAL> accessed 20 January 2017 (noting that investment decisions by multinational companies explicitly factor customs efficiencies when deciding locations for outsourced production).

[30] See ibid 25 (explaining how in the 1990s, Philips Electronics used its economic size to secure commitments from Hungary to improve export efficiencies from countries as part of an agreement to locate production facilities there).

[31] See WTO (n 3).

meagre exports, and attracted an average yearly intake of less than US$5 million in FDI.[32] Over the following few years, Rwanda made massive pro-trade reforms, including simplified laws to start a business, better protection for investors, and more flexible lending standards for creditors. Rwanda also implemented multiple customs procedures reforms, including enhanced customs cooperation, a single window for trading, and an electronic filing system for paying taxes, etc. The result was that total exports grew threefold from US$197 million to US$573 million in 2013.[33] In addition, Rwanda has gone from pre-reform FDI levels in US$ single digit millions to US$159 million for 2012.[34] Rwanda now ranks thirty-second in the ease of doing business.[35] More importantly, during this period Rwanda has been able to diversify and increase its export profile in areas where there is higher productivity and greater value added.[36]

To understand the potential dynamism unleashed by the TFA, it is important to analyse the effects as a whole package, and not just as a series of improvements worth a few percentage points each in growth. This potential dynamism is down to the fact that, for private enterprises, the decision to root elements of their supply chains in certain locations is not a gradual one, but is rather binary. As recent case studies demonstrate, domestic reforms may happen in pieces over the course of many years, but business decisions to build production facilities or incorporate existing SME exports into supply chains are the result of those reforms reaching a critical mass or 'tipping point' in favour of efficiency.[37] It is envisaged that the TFA will spur the simultaneous implementation of a whole package of pro-trade measures in the WTO Members. WTO Members, numbering 164 countries, are obliged to implement Trade Facilitation reforms as the Agreement has come into force subsequent to its ratification.[38] The precise timing of implementation for a particular measure may differ according to the special and differential treatment Provision provided in section 2 of the TFA. However, the finishing line for all countries would be the same, as all WTO Member States would eventually implement

[32] World Bank, 'Foreign Direct Investment, Net Inflows', <http://data.worldbank.org/indicator/BX.KLT.DINV.CD.WD> accessed 20 January 2017.

[33] Rwanda Development Board, 'Rwanda's Trend of International Trade Data for the Last 5 Years (2009–2013)' <http://www.rdb.rw/fileadmin/user_upload/Documents/TM/2013-UPDATED_TREND_OF_INTERNATIONAL_TRADE_DATA-_FOR_THE_LAST_5_YEARS.pdf> accessed 20 January 2017.

[34] See n 19.

[35] International Bank for Reconstruction and Development and World Bank, *Doing Business 2014. Understanding Regulations for Small and Medium-Size Enterprises* (International Bank for Reconstruction and Development/World Bank 2013) 3 <http://www.doingbusiness.org/~/media/WBG/DoingBusiness/Documents/Annual-Reports/English/DB14-Full-Report.pdf> accessed 20 January 2017.

[36] Rwanda Institute of Policy Analysis and Research, 'Rwanda Case Study on Economic Transformation' (2012) 18–19, 29–30 <http://www.afdb.org/fileadmin/uploads/afdb/Documents/Knowledge/Economic%20Transformation%20in%20Africa%20The%20Case%20of%20Rwanda.pdf> accessed 20 January 2017.

[37] See nn 15, 17.

[38] See WTO, 'Members and Observers' <https://www.wto.org/english/thewto_e/whatis_e/tif_e/org6_e.htm> accessed 20 January 2017.

all the measures included in the TFA upon acquisition of implementation capacity. Contrary to previous WTO Agreements, the TFA requires full implementation for all Members, but conditions the implementation of selected measures by developing countries and least-developed countries to the receipt of technical and financial assistance.[39]

The following subsections will first identify specific areas where SMEs—particularly developing country SMEs—have traditionally encountered export-related transaction costs; and second will explain, for each area, how proper implementation of the TFA can have a positive effect on reducing these costs.

## I. Reducing information asymmetries allows SMEs to export with confidence

Developing country SMEs are unlikely to have an office or subsidiary located in the export markets to which they would like to expand, and even less likely to have an internal department dedicated to export regulation compliance. This results in significant informational lacunae regarding the regulatory atmosphere of the target market. Given the historical variability of different countries' customs procedures and laws, SMEs have traditionally faced daunting barriers when attempting to expand beyond just one or two known export markets and adopting a regional or even international export strategy (i.e. limited access to information on export opportunities, challenges to meet mandatory and voluntary standards).[40]

The TFA addresses this problem in a number of ways. Articles 1 to 3 TFA (discussed below) set out clear requirements on WTO Members to publish information detailing the requirements and procedures necessary to clear goods through customs. Article 1 TFA contains basic publishing requirements which, when implemented, will provide developing country businesses greater access, not only to customs and other border regulations, but also to information regarding classification, valuation, rules of origin, preferential trade agreements, and available tariff quotas. SMEs will particularly benefit from Article 1 TFA as they often do not have the resources to search for and comprehend the requirements of export markets, particularly if requirements are available only in the form of legal acts or other technical documents and in a foreign language, and considering they typically have limited presence overseas. A study of the UN Economic and Social Commission for Asia and the Pacific found increased transparency and predictability tend to 'increase the probability of exporting by SMEs … as well as export propensity' because the costs and risks of doing business are lowered. It also concluded that improvements in policy predictability by one unit generate a 66 per cent increase in the probability of SMEs participating in export activities.[41]

39 See Art 14 TFA.

40 International Trade Centre (ITC), 'SME Competitive Outlook' (ITC 2015) 50–51.

41 Yue Li and John S Wilson, 'Trade Facilitation and Expanding the Benefits of Trade: Evidence from Firm Level Data' (UNESCAP Working Paper No 3/14, June 2009) <http://www.unescap.org/sites/default/files/AWP%20No.%2071.pdf> accessed 20 January 2017.

The TFA also calls for direct engagement with customs authorities. Article 1(3) TFA requires WTO Members to establish enquiry points where developing country SMEs can direct specific questions related to customs rules and procedures. For developing country SMEs with quick and easy questions, this option should be a very efficient tool. It will be especially helpful and eliminate documentary uncertainty, as it provides an official source from which to procure current customs forms and documents. Article 1(3.3) TFA even limits the fees that can be charged for the use of this service to the approximate cost of the service.

Article 2 TFA encourages WTO Members to create a consultative mechanism, through which traders can comment on draft regulations and meet directly with customs agents to discuss questions and problems. This is an oft-overlooked, but very important element of business-friendly trade policy, as it allows the government to learn from traders' experiences of dealing with other customs regimes. Because this consultative mechanism allows governments to monitor and enforce the customs commitments and the pace of reform of other TFA Members, yet predominantly utilizes the resources of private enterprises, governments gain a powerful tool at a relatively small cost. The private sector also benefits from this type of public–private dialogue, not only by influencing trade policy, but also by having time to adapt to customs changes before they are implemented. Although SMEs might not take advantage of this mechanism directly, they will likely benefit through trade associations and other organizations that will represent their opinion and inform them ahead of significant changes.

Article 3 TFA takes predictability even further. If after consulting with available resources a developing country SME is still uncertain as to how an export will be classified, or what origin it will be assigned, the exporter will be able to request official guidance from the customs authority as to how that exporter's products will be classified.[42] Under Article 3(9) the TFA requires, at a minimum, that these 'advance rulings' be available to determine the tariff classification and the origin of the good. However, it also encourages Member States to provide advance rulings on valuation, exemption from customs duties, and quota eligibility. Once issued, advance rulings are binding on the customs authority with respect to the party seeking the ruling for a reasonable period of time. The TFA explicitly recognizes the challenges encountered by SMEs and, in Article 3(9), it specifically requires the Member State, being requested to make an advance ruling, to exercise less stringent requirements on an SME appellant to comply with these requirements. However, the requirements shall be clear and transparent and not constitute a means of arbitrary or unjustifiable discrimination.[43]

Although securing an advance ruling will not be an efficient option for all export-related questions—it will take time to receive the answer, and is probably only useful for large or frequent shipments—it will provide predictability on how exports will be classified and treated by the customs authority. This provision delivers particular benefits to the SMEs whose limited financial resources do not allow them to

[42] See Arts 3(7), (9) and 4 TFA.

[43] See Art 3(9) TFA.

cope with unforeseen changes in the amount of duties and taxes they should pay. If these rulings are published, there will be additional benefits of increased uniformity and even reduced corruption. On the second point, if a trader knows the treatment that he is owed by the customs agency, there will be less to gain by slipping money to border agents to receive more favourable treatment. Instead of viewing a bad determination as the norm, and a good determination as something worth paying for, traders will feel entitled to the best published information.

As customs practices and related trade information become digitized and accessible over the internet,[44] it will only be a matter of time before third-party vendors create additional tools to help traders. It is not too far-fetched to speculate that there might even be a smart-phone app to assist enterprises with their informational needs.

## II. Simplifying regulatory requirements preserves the value added by the SME

The TFA contains numerous provisions[45] designed to simplify, coordinate, and automate customs and other border procedures across WTO Members, who will be required to use a 'single window' for the submission of documents and data to be used by all agencies involved in the import process.[46] Moreover, Article 10(1.1)(a) TFA goes so far as to mandate that documentary requirements be the 'least restrictive measure' available to achieve the objective.

The single-window concept can take many different forms, but at a minimum it involves a one-time submission of trade documents and the obligation to not request the same documents again. This combination will help eliminate duplicative and redundant border procedures. It is also complemented by coordinating border policies (eg customs, agriculture, health, and transportation) at the national level, as well as between the countries with adjacent borders, and synchronizing working hours and formalities of border agencies. It also involves reducing, unifying the required documents, and facilitating joint payments. The single-window concept can be especially helpful to SMEs, because it reduces time in transit, limits the information needed to export, and reduces the chance for delay due to lost paperwork or clerical error.

In 2009, Zambia and Zimbabwe implemented a 'one-stop' customs post at the Chirundu border crossing. This effort simplified border crossing for small traders through reduced trade formalities and coordinated procedures. The first effect was a reduction in waiting times, from an average of five days to two days (and sometimes just a couple of hours).[47] As exporters realized the efficiency gains, they were able

[44] See Art 2 TFA. [45] See Arts 6, 7, 8, 9, 10, 11, and 12 TFA.

[46] Note that Art 10(4) TFA requires Members to 'use their best endeavors to establish or maintain a single window'. It is expected that Members would make efforts to implement this provision in their own interest.

[47] See Barbara Rippel, 'Why Trade Facilitation Is Important for Africa' (Africa Trade Policy Notes, Note 27, November 2011) 6 <http://siteresources.worldbank.org/INTAFRREGTOPTRADE/Resources/trade_facilitation_note_nov11.pdf> accessed 20 January 2017.

to export more through this corridor, and the overall volume of goods that cleared Chirundu increased from US$132 million in 2008 to US$590 million in 2012.[48]

In its more advanced form, the single-window concept incorporates electronic submission of documents and automation of payments. Automation and electronic submission not only speed up the clearance process, but help curb corruption by limiting person-to-person contact between traders and border authorities. There will be no need to physically transfer money, and it will create an electronic record for both government inspectors and private sector auditors to monitor for signs of unusual payments.

These types of procedures also help ensure that the governments receive the revenue associated with importation, while also encouraging increased export traffic through these crossings. For example, when Ghana implemented its electronic exchange system, it saw a 49 per cent increase in revenue collected,[49] whereas Uganda realized a 24 per cent increase in revenues after it completed its payment-systems reforms in 2008.[50]

## III. Diversifying market participation through exports

Because of their small size and light capital structure, SMEs are less able to mitigate adverse effects from outside events or to navigate through macroeconomic and structural changes. Due to the concentration of SMEs in a small number of geographic and product markets (often just one), when adverse events occur in that market, the overall damage to business is likely to be severe. Tsunamis, hyperinflation, prolonged drought, or even changes in technology can render damage to SMEs from which they are not liquid enough to recover. In contrast, MNCs are generally more able to diversify income streams across multiple product and geographic markets. In addition, larger entities can access capital and even equity markets, and thus remain liquid in more strained economic circumstances, whereas SMEs consistently 'suffer from a lack of funding for working capital and investment needs'.[51]

Implementation of the TFA will have positive effects on diversification into new product and geographic markets for SMEs in developing countries. One study demonstrated that the full implementation of the TFA would lead to a 35.6 per cent increase in the number of products by destination for LDCs

48 UN Comtrade Database, Extract Data, <http://comtrade.un.org/data> accessed 20 January 2017.

49 See Luc De Wulf and José B Sokol, 'Customs Modernization Initiatives: Case Studies' (World Bank 2004) 19–21 <http://www-wds.worldbank.org/external/default/WDSContentServer/IW3P/IB/2004/10/06/000090341_20041006140229/Rendered/PDF/301120PAPER0Customs0case0studies.pdf> accessed 20 January 2017.

50 See International Bank for Reconstruction and Development and World Bank, *Doing Business 2010: Reforming through Difficult Times* (International Bank for Reconstruction and Development/World Bank 2009) 50 <http://www.doingbusiness.org/~/media/WBG/DoingBusiness/Documents/Annual-Reports/English/DB10-FullReport.pdf> accessed 20 January 2017.

51 See ITC (n 40).

and a 59.3 per cent increase in the number of destinations by product.[52] By expanding into different product and geographic markets, developing country SMEs become less vulnerable to adverse events or macroeconomic changes in one single market. In addition, for SMEs specializing in intermediate goods, the benefits of diversification are twofold: First, diversification is good for sales markets (eg if watches fall out of fashion, the diversified SME can slowly shift resources towards making precision pressure gauges). Second, it is also good for managing supply of critical parts (eg if an earthquake destroys the Islamabad factory from which the SME buys machined aluminium bezels, the diversified SME can begin to source bezels from its supplier in Ho Chi Minh City).

## IV. Limiting export cost uncertainty allows smaller shipments to be more competitive

SMEs generally export in smaller shipments. Because many export-related costs (both direct and indirect) are incurred in relation to shipments and not to individual goods, SME products will often be forced to internalize a larger pro-rata share of export costs into their price than would products exported in large shipments from larger enterprises.

The TFA can help small-shipment exporters in two distinct ways. First, it limits the ability for countries to maintain trade-prohibitive, customs-related fees that function as de facto tariffs. Second, it reduces the time exports spend in customs clearance, which in turn limits the risk that perishable items in transit or 'just-in-time' exports arrive too late.

Article 6(2) TFA specifically precludes customs processing fees and charges that are in excess of the approximate cost of the services rendered, and Article 6(3) limits the size and scope of penalties by requiring that they are only imposed on the party responsible for the breach and that the fee/penalty commensurates with the severity of the breach. Additionally, the TFA requires that WTO Members design penalty assessments to avoid any incentives to issue excessive penalties as a means to collect revenue for the customs authority.[53] Because developing countries historically rely more heavily on customs revenue to fund the government, these provisions prevent them from implementing customs infractions or imposing excessive processing fees in order to boost revenue in times of need.

These provisions will benefit developing country SMEs, because any additional fees applied to a shipment will disproportionately hurt the competitiveness of the SME product. Smaller enterprises are more likely to be squeezed by customs, as they lack the political capital to fight back. In addition, because SMEs must rely on

[52] WTO, 'Speeding up Trade: Benefit and Challenges of Implementing the WTO Trade Facilitation Agreement' (World Trade Report, 2015) 2 <http://www.wto.org/english/res_e/booksp_e/world_trade_report15_e.pdf> accessed 20 January 2017.

[53] See Art 6(3.4) TFA.

third parties to transport their goods, by limiting the penalty to the party that violated customs law, developing country SMEs can reduce uncertainty over customs liability by simply making sure their exports comply with the regulations when they leave the building. As these TFA provisions provide greater predictability as to the total costs of exporting, risk-averse SMEs will be more inclined to take the leap into new export markets.

Equally important, the TFA contains comprehensive instructions addressing the release and clearance of goods from the customs authority based on the mantra that goods do not need to wait in storage to accommodate delays in the customs process. Assuming there is not an issue requiring quarantine, the goods should be able to move on to customers while the customs authority makes its calculations and determinations. For example, Article 7(1) TFA requires WTO Members to incorporate pre-arrival processing (a mechanism providing traders with the facility to submit import documents prior to arrival of goods), and Article 7(3) TFA requires Member States to establish or maintain procedures allowing the release of goods prior to the final determination of customs duties, taxes, fees, and charges. It also authorizes reduced physical inspections based on risk management calculations and provides for even more expedited procedures for authorized operators.

Implementation of these provisions could be very helpful to SMEs in developing countries, especially those that export perishable goods or those seeking to implement a just-in-time supply strategy. The only reservation is that smaller SMEs may not be able to fully utilize some of these procedures, at least not to the same extent as larger exporters (see below).

## E. Good Domestic Policy Will Enhance TFA Benefits

Increasing the efficiency of trading goods across borders is beneficial to both exporters and importers. Because transaction costs add to the price, but do not make the product better, reducing them through trade facilitation will be a net gain for consumers. However, one concern voiced by TFA is that reducing logistical and procedural friction to trade might give greater benefits to MNCs over SMEs.[54] The argument is that unclogging trade infrastructure and streamlining custom procedures will not only allow developing country SMEs to access foreign markets, but will also allow MNCs to better access SME domestic markets where pre-TFA procedural barriers prevented competition from more efficient foreign producers. Regardless of the accuracy of this argument, there are a few policies that developing countries can adopt to ensure that the TFA benefits are felt by SMEs.

[54] See Hoekman and Shepherd (n 4) 14.

## I. Competitive trade logistic services further enhance export competitiveness

Increasing trade flows by improving the transactional aspects of trade could be augmented further by making the domestic trade policy a comprehensive and coordinated initiative. As a matter of fact, even with the reforms introduced by the TFA, exporting goods still relies on the physical act of transporting them from domestic producers to foreign markets. For developing country SMEs to capitalize on TFA implementation, they need to transport their goods to their final customers as economically as possible. In practice, this requires the coordination of a number of components, including packaging and loading, ground transportation, port services, warehousing, and information and document management. If the logistics services sector in the exporting country is competitive, then SMEs will realize gains to their efficiency in the form of increased profits (via reduced export costs) as the TFA reforms[55] begin to take place. But if the transportation and logistics sector is inefficient or uncompetitive, developing country SMEs will continue to incur higher *relative* export-related costs as compared to larger competitors (who have the ability to internalize transportation services at lower costs). Higher relative export-related costs will make their products less competitive in foreign markets. Moreover, if transport or logistics operators have market power, the gains in efficiency created by the TFA will be absorbed by these intermediary service providers and neither realized by developing country SME producers nor passed on to final customers.

Therefore, to ensure the competitiveness of SME exports in foreign markets, TFA implementation is necessary, but not sufficient. It is also important to implement reforms that provide for a competitive transport and logistics sector, even if it means opening it up to foreign providers. In 1994, Rwanda liberalized its trucking sector and saw dramatic decreases in the cost of shipping goods, on the scale of 75 per cent in real terms, as foreign competition entered and made the market more efficient. In fact, as the market reached equilibrium, the number of domestic operators eventually returned to the levels present in the market before the reforms.[56] A similar result occurred in Mexico, when the country deregulated its trucking sector in 1989 and saw the costs of transport decrease by 23 per cent in real terms, while realizing increased speed and reliability of service.[57]

## II. Public–private partnerships engender innovative and efficient solutions

SMEs in developing countries need soft infrastructure (eg TFA Article 10(4) requesting Member States to establish a single window), but it is not always

[55] See Sections A and B of this chapter.

[56] See Supee Teravaninthorn and Gaël Raballand, 'Transport Prices and Costs in Africa: A Review of the International Corridors' (World Bank 2009) 23–24, <https://openknowledge.worldbank.org/bitstream/handle/10986/6610/461810PUB0Box3101OFFICIAL0USE0ONLY1.pdf?sequence=1> accessed 20 January 2017.

[57] ibid 20–21.

possible for governments in developing countries to provide it. Unlike developed countries that can finance infrastructure projects through various debt markets, infrastructure in developing countries—especially least-developed economies—will need to be paid for in advance. However, governments may not have to bear the burden to finance infrastructure improvements alone. If the business climate is good and adequate rule of law protections are in place, developing countries may be able to benefit from innovation in the form of public–private partnerships (PPPs)[58]. PPPs provide for infrastructural efficiency through consultation, collaboration, and contracting with the private sector. PPPs are also part of a virtuous circle through which governments change their perspective from viewing the private sector as the target of customs controls, to seeing the private sector as a joint stakeholder in establishing efficient customs policies.

Ghana implemented a customs-processing PPP in 2000, combining a Swiss inspection company, a Ghanaian customs department, a private export association, and two commercial banks.[59] The efficiency of bringing all these components into one entity reduced clearance times for ships from fourteen days to between two and three days, and for air cargo from two to three days to less than four hours. The secondary effect of this PPP implementation brought Ghana from 108th to 61st place on the World Bank index for trading across borders,[60] bearing in mind that customs revenue collected during the first years of implementation grew by 170 per cent.[61]

## III. Targeted fiscal policies provide renewed FDI to fuel SME growth

As developing countries continue to look for ways to stimulate their domestic economies, and to create sustainable growth around greater participation in the global economy, it would be wise to adopt policies that direct foreign investment towards SMEs. By some estimates, every dollar that is invested in SMEs produces thirteen in the local economy.[62] This effort can range from simply facilitating the introduction of SME producers to larger outsourcing MNCs, to offering preferential financing or leasing terms for SME projects. It can include special management or technical skills training offered to SMEs, as well as giving preferential taxation

[58] World Customs Organization, 'Stronger Partnerships with the Private Sector for Successful Implementation of the WTO Trade Facilitation Agreement' (22 April 2015) <http://www.wcoomd.org/en/media/newsroom/2015/april/stronger-partnerships-with-the-private-sector.aspx> accessed 20 January 2017.

[59] ITC, 'Public–Private Collaboration for Export Success: Case Studies from Barbados, Ghana, India, Thailand and Malaysia' (ITC 2012) 29.

[60] ibid 33. [61] ibid 32.

[62] See Small Enterprise Assistance Fund, 'From Poverty to Prosperity: Continuing the Discussion of the Development Impact of SME Investing' (2011) 26 <http://seaf.com/wp-content/uploads/2014/10/SEAF-Development-Impact-Fact-Sheet-2011.pdf> accessed 20 January 2017 (SEAF is a privately run investment fund).

to profits that come from value-additive processes or profits that are reinvested in a specific sector or area.[63]

During the 1980s, the Government of Singapore utilized a few different mechanisms to direct FDI to SMEs. First, it offered financial assistance in various forms to SME start-ups and entrepreneurs, as well as to SMEs looking to internationalize or SMEs needing to conduct technologically advanced research and development.[64] It also created policies that encouraged MNCs to 'adopt' SMEs into their value chains and then to transfer technology, marketing, and business process knowledge.[65] These policies included linking MNCs with adequate SMEs, subsidizing training costs for SME workers, and working with SMEs to ensure their products could meet international quality standards. As a result of these and other efforts, Singapore has an SME network that is actively engaged in trade across the world.

## F. Conclusion

SMEs account for an overwhelming majority of firms: they constitute over 95 per cent of all firms and make up for approximately 50 per cent of GDP and 60 to 70 per cent of total employment. But on a relative basis, their contribution to exports remains limited, in particular in developing and least-developed countries. For example, in the Philippines, SMEs constitute 99.6 per cent of all businesses, but only account for 10 per cent of total exports.

The emergence of global value chains provides new opportunities for small businesses to participate in international trade by specializing in a few value-additive processes to be incorporated into MNCs' chain of supply. However, one of the prerequisites for SMEs to tap into GVCs and access export markets is their ability to import and export rapidly and at a reasonable cost.

This prerequisite is rarely met in developing countries and LDCs where the time and costs to trade are significantly higher than in developed economies. According to the World Bank, the cost to export in developing countries is 48 per cent higher than in developed economies and the time to export is 100 per cent higher.

SMEs are particularly vulnerable to these costs and delays. Because SMEs export in smaller volumes, they typically have higher per-unit export-related costs relative to MNCs, which means that SMEs are affected to a greater extent by trade barriers and volatility surrounding export-related costs. In addition, SMEs' exports are often concentrated in a small number of geographic and product markets, which limits their ability to mitigate their risks. Finally, SMEs are usually thinly capitalized, making them more risk-adverse and often reluctant to expand into markets where cross-border compliance costs are high due to procedural inefficiencies and lack of transparency.

[63] See generally UNCTAD, 'Best Practices in Investment for Development: How to Integrate FDI and Skill Development Lessons from Canada and Singapore' (UNCTAD Investment Advisory Series B, No 5, 2011) <http://unctad.org/en/Docs/diaepcb2010d5_en.pdf> accessed 20 January 2017.

[64] ibid 27.

[65] ibid 27.

In this context, the TFA, whose negotiations were concluded during the WTO ninth Ministerial conference in Bali, provides an opportunity to unleash SMEs' export potential. Upon entry into force, the TFA will introduce binding requirements for WTO Members to improve the efficiency and transparency of cross-border procedures, thus addressing some of the challenges faced by SMEs.

First, the TFA will contribute to reduce information asymmetries faced by SMEs by requesting Member States to establish, among others, online trade facilitation portals, enquiry points, and advance rulings, thus allowing businesses to engage in export operations with confidence. Then, the TFA implementation will translate into reduced transaction costs by simplifying the regulatory requirements through the implementation of trade-facilitative mechanisms such as the single window or by limiting the amount of fees and charges levied by border regulatory agencies. Overall, it is expected that the TFA will reduce transaction costs by up to 15 to 17 per cent of total trade costs in developing countries and LDCs, and contribute to diversify business exports both in terms of products and of destination markets. Although TFA benefits businesses irrespective of their size, it is expected to improve SMEs' relative ability to enter foreign markets.

The world is waking up to a fundamental truth about trade: logistical efficiency is just as important as productive capacity. Finding effective low-cost producers is meaningless if exporting from those producers' markets is cost-prohibitive. Investment decisions are based not only on the current but also the likely future trade-facilitative environment. For many investors looking to build production facilities in a developing country, it may not be sufficient that the current customs practices are acceptable. Instead, long-term investors will want to see a credible commitment to maintaining a trade-facilitative environment.

The WTO Trade Facilitation Agreement is not a cure-all instrument that will make trading fair for all developing country SMEs. Yet, if implemented correctly and expediently, it will provide increased opportunities for developing country SMEs to participate to a greater degree in the still expanding global economy.

## References

Ayyagari, M, Demirguc-Kunt, A, and Maksimovic, V, 'Small vs. Young Firms across the World: Contribution to Job Creation, Employment, and Growth' (Policy Research Working Paper 5631, World Bank, April 2011) <http://elibrary.worldbank.org/doi/pdf/10.1596/1813-9450-5631> accessed 20 January 2017

Bernhofen, DM, El-Sahli, Z, and Kneller, R, 'Estimating the Effects of the Container Revolution on World Trade' (CESifo Working Paper 4136, February 2013) <http://ssrn.com/abstract=2228625> accessed 20 January 2017

De Wulf, L and Sokol, JB, 'Customs Modernization Initiatives: Case Studies' (World Bank 2004) <http://www-wds.worldbank.org/external/default/WDSContentServer/IW3P/IB/2004/10/06/000090341_20041006140229/Rendered/PDF/301120PAPER0Customs0case0studies.pdf> accessed 20 January 2017

Dixit, A and Norman, V, *Theory of International Trade: A Dual, General Equilibrium Approach* (Cambridge University Press 1980)

Djankov, S, Freund, C, and Pham, CS, 'Trading on Time' (World Bank Policy Research Working Paper 3909, May 2006) <https://openknowledge.worldbank.org/bitstream/handle/10986/8674/wps3909.pdf?sequence=1> accessed 20 January 2017

Field, AM, 'Smaller Shippers Likely Beneficiaries of WTO Trade Facilitation Agreement' Journal of Commerce Online (Newark, 28 April 2015) <http://www.joc.com/regulation-policy/trade-agreements/international-trade-agreements/smaller-shippers-likely-beneficiaries-wto-trade-facilitation-agreement_20150428.html> accessed 20 January 2017

Hoekman, B, 'Adding Value' (2013) 50(4) Finance & Development 22 <http://www.imf.org/external/pubs/ft/fandd/2013/12/hoekman.htm> accessed 20 January 2017

Hoekman, B, 'Trade Policy, Trade Costs, and Developing Country Trade' (Policy Research Working Paper 4797, December 2008) <http://elibrary.worldbank.org/doi/pdf/10.1596/1813-9450-4797> accessed 20 January 2017

Hoekman, B and Shepherd, B, 'Who Profits from Trade Facilitation Initiatives?' (RSCAS, European University Institute Working Papers 07/2015)

International Bank for Reconstruction and Development and World Bank, *Doing Business 2010: Reforming through Difficult Times* (International Bank for Reconstruction and Development/World Bank 2009) <http://www.doingbusiness.org/~/media/WBG/DoingBusiness/Documents/Annual-Reports/English/DB10-FullReport.pdf> accessed 20 January 2017

International Bank for Reconstruction and Development and World Bank, *Doing Business 2014: Understanding Regulations for Small and Medium-Size Enterprises* (International Bank for Reconstruction and Development/World Bank 2013) <http://www.doingbusiness.org/~/media/WBG/DoingBusiness/Documents/Annual-Reports/English/DB14-Full-Report.pdf> accessed 20 January 2017

ITC, 'Public–Private Collaboration for Export Success: Case Studies from Barbados, Ghana, India, Thailand and Malaysia' (ITC 2012)

ITC, 'SME Competitive Outlook' (ITC 2015)

Lawrence, RZ, Hanouz, MD, and Doherty, S (eds), 'The Global Enabling Trade Report 2012: Reducing Supply Chain Barriers' (2012) <http://www3.weforum.org/docs/GETR/2012/GlobalEnablingTrade_Report.pdf> accessed 20 January 2017

Li, Y and Wilson, JS, 'Trade Facilitation and Expanding the Benefits of Trade: Evidence from Firm Level Data' (UNESCAP Working Paper No 3/14, June 2009) <http://www.unescap.org/sites/default/files/AWP%20No.%2071.pdf> accessed 20 January 2017

OECD, Working Party of the Trade Committee, 'The Economic Impact of Trade Facilitation' (Trade Policy Working Paper No 21, October 2005) <http://www.oecd.org/officialdocuments/publicdisplaydocumentpdf/?doclanguage=en&cote=td/tc/wp(2005)12/FINAL> accessed 20 January 2017

OECD, 'High-Growth Enterprises: What Governments Can Do to Make a Difference' (OECD Studies on Entrepreneurship, November 2010) <http://www.keepeek.com/Digital-Asset-Management/oecd/industry-and-services/high-growth-enterprises_9789264048782-en#page3> accessed 20 January 2017

OECD, 'The WTO Trade Facilitation Agreement – Potential Impact on Trade Costs' (February 2014) <http://www.oecd.org/trade/tradedev/OECD_TAD_WTO_trade_facilitation_agreement_potential_impact_trade_costs_february_2014.pdf> accessed 20 January 2017

Pandya, V, 'Comparative Analysis of Development of SMEs in Developed and Developing Countries' (2012 International Conference on Business and Management, 6–7 September 2012, Phuket, Thailand) <https://www.researchgate.net/publication/266594413_

Comparative_analysis_of_development_of_SMEs_in_developed_and_developing_countries> accessed 20 January 2017

Rippel, B, 'Why Trade Facilitation Is Important for Africa' (Africa Trade Policy Notes, Note 27, November 2011) <http://siteresources.worldbank.org/INTAFRREGTOPTRADE/Resources/trade_facilitation_note_nov11.pdf> accessed 20 January 2017

Rwanda Development Board, 'Rwanda's Trend of International Trade Data for the Last 5 Years (2009–2013)' <http://www.rdb.rw/fileadmin/user_upload/Documents/TM/2013-UPDATED_TREND_OF_INTERNATIONAL_TRADE_DATA-_FOR_THE_LAST_5_YEARS.pdf> accessed 20 January 2017

Rwanda Institute of Policy Analysis and Research, 'Rwanda Case Study on Economic Transformation' (2012) <http://www.afdb.org/fileadmin/uploads/afdb/Documents/Knowledge/Economic%20Transformation%20in%20Africa%20The%20Case%20of%20Rwanda.pdf> accessed 20 January 2017

Rwanda Ministry of Trade and Industry, 'Small and Medium Enterprises (SMEs) Development Policy' (June 2010) <http://fortuneofafrica.com/rwanda/micro-small-medium-enterprises-in-rwanda/> accessed 20 January 2017

Small Enterprise Assistance Fund, 'From Poverty to Prosperity: Continuing the Discussion of the Development Impact of SME Investing' (2011) <http://seaf.com/wp-content/uploads/2014/10/SEAF-Development-Impact-Fact-Sheet-2011.pdf> accessed 20 January 2017

Tanzanian Ministry of Industry and Trade, 'Small and Medium Enterprise Development Policy 2003' (Dar es Salaam, April 2003) <http://www.mit.go.tz/uploads/documents/sw/1455890063-SME-Development-Policy.pdf> accessed 20 January 2017

Teravaninthorn, S and Raballand, G, 'Transport Prices and Costs in Africa: A Review of the International Corridors' (World Bank 2009) <https://openknowledge.worldbank.org/bitstream/handle/10986/6610/461810PUB0Box3101OFFICIAL0USE0ONLY1.pdf?sequence=1> accessed 20 January 2017

UNCTAD, 'Best Practices in Investment for Development: How to Integrate FDI and Skill Development Lessons from Canada and Singapore' (UNCTAD Investment Advisory Series B, No 5, 2011) <http://unctad.org/en/Docs/diaepcb2010d5_en.pdf> accessed 20 January 2017

US Department of Commerce, 'National Export Initiative Fact Sheet' (2014) <http://trade.gov/nei/nei-fact-sheet.asp> accessed 20 January 2017

Westhead, P and Storey, D, 'Management Training and Small Firm Performance: Why Is the Link So Weak?' (1996) 14(4) International Small Business Journal 13

World Bank, 'Doing Business 2015: Going Beyond Efficiency' (2015) <http://www.doingbusiness.org/~/media/WBG/DoingBusiness/Documents/Annual-Reports/English/DB15-Full-Report.pdf> accessed 20 January 2017

World Bank, 'Small and Medium Enterprises (SMEs) Finance' (1 September 2015) <http://www.worldbank.org/en/topic/financialsector/brief/smes-finance> accessed 20 January 2017

World Customs Organization, 'Stronger Partnerships with the Private Sector for Successful Implementation of the WTO Trade Facilitation Agreement' (22 April 2015) <http://www.wcoomd.org/en/media/newsroom/2015/april/stronger-partnerships-with-the-private-sector.aspx> accessed 20 January 2017

World Economic Forum, 'Enabling Trade: Valuing Growth Opportunities' (Report from the World Economic Forum in collaboration with Bain & Company and the World Bank, Geneva 2013) <http://www3.weforum.org/docs/WEF_SCT_EnablingTrade_Report_2013.pdf> accessed 20 January 2017

WTO, 'Fourth Global Review of Aid for Trade 2013 Connecting to Value Chains' (Summary Report, July 2013)

WTO, 'Speeding Up Trade: Benefits and Challenges of Implementing the WTO Trade Facilitation Agreement' (World Trade Report, 2015) <http://www.wto.org/english/res_e/booksp_e/world_trade_report15_e.pdf> accessed 20 January 2017

WTO, 'WTO's Trade Facilitation Agreement enters into force' (22 February 2017) <https://www.wto.org/english/news_e/news17_e/fac_31jan17_e.htm> accessed 27 February 2017

WTO, 'Trade Facilitation Agreement: Easing the Flow of Goods across Borders' (2016) <https://www.wto.org/english/thewto_e/20y_e/wto_tradefacilitation_e.pdf> accessed 20 January 2017

# 3

# Rediscovering the Forgotten Article of the WTO Anti-Dumping Agreement

## How Article 6.13 Protects SMEs

*Karsten Pötschke*

### A. Introduction

The imposition of anti-dumping (AD) duties has become common practice.[1] Such duties are imposed by states to prevent the import of products at a lower price than their 'normal value', ie the price of the product when sold in the market of origin or in special circumstances the cost of its production. AD measures normally take the form of countrywide duties affecting all imports of the product under consideration. However, exporters that have cooperated shall be attributed an individual duty rate which reflects their own situation.[2]

Even though the possibility to introduce AD duties was already mentioned in the General Agreements on Tariffs and Trade of 1947 (GATT 1947)[3] and elaborated upon in the 1968 Anti-Dumping Code,[4] the use of AD duties only started to flourish with the establishment of the World Trade Organization (WTO) in 1994 and the entry into force of the Anti-Dumping Agreement (ADA). The agreement spells out in great detail the material and procedural requirements for conducting a domestic AD investigation and imposing AD duties. As a consequence, more than 3,000 AD measures have been imposed by WTO Members following 4,757

[1] Mark Wu, 'Antidumping in Asia's Emerging Giants' (2012) 53 Harvard International Law Journal 1; Wentong Zheng, 'Reforming Trade Remedies' (2013) 34 Michigan Journal of International Law 151.

[2] Peter van den Bossche and Werner Zdouc, *The Law and Policy of the World Trade Organization: Text, Cases and Materials* (3rd edn, Cambridge University Press 2013) 724–26; European Commission, 'Guide for EU Exporters: Trade Defence Instruments: Anti-Dumping Anti-Subsidy Safeguards' (Brussels 2010) 6, 8 <http://trade.ec.europa.eu/doclib/docs/2010/october/tradoc_146701.pdf> accessed 20 January 2017.

[3] Art II:2(b) GATT 1947.

[4] Agreement on Implementation of Article VI of the General Agreement on Tariffs and Trade (signed 30 June 1967) 19 UST 4348 (1968 Anti-Dumping Code).

national AD investigations conducted between 1995 and 2014.[5] AD measures are by far the most used trade defence instrument (TDI). The other two instruments permitted under WTO law to counter unfair trade practices—anti-subsidy and safeguard measures—account for merely 10 per cent of all TDIs.[6]

AD investigations not only affect large multinational companies, but also small and medium-sized enterprises (SMEs[7]).[8] This is because SMEs form a major part of every national economy and are becoming ever-more engaged in international trade. In the European Union, 99 per cent of all companies are SMEs.[9] They account for 60 per cent of the European Union's Gross Domestic Product (GDP).[10] One out of three European SMEs has some international business activity.[11] Half of those companies even trade beyond the European Single Market.[12] Moreover, even non-exporting SMEs can also be affected both positively and negatively by

[5] WTO, 'Statistics on Anti-Dumping: Measures by Reporting Member 01/01/1995–31/12/2014' (2014) <http://www.wto.org/english/tratop_e/adp_e/AD_MeasuresByRepMem.xls> accessed 20 January 2017; WTO, 'Statistics on Anti-Dumping: Initiations by Reporting Member 01/01/1995–31/12/2014' (2014) <http://www.wto.org/english/tratop_e/adp_e/AD_InitiationsByRepMem.xls> accessed 20 January 2017.

[6] Since the establishment of the WTO a total 380 anti-subsidy and 279 safeguard proceedings have been initiated. They resulted in 202 anti-subsidy and 136 safeguard measures. See WTO, 'Statistics on Subsidies and Countervailing Measures: Countervailing Initiations by Reporting Member 01/01/1995–31/12/2014' (2014) <http://www.wto.org/english/tratop_e/scm_e/CV_InitiationsByRepMem.xls> accessed 20 January 2017; WTO, 'Statistics on Subsidies and Countervailing Measures: Countervailing Measures by Reporting Member 01/01/1995–31/12/2014' (2014) <http://www.wto.org/english/tratop_e/scm_e/CV_MeasuresByRepMem.xls> accessed 20 January 2017; WTO, 'Statistics on Safeguard Measures: Initiations by Reporting Member 01/01/1995–30/04/2014' (2014) <http://www.wto.org/english/tratop_e/safeg_e/SG-Initiations_By_Reporting_Member.xls> accessed 20 January 2017; WTO, 'Statistics on Safeguard Measures: Measures by Reporting Member 01/01/1995–30/04/2014' (2014) <http://www.wto.org/english/tratop_e/safeg_e/SG-Measures_By_Reporting_Member.xls> accessed 20 January 2017.

[7] The criteria and thresholds to define SMEs vary significantly. Thus far no universally accepted SME definition has emerged. For the European Union, 'the category of micro, small and medium-sized enterprises (SMEs) is made up of enterprises which employ fewer than 250 persons and which have an annual turnover not exceeding €50 million, and/or an annual balance sheet total not exceeding €43 million'. European Commission, Commission Recommendation 2003/361/EC of 6 May 2003 concerning the definition of micro, small and medium-sized enterprises [2003] OJ L124/36, Arts 1–2. The WTO does not define the SME notion. Concerning the various definitions of SMEs, see also Rudolf Adlung and Marta Soprana in the Annex in this volume.

[8] The importance of TDIs for SMEs is also evidenced by the numerous EU documents that address this issue; see European Parliament, Resolution of 5 February 2009 on enhancing the role of European SMEs in international trade (2008/2205(INI)) [2009] P6_TA(2009)0048, paras 10–17; European Commission, 'Q&As: Modernisation of the EU's Trade Defence Instruments' (Press Release, 10 April 2013) MEMO/13/319 <http://europa.eu/rapid/press-release_MEMO-13-319_en.htm> accessed 20 January 2017; European Parliament, Resolution of 11 December 2012 on financing EU SMEs' trade and investment: facilitated access to credit in support of internationalisation (2012/2114(INI)) [2012] P7_TA-PROV(2012)0469, para 27; European Parliament, Resolution of 23 October 2012 on Small and Medium Size Enterprises (SMEs): competitiveness and business opportunities (2012/2042(INI)) [2012] P7_TA(2012)0387, para 19.

[9] Gide Loyrette Nouel, 'Study of the Difficulties Encountered by SMEs in Trade Defence Investigation and Possible Solutions' (Final Report, 30 November 2010) 8 <http://trade.ec.europa.eu/doclib/docs/2011/february/tradoc_147475.pdf> accessed 20 January 2017; European Commission, 'Small and Medium-Sized enterprises (SMEs): Website of the European Union' <http://ec.europa.eu/growth/smes> accessed 20 January 2017.

[10] Gide Loyrette Nouel (n 9) 8; European Commission (n 9). [11] ibid. [12] ibid.

AD duties. On the one hand, their production costs may rise if their production inputs are subject to AD duties. On the other hand, their competitive position in the domestic market may improve if foreign companies face AD duties.

A recent example of the negative impact of AD duties on SMEs is the solar panel dispute between China on the one side and the United States and the European Union on the other.[13] A number of European and American SMEs which install solar panels criticized the imposition of duties since they increased their input costs significantly.[14] Closely related to the solar panel dispute was the threat of China's Ministry of Commerce of starting an AD investigation into European wine exports to China.[15] The resulting AD duties would have had drastic consequences for European businesses, including the many small vineyards in France and Spain.[16] The investigation was, however, eventually stopped in March 2014 after an amicable agreement between China and the European Union had been reached.[17]

Taking part in TDI proceedings is particularly challenging for SMEs because meaningful participation generally requires 'a significant investment in terms of time, financial and human resources',[18] which SMEs frequently do not have at their disposal.[19] SMEs face particular difficulties in becoming aware of imminent TDI investigations that potentially affect them.[20] They also lack the knowledge on how

[13] European Commission, 'EU Imposes Provisional Anti-Dumping Duties on Chinese Solar Panels' (4 June 2013) MEMO-13-497 <http://europa.eu/rapid/press-release_MEMO-13-497_en.htm> accessed 20 January 2017; WTO, *United States—Countervailing Duty Measures on Certain Products from China*, Appellate Body Report (18 December 2014), WT/DS437/AB/R.

[14] Jennifer Runyon, 'Solar Panel Prices Expected to Rise in the US Due to New Tariffs on Chinese Panels' *Renewable Energy World.com* (28 July 2014) <http://www.renewableenergyworld.com/rea/news/article/2014/07/solar-panel-prices-expected-to-rise-in-the-us-due-to-new-tariffs-on-chinese-panels> accessed 20 January 2017.

[15] Keith Bradsher, 'China Aims at Europe's Wines after Solar Panel Action' *The New York Times* (New York, 6 June 2013) <http://www.nytimes.com/2013/06/06/business/global/china-to-investigate-eu-wine-after-subsidy-and-dumping-complaints.html?pagewanted=all&_r=0> accessed 20 January 2017.

[16] ibid.

[17] European Commission, 'European Commission Welcomes Agreement Reached between European and Chinese Wine Industries Which Will Put an End to China's Anti-Dumping and Anti-Subsidy Cases' (Press Release, 21 March 2014) <http://trade.ec.europa.eu/doclib/press/index.cfm?id=1048> accessed 20 January 2017.

[18] European Commission (n 2) 1, 19.

[19] See Jiju Antony, Maneesh Kumar, and Ashraf Labib, 'Gearing Six Sigma into UK Manufacturing SMEs: Results from a Pilot Study' (2008) 59 Journal of the Operational Research Society 482 <http://www.palgrave-journals.com/jors/journal/v59/n4/full/2602437a.html> accessed 20 January 2017, Table 1 ('Strengths and Weaknesses of SMEs'); Tom Gibson and Hubertus van der Vaart, 'Defining SMEs: A Less Imperfect Way of Defining Small and Medium Enterprises in Developing Countries' (2008) 11 <https://www.brookings.edu/research/defining-smes-a-less-imperfect-way-of-defining-small-and-medium-enterprises-in-developing-countries/> accessed 20 January 2017; Gide Loyrette Nouel (n 9) 9; Birgit Leick, Grit Leßmann, and Jens Nussbaum, 'Internationalisierungspfade mittelständischer Unternehmen in Osteuropa: Internationalisierungsprozess und Standorteffekte am Beispiel niedersächsischer KMU' (IfM-Materialien No 218, October 2012) 8 <http://www.ifm-bonn.org//uploads/tx_ifmstudies/IfM-Materialien-218_2012.pdf> accessed 20 January 2017; Edwin Vermulst and Olivier Prost, 'Modernization of the EU's Trade Defence Instruments (TDI)' (Workshop, April 2014), 42 <http://www.europarl.europa.eu/RegData/etudes/workshop/join/2014/433842/EXPO-INTA_AT%282014%29433842_EN.pdf> accessed 20 January 2017.

[20] Gide Loyrette Nouel (n 9) 19–21, 41–42; Cliff Stevenson Consulting, 'Research Project on the Impact of Anti-Dumping Investigations on UK Business' (Final Report, 12 July 2012) 12, 28 <https://

to participate effectively in TDI proceedings. At the same time, they are reluctant to hire external legal advisers given the considerable expense involved.[21] In addition, the collection, processing, and provision of information, which is required by the investigating authorities, represent a significant obstacle for SMEs.[22] The investigation authorities also frequently use only large companies as samples during TDI investigations.[23] Hence, SMEs are often subject to 'calculated duties' that sometimes do not correspond to their actual situation. Furthermore, small businesses are frequently not even aware of the consequences that TDI proceedings will have on them. They are therefore even more reluctant to dedicate their scarce resources towards monitoring and participating in such proceedings.[24] Overall, inherent capacity constraints hamper SMEs from participating adequately in TDI proceedings, leading to unfavourable outcomes for them.

With the growing recognition of the importance of SMEs for international trade, states have recently also shown more interest in addressing the difficulties of SMEs with regard to TDIs. For instance, the European Union has sponsored a study examining the difficulties encountered by SMEs in support of the reform of its TDIs.[25] A recent workshop of the EU Directorate-General on External Policies shows the diversity of reforms considered with a view to improving SME access to TDIs. The European Union is considering in particular strengthening SME help desks.[26] This measure is used by a number of WTO Members to support their own SMEs during an AD investigation.[27]

The state parties to the GATT attempted to address the issue of SME participation during the latest revision of the TDIs in the Uruguay Round (1986–1994). The most evident change in support of SMEs is the addition of Article 6.13 in the ADA and Article 12.11 in the Agreement on Subsidies and Countervailing Measures (SCM) in 1994. Both articles read: 'The authorities shall take due account of any

www.gov.uk/government/uploads/system/uploads/attachment_data/file/34580/12-1021-research-impact-anti-dumping-investigations-on-uk-business.pdf> accessed 20 January 2017.

[21] Cliff Stevenson Consulting (n 20) 14.

[22] Gide Loyrette Nouel (n 9) 24, 26–28, 37; International Trade Center (ITC), 'WTO Negotiations on the Agreement on Anti-Dumping Practices' (Business and the Multilateral Trade System, Technical Paper, 2005) 65 <http://www.economy.gov.tr/portal/content/conn/UCM/path/Contribution%20Folders/web/%C4%B0thalat/Ticaret%20Politikas%C4%B1%20Savunma%20Ara%C3%A7lar%C4%B1/T%C3%BCrk%20%C4%B0hra%C3%A7%20%C3%9Cr%C3%BCnlerine%20Y%C3%B6nelik%20Uygulanan%20TPSA%20%C3%96nlemleri/TPSA%20%C3%96nlemlerine%20%C4%B0li%C5%9Fkin%20Faydal%C4%B1%20Bilgiler/wtonegotiations.pdf> accessed 20 January 2017.

[23] Gide Loyrette Nouel (n 9) 36.

[24] ibid 19, 38.

[25] For example, Gide Loyrette Nouel (n 9); European Commission, 'Paper on Actions to Address the Difficulties Encountered by SMEs Involved in Trade Defence Instruments' (2011) <http://trade.ec.europa.eu/doclib/docs/2011/june/tradoc_148004.pdf> accessed 20 January 2017.

[26] Vermulst and Prost (n 19) 42.

[27] Examples are the Australian International Trade Remedies Advisory Service for SMEs <https://www.business.gov.au/advisory-services/international-trade-remedies-advisory-service> accessed 20 January 2017 and the European Union's SME Trade Defence Helpdesk (Gide Loyrette Nouel (n 9) 10, 14–15).

difficulties experienced by interested parties, in particular small companies, in supplying information requested, and shall provide any assistance practicable.'[28]

The two articles are of particular importance for SMEs since they are the only provisions in the agreements which mention small enterprises explicitly.

However, despite their significance for SMEs, Articles 6.13 ADA and 12.11 SCM have not received much attention. National AD and subsidy codes merely replicate their language without spelling out which special treatment and support schemes should be open to SMEs.[29] Moreover, neither article has yet been subject to litigation within the WTO with the notable exception of *US—Hot-Rolled Steel*,[30] which briefly referred to Article 6.13 ADA. In addition, academia largely seems to have turned a blind eye to the Articles. No papers have been written about them and commentaries on the ADA and the SCM merely rephrase the provisions without elaborating on them.[31] The recent EU-commissioned study on the difficulties of SMEs' use of TDIs is a notable exception.[32] The study even qualifies Article 6.13 ADA as the 'guiding legal principle' with regard to the treatment of SMEs during TDI proceedings.[33] However, the study does not provide a more extensive legal analysis of the specific consequences of this provision. In sum, the overall functioning and effects of Article 6.13 ADA remain obscure.

Against this backdrop, the present chapter attempts to shed some light on the unique provision of Article 6.13 ADA. It will be shown that the provision is undervalued and that it influences the application of other provisions of the TDI framework in situations involving SMEs.

The analysis focuses on the ADA because it governs more than 90 per cent of all trade defence measures.[34] Nevertheless, its results can be transposed by a large degree to the Subsidy and Countervailing Measures Agreement as both SME-specific provisions—Articles 6.13 ADA and 12.11 SCM—are identical and the agreements possess overall a very similar structure and language.[35]

[28] Art 6.13 ADA; Art 12.11 SCM.

[29] The European Union's basic AD regulation does not even copy Art 6.13 ADA nor makes any reference to SMEs. Council of the European Union, Council Regulation (EC) 1225/2009 of 30 November 2009 on protection against dumped imports from countries not members of the European Community [2009] OJ L343/51; see also Malaysia's Countervailing and Anti-Dumping Duties Act 1993 <http://www.miti.gov.my/miti/resources/fileupload/Countervailing_and_Anti-Dumping_Duties_Act_1993_[Act_504].pdf> accessed 20 January 2017.

[30] WTO, *United States—Anti-Dumping Measures on Certain Hot-Rolled Steel Products from Japan*, Appellate Body Report (24 July 2001), WT/DS184/AB/R (*US—Hot-Rolled Steel*, AB); WTO, *United States—Anti-Dumping Measures on Certain Hot-Rolled Steel Products from Japan*, Panel Report (28 February 2001), WT/DS184/AB/R (*US—Hot-Rolled Steel*, Panel).

[31] For example, Jean-Francois Bellis, 'Article 6 ADA' in Rüdiger Wolfrum, Peter-Tobias Stoll, and Michael Koebele (eds), *WTO: Trade Remedies*, vol 4 (Max Planck Commentaries on World Trade Law, Martinus Nijhoff 2008) 82–90; Edwin A Vermulst, *The WTO Anti-Dumping Agreement: A Commentary* (Oxford Commentaries on the GATT/WTO agreements, Oxford University Press 2005) 166.

[32] Gide Loyrette Nouel (n 9). In contrast, the 2012 research project on the impact of AD investigations on UK businesses does not reference once Art 6.13 ADA. Cliff Stevenson Consulting (n 20).

[33] Gide Loyrette Nouel (n 9) 15.

[34] Wu (n 1) 174.

[35] The WTO makes use of the similarity between ADA and SCM during the current Doha reform process. The Member States first discuss changes to the ADA with a view to subsequently transposing them, where appropriate, to the SCM. See WTO Negotiating Group on Rules, 'Possible Transposition of Texts on Anti-Dumping and Countervailing Measures' (18 June 2009) TN/RL/W/238, 12

Section B provides an overview of the procedure for conducting AD investigations in accordance with the WTO ADA. This will provide the context for the in-depth legal analysis of Article 6.13 ADA in the following parts. In Section C the scope of the obligations in Article 6.13 ADA and the limits of their application are explored. This section includes a discussion of the negotiation history of this provision. Finally, Section D discusses the radiating effect of this provision. It will show how Article 6.13 ADA serves as an interpretative guidance for other provisions of the ADA and how it hence affects the way in which SMEs need to be treated.

## B. An Overview of the WTO Anti-Dumping Agreement

In its eighteen Articles and two Annexes, the WTO Anti-Dumping Agreement sets out in detail the material and procedural requirements for the investigation, imposition, and review of AD duties. AD investigations are initiated after a complaint from the domestic industry has been received by the national authorities (Article 5.1 ADA) or in exceptional cases on the national investigating authorities' own initiative[36] (Article 5.6 ADA). The complainants need to include sufficient evidence to show that: (i) dumping takes place; (ii) the domestic industry has sustained an injury; and (iii) a causal link between the dumping and the injury exists (Article 5.2 ADA). If the national authorities are satisfied that the evidence is sufficient, an official investigation is started to 'verify whether the legal conditions to impose [AD] measures are fulfilled and to establish the level of the measures'[37] (Articles 5.1–5.2 ADA). After notifying the initiation of the investigation (Article 12.1 ADA), national authorities will register 'interested parties' who want to participate in it (Article 6.1 ADA), for example, exporters of an allegedly dumped product, local producers competing with the foreign product, or users of a dumped product or the government of an exporting Member (Article 6.11 ADA). During the investigation, the investigation authorities will collect information from various sources ranging from questionnaires (Article 6.1.1 ADA), which are provided to the interested parties, to optional on-site visits at the exporter's premises (Article 6.7 ADA). At the end of an investigation, the national authorities may impose a definitive AD duty (Article 9 ADA). If required, the authorities may impose provisional duties during the investigation to prevent injury to the domestic economy (Article 7 ADA). The authorities are required to disclose the final determination including their reasoning (Article 12.2 ADA) and provide interested parties with the opportunity to comment on their determination before imposing definitive measures. AD measures are normally imposed for five years, but can be extended for another

<https://docs.wto.org/dol2fe/Pages/FE_Search/DDFDocuments/69333/Q/TN/RL/W238.pdf> accessed 20 January 2017.

[36] This possibility was designed specifically with the needs of SMEs in mind. Vermulst and Prost (n 19) 9, 20.

[37] EU Commission (n 2) 9.

five-year period after a review investigation. However, AD duties shall remain in force only as long as and to the extent necessary (Article 11.1 ADA). The initial investigation shall, except in special circumstances, be concluded within one year and in no case later than eighteen months after its initiation (Article 5.10).

As an alternative to anti-dumping duties, an exporter may offer price undertakings (Article 8 ADA). This means it offers to export a product above a certain price limit. If such offer is accepted by the national authorities, this exporter can be exempt from punitive duties. However, such price undertaking offers need not be accepted by the authorities (Article 8.3 ADA) and even if accepted the exporter will be subject to a strict monitoring system and frequent reporting obligations (Article 8.6 ADA).

Decisions regarding AD measures can be challenged in a domestic court by those affected claiming that national legislation has not been applied correctly (Article 13 ADA). In addition, AD measures can also be challenged in WTO dispute settlement proceedings if it is considered that WTO provisions have not been applied correctly (Article 17 ADA and Annex II WTO Agreement). However, this procedure cannot be initiated by an individual company—only by WTO Members.

## C. Discovering the Meaning of Article 6.13 ADA

### I. The dual obligation

The ADA is designed to ensure cooperation between those who investigate, those who are investigated, and other parties who have an interest in the investigation. The Appellate Body (AB) and Panels have held in this context that the principle of good faith, which is a general principle of international law, is crucial for the ADA.[38] It informs the interpretation of the Agreement by requiring to strike a balance between the interests of all parties involved in the investigation, and by ensuring that no party suffers any serious disadvantage.[39]

Article 6.13 ADA can be seen as an expression of the principles of good faith, proportionality, and due process restating the premises on which the ADA is based.[40] This provision prevents the imposition of undue burdens upon interested parties due to their specific circumstances or capacity constraints. In *US—Hot-Rolled Steel*, the AB used Article 6.13 ADA to support its interpretation of paragraphs 2 and 5 of Annex II which, according to the AB, call for a careful balance between the interests of investigating authorities and interested parties.[41] The AB specified that while investigating authorities can expect a 'significant degree of effort' from interested

[38] *US—Hot-Rolled Steel* (AB), paras 100–02; WTO, *Egypt—Definitive Anti-Dumping Measures on Steel Rebar from Turkey*, Panel Report (8 August 2002) WT/DS211/R (*Egypt—Steel Rabar*), para 7.161.

[39] For instance, para 2 of Annex II, which prevents the investigating authorities from establishing unreasonable burdens when requesting evidence and to insist on absolute standards, has been described as a 'detailed expression of the principle of faith': see *US—Hot-Rolled Steel* (AB), para 101.

[40] Gide Loyrette Nouel (n 9) 16–17.

[41] *US—Hot-Rolled Steel* (AB), para 102; Gide Loyrette Nouel (n 9) 16, 43.

parties when cooperating with the authorities, the authorities need to refrain from 'insist[ing] upon *absolute* standards or impos[ing] *unreasonable* burdens upon them'.[42] Referring to Article 6.13 ADA directly, the AB added: 'Article 6.13 … underscores that "cooperation" is … a two-way process involving joint effort. [It] requires investigating authorities to make certain allowances for, or take action to assist, interested parties in supplying information.'[43]

The statement of the AB clarifies that Article 6.13 ADA places two distinct obligations upon the investigating authorities, namely an obligation to 'make … allowances for' and an obligation 'to assist' SMEs and other disadvantaged parties (the provision is not strictly limited to SMEs). Whereas the first obligation requires authorities to consider the impact of their actions such as requests for information directed to SMEs (and other disadvantaged parties) and adjust their actions accordingly, the second obligation requires the authorities to proactively apply measures in support of SMEs (and other disadvantaged parties) whenever practicable for them.

The wording of Article 6.13 ADA gives a first indication of the degree of effort expected from the investigating authorities. First, the wording '*shall* take due account' and '*shall* provide' indicates that the obligations are mandatory and not merely hortatory.[44] Second, the word 'any' in the phrase 'take due account of *any* difficulties' and 'provide *any* assistance practicable'[45] shows that the obligations placed upon the investigating authorities are extensive. In the first phrase, 'any' requires the authorities to consider all types of handicaps. This phrase contains no language limiting it only to the most severe capacity constraints. The inclusion of the word 'any' in the second phrase indicates that the provision refers to diverse types of assistance and that a high degree of assistance is required. However, the obligation to assist is limited by the word 'practicable', which balances the interest of the handicapped parties in participating in the investigation proceedings with the ability of the investigating authorities to offer special support. Overall, the language of Article 6.13 ADA seems to require substantial efforts on the part of the investigating authorities to accommodate the needs of SMEs during the investigation.

However, despite the mandatory language and the broad scope of the obligations, it is difficult to derive concrete and actionable obligations to support handicapped parties from the clause alone. Article 6.13 ADA does not define which support is required and how the difficulties for SMEs and other disadvantaged parties need to be taken into account. In the light of its vagueness, Edwin Vermulst even categorizes Article 6.13 ADA as merely a 'soft obligation'.[46]

The vagueness of the paragraph was also discussed during the Doha negotiations. Several proposals have been made to specify the obligations contained in Article

[42] *US—Hot-Rolled Steel* (AB) para 102 (emphases in original). [43] ibid, para 104.

[44] Emphases added. In *US—Stainless Steel (Korea)*, the Panel stated during the analysis of the wording 'should' in Art 2.4 ADA that 'shall' is mandatory language. Whereas 'should' only permits certain actions, 'shall' requires them. See WTO, *United States—Anti-Dumping Measures on Stainless Steel Plate in Coils and Stainless Steel Sheet and Strip from Korea*, Panel Report (22 December 2000), WT/DS179/R, para 6.93 and n 102.

[45] Emphases added. [46] Vermulst (n 31) 166.

6.13 ADA. The latest reform draft of 2011 notes that the duty to provide assistance includes, inter alia, the obligation to 'respond … in a timely manner to requests for clarification of questionnaires'.[47] In the earlier draft of 2008, some delegations suggested to specify that the authorities shall assist small enterprises to identify information that is needed by the authorities. The 2008 draft also proposed to introduce the term '(SME)' after 'small companies'.[48] However, even with those additions the scope of the obligation would not be clear. The proposals show, nevertheless, that Article 6.13 ADA is intended to require an increased interaction between the interested parties, in particular SMEs, and the investigating authorities.

It is unfortunate that the vagueness of the paragraph has not yet been further clarified via an explanatory note of the state parties or by WTO case law. The *US—Hot-Rolled Steel* case showed, however, that Article 6.13 ADA is not merely a 'paper tiger', but has a real impact on AD proceedings. In this case, the AB used Article 6.13 ADA to describe the type of cooperation required with regard to Article 6.8 ADA. The latter provision permits the investigating authorities to make assumptions on the basis of the facts available when they lack information because the investigated parties have not cooperated sufficiently. The AB concluded that: 'If the investigating authorities fail to "take due account" of genuine "difficulties" experienced by interested parties, and made known to the investigating authorities, they cannot … fault the interested parties concerned for a lack of cooperation.'[49]

It is noteworthy that the quote refers to 'genuine' difficulties, indicating difficulties specific to the interested parties. The AB hence clarifies that the term 'any difficulties' in Article 6.13 ADA only refers to difficulties stemming from the characteristics of the interested party.

It is difficult to deduce the exact normative content of Article 6.13 ADA from its wording and the sparse case law alone. For that reason, an analysis of the drafting history of this provision is particularly helpful.

## II. The genesis of Article 6.13 ADA

Article 6.13 ADA is an innovation which stems from the latest revision of the WTO anti-dumping framework during the Uruguay Round (1986–1994). Neither of the two prior versions of the ADA (1968[50] and 1979[51]) contained any provisions protecting SMEs and other disadvantaged parties.

[47] WTO Negotiating Group on Rules, 'Communication from the Chairman' (21 April 2011) TN/RL/W/254, 16 <https://www.wto.org/english/tratop_e/dda_e/chair_texts11_e/adp_subsidies_e.doc> accessed 20 January 2017.

[48] WTO Negotiating Group on Rules, 'Working Document from the Chairman: Annex A' TN/RL/W/232, A-67 <https://docs.wto.org/dol2fe/Pages/FE_Search/FE_S_S006.aspx?MetaCollection=WTO&SymbolList=%22TN/RL/W/232%22+OR+%22TN/RL/W/232/%22> accessed 20 January 2017.

[49] *US—Hot-Rolled Steel* (AB), para 104.

[50] 1968 Anti-Dumping Code (n 4).

[51] Agreement on Implementation of Art VI of the General Agreement on Tariffs and Trade (signed 12 April 1979) 1186 UNTS 2 (1979 Anti-Dumping Code).

The Uruguay negotiation documents show a broad recognition of the need to support small companies. They contain different proposals on how the situation of SMEs could be improved. While stressing that AD investigations should be company-specific, a number of delegations recognized at the same time that 'small companies [can] have genuine difficulties in responding to or participating fully in [those] investigations'.[52] The Hong Kong delegation explained that 'it was not the intention of the [Anti-Dumping] Code that companies which could not comply with the very technical requirements should be unfairly penalized'.[53] This statement, which is an unequivocal expression of the principle of good faith, was not challenged during the negotiation. Another delegation, whose statement also remained unopposed, added that 'flexibility should be shown' with regard to small companies.[54] A different delegation stated that such flexibility should apply to foreign exporters and complaining domestic companies alike since small companies of both sides face similar obstacles.[55]

During the negotiations, Hong Kong provided the most concrete proposals on how such flexibility could be achieved. Its first proposal aimed at improving the procedure for requesting information from SMEs. Hong Kong requested adding the following passage to Article 6.1 ADA:

> Any request for information by the authorities concerned shall be restricted to information essential to the investigation. When drawing up such request and when analysing the evidence received in response to such a request, the authorities concerned shall take special account of the difficulties which may be experienced by small producers in providing the evidence requested.[56]

Hong Kong explained that this text was intended to make special allowances for SMEs 'with regard to the *volume* and *detail* of information required from them'.[57] With its proposal Hong Kong advocated 'special measures, [such as] simplified questionnaire[s] [that] would enable small companies to participate in the investigation to the best of their ability'.[58]

The second proposal aimed at improving Article 8.2 ADA (today's Article 9.2 ADA), which deals with the imposition of AD duties and the acceptance of price undertakings.[59] Hong Kong proposed adding a subparagraph calling upon the investigating authorities to 'take into account the special situation of small companies which are unable to participate fully in the investigation due to lack of

[52] GATT Negotiating Group on Multilateral Trade Negotiations (MTN), 'Meeting of 31 January–2 February and 19–20 February 1990' (19 March 1990) MTN.GNG/NG8/15, 41.

[53] ibid. [54] ibid. [55] ibid.

[56] 'Addendum to Communication from the Delegation from Hong Kong: Amendments to the Anti-Dumping Code' (21 March 1990) MTN.GNG/NG8/W/51/Add.2, 5 <http://www.worldtradelaw.net/history/urad/w51a2.pdf> accessed 20 January 2017.

[57] ibid (emphases added).

[58] 'Addendum to Communication from the Delegation from Hong Kong: Amendments to the Anti-Dumping Code' (22 December 1989) MTN.GNG/NG8/W/51/Add.1, 5 <http://www.worldtradelaw.net/history/urad/w51a1.pdf> accessed 20 January 2017.

[59] Companies can avoid the imposition of AD duties by voluntarily raising their export prices. This voluntary price increase is called 'price undertaking'.

resources. Such companies shall provide, to the best possible extent, any available information required by the investigating authorities'.[60]

The delegation from Hong Kong clarified that this wording requires SMEs to be given '*sympathetic consideration* if they can provide evidence of their problems and demonstrate their willingness to furnish all the information within their means'.[61]

In the end, most of Hong Kong's proposals did not find their way into the new agreement. Instead of the specific and elaborate provisions proposed by Hong Kong, the only remaining reference to SMEs can be found in today's Article 6.13 ADA.

However, the lack of controversy about the proposals made by Hong Kong[62] and the inclusion of Article 6.13 ADA allows for four assumptions. First, the inclusion of Article 6.13 ADA to facilitate the participation of SMEs in AD proceedings was widely accepted. Second, the ideas put forward by Hong Kong and the text of Article 6.13 ADA did not oppose each other. Article 6.13 ADA was rather thought to be a simplification and bundling of Hong Kong's proposals in one specific paragraph. The delegations hoped that this single paragraph, in which they enshrined two general mandatory obligations, would suffice to guarantee proper treatment of SMEs throughout the entire ADA. Consequently, Article 6.13 ADA is of relevance for the interpretation of other provisions in the ADA. It should not be understood as a self-contained article. Third, the specific proposals made by Hong Kong provide an indication as to the interpretative effects Article 6.13 ADA should have. Fourth, the unchallenged statements of the negotiating parties on the objective, scope, and purpose of SME support clauses in the Uruguay draft text remain relevant for the interpretation of Article 6.13 ADA.

## III. The limits of Article 6.13 ADA

Whereas the previous two sections showed the extensiveness of the obligations contained in Article 6.13 ADA and the high ambition attached to the Article, the current section will examine the possible limitations of Article 6.13 ADA. The section will focus on three aspects. It will first explore the meaning of 'interested parties', ie to whom the provision applies, before considering the phrase 'in supplying information requested'. It will finally discuss whether the placement of the provision at the end of Article 6 limits its interpretative effect.[63]

### *1. The term 'interested parties'*

The term 'interested parties' is defined in Article 6.11 ADA. This provision explains that the term 'shall include' exporters and importers of a product under consideration, the government of an exporting Member, and domestic producers of a competing product in the importing state. In addition, WTO Members are not

60 Hong Kong (n 56) 6.
61 ibid (emphasis added).
62 Negotiating Group on MTN (n 52).
63 The meaning of the word 'practicable' at the end of the paragraph has already been addressed in Section C.I.

precluded 'from allowing domestic or foreign parties other than those mentioned [in the list] as interested parties'.[64] This shows that the benefits of Article 6.13 ADA are not limited to exporters only. This is particularly important for domestic SMEs which want to participate in AD investigations. Domestic SMEs may have an interest in the investigations either because they need to prevent AD duties that raise the costs of their production inputs or because they require the imposition of duties to protect their businesses against foreign competitors. This notion also finds support in the *travaux préparatoires*.[65]

## 2. *The term 'in supplying information requested'*

The understanding of the phrase 'in supplying information requested' is of key importance for determining the scope of the provision and defines which other provisions of the ADA are impacted by Article 6.13 ADA. Reading the phrase *stricto sensu* limits the application of this provision to situations where the authorities have directly asked interested parties to submit information—for example, the completion of the questionnaires sent to exporters (Article 6.1.1 ADA).[66] Such a strict interpretation would exclude the situation in which interested parties submit information *proprio motu* to the investigating authorities. For instance, Article 6.12 ADA provides users of allegedly dumped products with the opportunity to supply the authorities with information relevant to the investigation. The wording of Article 6.12 ADA does not require the authorities to proactively request such information. A reading of the phrase 'in supplying information requested' in Article 6.13 ADA *lato sensu* would, however, include the scenario covered by Article 6.12 ADA.

A closer examination of Article 6.13 ADA supports a broad understanding of the phrase 'in supplying information requested', despite the inclusion of the word 'requested', the dictionary meaning of which describes the 'act of asking politely or formally for something'.[67] The reading of the phrase 'information requested' as referring rather to 'information relevant to the investigation' or 'information submitted in conformity with the AD-Agreement' can be based on the structure, context, purpose, and historical origins of Article 6.13 ADA. First, the paragraph refers to the supply of information by 'interested parties', a term which includes in addition to exporters also other entities.[68] It would be illogical to use the term 'interested parties' if a strict reading of 'information requested' were to de facto limit the provision to exporters only, given that they are the only category of interested

[64] Art 6.11 Second Sentence ADA. See also Vermulst (n 31) 165.

[65] Negotiating Group on MTN (n 52) 40. See Section C.II. Therefore, the statement of Bellis in his commentary that 'Article 6.13 ADA aims at meeting the needs of small- and medium-sized companies of *exporting countries*' (emphasis added) is misguided; see Bellis (n 31) 121.

[66] Another example is Art 6.8 ADA which regulates the investigating authorities' options if requested information is not received.

[67] John Simpson and Edmund Weiner, 'Requested' in *Oxford English Dictionary: 20 Volume Set and CD-ROM* (Oxford University Press 2009).

[68] Art 6.11(iii) ADA.

parties subject to a proactive enquiry for information by the investigating authorities. The negotiation documents show that the provision was intended to address the difficulties of complaining and investigated companies.[69] Second, it does not make sense to limit a general provision designed to foster cooperation between SMEs and the investigating authorities to proactive information requests.[70] This would exclude a major source of information from the requirement to cooperate, ie *proprio motu* submissions. The negotiation history shows that Article 6.13 ADA was thought to address the 'genuine difficulties [of small companies to] respond ... to or *participat[e] fully in investigations*'.[71]

Considering these arguments, the phrase 'in supplying information requested' still retains a limiting effect. It confines the extensive obligations to assist and take into account difficulties to facilitating the *participation* of SMEs in the AD proceedings. In contrast, the obligations laid down in Article 6.13 ADA do not apply to the consideration whether to apply duties or whether to accept voluntary price undertakings. A proposal made by Hong Kong during the Uruguay Round to 'take into account the special situation of small companies which are unable to participate fully in the investigations due to lack of resources' during the *determination* of AD duties was not included in the current ADA.[72] This is the only instance where the wording of Article 6.13 ADA and the Hong Kong proposals are contradictory. The current text focuses only on facilitating the participation of SMEs in the investigation. It does not improve their position with regard to the actual determination whether or not to apply dumping duties.

### 3. *The positioning of paragraph 13 at the end of Article 6*

Another important determinant of the value of Article 6.13 ADA is the reach of its interpretative effect. It could be argued that the placement of the SME provision at the very end of Article 6 ADA suggests that it was designed to elaborate only on the prior paragraphs and should hence only be used for their interpretation. If the provision were intended to have a more general effect, it should have been enshrined in a separate Article in a similar manner to the provision supporting developing countries in Article 15 ADA.

Such limitation of the effect of Article 6.13 ADA is not appropriate for three reasons. First, the argument that a general provision should have been enshrined in a separate Article is weak because of the overall form and structure of the ADA. The Articles of the ADA form one coherent framework and rely upon each other. For instance, Article 5 ADA (Initiation and Subsequent Investigation) establishes the procedural sequence for the AD investigation in which Articles 2 (Determination of Dumping), 3 (Determination of Injury), 4 (Definition of Domestic Industry), and

[69] Negotiating Group on MTN (n 52) 41. [70] *US—Hot-Rolled Steel* (AB), para 104.

[71] Negotiating Group on MTN (n 52) 41 (emphasis added). See also explanatory note on Hong Kong's amendment proposal on Art 8.2 ADA: 'special consideration be given to small companies which have genuine difficulties in participating in the investigation', Hong Kong (n 56) 6.

[72] Hong Kong (n 56) 6.

6 ADA (Evidence) must be applied.[73] Second, the negotiating history reveals that it is the purpose of Article 6.13 ADA to facilitate the participation of handicapped parties (both investigated and complaining) in the AD proceedings based on the principle of good faith.[74] Paragraph 13 was designed as a general provision relevant to the entire AD investigation. This is highlighted by the fact that the paragraph was introduced instead of other provisions suggested for the benefit of SMEs which were scattered throughout the ADA.[75] Article 6.13 ADA replaced, for instance, drafts of provisions in Articles 5 and 8 ADA.[76] Third, the wording of Article 6.13 ADA does not limit its application. Unlike paragraphs 1, 2, and 6 of Article 6, no language limiting paragraph 13 to the investigation stage is included. In conclusion, the two obligations contained in Article 6.13 ADA reach beyond Article 6 and therefore affect the interpretation of provisions outside Article 6 ADA.[77]

In sum, the three issues examined do not significantly narrow the scope of Article 6.13 ADA. It provides an interpretative guidance for legal clauses beyond Article 6 ADA.[78] Its supporting function is not limited to the investigated exporters, but facilitates the participation of many different parties in the AD proceedings. Only the clause 'in supplying information requested' slightly limits the differential treatment of SMEs (and other disadvantaged parties). Because of this phrase, their capacity constraints are only relevant during participation in the AD investigation, but need not be taken into account when the authorities make the actual decision whether to impose duties or rather accept undertakings.

## IV. The effect of Article 6.13 ADA

The effect of Article 6.13 ADA on the AD proceedings is twofold. On the one hand, paragraph 13—taken by itself—defines 'the mindset' for the interaction between the investigating authorities and SMEs. It establishes a cooperative framework. However, because of the broad and unspecific language, it is difficult to deduce concrete and actionable obligations directly from the text.[79] On the other hand, Article 6.13 ADA provides an interpretative guideline for the numerous provisions relating to the supply of information in the ADA. It modifies their effect with a view to ensuring better treatment of SMEs.[80] In this way, Article 6.13 ADA functions like the first paragraph of Article III GATT. It is generally accepted that Article III:1 GATT merely postulates the general principle of national treatment,

[73] cf WTO, *European Communities—Anti Dumping Duties on Imports of Cotton Type Bed Linen from India—Recourse to Article 21.5 of the DSU*, Appellate Body Report (24 April 2003) WT/DS141/AB/RW, para 136. For instance, Arts 5.7 and 5.8 ADA directly refer to 'evidence' which is regulated in Art 6 ADA.

[74] See the previous Section C.I on the genesis of the Article.

[75] See Section C.II.

[76] Hong Kong (n 56) 5–7.

[77] See Section C.IV.

[78] In this respect, Art 6.13 ADA bears some similarities to 'principles' within the meaning of Robert Alexy's *Theory of Constitutional Rights*. Robert Alexy, *A Theory of Constitutional Rights* (Oxford University Press 2010) chs 5, 10.

[79] See Section D.I.

[80] It impacts in particular Arts 2.4, 5.2, 6.1, 6.2, 6.8, 6.9, 6.10, and 8.6 ADA. See Section D.

but has no direct legal effect in itself. The first paragraph only guides the interpretation of Articles III:2 and III:4 GATT which contain more specific national treatment regulations.[81]

This radiating effect is what makes Article 6.13 ADA most valuable for SMEs. It opens the door for a capacity-based interpretation of the ADA. This means that some provisions dealing with the supply of information are addressee-specific, ie the standard for the treatment of the businesses involved depends on their individual financial, personnel, and organizational resources.

Such capacity-based interpretation is possible where the language of the ADA is sufficiently flexible. Some provisions grant a broad margin of appreciation to the investigating authorities. For instance, Article 6.1.1 ADA requires the investigating authorities to give 'due consideration … to any request for an extension [of the timeframe provided to exporters to respond to questionnaires] … upon cause shown'. Other provisions contain undefined legal terms such as 'reasonable' or 'sufficient'. For example, Article 5.2 ADA uses the wording 'reasonably available' to describe the quality of the information to be submitted. Article 6.8 ADA calls for the provision of information by investigated exporters within a 'reasonable period'. In Article 6.9 ADA, investigating authorities are asked to provide 'sufficient' time for parties to defend their interest. Article 2.4 ADA prohibits the imposition of 'an unreasonable burden of proof' upon those parties asked to provide information relating to normal values and export prices. Moreover, Article 6.2 ADA grants a 'full opportunity for the defense of their interests' to all interested parties.

Because of Article 6.13 ADA, which focuses on the individual party, such flexible language must be understood as setting an addressee-specific rather than a fixed standard. This means that what is, for instance, 'reasonable' must not be assessed from a generic perspective, but depends on the capacity of the individual party. A capacity-based interpretation creates an individual standard. This subjective approach is supported by the idea that the interaction among the parties in the ADA should be based on the principles of good faith, proportionality, and due process.[82] No party should suffer significant disadvantages during the AD proceedings because of its individual constraints.[83]

The use of capacity-based provisions, ie provisions which require different actions depending on the individual capacity of those addressed by them, is not uncommon in international law.[84] WTO law contains several provisions to

[81] WTO, *European Communities—Measures Affecting Asbestos and Products Containing Asbestos*, Appellate Body Report (12 March 2001) WT/DS135/AB/R, 98; see also Christian Tietje, *Internationales Wirtschaftsrecht* (De Gruyter Recht 2015) § 3, para 77.

[82] *US—Hot-Rolled Steel* (AB), paras 100–102; *Egypt—Steel Rebar*, para 7.161.

[83] In *US—Hot-Rolled Steel* (AB), the AB pointed towards paragraph 2 of Annex II as an example for the principle of good faith. It stressed that in this context the objective was to strike a balance between the efforts of those involved in the investigation and their practical ability to deliver information. *US—Hot-Rolled Steel* (AB), para 101.

[84] The opposite are provisions which are 'absolute' and 'non-discriminatory', ie provisions which establish common standards for every addressed actor to comply with. An example is fixed deadlines.

support developing countries.[85] Article XI of the WTO Agreement states that least-developed nations 'will only be required to undertake commitments and concessions to the extent consistent with their individual development, financial and trade needs or their administrative and institutional capabilities'. The preamble of the OECD Convention asks developed nations to cooperate to the best of their abilities with countries in the process of economic development.[86] The UN Convention on the Rights of the Child also contains a capacity-based provision in Article 27. The Article holds that 'parents have the duty to ensure ... to the *best of their ability* [a standard of living for their child, which is adequate]'.[87] In addition, Article 5.2 of the Additional Protocol II to the Geneva Conventions requires that 'those who are responsible for the internment or detention of the persons referred to in Paragraph 1 shall also, *within the limits of their capabilities*, respect the following provisions relating to such persons ...'.[88] The capacity-based provisions in these examples prevent unreasonable burdens.[89] They reflect the idea that in absolute terms[90] a

[85] This type of discrimination is described as 'special and differential treatment'. Examples are Art XVIII of GATT 1947 which embraced Governmental Assistance to Economic Development, the General System of Preferences which was introduced to GATT in 1968, or the Enabling Clause introduced in 1979.

[86] Preamble Convention on the Organisation for Economic Co-operation and Development (signed 14 December 1960, entered into force 30 September 1961) 888 UNTS 180 (OECD Convention). Another example for capacity-based provisions relating to the capacity of states is Art 194.1 UN Convention on the Law of the Sea (16 November 1994) A/CONF.62/122 & Corrs (UNCLOS). The idea of capacity-based discrimination is also enshrined in the principle of common but differentiated responsibility. UN Environment Programme, 'Rio Declaration on Environment and Development' (Earth Summit on Sustainable Development, 14 June 1992) UN Doc A/CONF.151/26 (vol I) (Rio Declaration) Principle 7 <http://cil.nus.edu.sg/1992/1992-rio-declaration-on-environment-and-development> accessed 20 January 2017; United Nations, 'Decision 1/CP3 Adoption of the Kyoto Protocol to the United Nations Framework Convention on Climate Change' (Report of the Conference of the Parties on Its Third Session, Held at Kyoto from 1 to 11 December 1997, 25 March 1998) FCCC/CP/1997/7/Add.1 (Kyoto Protocol) Art 10 <http://unfccc.int/resource/docs/cop3/07a01.pdf> accessed 20 January 2017; UN Framework Convention on Climate Change (adopted 9 May 1992, entered into force 21 April 1994) 31 International Legal Materials 849 (UNFCCC) Preamble and Art 3.1. See also Rowena Maguire and Bridget Lewis, 'The Influence of Justice Theories on International Climate Policies and Measures' (2012) 8 Macquarie Journal of International and Comparative Environmental Law 16, 32; Council of Europe, *Manual on Human Rights and the Environment* (2nd edn, Council of Europe Publishing 2012) 132.

[87] Article 27 of the Convention on the Rights of the Child (signed 20 November 1989, entered into force 2 September 1990) 1577 UNTS 3 (emphasis added).

[88] Article 5.2 of the Protocol Additional to the Geneva Conventions of 12 August 1949, and Relating to the Protection of Victims of Non-International Armed Conflicts (Protocol II) (adopted 8 June 1977, entered into force 7 December 1978) 1125 UNTS 609 (emphasis added). See also Art 10.1 of the Protocol Additional to the Geneva Conventions of 12 August 1949, and Relating to the Protection of Victims of International Armed Conflicts (Protocol I) (adopted 8 June 1977, entered into force 7 December 1978) 1125 UNTS 3 (emphasis added).

[89] The notion is related to the concept of 'capacity-based noncompliance' discussed in Jacob K Cogan, 'Noncompliance and the International Rule of Law' (2005) 31 Yale Journal of International Law 189.

[90] See comments on Art 6.8 ADA in the following section. Absolute terms refer, for instance, to man power and monetary resources dedicated.

higher degree of effort can be expected from those who have more resources than from those with fewer resources.

The following section discusses in more depth how Article 6.13 ADA serves as interpretative guidance for the individual provisions of the ADA.

## D. The Specific Interpretative Effects of Article 6.13 ADA

Article 6.13 ADA provides the basis for interpreting the ADA's specific provisions related to the supply of information by the interested parties. It supports a capacity-based interpretation of such provisions that contain sufficiently flexible language.[91] The effects of Article 6.13 ADA on other provisions can be grouped in three categories: it relaxes the submission requirements for information;[92] requires investigating authorities to provide support proactively;[93] and prevents negative discrimination of handicapped parties.[94] The following three sections provide salient examples for all three categories.

### I. Relaxing submission requirements

Article 6.13 ADA relaxes the submission requirements through easing the time frames[95] and formal submission criteria.[96] It also relates to the acceptance of insufficiencies in the quality and quantity of information provided by the interested parties when such deficiencies result from capacity constraints.[97]

#### *1. Quality and quantity of information*

Provisions establishing a quality and quantity threshold for information submitted by the interested parties which are affected by Article 6.13 ADA include Articles 2.4, 5.2, 6.8, and 8.6 ADA.

*Article 6.8 ADA* allows the investigating authorities to make determinations based on 'facts available' if an 'interested party refuses' or 'otherwise does not provide necessary information' within 'a reasonable period'. It establishes a minimum standard for the quality, quantity, format, and timeliness of the information which interested parties need to provide. Its purpose is to permit the investigating authorities to continue the AD proceedings when 'the first best information', ie information provided by the parties, is not available.[98] Determinations on the basis of the facts available frequently hurt the parties which failed to provide information, as

[91] See the previous Section C.IV for the reasoning.
[92] For example, Arts 2.4, 5.2, 6.1.1, 6.8, 6.9, 6.12, and 8.6 ADA.
[93] For example, Arts 2.4, 6.8, and 6.9 ADA.
[94] For example, Art 6.10 ADA.
[95] For example, Arts 6.1.1, 6.8, 6.9, 6.12, and 8.6 ADA.
[96] For example, Art 6.8 ADA.
[97] For example, Arts 2.4, 5.2, and 8.6 ADA.
[98] *US—Hot-Rolled Steel* (Panel), paras 7.72, 7.55.

the investigative authorities tend to use information which is not optimal or even disadvantageous for the interested party.[99]

Annex II of the ADA specifies how Article 6.8 ADA needs to be applied.[100] In particular, its paragraphs 5 and 7 create an opening for a capacity-based interpretation benefitting small companies.

*Paragraph 5 of Annex II* prevents the authorities from disregarding information that 'may not be ideal in all respects', if the providing party has 'acted to the best of its ability'. The paragraph hence describes the degree of cooperation as well as the quality of information the investigating authorities can expect from interested parties.[101] The wording 'best of *its* ability' suggests—especially when read together with Article 6.13 ADA—that the specific cooperation required by paragraph 5 of Annex II is dependent on a party's individual capacity. Parties with limited personnel and financial resources, such as SMEs, are not expected to produce the same cooperation results as 'more capable' parties. In *Egypt—Steel Rebar*, the Panel noted during its analysis of paragraph 5:

> Information that is of a *very high quality, although not perfect*, must not be considered unverifiable solely because of its minor flaws, so long as the submitter has acted to the best of its ability. That is, so long as the level of good faith cooperation by the interested party is high, slightly imperfect information should not be dismissed as unverifiable.[102]

This statement also shows that the investigating authorities only need to accept minor deficiencies. Low quality and incomplete information need not be accepted, just because the providing party acted to the best of its abilities.[103] This is because 'an interested party's level of effort to submit certain information does not necessarily have anything to do with the substantive quality of the information submitted, and in any case is not the only determinant thereof'.[104]

Consequently, paragraph 5 of Annex II cannot 'save' SMEs in all instances. If SMEs fail to provide substantial information because of their capacity constraints despite acting to the best of their abilities, this provision does not prevent investigating authorities from making determinations on the basis of the facts available. Paragraph 5 of Annex II merely forces investigating authorities to accept

[99] For example, the US legislation allows authorities to use 'adverse facts available' (19 USC §1677e(b)), *US—Hot-Rolled Steel* (AB), paras 67, 94–95, nn 45 and 60. In practice, the paragraph is a 'powerful weapon' in the hands of the authorities, which can be easily abused. See Vermulst (n 31) 146.

[100] Article 6.8 ADA specifies that 'the provisions of Annex II shall be observed in the application of the paragraph'. The Annex forms an integral part of Art 6.8 ADA. *Egypt—Steel Rebar*, para 7.153; *US—Hot-Rolled Steel* (AB), para 75; WTO, *Argentina—Definitive Anti-Dumping Measures on Carton-Board Imports from Germany and Definitive Anti-Dumping Measures on Imports of Ceramic Tiles from Italy*, Panel Report (5 November 2001) WT/DS189/R (*Argentina—Ceramic Tiles*), paras 6.55, 6.67, 6.74.

[101] See also para 3 of Annex II.

[102] *Egypt—Steel Rebar*, para 7.161 (emphasis added). The statement also referred to para 3 of Annex II ADA.

[103] See interplay of para 5 with paras 2 and 3 of Annex II.

[104] *Egypt—Steel Rebar*, para 7.242. The Panel also referred to the AB in *US—Hot-Rolled Steel* (AB), which stated: 'The fact of "cooperating" is in itself not determinative of the end result of the cooperation.' *US—Hot-Rolled Steel* (AB), para 99.

information provided by SMEs which contains minor deficiencies caused by capacity constraints of interested parties if the party has acted to the best of its ability. It effectively combines an obligation of conduct (to cooperate) with an obligation of result (to produce sufficient information).

*Paragraph 7 of Annex II* regulates the manner in which the investigating authorities should select, check, and apply facts to fill information gaps, including those gaps which exist despite the interested parties acting to the best of their abilities. In principle, the investigating authorities need to base their decisions on the 'best information available'.[105] This means 'that information has to be not simply correct or useful per se, rather, it must be the most fitting or most appropriate information available in the case at hand'.[106] Where the authorities use secondary sources, they must do so with 'special circumspection', ie they must check their plausibility.[107] Using 'special circumspection' does not rule out that the authorities may have to choose among a number of equally credible options.[108]

A key question for SMEs is whether the authorities may knowingly select facts which are to their detriment—bearing in mind that AD measures are frequently (ab-)used for protectionist purposes.[109] The last sentence of paragraph 7 of Annex II indicates that parties which have 'not cooperate[d]' and hence have 'withheld … relevant information' from the authorities may face a situation which is 'less favourable' than if the party had cooperated. This sentence does not require the application of 'adverse facts', but merely allows it. Its wording indicates that the level of non-cooperation described in paragraph 7 is much lower than the degree of cooperation required in paragraph 5 of Annex II. It cannot be said that a party that 'does not cooperate to the *best of its abilities*' can be equated to a party that 'does not cooperate'. The word 'withheld' in paragraph 7 of Annex II suggests in this context that an interested party refuses to supply information in its possession.[110] Therefore, the last sentence of paragraph 7 applies to a situation where a party deliberately fails to provide information consciously. Moreover, reading this provision in conjunction with paragraph 5 of Annex II and Article 6.13 ADA shows that, if interested parties cooperate, investigating authorities should, wherever possible, fill information gaps with facts which are not to the detriment of the cooperating party. It is not possible to reconcile the principle of good faith and the obligation to take due account of the genuine difficulties of interested parties, with the application of 'adverse facts' against a party that has failed to provide sufficient information despite its utmost efforts.

In *US—Hot-Rolled Steel*, the AB had to decide precisely on the question of whether 'adverse facts' could be applied to an interested party who cooperated, but was unable to furnish requested documents. The AB commenced its analysis with

105 The title of Annex II ADA reads: 'Best information available in Terms of Paragraph 8 of Article 6'. See also WTO, *Mexico—Definitive Anti-Dumping Measures on Beef and Rice*, Appellate Body Report (29 November 2005), WT/DS295/AB/R (*Mexico—Anti-Dumping on Rice*, AB), para 289.

106 *Mexico—Anti-Dumping on Rice* (AB), 104, para 225.

107 Paragraph 7, sentences 1 and 2 of Annex II.

108 *Egypt—Steel Rebar*, para 7.305.

109 See n 99.

110 'Withhold' in *Oxford Dictionary* (n 67).

the statement that 'investigating authorities should not arrive at a "less favourable" outcome simply because an interested party fails to furnish requested information if, in fact, the interested party has "cooperated" '.[111]

It then used paragraph 2 of Annex II, which describes the form in which information should be provided to the authorities, and paragraph 5 of Annex II, as well as Article 6.13 ADA, to establish the degree of cooperation required under paragraph 7 of Annex II.[112] Referring to Article 6.13 ADA, the AB explained: 'If the investigating authorities fail to "take due account" of genuine "difficulties" experienced by interested parties, and made known to the investigating authorities, they cannot, in our view, fault the interested parties concerned for a lack of cooperation.'[113]

After analysing the substantial efforts made by the exporting company, the AB concluded that 'adverse facts available' should not be applied as the party had cooperated sufficiently.[114] In conclusion, investigating authorities are barred from knowingly applying 'adverse facts' available to parties that have cooperated to the best of their abilities. This applies with special force to SMEs.

*Article 5.2 ADA* is another central provision of the ADA that is affected by Article 6.13 ADA. It requires applicants requesting an AD investigation to provide relevant evidence of dumping, an injury to the domestic industry, and the causal link between the two. The long list of information that applicants need to submit[115] (Article 5.2(i)–(iv) ADA) presents a significant obstacle for SMEs.[116] The collection of information on product prices in exporting countries, the evolution of import volumes, and the effect of those imports on the domestic market is especially challenging for them. It requires significant resources and coordination among SMEs, if no trade associations or co-applicants with a larger resource pool help them in drafting the application.

The third sentence of Article 5.2 ADA alleviates the burden of collecting the relevant information[117] significantly. It states that the 'application shall contain such information as is *reasonably available* to the applicant'.[118] In *US—Softwood Lumber VI*, the Panel held that the 'reasonably available language was intended to avoid putting an *undue burden* on the applicant'[119] and that the applicant is merely

[111] *US—Hot-Rolled Steel* (AB), para 99. [112] ibid, paras 100–10.

[113] ibid, para 104. [114] ibid, paras 109–10; see also Vermulst (n 31) 157.

[115] The information required is limited to the four aspects mentioned in Art 5.2(i)–(iv) ADA and to the extent necessary to support the claim. WTO, *United States—Final Dumping Determination on Softwood Lumber from Canada*, Panel Report (13 April 2004), WT/DS264/R (*US—Softwood Lumber VI*), paras 7.53–7.56.

[116] bkp Development, Research & Consulting, 'Evaluation of the European Union's Trade Defence Instruments' (Final Evaluation Study, 27 February 2012) 354 <http://trade.ec.europa.eu/doclib/html/149236.htm> accessed 20 January 2017.

[117] Jurisprudence confirms that 'information' needs to be distinguished from 'analysis'. Article 5.2 only requires applicants to provide 'raw data' rather than an analysis supporting their allegations (which undoubtedly is helpful). See WTO, *Thailand—Anti-Dumping Duties on Angles, Shapes and Sections of Iron or Non-Alloy Steel and H Beams from Poland*, Panel Report (28 September 2000), WT/DS122/R (*Thailand—H-Beams*), paras 7.76–7.78.

[118] Emphasis added. [119] *US—Softwood Lumber VI*, para 7.54 (emphasis in original).

required to submit information '*to the extent* reasonably available to [him]'.[120] Such statements support a capacity-based interpretation of Article 5.2 ADA, which is called for by Article 6.13 ADA. Therefore, the amount and detail of information required in an application depends directly on the capacity of the applicant.

The second sentence of Article 5.2, which requires that the information provided in the application must still be sufficient to substantiate the claim of the applicant and make it more than a 'simple assertion',[121] does not alter the previous conclusion. It only sets a minimum quality requirement—albeit relatively low—for the information submitted.[122] In *Thailand—H-Beams*, the Panel, for instance, accepted that the submission of raw numerical data is permissible[123] and explained that submitted information must only be sufficient to support a prima facie[124] case.[125]

The more important de facto threshold for the quality and quantity of information submitted along with the application is Article 5.3 ADA. This provision requires the investigating authorities to examine the accuracy and adequacy of evidence in order to determine whether it is sufficient to start an AD investigation. In *Mexico—Corn Syrup*, the Panel emphasized that 'an application which is consistent with the requirements of Article 5.2 will not necessarily contain sufficient evidence to justify initiation [of an AD investigation] under Article 5.3'.[126]

*Article 2.4 ADA* requires the investigating authorities to compare the normal value and the export prices at the same level of trade and at nearly the same time. The last sentence of Article 2.4 ADA obligates the authorities to 'indicate[ ] to [the] parties ... what information is necessary to ensure a fair comparison' without imposing an 'unreasonable burden of proof'.[127] In *EC—Fasteners (China)*, the AB explained that 'the last sentence ... adds a procedural requirement to the general obligation of investigating authorities to ensure a fair comparison'.[128] It leads to 'a

[120] *US—Softwood Lumber VI*, para 7.55 (emphasis in original); see also Vermulst (n 31) 103: 'The phrase effectively is "a modulation of the requirement to provide such information [as listed in paragraph 2] in the light of its availability" '.

[121] See also Vermulst (n 31) 105.

[122] Jacques Bourgeois, 'Article 5 ADA' in Rüdiger Wolfrum, Peter-Tobias Stoll, and Michael Koebele (eds), *WTO: Trade Remedies*, vol 4 (Max Planck Commentaries on World Trade Law, Martinus Nijhoff 2008) 86.

[123] *Thailand—H-Beams*, para 7.77.

[124] Bourgeois points out that 'interestingly, the term prima facie evidence does not appear in art 5.2'. Bourgeois (n 122) 86.

[125] Therefore, the European Union should have no problem to include the suggestions of SMEs in its AD legislation. It is permissible to recognize prima facie evidence as sufficient to submit an application, to accept more sources and types of evidences, including macro-economic statistical data. Gide Loyrette Nouel (n 9) 24, 35.

[126] WTO, *Mexico—Anti-Dumping Investigation of High-Fructose Corn Syrup (HFCS) from the United States*, Panel Report (28 January 2000), WT/DS132/R, para 7.74; see also *US—Softwood Lumber VI*, para 7.74.

[127] Art 2.4 ADA; see also Terence P Stewart and David P Mueller, 'Article 2 ADA' in Rüdiger Wolfrum, Peter-Tobias Stoll, and Michael Koebele (eds), *WTO: Trade Remedies*, vol 4 (Max Planck Commentaries on World Trade Law, Martinus Nijhoff 2008) 38.

[128] WTO, *European Communities—Definitive Anti-Dumping Measures on Certain Iron or Steel Fasteners From China*, Appellate Body Report (15 July 2011), WT/DS397/AB/R (*EU—Fasteners*) para 489.

"dialogue" between the authority and the interested parties'.[129] Reading the last sentence together with Article 6.13 ADA indicates that the criterion of 'unreasonableness' depends on the capacity of the individual company to gather further information required. A situation where a party cannot obtain further information needed in order to make a fair comparison must be assessed with regard to the facts available according to the rules set out in Article 6.8 and Annex II.[130]

*Article 8.6 ADA* is another instance in which Article 6.13 ADA calls for a capacity-based interpretation. The provision permits investigating authorities to require any exporter with price undertakings to periodically submit information allowing the verification of its commitment. If an undertaking is violated, the authorities may take expeditious action including the immediate application of provisional AD duties.[131] The wording of this paragraph grants the authorities a broad margin of appreciation.[132] The use of the wording 'any' instead of 'all' exporters suggests that the authorities are free to differentiate among exporters. Hence, they can request information selectively from some and not from other exporters. The authorities may also determine the frequency and type of information required as long as the information is 'relevant to the fulfillment of such … undertaking[s]'. Article 6.13 ADA limits the authority's margin of appreciation in situations involving SMEs. Authorities must not overburden SMEs with regard to the frequency and amount of requested information. Importantly, whereas the wording of Article 8.6 ADA allows the imposition of provisional measures in response to any, even minor, violation—substantive or procedural—of the price undertaking, Article 6.13 ADA bars such a response in situations in which SMEs have violated procedural obligations due to capacity constraints—for example, by submitting information too late or incompletely. Investigating authorities should first enter into dialogue with such parties in an attempt to remedy the violation before imposing AD duties.

### 2. *Time criterion*

A capacity-based interpretation also allows SMEs more time to submit information and can even require the authorities to accept information that has been received after a set deadline.

SMEs benefit in particular from a capacity-based interpretation of *Article 6.1.1 ADA*. The Article states that exporters and foreign producers shall be given *at least* thirty days by the investigating authorities to reply to the initial questionnaires. Interested parties can request an extension of the deadline. The investigating authorities shall give due consideration to the request and shall grant an extension, upon

[129] ibid. [130] See above.

[131] Art 8.6 ADA: 'Authorities of an importing Member *may require* any exporter from whom an undertaking has been accepted to provide periodically information relevant to the fulfilment of such an undertaking … In case of violation of an undertaking, the authorities of the importing Member *may take* … expeditious actions which *may constitute* immediate application of provisional measures using the best information available …' (emphases added).

[132] See also Vermulst (n 31) 170.

causes shown, whenever practicable.[133] Reading the provision together with Article 6.13 ADA requires the authorities to grant more time to SMEs and other disadvantaged parties on a case-by-case basis if they consider that they cannot process the complex information requests[134] within thirty days.[135] The authorities also need to show a greater willingness to extend submission deadlines if SMEs request it. How much time needs to be granted depends on the complexity of the request and the capacity of the company to process it.[136] This conclusion is supported by the recommendation of the Committee on AD Practices '[c]oncerning an Indicative List of Elements Relevant to a Decision on a Request for Extension of Time to Provide Information'. The non-binding document recommends investigating authorities to take into account, inter alia, 'the ability of [a] party ... to respond to the request, in light of the nature and extent of the information requested, including the party's available resources, personnel, and technological capability', 'any unusual burdens ... incurred by the party ... in searching for, identifying and/or compiling the information requested', and whether 'any unforeseen circumstances affecting the ability of the party to provide the information [exist]'.[137]

Article 6.13 ADA also influences the interpretation of the notion of a 'reasonable period' in *Article 6.8 ADA*,[138] ie the time frame after which the authorities can resort to determinations on the basis of facts available.[139] Reading both Articles together shows that what is 'reasonable' depends on the capacity of the party that supplies the information. In principle, the authorities must not reject information submitted within a reasonable period, even if the submitting party failed to meet the original deadline set by the authorities.[140] This interpretation finds support in the AB's reasoning in *US—Hot-Rolled Steel.* Holding that 'what constitutes a reasonable period ... should be defined on a case-by-case basis, in the light of the specific circumstances of each investigation', the AB set out a list of factors that should be considered.[141] Those factors include the nature and quantity of information submitted, the difficulties encountered by an investigated exporter to obtain the information, and the number of days by which the exporter missed the deadlines.[142]

[133] Vermulst notes that 'while a similar rule for domestic producers and importers is lacking, presumably they should *ceteris paribus* nevertheless receive a longer time period'. ibid 127.

[134] cf *EU—Fasteners*, para 613.

[135] See Vermulst (n 31) 166. However, the time frame granted cannot be extended indefinitely as the authorities need to guarantee expeditious proceedings. Compare Arts 5.10 and 6.12. See also *Mexico—Anti-Dumping on Rice* (AB), para 282; WTO, *United States—Sunset Reviews of Anti-Dumping Measures on Oil Country Tubular Goods from Argentina*, Appellate Body Report (29 November 2004), WT/DS268/AB/R, para 242; *US—Hot-Rolled Steel* (AB), para 73.

[136] Vermulst (n 31) 128, 166. In *Mexico—Anti-Dumping on Rice*, the AB merely underlined that the minimum time limit of thirty days applies to all parties on a non-discriminatory basis. See *Mexico Anti-Dumping on Rice*, paras 280, 282.

[137] WTO Committee on Dumping Practices, 'Recommendation Concerning Indicative List of Elements Relevant to a Decision on a Request for Extension of Time to Provide Information' (1 May 2001) G/ADP/7 <http://docsonline.wto.org/imrd/directdoc.asp?DDFDocuments/t/G/ADP/7.doc> accessed 20 January 2017.

[138] See n 100 on content of Art 6.8.

[139] *US—Hot-Rolled Steel* (AB), para 77.

[140] ibid.

[141] ibid, paras 84–85.

[142] ibid, paras 84–85; Vermulst (n 31) 148; Bellis (n 31) 110.

The importance of Article 6.13 ADA and its interplay with Articles 6.1.1 and 6.8 ADA can be seen in the recent AD investigations of Australia regarding prepared or preserved tomatoes from Italy.[143] An Italian family business complained with the Australian AD Commission about its categorization as an uncooperative party, which resulted in a higher AD duty. The company claimed that Australia had acted against its obligation stemming from Article 6.13 ADA. It argued that Australia should have taken into account its efforts to cooperate and should have acknowledged its personnel constraints, language barriers, and IT difficulties in complying with the commission's request for information.[144] In particular, Australia should have accepted the request to extend the deadline for the submission of information by four days.

Another example for a modified time requirement is *Article 8.6 ADA*. Read together with Article 6.13 ADA, this provision prevents authorities from rejecting price undertakings immediately if handicapped parties fail to meet a deadline for the submission of information verifying compliance with their undertaking. Accordingly, the investigating authorities should also keep the capacity constraints of parties in mind when setting deadlines.[145]

### *3. Form criterion*

Article 6.13 ADA also affects the form in which SMEs need to submit information to the investigating authorities. This effect can be seen in *paragraphs 2 and 3 of Annex II*. Paragraph 2 allows authorities to request information in a particular medium and computer language. It also calls upon the authorities to 'consider the reasonable ability of the interested party to respond in the preferred medium' and prohibits requests which would place an 'unreasonable extra burden on the interested party'.[146] Paragraph 3 requires the authorities to take all adequate information into account, ie information which is (i) verifiable, (ii) which *can be used without undue difficulties*, (iii) which is supplied in a timely fashion, and (iv) which is supplied *using the requested medium*. In the light of Article 6.13 ADA, the authorities should first choose a medium which is easy to use for SMEs and second accept information even when its form makes it slightly difficult to use. The difficulties authorities must accept increase with the difficulties interested parties face in providing information in a different format. This is because Article 6.13 ADA requires the authorities to provide any assistance practicable to handicapped parties, which includes accepting greater difficulties in using information provided by such parties.

[143] Australian Government Anti-Dumping Commission, 'Dumping Investigation ADC 217: Tomato Products, Prepared or Preserved Exported from Italy' (8 May 2014) <http://www.adcommission.gov.au/cases/Pages/ArchivedCases/ADC217.aspx> accessed 20 January 2017.

[144] Van Bael & Bellis, 'Response to Statement of Essential Facts on Behalf of our Client Lodato Gennaro & C. S.p.A.: Anti-Dumping Investigation No. 217: Prepared or Preserved Tomatoes from Italy', 2 <http://www.adcommission.gov.au/cases/documents/078-Submission-Exporter-VanBaelandBellisonbehalfofLodatoGennaroandCSpa.pdf> accessed 20 January 2017.

[145] See n 133.

[146] See para 2 of Annex II.

## II. Calling for proactive support

The obligation in Article 6.13 ADA to 'provide any assistance practicable' also has a proactive component. It requires the investigating authorities to take action in support of SMEs (or other disadvantaged parties). Possible forms of action are manifold and depend on the capacity of both the investigating authorities and the interested party.[147] They include not only the prolongation of response periods for handicapped parties described in the previous section, but also the simplification of questionnaires[148] and the provision of more detailed and annotated responses to SMEs, which help them understand the authorities' reasoning.[149] In addition, authorities may need to provide SMEs with more detailed guidance on how the investigations are conducted and may need to allow for more time for personal consultations.[150] An EU study from 2012 contains recommendations for further measures that can facilitate the participation of SMEs in AD investigations.[151] Suggested measures include setting up SME help desks, assisting in the creation of ad-hoc associations to allow for better SME coordination, and visiting SMEs personally in order to explain what is at stake for them in the AD investigation, as well as the participatory rights.[152] However, it remains largely obscure which specific proactive support measures are *legally* required by virtue of Article 6.13 ADA.

*Article 2.4 ADA* provides a good illustration of the effect of Article 6.13 ADA. This provision obligates the authorities to indicate to the parties in question which information is required in order to compare normal values and export prices.[153] It hence contains an obligation for the investigating authorities to guide the interested parties in providing necessary information.[154] Because of Article 6.13 ADA, the authorities should be particularly elaborate in their instructions for SMEs.

This interpretation ties in well with *Article 6.1 ADA*, which requires that 'all interested parties ... shall be given notice of the information which the authorities require and ample opportunity to present ... evidence'. Such notice must be issued effectively to the interested parties, keeping their capacity to receive and process it in mind.[155] In *Mexico—AD Measures on Rice*, the Panel found that Mexico had failed to comply with this obligation, as it did not make a sufficient effort to identify exporters and reach them. The Panel stated:

> It is, in our view, the task of the investigating authority and not of the interested parties to inform all interested parties of the information that is required and to conduct a proper investigation. We are of the view that the investigating authority is not allowed to rely on the initiative of the interested parties for the fulfilment of obligations which are really its own.[156]

[147] See Sections C and D.
[148] For example, Art 2.4 ADA.
[149] For example, Art 6.9 ADA.
[150] For example, Art 6.2 ADA.
[151] bkp Development, Research & Consulting (n 116) 389, 398.
[152] ibid 389.
[153] Stewart and Mueller (n 127) 38.
[154] cf *EU—Fasteners*, paras 489–90, 512.
[155] cf *Argentina—Ceramic Tiles*, para 6.54.
[156] WTO, *Mexico—Definitive Anti-Dumping Measures on Beef and Rice*, Panel Report (6 June 2005), WT/DS295/R, para 7.199.

Article 6.13 ADA reinforces this jurisprudence by requiring the capacity of interested parties to be kept in mind when notifying them about the information required for the investigation and when providing them with an opportunity to present evidence. If SMEs are involved, the authorities must take particular care to identify affected SMEs and ensure that they are aware of what is required from them.

Moreover, the first sentence of *Article 6.2 ADA* contains a 'fundamental due process provision'[157] which requires the investigating authorities 'to *provide opportunities* for interested parties' to defend their interests.[158] The Panel in *Egypt—Steel Rebar* further explained that: 'Failure by respondents to take the initiative to defend their own interests in an investigation cannot be equated, through WTO dispute settlement, with failure by an investigating authority to provide opportunities for interested parties to defend their interests.'[159]

However, the very general language of Article 6.2 ADA 'provides no specific guidance as to what steps investigating authorities must take in practice'.[160] Yet, reading Articles 6.2 and 6.13 ADA together, it becomes clear that what constitutes a full opportunity for defence depends on the capacities of the parties. Weaker parties typically require more assistance to facilitate an equal level of protection. The next sentence of Article 6.2 ADA specifies that the authorities shall provide opportunities allowing interested parties with opposing interests to meet.[161] The provision of such opportunities must take account of the convenience to the parties.[162] This indicates, if read together with Article 6.13 ADA, that the authorities must bear in mind the difficulties of the interested parties to attend such meetings. It is debatable whether this obligation requires the authorities to make financial contributions in support of SMEs. Considering the high assistance requirements of Article 6.13 ADA, such an obligation is not implausible.

Finally, *Article 6.9 ADA* obligates investigating authorities to proactively inform all interested parties, before a final determination on AD measures is made, about the 'essential facts' on which they intend to base their determination.[163] This paragraph provides interested parties with a final opportunity to make any comments. In *Guatemala—Cement from Mexico II*, the Panel explicitly stated that simply copying all information in a file does not meet the requirements of Article 6.9 ADA.[164] The authorities must select and structure the information sufficiently. The 2011 Doha reform draft clarifies this obligation by stating that the authorities must provide a written report.[165] It hence prohibits the mere submission of a compilation of documents. Because of Article 6.13 ADA, the authorities must organize the

[157] WTO, *Guatemala—Definitive Anti-Dumping Measure on Grey Portland Cement from Mexico*, Panel Report (24 October 2000), WT/DS156/R (*Guatemala—Cement II*), para 8.179.

[158] *Egypt—Steel Rebar*, para 7.88 (emphasis added).

[159] ibid.

[160] *Guatemala—Cement II*, paras 8.162, 8.238.

[161] Art 6.2, sentence 2 ADA.

[162] Art 6.2, sentence 3 ADA.

[163] This selection of facts differentiates the obligation of para 9 from para 4, see *Guatemala—Cement II*, paras 8.229–8.230.

[164] *Guatemala—Cement II*, para 8.230; see also *Argentina—Ceramic Tiles*, para 6.125; see also Vermulst (n 31) 160.

[165] WTO Negotiating Group on Rules (n 47) 15.

information in a manner which is easy to access and to understand by SMEs in order to allow them to comment effectively. As with the previous provisions discussed, Article 6.13 ADA requires an SME-friendly interpretation of the obligations contained in Article 6.9 ADA.

## III. Prohibiting negative discrimination

Article 6.13 ADA not only requires a more beneficial treatment of SMEs, but also prohibits the investigating authorities from treating SMEs less favourably as a consequence of their capacity constraints.

A prominent example for this effect is *Article 6.10 ADA*, which allows the investigating authorities to limit their examination to a 'reasonable number of interested parties or products' by either using 'statistically valid' samples (method 1), or the largest percentage of exports from the country under investigation which can be reasonably investigated (method 2).[166] The authorities may only use sampling if the number of exporters or products is so large as to make an individual determination of dumping margins[167] impracticable. The selection of the sample is important for companies since only sampled exporters receive an individual dumping duty.[168] Therefore, it is problematic that SMEs are frequently excluded from individual examination because the authorities tend to focus on companies with larger export volumes.[169]

This practice of focusing on larger companies is questionable. It is true that Article 6.10 ADA provides investigating authorities with a substantive margin of appreciation on *whether*[170] and *how* to apply sampling. If authorities use sampling, it is left to them to decide who is to be included in the sample. However, their freedom of choice is not unlimited. The wording of this provision requires them to include a '*reasonable* number of interested parties or products by using … *statistically valid* [samples]' or the 'largest percentage [of exports] … which can *reasonably*

[166] See Vermulst (n 31) 162.

[167] Dumping margin describes the rate by which a company undersells its goods abroad as compared to the price in its home market. The dumping margin is the basis for the calculation of the dumping duty.

[168] The fact that sampled exporters do not furbish sufficient information shall 'not deprive them of the right to obtain an individual dumping margin'. Vermulst (n 31) 164; WTO, *Argentina—Definitive Anti-Dumping Measures on Poultry from Brazil*, Panel Report (22 April 2003) WT/DS241/R, para 7.216.

[169] Scott Flaherty, 'Commerce to Use Sampling to Pick Duty Case Respondents' (4 November 2013) <http://www.law360.com/articles/485902/commerce-to-use-sampling-to-pick-duty-case-respondents> accessed 20 January 2017; US Government Publishing Office 'Antidumping Proceedings: Announcement of Change in Department Practice for Respondent Selection in Antidumping Duty Proceedings and Conditional Review of the Nonmarket Economy Entity in NME Antidumping Duty Proceedings' (4 November 2013) 65964 <https://www.gpo.gov/fdsys/pkg/FR-2013-11-04/html/2013-26266.htm> accessed 20 January 2017; Gide Loyrette Nouel (n 9) 26–27, 35–36.

[170] The use of sampling is optional. The authorities may use it once the threshold criteria are met. However, they remain free to determine individual dumping margins, even if a large number of exporters and product types exist.

be investigated'.[171] Nothing in this language suggests that a certain category of companies should be excluded from the investigation. Moreover, the notion of statistical validity requires authorities to consider the different qualities of the samples chosen. Furthermore, in *EC—Salmon (Norway)*, the Panel denied that the reasonableness test used in method 2 is purely a numerical exercise. It rather stated:

> The volume of export sales that may be reasonable for an investigating authority … must be assessed on a case-by-case basis, taking into account all relevant facts that are before the investigating authority, including the *nature and type of interested parties*, the products involved and the investigating authority's own investigating capacity and resources.[172]

Moreover, reading Article 6.10 ADA together with paragraph 13 suggests that a quantitative approach to sampling is insufficient. Article 6.13 ADA requires the participation of SMEs (and other disadvantaged parties) in the investigation to be ensured. Hence, an interpretation of paragraph 10 to the effect that the authorities could specifically exclude SMEs is irreconcilable with paragraph 13. SMEs should not be discriminated against due to their capacity constraints, but rather be included in the investigation. Therefore, it would be incompatible with the ADA to consciously exclude SMEs because of the difficulties in cooperating with them. However, neither Article 6.13 ADA nor Article 6.10 ADA requires measures by the authorities which are 'impracticable'. Hence, they do not place an absolute obligation upon investigating authorities to use SMEs as samples, if this were to overstretch the authority's capacities.

## E. Conclusion

Article 6.13 ADA is an invaluable provision for SMEs as it can contribute to alleviating their inherent difficulties in participating in AD proceedings. This provision establishes a cooperative framework among the parties of the investigation and provides interpretative guidance as to the proper interpretation of several provisions of the ADA in favour of SMEs. It does so by lending support to a capacity-based interpretation of such provisions. Article 6.13 ADA in particular contributes to easing information submission requirements for SMEs (and other disadvantaged parties). It further urges states to implement proactive support mechanisms and prevents negative discrimination of SMEs. However, Article 6.13 ADA only informs the interpretation of those provisions regulating the submission of information of interested parties to the investigating authorities. Hence, the interpretative effect of Article 6.13 ADA applies only to the procedural aspects of an AD investigation, rather than to the actual determination of whether or not to apply dumping duties.

[171] Art 6.10 ADA (emphases added).

[172] WTO, *European Communities—Anti-Dumping Measure on Farmed Salmon from Norway*, Panel Report (16 November 2007), WT/DS337/R, para 7.188 (emphasis added).

Despite its significance for SMEs, Article 6.13 ADA has not received much attention since its introduction. The provision has hardly been discussed in WTO fora or at national level. Therefore, no guidance has been provided to date on how to implement this rather vague provision. Moreover, with the exception of *Hot-Rolled Steel*, neither a Panel nor the Appellate Body has made reference to Article 6.13 ADA. Likewise, academia has not yet explored its effect and limits.

It is only recently that Article 6.13 ADA appears to have been rediscovered. For instance, the European Union's efforts to promote SME participation in international trade and to reform its TDI mechanisms have created some attention for Article 6.13 ADA. It has been identified as the guiding principle for ensuring SME participation in AD investigations at WTO level.[173] The Union's TDI reform proposals contain several ideas that show how Article 6.13 ADA could be operationalized.

This new focus on Article 6.13 ADA may help to address its largest deficiency: its vagueness and the lack of any indication as to its implementation. When and how the investigating authorities need to take the capacity constraints of SMEs into account should be specified—if possible also in national AD regulations. It is important to clarify the criteria for determining adequate responses with regard to interested parties with capacity constraints. In addition, available support measures must be specified, without necessarily limiting the investigating authorities to such measures. This includes, for instance, developing a list of criteria to determine the amount of time to be granted to SMEs for answering the authority's requests for information, and an open list of measures for informing SMEs about AD proceedings and explaining to them how to participate in them effectively. In the end, what the investigating authorities are required to do will depend in each individual case on the capacity constraints of the company participating in AD investigations. However, further guidance for determining the adequacy of the investigating authority's actions as well as ideas for appropriate measures will significantly help with the implementation of Article 6.13 ADA.

Hopefully, future WTO case law will specify the obligations and options in support of SMEs. In the absence of such case law and the standstill of the Doha Round which could have clarified the meaning of Article 6.13 ADA, its effects may be specified in national or EU AD guidelines. The drafting of such guidelines could significantly reduce the uncertainty for interested parties and investigating authorities as to how to engage with SMEs (and other disadvantaged parties). In addition to increasing predictability and transparency, such guidelines could serve as a nucleus for future discussions at the international level on how best to respect the needs of SMEs.

It remains to be hoped that Article 6.13 ADA will receive the attention it deserves. It is a significant tool for keeping AD proceedings open to SMEs (and other disadvantaged parties). The importance of this provision is likely to increase

[173] Gide Loyrette Nouel (n 9) 16.

because ever-increasing numbers of SMEs are affected by an increasing number of AD proceedings.

## References


Alexy, R, *A Theory of Constitutional Rights* (Oxford University Press 2010)

Antony, J, Kumar, M, and Labib, A, 'Gearing Six Sigma into UK Manufacturing SMEs: Results from a Pilot Study' (2008) 59 Journal of the Operational Research Society 482 <http://www.palgrave-journals.com/jors/journal/v59/n4/full/2602437a.html> accessed 20 January 2017

Australian Government Anti-Dumping Commission, 'Dumping Investigation ADC 217: Tomato Products, Prepared or Preserved Exported from Italy' (8 May 2014) <http://www.adcommission.gov.au/cases/Pages/ArchivedCases/ADC217.aspx> accessed 20 January 2017

Bellis, J-F, 'Article 6 ADA' in Rüdiger Wolfrum, Peter-Tobias Stoll, and Michael Koebele (eds), *WTO: Trade Remedies*, vol 4 (Max Planck Commentaries on World Trade Law, Martinus Nijhoff 2008)

bkp Development, Research & Consulting, 'Evaluation of the European Union's Trade Defence Instruments' (Final Evaluation Study, 27 February 2012) <http://trade.ec.europa.eu/doclib/html/149236.htm> accessed 20 January 2017

Bourgeois, J, 'Article 5 ADA' in Rüdiger Wolfrum, Peter-Tobias Stoll, and Michael Koebele (eds), *WTO: Trade Remedies*, vol 4 (Max Planck Commentaries on World Trade Law, Martinus Nijhoff 2008)

Bradsher, K, 'China Aims at Europe's Wines after Solar Panel Action' *The New York Times* (New York, 6 June 2013) <http://www.nytimes.com/2013/06/06/business/global/china-to-investigate-eu-wine-after-subsidy-and-dumping-complaints.html?pagewanted=all&_r=0> accessed 20 January 2017

Cliff Stevenson Consulting, 'Research Project on the Impact of Anti-Dumping Investigations on UK Business' (Final Report, 12 July 2012) <https://www.gov.uk/government/uploads/system/uploads/attachment_data/file/34580/12-1021-research-impact-anti-dumping-investigations-on-uk-business.pdf> accessed 20 January 2017

Cogan, JK, 'Noncompliance and the International Rule of Law' (2005) 31 Yale Journal of International Law 189

Council of Europe, *Manual on Human Rights and the Environment* (2nd edn, Council of Europe Publishing 2012)

European Commission, 'Guide for EU Exporters: Trade Defence Instruments: Anti-Dumping Anti-Subsidy Safeguards' (European Union 2010) <http://trade.ec.europa.eu/doclib/docs/2010/october/tradoc_146701.pdf> accessed 20 January 2017

European Commission, 'Paper on Actions to Address the Difficulties Encountered by SMEs Involved in Trade Defence Instruments' (2011) <http://trade.ec.europa.eu/doclib/docs/2011/june/tradoc_148004.pdf> accessed 20 January 2017

European Commission, 'Q&As: Modernisation of the EU's Trade Defence Instruments' (Press Release, 10 April 2013) MEMO/13/319 <http://europa.eu/rapid/press-release_MEMO-13-319_en.htm> accessed 20 January 2017

European Commission, 'Memo: EU Imposes Provisional Anti-Dumping Duties on Chinese Solar Panels' (4 June 2013) MEMO-13-497 <http://europa.eu/rapid/press-release_MEMO-13-497_en.htm> accessed 20 January 2017

European Commission, 'European Commission Welcomes Agreement Reached between European and Chinese Wine Industries Which Will Put an End to China's Anti-Dumping and Anti-Subsidy Cases' (Press Release, 21 March 2014) <http://trade.ec.europa.eu/doclib/press/index.cfm?id=1048> accessed 20 January 2017

European Commission, 'Small and Medium-Sized enterprises (SMEs): Website of the European Union' <http://ec.europa.eu/growth/smes> accessed 20 January 2017

Flaherty, S, 'Commerce to Use Sampling to Pick Duty Case Respondents' (4 November 2013) <http://www.law360.com/articles/485902/commerce-to-use-sampling-to-pick-duty-case-respondents> accessed 20 January 2017

Gibson, T and van der Vaart, H, 'Defining SMEs: A Less Imperfect Way of Defining Small and Medium Enterprises in Developing Countries' (2008) <https://www.brookings.edu/research/defining-smes-a-less-imperfect-way-of-defining-small-and-medium-enterprises-in-developing-countries/> accessed 20 January 2017

Gide Loyrette Nouel, 'Study of the Difficulties Encountered by SMEs in Trade Defence Investigation and Possible Solutions' (Final Report, 30 November 2010) <http://trade.ec.europa.eu/doclib/docs/2011/february/tradoc_147475.pdf> accessed 20 January 2017

ITC, 'WTO Negotiations on the Agreement on Anti-Dumping Practices' (Business and the Multilateral Trade System, Technical Paper, June 2005) <http://www.economy.gov.tr/portal/content/conn/UCM/path/Contribution%20Folders/web/%C4%B0thalat/Ticaret%20Politikas%C4%B1%20Savunma%20Ara%C3%A7lar%C4%B1/T%C3%BCrk%20%C4%B0hra%C3%A7%20%C3%9Cr%C3%BCnlerine%20Y%C3%B6nelik%20Uygulanan%20TPSA%20%C3%96nlemleri/TPSA%20%C3%96nlemlerine%20%C4%B0li%C5%9Fkin%20Faydal%C4%B1%20Bilgiler/wtonegotiations.pdf> accessed 20 January 2017

Leick, B, Leßmann, G, and Nussbaum, J, 'Internationalisierungspfade mittelständischer Unternehmen in Osteuropa: Internationalisierungsprozess und Standorteffekte am Beispiel niedersächsischer KMU' (IfM-Materialien No 218, October 2012) <http://www.ifm-bonn.org//uploads/tx_ifmstudies/IfM-Materialien-218_2012.pdf> accessed 20 January 2017

Maguire, R and Lewis, B, 'The Influence of Justice Theories on International Climate Policies and Measures' (2012) 8 Macquarie Journal of International and Comparative Environmental Law 16

Runyon, J, 'Solar Panel Prices Expected to Rise in the US Due to New Tariffs on Chinese Panels' *Renewable Energy World.com* (28 July 2014) <http://www.renewableenergyworld.com/rea/news/article/2014/07/solar-panel-prices-expected-to-rise-in-the-us-due-to-new-tariffs-on-chinese-panels> accessed 20 January 2017

Simpson, J and Weiner, E, *Oxford English Dictionary: 20 Volume Set and CD-ROM* (Oxford University Press 2009)

Stewart, TP and Mueller, DP, 'Article 2 ADA' in Rüdiger Wolfrum, Peter-Tobias Stoll, and Michael Koebele (eds), *WTO: Trade Remedies*, vol 4 (Max Planck Commentaries on World Trade Law, Martinus Nijhoff 2008) 7

Tietje, C, *Internationales Wirtschaftsrecht* (De Gruyter Recht 2015)

US Government Publishing Office, 'Antidumping Proceedings: Announcement of Change in Department Practice for Respondent Selection in Antidumping Duty Proceedings and Conditional Review of the Nonmarket Economy Entity in NME Antidumping Duty Proceedings' (4 November 2013) <https://www.gpo.gov/fdsys/pkg/FR-2013-11-04/html/2013-26266.htm> accessed 20 January 2017

Van Bael & Bellis, 'Response to Statement of Essential Facts on Behalf of our Client Lodato Gennaro & C. S.p.A.: Anti-Dumping Investigation No. 217: Prepared or

Preserved Tomatoes from Italy' <http://www.adcommission.gov.au/cases/documents/078-Submission-Exporter-VanBaelandBellisonbehalfofLodatoGennaroandCSpa.pdf> accessed 20 January 2017

van den Bossche, P and Zdouc, W, *The Law and Policy of the World Trade Organization: Text, Cases and Materials* (3rd edn, Cambridge University Press 2013)

Vermulst, EA, *The WTO Anti-Dumping Agreement: A Commentary* (Oxford Commentaries on the GATT/WTO Agreements, Oxford University Press 2005)

Vermulst, EA and Prost, O, 'Modernization of the EU's Trade Defence Instruments (TDI)' (Workshop, April 2014) <http://www.europarl.europa.eu/RegData/etudes/workshop/join/2014/433842/EXPO-INTA_AT%282014%29433842_EN.pdf> accessed 20 January 2017

WTO, 'Statistics on Anti-Dumping: Initiations by Reporting Member 01/01/1995–31/12/2014' (2014) <http://www.wto.org/english/tratop_e/adp_e/AD_InitiationsByRepMem.xls> accessed 20 January 2017

WTO, 'Statistics on Anti-Dumping: Measures by Reporting Member 01/01/1995–31/12/2014' (2014) <http://www.wto.org/english/tratop_e/adp_e/AD_MeasuresByRepMem.xls> accessed 20 January 2017

WTO, 'Statistics on Safeguard Measures: Initiations by Reporting Member 01/01/1995–30/04/2014' (2014) <http://www.wto.org/english/tratop_e/safeg_e/SG-Initiations_By_Reporting_Member.xls> accessed 20 January 2017

WTO, 'Statistics on Safeguard Measures: Measures by Reporting Member 01/01/1995–30/04/2014' (2014) <http://www.wto.org/english/tratop_e/safeg_e/SG-Measures_By_Reporting_Member.xls> accessed 20 January 2017

WTO, 'Statistics on Subsidies and Countervailing Measures: Countervailing Initiations by Reporting Member 01/01/1995–31/12/2014' (2014) <http://www.wto.org/english/tratop_e/scm_e/CV_InitiationsByRepMem.xls> accessed 20 January 2017

Wu, M, 'Antidumping in Asia's Emerging Giants' (2012) 53 Harvard International Law Journal 1

Zheng, W, 'Reforming Trade Remedies' (2013) 34 Michigan Journal of International Law 151

# 4

# The South African Walmart/Massmart Case

## SME-Friendly Domestic Competition Laws in the Light of International Economic Law

*Tilman Michael Dralle*

### A. Introduction

The Walmart/Massmart case[1] is exemplary and instructive for the way in which international economic law affects the policy space of states to enact domestic regulation supportive of small and medium-sized enterprises (SMEs). The case revolves around the acquisition of the South African company Massmart by the US-American retail giant Walmart. The merger sparked much controversy in South Africa and beyond.[2] Opponents of the takeover, among which were three government ministers, expressed concern that the merger would have negative effects on South African SMEs. As the South African Competition Act explicitly mandates consideration of SME interests,[3] the critics demanded the prohibition of the transaction or, in the alternative, that certain performance requirements should be imposed as a condition of merger approval. In contrast, the merging parties argued before the South African competition authorities that the imposition of performance requirements would violate the country's international law obligations.

For a number of reasons, an analysis of the Walmart/Massmart merger is highly useful for an examination of the role of SMEs in international economic law. Most importantly, it serves as a high-profile example of the tension between domestic regulation that expressly protects the interests of SMEs, on the one hand, and the requirements of international economic law, on the other. Furthermore, the

[1] Competition Tribunal of South Africa, *Walmart Stores Inc and Massmart Holdings Ltd*, Case No 73/LM/Nov10, Order (31 May 2011); ibid, Reasons for Decision (29 June 2011); Competition Appeal Court of South Africa, *Wal-Mart Stores Inc*, Case Nos 110/CAC/Jul11 and 111/CAC/Jun11, Judgment (9 March 2012); ibid, Judgment (9 October 2012).

[2] For an excellent account, see Laurence Boulle, 'Balancing Competing Interests in FDI Policy: A Developing Country Perspective' (2012) 7 Asian Journal of WTO & International Health Law & Policy 315, 319–26, *passim*.

[3] Section 12A(1)(a)(ii) and (1)(b) in conjunction with s 12A(3)(c) of the Competition Act 89 of 1998 (South Africa), as amended. See also ibid, s 2(e).

proceedings before the South African competition authorities provide an insightful compilation of the benefits and the adverse effects that are associated with the market entry of a multinational corporation with superior buying power in the retail sector from the perspective of SMEs. Moreover, the South African situation is by no means an isolated case. India and Malaysia have had similar experiences regarding the interface between international trade and investment obligations and SME development imperatives.[4]

The structure of this chapter will be as follows: First, the Walmart/Massmart case will be introduced (Section B). Subsequently, the case will be analysed in the light of international economic law. For this purpose, Section C addresses the law of the World Trade Organization (WTO), in particular the General Agreement on Tariffs and Trade (GATT)[5] and the General Agreement on Trade in Services (GATS).[6] In Section D, the compatibility of SME-supportive measures with international investment law will be examined. Section E provides a comparison with the Indian and Malaysian cases. Finally, some conclusions will be presented in Section F.

## B. The Walmart/Massmart Case—Background

Massmart Holdings Ltd is a South African retail and wholesale distributor. According to its own information, it is the second-largest distributor of consumer goods in Africa, the leading retailer of general merchandise, liquor, home improvement, and building supplies, and the leading food wholesaler.[7] Wal-Mart Stores, Inc, for its part, is the world's biggest retailer and has an annual revenue that exceeds the gross domestic product of South Africa. In September 2010, Walmart's intention to acquire a controlling interest in Massmart was made public. Walmart had made a US$4.6 billion offer to take over Massmart.[8] In the end, Walmart acquired a 51 per cent share in Massmart for US$2.4 billion.[9] The acquisition of Massmart is part and parcel of Walmart's global expansion strategy. Being one of the biggest economies of Africa, South Africa has a large consumer market with great potential

[4] See Section E below.

[5] General Agreement on Tariffs and Trade (adopted 15 April 1994, entered into force 1 January 1995) 1867 UNTS 187.

[6] General Agreement on Trade in Services (adopted 15 April 1994, entered into force 1 January 1995) 1869 UNTS 183.

[7] See Massmart's website <http://www.massmart.co.za/investor-center/overview> accessed 20 January 2017.

[8] Miguel Bustillo, Robb M Stewart, and Paul Sonne, 'Wal-Mart Bids $4.6 Billion for South Africa's Massmart' *The Wall Street Journal* (New York, 28 September 2010) <http://online.wsj.com/articles/SB10001424052748704654004575517300108186976> accessed 20 January 2017; Sarah Shannon, Nasreen Seria, and Matthew Boyle, 'Wal-Mart Seeks to Enter Africa with $4.6 Billion Deal' *Bloomberg* (New York, 27 September 2010) <http://www.bloomberg.com/news/2010-09-27/wal-mart-offers-to-buy-south-africa-s-massmart-holdings-for-21-08-a-share.html> accessed 20 January 2017.

[9] Wal-Mart Stores Inc, 'Walmart Closes Investment in 51% Stake in Massmart' (20 June 2011) <http://corporate.walmart.com/_news_/news-archive/investors/walmart-closes-investment-in-51-stake-in-massmart-1576044> accessed 20 January 2017; UNCTAD, *World Investment Report 2014* (United Nations 2014) 17.

for growth. Besides, Massmart also functions as an important 'door-opener', because the company operates in twelve sub-Saharan countries.[10]

As South Africa had no general investment screening law in place,[11] the proposed merger was scrutinized only on the basis of South Africa's Competition Act of 1998. By and large, the principles of South Africa's competition law resemble those of other major jurisdictions such as the European Union and the United States. An unusual feature of the Competition Act, however, is that it empowers the authorities not only to carry out an assessment of the competition concerns that may be raised with respect to a specific merger or acquisition, but also to prohibit or impose conditions on a proposed transaction on the basis of public interest criteria. According to section 12A of the Competition Act, the national authorities *must* determine whether the merger 'can or cannot be justified on *substantial public interest grounds*'.[12] In this context, the effect on the 'ability of small businesses ... to become competitive' is explicitly mentioned as one of the relevant criteria.[13] What is more, section 2 stipulates that it is the purpose of the Act to, inter alia, 'ensure that small and medium-sized enterprises have an equitable opportunity to participate in the economy'.[14] South African courts have recognized that the effect of these provisions is to 'protect' the interests of small and medium-sized businesses in South Africa.[15] Section 12A thus served as the portal through which issues not related to competition policy came to be relevant for the authorities' decision on the Walmart/Massmart merger.[16]

Under the South African Competition Act, three institutions are responsible for handling merger proceedings: the Competition Commission, the Competition Tribunal, and, finally, the Competition Appeal Court. The Walmart/Massmart merger was reviewed by all three institutions. The Commission issued its report on 11 February 2011, followed by the order of the Competition Tribunal on 31 May 2011 and two judgments of the Competition Appeal Court dated 9 March and 9 October 2012.

[10] See Massmart's website (n 7).

[11] Department of Trade and Industry of the Republic of South Africa, 'South Africa: Investor's Handbook 2014/15' (2015) 61 <http://www2.deloitte.com/content/dam/Deloitte/za/Documents/tax/ZA_DTI-InvestinginSA_2014-15.pdf> accessed 20 January 2017; National Treasury of the Republic of South Africa, 'A Review Framework for Cross-Border Direct Investment in South Africa' (2011) 13 <http://www.treasury.gov.za/documents/national%20budget/2011/A%20review%20framework%20for%20cross-border%20direct%20investment%20in%20South%20Africa.pdf> accessed 20 January 2017.

[12] s 12A(1)(a)(ii) and (1)(b) in conjunction with s 12A(3) of the Competition Act 89 of 1998 (SA) (emphasis added).

[13] s 12A(3)(c) of the Competition Act 89 of 1998 (SA).

[14] s 2(e) of the Competition Act 89 of 1998 (SA).

[15] Competition Appeal Court (n 1) Judgment (9 March 2012) para 162. The term 'small business', as used in the Competition Act, is defined by reference to the National Small Business Act 102 of 1996 (South Africa), as amended.

[16] For a general account, see Kim Kampel, 'The Role of South African Competition Law in Supporting SMEs' in Paul Cook, Raul Fabella, and Cassey Lee (eds), *Competitive Advantage and Competition Policy in Developing Countries* (Edward Elgar 2007).

In the first phase of the process, the Competition Commission conducted an investigation into the merger and finally concluded that the merger is unlikely to substantially lessen or prevent competition. This finding was rather uncontroversial and not overruled in the subsequent stages of the proceedings.[17] From its very inception, therefore, the entire legal dispute centred on the public interest concerns. As the takeover was a 'large merger' within the meaning of the Competition Act,[18] the Competition Commission had no decision-making power.[19] Instead, as it did not see any public interest concerns at the time, it issued a recommendation to the Competition Tribunal that the merger be approved without conditions. Later, as new evidence emerged, the Commission changed its position on this issue.[20]

The second round of proceedings took place before the Competition Tribunal. Four trade unions (SACCAWU and others[21]), three government ministers, and the South African Small Medium and Micro Enterprise Forum (SMMEF) sought to demonstrate that the merger raised substantial public interest concerns. The main objections related to possible retrenchments, Walmart's attitude towards collective bargaining rights, and the substitution of domestic procurement with imports from foreign producers.[22] As regards procurement, the opponents of the merger sought to show that the merged entity would lower its prices by sourcing its goods from overseas rather than buying them from local suppliers. Such a substantial shift in procurement practices, away from South African manufacturers to foreign low-cost producers, particularly from China, was feared to cause considerable harm to domestic suppliers, especially SMEs. As a remedy, the opponents suggested the imposition of a local procurement quota.[23] The SMMEF, for example, demanded that the merged entity should 'maintain current levels of procurement of products ... from [small, medium, and micro enterprises] at the date of the merger for a period of at least three years'.[24] The proposed domestic procurement condition was one of the most controversial issues before the Competition Tribunal. The merging parties even threatened to 'walk away from the transaction'[25] and to push for WTO action against South Africa[26] if such a condition was imposed. In

[17] See Competition Tribunal (n 1) Competition Commission's Submissions (16 May 2011) paras 4–5; ibid, Reasons for Decision (29 June 2011) paras 26–27.

[18] s 11(5) of the Competition Act 89 of 1998 (SA); Competition Commission of South Africa, 'Merger Thresholds' <http://www.compcom.co.za/merger-thresholds> accessed 20 January 2017.

[19] See s 14A(1) of the Competition Act 89 of 1998 (SA).

[20] Competition Tribunal (n 1) Competition Commission's Submissions (16 May 2011) paras 9–19.

[21] South African Commercial Catering and Allied Workers Union (SACCAWU), the Congress of South African Trade Unions (COSATU), the Food and Allied Workers Union (FAWU), and the National Union of Metal Workers in South Africa (NUMSA).

[22] For a general critical account of Walmart's impact on local communities, see Jane Kelsey, *Serving Whose Interests? The Political Economy of Trade in Services Agreements* (Routledge-Cavendish 2008) 270–76.

[23] Competition Tribunal (n 1) Reasons for Decision (29 June 2011) para 75.

[24] Competition Tribunal (n 1) Submissions of the South African Small Medium and Micro Enterprise Forum (16 May 2011) para 69.

[25] Competition Tribunal (n 1) The Merging Parties' Position on Conditions (16 May 2011) para 2.3.

[26] Ann Crotty, 'Walmart "Could Seek WTO Relief" ' *Independent Online* (Pretoria, 24 October 2011) <http://www.iol.co.za/business/news/walmart-could-seek-wto-relief-1162964> accessed 20 January 2017.

an effort to counter the public interest concerns, Walmart and Massmart proposed certain undertakings: first, a moratorium on merger-related retrenchments for a period of two years; second, the recognition of existing labour agreements and of SACCAWU's position within the company for at least three years; and third, the setting up of a fund with the amount of R100 million (more than US$6 million) to support small and medium-sized South African suppliers (the so-called 'investment remedy').[27] The Competition Tribunal was satisfied that these voluntary undertakings were adequate and approved the merger accordingly.[28]

Subsequently, the Competition Tribunal's decision was appealed, bringing the merger before the Competition Appeal Court. In its March 2012 judgment, the Competition Appeal Court largely confirmed the conditions imposed by the Competition Tribunal.[29] However, it held that the Tribunal had only insufficiently examined whether the proposed investment remedy was in fact appropriate to address the merger-related implications for SMEs.[30] Therefore, it commissioned a study regarding the exact parameters (framework, operation, size) of the fund.[31] In its second judgment of October 2012, the Competition Appeal Court then directed the establishment of a R200 million fund (almost US$13 million), the purpose of which is, in the words of the court, 'to minimize the risks to micro, small and medium sized producers of South African products caused or which may be caused by Massmart's merger with Wal-Mart'.[32] Meanwhile, the fund has been established under the name 'Supplier Development Fund'.[33]

## C. World Trade Law

The facts of the Walmart/Massmart case give rise to a number of questions under WTO law which will be addressed in this section. First, it is necessary to make some general remarks on the application of WTO law to domestic competition laws and decisions. Second, it will be discussed whether South Africa was allowed, under WTO law, to prohibit the merger on the basis of SME-specific concerns (which it did not) or to condition approval on compliance with certain SME-friendly performance requirements (which it did).

[27] Competition Tribunal (n 1) The Merging Parties' Position on Conditions (16 May 2011).

[28] Competition Tribunal (n 1) Order (31 May 2011) paras 1.1–1.4.

[29] In addition, it ordered the reinstatement of 503 employees that were laid off in the run-up to the Walmart/Massmart merger.

[30] Competition Appeal Court (n 1) Judgment (9 March 2012) paras 165–68.

[31] ibid 108–10. [32] ibid, Judgment (9 October 2012) 30.

[33] The first two annual reports are available online, see Massmart Holdings Ltd, 'Supplier Development Fund: Annual Report 2013' <http://www.massmart.co.za/wp-content/uploads/2014/03/SDF-2013-Condensed-Report.pdf> accessed 20 January 2017; ibid, 'Supplier Development Fund: Annual Report 2014' <http://www.massmart.co.za/wp-content/uploads/2014/08/Massmart-SDF-2014.pdf> accessed 20 January 2017.

## I. Application of WTO law to domestic competition laws and decisions

As a first step, it needs to be determined whether WTO law applies to domestic competition laws and decisions, such as the South African Competition Act of 1998 and the corresponding decisions of the South African Competition Tribunal and Competition Appeal Court. The application of WTO law to competition issues is politically very sensitive. In particular, there are strong political reservations about the application of the WTO dispute settlement procedure to individual competition decisions. On several occasions, the European Union, for instance, expressed the view that 'there should be no dispute settlement review of individual decisions'.[34] Furthermore, the application of WTO law to domestic competition laws and decisions is also politically controversial, because there is no carve-out for SME development policies under current WTO law with respect to national competition regimes. Many developing countries have demanded such an SME exception.[35] They called for a flexible approach in the application of competition policy with respect to SMEs, in particular regarding exceptions from the principle of non-discrimination.[36]

From a legal perspective, however, it is clear that competition issues are not excluded a priori from the scope of WTO law. In an article of 2002, Ehlermann and Ehring have demonstrated that the GATT fully applies to competition laws and to individual competition decisions.[37] As will be explained below, this finding holds equally true for the GATS. Therefore, while WTO Members will be rather reluctant to initiate a review in practice, competition-related cases such as the Walmart/Massmart merger may, in principle, be challenged through the WTO dispute settlement system.

[34] WTO, 'Preparations for the 1999 Ministerial Conference, EC Approach to Trade and Competition: Communication from the European Communities' (2 June 1999) WT/GC/W/191, para 4. See also WTO, Working Group on the Interaction between Trade and Competition Policy, 'Communication from the European Community and Its Member States' (12 July 1999) WT/WGTCP/W/130, 6; WTO, Working Group on the Interaction between Trade and Competition Policy, 'Communication from the European Community and its Member States' (14 March 2001) WT/WGTCP/W/160, 3, 5.

[35] Such demands were voiced during the discussions on the development of a multilateral framework on competition policy in the WTO; see WTO, 'Report (1998) of the Working Group on the Interaction between Trade and Competition Policy to the General Council' (8 December 1998) WT/WGTCP/2, paras 26, 37–38, 48, 134; WTO, 'Report (1999) of the Working Group on the Interaction between Trade and Competition Policy to the General Council' (11 October 1999) WT/WGTCP/3, para 76; WTO, 'Report (2001) of the Working Group on the Interaction between Trade and Competition Policy to the General Council' (8 October 2001) WT/WGTCP/5, paras 21, 39, 49; WTO, 'Report (2002) of the Working Group on the Interaction between Trade and Competition Policy to the General Council' (9 December 2002) WT/WGTCP/6, paras 25, 37, 42, 44; WTO, 'Report (2003) of the Working Group on the Interaction between Trade and Competition Policy to the General Council' (17 July 2003) WT/WGTCP/7, para 31.

[36] ibid.

[37] Claus-Dieter Ehlermann and Lothar Ehring, 'WTO Dispute Settlement and Competition Law: Views from the Perspective of the Appellate Body's Experience' (2002) 26(6) Fordham International Law Journal 1505.

## II. Market access rights for Walmart

Given that some of the merger's opponents called for its prohibition on the basis of the public interest test contained in section 12A of the Competition Act, it is apposite to examine whether the Competition Tribunal and the Competition Appeal Court would have been at liberty, under international law, to prohibit the transaction by reason of the adverse effects on SMEs.

A prohibition decision could conflict with establishment rights under international economic law. In particular, such rights could arise under the GATS. Indeed, one commentator suggested that '[s]hould Walmart's entry into the South African market be refused … South Africa will in principle be violating its GATS obligations'.[38] Article XVI of the GATS is of relevance in this context. It prohibits the adoption or maintenance of certain measures, which are defined as market access barriers.

Prior to a closer analysis of Article XVI GATS, the general application of the GATS to the Walmart/Massmart merger decision needs to be addressed. According to Article I:1 GATS, the agreement 'applies to measures by Members affecting trade in services'. The definition of 'measure' is all-encompassing, including laws, regulations, rules, procedures, decisions, and administrative action.[39] Acts of the judiciary are covered by this definition.[40] The South African Competition Act clearly is a 'law', the order of the Competition Tribunal can be classified as a 'decision' or 'administrative action', and the judgments of the Competition Appeal Court, which is part of the judicial system of South Africa,[41] constitute judicial acts. Furthermore, the term 'affecting' has been given a broad interpretation in WTO jurisprudence.[42] Trade in services includes, inter alia, the supply of a service 'by a service supplier of one Member, through commercial presence in the territory of any other Member'.[43] This is the so-called mode 3 of the GATS. Notably, the term 'commercial presence' includes the acquisition of a juridical person.[44] In this light, it can be assumed that the GATS covers investment in services.[45]

Article XVI GATS only applies where specific liberalization commitments have been undertaken. Such commitments are recorded in the Schedule of Specific Commitments of each WTO Member. As South Africa has undertaken

38 Paul Kruger, 'The Impact of WTO Law on Foreign Investment: The Walmart/Massmart Merger' (tralac Working Paper S12WP03/2012, 2012), 9–10 <http://www.tralac.org/files/2012/02/S12WP032012-Kruger-Impact-WTO-law-foreign-investment-WalmartMassmart-merger-FIN.pdf> accessed 20 January 2017.

39 cf Art XXVIII(a) GATS.

40 Clemens Feinäugle, 'Article XXVIII GATS: Definitions' in Rüdiger Wolfrum, Peter-Tobias Stoll, and Clemens Feinäugle (eds), *WTO: Trade in Services* (Martinus Nijhoff 2008) para 4.

41 cf s 36(1)(a) of the Competition Act 89 of 1998 (SA) in conjunction with s 166(e) of the Constitution of the Republic of South Africa (1996).

42 WTO, *European Communities—Regime for the Importation, Sale and Distribution of Bananas*, Report of the Appellate Body (9 September 1997), WT/DS27/AB/R (*EC—Bananas* (AB)) para 220.

43 Art I:2(c) GATS.

44 Art XXVIII(d)(i) GATS.

45 For a general overview, see Martín Molinuevo, *Protecting Investment in Services: Investor-State Arbitration versus WTO Dispute Settlement* (Kluwer Law International 2012); Karl Sidhu, *Die Regelung von Direktinvestitionen in der WTO: Das TRIMs-Abkommen und das GATS* (V&R unipress 2004).

a commitment on mode 3 in the wholesale and retailing sector with respect to market access,[46] the Walmart/Massmart merger is subject to review under Article XVI GATS. The question now arises as to whether a denial of authorization for a specific merger, which allegedly has detrimental effects on domestic SMEs, constitutes a market access barrier in violation of Article XVI GATS. A similar question arises in connection with decisions by investment screening agencies, which may reject 'undesirable' investments from abroad. To give an answer to this question, it is important to note that Article XVI GATS does not guarantee full market access as commonly understood, ie the absence of any obstacles to the inflow of foreign direct investment (FDI), but rather prohibits the adoption or maintenance of an exhaustive list of market access restrictions.[47] The most relevant provision in this context is Article XVI:2(a) GATS, which prohibits 'limitations on the number of service suppliers whether in the form of numerical quotas, monopolies, exclusive service suppliers or the requirements of an economic needs test'.

One could argue that the prohibition of the Walmart/Massmart merger qualifies as a 'limitation on the number of service suppliers ... *in the form of ... the requirements of an economic needs test*'.[48] Economic needs tests (ENTs) are indeed quite a frequent phenomenon, not least in the retail sector.[49] Roughly half of all WTO Member States have scheduled such tests.[50] Notably, some of these scheduled ENTs explicitly relate to SMEs.[51] Unfortunately, the concept of 'economic needs test' lacks a definition in the GATS.[52] It is therefore highly difficult to determine which measures amount to an ENT within the meaning of Article XVI GATS. Broadly speaking, ENTs condition market access based on an assessment of the 'needs' of the domestic market, which are frequently defined in accordance with national public policy objectives.[53] Such needs could conceivably relate, for instance, to the promotion of SMEs. Where investment authorization is granted based on economic criteria relating to 'the effect that [a given] merger will have on the ability of small businesses ... to become competitive',[54] to quote the South African Competition Act, this may prima facie amount to an ENT.

What militates against this, however, is the statement of the WTO Secretariat that 'the *quantitative nature* of measures in the form of ENTs means that ... these are measures based on criteria the fulfillment of which is *beyond the control* of the affected service supplier'.[55] It should be pointed out in this respect that the Competition Act

[46] WTO, 'South Africa—Schedule of Specific Commitments' (15 April 1994) GATS/SC/78, 16.

[47] Molinuevo (n 45) 84. [48] Emphasis added.

[49] cf UNCTAD, 'Lists of Economic Needs Tests in the GATS Schedules of Specific Commitments' (6 September 1999) UNCTAD/ITCD/TSB/8, para 6.

[50] ibid, para 4.

[51] See also Rudolf Adlung and Marta Soprana, Chapter 1 of this volume, text accompanying n 23.

[52] WTO, 'Economic Needs Tests: Note by the Secretariat' (30 November 2001) S/CSS/W/118, para 4.

[53] OECD, Working Party of the Trade Committee, 'Assessing Barriers to Trade in Services: The Scheduling of Economic Needs Tests in the GATS: An Overview' (10 November 2000) TD/TC/WP(2000)11/FINAL, para 3.

[54] s 12A(3)(c) of the Competition Act 89 of 1998 (SA).

[55] WTO (n 52) para 6 (emphases in the original).

does not set any fixed quantitative limit, but instead prescribes a flexible case-by-case approach. Furthermore, the fulfilment of the relevant criterion—consideration of the interests of SMEs—is not entirely beyond the control of the merging parties. They are in fact in a position to take appropriate steps to ensure that SMEs are not significantly harmed as a result of the merger. It is thus doubtful whether a denial of the Walmart/Massmart merger on SME-related grounds could be characterized as an ENT within the meaning of Article XVI GATS.

On a more general note, it is unclear whether the market access provision can be invoked to challenge measures affecting only a single service supplier as opposed to general measures that affect a large indefinite number of service suppliers.[56] Moreover, a violation of Article XVI GATS could be justified in any event under the general exception clause of Article XIV GATS.[57] This issue is addressed further below in the context of the discussion of the national treatment principle of the GATS.[58]

## III. Imposition of performance requirements

### 1. *Introductory remarks*

Apart from the question of whether international economic law precludes states from prohibiting mergers on SME-related grounds, the legality of the imposition of SME-friendly performance requirements as a precondition for merger approval was a key issue in the Walmart/Massmart case. For the following analysis, it is useful to distinguish between goods-related and services-related performance requirements.

With respect to the former, Walmart and Massmart argued vigorously throughout the proceedings that the imposition of a local sourcing requirement would constitute a breach of WTO law. Indeed, an appreciable part of the merging parties' written and oral submissions was dedicated to this issue.[59] The merging parties relied mainly on Article III:4 GATT and Article 2 of the Agreement on Trade-Related Investment Measures (TRIMs),[60] but also cited a host of other

[56] See Bart De Meester, *Liberalization of Trade in Banking Services: An International and European Perspective* (Cambridge University Press 2014) 227–30 (discussing under which circumstances art XVI GATS gives rise to market access rights of individual service suppliers). See also Bart De Meester and Dominic Coppens, 'Mode 3 of the GATS: A Model for Disciplining Measures Affecting Investment Flows?' in Zdenek Drabek and Petros C Mavroidis (eds), *Regulation of Foreign Investment: Challenges to International Harmonization* (World Scientific Publishing 2013) 112–18. In addition, some authors have stated that the GATS does not place any restrictions on investment screening, see Molinuevo (n 45) 84; Americo B Zampetti and Pierre Sauvé, 'International Investment' in Andrew T Guzman and Alan O Sykes (eds), *Research Handbook in International Economic Law* (Edward Elgar 2007) 256: 'The GATS does not contain provisions dealing directly with matters of investment screening ... which may be subject to terms and conditions inscribed in national schedules'.

[57] Art XIV(c) GATS. [58] See Section C.III.3 below.

[59] Competition Tribunal (n 1) Merging Parties' Written Submissions (16 May 2011) 67–74; ibid, Transcript of Hearing (12 May 2011) 606–13; ibid, Transcript of Hearing (16 May 2011) 1004–09; Competition Appeal Court (n 1) Merged Firm's Written Submissions (10 October 2011) 77–96.

[60] Agreement on Trade-Related Investment Measures (adopted 15 April 1994, entered into force 1 January 1995) 1868 UNTS 186.

provisions.[61] These international law arguments, however, were avoided by the trade unions and the government ministers in their written submissions.[62] During the oral hearing, the team representing the government ministers accepted that, depending on their design, procurement conditions in favour of SMEs 'might indeed infringe Article III:4 of GATT' and focused on the general exceptions under Article XX GATT.[63]

Although the Competition Tribunal dismissed the domestic procurement requirement mainly for reasons of practicality, its dubious legality in terms of international law certainly played a role. Indeed, the Competition Tribunal observed that the legal objections raised by the merging parties 'may well be correct and add to the problems associated with this proposed remedy'.[64] Furthermore, it is noteworthy that the Competition Appeal Court, recapitulating the findings of the Competition Tribunal, understood the Tribunal's decision to mean that 'the procurement condition would be impermissible as it would render the country in breach of trade obligations under several international trade agreements to which South Africa was a party'.[65] However, the Competition Appeal Court refrained from pronouncing itself on the validity of the international law arguments. It merely stated that 'it is unnecessary, at this stage to engage with the interesting arguments raised in respect of conditions and relevant provisions of international law, particularly GATT'.[66]

The merging parties' international law arguments were not exclusively geared towards trade in goods, but also addressed possible services-related performance requirements. For example, it was asserted that the following measures would violate international law: (1) limitations on foreign ownership; (2) limitations on the scale of operations; (3) mandatory compliance with 'broader economic strategies'; (4) recognition of union contracts; (5) restricting retail stores to the outskirts of cities; and (6) restricting expansion.[67] For obvious reasons, however, the lawfulness

[61] Arts III:5 and XI GATT; Arts II, XVI, and XVII GATS; Art 2.1 of the Agreement on Technical Barriers to Trade (adopted 15 April 1994, entered into force 1 January 1995) 1868 UNTS 120; Art 3 of the Agreement on Subsidies and Countervailing Measures (adopted 15 April 1994, entered into force 1 January 1995) 1867 UNTS 14.

[62] Competition Tribunal (n 1) Heads of Argument for SACCAWU and others (May 2011) 13, para 3.4.1; ibid, Heads of Argument on Behalf of the Government Departments (May 2011) 103, para 209; Competition Appeal Court (n 1) The Ministers' Submissions (3 October 2011) para 253.2. It seems that the government's legal team produced a separate note dealing with the pertinent issues under international trade law. However, this document is not publicly available.

[63] Competition Tribunal (n 1) Transcript of Hearing (16 May 2011) 1102–03.

[64] Competition Tribunal (n 1) Reasons for Decision (29 June 2011) paras 111–12.

[65] Competition Appeal Court (n 1) Judgment (9 March 2012) para 25. See also, in this regard, David Lewis, *Enforcing Competition Rules in South Africa: Thieves at the Dinner Table* (Edward Elgar 2013) 124: 'Although the Tribunal did not finally have to decide this point, it ... appeared to accept that the imposition of a procurement-related condition of the kind sought would be contrary to South Africa's international trade obligations.'

[66] Competition Appeal Court (n 1) Judgment (9 March 2012) para 171. Boulle noted in this respect that 'all phases of the merger approval process neatly circumvented the issue of possible non-compliance with the country's international economic obligations', see Boulle (n 2) 325.

[67] Competition Tribunal (n 1) Merging Parties' Written Submissions (16 May 2011) paras 170–71; Competition Appeal Court (n 1) Merged Firm's Written Submissions (10 October 2011) paras 232–33.

of those merger conditions that Walmart and Massmart themselves had proposed[68] (including notably the investment remedy), and that were subsequently imposed by the Competition Tribunal, was not challenged. This could explain why the Competition Tribunal noted, without further elaboration, that the requirement to establish an SME fund 'does not raise the concerns that the procurement remedy does'.[69]

The foregoing demonstrates that great uncertainty remains as to which performance requirements can be lawfully imposed under international economic law with a view to protecting domestic SMEs.

## 2. *Local procurement condition*

In what follows, the SME-friendly domestic procurement condition will be analysed. The inclusion of such a goods-related performance requirement into an individual competition decision could primarily raise issues of inconsistency with the GATT, in particular the national treatment principle in Article III:4 GATT. Article III:4 GATT reads:

> The products of the territory of any contracting party imported into the territory of any other contracting party shall be accorded treatment no less favourable than that accorded to like products of national origin in respect of all laws, regulations and requirements affecting their internal sale, offering for sale, purchase, transportation, distribution or use.

In *Korea—Various Measures on Beef*,[70] the Appellate Body held that Article III:4 GATT involves a three-tier test: The internal regulation must be a law, regulation, or requirement affecting the internal sale, offering for sale, purchase, transportation, distribution, or use of products; the imported and domestic products must be 'like products'; and the imported products must be accorded 'less favourable' treatment than that accorded to like domestic products.[71] Regarding the first part of the test, Ehlermann and Ehring have pointed out that individual decisions of competition authorities can be considered to fall into the category of 'requirements'.[72] Indeed, in the *Canada—Administration of the Foreign Investment Review Act*[73] case, the Panel held that 'in judging whether a measure is contrary to obligations under Article III:4, it is not relevant whether it applies across-the-board or only in isolated cases. Any interpretation which would exclude case-by-case action would, in the view of the Panel, defeat the purposes of Article III:4'.[74] Regarding the second part of the test, it is not necessary to carry out an in-depth analysis of likeness in the case

[68] cf Competition Tribunal (n 1) The Merging Parties' Position on Conditions (16 May 2011).

[69] Competition Tribunal (n 1) Reasons for Decision (29 June 2011) para 121.

[70] WTO, *Korea—Measures Affecting Imports of Fresh, Chilled and Frozen Beef*, Reports of the Appellate Body (11 December 2000), WT/DS161/AB/R, WT/DS169/AB/R (*Korea—Beef*).

[71] ibid, para 133.

[72] Ehlermann and Ehring (n 37) 1526.

[73] GATT, *Canada—Administration of the Foreign Investment Review Act*, Report of the Panel (7 February 1984) BISD 30S/140.

[74] ibid, para 5.5. See also Peter Van den Bossche and Werner Zdouc, *The Law and Policy of the World Trade Organization* (3rd edn, Cambridge University Press 2013) 385.

of the Walmart/Massmart merger. WTO case law has confirmed that the likeness criterion is met where a measure makes a clear origin-based distinction.[75] As the proposed procurement condition distinguishes between domestic and imported products merely by virtue of their origin, the 'like products' requirement in Article III:4 GATT is satisfied. Also, imported products are clearly treated less favourably than domestic products within the meaning of Article III:4 GATT, because the procurement condition would modify the conditions of competition in the relevant market to the detriment of imported products.[76] As a result, the proposed procurement condition would violate Article III:4 GATT.

The procurement condition would also be prohibited by the TRIMs Agreement. Article 2.1 of the agreement outlaws all trade-related investment measures 'which are mandatory or enforceable under domestic law or under administrative rulings … and which require the purchase or use by an enterprise of products of domestic origin or from any domestic source'.[77] The procurement condition clearly matches this definition. It should be noted that the South African Government takes the position that, under the TRIMs Agreement, 'the [Republic of South Africa] cannot give national investors any preferential treatment over foreign investors *once they are established in the country*'.[78] This legal statement is certainly inaccurate,[79] but it might explain why the government believed that the procurement condition was in line with the TRIMs Agreement.[80]

The violation of Article III:4 GATT and Article 2.1 TRIMs Agreement could be justified under Article XX GATT.[81] Although SMEs are not explicitly mentioned in the general exception provision of the GATT,[82] Article XX could nevertheless

[75] See WTO, *Argentina—Measures Relating to Trade in Goods and Services*, Report of the Appellate Body (14 April 2016) WT/DS453/AB/R, para 6.36 (with further references); Van den Bossche and Zdouc (n 74) 393–94.

[76] cf WTO, *European Communities—Measures Prohibiting the Importation and Marketing of Seal Products*, Reports of the Appellate Body (22 May 2014), WT/DS400/AB/R, WT/DS401/AB/R, para 5.101.

[77] Art 2.1 of the TRIMs Agreement in conjunction with Art 2.2 and the Annex.

[78] Department of Trade and Industry of the Republic of South Africa, 'Bilateral Investment Treaty Policy Framework Review: Government Position Paper' (2009) 48 <http://www.pmg.org.za/policy-documents/2009/06/25/bilateral-investment-treaty-policy-framework-review> accessed 20 January 2017 (emphasis added).

[79] See Rudolf Dolzer and Christoph Schreuer, *Principles of International Investment Law* (2nd edn, Oxford University Press 2012) 90–92; August Reinisch, '§ 8: Internationales Investitionsschutzrecht' in Christian Tietje (ed), *Internationales Wirtschaftsrecht* (De Gruyter 2009) 355–56 (who discuss performance requirements and the TRIMs Agreement as part of the admission and establishment of investments).

[80] cf Competition Tribunal (n 1) Transcript of Hearing (16 May 2011) 1114.

[81] Art XX GATT can also justify violations of the TRIMs Agreement; see Art 3 of the TRIMs Agreement.

[82] See Petros C Mavroidis, *Trade in Goods: The GATT and the Other WTO Agreements Regulating Trade in Goods* (Oxford University Press 2012) 333: '… recall [art XX GATT] is an exhaustive list and, if the regulating state pursues an objective other than those mentioned in its list (*e.g. protection of small and medium enterprises*), it can find itself unable to defend its measures' (emphasis added); ibid 307: 'Another example would be domestic taxation that treats products originating from small and medium enterprises more favourably than products of bigger players…. *The defendant would then have a hard time justifying its measures under Art. XX GATT*' (emphasis added).

be invoked in the present context. The first possible justification is Article XX(d) GATT, which permits Member States to derogate from their WTO obligations when they adopt measures 'necessary to secure compliance with laws or regulations which are not inconsistent with the provisions of [the GATT]'.[83] In addition, such measures must comply with the Chapeau of Article XX GATT.

First of all, the decisions of the Competition Tribunal and the Competition Appeal Court are clearly designed to enforce specific rules and requirements of the South African Competition Act, namely section 12A thereof. Thus, they can be said to 'secure compliance' with that law.[84] Furthermore, the Competition Act is in conformity with the national treatment obligation of the GATT. There is no obvious reason why it should modify the conditions of competition between imported and like domestic products to the detriment of the former. Finally, in order to invoke Article XX(d) GATT, the measure at issue must also be 'necessary' to secure compliance with a GATT-consistent law or regulation. Following well-established WTO jurisprudence, the necessity analysis involves 'a process of weighing and balancing a series of factors', which include

> the relative importance of the common interests or values that the law or regulation to be enforced is intended to protect (the more vital or important those common interests or values are, the easier it would be to accept as 'necessary' a measure designed as an enforcement instrument); the extent to which the measure contributes to the realization of the end pursued, the securing of compliance with the law or regulation at issue (the greater the contribution, the more easily a measure might be considered to be 'necessary'); and, the restrictive impact of the measure on imported goods (a measure with a relatively small impact upon imported products might more easily be considered as 'necessary' than a measure with intense or broader restrictive effects).[85]

Based on these parameters, a number of observations can be made. With respect to the importance of the interests or values, it can be said, on the one hand, that the objective to support SMEs—primarily an economic interest—is not as important as, for instance, the protection of human life and health against a life-threatening health risk.[86] On the other hand, it has been recognized in WTO jurisprudence that an assessment of the importance of the interests or values must take into account the 'prevailing circumstances' and 'particular realities' faced by the respective WTO

[83] The possibility to invoke Art XX(d) GATT in order to justify individual decisions of competition authorities is highlighted by Ehlermann and Ehring (n 37) 1529.

[84] cf WTO, *Argentina—Measures Relating to Trade in Goods and Services*, paras 6.202–6.203; WTO, *Korea—Beef*, para 157.

[85] WTO, *Dominican Republic—Measures Affecting the Importation and Internal Sale of Cigarettes*, Report of the Panel (26 November 2004) WT/DS302/R (*Dominican Republic—Cigarettes*) para 7.214 (referring to WTO, *Korea—Beef*, paras 162–63). This approach towards assessing the 'necessity' of a measure was recently confirmed in WTO, *United States—Measures Relating to Shrimp from Thailand*, Report of the Appellate Body (16 July 2008), WT/DS343/AB/R, para 316; and WTO, *United States—Customs Bond Directive for Merchandise Subject to Anti-Dumping/Countervailing Duties*, Report of the Appellate Body (16 July 2008), WT/DS345/AB/R, para 316.

[86] cf WTO, *Canada—Measures Relating to Exports of Wheat and Treatment of Imported Grain*, Report of the Appellate Body (30 August 2004), WT/DS276/AB/R, paras 6.224, 6.303.

Member.[87] The protection of SMEs is certainly relatively more important for South Africa than for many other (developed) countries. With respect to the second criterion—the extent to which the measure contributes to the realization of the end pursued—one should note that the Competition Tribunal itself recognized the 'dubious utility' of the domestic procurement condition.[88] In this light, there are grounds for doubting the effectiveness of the measure. Lastly, with respect to the measure's trade-restrictiveness, it will be recalled that the procurement condition would freeze Walmart's level of local procurement for a certain period of time and would thus, in effect, constitute a restriction on importation. Considering all these factors, it appears that it would be difficult for the South African Government to establish the necessity of the domestic procurement condition.[89]

Furthermore, the Appellate Body has stated that the availability of a WTO-consistent alternative measure, which the Member concerned could 'reasonably be expected to employ', also has an important bearing on the necessity analysis.[90] In a WTO dispute, the complaining Member could argue that the requirement to establish a fund for the benefit of SMEs is sufficient to address the public interest concerns in accordance with the South African Competition Act. Indeed, the Competition Tribunal and the Competition Appeal Court accepted that the public interest concerns could be 'adequately remedied' by, inter alia, the establishment of such a fund.[91] Under the assumption that this 'investment remedy' is WTO/GATS-consistent,[92] a claim that the domestic procurement condition is necessary would hardly be sustainable.

Another possible justification is provided by Article XX(a) GATT. It allows WTO Member States to adopt measures 'necessary to protect public morals'. The exception provided in Article XX(a) GATT was invoked by the South African Government in the hearing before the Competition Tribunal[93] and subsequently discussed in the merged firm's written submissions before the Competition Appeal Court.[94] In *China—Publications and Audiovisual Products*, the Panel stated that the term 'public morals' signifies 'standards of right and wrong conduct maintained by or on behalf of a community or nation'.[95] According to the Panel, this includes

[87] WTO, *Colombia—Indicative Prices and Restrictions on Ports of Entry*, Report of the Panel (27 April 2009) WT/DS366/R, paras 7.562–7.566. See also WTO, *Dominican Republic—Cigarettes*, para 7.215.

[88] Competition Tribunal (n 1) Reasons for Decision (29 June 2011) para 110.

[89] It is telling that the Competition Tribunal itself concluded that a local procurement condition would not be 'proportional', see ibid, para 117.

[90] WTO, *Korea—Beef*, para 165 (referring to WTO, *United States—Section 337 of the Tariff Act of 1930* (16 January 1989) BISD 36S/345, para 5.26).

[91] See Competition Appeal Court (n 1) Judgment (9 March 2012) para 1.

[92] This question will be addressed below in section C.III.3.

[93] Competition Tribunal (n 1) Transcript of Hearing (16 May 2011) 1102–03.

[94] Competition Appeal Court (n 1) Merged Firm's Written Submissions (10 October 2011) paras 218–28.

[95] WTO, *China—Measures Affecting Trading Rights and Distribution Services for Certain Publications and Audiovisual Entertainment Products*, Report of the Panel (12 August 2009) WT/DS363/R, para 7.759 (referring to WTO, *United States—Measures Affecting the Cross-Border Supply of Gambling and Betting Services*, Report of the Panel (10 November 2004), WT/DS285/R (*US—Gambling*) para 6.465).

'prevailing social, cultural, ethical and religious values'.[96] On the basis of this definition, it seems plausible that Article XX(a) GATT covers measures relating to pornography, drugs, narcotics,[97] gambling and betting,[98] seal welfare,[99] and violations of core labour or human rights standards.[100] In contrast, it seems difficult to justify purely economically motivated governmental action which is aimed at supporting SMEs. It might, however, be possible to subsume the South African Black Economic Empowerment (BEE) legislation under the type of policies encompassed by Article XX(a) GATT.[101] Before the Competition Tribunal, the South African Government argued that the public morals exception in Article XX(a) GATT 'will in all likelihood apply' and that '[a] persuasive case could be mounted that such a measure is necessary to protect public morals in order to eradicate the after effects of apartheid'.[102] Indeed, the Competition Act of 1998 is one piece of legislation introduced after the end of the apartheid era in 1994 which sought to redress the injustices of apartheid.[103] In South Africa, the BEE legislation and the promotion of SMEs are closely intertwined.[104] Still, as under Article XX(d) GATT, it would need to be demonstrated that the domestic procurement condition is 'necessary' for the attainment of BEE objectives.

In summary, mandatory local procurement requirements in individual competition decisions, which are imposed to remedy SME-specific concerns, are in principle inconsistent with WTO law. Therefore, the Competition Tribunal and the Competition Appeal Court were right to approach the issue with caution.

[96] ibid.

[97] Mark Wu, 'Free Trade and the Protection of Public Morals: An Analysis of the Newly Emerging Public Morals Clause Doctrine' (2008) 33 Yale Journal of International Law 215, 250–51.

[98] WTO, *US—Gambling*, paras 6.479–6.487.

[99] WTO, *European Communities—Measures Prohibiting the Importation and Marketing of Seal Products*, Reports of the Panel (25 November 2013) WT/DS400/R, WT/DS401/R, paras 7.409–7.410 (subsequently upheld by the Appellate Body).

[100] Nicola Wenzel, 'Article XX lit. a GATT' in Rüdiger Wolfrum, Peter-Tobias Stoll, and Holger P Hestermeyer (eds), *WTO: Trade in Goods* (Martinus Nijhoff 2011) paras 23–30.

[101] See on this Paul Kruger, 'Empowerment Policies in SADC and Their Effect on Agreement Design' (tralac Trade Brief S11TB10/2011, 2011) 14–16 <http://www.tralac.org/publications/article/4610-empowerment-policies-in-sadc-and-their-effect-on-agreement-design.html> accessed 20 January 2017.

[102] Competition Tribunal (n 1) Transcript of Hearing (16 May 2011) 1103.

[103] Department of Trade and Industry of the Republic of South Africa, 'South Africa's Economic Transformation: A Strategy for Broad-Based Black Economic Empowerment' (2003) paras 2.4.1–2.4.4.4 <http://www.thedti.gov.za/economic_empowerment/bee-strategy.pdf> accessed 20 January 2017.

[104] OECD, 'Competition Law and Policy in South Africa: An OECD Peer Review' (2003) 52 <http://www.oecd.org/daf/competition/prosecutionandlawenforcement/2958714.pdf> accessed 20 January 2017: 'Support for small business is closely related to the policy of empowering historically disadvantaged populations, as their business operations are often small ones'; Department of Trade and Industry of the Republic of South Africa, 'White Paper on National Strategy for the Development and Promotion of Small Business in South Africa' (1995) <http://www.thedti.gov.za/sme_development/docs/White_paper.pdf> accessed 20 January 2017; Neo Chabane, 'An Evaluation of the Influence of BEE on the Application of Competition Policy in South Africa' (2003) 7–8 <http://www.tips.org.za/research-archive/annual-forum-papers/2003/item/371-an-evaluation-of-the-influence-of-bee-on-the-application-of-competition-policy-in-south-africa> accessed 20 January 2017.

### 3. *Establishment of an SME fund*

As already mentioned, the Walmart/Massmart merger was eventually approved under several conditions, the most prominent of which relates to the establishment of a fund for the benefit of SMEs. This investment remedy, like other services-related performance requirements in favour of SMEs, could violate the national treatment obligation of the GATS. According to Article XVII GATS, South Africa is obliged to accord to services and service suppliers of any other Member, in respect of all measures affecting the supply of services, treatment no less favourable than it accords to its own like services and service suppliers.

In order to establish a breach of Article XVII GATS, the following four-pronged test applies: First, South Africa needs to have made a commitment on national treatment in the relevant sector and mode of supply. Second, the order to establish a fund for the benefit of SMEs must be a 'measure affecting the supply of services' in the relevant sector and mode of supply. Third, it needs to be established whether foreign services or service suppliers are 'like' domestic services or service suppliers. Fourth, the performance requirements must be shown to accord less favourable treatment to the foreign services or service suppliers than to the like domestic services or service suppliers.

As to the first requirement, South Africa has undertaken a full commitment on mode 3 in the wholesale and retailing sector with respect to national treatment.[105] As to the second requirement, the relevant terms have already been interpreted in the context of Article XVI GATS.[106] Based on the above observations, it seems uncontroversial that the respective administrative and judicial decisions are 'measures affecting the supply of services' through mode 3 in the wholesale and retail sector.[107] Some authors, however, argue that extending national treatment to market access restrictions would render certain elements of the market access provision superfluous.[108] In particular, this objection applies to market access restrictions which only exist in a discriminatory form, such as limitations on the participation of foreign capital (Article XVI:2(f)). As a consequence, these authors advocate a different interpretation of Article XVII GATS, according to which the national treatment provision would not apply to market access restrictions.[109] This interpretation regarding the scope of the national treatment provision conflicts, however, with the unequivocal wording of Article XVII GATS ('in respect of *all* measures affecting the supply of services'[110]). In

[105] WTO (n 46) 16. [106] See above nn 39–45 and accompanying text.

[107] Kruger (n 38) 10–11; Ehlermann and Ehring (n 37) 1519 (stating that their reasoning regarding the applicability of Art III:4 GATT to competition laws and individual competition decisions also applies '*mutatis mutandis*' to Art XVII GATS).

[108] Markus Krajewski and Maika Engelke, 'Article XVII GATS: National Treatment' in Rüdiger Wolfrum, Peter-Tobias Stoll, and Clemens Feinäugle (eds), *WTO: Trade in Services* (Martinus Nijhoff 2008) para 60.

[109] ibid, paras 62–65; Markus Krajewski, *National Regulation and Trade Liberalization in Services: The Legal Impact of the General Agreement on Trade in Services (GATS) on National Regulatory Autonomy* (Kluwer Law International 2003) 114–16; Felix Geiger, *Beschränkungen von Direktinvestitionen aus Drittstaaten* (Nomos 2013) 274–75.

[110] Emphasis added.

this light, preference must be given to a textual reading of Article XVII GATS. Thus, the correct view is that Article XVII GATS also covers market access restrictions.[111] It follows that performance requirements fall within the scope of application of Article XVII GATS.

Regarding the third requirement, much ambiguity still remains about the concept of likeness in the GATS.[112] What is clear is that the criteria flowing from the GATT jurisprudence cannot be transposed to the GATS context in a mechanistic fashion.[113] This is mainly due to the fact that services are—in contrast to goods—intangible and that the GATS refers to 'like services *and service suppliers*',[114] whereas the GATT only mentions 'like products'. In line with recent GATS case law, however, it is the competitive relationship between services and service suppliers which is crucial for the likeness analysis under the GATS.[115] The services provided by Walmart and the services provided by South-African-based retailers are beyond doubt essentially the same in competitive terms. Therefore, the likeness criterion is fulfilled.

The test of whether the national treatment obligation has been violated thus centres on the last requirement, ie whether the investment remedy accords *less favourable treatment* to the foreign services or service suppliers than to the like domestic services or service suppliers. Some authors have raised doubts about the possibility of challenging individual decisions relating to a particular investment by virtue of the national treatment obligation in the GATS.[116] To illustrate their argument, they specifically refer to the Walmart/Massmart merger, arguing that 'when a competent authority in a WTO Member would decide, after an assessment of the public interest considerations, that an investment can only take place provided the investor accepts certain undertakings, it is not clear whether such decision could violate the obligation of national treatment'.[117] As a basis for their argument, they cite an *obiter dictum* from the Appellate Body report in *EC—Asbestos*. The Appellate Body had stated in that case that

> even if two products are 'like', that does not mean that a measure is inconsistent with Article III:4 [of GATT 1994]. A complaining Member must still establish that the measure accords

[111] Joost Pauwelyn, 'Rien Ne Va Plus? Distinguishing Domestic Regulation from Market Access in GATT and GATS' (2005) 4(2) World Trade Review 131, 148–50; Aaditya Mattoo, 'National Treatment in the GATS: Corner Stone or Pandora's Box?' (1997) 31(1) Journal of World Trade 107, 113–17; Sidhu (n 45) 257–59.

[112] See Mireille Cossy, 'Some Thoughts on the Concept of "Likeness" in the GATS' in Marion Panizzon, Nicole Pohl, and Pierre Sauvé (eds), *GATS and the Regulation of International Trade in Services* (Cambridge University Press 2008).

[113] WTO, *Argentina—Measures Relating to Trade in Goods and Services*, paras 6.30–6.32; WTO, *China—Certain Measures Affecting Electronic Payment Services*, Report of the Panel (16 July 2012) WT/DS413/R, para 7.698.

[114] Emphasis added.

[115] WTO, *Argentina—Measures Relating to Trade in Goods and Services*, para 6.25 (citing WTO, *China—Certain Measures Affecting Electronic Payment Services*, para 7.700).

[116] De Meester and Coppens (n 56) 120–22.

[117] ibid 120 (footnotes omitted).

to the *group* of 'like' imported products 'less favourable treatment' than it accords to the *group* of 'like' domestic products.[118]

The Appellate Body's statement on the 'less favourable treatment' test clarifies the scope of de facto discrimination under Article III:4 GATT. It suggests that de facto discrimination does not occur solely on the basis that *any* imported product is treated less favourably compared to *any* like domestic product.[119] In contrast, an origin-neutral rule is de facto discriminatory only if imported products as a whole bear a heavier overall burden than the like domestic products as a whole.[120] In academic writing, it has been observed that such an approach effectively 'limits the scope of the WTO non-discrimination obligations to a ban on protection in general, *while disregarding individual instances of distorted competition between like or competitive products*'.[121]

Now the question arises whether this approach is also applicable to the GATS. Some commentators have indeed accepted that an analysis of 'treatment no less favourable' under the GATS must focus on whether the respective measure accords to the *group* of foreign services or service suppliers less favourable treatment than it accords to the *group* of like domestic services or service suppliers.[122] Therefore, a measure relating to only a single foreign service supplier (in casu, Walmart) cannot be said to result in a heavier burden for foreign service suppliers *as a whole*.[123] It does not disfavour *predominantly* foreign services or service suppliers in comparison to like domestic services or service suppliers. In fact, such a measure would fall precisely into the above-mentioned category of 'individual instances of distorted competition'. Any other interpretation would overstretch the boundaries of the national treatment obligation under the GATS at the expense of national regulatory autonomy. Thus, it is contended that the national treatment principle of the GATS is in principle unsuitable to be applied to individual competition decisions affecting only a single service supplier.[124] A violation of Article XVII GATS could

[118] WTO, *European Communities—Measures Affecting Asbestos and Asbestos-Containing Products*, Report of the Appellate Body (12 March 2001), WT/DS135/AB/R, para 100 (emphasis in the original removed, emphases added).

[119] Jochem Wiers and James Mathis, 'The Report of the Appellate Body in the Asbestos Dispute: WTO Appellate Body Report 12 March 2001, WT/DS135/AB/R, European Communities—Measures Affecting Asbestos and Asbestos-Containing Products' (2001) 28(2) Legal Issues of Economic Integration 211, 222–23.

[120] See on this Lothar Ehring, 'De Facto Discrimination in World Trade Law: National and Most-Favoured-Nation Treatment—or Equal Treatment?' (2002) 36(5) Journal of World Trade 921.

[121] ibid 973 (emphasis added).

[122] See Krajewski and Engelke (n 108) para 44 (referring to WTO, *European Communities—Regime for the Importation, Sale and Distribution of Bananas*, Report of the Panel (22 May 1997), WT/DS27/R/ECU (*EC—Bananas* (Panel)) paras 7.332–7.338); Nicolas F Diebold, *Non-Discrimination in International Trade in Services: 'Likeness' in WTO/GATS* (Cambridge University Press 2010) 37–45.

[123] See Piet Eeckhout, 'Constitutional Concepts for Free Trade in Services' in Gráinne de Búrca and Joanne Scott (eds), *The EU and the WTO: Legal and Constitutional Issues* (Hart Publishing 2001) 233–34.

[124] De Meester (n 56) 231–36.

exceptionally be envisaged in situations where there is manifest protectionism,[125] but this is clearly not the case here.

Furthermore, even if the requirement to establish a fund for the benefit of SMEs were to be found to violate the national treatment principle, GATS-inconsistent individual competition decisions could be justified under Article XIV(c) GATS, which exempts measures 'necessary to secure compliance with laws or regulations which are not inconsistent with the provisions of [the GATS]'. This provision is analogous to Article XX(d) GATT which has already been examined above in the context of the domestic procurement condition. The observations pertaining to the interpretation of Article XX(d) GATT also apply to Article XIV(c) GATS, since both provisions are textually almost identical.[126]

In order to invoke the justification under Article XIV(c) GATS, the South African Competition Act would need to be GATS-consistent. The national treatment obligation is the most relevant provision in this respect. It covers both de jure and de facto discrimination.[127] It will be recalled that the Competition Act mandates to consider the interests of SMEs in South Africa in every merger transaction.[128] This 'substantial public interest' test is applied even-handedly to foreign and domestic mergers[129] and usually results in the imposition of conditions on South African companies.[130] In this respect, there is no asymmetric impact on foreign services or service suppliers. There is, however, another aspect that could be problematic. While the SME provisions under section 12A of the Competition Act are facially neutral,[131] the 'beneficiaries' could predominantly be South African service providers, assuming that foreign service suppliers in South Africa will typically not meet the definition of an SME. If 'small' and 'big' companies are considered

[125] ibid 234–36; Bart De Meester, 'The Global Financial Crisis and Government Support for Banks: What Role for the GATS' (2010) 13(1) Journal of International Economic Law 27, 51; Ehlermann and Ehring (n 37) 1529.

[126] See WTO, *US—Gambling*, para 6.537.

[127] WTO, *Argentina—Measures Relating to Trade in Goods and Services*, para 6.105 (referring to WTO, *EC—Bananas* (AB), para 233).

[128] See above nn 12–14 and accompanying text.

[129] National Treasury of the Republic of South Africa (n 11) 15: 'There are no formal distinctions drawn between foreign and domestic mergers under the [Competition Act].'

[130] See, for instance, Competition Tribunal of South Africa, *Hyprop Investments Ltd and Sycom Property Fund Managers Ltd in Respect of the Property Letting Enterprise Known as 'Somerset Mall' and in Somerset Mall Property Management Company (Pty) Ltd*, Decision (7 August 2013) Case No 016683, paras 16–21; Competition Tribunal of South Africa, *Accelerate Property Fund Ltd and 15 Letting Enterprises Being Sold by Fourways Precinct (Pty) Ltd*, Decision (17 April 2013) Case No 016170, paras 10–14; Competition Tribunal of South Africa, *Synergy Income Fund Ltd and Khuthala Alliance (Pty) Ltd*, Reasons for Decision (20 July 2012) Case No 11/AM/Jan12, paras 12–14; Competition Tribunal of South Africa, *Media24 Ltd, Paarl Coldset (Pty) Ltd and The Natal Witness Printing and Publishing Company (Pty) Ltd*, Reasons for Decision (5 July 2012) Case No 15/LM/Jun11, paras 145–54.

[131] See n 15. Policies which favour only domestic SMEs are clearly inconsistent with Art XVII GATS. For this reason, Mexico included a horizontal reservation in the national treatment column under mode 3 for 'research and development subsidies and incentives to small service enterprises owned by Mexican nationals': see WTO, 'Mexico—Schedule of Specific Commitments' (15 April 1994) GATS/SC/56, 1.

to be 'like',[132] does this amount to de facto discrimination within the meaning of Article XVII GATS?[133] Given that the SME test under the Competition Act will be applied on a case-by-case basis in very different factual situations and will only occasionally lead to the imposition of merger conditions that could be considered to actually privilege SMEs (such as the 'investment remedy'), it will be extremely difficult for a complainant to make a convincing case that the conditions of competition in a specific sector are modified to the detriment of services or service suppliers of its origin. In this light, the Competition Act is, at least prima facie, GATS-consistent.

Finally, the requirement to set up an SME fund must also be 'necessary' to secure compliance with the SME-supportive public interest test of the Competition Act. The meaning of 'necessary' has already been analysed in the context of goods-related performance requirements under Article XX(d) GATT.[134] In that context, it was concluded that the domestic procurement condition is *not* 'necessary' to secure compliance with the Competition Act. The obligation to establish an SME fund, however, appears to meet the necessity test. Notably, in terms of the effectiveness of the measure, the fund enables the realization of targeted support measures for SMEs. Moreover, the ensuing trade-restrictive impact is marginal due to the limited duration of the fund (five years).

In conclusion, the obligation imposed on Walmart/Massmart by the South African Competition Appeal Court to establish a fund for the benefit of SMEs is not inconsistent with South Africa's obligations under Article XVII of the GATS. Therefore, while WTO rules effectively ban SME-friendly local procurement quotas, they permit the adoption of carefully drafted, well-balanced, services-related performance requirements in favour of SMEs. It is interesting to note in this connection that the current South African Minister of Economic Development, Ebrahim Patel, recently stated that the creation of an SME fund as part of the Walmart/Massmart deal has set the 'benchmark' for how multinational corporations should be treated in South Africa and in developing countries in general.[135]

[132] See Cossy (n 112) 337 (arguing that 'it is not clear why the size of a company … should matter, when the services they supply compete on a given market'). But see Krajewski (n 109) 105.

[133] This issue has been raised in the following fora: WTO, Working Group on the Interaction between Trade and Competition Policy, 'Communication from the United States' (6 November 2002) WT/WGTCP/W/218, 3; WTO, Working Group on the Interaction between Trade and Competition Policy, 'Report on the Meeting of 5–6 July 2001: Note by the Secretariat' (14 August 2001) WT/WGTCP/M/15, para 43; OECD, 'Core Principles of Non-Discrimination, Transparency and Procedural Fairness in a Multilateral Framework on Competition' (23 April 2003) CCNM/GF/COMP/TR(2003)6, paras 7–9. Some WTO Members seem to take the view that such measures could fall under Art XVII GATS. Laos, for example, included a horizontal reservation in its national treatment column under mode 3 providing that '[t]ax measures, generally pertaining to small and medium enterprises may result in a difference of treatment in favour of Lao PDR services and service suppliers': see WTO, 'Lao PDR—Schedule of Specific Commitments' (22 April 2013) GATS/SC/150, 2.

[134] See n 84 and accompanying text.

[135] This statement was made at the Fourth BRICS International Competition Conference in Durban in November 2015: see Nompumelelo Magwaza, 'SA's Walmart Deal "Set Brics Standard"' *Business Day Live* (13 November 2015) <http://www.bdlive.co.za/national/2015/11/13/sas-walmart-deal-set-brics-standard> accessed 20 January 2017; John Oxenham, Andreas Stargard, and Michael-James Currie, 'Developments in South African Merger Control: Ministerial Interventionism and the

## D. International Investment Law

International investment law may also have an impact on the ability of states to impose performance requirements on foreign companies for the purpose of attenuating negative effects on SMEs. However, in the absence of a bilateral investment agreement (BIT) between the United States (the home state of Walmart) and South Africa (the host state),[136] international investment law played no significant role in the Walmart/Massmart saga.[137] Nevertheless, the following generally applicable remarks can be made.

Most BITs contain an obligation pursuant to which the host state shall accord to investors of the home state treatment no less favourable than that it accords to its own investors. Referring to the national treatment standard, the South African Government expressed concerns that states might be prevented from imposing performance requirements, such as local purchase requirements, on foreign investors.[138] Although the apprehensions of the South African Government are not completely unwarranted, it is essential to distinguish between the pre- and post-establishment phase in this regard. While the post-establishment phase refers to the treatment of investments *after* their admission, the pre-establishment phase relates to the *making* of *new* investments. Performance requirements like those in the Walmart/Massmart case fall into the pre-establishment phase. BITs, however, do not always cover this stage of the investment process. For instance, the BITs of EU Member States traditionally focused on the treatment of investors 'post-admission' only.[139] Where BITs provide for national treatment post-establishment only, the host state has total discretion to determine the conditions on which foreign investors will be allowed to enter the domestic market.[140] In contrast, Canadian and US BITs frequently extend national treatment and most-favoured-nation treatment to the establishment and acquisition of investments.[141] In such cases, performance requirements may not be applied in a discriminatory way.[142]

Impact on Timing and Certainty' (2016) 17 <https://africanantitrust.files.wordpress.com/2016/04/aba-final-merger-control-south-africa-mc-edits-18-04-2016.pdf> accessed 20 January 2017.

[136] Boulle (n 2) 325.

[137] Other agreements with the United States establish consultation and cooperation mechanisms relating to investment issues, but do not contain any binding treatment standards. See, for example, the Agreement concerning the Development of Trade and Investment between the Government of the Republic of South Africa and the Government of the United States of America (concluded 18 February 1999); Cooperative Agreement between the United States of America and the Southern African Customs Union to Foster Trade, Investment and Development (concluded 16 July 2008).

[138] Department of Trade and Industry of the Republic of South Africa (n 78) 36–37.

[139] Thomas Pollan, *Legal Framework for the Admission of FDI* (Eleven International 2006) 74–75; European Commission, 'Towards a Comprehensive European International Investment Policy' (2010) COM(2010)343 final, 5.

[140] UNCTAD, *Bilateral Investment Treaties 1995–2006: Trends in Investment Rulemaking* (United Nations 2007) 65; Prabhash Ranjan, 'FDI in Multi-Brand Retail Trading and India's Bilateral Investment Treaties' (2013) 5(1) Trade, Law and Development 198, 204–05.

[141] See Art 3(1) and (2) of the 2012 US Model BIT <http://www.state.gov/documents/organization/188371.pdf> accessed 20 January 2017; Art 3(1) and (2) of the 2004 Canadian Model BIT <http://www.italaw.com/documents/Canadian2004-FIPA-model-en.pdf> accessed 20 January 2017.

[142] Pollan (n 139) 77.

Several BITs concluded after the entry into force of the TRIMs Agreement also contain an explicit prohibition of certain performance requirements such as export undertakings, local content requirements, and commitments to transfer a particular technology or production process.[143] Examples are the BITs of Canada and the United States,[144] the CAFTA-DR,[145] and the NAFTA.[146]

Thus, whether BITs or other international investment agreements restrict the use of SME-friendly performance requirements depends primarily on the exact wording of the national treatment obligation and on the inclusion of specific prohibitions to that effect.

## E. The Indian and Malaysian Cases

The Walmart/Massmart case aptly illustrates the implications of international trade and investment agreements for the policy space available to governments to adopt measures which are designed to support SMEs. This phenomenon is, however, not confined to South Africa or, for that matter, to the African continent. India and Malaysia have made similar experiences.

The Indian Government takes a cautious stance towards letting foreign companies like Walmart or Tesco enter the Indian multi-brand retail market. In 2012, after a review of the policy on foreign direct investment, the government decided to allow FDI up to 51 per cent in multi-brand retail trading.[147] One of the conditions for foreign retail companies is that '[a]t least 30% of the value of procurement of manufactured/processed products purchased shall be sourced from Indian micro, small and medium industries'.[148] This closely resembles the domestic procurement requirement, which was so fiercely disputed in the Walmart/ Massmart merger. After the government's decision, politicians from the Bharatiya Janata Party (BJP) raised doubts regarding the compatibility of such conditions with India's obligations under international investment agreements.[149] In reaction to these statements, the Indian Ministry of Commerce & Industry felt

[143] See UNCTAD (n 140) 66–69.

[144] Art 8 US Model BIT; Art 7 Canadian Model BIT.

[145] Art 10.9 of the Dominican Republic–Central America–United States Free Trade Agreement (CAFTA-DR) (signed 5 August 2004, entered into force 1 March 2006 [US, El Salvador], 1 April 2006 [Honduras, Nicaragua], 1 July 2006 [Guatemala], 1 March 2007 [Dominican Republic], 1 January 2009 [Costa Rica]) available at <https://ustr.gov/trade-agreements/free-trade-agreements/cafta-dr-dominican-republic-central-america-fta/final-text> accessed 20 January 2017.

[146] Art 1106 of the North American Free Trade Agreement (NAFTA) (adopted 17 December 1992, entered into force 1 January 1994) (1993) 32 International Legal Materials 605.

[147] Government of India, Ministry of Commerce & Industry, Department of Industrial Policy & Promotion, 'Review of the Policy on Foreign Direct Investment: Allowing FDI in Multi-Brand Retail Trading' (2012) <http://dipp.nic.in/english/acts_rules/Press_Notes/pn5_2012.pdf> accessed 20 January 2017. See also ibid, 'Consolidated FDI Policy Circular of 2015' (2015) 65–67 <http://dipp.gov.in/English/Policies/FDI_Circular_2015.pdf> accessed 20 January 2017.

[148] Government of India, 'Consolidated FDI Policy Circular of 2015' (n 147) 65.

[149] 'Retail Companies Opening Stores in India Can't Be Made Conditional: BJP' *The Economic Times* (New Delhi, 17 September 2012) <http://articles.economictimes.indiatimes.com/2012-09-17/news/33902717_1_multi-brand-fdi-retail-companies> accessed 20 January 2017. See also 'States Not

compelled to clarify India's international law commitments. In a public statement, it asserted that the new FDI policy on multi-brand retail trading is in full conformity with Bilateral Investment Promotion and Protection Agreements (BIPAs), Comprehensive Economic Cooperation Agreements (CECAs), Comprehensive Economic Partnership Agreements (CEPAs), and multilateral obligations arising from India's membership in the WTO.[150] As may be surmised from the statement, the ministry apparently takes the view that the GATT and the TRIMs Agreement are not applicable. The press release claims that '[i]nvestment is not a part of WTO disciplines except through Mode 3 under GATS'.[151] It adds that as India has not undertaken any specific commitments under the GATS in the relevant sector, 'there is no impact of the policy on our commitments under the WTO'.[152] The ministry's legal position on this issue is, however, untenable. First, as has been shown above, investment-related measures are not exclusively subject to the GATS, but may also come into conflict with the GATT or the TRIMs Agreement.[153] Second, the WTO dispute settlement organs have repeatedly held that the GATS and the GATT are not mutually exclusive and can apply simultaneously to the same set of facts.[154] Therefore, the Indian FDI policy in the area of multi-brand retail trading is, in principle, open to challenge under Article III:4 GATT and Article 2.1 TRIMs Agreement.[155]

In February 2016, the Indian Government announced that it plans to allow 100 per cent FDI in multi-brand retail in the food processing sector. However, the food products will have to be produced and manufactured in India: a 100 per cent local sourcing condition applies.[156] While the final policy guidelines have not yet been released, big players such as Walmart have already expressed an interest in taking advantage of the new policy.[157]

in a Position to Stop FDI in Retail: BJP' *The Economic Times* (New Delhi, 18 September 2012) <http://articles.economictimes.indiatimes.com/2012-09-18/news/33926082_1_multi-brand-retail-chains-fdi> accessed 20 January 2017.

150 Government of India, 'FDI Policy on Multi Brand Retail Trading and India's Commitments under International Investment Agreements' (Press Information Bureau, Release ID 87836, 18 September 2012) <http://pib.nic.in/newsite/erelease.aspx?relid=87836> accessed 20 January 2017.

151 ibid. 152 ibid. 153 See section C.III.2 above.

154 WTO, *EC—Bananas* (AB), para 221.

155 In contrast, given that India's BITs generally apply to the post-establishment phase only, the SME-friendly FDI policy is in conformity with India's obligations under these international investment agreements. See Ranjan (n 140) 204–05.

156 Rasul Bailay, 'Budget 2016: 100% FDI to Be Allowed in Food Products Produced and Marketed in India' *The Economic Times* (New Delhi, 29 February 2016) <http://economictimes.indiatimes.com/news/economy/policy/budget-2016-100-fdi-to-be-allowed-in-food-products-produced-and-marketed-in-india/articleshow/51188793.cms> accessed 20 January 2017; Government of India, 'Food Processing Industries Minister Welcomes 100% FDI in Marketing of Food Produced and Manufactured in India' (Press Information Bureau, Release ID 137137, 1 March 2016) <http://pib.nic.in/newsite/erelease.aspx?relid=137137> accessed 20 January 2017; Government of India, '100 Percent FDI in Multi Brand Marketing of Food to Act as Catalyst for the Food Processing Sector—Harsimrat Kaur Badal' (Press Information Bureau, Release ID 137412, 7 March 2016) <http://pib.nic.in/newsite/erelease.aspx?relid=137412> accessed 20 January 2017.

157 See, for example, Sagar Malviya and Chaitali Chakravarty, 'Walmart Wants to Sell Food Products in India via Both Brick-and-Mortar and Online Stores' *The Economic Times* (Mumbai/

Malaysia has also taken steps to promote domestic SMEs. In Malaysia, SME favourable regulation is part of an overarching effort to support the ethnic Malay community (*bumiputera*), which makes up approximately 67 per cent of Malaysia's total population. The affirmative action measures were set out in the New Economic Policy (NEP) and the National Development Policy (NDP). One area where preferential treatment is granted to the *bumiputera* population is public procurement.[158] This raises issues relating to the WTO Government Procurement Agreement, which have been addressed elsewhere.[159] Apart from the Malaysian Government's procurement policy, preferential treatment extends also to other areas. All hypermarkets, department stores, and superstores must allocate at least 30 per cent of their shelf space to 'Bumiputera SMEs goods/products' in each outlet.[160]

The Malaysian measures could potentially be justified under the public morals exception in Article XX(a) GATT.[161] Under the GATS, Malaysia has not undertaken any commitments in the distribution sector.[162] In any event, Malaysia has inscribed a limitation relating to measures designed to achieve the objectives of the NEP and NDP.[163] This reservation is also a consistent feature of Malaysia's services negotiations in the regional context—for instance, under the Association of South-East Asian Nations Framework Agreement on Services (AFAS).[164]

## F. Conclusions

On the basis of the Walmart/Massmart merger, this chapter analysed whether SME-supportive domestic competition decisions are in conformity with the requirements

New Delhi, 29 April 2016) <http://articles.economictimes.indiatimes.com/2016-04-29/news/72704262_1_food-products-food-marketing-food-items> accessed 20 January 2017.

[158] Christopher McCrudden and Stuart G Gross, 'WTO Government Procurement Rules and the Local Dynamics of Procurement Policies: A Malaysian Case Study' (2006) 17(1) European Journal of International Law 151, 162–70.

[159] See John Linarelli, 'The Limited Case for Permitting SME Procurement Preferences in the Agreement on Government Procurement' in Sue Arrowsmith and Robert Anderson (eds), *The WTO Regime on Government Procurement: Challenge and Reform* (Cambridge University Press 2011); see also Caroline Nicholas and Anna C Müller, Chapter 5 of this volume.

[160] Government of Malaysia: Ministry of International Trade & Industry (MITI), 'Malaysia: Investment in the Services Sector: Distributive Trade' (October 2012) 4, 6, 8 <http://www.mida.gov.my/env3/uploads/Publications_pdf/Malaysia_InvestmentinTheServicesSector/2012/08%20DistributiveTrade.pdf> accessed 20 January 2017; WTO, 'Trade Policy Review: Malaysia: Report by the Secretariat' (27 January 2014) WT/TPR/S/292, 103; WTO, 'Distribution Services: Background Note by the Secretariat' (29 October 2010) S/C/W/326, para 83.

[161] Kruger (n 38) 14–17. See also above nn 92–103 and accompanying text.

[162] WTO, 'Malaysia—Schedule of Specific Commitments' (15 April 1994) GATS/SC/52.

[163] ibid 1, 15–19, 28, 58. See also WTO, 'Malaysia—Schedule of Specific Commitments' (26 February 1998) GATS/SC/52/Suppl.3, 2.

[164] See ASEAN, 'Malaysia: Horizontal Commitments under the AFAS' (2016) <http://investasean.asean.org/files/upload/AFAS%208%20HC%20-%20MY%204.pdf> accessed 20 January 2017; ASEAN, 'Malaysia: Specific Commitments under the AFAS' (2016) <http://investasean.asean.org/files/upload/AFAS%208%20Schedule%20-%20Malaysia%20%2820Oct10%29%20CLEAN.pdf> accessed 20 January 2017.

of WTO law, in particular the GATT and the GATS, and international investment law. The results may be summarized as follows.

Competition authorities can prohibit takeovers by foreign companies on SME-related grounds without violating the market access obligation in Article XVI GATS, even if specific commitments have been undertaken. WTO law does, however, limit the possibility of imposing SME-friendly performance requirements as a precondition for merger approval. Local procurement quotas, which had been advocated by the opponents of the Walmart/Massmart merger, are in breach of Article III:4 GATT and Article 2.1 TRIMs Agreement. It does not matter whether such requirements are contained in individual competition decisions, as in the South African situation, or generally applicable laws, as in India. Depending on the factual circumstances of the particular case, it may be possible to justify such measures as part of a broader effort to support disenfranchised or disadvantaged groups of society (Article XX(a) GATT). It is rather unrealistic that the WTO Dispute Settlement Body will accept that such goods-related performance requirements are 'necessary' to enforce otherwise WTO-consistent competition laws (Article XX(d) GATT). Theoretically, there is also the possibility to permit SME-friendly trade measures *de lege ferenda*. During the Doha Round, Brazil and India, for example, tried to garner support for the proposition that developing countries should be allowed to use trade-related investment measures 'in order to promote small and medium-sized enterprises as they contribute to employment generation'.[165] It is, however, very doubtful whether such proposals are capable of obtaining a majority within the WTO.

The picture is different for services-related performance requirements designed to support SMEs. The obligation to establish an SME fund is in line with the national treatment obligation in Article XVII GATS. This is due to the fact that in the absence of manifest protectionism, the national treatment principle cannot be applied to individual competition decisions. In any event, as long as such individual decisions are adopted in pursuance of a GATS-consistent legislative instrument like the South African Competition Act, they will be justified under Article XIV(c) GATS. Thus, as the law stands, WTO Members do not need to schedule SME-supportive competition laws in order to retain their right to regulate.

Regarding international investment law, no one-size-fits-all answer can be given. BITs with pre-establishment provisions may limit a state's regulatory power to impose performance requirements in a cross-border investment context, inter alia, through competition laws. BITs that only guarantee national treatment post-establishment leave a state's regulatory freedom unfettered in that respect. In their bilateral investment practice, states could in future include reservations carving out SME-related measures.[166]

165 WTO, Council for Trade in Goods, Committee on Trade-Related Investment Measures, 'Communication from Brazil and India' (9 October 2002) G/C/W/428, G/TRIMS/W/25, para 12(g).

166 UNCTAD, *World Investment Report 2012* (United Nations 2012) 146, 150; Boulle (n 2) 337–38.

In conclusion, international economic law puts some limits on the range of permissible SME-supportive measures. By and large, however, international trade and investment law is sufficiently deferential towards domestic competition laws that seek to promote the interests of SMEs. Therefore, the SME support provisions of the South African Competition Act, which took centre stage in the Walmart/Massmart case, can be utilized to their full potential, while not violating international trade and investment rules.

## References

ASEAN, 'Malaysia: Horizontal Commitments under the AFAS' (2016) <http://investasean.asean.org/files/upload/AFAS%208%20HC%20-%20MY%204.pdf> accessed 20 January 2017

ASEAN, 'Malaysia: Specific Commitments under the AFAS' (2016) <http://investasean.asean.org/files/upload/AFAS%208%20Schedule%20-%20Malaysia%20%2820Oct10%29%20CLEAN.pdf> accessed 20 January 2017

Bailay, R, 'Budget 2016: 100% FDI to Be Allowed in Food Products Produced and Marketed in India' *The Economic Times* (New Delhi, 29 February 2016) <http://economictimes.indiatimes.com/news/economy/policy/budget-2016-100-fdi-to-be-allowed-in-food-products-produced-and-marketed-in-india/articleshow/51188793.cms> accessed 20 January 2017

Boulle, L, 'Balancing Competing Interests in FDI Policy: A Developing Country Perspective' (2012) 7 Asian Journal of WTO & International Health Law & Policy 315

Bustillo, M, Stewart, RM, and Sonne, P, 'Wal-Mart Bids $4.6 Billion for South Africa's Massmart' *The Wall Street Journal* (New York, 28 September 2010) <http://online.wsj.com/articles/SB10001424052748704654004575517300108186976> accessed 20 January 2017

Chabane, N, 'An Evaluation of the Influence of BEE on the Application of Competition Policy in South Africa' (2003) <http://www.tips.org.za/research-archive/annual-forum-papers/2003/item/371-an-evaluation-of-the-influence-of-bee-on-the-application-of-competition-policy-in-south-africa> accessed 20 January 2017

Cossy, M, 'Some Thoughts on the Concept of "Likeness" in the GATS' in Marion Panizzon, Nicole Pohl, and Pierre Sauvé (eds), *GATS and the Regulation of International Trade in Services* (Cambridge University Press 2008)

Crotty, A, 'Walmart "Could Seek WTO Relief"' *Independent Online* (Pretoria, 24 October 2011) <http://www.iol.co.za/business/news/walmart-could-seek-wto-relief-1162964> accessed 20 January 2017

De Meester, B, 'The Global Financial Crisis and Government Support for Banks: What Role for the GATS?' (2010) 13(1) Journal of International Economic Law 27

De Meester, B, *Liberalization of Trade in Banking Services: An International and European Perspective* (Cambridge University Press 2014)

De Meester, B and Coppens, D, 'Mode 3 of the GATS: A Model for Disciplining Measures Affecting Investment Flows?' in Zdenek Drabek and Petros C Mavroidis (eds), *Regulation of Foreign Investment: Challenges to International Harmonization* (World Scientific Publishing 2013)

Department of Trade and Industry of the Republic of South Africa, 'White Paper on National Strategy for the Development and Promotion of Small Business in South Africa'

(1995) <http://www.thedti.gov.za/sme_development/docs/White_paper.pdf> accessed 20 January 2017

Department of Trade and Industry of the Republic of South Africa, 'South Africa's Economic Transformation: A Strategy for Broad-Based Black Economic Empowerment' (2003) <http://www.thedti.gov.za/economic_empowerment/bee-strategy.pdf> accessed 20 January 2017

Department of Trade and Industry of the Republic of South Africa, 'Bilateral Investment Treaty Policy Framework Review: Government Position Paper' (2009) <http://www.pmg.org.za/policy-documents/2009/06/25/bilateral-investment-treaty-policy-framework-review> accessed 20 January 2017

Department of Trade and Industry of the Republic of South Africa, 'South Africa: Investor's Handbook 2014/15' (2015) <http://www2.deloitte.com/content/dam/Deloitte/za/Documents/tax/ZA_DTI-InvestinginSA_2014-15.pdf> accessed 20 January 2017

Diebold, NF, *Non-Discrimination in International Trade in Services: 'Likeness' in WTO/GATS* (Cambridge University Press 2010)

Dolzer, R and Schreuer, C, *Principles of International Investment Law* (2nd edn, Oxford University Press 2012)

Eeckhout, P, 'Constitutional Concepts for Free Trade in Services' in Gráinne de Búrca and Joanne Scott (eds), *The EU and the WTO: Legal and Constitutional Issues* (Hart Publishing 2001)

Ehlermann, C-D and Ehring, L, 'WTO Dispute Settlement and Competition Law: Views from the Perspective of the Appellate Body's Experience' (2002) 26(6) Fordham International Law Journal 1505

Ehring, L, 'De Facto Discrimination in World Trade Law: National and Most-Favoured-Nation Treatment—or Equal Treatment?' (2002) 36(5) Journal of World Trade 921

European Commission, 'Towards a Comprehensive European International Investment Policy' COM(2010) 343 final

Feinäugle, C, 'Article XXVIII GATS: Definitions' in Rüdiger Wolfrum, Peter-Tobias Stoll, and Clemens Feinäugle (eds), *WTO: Trade in Services* (Martinus Nijhoff 2008)

Geiger, F, *Beschränkungen von Direktinvestitionen aus Drittstaaten* (Nomos 2013)

Government of India, 'FDI Policy on Multi Brand Retail Trading and India's Commitments under International Investment Agreements' (Press Information Bureau, Release ID 87836, 18 September 2012) <http://pib.nic.in/newsite/erelease.aspx?relid=87836> accessed 20 January 2017

Government of India, 'Food Processing Industries Minister Welcomes 100% FDI in Marketing of Food Produced and Manufactured in India' (Press Information Bureau, Release ID 137137, 1 March 2016) <http://pib.nic.in/newsite/erelease.aspx?relid=137137> accessed 20 January 2017

Government of India, '100 Percent FDI in Multi Brand Marketing of Food to Act as Catalyst for the Food Processing Sector—Harsimrat Kaur Badal' (Press Information Bureau, Release ID 137412, 7 March 2016) <http://pib.nic.in/newsite/erelease.aspx?relid=137412> accessed 20 January 2017

Government of India, Ministry of Commerce & Industry, Department of Industrial Policy & Promotion, 'Review of the Policy on Foreign Direct Investment: Allowing FDI in Multi-Brand Retail Trading' (2012) <http://dipp.nic.in/english/acts_rules/Press_Notes/pn5_2012.pdf> accessed 20 January 2017

Government of India, Ministry of Commerce & Industry, Department of Industrial Policy & Promotion, 'Consolidated FDI Policy Circular of 2015' (2015) <http://dipp.gov.in/English/Policies/FDI_Circular_2015.pdf> accessed 20 January 2017

Government of Malaysia, Ministry of International Trade & Industry (MITI), 'Malaysia: Investment in the Services Sector: Distributive Trade' (October 2012) <http://www.mida.gov.my/env3/uploads/Publications_pdf/Malaysia_InvestmentinTheServicesSector/2012/08%20DistributiveTrade.pdf> accessed 20 January 2017

Kampel, K, 'The Role of South African Competition Law in Supporting SMEs' in Paul Cook, Raul Fabella, and Cassey Lee (eds), *Competitive Advantage and Competition Policy in Developing Countries* (Edward Elgar 2007)

Kelsey, J, *Serving Whose Interests? The Political Economy of Trade in Services Agreements* (Routledge-Cavendish 2008)

Krajewski, M, *National Regulation and Trade Liberalization in Services: The Legal Impact of the General Agreement on Trade in Services (GATS) on National Regulatory Autonomy* (Kluwer Law International 2003)

Krajewski, M and Engelke, M, 'Article XVII GATS: National Treatment' in Rüdiger Wolfrum, Peter-Tobias Stoll, and Clemens Feinäugle (eds), *WTO—Trade in Services* (Martinus Nijhoff 2008)

Kruger, P, 'Empowerment Policies in SADC and Their Effect on Agreement Design' (tralac Trade Brief S11TB10/2011, 2011) <http://www.tralac.org/publications/article/4610-empowerment-policies-in-sadc-and-their-effect-on-agreement-design.html> accessed 20 January 2017

Kruger, P, 'The Impact of WTO Law on Foreign Investment: The Walmart/Massmart Merger' (tralac Working Paper S12WP03/2012, 2012) <http://www.tralac.org/files/2012/02/S12WP032012-Kruger-Impact-WTO-law-foreign-investment-WalmartMassmart-merger-FIN.pdf> accessed 20 January 2017

Lewis, D, *Enforcing Competition Rules in South Africa: Thieves at the Dinner Table* (Edward Elgar 2013)

Linarelli, J, 'The Limited Case for Permitting SME Procurement Preferences in the Agreement on Government Procurement' in Sue Arrowsmith and Robert Anderson (eds), *The WTO Regime on Government Procurement: Challenge and Reform* (Cambridge University Press 2011)

Magwaza, N, 'SA's Walmart Deal "Set Brics Standard"' *Business Day Live* (13 November 2015) <http://www.bdlive.co.za/national/2015/11/13/sas-walmart-deal-set-brics-standard> accessed 20 January 2017

Malviya, S and Chakravarty, C, 'Walmart Wants to Sell Food Products in India via Both Brick-and-Mortar and Online Stores' *The Economic Times* (Mumbai/New Delhi, 29 April 2016) <http://articles.economictimes.indiatimes.com/2016-04-29/news/72704262_1_food-products-food-marketing-food-items> accessed 20 January 2017

Massmart Holdings Ltd, 'Supplier Development Fund: Annual Report 2013' <http://www.massmart.co.za/wp-content/uploads/2014/03/SDF-2013-Condensed-Report.pdf> accessed 20 January 2017

Massmart Holdings Ltd, 'Supplier Development Fund: Annual Report 2014' <http://www.massmart.co.za/wp-content/uploads/2014/08/Massmart-SDF-2014.pdf> accessed 20 January 2017

Massmart's website, <http://www.massmart.co.za/investor-center/overview> accessed 20 January 2017

Mattoo, A, 'National Treatment in the GATS: Corner Stone or Pandora's Box?' (1997) 31(1) Journal of World Trade 107

Mavroidis, PC, *Trade in Goods: The GATT and the Other WTO Agreements Regulating Trade in Goods* (Oxford University Press 2012)

McCrudden, C and Gross, SG, 'WTO Government Procurement Rules and the Local Dynamics of Procurement Policies: A Malaysian Case Study' (2006) 17(1) European Journal of International Law 151

Molinuevo, M, *Protecting Investment in Services: Investor-State Arbitration versus WTO Dispute Settlement* (Kluwer Law International 2012)

National Treasury of the Republic of South Africa, 'A Review Framework for Cross-Border Direct Investment in South Africa' (2011) <http://www.treasury.gov.za/documents/national%20budget/2011/A%20review%20framework%20for%20cross-border%20direct%20investment%20in%20South%20Africa.pdf> accessed 20 January 2017

OECD, Working Party of the Trade Committee, 'Assessing Barriers to Trade in Services: The Scheduling of Economic Needs Tests in the GATS: An Overview' (10 November 2000) TD/TC/WP(2000)11/FINAL

OECD, 'Competition Law and Policy in South Africa: An OECD Peer Review' (2003) <http://www.oecd.org/daf/competition/prosecutionandlawenforcement/2958714.pdf> accessed 20 January 2017

OECD, Joint Global Forum on Trade and Competition, 'Core Principles of Non-Discrimination, Transparency and Procedural Fairness in a Multilateral Framework on Competition' (23 April 2003) CCNM/GF/COMP/TR(2003)6

Oxenham, J, Stargard, A, and Currie, M-J, 'Developments in South African Merger Control: Ministerial Interventionism and the Impact on Timing and Certainty' (2016) <https://africanantitrust.files.wordpress.com/2016/04/aba-final-merger-control-south-africa-mc-edits-18-04-2016.pdf> accessed 20 January 2017

Pauwelyn, J, 'Rien Ne Va Plus? Distinguishing Domestic Regulation from Market Access in GATT and GATS' (2005) 4(2) World Trade Review 131

Pollan, T, *Legal Framework for the Admission of FDI* (Eleven International 2006)

Ranjan, P, 'FDI in Multi-Brand Retail Trading and India's Bilateral Investment Treaties' (2013) 5(1) Trade, Law and Development 198

Reinisch, A, '§ 8: Internationales Investitionsschutzrecht' in Christian Tietje (ed), *Internationales Wirtschaftsrecht* (De Gruyter 2009)

'Retail Companies Opening Stores in India Can't Be Made Conditional: BJP' *The Economic Times* (New Delhi, 17 September 2012) <http://articles.economictimes.indiatimes.com/2012-09-17/news/33902717_1_multi-brand-fdi-retail-companies> accessed 20 January 2017

Shannon, S, Seria, N, and Boyle, M, 'Wal-Mart Seeks to Enter Africa with $4.6 Billion Deal' *Bloomberg* (New York, 27 September 2010) <http://www.bloomberg.com/news/2010-09-27/wal-mart-offers-to-buy-south-africa-s-massmart-holdings-for-21-08-a-share.html> accessed 20 January 2017

Sidhu, K, *Die Regelung von Direktinvestitionen in der WTO: Das TRIMs-Abkommen und das GATS* (V&R unipress 2004)

'States Not in a Position to Stop FDI in Retail: BJP' *The Economic Times* (New Delhi, 18 September 2012) <http://articles.economictimes.indiatimes.com/2012-09-18/news/33926082_1_multi-brand-retail-chains-fdi> accessed 20 January 2017

UNCTAD, *World Investment Report 2014* (United Nations 2014)

Van den Bossche, P and Werner Zdouc, W, *The Law and Policy of the World Trade Organization* (3rd edn, Cambridge University Press 2013)

Wal-Mart Stores Inc, 'Walmart Closes Investment in 51% Stake in Massmart' (20 June 2011) <http://corporate.walmart.com/_news_/news-archive/investors/walmart-closes-investment-in-51-stake-in-massmart-1576044> accessed 20 January 2017

Wenzel, N, 'Article XX lit. a GATT' in Rüdiger Wolfrum, Peter-Tobias Stoll, and Holger P Hestermeyer (eds), *WTO: Trade in Goods* (Martinus Nijhoff 2011)

Wiers, J and Mathis, J, 'The Report of the Appellate Body in the Asbestos Dispute: WTO Appellate Body Report 12 March 2001, WT/DS135/AB/R, European Communities—Measures Affecting Asbestos and Asbestos-containing Products' (2001) 28(2) Legal Issues of Economic Integration 211

Wu, M, 'Free Trade and the Protection of Public Morals: An Analysis of the Newly Emerging Public Morals Clause Doctrine' (2008) 33 Yale Journal of International Law 215

Zampetti, AB and Sauvé, P, 'International Investment' in Andrew T Guzman and Alan O Sykes (eds), *Research Handbook in International Economic Law* (Edward Elgar 2007)

# 5

# SME Participation in Government Procurement Markets

## Legal and Policy Considerations under the WTO Agreement on Government Procurement and the UNCITRAL Model Law on Public Procurement

*Caroline Nicholas and Anna Caroline Müller**

### A. Introduction

Access to and participation in public procurement[1] markets[2] by small and medium-sized enterprises (SMEs)[3] has been identified by many governments as a crucial element in fostering sustainable economic development and prosperity worldwide.

First, SMEs have been described as the 'backbone' of many economies and governments increasingly recognize the role of SMEs and entrepreneurship as drivers of growth and job creation, and as effective tools for poverty alleviation.[4] According to studies of the Organisation for Economic Co-operation and Development (OECD), SMEs are the dominant form of business organisation, accounting, on average, for between 95 and 99 per cent of all enterprises. They are responsible for between 60 and 70 per cent of net job creation in OECD member countries and over two-thirds of EU gross domestic product (GDP).[5] This suggests—as

* The views expressed in this chapter are the authors' personal responsibility and are not to be viewed as representing official views of the United Nations or of the WTO, including their Secretariats and their members.

[1] Referred to throughout as 'procurement'.

[2] 'Public procurement' or 'government procurement' refers to the purchase by governments and state-owned enterprises of goods, services, and works.

[3] There are varying definitions of SMEs. See OECD and UNIDO, 'Effective Policies for Small Business: A Guide for the Policy Review Process and Strategic Plans for Micro, Small and Medium Enterprise Development' (2004) 20 <https://www.unido.org/fileadmin/user_media/Publications/Pub_free/Effective_policies_for_small_business.pdf> accessed 20 January 2017. See also the in-depth analysis of this issue by Rudolf Adlung and Marta Soprana in the Annex of this volume.

[4] See, for example, OECD, The Bologna Charter on SME Policies (adopted on 15 June 2000) <http://www.oecd.org/cfe/smes/thebolognacharteronsmepolicies.htm> accessed 20 January 2017.

[5] OECD, *Regions and Innovation Policy* (OECD Reviews of Regional Innovation, OECD 2011) <http://dx.doi.org/10.1787/9789264097803-en> accessed 20 January 2017.

*SME Participation in Government Procurement Markets: Legal and Policy Considerations under the WTO Agreement on Government Procurement and the UNCITRAL Model Law on Public Procurement.* Caroline Nicholas and Anna Caroline Müller.  Published 2017 by Oxford University Press.

the logic underlying government programmes fostering SME participation in the economy—that what is good for SME growth will also help governments achieve overall economic policy goals.[6]

Second, government procurement markets capture an important share of economic activity worldwide and represent a significant amount of government expenditure. In 2013, OECD governments spent, on average, 29 per cent of the total general government expenditure on public procurement compared to an average level of 30 per cent in 2009. In terms of GDP, OECD countries reported an average share of 12.1 per cent spent on public procurement in 2013 (excluding procurement by state-owned utilities).[7] When purchases of procurement contracts issued by state-owned utilities are also accounted for, the size of procurement markets increases by an additional 2 to 13 percentage points of GDP,[8] meaning that procurement markets can potentially capture up to around 25 per cent of GDP or more. Variations in the size of procurement markets reflect the different size of the state, its role in the economy, and the existence of high-value spending projects (eg infrastructure investments).

Certain characteristics of procurement markets make them potentially attractive for SMEs, and increasingly so. For example, public procurement at the state and local levels accounts on average for 63 per cent of total procurement spending across OECD countries, with the share going up to 87 per cent in federal states, such as Canada, and 78 per cent in other states, such as Italy.[9] This may mean that 'local' SMEs that are familiar with the conditions prevailing in the relevant regions may have a competitive advantage over larger firms located elsewhere.[10] Furthermore, even when public demand is aggregated through centralized purchasing, the increased use of framework agreements which allow for smaller 'call-offs' may mean that procurement markets are still attractive for SMEs.[11] Overall,

[6] For a critical discussion of whether economic evidence confirms this premise, see Thorsten Beck, Asil Demirguc-Kunt, and Ross Levine, 'SMEs, Growth, and Poverty: Cross-Country Evidence' (2005) 10 Journal of Economic Growth 199.

[7] Figures range from 5.2 per cent in Mexico to 20.8 per cent in the Netherlands. OECD, *Government at a Glance 2011* (OECD 2011) 148 f <http://dx.doi.org/10.1787/gov_glance-2011-en> accessed 20 January 2017.

[8] See OECD, *Government at a Glance 2015* (OECD 2015) 136 f <http://dx.doi.org/10.1787/gov_glance-2015-42-en> accessed 20 January 2017.

[9] See OECD (n 7) 148 f.

[10] This is not necessarily the case, however. A 2014 study on the EU market found that the proportion of public procurement contracts awarded to SMEs was highest for contracts issued by central governments and utilities (43 and 46 per cent of the total respectively) and lowest in contracts issued by local governments (35 per cent of the total). See Technopolis, 'Evaluation of SMEs' Access to Public Procurement Markets in the EU' (2014) <http://ec.europa.eu/DocsRoom/documents/2153/attachments/1/translations/en/renditions/pdf> accessed 20 January 2017.

[11] See, for example, European Commission, 'SMEs' Access to Procurement Markets and Aggregation of Demand in the EU' (DG Internal Market and Services, February 2014) <http://ec.europa.eu/internal_market/publicprocurement/docs/modernising_rules/smes-access-and-aggregation-of-demand_en.pdf> accessed 20 January 2017. The study reports that the use of framework agreements has increased in recent years and that more than half of all centralized purchasing arrangements (25 per cent of the total value of all contracts and 5 per cent of all contracts [in terms of number of awards] awarded above the EU thresholds) are through framework agreements.

therefore, even though public procurement is often thought of as high-value contracts and projects that may be difficult to obtain for SMEs, evidence suggests that this should not necessarily be the case. Yet SMEs are routinely found to underperform in public procurement markets in that the percentage of public procurement contracts they win is lower than their proportionate participation in the economies concerned.[12] For example, a recent EU study finds that the 29 per cent share of the procurement market that European SMEs secured in the 2009 to 2011 period was 29 per cent lower than it would have been (ie 58 per cent) had the share of public procurement that they won equalled the SME share of the total gross value added produced in the business economy.[13]

These facts and figures, combined with the fact that public procurement markets are subject to detailed procedural rules and regulations, make government procurement an obvious target for governments trying to stimulate overall economic growth and prosperity through SME participation in the economy.[14] Overall, public procurement is often described as a powerful 'tool' to promote socioeconomic objectives, such as SME participation, because it operates at the intersection of the government's regulatory and buying powers.[15] In line with this, 62.1 per cent of OECD countries have developed strategies or policies to support SMEs.[16] The fact that public procurement is often used to also support innovation,[17] an area of economic activity in which SMEs may have a comparative advantage,[18] may be particularly good news for SMEs. The argument is also advanced that it is economically sensible for governments to buy from SMEs and encourage their participation in procurement markets: SMEs can add comparative advantage and add value in innovation and responsiveness to government needs.[19] They can also help overcome

[12] In that regard, it is crucial to distinguish between the level of SME participation in terms of value of contracts and in terms of the number of contracts. A recent survey among GPA parties resulted in the finding that among the six parties that were able to report on relevant statistics, only three were able to provide data on the number of contracts awarded to SMEs. The results in terms of number of contracts ranged from 56 to 80 per cent of contracts, while the results in terms of value of contracts ranged from 25 to 64 per cent of public procurement spending.

[13] See n 11. Behind these aggregated data, however, the position varies as between micro, small, and medium-sized enterprises.

[14] See, for a discussion of the economic rationale behind SME policies, how they may be pursued through public procurement, and whether and how their effectiveness can be evaluated, Caroline Nicholas and Michael Fruhmann, 'Small and Medium-Sized Enterprises Policies in Public Procurement: Time for a Rethink?' (2014) 14 Journal of Public Procurement 328.

[15] Christopher McCrudden, 'Using Public Procurement to Achieve Social Outcomes' (2004) 28 Natural Resources Forum 257.

[16] OECD (n 8) 138 f <http://dx.doi.org/10.1787/gov_glance-2015-43-en> accessed 20 January 2017. Strategies and measures may differ significantly. On the different ways of using government procurement to implement secondary policies, see Sue Arrowsmith, 'Horizontal Policies in Government Procurement: A Taxonomy' (2010) 10 Journal of Public Procurement 149.

[17] This is the case in 39.3 per cent of OECD countries. See OECD (n 8) 138 f.

[18] See, for example, OECD, The Istanbul Ministerial Declaration on Fostering the Growth of Innovative and Internationally Competitive SMEs (June 2004) <http://www.oecd.org/cfe/smes/theistanbulministerialdeclarationonfosteringthegrowthofinnovativeandinternationallycompetitivesmes.htm> accessed 20 January 2017.

[19] Jurong Zheng, Helen Walker, and Christine Harland, 'The Role of SMEs in Public Procurement: A Review of Literature and Research Agenda' (2006) <https://www.researchgate.net/

and respond to supply market dominance and fragmentation, and enhance overall competition in procurement markets.[20]

A perfect fit, then? Not as perfect as it may seem at first glance, at least in some respects. First, the integration of socioeconomic policy goals in the procurement process may shift the focus of procurement policies away from their 'primary' purpose: transparency, integrity, and competition in public purchasing, in order to ensure value for money, efficiency, and safeguard the public interest.[21] Achieving the primary goals of procurement is a key factor in achieving economic well-being and growth, as government procurement often is crucial for the fulfilment of essential public functions, such as the delivery of basic infrastructure, health care, or education.[22] Getting procurement policy right therefore transcends the mere goal of avoiding wasteful spending of public monies. As a consequence, commentators recognize that a balance needs to be struck between the achievement of primary procurement goals and secondary policy objectives.[23] Ideally, they coincide, as enhanced SME participation may increase competition in procurement markets, and therefore result in enhanced value for money and innovation.[24] However, this may not always be the case.

Second, the factual background and effectiveness of different measures taken is often unclear.[25] The OECD, reporting on the results of its latest surveys, finds that nowhere near all countries implementing such a programme measure the impact of their policy or strategy to provide support for SMEs (only 62.1 per cent).[26] For

publication/239950830_The_Role_of_SMEs_in_public_procurement_a_Review_of_Literature_and_Research_Agenda> 29 August 2016.

20 Nigel D Caldwell and others, 'Promoting Competitive Markets: The Role of Public Procurement' (2005) 11 Journal of Purchasing Supply Management 242.

21 For a discussion of the objectives of public procurement regulations, see Steven L Schooner, 'Desiderata: Objectives for a System of Government Contract Law' (2002) 11 Public Procurement Law Review 103.

22 See, for example, Robert D Anderson and Anna Caroline Müller, 'The Revised WTO Agreement on Government Procurement: An Emerging Pillar of the World Trading System: Recent Developments' (2015) 7 Trade Law and Development 229.

23 Such policies are also known in the procurement context as socio-economic policies (in UNCITRAL), secondary, or horizontal policies (in the European Union). For a comprehensive discussion in the EU context, see Sue Arrowsmith and Peter Kunzlik (eds), *Social and Environmental Policies in EC Procurement Law: New Directives and New Directions* (Cambridge University Press 2009).

24 See, for example, Anne Glover, *Accelerating the SME Economic Engine: Through Transparent, Simple and Strategic Procurement* (HM Treasury 2008) <https://web.archive.org/web/20100602051331/http://webarchive.nationalarchives.gov.uk/+/http:/www.hm-treasury.gov.uk/d/pbr08_economicengine_2390.pdf> accessed 20 January 2017.

25 McCrudden (n 15) provides an overview of different initiatives over time, and states: 'The use of public procurement to achieve social outcomes is widespread, but detailed information about how it operates is often sketchy and difficult to find.' See also Allan Gibb, 'SME Policy, Academic Research and the Growth of Ignorance, Mythical Concepts, Myths, Assumptions, Rituals and Confusions' (2000) 18 International Small Business Journal 13; Andrew Freeman, *Challenging Myths about the Funding of Small Businesses ... : Finance for Growth* (Demos 2013) <http://www.demos.co.uk/files/DF_-_Finance_for_Growth_-_web.pdf?137821> accessed 20 January 2017. The author finds that 'a close examination of the academic, regulatory, and commercial literature regarding SMEs and their role in the economy remains riddled with poor thinking and muddled conclusions, problems compounded by a plethora of issues relating to the availability and quality of relevant data'.

26 See OECD 'Survey on Public Procurement' (2014) <http://dx.doi.org/10.1787/888933249069> accessed 20 January 2017; also quoted in OECD (n 8) 138 f.

those countries that are not measuring the results of their strategies, the main challenges include the lack of data, as well as the lack of an appropriate methodology to measure the impact of their policies. Therefore, some question the empirical viability of SME support measures. In the worst case, corruption enabled by complex exceptions to procurement rules diverts scarce public resources to socially wasteful contracts.[27]

The significance of international trade rules and instruments for the participation of SMEs in procurement markets has been characterized in contrasting ways. On the one hand, general transparency and non-discrimination measures can be an important factor in limiting the scope for cronyism and thereby fostering the participation of new entrepreneurs, in particular SMEs. Furthermore, the beneficial effects of the integration of SMEs in procurement markets on economic growth and development may be multiplied if international trade is added to the mix.[28] Economic research suggests that for SMEs there is a strong positive relationship between export and growth, as well as exports and innovation.[29] Particularly for SMEs located in smaller or less developed economies, market opportunities in larger economies can therefore be of considerable importance in harnessing their potential. Therefore, to the extent that governments choose to support SME participation with measures that are generally conducive to increased participation in procurement markets, the objectives of trade instruments, primary and secondary procurement policies may go hand-in-hand.

On the other hand, global markets created by international trade rules are sometimes perceived as a threat to SMEs, and international economic and trade rules with their liberalization goals are often viewed as—at least potentially—constraining 'policy space' with regard to the integration of secondary policy goals, such as SME participation.[30] And indeed, most governments' dedicated *preferential* policies to support SMEs in public procurement, where they exist, are targeted at domestic SMEs. This may create an inherent tension with the non-discrimination

[27] See, for example, John Linarelli, 'The Limited Case for Permitting SME Procurement Preferences in the Agreement on Government Procurement' in Sue Arrowsmith and Robert D Anderson (eds), *WTO Regime on Government Procurement: Challenge and Reform* (Cambridge University Press 2011) 453: 'The bad story is that some governments have used public procurement as an enclave in which politics predominates over market-based considerations, to protect favoured industries or even to dispense patronage to political friends. In the worst case, corruption diverts scarce public resources to socially wasteful contracts.'

[28] The removal of trade barriers for SMEs has been identified as one of the goals of international efforts to increase SME growth. See, for example, OECD, *Removing Barriers to SME Access to International Markets* (OECD 2008) <http://dx.doi.org/10.1787/9789264045866-en> accessed 20 January 2017.

[29] See Elena Golovko and Giovanni Valentini, 'Exploring the Complementarity between Innovation and Export for SMEs' Growth' (2011) 42 Journal of International Business Studies 362; James H Love and Stephan Roper, 'SME Innovation, Exporting and Growth: A Review of Existing Evidence' (2015) 33 International Small Business Journal 28.

[30] See, for example, Simona Morettini, 'Public Procurement and Secondary Policies in EU and Global Administrative Law' in Edoardo Chiti and Bernardo Giorgio Mattarella (eds), *Global Administrative Law and EU Administrative Law* (Springer 2011).

principles contained in trade instruments, and, to some extent, with primary procurement objectives.

Rather than attempting to decide or even enter the policy debate as to whether and what measures should be taken by governments in furthering SME participation in procurement markets, this chapter will consider how the participation of SMEs in public procurement is and can be facilitated under, respectively, the World Trade Organization's Agreement on Government Procurement (GPA) and the Model Law on Public Procurement issued by the UN Commission on International Trade Law (UNCITRAL Model Law).[31]

The WTO and UNCITRAL have both undertaken work in public procurement as a matter of trade policy, with the explicit aim of encouraging cross-border participation in public procurement procedures. And given the large share of the world economy that SMEs represent, making international procurement markets work for SMEs by enhancing cross-border procurement from SMEs may well be key to rendering the WTO and UNCITRAL instruments, as well as others, effective in that regard.[32] Recognizing the importance of facilitating the participation of SMEs in government procurement, the WTO Committee on Government Procurement (the Committee) has embarked upon on a Work Programme on SMEs with the aim of reviewing and identifying best practices on expanding the participation of SMEs of the parties to the GPA in government procurement.[33]

This section considers how and why the GPA and the UNCITRAL Model Law seek to enhance participation of foreign suppliers in public procurement, and how these texts can complement and/or accommodate national SME support policies. It will not analyse social and political justifications for SME policies per se, though it is acknowledged that correcting historical disadvantage and supporting minorities in public procurement can also have consequential economic benefits.[34] It comments on the areas of coherence and of tension between SME support and many broader public procurement objectives, and the implications of the observation that both SME and cross-border success in public procurement remain work-in-progress.[35]

[31] For further information on the UNCITRAL Model Law, see UNCITRAL, 'UNCITRAL Model Law on Public Procurement' (2011) <http://www.uncitral.org/uncitral/uncitral_texts/procurement_infrastructure/2011Model.html> accessed 20 January 2017. For further information on the GPA, see WTO, 'Agreement on Government Procurement' (2016) <https://www.wto.org/english/tratop_e/gproc_e/gp_gpa_e.htm> accessed 20 January 2017.

[32] Recent studies suggest that international direct cross-border procurement is low, even among GPA participants. For findings on the EU procurement market, as part of the GPA-covered market, see European Commission, 'EU Public Procurement Legislation: Delivering Results: Summary of Evaluation Report' (2011) <http://ec.europa.eu/internal_market/publicprocurement/docs/modernising_rules/executive-summary_en.pdf> accessed 20 January 2017. See also, on the lack of available data: Lucian Cernat and Zornitsa Kutlina-Dimitrova, 'International Public Procurement: From Scant Facts to Hard Data' (2014) <http://trade.ec.europa.eu/doclib/docs/2015/april/tradoc_153347.pdf> accessed 20 January 2017.

[33] See WTO, Committee on Government Procurement (2 April 2012) GPA/113, Appendix 2, Annex C. For further details on the Work Programme, see Section C.I.1.

[34] See for a discussion Christopher McCrudden, *Buying Social Justice: Equality, Government Procurement, & Legal Change* (Oxford University Press 2007).

[35] See, for example, OECD, *Government at a Glance 2013* (OECD Publishing 2013) 136 f <http://dx.doi.org/10.1787/gov_glance-2013-47-en> accessed 20 January 2017.

The section concludes with some recommendations—drawn from the evaluation of certain measures to support SMEs in public procurement—as to how those measures might also facilitate their cross-border participation in public procurement.

## B. The GPA and the UNCITRAL Model Law as International Instruments Shaping Procurement Policies and Legislation Worldwide

The GPA and the UNCITRAL Model Law are two complementary but distinct instruments, created by two different international institutions.[36] While the WTO, an independent international organization created in 1994/95, deals with state-to-state negotiations of binding and enforceable trade agreements (and resolves disputes pertaining to those rules), UNCITRAL is the main legal body of the UN system in the field of international trade law, with a general mandate to further the progressive harmonization and unification of the law of international trade, primarily through the issuing of conventions and model laws.

This section briefly sets out the main characteristics of the GPA and the UNCITRAL Model Law that are of relevance to the discussion of SME participation in public procurement markets. Their 'common denominator' is the objective of harnessing the potential for international trade in the public procurement market as an efficiency goal.

### I. The GPA

The GPA (also referred to as 'the Agreement') is a binding international agreement that (1) promotes value for money in government procurement, by (2) establishing the right of foreign suppliers to participate in procurement markets based on the principle of non-discrimination, and thereby (3) promotes the mutual opening of government procurement markets to international competition by the participating WTO members.[37] It does so by establishing minimum rules regarding integrity, transparency, and procedural fairness in covered procurement and is an instrument that can potentially deliver both good governance benefits and market access for participating countries.[38] As a result of several rounds of negotiations, the GPA parties have opened procurement activities worth an estimated US$1.7 trillion

[36] On the synergies between the work of the WTO and UNCITRAL on government procurement, see Caroline Nicholas, 'Work of UNCITRAL on Government Procurement: Purpose, Objectives and Complementarity with the Work of the WTO' in Sue Arrowsmith and Robert D Anderson (eds), *WTO Regime on Government Procurement: Challenge and Reform* (Cambridge University Press 2011).

[37] Parts of this section draw on Robert D Anderson and Anna Caroline Müller, 'WTO Accession and Accession to the Agreement on Government Procurement (GPA): What Is the Relationship? Why Should WTO Accession Candidates Also Consider GPA Accession? What Are the Pros and Cons?' in Chiedu Osakwe and Dadush Uri (eds), *WTO Accessions and Trade Multilateralism: Case Studies and Lessons* (WTO and Cambridge University Press 2015).

[38] See Anderson and Müller (n 22).

annually to international competition (ie to suppliers from GPA parties offering goods, services, or construction services).[39]

The GPA is a plurilateral agreement, meaning that it comprises only a subset of the full membership of the WTO. Currently, the GPA binds forty-seven WTO Members which formally constitute nineteen 'parties' (the European Union and its twenty-eight Member States are counted as a single party).[40] Ukraine and Moldova are the latest WTO Members to have become GPA parties, in 2016. Another nine WTO Members are in the process of acceding.[41] Six other WTO Members have undertaken commitments, in their WTO accession protocols, to eventually initiate accession to the GPA.[42] Just as the GPA only binds the parties, the benefits available under the Agreement are exclusively available to suppliers, goods, and services from GPA parties.

The GPA is composed of two principal parts: the text of the GPA and the parties' market access commitments, which are set out in detailed schedules known as the 'Appendix I Annexes'. The text of the Agreement establishes rules requiring that open, fair, and transparent conditions of competition be ensured in government procurement.

The Agreement embodies the following main elements:

- general rules guaranteeing national treatment, non-discrimination, and transparency with respect to each party's 'covered procurement markets'. Additional specific requirements regarding the transparency of procurement-related information (eg relevant statutes and regulations; evaluation criteria and contract awards);
- minimum standards (based on international best practices and incorporating significant flexibility) on aspects of the procurement process, to ensure transparent and open conditions of competition. These include provisions on:
    - tendering procedures;
    - qualification of suppliers;
    - time limits, documentation, opening of tenders, and contract award procedures;

[39] See Robert D Anderson and others, 'Assessing the Value of Future Accessions to the WTO Agreement on Government Procurement (GPA): Some New Data Sources, Provisional Estimates, and an Evaluative Framework for Individual WTO Members Considering Accession' (WTO Staff Working Paper ERSD-2011-15, 2011) <https://www.wto.org/english/res_e/reser_e/ersd201115_e.htm> accessed 20 January 2017.

[40] The nineteen parties currently are: Armenia; Canada; the European Union with its twenty-eight Member States; Hong Kong, China; Iceland; Israel; Japan; Korea; Liechtenstein; Moldova; Montenegro; the Netherlands with respect to Aruba; New Zealand; Norway; Singapore; Switzerland; Chinese Taipei; Ukraine; and the United States.

[41] These are Albania, Australia, China, Georgia, Jordan, Kyrgyz Republic, Oman, the Russian Federation, and Tajikistan.

[42] They are Afghanistan, Kazakhstan, Mongolia, Saudi Arabia, Seychelles, and the former Yugoslav Republic of Macedonia. For further, up-to-date information, see WTO, 'Parties, Observers and Accessions' (2016) <http://www.wto.org/english/tratop_e/gproc_e/memobs_e.htm> accessed 20 January 2017.

- provisions relating to the establishment of independent domestic review procedures and application of the WTO Dispute Settlement ('enforcement tools');
- provisions regarding accession to the GPA and the availability of 'transitional measures' for developing countries that join the GPA; and
- a 'built-in agenda' for improvement of the GPA, extension of coverage, and elimination of remaining discriminatory measures applied by parties;
- detailed schedules ('Appendix I Annexes') setting out the range of each party's procurements covered by the Agreement. The schedules set out covered entities, thresholds, covered services, specific exclusions, etc. The Agreement also incorporates built-in procedures for modification of parties' coverage in response to relevant developments (eg the privatization of covered entities).

It should be emphasized that the GPA's rules do not automatically apply to *all* procurement activities of each party. Rather, the coverage schedules play a critical role in determining whether or not a procurement activity is covered by the Agreement. Only those procurement activities that are carried out by covered entities purchasing listed goods, services, or construction services of a value exceeding specified threshold values are covered by the GPA. The coverage is specified in each party's market access schedules.

On 6 April 2014, a revised version of the GPA entered into force.[43] The GPA renegotiation was, first and foremost, an international trade negotiation; as such, the expansion of access to the parties' procurement markets by their respective suppliers was central to the process and to the agreement reached. The package of additions to market access adopted in the conclusion has been valued by the WTO Secretariat as being worth in the range of US$80 to 100 billion annually.[44]

The second element of the renegotiation, the revised GPA text, is based on the same principles and contains the same main elements as the existing Agreement. It nonetheless improves on the existing text in multiple significant ways. For example, the revised text reflects, streamlines, and updates the original Agreement to take into account developments in current government procurement practice, notably the use of electronic tools. In an important additional change, the transitional measures ('special and differential treatment' or 'S&D') that are available to developing countries that accede to the Agreement have been clarified and improved.[45]

Another significant element of the revised GPA consists in a specific new requirement for participating governments and their relevant procuring entities to conduct

[43] For information on the date of entry into force of and accession to the Agreement for individual parties, see ibid.

[44] See, for relevant details, Robert D Anderson, 'The Conclusion of the Renegotiation of the WTO Agreement on Government Procurement: What It Means for the Agreement and for the World Economy' (2012) 21 Public Procurement Law Review 83.

[45] See, for elaboration, Anna Caroline Müller, 'Special and Differential Treatment and Other Special Measures for Developing Countries under the Agreement on Government Procurement: The Current Text and New Provisions' in Sue Arrowsmith and Robert D Anderson (eds), *WTO Regime on Government Procurement: Challenge and Reform* (Cambridge University Press 2011).

their procurements in ways that avoid conflicts of interest and prevent corrupt practices. This provision is unique in the context of WTO treaty obligations.[46] The significance of this new provision is reinforced by new language, in the Preamble to the GPA, recognizing the GPA's significance for good governance and the fight against corruption.[47] Together, these elements signal a belief on the part of the parties that the GPA, while first and foremost an international trade agreement, is directly relevant to the global struggle for good governance.

As an integral part of the renegotiation of the Agreement, the parties to the GPA agreed on the initiation of a set of Work Programmes on issues of common interest and/or concern. These, importantly, include a Work Programme on SMEs.[48] The relevant decision entered into force on 6 April 2014, together with the Protocol Amending the GPA.

In the decision, parties recognize: (1) the importance of facilitating the participation of SMEs in government procurement; and (2) that parties have agreed in Article XXII:6 to seek to avoid introducing or continuing discriminatory measures that distort open procurement.

The Committee is given the mandate to review measures and policies for SMEs that the parties use to assist, promote, encourage, or facilitate participation by SMEs in government procurement and to identify the measures and policies that it considers to be best practices for promoting and facilitating the participation of SMEs of the GPA parties in government procurement.

The work is carried out on the basis of a transparency programme consisting of replies to a survey and related exchanges, questions, and comments. Questions addressed in the survey relate to: (1) the measures and policies used to promote, encourage, or facilitate participation by SMEs in government procurement; (2) the definition of SMEs; (3) the existence of agencies or institutions to assist SMEs with respect to government procurement; (4) information (including statistics, if available) on the level of participation by SMEs in government procurement in terms of both value and number of contracts awarded to SMEs; (5) measures and policies related to SME subcontracting; (6) facilitation of SME participation in joint bidding; (7) measures related to enhanced transparency, simplifying qualification requirements, reducing contract sizes, and ensuring timely payments; and (8) measures and policies to stimulate SME innovation.

[46] See Sue Arrowsmith, 'The Revised Agreement on Government Procurement: Changes to the Procedural Rules and Other Transparency Provisions' in Sue Arrowsmith and Robert D Anderson (eds), *WTO Regime on Government Procurement: Challenge and Reform* (Cambridge University Press 2011) 285; see also Robert D Anderson, Steven L Schooner, and Collin D Swan, 'The WTO's Revised Government Procurement Agreement: An Important Milestone Toward Greater Market Access and Transparency in Global Public Procurement Markets' (GWU Legal Studies Research Paper No 2012-7, 2012) <http://ssrn.com/abstract=1984216> accessed 20 January 2017.

[47] See also Robert D Anderson, William E Kovacic, and Anna Caroline Müller, 'Promoting Competition and Deterring Corruption in Public, Procurement Markets: Synergies with Trade Liberalization' (Think Piece, E15 Expert Group on Competition Policy and the Trade System, ICTSD, World Economic Forum 2015) <http://e15initiative.org/wp-content/uploads/2015/09/E15-Competition-Anderson-Muller-Kovacic-Final.pdf> accessed 20 January 2017.

[48] See WTO (n 33).

After two years, the Committee is to review the effect of the best practices on expanding the participation of SMEs of the parties in government procurement, and to consider whether other practices would further enhance participation by SMEs.

The decision also states that the parties shall avoid introducing discriminatory measures that favour only domestic SMEs and shall discourage the introduction of such measures and policies by acceding parties.

## II. The UNCITRAL Model Law

UNCITRAL is a UN commission, the mandate of which is to remove barriers to commercial relationships that can arise under the substantive *private* law rules governing cross-border trade, including procurement contracts entered into by governmental and other public bodies.[49] UNCITRAL's decision to issue a Model Law on Public Procurement,[50] in addition to opening up the international market concerned, was motivated by a wish to address inadequate or outdated legislation in many countries, which was itself impeding the efficient and effective provision of public services by governments. Furthermore, it was considered that divergent national laws hampered the ability of firms to sell to foreign governments, and that harmonizing those laws through the use of a model would be beneficial in practice. The UNCITRAL Model Law is consequently designed to ensure that the government purchaser will obtain value for money in spending public funds and, in addition, that there is integrity in the process. Integrity in this sense means more than a lack of abuse or corruption: it involves government purchasers acting ethically and fairly, and in accordance with the values of the system as expressed through its objectives.

The UNCITRAL Model Law is, as its name implies, a non-binding template for national legislation on public procurement. It therefore differs in its objective from the GPA, which contains binding minimum rules at the international level. It is accompanied by a Guide to Enactment,[51] intended as a reference tool for policymakers and users of a procurement system based on the Model Law (eg regulators and

[49] In this regard, UNCITRAL furthers the 'progressive harmonization and unification of the law of international trade'. See, further, UNCITRAL, 'Origin, Mandate and Composition of UNCITRAL' (2016) <http://www.uncitral.org/uncitral/en/about/origin.html> accessed 20 January 2017. UNCITRAL's mandate under General Assembly Resolution 37/106 refers to the 'body of rules governing commercial relationships of a private nature involving different countries', UN General Assembly, 'Report by the Secretary-General' (23 September 1966) UN Doc A/6396, para 10, A/6396/Add.1, and A/6396/Add.2.

[50] UNCITRAL Model Law on Public Procurement (adopted 1 July 2011) <http://www.uncitral.org/uncitral/uncitral_texts/procurement_infrastructure.html> accessed 20 January 2017. The Model Law addresses the award of contracts for goods, construction, and services by governmental and other public bodies.

[51] UNCITRAL, 'Guide to Enactment of the UNCITRAL Model Law on Public Procurement' (2012) <http://www.uncitral.org/uncitral/en/uncitral_texts/procurement_infrastructure/2012Guide.html> accessed 20 January 2017.

public procurement agencies), explaining the policy choices made by UNCITRAL in drafting the Model Law and how it is envisaged they be implemented.

The Model Law was negotiated in an intergovernmental forum, as are all UNCITRAL texts, with the participation of all UN Member States, together with a variety of intergovernmental organizations and non-governmental organizations which represent different legal traditions and levels of economic development. The text, adopted by consensus, is considered to be widely acceptable in offering solutions appropriate for all governments.[52] It was also designed to be consistent with the GPA to allow national governments to use the UNCITRAL Model Law towards fulfilling their legal obligations under the GPA.[53]

The Model Law contains a statement of its objectives (set out in a Preamble to the main text), namely:

- achieving economy and efficiency;
- wide participation by suppliers and contractors, with procurement open to international participation as a general rule;
- maximizing competition;
- ensuring fair, equal, and equitable treatment;
- assuring integrity, fairness, and public confidence in the procurement process; and
- promoting transparency.

These objectives are, to a large extent, mutually supporting and reinforcing. Competition, objectivity, and transparency in the procurement process, in turn, facilitate fair, equal, and equitable treatment and public confidence in the system, and thus the achievement of value for money and integrity in the procurement process. They are also important in the fight against corruption and abuse.

The parallel with the main GPA objectives is clear and, indeed, there is broad international consensus that these objectives should underpin all public procurement systems. The Model Law places a high premium on transparency, a lack of which has been identified as a major barrier to SMEs in public procurement.[54] Transparency in this context involves five main elements: the public disclosure of the rules that apply in the procurement process; the publication of procurement opportunities; the prior determination and publication of what is to be procured and how tenders are to be considered; the visible conduct of procurement according

[52] See, for example, Christopher R Yukins, 'Integrating Integrity and Procurement: The United Nations Convention Against Corruption and the UNCITRAL Model Procurement Law' (2007) 36 Public Contract Law Journal 307; Christopher R Yukins, 'A Case Study in Comparative Procurement Law: Assessing UNCITRAL's Lessons for U.S. Procurement' (2006) 35 Public Contract Law Journal 457.

[53] Both texts, in addition, are designed to comply with the procurement-related aspects of the UN Convention Against Corruption set out in its Art 9. See UN Convention Against Corruption (adopted 31 October 2003, entered into force 14 December 2005) 2349 UNTS 41.

[54] See, for example, Glover (n 24).

to the prescribed rules and procedures; and the existence of a system to monitor that these rules are being followed and to enforce them if necessary.

The Model Law's objectives are not self-enforcing, and so the Model Law sets out the main principles and procedures required to implement them. At a more detailed level, the default rules under the Model Law require:

- universal eligibility and set out permissible criteria for determining the suppliers that are qualified to participate in a procurement procedure;
- a comprehensive description of what is to be procured to provide a common basis upon which firms are to prepare their tenders so that they can be compared objectively;
- full disclosure of the criteria to be used in identifying the successful tender;
- the strict prohibition of negotiations on tenders, once submitted;
- the public opening of tenders at the deadline for submission; and
- the disclosure of any formalities required for entry into force of the procurement contract.

There is, in contrast to the GPA and reflecting the different scope of the two texts, no de minimis threshold for the application of the UNCITRAL Model Law: it applies to all public procurement (with flexibility for enacting states to set the dividing line between public and private firms in their jurisdiction). As a non-binding instrument, the UNCITRAL Model Law and the related Guide to Implementation are also not geographically limited in their application in any way: it is available as a source of inspiration and guidance to governments worldwide. While governments are therefore free to enact (elements of) it as they see fit, the UNCITRAL Model Law is conceived as a template, so that its potential benefits are largely proportional to the extent that it is implemented as a whole.

The Model Law, therefore, while a template for national legislation going beyond the minimum rules provided by the GPA, does not provide a comprehensive, predefined set of rules, but rather a flexible legislative framework for a public procurement system. Effective use of the Model Law requires more detailed rules, together with implementation support and guidance (as further explored below). This approach provides enacting states with sufficient policy space in implementing the main principles and procedures in practice.

## III. Harnessing the potential for international trade in the public procurement market

In their approach, both the GPA and the UNCITRAL Model Law encourage the widest possible participation in procurement markets and therefore are designed to help governments attract the best possible suppliers offering their goods and services at the most competitive prices. The idea behind both instruments is that governments benefit as they achieve the best value for money, and suppliers benefit as they gain access to markets that were previously closed to them, whether due to formal reasons such as discriminatory policies, or practical obstacles, such as a lack of transparency regarding opportunities and conditions for participation.

The GPA and the UNCITRAL Model Law are complementary in that the GPA's rules, while setting minimum standards and principles, are not designed to provide a full set of legislative rules applying to government procurement. The UNCITRAL Model Law and the Guide to Implementation fill that gap to a significant extent, by providing a model for possible legislative provisions and approaches, as well as non-binding guidance for governments seeking to apply international best practices. While ratification of the GPA and implementation of the UNCITRAL Model Law by no means necessarily coincide, the UNCITRAL Model Law, with its toolbox approach, is one way of ensuring GPA-compliant legislation at the national level.

Their role in facilitating the integration of SMEs in procurement markets is important in two respects. First, both instruments ultimately derive their *raison d'être* from their usefulness in facilitating private sector suppliers' access to procurement markets abroad. In that regard, SMEs represent an important factor in rendering them effective, as SMEs represent a large majority of firms worldwide. Second, both instruments are part of and derived from an emerging standard of international best practices in government procurement, and seek to increase good governance and the efficiency of public procurement systems for the benefit of governments and their citizens. Therefore, they arguably need to offer appropriate solutions and/or flexibilities to governments seeking to integrate SMEs in their supplier base in the best possible ways. In order for these goals to be achieved and to increase the effectiveness of procurement systems worldwide, the barrier-reducing measures proposed by the GPA and the UNCITRAL Model Law need to work in tandem with SME support measures.

## C. Encouraging SME Participation under the GPA and the UNCITRAL Model Law

How do the GPA and the UNCITRAL Model Law then address SME participation in procurement markets? In that regard, a first important point to note is that neither the GPA nor the UNCITRAL Model Law contain specific provisions on the issue as part of their core provisions.

The revised text of the GPA, while specifically stating the parties' right to adopt technical specifications to promote the conservation of natural resources or protect the environment, only refers to SMEs in its Article XXII:8, under the heading of 'Future Negotiations', and establishes the work programme on SMEs described above.

Similarly, the Model Law does not take a position on whether secondary policies are appropriately or best pursued through a procurement system, reflecting a long-standing policy approach in UNCITRAL. When first considering revisions to an earlier version of the Model Law in 2004,[55] an UNCITRAL intergovernmental

[55] See UNCITRAL Model Law on Procurement of Goods, Construction and Services (adopted

Working Group (the Group) noted that sustainable development policy should include long-term planning and the consideration of social, economic, and environmental impacts beyond the local area (regional, national, and international impacts). However, when reviewing the scope of the reform programme for the 1994 Model Law, the Group noted that while using procurement to achieve other policy goals might be considered appropriate, such use might in some cases undermine the main objectives of the procurement process (as described in Section B above).[56]

Therefore, a main focus of this section is to identify ways to pursue SME policies that are in harmony with the general procurement policy goals and rules established by the two instruments, and to discuss how to legally include and mitigate negative effects of policies that have the potential to conflict with those goals. In line with the preferences expressed by many governments worldwide, the underlying assumption is that policies are needed to address obstacles faced by SMEs in procurement markets, and to create conditions in which potential factors enabling SMEs to fully utilize a possible competitive advantage over other enterprises are maximized.

The following sections identify three areas of interaction between the GPA and the UNCITRAL Model Law with regard to national efforts to increase participation of SMEs in procurement markets. First, we address measures to improve general features of procurement legislation and systems relating to transparency, integrity, and competition. These 'level the playing field' among all potential suppliers, as a first step. The second area concerns more specific measures relating to procurement practices that can be taken in the application of general rules in order to facilitate SME participation. These are needed to overcome potential barriers to SME participation that may persist despite a generally open and transparent system. The final subsection concerns preferential measures or programmes designed to give SMEs privileged access to procurement contracts. For each of these types of measures, the approach taken by the GPA and the UNCITRAL Model Law is set out.

## I. Improving procurement legislation and systems: Lack of transparency, integrity, and inclusiveness as potential barriers to SME participation

A first fundamental contribution that the GPA and the UNCITRAL Model Law have to make in improving SME access to procurement markets, whether at the local, regional, national, or international level, lies in their potential to help governments increase the transparency, integrity, and supplier inclusiveness of their procurement systems.

15 June 1994) <http://www.uncitral.org/uncitral/en/uncitral_texts/procurement_infrastructure/1994Model.html> accessed 20 January 2017.

[56] See UN Commission on International Trade Law, Report of Working Group I (Procurement) on the Work of its Sixth Session (Vienna, 30 August–3 September 2004) A/CN.9/568, paras 94–101.

Indeed, SMEs can be expected to be less likely to overcome barriers to procurement markets related to insufficient availability of information on procurement opportunities, cronyism, and/or corruption, whether at the national or the international level. With regard to transparency, a paper by the International Trade Centre (ITC) points out:

> SMEs face considerable barriers to entry because of the costs of obtaining information on goods, works and services being sought by governments. Information costs may be sufficiently onerous so as to preclude SME involvement in public procurement. The difficulty of acquiring information is more significant in the international context. Large firms, especially multinationals, have easier access to information about invitations to tender in foreign countries than do SMEs. Potentially, the lack of information is damaging particularly to firms in developing and transitioning economies. Lowering the costs of information will remove or lessen a significant impediment to SME participation in public procurement.[57]

Indeed, inadequate information on procurement regulations and requirements as well as on procurement opportunities has been identified as a major impediment to SME participation in procurement.[58] The increasingly widespread use of electronic procurement systems holds the potential to offer promising solutions with regard to transparency of procurement information at low cost, and its usefulness for SMEs has been noted.[59]

With regard to corruption, SMEs have been described as more vulnerable than large firms to corrupt practices in their effort to win government contracts, with this trend being relatively more prominent in the developing world.[60] Measures to ensure appropriate competition in procurement markets are also needed to complement anti-corruption strategies.[61] Where corruption dominates, one of its effects

[57] International Trade Centre, 'SMEs and Export-Led Growth: Are There Roles for Public Procurement Programmes? A Practical Guide for Assessing and Developing Public Procurement Programmes to Assists SMEs' (presented at the WTO/World Bank regional workshop on procurement reforms and transparency in public procurement for Anglophone African countries, Dar es Salaam, Tanzania, 14–17 January 2003).

[58] See Eliezer Mishory, 'Leveling Asymmetry: The Information-Leveling Model of Transparency in Government Procurement' (2013) <http://dx.doi.org/10.2139/ssrn.2365092> accessed 20 January 2017. See also Ruth Fee, Andrew Erridge, and Sean Hennigan, 'SMEs and Government Purchasing in Northern Ireland: Problems and Opportunities' (2002) 14 European Business Review 326; Katri Karjalainen and Katariina Kemppainen, 'The Involvement of Small- and Medium-Sized Enterprises in Public Procurement: Impact of Resource Perceptions, Electronic Systems and Enterprise Size' (2008) 14 Journal of Purchasing and Management 230.

[59] See, for example, the EU Commission's explanation of the rationales for the new EU rules on e-procurement: 'The use of electronic tools in public procurement offers a range of important benefits such as new business opportunities by improving the access of enterprises, including small and medium-sized enterprises (SMEs) to public procurement markets'. European Commission, 'E-Procurement' (2016) <http://ec.europa.eu/growth/single-market/public-procurement/e-procurement/index_en.htm> accessed 20 January 2017.

[60] See Lea Kaspar and Andrew Puddephatt, 'Benefits of Transparency in Public Procurement for SMEs: General Lessons for Egypt' (Global Partners and Associates 2012) <http://www.gp-digital.org/wp-content/uploads/pubs/Benefits-of-transparency-in-PP-for-SMEs.pdf> accessed 20 January 2017.

[61] See Anderson and others (n 47); see also Robert D Anderson and William E Kovacic, 'Competition Policy and International Trade Liberalisation: Essential Complements to Ensure Good Performance in Public Procurement Markets' (2009) 18 Public Procurement Law Review 67.

may be the exclusion of SMEs from procurement markets via the endogenous creation of cartels among 'established' large suppliers.[62]

Overly restrictive qualification requirements and technical specifications also particularly harm SMEs. SMEs may offer innovative solutions, but risk aversion on the part of procurement officials may prevent them from harnessing their potential. From a design perspective, ensuring that excessive 'standard' requirements are avoided and setting this out clearly in the initial publicity may therefore assist in enhancing interest from SME bidders.[63] Furthermore, SMEs are less experienced bidders: allowing them sufficient time to bid in new opportunities and engaging in outreach to build capacity in how to draft and present a bid may also yield benefits.[64]

In sum, measures to ensure the broadest possible participation of suppliers in procurement markets can generally be considered as a positive contribution to SME participation. Importantly, such measures are not only in the interest of SMEs trying to win contracts: they are fully in line with the broader goals of procurement systems outlined above. Essentially, they can be expected to favour successful participation not only of SMEs 'per se', but in particular of those SMEs that are competitive in the sense that they offer advantages to the government as buyer.

Such measures are also actively encouraged by both the GPA and the UNCITRAL Model Law: in all respects addressed above, SMEs may be disadvantaged in a way that is very similar to international suppliers, whose participation in procurement markets both the GPA and UNCITRAL Model Law are designed to facilitate. Consequently, the goals and specific procedural rules established by the two instruments, in encouraging broad participation and competition in procurement markets, are fully compatible with the goal of favouring the inclusion of SMEs in the supplier base of governments by such means.

The following subsections highlight particular provisions of the GPA and the UNCITRAL Model Law that can be expected to be of particular relevance in this regard.

### 1. *The GPA*

As a basic rule, Article IV:4 provides that a procuring entity shall conduct covered procurement in a transparent and impartial manner using methods such as open tendering, selective tendering, and limited tendering that avoids conflicts of interest and prevents corrupt practices. The GPA therefore promotes open, transparent procurement procedures and integrity as a basic prerequisite for SME participation in procurement markets.

With regard to the publication of notices, the revised GPA goes beyond mere transparency requirements in terms of the information to be contained in notices,

[62] See Gustavo Piga, 'A Fighting Chance Against Corruption in Government Procurement' in Susan Rose-Ackerman and Tina Soreide (eds), *International Handbook on the Economics of Corruption* (Edward Elgar 2011).

[63] See Nicholas and Fruhmann (n 14), and references quoted therein.

[64] ibid.

and encourages the publication of electronic notices available free of charge and through a single point of access (see Article VII:1). The resulting enhanced availability of information on procurement opportunity can be expected to be especially beneficial to SMEs and other companies with limited staff and resources to search multiple information outlets for relevant information.

Furthermore, Article VIII:1 contains an obligation for procuring entities to limit any conditions for participation in a procurement to those that are essential to ensure that a supplier has the legal and financial capacities and the commercial and technical abilities to undertake the relevant procurement. In this regard, the GPA makes it clear that only essential requirements are considered legitimate and thereby opens possibilities for participation of SMEs.

Similarly, Article IX:2 and 3 obliges GPA parties to seek to minimize differences and unnecessary obstacles to participation in qualification procedures and registration systems. Again, such obstacles and differences, where they exist, can be expected to place a particular burden on SME suppliers due to their resource constraints.

Article X on technical specifications and tender documentation safeguards the interest of SMEs in seeing unnecessary technical specifications removed, and in obtaining tender documentation in time in order to permit them to submit a responsive tender. With regard to timelines, Article XI establishes minimum rather than maximum time periods, thereby protecting SMEs' interests in being allowed sufficient time to prepare tenders. Subsequent Articles guarantee the transparent and fair conduct of procurement procedures related to negotiations and electronic auctions, as well as to the award of the contract.

Importantly for SMEs as potential newcomers, Article XVI:1 provides unsuccessful SMEs with the right to request (and receive) an explanation of the reasons why the entity did not select its tender and the relative advantages of the successful supplier's tender. This right to be debriefed is particularly valuable to SMEs with little experience in submitting tenders and ensures that their chances of winning can increase over time.

Finally, all these rights are made enforceable in Article XVIII through domestic review procedures.[65]

While these minimum rules and standards relating to the transparency and procedural fairness of procurement procedures in the GPA were designed with international suppliers generally—rather than SMEs in particular—in mind, the potential meaning and impact of their existence on the participation of SMEs in the GPA parties' procurement markets should not be underestimated. This view is corroborated by the GPA parties' answers to the survey carried out as part of the GPA Committee's Work Programme on SMEs.[66] A vast majority of parties

[65] On the importance of domestic review procedures, and related policy considerations, see Daniel I Gordon, 'Bid Protests: The Costs Are Real, But the Benefits Outweigh Them' (2013) 42 Public Contract Law Journal 3; and Daniel I Gordon, 'Constructing a Bid Protest Process: Choices Every Procurement Challenge System Must Make' (2006) 35 Public Contract Law Journal 3.

[66] For the topics addressed in the survey, see Section B.I.

confirm therein that they use their general transparency instruments implementing GPA provisions to make government procurement information available to SMEs. Three parties enhance them with special portal sites that are relevant to SMEs' participation in government procurement. Similarly, nine parties expressly confirm that their implementing legislation takes into consideration the needs of SMEs in simplifying qualification requirements.

Furthermore, while little, if any, data exist to measure whether GPA accession has an impact on SME participation in covered procurement markets, it can by no means be assumed that non-GPA parties, especially if not implementing the UNCITRAL Model Law standards or other applicable international best practices, necessarily follow such rules.

### 2. *The UNCITRAL Model Law*

While the UNCITRAL Model Law includes requirements that reflect the provisions of the GPA described in the preceding paragraphs,[67] some additional provisions are designed to support wide participation of suppliers in public procurement under the Model Law.

A key rule under the UNCITRAL Model Law is unrestricted eligibility to participate for all qualified suppliers, with the limited exemptions under the Model Law requiring justification. This principle is given effect through an express prohibition against discrimination:

> Except when authorized or required to do so by the procurement regulations of other provisions of law of this State, the procuring entity shall establish no other requirement aimed at limiting the participation of suppliers ... in procurement proceedings that discriminates against or among suppliers ... or against categories thereof.[68]

This rule operates also to establish a default rule in favour of international participation in any procurement process, and it is supported by a requirement that prior announcements of procurement proceedings under the Model Law be published internationally. A general non-discrimination rule in almost identical terms is also expressly applied to the determination of which suppliers are considered qualified to supply the subject matter of the procurement to the government in Article 9; to the description of the subject matter of the procurement at issue in Article 10; and to rules on designing and applying the evaluation criteria that will be used to determine the winner of the procurement contract concerned in Article 11.

[67] See Section B.II. For readers wishing to consider the complementarity of the two texts further, Art IV:4 GPA is reflected in Art 28 of the Model Law; the recommendations of Art VII:1 are reflected in the Guide to Enactment discussion of solicitation in chapter II, part II of the Model Law; the requirements of Arts VIII:1 and IX:2 and 3 are reflected in Arts 9 and 18 of the Model Law; those of Art X in Art 10 of the Model Law; debriefings are encouraged in the commentary to Art 22 of the Model Law, and chapter VIII of the Model Law also contains enforcement procedures through its challenge mechanism.

[68] Article 8 of the UNCITRAL Model Law.

Therefore, as stated above, the UNCITRAL Model Law promotes reforms aimed at creating open, transparent, and inclusive procurement legislation and systems that encourage the widest possible participation in procurement markets.

Overall, both the UNCITRAL Model Law and the GPA actively encourage measures needed in order for SMEs to overcome barriers to participation in public procurement: in all regards addressed above, SMEs are very similar to international suppliers, whose participation in procurement markets both the GPA and UNCITRAL Model Law are designed to facilitate. Consequently, the goals and specific procedural rules established by the two instruments, in encouraging broad participation and competition in procurement markets, are fully compatible with the goal of favouring the inclusion of SMEs in the supplier base of governments by such means.

## II. Reforming procurement practices and systems to enhance SME participation

A second contribution that the work of the WTO and of UNCITRAL can make to the integration of SMEs in procurement markets lies in providing policy space, as well as guidance and advice, where needed, on 'optional' features and characteristics of procurement systems that can have an impact on SME participation.

In that regard, the extent to which procurement is disaggregated, the use of framework agreements and e-procurement systems, the design of standard procurement documentation to reduce transaction costs, and other procurement practices come to mind. Furthermore, the creation of institutions or other instruments to provide information and training on procurement opportunities for SMEs and to monitor their success may have a positive impact. Similarly, possibilities for SMEs to act as subcontractor or to participate in joint bidding may be encouraged and impacted on through procurement practices. Ensuring prompt payment of suppliers may have a particular impact on SMEs that dispose of less cash-flow reserves than larger enterprises.

In this regard, the basic approach of both instruments is to leave options for each government to decide on, as long as general principles of transparency and non-discrimination are complied with. Such choices are left to governments as the measures in question are not considered as generally conflicting with the primary goals of the procurement function as described above, or per se problematic with regard to the participation of international suppliers. Nevertheless, the choices and solutions adopted can have a significant impact on SME procurement and the efficiency of the procurement system as a whole, and therefore need to be reflected upon. For example, recent research shows that both high individual contract values and centralized purchasing have a considerable negative effect on SME access.[69] However, the efficiency gains achieved for the public sector may also be non-negligible. While SME participation may be encouraged by a more flexible

[69] See n 11.

approach to subcontracting and joint bidding, some measures—such as allowing temporary consortia between suppliers—may carry the risk of making a cartel or collusive agreement in the form of bid rotation more feasible or raise other integrity issues.

While it may therefore not be appropriate to determine across-the-board solutions in either the GPA or the UNCITRAL Model Law, the two instruments do not entirely ignore the relevance of such issues. While the GPA, as a binding instrument, carefully carves out policy space in this regard, the Work Programme on SMEs established by the GPA Committee permits related policy discussions. Similarly, the Guide to Enactment of the UNCITRAL Model Law raises issues and addresses advantages and disadvantages of policy choices to be made in this regard.

### *1. The GPA*

As explained above, the GPA establishes minimum rules in the sense that it only addresses those aspects and features that are considered essential in safeguarding the rights of foreign suppliers to participate in covered procurement under conditions of transparency and non-discrimination. In many respects, the interests of foreign suppliers and those of SMEs are aligned.

This, furthermore, means that the GPA provides ample policy space with regard to many choices governments can make, and that are essential in determining SME participation in markets. For example, while the GPA does contain provisions on the valuation of procurements in order to avoid the circumvention of commitments by artificially splitting procurements,[70] it does not contain any limitation with regard to the awarding of smaller lots within a covered procurement. As SMEs are more likely to apply for and win smaller contracts, government choices in this regard can have a significant impact on SME participation.

Similarly, the GPA simply reflects, in its Annexes, choices individual economies make as to the number of procuring entities and resulting aggregation or disaggregation of the procurement function. In that regard, the GPA's Annex structure is flexible enough to accommodate different models and therefore does not interfere with or contain any restrictions of parties' choices in this regard.

The GPA also does not contain any provisions either encouraging or prohibiting the use of framework agreements. While it regulates some aspects of the use of 'multi-use lists' to encourage possibilities for inclusion on such lists by new suppliers and make them transparent, it does not indicate under what circumstances and to what extent they are to be used. And while the GPA generally recognized the transparency, governance, and efficiency benefits of e-procurement systems, it leaves many choices as to the mandatory nature and the exact extent of their use to its parties. The use of standard documentation is not addressed in the GPA,[71] and neither is subcontracting or joint bidding.

[70] See Arts II:6–8 GPA.

[71] The GPA parties have, however, decided to conduct future work on the advantages and disadvantages of developing standardized notices. See WTO (n 33) Annex B.

Furthermore, while the GPA contains reporting requirements with regard to procurement statistics, it does not establish an obligation to include information on SME participation in these. Technical assistance envisaged under the Agreement is directed at developing WTO members generally, without specific reference to SMEs—even though inclusion of such topics is possible upon request of the receiving WTO member(s). No requirements relating to post-award contract management and/or payment of suppliers are contained in the GPA.

In sum, the GPA leaves significant 'policy space' for its parties to either establish procurement practices with SME inclusion as a goal in mind, or not—depending on the preference of the GPA party in question. The current lack of restrictive rules on such procurement practices impacting on SME inclusion may mean that GPA parties have in the past considered such issues predominantly as areas of domestic policy, which would make a lack of binding rules on the matter most appropriate. However, given the above-mentioned importance of SMEs in the global economy, the lack of guidance on the issue in the GPA can also be considered a *lacuna* that could lead to both governments and SMEs forgoing the potential benefits of SME participation in international procurements.

The Work Programme on SMEs established by the GPA Committee may help in either confirming the adequacy of the current approach, or in finding different, appropriate solutions. In any case, it permits policy discussion with a view to the parties agreeing on (non-binding) best practices. Under the Work Programme, the parties have, in the past months, exchanged information on many of the issues raised above.[72] This is certainly a helpful first step in increasing transparency and creating a basis for discussion in the Committee.

## 2. *The UNCITRAL Model Law*

The non-discrimination provisions of the UNCITRAL Model Law outlined above are designed to ensure that SMEs are not deliberately prevented from accessing the public procurement markets. They are subject to a caveat: procuring entities may not discriminate among suppliers 'except when authorized or required to do so by the procurement regulations or by other provisions of law of this State'. As the Guide to Enactment explains, the purpose of this provision is to allow the procuring entity, solely in order to promote a government's declared national policies as reflected in other laws or the procurement regulations, to restrict procurement to and/or to prefer tenders from certain groups of suppliers.[73] The exceptional use of such policies—the intended effect of which is to discriminate against, for example, larger suppliers—is discussed further in Section III below.

However, as also explained in the Guide to Enactment, there may be unintended barriers to SME participation in public procurement markets, perhaps explaining

[72] Publicly available documents are published online at <https://docs.wto.org/> accessed 20 January 2017.

[73] See UNCITRAL (n 51) 5 ff and 222.

why SMEs are often considered to underperform in public procurement markets. These barriers might arise due to factors such as the aggregation of public procurement demand, or technical, health and safety, sustainability, equality, and diversity policies that may put the contracts beyond SMEs. Elements of procurement procedures themselves, as applied in practice, may also operate to create unintended barriers to access. These unintended barriers are the focus of the following paragraphs, which set out some of the guidance provided by the UNCITRAL Model Law and the Guide to Enactment on these topics.

As a matter of design of the procurement process, the UNCITRAL Model Law starts from the premise that the procuring entity should have the flexibility to choose how to determine and express its needs, and how to conduct the procurement procedure in a way that will meet them. Article 9 governing qualification therefore provides that the procuring entity can apply any of the listed criteria that are considered appropriate and relevant in the circumstances of the procurement, to ensure that potential suppliers have the necessary professional, technical, and environmental qualifications, and financial and other necessary resources, to fulfil the procurement contract envisaged, that they meet ethical and legal standards, and that they have paid applicable taxes and social security contributions. How these rules are applied in practice requires the procuring entity to balance meeting its needs in the most effective way possible with opening up the procurement procedure to potential suppliers without previous experience in supplying the government.

The Guide to Enactment, when discussing Article 9, encourages enacting states to carefully consider the procedures and requirements for each procurement contract, in order to seek to eliminate unnecessary barriers.[74] For example, a common requirement for a minimum of five years' audited accounts and previous relevant experience may prevent new and innovative suppliers from participating. Technical qualifications may be, similarly, excessively stringent,[75] or primarily aimed at mitigating the government's reputational risk or reducing the administrative burden on procurement officials in assessing marginal tenders.

In addition, it is routinely noted that the law governing procurement, and other applicable rules, are highly complex: they may also not be easily available or comprehensible, and learning to use them may involve considerable time and effort; information about procurement opportunities may be poor or lacking entirely; tender documents are often unclear, ambiguous, expressed in jargon, and/or not issued in timely fashion. In terms of transparency, poorly worded requirements in tender documents mean that the procurement may be accessible only to those familiar

[74] See UNCITRAL (n 51) 78 ff.

[75] See, for example, European Parliament and Council of the European Union, Directive 2014/24/EU of the European Parliament and of the Council of 26 February 2014 on public procurement and repealing Directive 2004/18/EC [2014] OJ L94/65, which introduces self-declarations in qualification, and limits the evidence of financial capacity of the supplier that can be required (eg turnover requirements may not exceed a maximum of twice the estimated value of the contract). It has been noted that the latter requirement may be of limited assistance, and that a limit by reference to the annual cost might enhance the impact.

with the procuring entity's requirements or who have the resources to investigate them. As the Guide to Enactment points out, these issues can be particularly disruptive to SMEs, which generally do not have experience in tendering or specialized tender-writing departments (unlike some large government suppliers). Therefore, the Guide to Enactment recognizes the helpful role of rationalization and standardization of procurement and of procurement practices in facilitating SME participation.[76]

The Guide to Enactment also points out that enacting states should ensure consistent terminology across their legislation to avoid confusion and ensure consistency in interpretation and application.[77] Using standard terminology in specifications and other elements of descriptions of what is to be procured (such as the EU Common Procurement Vocabulary, CPV,[78] and the UN Standard Products and Services Code[79]) may assist in some markets where SMEs tend not to participate (or, conversely, be barriers in others).

The UNCITRAL Model Law, too, has provisions on many procurement methods (including framework agreements) that allow suppliers to compete for only a part of a procurement contract, and it permits the use of multi-supplier framework agreements, both of which techniques can facilitate SME access. In helping enacting states address barriers related to contract size, Article 39(g) of the UNCITRAL Model Law allows partial tenders as a general rule, and the Guide to Enactment points out that permitting partial tenders may facilitate participation by SMEs, which may have the capacity to submit tenders only for certain portions of the procurement.[80] With regard to framework agreements, the Guide to Enactment states expressly that placing smaller orders within the framework agreement may allow smaller suppliers or contractors to participate and discusses the risk of restricting market access, particularly to SMEs, through bundling several requirements.[81]

The UNCITRAL Model Law also contains several features to support innovation in procurement as an area in which SMEs may have a potential competitive advantage over larger firms—for example, through advance notices, appropriately open tender specifications through use of output-based descriptions and terms and conditions for the procurement, and the choice of procurement methods, all of which can encourage SME participation.[82] In particular, an over-emphasis on price over quality in evaluation criteria can disadvantage SMEs and discourage participation.

A second set of barriers relates to the costs of participation in the procurement process—both in terms of time and money—which may operate as a disincentive to participation. SMEs are disproportionately affected by the costs involved, many of which are fixed. Estimates indicate that these costs may be 10 to 50 per cent

[76] See UNCITRAL (n 51) 20. [77] ibid 48.

[78] See European Commission, Commission Regulation (EC) No 213/2008 of 28 November 2007 amending Regulation (EC) No 2195/2002 of the European Parliament and of the Council on the Common Procurement Vocabulary (CPV) and Directives 2004/17/EC and 2004/18/EC of the European Parliament and of the Council on public procurement procedures, as regards the revision of the CPV [2008] OJ L74/1.

[79] See <https://www.unspsc.org/> accessed 20 January 2017.

[80] See UNCITRAL (n 51) 148. [81] ibid 255, 262.

[82] See, for example, ibid 68, 84, 194.

higher in public procurement as compared with comparable projects in the private sector.[83] For example, tender securities, performance bonds, licences, and other fees can be disproportionately expensive for SMEs. Here, the Guide to Enactment encourages a case-by-case analysis of the costs and benefits of imposing these requirements.[84] In low-value procurement, the risks of delivery or performance faced by the procuring entity and its potential losses are generally low, and the cost of providing a tender security—which will normally be reflected in the contract price and may discourage SMEs from participating in the tender—will be less justified. The Guide to Enactment also encourages implementing states to consider, inter alia, the negative effect of charges for solicitation documents on the participation of suppliers or contractors, in particular SMEs.[85]

Once a contract is awarded, a winning supplier will probably be confronted with complex contract management procedures and dispute resolution processes, and the cash-flow implications of funding the contracts concerned until payment, noting that the payment period in the public sector is significantly longer than in the private sector.[86] Addressing the financial cost of contract performance, through reducing times for the payment under procurement contracts and providing direct financing measures, may be desirable, but there are indications that some governments under financial pressure may be reluctant to implement this in practice.[87]

Supporting these regulatory and design measures, governments can also seek to enhance capacity to participate in procurement and SME ability to supply governments through capacity-building.[88] Measures can include improving SME visibility in procurement (promoting the use of SMEs vis-à-vis procuring entities); improving communications and interaction between SMEs and procuring entities; targeting information as noted above at SMEs, which may not be aware of the potential for supplying the government; enhancing tender-drafting abilities (as SMEs suffer from inexperience in writing tenders); building capacity in using new procurement tools (e-procurement tools such as electronic reverse auctions), so that they do not become a new barrier to access; and addressing SME weaknesses in terms of technical and financial capacity by allowing SMEs to combine or subcontract to reach minimum turnover requirements, or to be able to offer complementary components.

Similar to the GPA, the UNCITRAL Model Law therefore provides a large degree of flexibility to implementing governments with regard to many issues that can be of considerable importance for SME participation in procurement. The

[83] See Nicholas and Fruhmann (n 14) citing Fee and others (n 58); Karjalainen and Kemppainen (n 58); Peter Smith and Adam Hobbs, 'SMEs and Public Sector Procurement' (January 2001) Shreeveport Management Consultancy, 704/V07; UK Government, Department for Business, Innovation and Skills and others, 'Analysis of Responses to the Consultation on Making Public Sector Procurement More Accessible to Small and Medium Sized Enterprises' (2013) <https://www.gov.uk/government/uploads/system/uploads/attachment_data/file/264101/LYCons_response3final.pdf> accessed 20 January 2017.

[84] See UNCITRAL (n 51) 99.

[85] See ibid 146.

[86] See, further, Nicholas and Fruhmann (n 14).

[87] See UNCITRAL (n 51) 25.

[88] See ibid.

Guide to Enactment is a useful reference tool for policymakers and procuring entities in determining appropriate solutions to the issues raised. Of course, there is no guarantee that the flexibilities offered by the UNCITRAL Model Law or the guidance provided by the Guide to Enactment will be taken up in practice. Problems in take-up and related negative effects on SME participation in public procurement may well be related to risk-aversion of procurement officials who may be reluctant to depart from tried-and-tested solutions. In that regard, policymakers should be aware of the fact that the way in which procurement officials' performance is measured may have an impact on their attitude to taking the risks that contracting with untried-and-untested SMEs may involve.

Any review of potential successes and failures presupposes first and foremost that transparency is created with regard to the impact of choices to be made on procurement outcomes. In the current absence of sufficiently precise and complete data in most economies, many countries will have to rely on more general policy guidance based on experience gained in other countries in this regard. Therefore, policy discussions and technical assistance may be helpful for many countries in the process of setting or reviewing procurement policies with regard to SMEs.

Both UNCITRAL and the WTO engage in demand-driven technical assistance in support of their published texts. They often work together with other international institutions and have established dedicated cooperation programmes on public procurement with the European Bank for Reconstruction and Development.[89] They also partner with organizations such as the World Bank and the OECD in order to be able to respond to the needs of developing and transition economies. Again, the barriers with regard to procurement practices to be overcome by SMEs as 'newcomers' to public procurement often resemble those faced by foreign suppliers. Therein lies an opportunity for governments to address unintended barriers for both SMEs and (other) international suppliers at the same time—with the benefit of rendering their procurement system more efficient. This can be done through the implementation of the policy approach of the GPA and the UNCITRAL Model Law—both of which require more detailed elaboration at the national level in order to be rendered effective.

## III. Preferential programmes

The third range of measures that can be taken by governments to support SME participation in procurement markets concerns preferential programmes designed to alter the outcome of procurement processes and tip the balance in favour of SMEs, thereby creating incentives for them to participate.

[89] For further information on the EBRD UNCITRAL Public Procurement Initiative, see European Bank for Reconstruction and Development, 'EBRD UNCITRAL Public Procurement Initiative' (2011) <https://www.ppi-ebrd-uncitral.com> accessed 20 January 2017. For further information on the EBRD GPA Technical Cooperation Facility, see European Bank for Reconstruction and Development, 'EBRD GPA Technical Cooperation Facility' (2016) <http://ebrd-gpa-facility.com/?id=1&PHPSESSID=2c64554d0cf9719558ad063184477748> accessed 20 January 2017.

Such programmes can take a variety of forms: they can consist of set-asides, price preference margins, or offset requirements relating to SME inputs or subcontracting, or a combination of the above.[90] Some systems—such as in the United States and South Africa, which base their SME policies on targeted assistance for economic and social reasons—set targets for awards to SMEs using a flexible combination of price preferences and set-asides, and in the case of the United States require procuring entities to justify deviations from the policies concerned.[91] According to OECD statistics, a third of OECD member countries (33 per cent) have put in place specific legislative provisions or policies, including set-asides, to encourage participation from SMEs in procurement—worldwide statistics as to the prevalence of such measures are hard to find, but anecdotal evidence suggests that a number of countries implement such programmes.[92] Where such assistance programmes are permitted, the advantages cited are that they support SMEs directly through creating and sustaining demand, and provide quick and visible benefits to SMEs.[93]

In the decision about whether or not to implement such measures, several factors can play a role. Arguments in favour of preferential programmes, such as social justice, industrial policy objectives, and potential efficiency gains, inter alia, due to enhanced SME participation, have to be balanced against potential drawbacks. Set-asides, by their very nature, exclude non-targeted tenderers from procurements, and may therefore lead to reduced competition, with potential effects on the value for money of the goods and services procured.[94] Price preference margins may raise the cost of procurement and therefore have important budget implications or reduce the quantity of goods and services that can be procured out of the public purse.[95] Offset requirements may have similar effects by making it more difficult for suppliers to comply with tender requirements.[96] Furthermore, the administration of such programmes may, under some circumstances, be burdensome and

[90] For a concise overview, see Asian Bank of Development, 'SME Development: Government Procurement and Inclusive Growth' (2012) <http://www.adb.org/publications/sme-development-government-procurement-and-inclusive-growth> accessed 20 January 2017.

[91] ibid.

[92] See, for example, Linarelli (n 27) citing examples from the United States, South Africa, and Malaysia. See also McCrudden (n 15).

[93] See Nicholas and Fruhmann (n 14).

[94] See Arrowsmith (n 16). For a study with contrary findings, using data on US federal procurement of dredging services, see Thomas A Denes, 'Do Small-Business Set-Asides Increase the Cost of Government Contracting?' (1997) 57 Public Administration Review 441.

[95] See Arrowsmith (n 16). On potential efficiencies of price preferences in a trade context and under certain circumstances, see Simon Evenett, 'Government Procurement' in Kenneth A Reinert and Ramkishen S Rajan (eds), *The Princeton Encyclopedia of the World Economy* (Princeton University Press 2009), citing Preston R McAffee and John McMillan, 'Government Procurement and International Trade' (1989) 26 Journal of International Economics 291.

[96] See Arrowsmith (n 16): 'Policies directed at, or affecting, behaviour outside government contracts often impose a greater burden on contractors than policies limited to the contract, especially when they extend to all the contractor's activities. As a result, there are also potentially greater costs for the procurement process. These arise both because of the costs of compliance reflected in tenders, and because (especially with contract conditions laid down by government) these policies may reduce the pool of contractors.'

create opportunities for collusion and corruption.[97] Finally, they may not create the desired economic benefits: they may involve awards to less efficient firms, or be applied in sectors where they are not needed.[98] It therefore seems prudent for governments that decide in favour of such programmes to monitor both costs and outcomes in order to target them well, and encourage effective and beneficial participation of innovative and competitive SMEs.[99]

Perhaps due to the potential costs, and in line with the political economy and industrial policy goals of such measures, such programmes, where implemented, are almost exclusively, if not entirely, aimed at *domestic* SMEs as beneficiaries. They therefore have important implications for the objectives of the GPA and the UNCITRAL Model Law to encourage the widest possible participation in procurement markets.

### 1. *Preferential programmes under the GPA*

The GPA, as a matter of principle, prohibits discrimination of foreign suppliers, goods, and services from GPA parties, as well as offsets with regard to covered procurement.[100] Furthermore, it restricts the conditions for participation to those that are essential to ensure that a supplier is capable and able to undertake the relevant procurement (see Article VIII). On this basis, one commentator, Linarelli, expresses the view that, as a matter of principle, 'GPA non-market access provisions do not permit SME ... preference policies. Going further, SME preference policies probably violate several GPA provisions.'[101] As Linarelli also points out, it is, in any case, still possible for GPA parties to implement preferential programmes without breaching their obligations under the Agreement.

As explained above, GPA obligations only apply to covered procurement, namely, procurement that is specified by the party in question in its Appendix I to the Agreements and satisfies several other conditions spelled out in Article II of the Agreement. For each GPA Party, Appendix I is divided into six Annexes which deal, respectively, with: (1) central government entities covered by the Agreement; (2) covered sub-central government entities; (3) 'other' covered entities (eg utilities and state-owned enterprises, SOEs); (4) coverage of goods; (5) services coverage; (6) coverage of construction services; and (7) any general notes.

[97] See, for example, Louisa Fluker, Julia Muravska, and Mark Pyman, 'Due Diligence and Corruption Risk in Defence Industry Offset Programmes' (Transparency International 2012) <https://issuu.com/tidefence/docs/2012-02_duediligenceandcorruptionri/12> accessed 20 January 2017: 'Besides the risk of bribery in offsets contracts, there is an additional risk that main supplier companies may be using the offsets package as a vehicle to offer benefits to individuals in return for undue influence or access to ... contracts.'

[98] See Arrowsmith (n 16).

[99] See the discussion in Nicholas and Fruhmann (n 14) with reference to Paul Nightingale and Alex Coad, 'Muppets and Gazelles: Political and Methodological Biases in Entrepreneurship Research' (University of Sussex, September 2011) <http://sro.sussex.ac.uk/49180/1/Ind_Corp_Change-2014-Nightingale-113-43.pdf> accessed 20 January 2017. See also UNCITRAL (n 51) 6.

[100] See Arts IV:1–2 and 6, as well as Art XIII:1 of the revised GPA.

[101] Linarelli (n 27) 453.

**Table 5.1** General threshold values under the GPA (in Special Drawing Rights, SDR)[i]

| | Annex 1: Central government entities | Annex 2: Sub-central government entities | Annex 3: Other entities |
|---|---|---|---|
| Goods and services | 130,000 SDR | 200,000 SDR | 400,000 SDR |
| Construction services | 5,000,000 SDR | 5,000,000 SDR | 5,000,000 SDR |

Notes:
[i] Not all parties apply the threshold levels as indicated. Source: WTO, e-GPA Portal <https://e-gpa.wto.org/en/ThresholdNotification/FrontPage> accessed 20 January 2017.

The Annexes also specify the threshold values above which individual procurements are subject to the GPA disciplines. In addition, the Annexes of most parties contain notes that qualify the application of the Agreement. In principle, all goods are covered if procured by a covered entity and not excluded specifically.

By virtue of the rules on coverage specified in the GPA, a procurement only falls within the ambit of the GPA's rules if the procuring entity is covered, if the service or good procured is included in the relevant party's commitments, and if the value of the procurement in question is above the threshold levels indicated in the relevant party's schedules.[102] This leaves a possibility to apply preferential SME programmes below the threshold values of the GPA—in other words with regard to smaller value procurements, which may be particularly attractive to SMEs (see Table 5.1 for general threshold values applied by most GPA parties). As all parties apply thresholds and do not open up small-value procurement to international competition, this does not require extensive negotiation of 'policy space'.

Furthermore, parties can negotiate specific exclusions to their above-threshold coverage. Apart from targeted procurement by non-covered entities, or SME programmes applicable only to non-covered sectors (goods, services, or construction services), it is possible for parties to indicate exceptions from coverage in notes to specific Annexes and in the General Notes in Annex 7. Several parties, including Canada, Japan, Korea, and the United States, have negotiated relevant exceptions from coverage and apply SME preferences in this way.

Linarelli points out that these 'negotiated' exclusions may lead to inequalities between GPA parties. According to him, 'the extent of a GPA contracting party's autonomy to pursue its own domestic justice policies depends on its market power, on its ability to offer up on the GPA negotiating table substantial other procurements unaffected by preference programmes. Thus, in the GPA context, only

[102] See also Robert D Anderson, Anna Caroline Müller, and Philippe Pelletier, 'Regional Trade Agreements and Procurement Rules: Facilitators or Hindrances?' (Research Paper No RSCAS 2015/81, 2015) <http://papers.ssrn.com/sol3/papers.cfm?abstract_id=2707219> accessed 20 January 2017; Robert D Anderson and others, 'The Relationship between Services Trade and Government Procurement Commitments: Insights from Relevant WTO Agreements and Recent RTAs' (WTO Working Paper ERSD-2014-21, 2014) <http://www.wto.org/english/res_e/reser_e/ersd201421_e.pdf> accessed 20 January 2017.

contracting parties with substantial import markets in public procurement have substantial policy autonomy'.[103] This concern identified by Linarelli with regard to the situation prevailing under the GPA 1994 may have been alleviated to some extent by the provisions of the revised GPA.

As noted above, the revised GPA introduces a completely redesigned provision on developing countries,[104] expressly permitting them to adopt or maintain price-preference programmes and offsets, as well as higher initial thresholds as transitional measures, based on their development needs and subject to transparency requirements.[105] While these still need to be negotiated by the country in question—the measures are subject to the agreement of existing GPA parties—this provision can arguably be seen as an attempt by GPA parties to 'level the playing field' to some extent and introduce the flexibilities required in order for less developed and/or smaller economies to join the Agreement. In any case, the provision can reinforce the negotiating position of developing or transition economies wishing to use targeted preferential SME programmes in government procurement for economic development.

Furthermore, the submissions of GPA parties under the Work Programme on SMEs have helped in further increasing transparency as to the implementation of negotiated exceptions to the GPA in practice. The Work Programme commits parties to a discussion on best practices in this regard.

Overall, the GPA therefore recognizes the need to provide flexibilities to allow for preferential treatment of SMEs and other 'secondary' or 'horizontal' policies and makes it a subject matter of negotiation and discussion.

### 2. *Preferential programmes under the UNCITRAL Model Law*

While the UNCITRAL Model Law, as a non-binding instrument, does not limit a government's choices with regard to preferential SME programmes by establishing prescriptive rules, the general approach promoted under it and the guidance provided for its implementation go in a similar direction.

As pointed out above, the non-discrimination provisions of the UNCITRAL Model Law outlined above are designed to ensure that SMEs are not deliberately prevented from accessing the public procurement markets. They are subject to a caveat: procuring entities may not discriminate among suppliers 'except when authorized or required to do so by the procurement regulations or by other provisions of law of this State'. As the Guide to Enactment explains, the purpose of this provision is to allow the procuring entity, solely in order to promote a government's declared national policies as reflected in other laws or the procurement regulations, to restrict procurement to, and/or to prefer tenders from, certain groups of suppliers.[106]

The caveat to the non-discrimination provisions in the Model Law[107] allows the government, through the procurement regulations or other laws, to limit eligibility to participate in procurement to particular groups, such as SMEs, so that a

[103] Linarelli (n 27).
[104] See Article V of the revised GPA.
[105] See for further detail Müller (n 45).
[106] See UNCITRAL (n 51) 5 ff, 222.
[107] See Section C.II.2.

procurement may be set aside for those groups, as well as allowing them to receive preferential treatment, and/or requiring or allowing credit in a tender for engaging SMEs as sub-contractors. Without the caveat, however, targeted procurement of this type would be prohibited under the Model Law.

A further option under Article 11 allows procuring entities to grant a margin of preference to suppliers on the basis of their nationality or on the basis of the origin of the subject matter of procurement (in practice, applying to domestic suppliers or domestically produced or provided items or services). The effect in practice is to provide a discount on the offered tender price in favour of, for example, SMEs. It is important to note, in this regard, that Article 11 does not limit preferences to domestic suppliers or contractors or to domestically produced goods, but also allows for any other preference.[108]

It should be emphasized that while UNCITRAL recognizes that governments may wish to pursue SME policies (and other secondary policies), it does not take a position on whether those policies are appropriately or best pursued through a procurement system, reflecting the long-standing policy approach referred to above.[109] The Guide to Enactment, however, provides the following commentary:

> The pursuit and implementation of these policies may have an impact on the performance of the procurement system itself, as, in essence, they are implemented through restrictions on competition for a particular procurement. For this reason, the pursuit of socio-economic policies involves exceptions to the principle of full and open competition and can bring additional costs to procurement, as it may increase the ultimate price paid. Additionally, the cost of monitoring compliance with government policies may add to administrative or transaction costs, which may have a negative effect on efficiency. On the other hand, some policies of this type may open the procurement market to groups or sectors that have traditionally been excluded from procurement contracts (such as SMEs) and may increase participation and competition, though in the longer term such benefits may not persist (eg if suppliers or contractors choose artificially to remain SMEs). Consequently, the pursuit and implementation of socio-economic policies through procurement should be carefully weighed against the costs that the policies may involve in both the short and long term (footnote omitted). In this regard, while there are indications that the results from the use of some preference policies (such as the use of evaluation criteria to prefer a defined group) tend to be more positive than from set-aside policies (such as restricting qualification or requiring subcontracting to a defined group, or resorting to domestic procurement), the main concern is that total insulation from competition for an extended period of time or beyond the point that suppliers or contractors can compete freely can also frustrate the capacity development that such policies are designed to achieve. Consequently, such policies may be considered to be appropriate as transitory measures, only for the purposes of granting market access to emergent suppliers or contractors, opening the national economy, such as through capacity-building, and should not be used as a form of protectionism. The policies should accommodate a progressive exposure to unlimited competition.[110]

Furthermore, these measures are all made subject to three caveats. First, the UNCITRAL Model Law requires an overall targeted policy in requiring that

[108] See UNCITRAL (n 51) 359. [109] See Section B.II. [110] See UNCITRAL (n 51) 6.

socio-economic policies be made part of the legislation on government procurement so that procuring entities are not permitted to create exemptions on an ad hoc basis. Second, it also establishes rigorous transparency standards, so that the impact of the measures is predetermined and pre-disclosed as for any other applicable term of a procurement procedure.[111] Third, enacting states may use them only where their international obligations—for example, those under the GPA—permit.[112]

The Guide to Enactment also encourages states to make use of the transparency rules and other benchmarks to assess any premium paid for set-asides or preferences, and to balance it against the benefits to be derived, though it is considered that a full empirical assessment of costs and results is likely to be difficult.[113]

In sum, it can be concluded that both the GPA and the UNCITRAL Model Law offer flexibilities for governments wishing to implement preferential programmes. As such programmes can create significant tensions with the general objectives of both instruments, they permit them only as targeted exceptions to the open and non-discriminatory procurement procedures that are encouraged as matter of principle. In regulating their use, they establish transparency and other requirements designed to encourage the careful design and monitoring of policies by implementing governments.

## D. Conclusions

This chapter has discussed the role of the GPA and the UNCITRAL Model Law in facilitating the participation of SMEs in public procurement, in light of the fact that access to and participation in public procurement markets by SMEs has been identified, by many governments, as a crucial element in fostering sustainable economic development and prosperity worldwide.

In their approach, both the GPA and the UNCITRAL Model Law encourage the widest possible participation in procurement markets and therefore are designed to help governments attract the best possible suppliers offering their goods and services at the most competitive prices. The idea behind both instruments is that governments benefit as they achieve best value for money, and suppliers benefit as they gain access to markets that were previously closed to them, whether due to formal reasons such as discriminatory policies, or practical obstacles, such as a lack of transparency regarding opportunities and conditions for participation.

Their role in facilitating the integration of SMEs in procurement markets is important in two respects. First, both instruments ultimately derive their *raison d'être* from their usefulness in facilitating private sector suppliers' access to procurement markets abroad. In that regard, SMEs represent an important factor in rendering them effective, as SMEs represent a large majority of firms worldwide.

[111] ibid 7. [112] ibid 6.

[113] ibid 7. Included in the costs of such measures will be the additional cost of monitoring that SMEs fulfil the criteria to define them as such.

Second, both instruments are part of and derived from an emerging standard of international best practices in government procurement, and seek to increase good governance and the efficiency of public procurement systems for the benefit of governments and their citizens. Therefore, they arguably need to offer appropriate solutions and/or flexibilities to governments seeking to integrate SMEs in their supplier base in the best possible ways. In order for these goals to be achieved and to increase the effectiveness of procurement systems worldwide, the barrier-reducing measures that the GPA and the UNCITRAL Model Law propose need to work in tandem with SME support measures. Neither the GPA nor the UNCITRAL Model Law contain specific provisions on the issue as part of their core provisions. However, both instruments are of relevance, and should usefully be considered by governments seeking to devise SME policies in public procurement in three respects.

First, they are helpful in identifying measures to improve general features of procurement legislation and systems relating to transparency, integrity, and competition. These 'level the playing field' among all potential suppliers, and can be expected to remove obstacles to participation of particular relevance of SMEs as a first step. Important synergies therefore exist between SME policies and the objectives, rules, and principles of the GPA and the UNCITRAL Model Law. Both the UNCITRAL Model Law and the GPA actively encourage measures related to transparency, openness, and integrity needed in order for SMEs to overcome barriers to participation in public procurement: in these regards, SMEs are very similar to international suppliers whose participation in procurement markets the two instruments are designed to facilitate. Consequently, the goals and specific procedural rules established by the two instruments, in encouraging broad participation and competition in procurement markets, are fully compatible with the goal of favouring the inclusion of SMEs in the supplier base of governments by such means.

The second area concerns more specific measures relating to procurement practices that can be taken in the application of general rules in order to facilitate SME participation. Examples include the disaggregation of demand, appropriate use of framework agreements and e-procurement systems, creation of opportunities for subcontracting and joint bidding, prompt payment of suppliers, and the provision of training. Such measures may be needed to overcome potential barriers to SME participation that may persist despite a generally open and transparent system. In this regard, the basic approach of both instruments is to leave options for each government to decide on, as long as general principles of transparency and non-discrimination are complied with. Such choices are left to governments as the measures in question are not considered as generally conflicting with the primary goals of the procurement function as described above, or per se problematic with regard to the participation of international suppliers. Nevertheless, the choices and solutions adopted can have a significant impact on SME procurement and the efficiency of the procurement system as a whole, and therefore need to be reflected upon. The two instruments therefore do not ignore the relevance of such issues. While the GPA, as a binding instrument, carefully carves out policy space in this regard, the Work Programme on SMEs established by the GPA Committee permits related policy discussions. Similarly, the Guide to Enactment of the UNCITRAL Model Law raises issues and addresses advantages and disadvantages of policy choices to be made in this regard.

The third area of interaction concerns preferential measures or programmes designed to give SMEs privileged access to procurement contracts. In that regard, both the GPA and the UNCITRAL Model Law, even if in varying degrees, offer flexibilities for governments wishing to implement preferential programmes that discriminate against some suppliers or categories of suppliers. As such programmes can create significant tensions with the general objectives of both instruments, they permit them only as targeted exceptions to the open and non-discriminatory procurement procedures that are encouraged as a matter of principle. In regulating their use, they establish transparency and other requirements designed to encourage the careful design and monitoring of such policies by implementing governments.

Overall, therefore, the synergies that exist between the two instruments and policies to encourage SME participation in procurement markets may well exceed conventional perceptions in this regard. Recent developments, including the entry into force of the revised GPA in 2014, the initiation of Work Programme on SMEs, and the new, 2011 UNCITRAL Model Law, provide a convenient point of departure for relevant discussions.

In that regard, it may be most striking that statistics and data on the use and effectiveness of the different types of measures are extremely hard to find, and where national data exist, international comparisons are difficult. The GPA and the UNCITRAL Model Law, as tested instruments designed to identify international best practices in government procurement, may be helpful in reminding policymakers of guidelines to be followed.

With this in mind, and in line with the findings set out in this chapter, the following observations seem relevant. First, there is potential to further harness the synergies that can be created between general reform and liberalization efforts and SME participation measures. The GPA and the UNCITRAL Model Law can be helpful instruments in this regard, whether implemented directly or as general guidelines. Second, many choices governments can make while fully respecting non-discrimination and transparency principles under both instruments can be expected to have a positive impact on SME participation. In this respect, the possibilities for information sharing and technical assistance opened up by the work of the WTO and UNCITRAL may be helpful in further contributing to the development of international best practices. Finally, while both instruments recognize that it is up to each government to decide on the usefulness of preferential programmes to foster SME participation, such programmes would ideally be designed as effective and targeted measures subject to rigorous transparency standards that allow a cost-benefit analysis.

Recent economic analysis suggests that both SME and cross-border success in public procurement remain work-in-progress. It is therefore only natural that neither the GPA nor the UNCITRAL Model Law offer all relevant answers. What seems crucial, however, is that the principle of transparency that is embodied in both instruments is integrated into policy discussions on the subject matter—and potentially into future rules of international economic law governing it.

## References

Anderson, RD, 'The Conclusion of the Renegotiation of the WTO Agreement on Government Procurement: What It Means for the Agreement and for the World Economy' (2012) 21 Public Procurement Law Review 83

Anderson, RD and Kovacic, WE, 'Competition Policy and International Trade Liberalisation: Essential Complements to Ensure Good Performance in Public Procurement Markets' (2009) 18 Public Procurement Law Review 67

Anderson, RD, Kovacic, WE, and Müller, AC, 'Promoting Competition and Deterring Corruption in Public, Procurement Markets: Synergies with Trade Liberalization' (Think Piece, E15 Expert Group on Competition Policy and the Trade System, ICTSD, World Economic Forum 2015) <http://e15initiative.org/wp-content/uploads/2015/09/E15-Competition-Anderson-Muller-Kovacic-Final.pdf> accessed 20 January 2017

Anderson, RD and Müller, AC, 'The Revised WTO Agreement on Government Procurement: An Emerging Pillar of the World Trading System: Recent Developments' (2015) 7 Trade Law and Development 229

Anderson, RD and Müller, AC, 'WTO Accession and Accession to the Agreement on Government Procurement (GPA): What is the Relationship? Why Should WTO Accession Candidates Also Consider GPA Accession? What Are the Pros and Cons?' in Chiedu Osakwe and Dadush Uri (eds), *WTO Accessions and Trade Multilateralism: Case Studies and Lessons* (WTO and Cambridge University Press 2015)

Anderson, RD, Müller, AC, and Pelletier, P, 'Regional Trade Agreements and Procurement Rules: Facilitators or Hindrances?' (Research Paper No RSCAS 2015/81, 2015) <http://papers.ssrn.com/sol3/papers.cfm?abstract_id=2707219> accessed 20 January 2017

Anderson, RD, Pelletier, P, Osei-Lah, K, and Müller, AC, 'Assessing the Value of Future Accessions to the WTO Agreement on Government Procurement (GPA): Some New Data Sources, Provisional Estimates, and an Evaluative Framework for Individual WTO Members Considering Accession' (WTO Staff Working Paper ERSD-2011-15, 2011) <https://www.wto.org/english/res_e/reser_e/ersd201115_e.htm> accessed 20 January 2017

Anderson, RD, Locatelli, C, Müller, AC, and Pelletier, P, 'The Relationship between Services Trade and Government Procurement Commitments: Insights from Relevant WTO Agreements and Recent RTAs' (WTO Working Paper ERSD-2014-21, 2014) <http://www.wto.org/english/res_e/reser_e/ersd201421_e.pdf> accessed 20 January 2017

Anderson, RD, Schooner, SL, and Swan, CD, 'The WTO's Revised Government Procurement Agreement: An Important Milestone Toward Greater Market Access and Transparency in Global Public Procurement Markets' (GWU Legal Studies Research Paper No 2012-7, 2012) <http://ssrn.com/abstract=1984216> accessed 20 January 2017

Arrowsmith, S, 'Horizontal Policies in Government Procurement: A Taxonomy' (2010) 10 Journal of Public Procurement 149

Arrowsmith, S, 'The Revised Agreement on Government Procurement: Changes to the Procedural Rules and Other Transparency Provisions' in Sue Arrowsmith and Robert D Anderson (eds), *WTO Regime on Government Procurement: Challenge and Reform* (Cambridge University Press 2011)

Arrowsmith, S and Kunzlik, P (eds), *Social and Environmental Policies in EC Procurement Law: New Directives and New Directions* (Cambridge University Press 2009)

Asian Bank of Development, 'SME Development: Government Procurement and Inclusive Growth' (2012) <http://www.adb.org/publications/sme-development-government-procurement-and-inclusive-growth> accessed 20 January 2017

Beck, T, Demirguc-Kunt, A, and Levine, R, 'SMEs, Growth, and Poverty: Cross-Country Evidence' (2005) 10 Journal of Economic Growth 199

Caldwell, ND, Walker, H, Harland, C, Knight, L, Zheng, J, and Wakeley, T, 'Promoting Competitive Markets: The Role of Public Procurement' (2005) 11 Journal of Purchasing Supply Management 242

Cernat, L and Kutlina-Dimitrova, Z, 'International Public Procurement: From Scant Facts to Hard Data' (2014) <http://trade.ec.europa.eu/doclib/docs/2015/april/tradoc_153347.pdf> accessed 20 January 2017

Denes, TA, 'Do Small-Business Set-Asides Increase the Cost of Government Contracting?' (1997) 57 Public Administration Review 441

European Bank for Reconstruction and Development, 'EBRD UNCITRAL Public Procurement Initiative' (2011) <https://www.ppi-ebrd-uncitral.com> accessed 20 January 2017

European Bank for Reconstruction and Development, 'EBRD GPA Technical Cooperation Facility' (2016) <http://ebrd-gpa-facility.com/?id=1&PHPSESSID=2c64554d0cf9719558ad063184477748> accessed 20 January 2017

European Commission, 'EU Public Procurement Legislation: Delivering Results—Summary of Evaluation Report' (2011) <http://ec.europa.eu/internal_market/publicprocurement/docs/modernising_rules/executive-summary_en.pdf> accessed 20 January 2017

European Commission, 'SMEs' Access to Procurement Markets and Aggregation of Demand in the EU' (DG Internal Market and Services, February 2014) <http://ec.europa.eu/internal_market/publicprocurement/docs/modernising_rules/smes-access-and-aggregation-of-demand_en.pdf> accessed 20 January 2017

European Commission, 'E-Procurement' (2016) <http://ec.europa.eu/growth/single-market/public-procurement/e-procurement/index_en.htm> accessed 20 January 2017

Evenett, S, 'Government Procurement' in Kenneth A Reinert and Ramkishen S Rajan (eds), *The Princeton Encyclopedia of the World Economy* (Princeton University Press 2009)

Fee, R, Erridge, A, and Hennigan, S, 'SMEs and Government Purchasing in Northern Ireland: Problems and Opportunities' (2002) 14 European Business Review 326

Fluker, L, Muravska, J, and Pyman, M, 'Due Diligence and Corruption Risk in Defence Industry Offset Programmes' (Transparency International 2012) <https://issuu.com/tidefence/docs/2012-02_duediligenceandcorruptionri/12> accessed 20 January 2017

Freeman, A, 'Challenging Myths about the Funding of Small Businesses … : Finance for Growth' (Demos 2013) <http://www.demos.co.uk/files/DF_-_Finance_for_Growth_-_web.pdf?137821> accessed 20 January 2017

Gibb, A, 'SME Policy, Academic Research and the Growth of Ignorance, Mythical Concepts, Myths, Assumptions, Rituals and Confusions' (2000) 18 International Small Business Journal 13

Glover, A, 'Accelerating the SME Economic Engine: Through Transparent, Simple and Strategic Procurement' (HM Treasury 2008) <https://web.archive.org/web/20100602051331/; http://webarchive.nationalarchives.gov.uk/+/http:/www.hm-treasury.gov.uk/d/pbr08_economicengine_2390.pdf> accessed 20 January 2017

Golovko, E and Valentini, G, 'Exploring the Complementarity between Innovation and Export for SMEs' Growth' (2011) 42 Journal of International Business Studies 362

Gordon, DI, 'Constructing a Bid Protest Process: Choices Every Procurement Challenge System Must Make' (2006) 35 Public Contract Law Journal 3

Gordon, DI, 'Bid Protests: The Costs Are Real, But the Benefits Outweigh Them' (2013) 42 Public Contract Law Journal 3

International Trade Centre, 'SMEs and Export-Led Growth: Are There Roles for Public Procurement Programmes? A Practical Guide for Assessing and Developing Public Procurement Programmes to Assists SMEs' (presented at the WTO/World Bank regional workshop on procurement reforms and transparency in public procurement for Anglophone African countries, Dar es Salaam, Tanzania, 14–17 January 2003)

Karjalainen, K and Kemppainen, K, 'The Involvement of Small- and Medium-Sized Enterprises in Public Procurement: Impact of Resource Perceptions, Electronic Systems and Enterprise Size' (2008) 14 Journal of Purchasing and Management 230

Kaspar, L and Puddephatt, A, 'Benefits of Transparency in Public Procurement for SMEs: General Lessons for Egypt' (Global Partners and Associates 2012) <http://www.gp-digital.org/wp-content/uploads/pubs/Benefits-of-transparency-in-PP-for-SMEs.pdf> accessed 20 January 2017

Linarelli, J, 'The Limited Case for Permitting SME Procurement Preferences in the Agreement on Government Procurement' in Sue Arrowsmith and Robert D Anderson (eds), *WTO Regime on Government Procurement: Challenge and Reform* (Cambridge University Press 2011)

Love, JH and Roper, S, 'SME Innovation, Exporting and Growth: A Review of Existing Evidence' (2015) 33 International Small Business Journal 28

McAffee, PR and McMillan, J, 'Government Procurement and International Trade' (1989) 26 Journal of International Economics 291

McCrudden, C, 'Using Public Procurement to Achieve Social Outcomes' (2004) 28 Natural Resources Forum 257

McCrudden, C, *Buying Social Justice: Equality, Government Procurement, & Legal Change* (Oxford University Press 2007)

Mishory, E, 'Leveling Asymmetry: The Information-Leveling Model of Transparency in Government Procurement' (2013) <http://dx.doi.org/10.2139/ssrn.2365092> accessed 20 January 2017

Morettini, S, 'Public Procurement and Secondary Policies in EU and Global Administrative Law' in Edoardo Chiti and Bernardo Giorgio Mattarella (eds), *Global Administrative Law and EU Administrative Law* (Springer 2011)

Müller, AC, 'Special and Differential Treatment and Other Special Measures for Developing Countries under the Agreement on Government Procurement: The Current Text and New Provisions' in Sue Arrowsmith and Robert D Anderson (eds), *WTO Regime on Government Procurement: Challenge and Reform* (Cambridge University Press 2011)

Nicholas, C, 'Work of UNCITRAL on Government Procurement: Purpose, Objectives and Complementarity with the Work of the WTO' in Sue Arrowsmith and Robert D Anderson (eds), *WTO Regime on Government Procurement: Challenge and Reform* (Cambridge University Press 2011)

Nicholas, C and Fruhmann, M, 'Small and Medium-Sized Enterprises Policies in Public Procurement: Time for a Rethink?' (2014) 14 Journal of Public Procurement 328

Nightingale, P and Coad, A, 'Muppets and Gazelles: Political and Methodological Biases in Entrepreneurship Research' (University of Sussex, September 2011) <http://sro.sussex.ac.uk/49180/1/Ind_Corp_Change-2014-Nightingale-113-43.pdf> accessed 20 January 2017

OECD, *Removing Barriers to SME Access to International Markets* (OECD 2008) <http://dx.doi.org/10.1787/9789264045866-en> accessed 20 January 2017

OECD, *Regions and Innovation Policy* (OECD Reviews of Regional Innovation, OECD 2011) <http://dx.doi.org/10.1787/9789264097803-en> accessed 20 January 2017

OECD, *Government at a Glance 2011* (OECD 2011) <http://dx.doi.org/10.1787/gov_glance-2011-en> accessed 20 January 2017

OECD, *Government at a Glance 2013* (OECD 2013) <http://dx.doi.org/10.1787/gov_glance-2013-47-en> accessed 20 January 2017

OECD, 'Survey on Public Procurement' (2014) <http://dx.doi.org/10.1787/888933249069> accessed 20 January 2017

OECD, *Government at a Glance 2015* (OECD 2015) <http://dx.doi.org/10.1787/gov_glance-2015-43-en> accessed 20 January 2017

OECD and UNIDO, 'Effective Policies for Small Business: A Guide for the Policy Review Process and Strategic Plans for Micro, Small and Medium Enterprise Development' (2004) <https://www.unido.org/fileadmin/user_media/Publications/Pub_free/Effective_policies_for_small_business.pdf> accessed 20 January 2017

Piga, G, 'A Fighting Chance Against Corruption in Government Procurement' in Susan Rose-Ackerman and Tina Soreide (eds), *International Handbook on the Economics of Corruption* (Edward Elgar 2011)

Schooner, SL, 'Desiderata: Objectives for a System of Government Contract Law' (2002) 11 Public Procurement Law Review 103

Smith, P and Hobbs, A, 'SMEs and Public Sector Procurement' (January 2001) Shreeveport Management Consultancy, 704/V07

Technopolis, 'Evaluation of SMEs' Access to Public Procurement Markets in the EU' (2014) <http://ec.europa.eu/DocsRoom/documents/2153/attachments/1/translations/en/renditions/pdf> accessed 20 January 2017

UK Government, Department for Business, Innovation and Skills, Department for Committees and Local Government, Department for Education, Department of Health and Home Office, 'Analysis of Responses to the Consultation on Making Public Sector Procurement More Accessible to Small and Medium Sized Enterprises' (2013) <https://www.gov.uk/government/uploads/system/uploads/attachment_data/file/264101/LYCons_response3final.pdf> accessed 20 January 2017

UNCITRAL, 'UNCITRAL Model Law on Public Procurement' (2011) <http://www.uncitral.org/uncitral/uncitral_texts/procurement_infrastructure/2011Model.html> accessed 20 January 2017

UNCITRAL, 'Guide to Enactment of the UNCITRAL Model Law on Public Procurement' (2012) <http://www.uncitral.org/uncitral/en/uncitral_texts/procurement_infrastructure/2012Guide.html> accessed 20 January 2017

UNCITRAL, 'Origin, Mandate and Composition of UNCITRAL' (2016) <http://www.uncitral.org/uncitral/en/about/origin.html> accessed 20 January 2017

WTO, 'Agreement on Government Procurement' (2016) <https://www.wto.org/english/tratop_e/gproc_e/gp_gpa_e.htm> accessed 20 January 2017

WTO, 'Parties, Observers and Accessions' (2016) <http://www.wto.org/english/tratop_e/gproc_e/memobs_e.htm> accessed 20 January 2017

WTO, 'Thresholds Indicated in Annexes 1, 2 and 3 of Appendix I to the Revised GPA' (2016) <https://e-gpa.wto.org/en/ThresholdNotification/FrontPage> accessed 20 January 2017

Yukins, CR, 'A Case Study in Comparative Procurement Law: Assessing UNCITRAL's Lessons for U.S. Procurement' (2006) 35 Public Contract Law Journal 457

Yukins, CR, 'Integrating Integrity and Procurement: The United Nations Convention Against Corruption and the UNCITRAL Model Procurement Law' (2007) 36 Public Contract Law Journal 307

Zheng, J, Walker, H, and Harland, C, 'The Role of SMEs in Public Procurement: A Review of Literature and Research Agenda' (2006) <https://www.researchgate.net/publication/239950830_The_Role_of_SMEs_in_public_procurement_a_Review_of_Literature_and_Research_Agenda> 20 January 2017

# PART II

# REGIONAL AND TRANSREGIONAL TRADE LAW

# 6

# SME Provisions in Trade Agreements and the Case of TTIP

*Martina Lodrant and Lucian Cernat**

## A. Introduction

With the effects of the 2008 financial crisis still weighing on their economies and multilateral trade negotiations largely stalled, the European Union and the United States in 2011 decided to consider bilateral options for increasing trade and investment in order to lift economic growth, create jobs, and render European and American businesses more competitive on the global stage. This led to the launch in 2013 of negotiations on a comprehensive trade and investment agreement named the Transatlantic Trade and Investment Partnership (TTIP).

To deliver the full economic benefits, this agreement must work for small and medium-sized enterprises (SMEs). In both constituencies, SMEs account not only for the vast majority of all companies, but also for the bulk of economic output and employment. Over 99 per cent of all businesses in the European Union are SMEs and they generated a large share of gross domestic product (GDP) (61 per cent) and employment (70 per cent). Similarly, US SMEs accounted for 50 per cent of GDP and employment and for the majority of new job creation in recent years.[1]

The empirical literature provides extensive evidence that SMEs with international activities—whether importing, exporting, or investing abroad—are more innovative, more productive, and grow revenue and employment at a faster rate.[2] While causality may run both ways, this indicates that increasing the participation

* The views expressed herein are those of the authors and not necessarily those of the European Commission. The authors would like to thank Ana Duch T-Figueras, Federica Pesce, and Desislava Borisova for their research assistance and numerous other colleagues for their useful comments.

[1] Iza Lejárraga and others, 'Small and Medium-Sized Enterprises in Global Markets: A Differential Approach for Services?' (OECD Trade Policy Papers No 165, 2014) 9 <http://dx.doi.org/10.1787/5jz17jtfkmzt-en> accessed 20 January 2017.

[2] EIM Business & Policy Research, 'Opportunities for the Internationalisation of European SMEs' (Directorate-General for Enterprise and Industry, European Commission, 2011); US International Trade Commission (USITC), 'Small and Medium-Sized Enterprises: Characteristics and Performance' (USITC Publication 4189, Investigation No 332-510, November 2010) <http://www.usitc.gov/publications/332/pub4189.pdf> accessed 20 January 2017; Lejárraga and others (n 1).

of SMEs in international trade and investment can be a powerful driving force for more robust and inclusive growth.

Millions of EU- and US-based SMEs are already doing business abroad and many more SMEs are involved in trade indirectly by supplying intermediate inputs to exporters. At the same time, SMEs still seem far from reaching their potential in international trade and transatlantic trade specifically. In 2012, less than 250,000 EU SMEs imported US products, while around 150,000 European SMEs exported their products directly to the United States.[3]

In this chapter, we will discuss why fewer small firms make the leap into foreign markets and how international agreements can help rectify this and thereby increase SME contribution to economic growth and employment. We will examine in particular to what extent trade and investment agreements such as TTIP should and could be tailored to enhance SME participation in the international economy.

The remainder of this chapter is divided into three sections. We first adopt a conceptual framework concerning SMEs and trade agreements. We introduce a taxonomy of trade barriers facing SMEs and in corresponding policy responses we discuss the role of trade agreements, making a distinction between general provisions and provisions specific to SMEs. In the subsequent section, we review past practice of the European Union and the United States concerning SME-specific provisions in trade agreements. We then apply our framework to the TTIP example. We begin by highlighting the potential for SMEs to benefit from this agreement and the main barriers reported by SMEs from both sides. Then we outline provisions in TTIP that could address them, highlighting opportunities to consider provisions specific to SMEs. Finally, we draw some conclusions on the treatment of SME issues in future trade agreements.

## B. SMEs and Trade Agreements: A General Framework

### I. Barriers to trade for SMEs

Multiple factors lie behind the relatively low share of SMEs observed in the international economy. It is partly accounted for by a high concentration of SMEs in less tradable industries. It also reflects a choice: some small business owners do not prioritize growth and therefore do not look for international expansion opportunities. However, it is also the case that SMEs are more affected by obstacles to trade than their larger counterparts. Successful exporting requires having a competitive product or service and access to foreign markets, finding foreign partners and customers, navigating the trade process and requirements, securing payment, and handling liability issues. Importing involves some similar steps. SMEs can be disadvantaged in this regard due to a combination of internal and external barriers:[4]

[3] Eurostat, 'Trade by Enterprise Characteristics Database (TEC)' (Luxembourg: Eurostat 2014).

[4] Lucian Cernat, Ana Norman-López, and Ana Duch T-Figueras, 'SMEs Are More Important Than You Think! Challenges and Opportunities for EU Exporting SMEs' (September 2014) 3 DG TRADE

- *Internal barriers* are related to the inherent and distinguishing characteristics of small firms. Small production volumes make economies of scales unavailable to SMEs, which are therefore less able to compete on cost and must instead find a niche, innovate, and offer better quality.[5] Being small also implies several types of resource constraints: *informational* (asymmetric information about foreign markets, business opportunities, rules, and regulations), *human* (lack of managerial and technical skills, qualifications, knowledge, and time), and *financial* (shortage of capital, difficulties in accessing loans or financial markets).[6]
- *External barriers* exist outside the firm and can be related to geographical, cultural, or market circumstances or to government policy and practices. Some emanate from the *domestic environment* (such as macroeconomic instability, poor infrastructure, lack of transparency, limited skills and capital availability, burdensome regulations, unfair business practices, inadequate intellectual property protection, inefficient administration and law enforcement). These barriers often have no deliberate protectionist intention and may hinder business in general or affect international trade simply as a result of differences in the conditions between the home and the target market (geographical, linguistic, cultural, or 'regulatory distance').[7] Others are related to the *trade and investment regime* as such (tariffs, quotas, rules of origin, and other non-tariff measures discriminating between domestic and foreign suppliers of goods or services).

While these barriers affect all businesses, many fall disproportionally on small firms without the in-house resources to deal with them and unable to spread the fixed cost of these outside barriers over large volumes. For instance, the cost of collecting information to enter a foreign market is unrelated to potential sales and may discourage small businesses from even exploring opportunities abroad.[8] Additional product testing or certification often required to comply with foreign technical regulations, paperwork, and fees for customs processing, enforcing contracts, or protecting intellectual property all generate fixed costs which make it less likely for SMEs to find profitable trades. Even ad-valorem tariffs can be more consequential for small companies when they already operate

Chief Economist Note 9 <http://trade.ec.europa.eu/doclib/docs/2014/september/tradoc_152792.pdf> accessed 20 January 2017; Lejárraga and others (n 1).

[5] Fabio Antoldi, 'Can European SMEs Really Intercept the Internationalisation Paths of Fast Growth?' in Fabio Antoldi, Magdolna Sass, and David Smallbone (eds), 'European SMEs and International Trade' (Workshop Expo Committee on International Trade, European Parliament, February 2012) <http://www.europarl.europa.eu/RegData/etudes/workshop/join/2012/457104/EXPO-INTA_AT(2012)457104_EN.pdf> accessed 20 January 2017. It should be noted nevertheless that trade can also be a way of increasing efficiency of small firms: importing can provide access to cheaper inputs, while exporting enables higher and thus more efficient volumes.

[6] Lejárraga and others (n 1) 49. [7] ibid. [8] ibid.

at a less efficient scale and with smaller profit margins. When tariff reductions or exemptions are granted but come with stringent rules of origin and high documentation cost of proving the nationality of the product, these may remain inaccessible to SMEs.[9]

In sum, as a result of their internal constraints of small size, external barriers that merely raise costs for large companies may inhibit trade by SMEs altogether if such barriers are of fixed-cost nature.

## II. Policy responses: Cross-cutting linkages

SMEs may be able to overcome obstacles to entering foreign markets by using different strategies (eg forming clusters, relying on wholesalers and distributors, e-commerce, and logistics firms) or sometimes SMEs are already 'born global', relying on foreign partners and joint ventures.[10]

Nevertheless, there is room for various domestic policies to foster the internationalization process where barriers result from government intervention (including the trade and investment regime as a whole) or are linked to the existence of market failures such as information asymmetries which governments can correct (for instance, transparency, skills, and capital shortages). Furthermore, governments can accelerate the adoption of new technologies and market-based solutions to trade barriers (such as e-commerce).

Governments may enhance international trade indirectly through measures aimed at improving the domestic business environment, enterprise competitiveness, and innovation capacity, which in turn help increase participation in international trade. We will focus on trade policy in a more direct sense, although the line is blurred in practice. Trade policy combines distinct but interrelated categories of trade liberalization, regulatory cooperation and harmonization, facilitation, and promotion. The first three correspond to reducing external trade barriers, while promotion aims at easing internal constraints and supporting firms so they can overcome external barriers. Trade promotion can thus be seen in part as a substitute for the other three types of policy measures. Trade liberalization, harmonization, and facilitation are established areas of international trade negotiations. Promotion policies, on the other hand, are normally conducted at the domestic level except in development contexts where international cooperation serves as a vehicle to transfer expertise and financing for trade promotion from donors to developing country recipients. However, international agreements can also provide a useful platform for achieving synergies in these activities through exchange of best practices, mutual access to assistance schemes, or joint programming. Covering all strands of trade policy within an international agreement also serves to enhance comprehensiveness and coherence.

[9] USITC (n 2) 6–26; Antoldi (n 5).
[10] USITC (n 2) 4–2; Lejárraga and others (n 1) 20, 55.

## III. SME-specific provisions in trade agreements: Economic needs and legal challenges

Before engaging in a review of SME provisions in trade agreements, certain general points need to be considered, with regard to their economic rationale and the legal framework under which such provisions need to be conceived.

Provisions in trade agreements that address issues of relevance to SMEs could be either de facto or de jure SME-targeted and could take the form of either:

- *generalized provisions* that make no distinction between operators based on size. The large majority of provisions will be of this kind. Whether any reference is made to SMEs or not, such provisions can still be particularly important for them; or
- *SME-specific provisions* that apply only to SMEs, introducing positive discrimination or action in their favour, and complement generalized provisions.

It goes without saying that specific provisions for SMEs need only be considered insofar as general trade policy and agreements cannot substantially reduce the trade barriers affecting SMEs. As long as standard trade liberalization, harmonization, and facilitation provisions effectively tackle external barriers, they will help traders regardless of their size. When barriers reduced in this way involve a fixed cost, small firms benefit proportionally more without any special provisions simply because such barriers fall more heavily on them. However, the minimum threshold to which external barriers need to be lowered to make trade profitable is lower for small companies. Therefore, measures must be more ambitious to trigger trade by SMEs.

Negotiators should therefore explore whether an extra degree of liberalization or facilitation could be agreed at least for SMEs—for instance, if such limited concessions would be less politically sensitive. Certain clear examples of these types of SME-related actions come to mind. Domestic regulatory policies sometimes differentiate in favour of SMEs where they risk being disproportionally burdened. Trade agreements should extend such preferential treatment in domestic rules relevant to trade and investment to foreign SMEs. With regard to the trade and investment regime, additional goods and services market access commitments and extra facilitations such as reduced customs formalities and fees for SMEs could be envisaged or priority treatment of visa requests from small foreign services providers.

As regards tackling external trade barriers, provisions specific to SMEs may therefore in some instances be developed as a fall-back solution. Such 'affirmative action' in favour of exporting SMEs may be more feasible in relation to the procedural aspects (cutting red tape and the administrative burden of customs and regulatory compliance) as opposed to substantive requirements. Since trade promotion measures target capacity constraints that are a distinct feature of SMEs, they lend themselves more naturally to SME-specific provisions.

When considering such SME-specific provisions, their legal aspects must nevertheless be carefully assessed. As further discussed in Section D.II, one challenge in the context of international negotiations is that there is currently no common definition of SMEs.[11] Second, the discriminatory element in these provisions could raise questions about their compatibility with existing international trade rules. Preferences in terms of market access and related formalities extended to SMEs but not to large companies need to be checked against both the general provisions in the law of the World Trade Organization (WTO) with regard to non-discrimination and the special requirements of Article XXIV of the General Agreement on Tariffs and Trade (GATT) and Article V of the General Agreement on Trade in Services (GATS) concerning regional arrangements. Trade promotion measures involving subsidies for SMEs would need to comply with the provisions laid out in the WTO Agreement on Subsidies and Countervailing Measures (SCM Agreement) to avoid the risk of legal challenges. Although there is no applicable precedent in WTO jurisprudence yet, legal constraints may reduce the options available of setting forth and implementing SME-specific provisions, but do not in principle exclude the possibility of such provisions complying with WTO rules. Certain authors, for example, claim that the GATS architecture clearly allows for differentiation in terms of trade rules by enterprise characteristics such as size.[12] However, particularly with regard to trade liberalization and facilitation, parties negotiating a trade agreement would still need to weigh the efficiency of maintaining parallel regimes for different segments of companies and the procedure for determining eligibility.

## C. SME-Specific Provisions in EU and US Free Trade Agreements: Practice to Date

The generic arguments in favour of SME-specific provisions discussed in the previous section are not just hypothetical. Such provisions have already been incorporated in many EU and US free trade agreements (FTAs) (see Table 6.1).

We have found them in twenty-one such agreements concluded by the European Union and eight by the United States between 1990 and 2014.[13] They come on top of the generalized content of these agreements which has evolved over time in ways that should a priori be seen as positive from the standpoint of internationalizing SMEs even if not targeting them specifically. Recent FTAs address not only tariffs, but also non-tariff barriers, regulations, and procedures affecting trade in goods, services, and investment, as well as intellectual property rights (IPR) protection, subsidies, and competition policy, and also labour, environment, and governance standards. In the categorization introduced above, these agreements combine trade liberalization, harmonization, and facilitation. At the same time, EU FTAs with neighbouring countries and countries of the African, Caribbean, and Pacific (ACP)

[11] Lejárraga and others (n 1) 53.

[12] Rudolf Adlung and Sébastien Miroudot, 'Poison in the Wine? Tracing GATS-Minus Commitments in Regional Trade Agreements' (2012) 4 WTO Staff Working Papers 1–25; Adlung and Soprana, Chapter 1 of this volume.

[13] The full list of these FTAs is included in Table 6.1.

**Table 6.1** Overview of EU and US FTAs negotiated 1990–2016, including dedicated SME provisions by topic[i]

| | FTA[ii] | |
|---|---|---|
| Issue | EU | US |
| Enterprise development | EU–Palestinian Authority (1997)<br>EU–Lebanon (2002)<br>EU–Macedonia (2001)<br>EU–Algeria (2002)<br>EU–Montenegro (2007)<br>EU–Cameroon (2009)<br>EU–CARIFORUM (2008)[iii]<br>EU–Albania (2006)<br>EU–South Africa (1999)<br>EU–Georgia (2014)<br>EU–Moldova (2014)<br>EU–Eastern and South African (ESA) region (2009) | US–Peru (2006)[iv]<br>US–Colombia (2006)[iv]<br>US–Korea (2007) |
| Access to finance | EU–Palestinian Authority (1997)<br>EU–Lebanon (2002)<br>EU–Cameroon (2009)<br>EU–South Africa (1999)<br>EU–ESA region (2009) | — |
| Innovation | EU–Palestinian Authority (1997)<br>EU–Lebanon (2002)<br>EU–CARIFORUM (2008)<br>EU–ESA region (2009) | — |
| Cross-border business networking | EU–Palestinian Authority (1997)<br>EU–Jordan (1997)<br>EU–Lebanon (2002)<br>EU–South Africa (1999) | — |
| Investment Promotion | EU–Palestinian Authority (1997)<br>EU–Tunisia (1995)<br>EU–Morocco (1996)<br>EU–Jordan (1997)<br>EU–Lebanon (2002)<br>EU–Egypt (2001)<br>EU–Algeria (2002)<br>EU–ESA region (2009)<br>EU–South Africa (1999)[v] | — |
| E-commerce | EU–Colombia & Peru (2012)<br>EU–Canada (2016) | US–Dominican Republic & Central America (2004)<br>US–Panama (2007) |
| Customs | EU–Cameroon (2009)<br>EU–Ivory Coast (2008)<br>EU–Colombia & Peru (2012)<br>EU–Moldova (2014) | — |
| Labour and environment issues | — | US–Chile (2003)<br>US–Peru (2006)<br>US–Colombia (2006) |

(*Continued*)

**Table 6.1** Continued

| | FTA[ii] | |
|---|---|---|
| Issue | EU | US |
| Subsidies | EU–South Africa (1999)<br>EU–Korea (2010) | — |
| Public procurement | EU–South Africa (1999)<br>EU–Korea (2010)<br>EU–Colombia & Peru (2012)<br>EU–Central America (2012) | US–Canada & Mexico (1992)<br>US–Chile (2003)<br>US–Australia (2004)<br>US–Colombia (2006)<br>US–Peru (2006)<br>US–Korea (2007) |
| Investment Protection | EU–Canada (2016) | |
| FTA implementation | EU–Colombia & Peru (2012) | |

Notes:
[i] Authors' analysis based on the screening of EU and US FTAs negotiated between 1990 and 2014. The texts of all EU FTAs can be accessed at <http://ec.europa.eu/trade/policy/countries-and-regions/agreements> accessed 20 January 2017 and US FTAs at <https://ustr.gov/trade-agreements/free-trade-agreements> accessed 20 January 2017.
[ii] The indicated year is the year of signature.
[iii] The provision is limited to the tourism services sector.
[iv] The agreement provides for possible cooperation measures to be agreed in the course of implementation.
[v] The provision is limited to the mining sector.

Group of States, which are broader in scope, also integrate promotion activities to support enterprise development backed with EU aid.[14]

We have analysed the provisions that make reference to SMEs in above-mentioned EU and US FTAs negotiated since the 1990s in terms of their scope and nature. The results arranged by thematic area are captured in Figure 6.1.[15]

From this analysis we can draw some stylized observations, which tend to corroborate some of the arguments reviewed in the previous sections:

- Many EU and US agreements already contain some SME-specific provisions. The EU FTAs cover a wider thematic variety of SME-specific provisions than US agreements, mostly on account of the EU practice of broader agreements covering industrial cooperation where SMEs are typically singled out.[16]

[14] See European Commission, 'Trade, Growth and Development: Tailoring Trade and Investment Policy for Those Countries Most in Need' (COM(2012) 22 final, Luxemburg 2012) 12 f.

[15] For more detailed information, see Table 6.1, which shows which FTAs contain SME-specific provisions in each thematic area.

[16] For instance, the interim Economic Partnership Agreement (EPA) between the European Union and the Eastern and Southern Africa states (ESA) has a chapter on Economic and Development Cooperation, including a dedicated Article on SMEs (Art 42), which covers several SME-specific areas: enterprise development, access to finance, trade and investment promotion, capacity building and institutional support, technology transfer and innovation, information exchange and networking, etc.

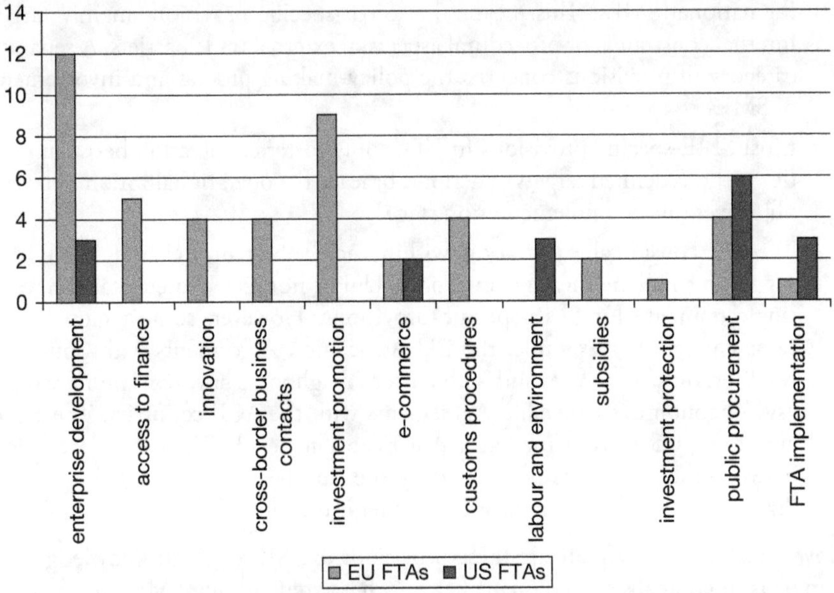


**Figure 6.1** Thematic range of SME-specific provisions in existing EU and US FTAs, by number of FTAs

Source: Authors' compilation based on the screening of EU and US FTAs concluded from the 1990s to 2014. The frequency count comprises both cooperation clauses (the predominant type of SME provisions in existing FTAs) and disciplines, notably in the most recent FTAs signed both by the United States and the European Union. In some cases, provisions are limited to one sector (eg tourism services, mining).

- The most common SME-specific provisions are horizontal, that is, they stipulate support for SMEs that is not limited to a specific barrier, but could apply to any aspect of their growth and participation in trade.[17] Other SME-specific provisions address barriers to trade in a particular sector such as those on the participation of SMEs in public procurement or on e-commerce.
- Insofar as SME-specific provisions relate to particular policy measures, they predominantly stipulate promotion activities and to a lesser extent also facilitation measures. We find no 'offensive' type of SME-specific provisions that would offer SMEs a more preferential level of trade liberalization. On the other hand, some agreements create 'defensive' carve-outs from liberalization commitments to preserve the existing subsidies for domestic SMEs or to allow FTA parties to maintain public procurement preferences and set-asides

[17] These are provisions we label as covering 'enterprise development' in Figure 6.1. For instance, the EU interim EPA with ESA referred to in n 16 contains a broad commitment to promote a favourable environment for SMEs (Chapter IV, Art 42). US FTAs with Peru and Colombia also envisage that action in favour of SMEs could be taken on any issue related to trade and the use of the FTA depending on the needs identified in the course of the FTA implementation.

for national SMEs. This means that SME-specific provisions mainly target internal constraints or procedural aspects of external trade barriers. A separate category of provisions concerns the policy-making process and involvement of SMEs.

- Most SME-specific provisions in FTAs only foster cooperation between parties without defined targets or actions, or leave the operationalization of broad objectives for the implementation stage.
- There is considerable variation within each subset of EU and US FTAs, suggesting that neither the European Union nor the United States have a single template for SME-specific provisions. However, some regional patterns emerge. For example, the EU Association Agreements with Southern Mediterranean countries and with Eastern neighbours have common features, as do Economic Partnership Agreements with the ACP countries. The same applies to US FTAs with Latin American partners.[18] There is also overlap between the provisions negotiated by the European Union and the United States, particularly where the FTA partner is the same.[19]

How valuable and adequate are these provisions to SMEs? To our knowledge, no study has so far analysed and quantified to what extent adding SME-specific provisions to FTAs has increased the number of exporting SMEs or increased their exports. Going forward, it will be important to better document these effects. However, given the important untapped potential for SMEs' trade, we see room overall for a more systematic, comprehensive, and legally enforceable approach to such provisions. In the next section, we examine how such an approach could be developed in the TTIP negotiations.

## D. SMEs and TTIP

### I. Potential and barriers for SMEs in transatlantic trade

The important economic stakes involved in the current transatlantic negotiations triggered a strong interest in the business sector. This interest is also present among EU SMEs, and quite rightly so. Numerous SMEs across the European Union are suppliers of exporters and stand to benefit indirectly from any boost TTIP would give to transatlantic trade conducted by these companies they supply. But SMEs

[18] For instance, the EU agreements with the Cariforum and ECA region have similar provisions on SMEs' development, technological cooperation, and innovation. The European Union's Mediterranean Association Agreements (with Egypt, Morocco, Tunisia, etc) have similar SME provisions concerning investment promotion. Similarly, US FTAs with Colombia and Peru have similar SME provisions on facilitating access to government procurement and support for implementation of labour and environmental standards.

[19] For example, both the EU and US agreements with Peru and Colombia refer to facilitating SMEs' access to government procurement and assessing the impact of the agreement on SMEs.

also have a large direct stake in TTIP. The following observations provide some evidence:[20]

First, while only a small proportion of SMEs is directly engaged in international trade, more than 80 per cent of EU exporters are SMEs. This amounted to over 600,000 exporting firms in 2012.[21] This makes for a significant small firm constituency that stands immediately to benefit from EU trade policy initiatives, not counting SMEs that might only start exporting as a result of them.

Second, the value of SME exports is larger than commonly assumed. With over €500 billion of merchandised exports, SMEs account for over a third of EU exports and employ more than 6 million people throughout Europe. In certain sectors, SMEs account for more than 50 per cent of EU exports.[22]

Third, as can be seen from Figure 6.2, EU SMEs are also already quite active in transatlantic trade. Noteworthy is the much larger number of importing SMEs as a share of total firms importing from the United States, considerably higher than the average share of SMEs in total EU imports. However, on the exporting side, it seems that EU SME exporters are less successful in selling to the United States than to other markets, both in terms of number of firms and share in trade values. This relative difference may be interpreted as an indication for further potential for EU SMEs in increasing their exports to the United States into which TTIP could tap.

Based on a simple 'proportionality assumption' that EU-exporting SMEs could reach the same proportion in transatlantic trade as they currently hold in total EU exports (34 per cent), a rough 'static' order of magnitude of the current lost transatlantic SME trade potential would be in the range of €7 to 8 billion, equivalent to around a tenth of current EU SMEs' transatlantic exports. Clearly, such a crude comparison is prone to error since the SME 'transatlantic gap' vis-à-vis their share in EU total trade is driven, as discussed in Section B.II, by multiple intrinsic and external barriers not all of which are within reach of trade agreements. Nevertheless, feedback from SMEs suggests that TTIP could help tackle many persisting barriers that currently hamper the ability of EU SMEs to penetrate the US market.

A recent SME survey run by the European Commission brings the message home.[23] It reminds that, while tariffs in the European Union and United States are low on average, they are still a significant barrier for SMEs, particularly as remaining peaks are found in sectors with high SME concentration such as apparel and footwear. Many SMEs that participated in this survey and reported that certain barriers prevent them from exporting to the United States found certain US tariffs prohibitive. Moreover, reinforcing previous findings of the Centre of Economic Policy Research (CEPR),[24] the survey points to the dominant role

[20] Cernat and others (n 4). [21] ibid 3. [22] ibid 6.

[23] European Commission, 'Small and Medium Sized Enterprises and the Transatlantic Trade and Investment Partnership' (European Union 2015) <http://trade.ec.europa.eu/doclib/docs/2015/april/tradoc_153348.pdf> accessed 20 January 2017.

[24] Joseph Francois and others, 'Reducing Transatlantic Barriers to Trade and Investment' (Final Project Report, Centre for Economic Policy Research, March 2013) <http://trade.ec.europa.eu/doclib/docs/2013/march/tradoc_150737.pdf> accessed 20 January 2017.

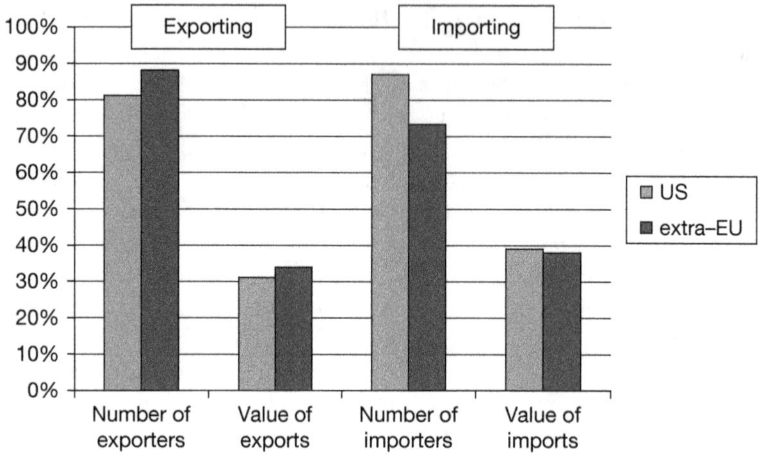


**Figure 6.2** The share of EU SMEs in exporting and importing activities, by number of firms and value of trade

Source: Eurostat TEC database, 2011 data.

played by regulatory issues as an impediment in transatlantic trade. Over a third of surveyed SMEs that were prevented from exporting to the United States attributed this to the extra costs caused by differences in standard-related measures, including technical, phytosanitary, and labelling regulations. SMEs also report challenges in dealing with customs paperwork and procedures, as well as the high cost of protecting IPR.

To give a few sectoral examples, for SMEs exporting EU food and beverages, tariffs and SPS barriers were key obstacles. Many SMEs exporting textiles and furniture products similarly cited both tariffs and technical and labelling requirements. In the case of products with a Geographical Indication (GI) exported by many European SMEs, adequate protection of this type of IPR is absent in the United States. For services-exporting SMEs, the lack of mutual recognition of licences and credentials for professional services providers and the procedures to obtain short-term business visas were particularly detrimental to their ability to export services to the United States. Exporting-services SMEs have ranked addressing restrictions on the movement of natural persons (so-called mode 4 of services trade under the GATS) high on their list of expectations from TTIP negotiations.[25] This is consistent with existing literature[26] which finds that, although in general commercial presence (mode 3) represents one of the main drivers of services exports, services SMEs are less likely to establish a commercial presence abroad and hence they have a higher propensity for their exports to take place under other modes of supply such as online sales (mode 1) or movement of natural persons (mode 4). Traditionally, these two modes of supply are less subject to multilateral commitments and rely on

[25] See n 22. [26] Lejárraga and others (n 1) 18.

bilateral agreements.[27] The US procurement market also remains relatively closed, although European SMEs provide many goods and services typically purchased by the authorities.

Overall, and in contrast to their larger counterparts, small firms consistently face difficulties in accessing useful information about the various legal requirements and procedures, but also relevant government assistance for internationalization.[28] Remarkably, US-based SMEs express very similar concerns in terms of exporting to the EU market.[29]

## II. The role of TTIP negotiations

How should the TTIP respond to these concerns? The overall objective of the TTIP negotiations is twofold: first, the agreement should tackle the remaining obstacles that inhibit trade between the European Union and the United States; second, it should also set a high standard for trade and investment rules that could contribute to the development of global rules and help parties address common barriers encountered by European and American companies in third countries.[30]

The talks have therefore embraced a comprehensive agenda around three clusters of issues: market access, regulatory coherence, and trade-related rules.[31] The market access pillar includes reciprocally eliminating duties on imported goods, liberalizing services, and liberalizing and ensuring the protection of foreign investment against expropriation or unfair and inequitable treatment, as well as opening public procurement. The negotiations within the regulatory pillar are aimed at cutting unnecessary costs of complying with regulatory requirements, particularly those stemming from divergences in standards, regulations, and related compliance procedures. This would be achieved through strengthened cooperation to achieve common international standards; where possible, harmonization, equivalence, or mutual recognition of existing regulations, and conformity assessments so that goods and services originating from one party in accordance with its regulatory requirements could ultimately be marketed in the other party without adaptation or additional testing; consolidation of good regulatory practices; and setting up of a framework for future upstream regulator-to-regulator cooperation with a view

[27] Martin Roy, Juan Marchetti, and Aik Hoe Lim, 'The Race Towards Preferential Trade Agreements in Services: How Much Market Access is Really Achieved?' in Marion Panizzon, Nicole Pohl, and Pierre Sauvé (eds), *GATS and the Regulation of International Trade in Services* (Cambridge University Press 2008).

[28] Also a main finding in other studies such as EIM Business & Policy Research (n 2) 88.

[29] See a recent comprehensive report on trade barriers in the European Union as perceived by American SMEs by the USITC. USITC, 'Trade Barriers that U.S. Small and Medium-Sized Enterprises Perceive as Affecting Exports to the European Union' (USITC Publication 4455, Investigation No 332-541, March 2014) <https://www.usitc.gov/publications/332/pub4455.pdf> accessed 20 January 2017.

[30] European Commission, 'European Union and United States to Launch Negotiations for a Transatlantic Trade and Investment Partnership' (13 February 2013) MEMO/13/94.

[31] EU–US High Level Working Group on Jobs and Growth (HLWG), 'Final Report' (11 February 2013) <http://trade.ec.europa.eu/doclib/docs/2013/february/tradoc_150519.pdf> accessed 20 January 2017.

to making new regulations more efficient and compatible. Finally, the trade rules pillar is about underpinning a level playing field in the transatlantic and third-country markets. It encompasses disciplines, principles, and cooperation in areas such as customs procedures, trade in raw materials, competition policy, State aid and state-owned enterprises, localization requirements, intellectual property rights, environmental and labour standards, and transparency. A structure of committees, a mediation, and a dispute-settlement mechanism would also be set up to support effective implementation of the TTIP agreement.

Juxtaposing this agenda against the trade concerns of European and American SMEs demonstrates that many of these could be addressed in the ordinary course of negotiations across different pillars, although negotiators need to take extra care to ensure that solutions are accessible to SMEs. Whether generalized or SME-specific, provisions across the TTIP agreement promise to open new opportunities for small companies to trade directly across the Atlantic and also as suppliers in value chains of exporting firms. Thus, a wide array of these provisions may in effect qualify as SME provisions.

At the same time, TTIP will also feature a chapter dedicated to SMEs, the purpose of which is to complement provisions in other parts of the agreement in areas where SMEs need extra help to take advantage of those improved trade and investment opportunities.[32] Three core components of this chapter have already been identified in the ongoing negotiations on SMEs. First, the chapter will solidify mechanisms for cooperation and the exchange of best practices between the two sides with a view to enhancing the competitiveness of SMEs and their ability to participate in trade. Second, it will commit parties to make available information useful to those who wish to benefit from the TTIP agreement and to do business in the transatlantic space. Third, it is envisaged that a dedicated body will be set up to deal with SME issues throughout the implementation stage.

This agenda indicates that the TTIP negotiations—while still ongoing—are set to go further than any previous trade agreement of the two parties in catering for the needs of SMEs through all strands of trade policy. Considering the disproportionately strong effect external trade barriers can have on SMEs, it will be particularly critical for them that the final agreement on the one hand embodies a high level of ambition in trade liberalization, regulatory alignment, and facilitation while preserving the right of parties to regulate at the appropriate level to ensure the protection of health, safety, consumer and labour rights, and the environment. On the other hand, the final agreement will have to help in making trade promotion activities, where they are needed, more effective and efficient.

In the following sections, we examine in more detail some key areas for SMEs in the TTIP negotiations and highlight provisions that could deliver the most value, including possible opportunities to top up baseline commitments with

[32] European Commission, 'Inside TTIP: An Overview and Chapter-by-Chapter Guide in Plain English' (European Union 2015) <http://trade.ec.europa.eu/doclib/docs/2015/july/tradoc_153635.pdf> accessed 20 January 2017.

SME-specific elements. Based on the preceding analysis, we will be looking for such SME-specific opportunities particularly with respect to trade facilitation and promotion measures. The issue of the definition of SMEs clearly arises. In the European Union, SMEs are defined as companies with fewer than 250 employees, an annual turnover of less than €50 million, or an annual balance sheet less than €43 million which are independent from larger companies.[33] On the other hand, in the United States, the 'size standard'—the largest size to be classified as a small business concern—varies across sectors of the economy and is set at 500 employees for most manufacturing and mining industries and US$7 million in average annual receipts for most non-manufacturing industries.[34]

TTIP negotiators will also face challenges related to the substance rather than SME-specificity of certain provisions. Aside from purely political concerns, the differences in the respective legal and regulatory systems in the European Union and the United States, and in particular the distribution of competences across different levels of government, need to be considered. For example, trade promotion in the European Union remains the competence of Member States[35] and in the United States many promotion activities are also conducted by states,[36] limiting the power of the federal level to negotiate on these issues.

### *1. Tariffs, rules of origin, and customs procedures*

The envisaged general elimination of customs duties will boost the competitive position of small manufacturers from Europe in the US market and vice versa, above all in SME-dominated sectors such as textiles, apparel, footwear, or food and beverages with current tariff peaks. To make this preferential or duty-free tariff treatment accessible to the largest number of SMEs, it will also be necessary to negotiate sufficiently flexible rules of origin and an efficient process to establish the origin of the product, since many exporting SMEs need to import key intermediate inputs. An SME-friendly solution to the issuance of certificates of origin would be the acceptance by the respective customs authorities of a self-declaration by the supplier as proof of origin.

Tariff dismantling should also be accompanied by provisions on facilitation measures that will reduce the paperwork and simplify the procedural steps in the clearance of goods for importation and exportation. A number of practices, normally

[33] European Commission, Commission Recommendation 2003/361/EC of 6 May 2003 concerning the definition of micro, small and medium-sized enterprises [2003] OJ L124/36, Art 2(1); cf the Annex of this volume, Table.

[34] Size Standards Division Office of Government Contracting & Business Development, 'SBA Size Standards Methodology' (April 2009) 1 <https://www.sba.gov/sites/default/files/articles/size_standards_methodology.pdf> accessed 20 January 2017.

[35] Trade promotion is outside the scope of EU trade policy as defined by Art 207 of the Treaty on the Functioning of the European Union.

[36] US Government Accountability Office, 'Export Promotion: Trade Agencies Should Enhance Collaboration with State and Local Partners' (21 May 2014) <http://www.gao.gov/products/GAO-14-393> accessed 20 January 2017.

captured in generalized commitments, would mostly benefit SMEs which often make low-value shipments (without being able to fill an entire standard container) and cannot afford hiring specialists to handle border formalities. Such facilitations measures include:

- free advanced rulings on conditions that will apply to the shipped goods, a single, electronic, and standardized goods declaration with not more than the necessary risk-related data elements and supporting documents;
- a single window online facility allowing traders to submit data and obtain release and clearance through a single point rather than having to communicate with multiple government agencies;
- risk-based and coordinated controls;
- prompt release of goods;
- waived customs and related fees, proportional penalties;
- easy duty and tax payment methods; and
- fast and inexpensive appeal of administrative decisions.

Providing for such a level of facilitation without lowering compliance with applicable legislation (concerning taxation, product safety, animal health, IPR, or security) presupposes that operators can be trusted, which in turn may require their prior verification. Insofar as certain simplifications can only be offered to approved traders, this status must also be available to SMEs. To this end, SME-specific provisions could be envisaged concerning both the substantive requirements to be approved and the approval process. For instance, SMEs could be exempted from certain information requirements or be subjected to less frequent re-approval.

## 2. *Services*

Exporting SMEs are not only present in the goods sector, but also in many services areas.[37] However, SMEs exporting services face specific challenges. Hence, any trade initiative supporting services SMEs (eg through greater use of the internet, and especially of e-commerce) would be beneficial for many exporting SMEs as this lowers barriers for internationalization for smaller companies across many sectors. The EU FTA 'standard' provides for dialogue on regulatory matters involved, such as recognition of electronic signatures, liability of intermediary services providers with regard to transmission or storage of information, consumer protection, etc.[38] Similarly, reducing the administrative barriers against short-term movement of personnel (mode 4) would be of particular importance for SMEs exporting services, notably for engineering and IT-consulting SMEs.

[37] On SMEs and trade in services, see also Adlung and Soprana, Chapter 1 of this volume; and Dralle, Chapter 4 of this volume.

[38] These are provisions found in the EU–Korea FTA and the agreed text for an EU–Canada FTA (CETA).

Another way in which small services companies can become indirect exporters is to become part of global supply chains. The indirect participation in exporting activities as suppliers of parts and components is found to be very important for SMEs exporting goods. In the case of SMEs exporting services, the indirect export of intermediate services as part of finished products is not only equally important, but also leads to a conceptually new 'mode 5' of indirect services exports.[39] While the share of SMEs in total 'mode 5' services exports cannot easily be estimated, the important size of overall 'mode 5' services exports for total EU trade (estimated at over €300 billion in 2009) renders 'mode 5' among the predilect modes of tapping into foreign markets by SME services exporters, alongside modes 1 and 4. For instance, the textile and apparel sector (an area where SMEs hold a large share of total EU exports) is the second most intensive 'mode 5' sector.

The nature of indirect 'mode 5' services exports as a complex bundle of goods and services raises a number of additional policy questions that makes them relevant for TTIP negotiations. The fact that ultimately 'mode 5' indirect services exports take place 'in a container' subjects such services exports to GATT rules rather than traditional GATS modes of supply.[40] Under GATT, being part of a finished product, 'mode 5' indirect services exports pay duties. Those SMEs exporting intermediate services that are prone to be exported under 'mode 5' (eg design, testing, engineering, IT, etc) along global supply chains could therefore benefit from an amendment of existing customs valuation rules which, under certain conditions, already allow such services to be deducted from the value on which duties are due. Hence, while TTIP may not remove all restrictions in transatlantic trade in services, the negotiations could nevertheless provide an opportunity for more liberal SME-specific preferences.

### 3. *Standards and regulatory issues*

TTIP negotiations are also putting a strong emphasis on behind-the-border regulatory issues with the aim of reducing unnecessary regulatory burdens which add to the cost of transatlantic trade. These efforts respond directly to a prime concern expressed by SMEs on both sides of the Atlantic for which non-tariff barriers (NTBs) pose a big, if not at times insurmountable, challenge.[41]

One approach pursued in order to address this issue is to agree on a set of good domestic regulatory practices, such as impact assessments of new regulations under consideration, transparency and stakeholder consultation, selection of the least burdensome and trade-restrictive measures, ex-post assessments and periodic reviews of regulations, and the use of international standards. An SME-specific angle could be appended to these provisions by reflecting the European Union's 'think small'

[39] Lucian Cernat and Zornitsa Kutlina-Dimitrova, 'Thinking in a Box: A "Mode 5" Approach to Service Trade' (2014) 48 Journal of World Trade 1109.

[40] ibid. [41] See Section D.I.

regulatory principle[42] and the equivalent US concept of regulatory flexibility,[43] which in domestic contexts stipulates departing from one-size-fits-all rules when SMEs would be unduly affected. Concretely, the agreement could enshrine obligations to assess the impact of proposed legislation on SMEs, publish these assessments, allow inputs from SMEs, consider mitigating measures when appropriate (such as transition periods to comply with regulations or derogations and exemptions, particularly in terms of reporting requirements), and also pay special attention to SME concerns in subsequent reviews and ex-post assessments.

A second approach followed in the TTIP negotiations in the regulatory area is cooperation on existing and forthcoming regulations targeted at divergences that impose a high but avoidable cost on traders. Work is already underway in a number of sectors where negotiators hope to achieve greater alignment of regulatory requirements and reduce duplication of approval procedures. It will be important to ensure that such 'red-tape' priority sectors also include some of those where SMEs are major exporters (eg textile, leather, wood, metal products, but also in selected services sectors), in addition to those sectors that are already high on the negotiating agenda. Common certification and joint standard schemes in some selected subsectors with a high SME export intensity (such as, for instance, organic product standardization) could provide a valuable export platform for thousands of SMEs.

## 4. *Public procurement*

Public procurement is another area that SMEs are interested in, but where particularly EU SMEs also disproportionally report facing barriers.[44] There is room for liberalization, facilitation, and promotion provisions, some of which might be dedicated to SMEs. First, SMEs would benefit if TTIP increased legal certainty and expanded access to each other's procurement markets at federal and sub-federal level by committing additional government entities and removing or modifying local content requirements (for instance, the 'buy America' requirement could be turned into 'buy transatlantic'). Insofar as the opening of public procurement remains partial, negotiators could maximize the value for SMEs by prioritizing entities that buy items where SMEs are very competitive exporters (eg textiles and apparel, basic metals, certain services) or allow at least foreign SMEs to bid for contracts.

Current US and EU procurement policies providing preferences for domestic SMEs could also be extended reciprocally to the SMEs of the other party based on the principle of national treatment.[45]

[42] Introduced by the 2008 Small Business Act. European Commission, Communication from the Commission to the Council, the European Parliament, the European Economic and Social Committee and the Committee of the Regions: '"Think Small First": A "Small Business Act" for Europe' (25 June 2008) COM(2008) 394 final.

[43] See 1980 Regulatory Flexibility Act, 5 USC 601–12.

[44] Cernat and others (n 4); see also Caroline Nicholas and Anna C Müller, Chapter 5 of this volume.

[45] In the United States, the Small Business Act mandates that overall at least 23 per cent of all prime government contract dollars must be awarded to US-based small businesses.

Furthermore, the European Union and the United States have introduced in their domestic laws various simplifications of the procurement procedures which could be taken up by TTIP in view of their special importance for SMEs, such as online publication of all tenders and handling of contracting (e-procurement), acceptance of self-declarations from bidders that they meet the requirements instead of full documentary evidence, standardized self-declaration forms, unbundling of contracts, or limits on required turnover to participate in public procurement.[46] Another simple possibility that could increase transparency in public procurement markets and greater participation by SMEs would be to streamline the various online portals where tenders are published to provide a 'one-stop shop' for SMEs interested in public procurement.

Finally, parties may also agree to extend access to relevant training and other support measures to each other's SMEs wishing to participate in the public procurement market.

## *5. IPR provisions*

Similar possibilities could be explored in the area of IPR. Making provisions on IPR relevant to SMEs means in particular making protection and enforcement of IPR (patents, trademarks, copyright, geographical indications, trade secrets, etc) accessible and affordable. In this regard, the case for provisions to limit related fees for SMEs should be explored. At the same time, numerous EU SMEs selling GI products are counting on TTIP to fill the gap in legal protection for this category of IPRs in the United States.

Cooperation on enforcement in third countries with less developed IPR systems, where IPR violations pose an even more serious problem for SMEs than in the EU–US context, could also be embedded in TTIP.[47] The aim would be to solidify existing cooperation in this area under the EU–US IPR Action Strategy,[48] including deployment of dedicated tools and capacity-building to help SME rightsholders better protect their intellectual property abroad.

## *6. Transparency*

Given the evidence that SMEs are missing out on cross-border business opportunities because they lack the necessary information to identify and pursue them,

[46] These are some of the features of the new EU rules on public procurement set out in European Parliament and Council of the European Union, Directive 2014/24/EU of the European Parliament and of the Council of 26 February 2014 on public procurement and repealing Directive 2004/18/EC [2014] OJ L94/65 and European Parliament and Council of the European Union, Directive 2014/25/EU of the European Parliament and of the Council of 26 February 2014 on procurement by entities operating in the water, energy, transport and postal services sectors and repealing Directive 2004/17/EC [2014] OJ L94/243.

[47] European Commission, 'TTIP, Towards an EU–US Trade Deal: Intellectual Property, EU Position Paper' (20 March 2015) <http://trade.ec.europa.eu/doclib/docs/2015/april/tradoc_153331.7%20IPR%20EU%20position%20paper%2020%20March%202015.pdf> accessed 20 January 2017.

[48] EU–US IPR Action Strategy provides for three areas of cooperation: engagement on IPR issues in third countries, customs cooperation, and public-private partnerships.

trade agreements such as TTIP should help create a more transparent business environment. While EU and US FTAs consistently include certain requirements for governments to ensure transparency of trade-related rules and measures,[49] SMEs necessitate still more ambitious transparency provisions.[50] They should cover all tariff and regulatory requirements and related procedures applicable to importing goods into the respective markets whether at the federal or sub-federal level, as well as available support mechanisms for small traders. They could also extend to information about market opportunities, particularly databases of potential business partners for SMEs looking to expand abroad, as well as of public procurement tenders. Furthermore, these provisions should ensure that information and resources are easy to find and comprehend. Parties negotiating TTIP should work towards a single, free-of-charge, web-based information portal, including search tools and a helpline.[51]

While it makes little sense to reserve such transparency rules for SMEs, they would nevertheless be the main beneficiaries. Some aspects of these provisions, such as the exemption from charges or assistance and training on the use of available information tools, may also take the form of SME-specific provisions.

## 7. *Support schemes*

One set of further commitments that could be considered concerns reciprocally opening trade-related support schemes to SMEs from the other side—for example, funding for research in light of the close link between innovation and trade. Alternatively, TTIP could provide for joint support initiatives, including the aggregation of information or other measures aimed at assisting European and American SMEs in entering those third-country markets where they face the same obstacles. Insofar as TTIP were to introduce additional disciplines and prohibitions concerning State aid, SME-specific exemptions from such provisions would need to be considered in order to allow the continuation of SME support schemes qualifying as subsidies.

## 8. *Investment protection*

Investment abroad is the most sophisticated form of internationalization which SMEs usually pursue only as a subsequent stage after exporting.[52] Nevertheless, numerous

[49] For instance, the EU–Korea FTA contains a chapter on transparency as well as dedicated provisions to make available information about technical regulations, SPS measures, customs laws and procedures, services regulations, subsidies, etc.

[50] cf Rudolf Adlung and Marta Soprana, Chapter 1 of this volume, Section C.VI; Caroline Nicholas and Anna C Müller, Chapter 5 of this volume, Section C.I; Heng Wang, Chapter 7 of this volume, Section B.III.1.

[51] European Commission (n 32).

[52] USITC (n 2); EIM Business & Policy Research (n 2).

European SMEs have invested or may invest in the United States, and vice versa. For those who take that step, effective access to protection of their foreign investments is important as smaller firms are more vulnerable to unfair and discriminatory treatment in their host country.[53]

Investment protection and investor-state arbitration provisions typically found in international investment treaties have come under fire for allegedly, albeit unintentionally, giving multinational corporations the power to overturn legitimate government regulation. However, among investors from the United States, SMEs rather than big multinational corporations appear to be the predominant users of investor-state dispute settlement.[54] SMEs rely on such procedures to address grievances against foreign governments because alternative means, such as diplomatic protection by their home state, are often unavailable when the investment at stake is small. Therefore, as TTIP negotiators seek to strike a balance between protecting investors' rights and safeguarding a state's ability to regulate in the public interest, they should also keep the needs of SMEs in mind. Specifically, this would mean providing for an investor-to-state dispute settlement mechanism that is not only neutral, but also affordable and quick.[55] Procedural deadlines and simplifications, such as the possibility of filing relatively low-value claims to a single judge, would speed up the proceedings and put a lid on the costs, to the benefit of SMEs. SME-specific limits on the costs to be paid by plaintiffs would facilitate access to redress for small investors while keeping the risk of excessive litigation at bay. Moreover, TTIP parties may wish to encourage recourse to mediation to resolve disputes amicably and thus save the cost of litigation.[56]

## E. Conclusion

The main issue dealt with in this chapter was whether trade agreements—and the Transatlantic Trade and Investment Partnership specifically—need to be, and whether they can be, adapted for the purpose of SMEs interested in expanding their trade and investment linkages across the Atlantic. The present study offers a nuanced answer. We expect that the best response to trade barriers faced by SMEs

[53] See Joachim Karl, Chapter 9 of this volume.

[54] For instance, about two-thirds of American investors who filed disputes at the International Centre for Settlement of Investment Disputes were individuals or SMEs. See Scott Miller and Greg Hicks, 'Investor-State Dispute Settlement: A Reality Check' (Report by the Scholl Chair in International Business at CSIS, Working Paper, October 2014) <http://csis.org/files/publication/141029_investor_state_dispute_settlement.pdf> accessed 20 January 2017. Globally, only 15 per cent of claimants in investor-state dispute settlement are SMEs: see Joachim Karl, Chapter 9 of this volume.

[55] See Alexander Gebert, Chapter 11 of this volume.

[56] See European Commission, 'The European Union's Proposal for Investment Protection and Resolution of Investment Disputes in the Transatlantic Trade and Investment Partnership' (12 November 2015) <http://trade.ec.europa.eu/doclib/docs/2015/november/tradoc_153955.pdf> accessed 20 January 2017.

will be a mix of generalized and SME-specific provisions. An SME-friendly design of these agreements can be summarized as follows:

- The role of SMEs in EU external trade performance is more important than previously thought, not only in terms of the share of SMEs in the total number of EU-exporting firms, but most importantly in terms of their share in the total value of EU exports. With around one-third of the total value of worldwide exports of the European Union being generated by EU SMEs, they are a non-negligible player in supporting EU trade competitiveness and job creation, with more than 6 million jobs depending on the ability of SMEs to export.[57]
- SMEs essentially face the same external barriers to trade as larger firms (both in terms of tariffs and regulatory barriers), but they are less able to deal with them because they have fewer resources. This is particularly true with respect to barriers such as lack of transparency or complex and divergent regulatory requirements. Therefore, to serve SMEs, trade agreements need to be more comprehensive and ambitious in removing these barriers by means of liberalization, regulatory harmonization, information-sharing, and facilitation provisions.
- At the same time, these provisions need not be specific to SMEs. Helping SMEs to trade across borders is not about denying the benefits of an open trade regime to large companies. Therefore, trade agreements can normally tackle external obstacles to SMEs' trade through generalized provisions that do not differentiate traders by size even if such differentiation is technically and legally feasible.
- An SME-specific approach should nevertheless be considered whenever this could help reduce market access barriers for SMEs beyond what negotiators could concede for all traders.
- Another way of maximizing the value of trade agreements for SMEs is to prioritize sectors with high SME trade potential and to reduce barriers found to have the most disproportionate effect on small traders.
- By lowering external barriers, trade agreements will automatically render small size less disadvantageous. To the extent that this cannot be achieved, trade agreements also have a role to play in putting in place the necessary support measures that will compensate for SME-inherent constraints and allow them to overcome those remaining obstacles in the trading environment. Provisions concerning such trade promotion activities lend themselves to a strong if not exclusive focus on SMEs.
- Furthermore, trade agreements should lock in the practice of monitoring and assessing their impact on SMEs with a view to adapting or complementing their provisions where internationalizing SMEs continue to experience

[57] Cernat and others (n 4) 4.

difficulties. Moreover, in the course of negotiations and during implementation, SMEs should be given the opportunity to voice their issues and concerns.

- The review of past EU and US FTAs demonstrates an awareness of particular needs of SMEs, but also suggests that more could be done to address them in trade agreements. The TTIP negotiations offer an opportunity to take a more systematic and creative approach and to make TTIP a prototype for a modern SME-friendly agreement which would both create new opportunities for trade and ensure that small firms are able to seize them.

## References

Adlung, R and Miroudot, S, 'Poison in the Wine? Tracing GATS-Minus Commitments in Regional Trade Agreements' (2012) 4 WTO Staff Working Papers 1

Antoldi, F, 'Can European SMEs Really Intercept the Internationalisation Paths of Fast Growth?' in Fabio Antoldi, Magdolna Sass, and David Smallbone (eds), 'European SMEs and International Trade' (Workshop Expo Committee on International Trade, European Parliament, February 2012) <http://www.europarl.europa.eu/RegData/etudes/workshop/join/2012/457104/EXPO-INTA_AT(2012)457104_EN.pdf> accessed 20 January 2017

Cernat, L and Kutlina-Dimitrova, Z, 'Thinking in a Box: A "Mode 5" Approach to Service Trade' (2014) 48 Journal of World Trade 1109

Cernat, L, Norman-López, A and Duch T-Figueras, A, 'SMEs Are More Important Than You Think! Challenges and Opportunities for EU Exporting SMEs' (September 2014) 3 DG TRADE Chief Economist Note 9 <http://trade.ec.europa.eu/doclib/docs/2014/september/tradoc_152792.pdf> accessed 20 January 2017

EIM Business & Policy Research, 'Opportunities for the Internationalisation of European SMEs' (Directorate-General for Enterprise and Industry, European Commission, 2011)

European Commission, 'European Union and United States to Launch Negotiations for a Transatlantic Trade and Investment Partnership' (13 February 2013) MEMO/13/94

European Commission, 'Inside TTIP: An Overview and Chapter-by-Chapter Guide in Plain English' (European Union 2015) <http://trade.ec.europa.eu/doclib/docs/2015/july/tradoc_153635.pdf> accessed 20 January 2017

European Commission, 'Small and Medium Sized Enterprises and the Transatlantic Trade and Investment Partnership' (European Union 2015) <http://trade.ec.europa.eu/doclib/docs/2015/april/tradoc_153348.pdf> accessed 20 January 2017

European Commission, 'The European Union's Proposal for Investment Protection and Resolution of Investment Disputes in Transatlantic Trade and Investment Partnership' (12 November 2015) <http://trade.ec.europa.eu/doclib/docs/2015/november/tradoc_153955.pdf> accessed 20 January 2017

European Commission, '"Think Small First": A "Small Business Act" for Europe' (Communication, 25 June 2008) COM(2008) 394 final

European Commission, 'Trade, Growth and Development: Tailoring Trade and Investment Policy for Those Countries Most in Need' COM(2012) 22 final

European Commission, 'TTIP, Towards an EU–US Trade Deal: Intellectual Property, EU Position Paper' (20 March 2015) <http://trade.ec.europa.eu/doclib/docs/2015/april/

tradoc_153331.7%20IPR%20EU%20position%20paper%2020%20March%202015.pdf> accessed 20 January 2017

Eurostat, 'Trade by Enterprise Characteristics Database (TEC)' (Luxembourg: Eurostat 2014)

EU–US High Level Working Group on Jobs and Growth (HLWG), 'Final Report' (11 February 2013) <http://trade.ec.europa.eu/doclib/docs/2013/february/tradoc_150519.pdf> accessed 20 January 2017

Francois, J, Manchin, M, Norberg, H, Pindyuk, O, and Tomberger, P, 'Reducing Transatlantic Barriers to Trade and Investment' (Final Project Report, Centre for Economic Policy Research, March 2013) <http://trade.ec.europa.eu/doclib/docs/2013/march/tradoc_150737.pdf> accessed 20 January 2017

Lejárraga, I, López Rizzo, H, Oberhofer, H, Stone, S, and Shepherd, B, 'Small and Medium-Sized Enterprises in Global Markets: A Differential Approach for Services?' (OECD Trade Policy Papers No 165, 2014) <http://dx.doi.org/10.1787/5jz17jtfkmzt-en> accessed 20 January 2017

Miller, S and Hicks, G, 'Investor-State Dispute Settlement: A Reality Check' (Report by the Scholl Chair in International Business at the CSIS, Working Paper, October 2014) <http://csis.org/files/publication/141029_investor_state_dispute_settlement.pdf> accessed 20 January 2017

Roy, M, Marchetti, J, and Lim, AH, 'The Race Towards Preferential Trade Agreements in Services: How Much Market Access is Really Achieved?' in Marion Panizzon, Nicole Pohl, and Pierre Sauvé (eds), *GATS and the Regulation of International Trade in Services* (Cambridge University Press 2008)

Size Standards Division Office of Government Contracting & Business Development, 'SBA Size Standards Methodology' (April 2009) <https://www.sba.gov/sites/default/files/articles/size_standards_methodology.pdf> accessed 20 January 2017

US International Trade Commission, 'Small and Medium-Sized Enterprises: Characteristics and Performance' (USITC Publication 4189, Investigation No 332–510, November 2010) <http://www.usitc.gov/publications/332/pub4189.pdf> accessed 20 January 2017

US International Trade Commission, 'Trade Barriers that U.S. Small and Medium-Sized Enterprises Perceive as Affecting Exports to the European Union' (USITC Publication 4455, Investigation No 332-541, March 2014) <https://www.usitc.gov/publications/332/pub4455.pdf> accessed 20 January 2017

US Government Accountability Office, 'Export Promotion: Trade Agencies Should Enhance Collaboration with State and Local Partners' (21 May 2014) <http://www.gao.gov/products/GAO-14-393> accessed 20 January 2017

# 7

# An Asian Perspective on SMEs in International Economic Law

## Opportunities and Challenges Arising from the TPP

*Heng Wang**

## A. Introduction

Small and medium-sized enterprises (SMEs) play an increasingly important role in international trade and investment. For instance, more jobs will be created if SMEs increase their transboundary trade and investment. While large businesses are in a position to spread overhead costs over a large number of products, various export markets, and subsidiaries or affiliated companies, SMEs are rarely able to do so. Due to inherent capacity constraints, they are more intensely affected by trade and investment barriers. Taking the United States as an example, SMEs may in particular encounter: (1) domestic barriers, including US Government regulation (eg export controls, visas, and tariffs on imported intermediate inputs), domestic transport costs; and (2) foreign barriers, including foreign government regulations (eg different labelling, certification, quality, and design requirements, costly sanitary and phytosanitary (SPS) regulations, insufficient intellectual property protection, time-consuming customs clearance, tariff and non-tariff restrictions), and language and cultural barriers.[1] SMEs in other countries encounter similar barriers. SMEs are therefore vulnerable to trade and investment barriers, and accordingly have often not been able to gain optimal benefits from trade agreements.

SMEs are particularly affected by international trade law and have in recent years received more attention in that context. While the generally applicable norms of the World Trade Organization (WTO) have benefitted SMEs in certain ways,

* An earlier version of this chapter has been previously published under the title 'The Implications of the Trans-Pacific Partnership for SMEs: Opportunities and Challenges' (2016) 6 KLRI Journal of Law and Legislation 45.

[1] US International Trade Commission, 'Small and Medium-Sized Enterprises: U.S. and EU Export Activities, and Barriers and Opportunities Experienced by U.S. Firms' (Investigation No 332-509, USITC Publication 4169, July 2010) xvi <http://www.usitc.gov/publications/332/pub4169.pdf> accessed 20 January 2017.

including enhanced stability, confidence, predictability, market access, and access to information,[2] WTO negotiations have also involved specific SME issues. In the WTO negotiations on services, both developed countries and developing countries are concerned with trade barriers that are particularly burdensome to services SMEs, and internationalization of SMEs has become a permanent WTO services negotiation issue.[3]

Moreover, free trade agreements (FTAs) and in particular 'mega-regionals' have become increasingly relevant to SMEs. With respect to ongoing mega-FTA negotiations, SME issues play an important role in the negotiations of the Transatlantic Trade and Investment Partnership (TTIP).[4] The Trans-Pacific Partnership (TPP) negotiations were concluded in 2015 and the TPP was signed on 4 February 2016. It has not yet entered into force since ratification by the TPP members has not been finalized. As indicated in its preamble, the TPP builds on the rights and obligations under WTO law, and is becoming increasingly relevant to SMEs. In general, it sets much stricter requirements than WTO law, and also enters WTO-extra areas, including investment, state-owned enterprises (SOEs), designated monopolies, labour, and the environment. Attracting great attention, SME issues were among the cross-cutting trade issues in the TPP,[5] and part of 'horizontal' issues in the TPP negotiations.[6] In particular, SME issues have been highlighted by the United States in the TPP negotiations:

> Since the launch of the TPP talks, one of the United States' core goals has been to promote and support American small and medium-sized enterprises entering global trade, and to address barriers that pose disproportionate challenges to small business exports. These include issues such as inaccessible or overly complex trade paperwork, opaque regulatory processes and corruption, inefficiency of customs administration, restrictions on Internet data flows, weak logistics services that raise costs, and slow delivery of small shipments.[7]

The TPP is the first agreement negotiated by the United States that contains a specific chapter on SMEs. The SME chapter was also the only chapter the completion of which had been publicly announced by TPP parties by 2013.[8] According to data of the US International Trade Administration, 97 per cent of exporters to

[2] Kitsuron Sangsuvan, 'Small Businesses in the WTO: Small Fish in a Big Pond or Globalization 3.0' (2015) 23 Michigan State International Law Review 372–77.

[3] Daniela Persin, 'Market Access for Small versus Large Service Enterprises: The Preferential and Multilateral Trade Liberalization Tracks Compared' (2011) 45 Journal of World Trade 785, 786.

[4] European Commission Directorate General for Trade, 'EU, U.S. Trade: Negotiators Explore Ways to Help SMEs Take Advantage of TTIP, as Fourth Round of Talks Ends in Brussels' (1 May 2014) <http://trade.ec.europa.eu/doclib/press/index.cfm?id=1041> accessed 20 January 2017.

[5] Office of the US Trade Representative, 'Outlines of TPP' (2016) <https://ustr.gov/tpp/outlines-of-TPP> accessed 20 January 2017.

[6] Deborah Kay Elms, 'The Trans-Pacific Partnership Trade Negotiations: Some Outstanding Issues for the Final Stretch' (2013) 8 Asian Journal of WTO & International Health Law and Policy 379, 391.

[7] Office of the US Trade Representative, 'The Trans-Pacific Parnership: Leveling the Playing Field for American Workers & American Businesses' (2016) Chapter 24 <https://ustr.gov/tpp/> accessed 20 January 2017.

[8] 'TPP SME Chapter Includes Commitments to Set Up Websites, Committee' (2013) Inside US Trade 31.

TPP nations have fewer than 500 employees.[9] As the only mega FTA for which the negotiations have been concluded, the TPP covers around 40 per cent of the world economy[10] and is likely to have a substantial effect on SMEs. At the same time, the important contribution of SMEs to economic growth and employment is explicitly acknowledged by the TPP.[11] It is safe to conclude that SMEs will be significantly affected by the TPP if it is approved. Even if the TPP is not ratified, the SMEs rules of the TPP may be relevant to the future trade agreements negotiated by the United States and other TPP countries, since these rules reflect the consensus in this respect.

A wide range of areas are identified by the TPP as relevant for SMEs, including customs, intellectual property, technical regulations, SPS measures, investment, business registration, employment, and taxation.[12] This is not an exhaustive list, as other areas (eg market access and the movement of business persons) are also closely related to SMEs. Issues related to SMEs are addressed in a variety of TPP chapters, including customs administration and trade facilitation, e-commerce, intellectual property, SPS measures, technical barriers to trade (TBT), competitiveness and business facilitation, and rules of origin, to name but a few.

The TPP could play an important role for SMEs in opening up new business opportunities and providing assistance. However, it could also pose challenges to SMEs, including the increase of competition from abroad. Since little research has been conducted regarding the effect of FTAs on SMEs, and in particular on their export performance,[13] this chapter will analyse a number of questions that may arise in this context: What are the opportunities the TPP may hold for SMEs from TPP countries? What are the challenges encountered by SMEs under the TPP? Research concerning the implications of the TPP for SMEs will be of great significance even if the TPP is not approved, since the TPP will have long-term effects on the development of FTAs and the TPP text could be seriously considered in future trade negotiations. The focus of this chapter[14] is not on assessing the substantive merits of the TPP rules,[15] but rather on an examination of the opportunities and challenges arising for SMEs. The implications of the TPP for SMEs outside the free trade area of the TPP will only be discussed when appropriate.

[9] Raymond J Keating, 'What the Trans-Pacific Partnership (TPP) Means for U.S. Economic Growth and Small Business' (6 October 2015) <http://www.sbecouncil.org/2015/10/06/what-the-trans-pacific-partnership-tpp-means-for-the-u-s-economy-and-small-business/> accessed 20 January 2017.

[10] David Ramli and Jared Lynch, 'TPP: What it Means for Australian Business' *The Sydney Morning Herald* (Sydney, 6 October 2015).

[11] Art 15.21.1 TPP. The version of the TPP text cited in the chapter is available at <https://www.tpp.mfat.govt.nz/text> accessed 20 January 2017.

[12] Art 24.1.3 TPP.

[13] US International Trade Commission (n 1) E-8.

[14] The analysis here focuses on the main text of the TPP rather than annexes and associated documents.

[15] The TPP arouses concerns such as the criminalization of trade secret law and the extension of copyright terms, which may potentially affect the use of intellectual property by SMEs. See, for example, Terry Lavender, 'Not too Late to Mitigate TPP Effects, Minister of International Trade Chrystia Freeland Told' *University of Toronto News* (19 January 2016) <http://news.utoronto.ca/not-too-late-mitigate-tpp-effects-minister-international-trade-chrystia-freeland-told> accessed 20 January 2017.

## B. Opportunities

Several TPP provisions address, to a greater or lesser degree, the specific concerns of SMEs. These include the preamble and the chapters on SMEs, customs administration and trade facilitation, government procurement, electronic commerce, intellectual property, labour, regulatory coherence, development, transparency, environment, cooperation and capacity building, competitiveness, and business facilitation. The TPP will bring opportunities to SMEs to access a much larger market with better conditions. These opportunities include cooperation to support SMEs and tariff elimination or reduction, as well as the reduction of non-tariff barriers (NTBs). This section will analyse the opportunities for SMEs from TPP countries. It should be noted, however, that some opportunities are largely limited to SMEs from specific TPP countries, such as the non-conforming measures permitted to Vietnam under the TPP SOE chapter aiming to assist SMEs.[16] In practice, only the SMEs of Vietnam rather than those of other countries are likely to benefit from these measures.

### I. Cooperation to support SMEs

The preamble of the TPP emphasizes support for the development of SMEs by enhancing their capacity to participate in and benefit from the TPP. Since the participation of the private sector is essential in cooperation and capacity building, the TPP recognizes that SMEs may need assistance in participating in world markets.[17]

A number of institutional arrangements are in place under the TPP, in particular the Committee on SMEs (SMEs Committee). The role of the SMEs Committee is to identify ways to help SMEs to explore commercial opportunities arising from the TPP.[18] It will also provide other assistance to SMEs, including seminars and workshops to inform SMEs how to benefit from the TPP.[19] Furthermore, the SMEs Committee will be involved in monitoring the implementation of SME-related obligations under the TPP.[20] In addition, the Committee on Government Procurement will meet upon request to facilitate the participation by SMEs in government procurement.[21] The Committee on Competitiveness and Business Facilitation (CCBF) will: (1) provide recommendations to the TPP Commission ('Commission') to promote the participation of SMEs in supply chains in the free trade area;[22] and (2) provide recommendations and encourage capacity-building activities to assist SMEs' participation in the regional supply chains.[23] With respect to the latter, the CCBF will collaborate with experts such as private sector and

[16] Sean Miner, 'Commitments on State-Owned Enterprises' in Jeffrey J Schott and Cathleen Cimino-Isaacs (eds), *Assessing the Trans-Pacific Partnership*, Vol 2: *Innovations in Trading Rules* (Peterson Institute for International Economics 2016) 98.

[17] Art 21.1.3 TPP. [18] Art 24.2.2(a) TPP. [19] Art 24.2.2(c) TPP.

[20] Art 24.2.2(h) TPP. [21] Art 15.23(b) TPP. [22] Art 22.2.3(c) TPP.

[23] Art 22.3.2 TPP.

international donor organizations.[24] It remains to be seen whether these recommendations are directed at other actors or at SMEs. The relationship between these two categories of recommendations is not clarified in the TPP.

In addition, cooperation among TPP countries is aimed at supporting SMEs in electronic commerce, labour, government procurement, and development. TPP members are encouraged to help SMEs overcome obstacles in using electronic commerce[25] and to cooperate in promoting improvements in business and labour productivity, particularly with regard to SMEs.[26] The TPP highlights the importance of increasing the participation of SMEs in government procurement,[27] and provides for facilitation measures and cooperation. SMEs' participation in government procurement as suppliers will also be encouraged.[28] Moreover, for broad-based economic growth, TPP parties may pursue policies associated with the promotion of market-based approaches to improve trading conditions and access to finance for SMEs.[29] This is a soft obligation and it will need to be seen whether and how these market-based approaches will benefit SMEs.

Entities other than governments can also be involved in providing support for SMEs. TPP parties may take action to encourage other actors (such as professional associations and other non-governmental organizations), if appropriate, to help SMEs develop internal controls or other measures to prevent bribery and corruption in trade and investment.[30] Private sector and international donor organizations may be involved in capacity-building activities to assist SMEs' participation in supply chains in the TPP area, which may take the form of seminars or workshops.[31] With regard to the rules on development, joint development activities include the promotion of public–private partnerships that would enable SMEs to utilize their capacities in cooperative ventures with governmental bodies in order to support development goals.[32] Such joint development activities may also involve multilateral institutions.[33] Among the joint development activities, capacity building is likely to be the key. SMEs may thus benefit directly through capacity building,[34] or indirectly from the capacity building of TPP parties with regard to SME export advice, assistance, and training programmes.[35]

## II. Tariff elimination or reduction

Trade barriers are disproportionately burdensome for SMEs because they have fewer resources to overcome them than larger businesses, and even a small increase in the cost of a good due to tariffs may lead to the loss of a sale for small firms in a competitive market.[36] Tariff reductions under previous FTAs concluded by the

[24] ibid. [25] Art 14.15(a) TPP. [26] Art 19.10.6(f) TPP.
[27] Art 15.21.1 TPP. [28] Art 15.22.2(a) TPP. [29] Art 23.3.4 TPP.
[30] Art 26.10.1(b) TPP. [31] Art 22.3.2 TPP. [32] Art 23.6.2(c) TPP.
[33] Art 23.6.2 TPP. [34] Art 22.3.2 TPP. [35] Art 24.2.2(d) TPP.
[36] Office of the US Trade Representative, 'Transatlantic Trade & Investment Partnership: Opportunities for Small and Medium-Sized Enterprises' (2015) <https://ustr.gov/sites/default/files/TTIP%20Brochure%20v3%20%284-16-15%29FINAL.pdf> accessed 20 January 2017.

United States, for example, have substantially benefitted American SMEs in terms of market access.[37] Under the TPP, tariff eliminations or reductions are provided for in the rules for trade in goods, in particular in the chapters on national treatment and market access for goods,[38] and on electronic commerce. In certain circumstances, SMEs may be given special consideration. Customs duties will not be assessed on express shipments valued at or below a fixed amount set under TPP parties' domestic law. In the periodical review of this amount, the impact on SMEs may be considered as a relevant factor.[39]

In electronic commerce, the TPP prohibits the imposition of customs duties on electronic transmissions[40] and the use of local computing facilities as a condition for conducting business in a TPP country.[41] These rules should particularly help competitive SMEs thriving in online markets.

The tariff benefits granted under the TPP will be much larger than those granted under bilateral FTAs. In contrast to a typical bilateral FTA, the TPP involves twelve signatories and will probably be acceded to by other countries (eg Korea) in the near future if everything goes smoothly. SMEs may therefore benefit from tariff reduction or elimination from multiple foreign markets. For instance, the import taxes on US textiles and apparel exports imposed by Japan, Vietnam, Malaysia, and New Zealand will be eliminated immediately or within a set time period.[42] Both SMEs and larger businesses will benefit from such tax elimination. However, the effect of tariff reductions on SMEs should not be overestimated. SMEs conducting international trade, for instance, may have already managed to avoid tariffs (eg by categorizing products differently or by exporting free-on-board shipping to require buyers to pay for possible duties), and therefore in certain circumstances tariffs are not their main concern.[43]

## III. Reduction of non-tariff barriers

Tariff reductions mainly affect trade in goods since services trade and investment per se are not usually subject to tariffs. In contrast, NTBs affect not only goods, but also services trade and investment.[44] Complex regulations and opaque procedures

[37] US International Trade Commission (n 1) 5–5, 5–6.

[38] See, for instance, Art 2.4.2 and Annex 2-D TPP (most tariff elimination in industrial goods will be implemented immediately, with tariff elimination of certain products to be implemented over longer time frames), Art 2.5 TPP (tariff benefits, new or existing ones, will not be contingent on the local content percentage and other performance requirements), Art 2.15 TPP (export duties, taxes or other charges are generally proscribed unless otherwise provided).

[39] Art 5.7.1(f) TPP. [40] Art 14.3.1 TPP. [41] Art 14.13.2 TPP.

[42] US Department of Commerce, International Trade Administration, 'Opportunities for the U.S. Textiles and Apparel Sector' (November 2015) <http://trade.gov/fta/tpp/industries/pdfs/textile.pdf> accessed 20 January 2017.

[43] Martina Battisti and Perry Martin, 'Creating Opportunity for Small-Firm Exporters through Regional Free Trade Agreements: A Strategic Perspective from New Zealand' (2008) 14 Australasian Journal of Regional Studies 275, 281.

[44] For instance, the EU–Singapore FTA contains a stand-alone on NTBs to trade and investment in renewable energy generation. See, for instance, EU–Singapore FTA, Chapter 7: Non-Tariff Barriers to Trade and Investment in Renewable Energy Generation, Art 7.4.

can be particularly burdensome for small firms and the clarity and certainty of market access rules are frequently a greater concern than tariff rates.[45] The reduction of NTBs is therefore of enormous significance to SMEs. The following analysis concerns the main forms of NTB reduction that are relevant for SMEs and their implications. Although the reduction of NTBs can be found throughout the TPP, it is argued that the opportunities provided for SMEs by reducing NTBs are mainly attributable to specific and general transparency rules, procedural fairness, regulatory coherence, and other requirements.

To ensure effectiveness in reducing NTBs, dispute settlement procedures are highlighted in the TPP. These dispute settlement mechanisms help businesses, including SMEs, to manage their risks. With regard to investment, the dispute settlement system covers general investor–state investment arbitration,[46] and investment disputes in financial services,[47] although investment is often made by larger businesses. With a view to promoting fair competition, the TPP competition rules explicitly provide for the private right of action,[48] under which businesses such as SMEs can benefit by having legal redress against the violation of national competition laws. Procedures are also in place to address complaints by a supplier about the violation of TPP government procurement rules.[49] According to the chapter on SOEs, the courts of a TPP party will have jurisdiction over civil claims against an enterprise controlled by a foreign country arising from a commercial activity in the territory of the TPP party in question.[50]

### 1. *Transparency*

Transparency rules will reduce the information acquisition costs and help SMEs to obtain contact information for relevant agencies of different TPP parties. Meanwhile, transparency requirements will also relieve SMEs of the potential costs of trading and investing resulting from the lack of access to necessary information.

#### (a) General transparency rules

The TPP transparency standards are the strictest among FTAs.[51] Transparency requirements are stipulated in a separate chapter,[52] but can also be found in nearly all other chapters.[53] By virtue of the transparency requirements described below, SMEs are given the opportunity to participate in rule-making in connection with certain matters affecting trade and investment. This may offer them the chance to

[45] Battisti and Martin (n 43) 284. [46] Chapter 9, Section B TPP.
[47] Art 11.22 TPP. [48] Art 16.3 TPP. [49] Art 15.19 TPP. [50] Art 17.5.1 TPP.
[51] Ministry of Trade and Industry of Singapore, 'Trans Pacific Partnership Free Trade Agreement (TPP): 7 Things You Should Know' (2016) <https://www.mti.gov.sg/MTIInsights/SiteAssets/Pages/TPP/Seven%20things%20you%20should%20know%20about%20the%20TPP%20(Final).pdf> accessed 20 January 2017.
[52] Chapter 26, Section B TPP.
[53] For instance, Arts 2.32, 2.28.3, 5.11, 7.13, 11.13, 12.6, 16.7, 17.10, 18.9 TPP.

comment on proposed measures, which, in turn, could lead to more serious consideration of their interests, and enable closer interaction with regulators.

Transparency is generally required for trade in goods and services, as well as intellectual property. For instance, information regarding trade in goods needs to be promptly published, including information relating to import and export procedures, duty rates, classification rules, fees, and charges.[54] Transparency requirements also expand to areas such as government procurement, competition (eg publication of final decisions in competition law proceedings with findings of fact and reasoning[55]), and investment (eg transparency of investment arbitral proceedings[56]). In addition, transparency rules target regulatory measures and administrative procedures such as the public availability of licensing requirements for public telecommunications[57] and documentation required for applications to supply financial services.[58]

Although general transparency rules apply equally regardless of the size of businesses, certain new developments may be particularly important for SMEs, in particular public input requirements and heightened requirements on information provision.

Public input requirements consist of the following provisions: (1) notice and comment opportunities; (2) the response to comments received; and (3) public submission and engagement opportunities. The notice and comment requirement is imposed as a best endeavour clause in the transparency chapter, which should apply across the TPP.[59] In several areas, similar or stricter requirements are provided. TPP members should seek to provide for interested persons opportunities to comment regarding proposed financial regulations.[60] Such comment opportunities are also required for other areas, including science and risk analysis,[61] as well as proposed measures regarding SPS,[62] TBT,[63] and telecommunications issues.[64] With regard to SPS measures, any written comments received need to be made publicly available either in full or in summary form.[65]

Furthermore, a response to comments received may be necessary. Regarding proposed TBT measures, the responses to key issues presented in comments have to be made publicly available.[66] TPP parties are also encouraged to respond in writing to substantive comments from interested persons on proposed financial services regulations.[67]

The TPP also provides for public submission and engagement opportunities. In accordance with domestic procedures, persons of TPP parties may make written

[54] Art 2.16 TPP. [55] Art 16.7.4 TPP. [56] Art 9.24 TPP.
[57] Art 13.18.1 TPP. [58] Art 11.13.8 TPP. [59] Art 26.2.2 TPP.
[60] Art 11.13.3(b), Annex 11-B, Section E TPP. [61] Art 7.9.4(b) TPP.
[62] Arts 7.13.1, 7.13.4 TPP.
[63] Arts 8.7.14, 8.7.15 TPP (the parties are encouraged to provide a sufficient time interval between the comment period and the adoption of any TBT measures to consider the comments).
[64] Art 13.22.1 TPP. [65] Art 7.13.5 TPP.
[66] Art 8.7.18(c) TPP (public availabilty of 'responses to significant or substantive issues presented in comments received').
[67] Art 11.13.4 TPP.

submissions on labour matters, identifying the issue directly associated with the labour chapter and the way in which it affects trade or investment.[68] The relevant provisions demand consideration of the submission and a timely response from the TPP member in question.[69] Similar public submissions are possible regarding environmental issues.[70] In addition, public engagement is provided for labour matters[71] and competitiveness and business facilitation,[72] as well as regulatory coherence.[73] Taking regulatory coherence as an example, the input from interested persons shall be taken into consideration when regulatory measures are developed,[74] and engagement with interested persons shall be established in order to collect input with a view to improving regulatory coherence.[75] Public engagement procedures differ from public submissions. For instance, public engagement can be conducted by both the TPP parties and a Labour Council established by the TPP members.[76] Public submissions are only collected and considered by the TPP parties.[77] However, the relationship between public engagement and public submissions will need to be further elaborated.

Heightened requirements on information provision pertain, among others, to the clarity and sufficiency of information regarding procedures concerning geographical indications,[78] the online publication, if possible, of explanatory material regarding temporary entry requirements for business persons,[79] the response to enquiries from interested persons on measures concerning financial services,[80] and, to the extent possible, an explanation of the purpose and rationale of a proposed or final regulation likely to affect trade or investment.[81] With regard to trade facilitation, an importer, an exporter, or a producer may request advice or information concerning issues such as quotas and duty drawbacks. The TPP members shall expeditiously respond to such requests.[82] For the regulatory coherence, subject to domestic laws, TPP parties should ensure that the information on new regulatory measures is available to the public, and where practicable online.[83] In the same vein, TPP members are encouraged to provide an annual public notice of all regulatory measures that they expect to adopt within the following twelve-month period.[84]

### (b) Specific transparency rules

Rules to provide information for SMEs are set forth in the chapters on SMEs and government procurement. The specifically applicable information requirements will reduce the cost of identifying the regulatory requirements in trade and investments by providing easier access to information. As a key component of the SME chapter, TPP members must provide a special website to provide information directly and indirectly to SMEs.

[68] Arts 19.9.1, 19.9.2(a), 19.9.2(c) TPP. [69] Art 19.9.3(a) TPP.
[70] Art 20.9 TPP. [71] Art 19.14 TPP. [72] Art 22.4 TPP. [73] Art 25.8 TPP.
[74] Art 25.2.2(d) TPP. [75] Art 25.8 TPP. [76] Arts 19.14.1, 19.14.2 TPP.
[77] For instance, Art 19.9.1 TPP.
[78] Art 18.31(c) TPP (the procedures being 'clearly' set out), Art 18.31(d) TPP (sufficient information for the public understanding of procedures).
[79] Art 12.6(a)(i) TPP. [80] Art 11.13.7 TPP. [81] Arts 26.2.4(c), 26.2.5(b) TPP.
[82] Art 5.4 TPP. [83] Art 25.5.5 TPP. [84] Art 25.5.7 TPP.

With regard to the direct provision of information, the website must publicize the TPP text, including all annexes, tariff schedules, product-specific origin rules, and a summary of the TPP.[85] In particular, the website needs to offer information 'designed for SMEs', including the description of TPP provisions relevant to SMEs, and any additional information that the party deems useful for SMEs to reap the TPP opportunities.[86] In reality, the provision of such additional information may in turn depend on the capacity of the TPP countries.

Information shall be indirectly provided through weblinks to equivalent websites of other TPP countries[87] and the websites of its government bodies or entities that offer information deemed useful for actors in trade, investment, or business.[88] With regard to the latter, the information may include tax information, business registration procedures, and regulations concerning several areas (ie customs, intellectual property rights, investment, technical barriers to trade, SPS issues, and employment).[89] Procedures in relation to customs and intellectual property rights may be included too.[90] Both direct and indirect information sharing needs to be kept updated and correct, and shall be regularly reviewed by the TPP members.[91]

In government procurement, any potential measure maintained by a Contracting Party granting preferential treatment to SMEs, including its eligibility criteria, needs to be transparent.[92] A 'best endeavours' clause calls for the provision of comprehensive information relating to procurement, including a definition of SMEs in a single electronic portal.[93]

## 2. *Procedural fairness*

General requirements of procedural fairness in the TPP apply to administrative proceedings as well as the review and appeal process, including the right of the parties to these proceedings to a reasonable opportunity to support and defend their positions.[94] Sector-specific procedural fairness provisions pertain in particular to import licensing,[95] tariff rate quotas (TRQs) administration,[96] telecommunications licensing,[97] financial services,[98] competition law enforcement,[99] government procurement (eg time period[100]), labour law enforcement,[101] trademark examination and registration procedures,[102] the listing for new pharmaceutical products or medical devices for reimbursement purposes,[103] procurement process,[104] trade

[85] Arts 24.1(a), 24.1(b) TPP. [86] Art 24.1.1(c)(i) TPP. [87] Art 24.1.2(a) TPP.
[88] Art 24.1.2(b) TPP. [89] Art 24.1.3 TPP. [90] Arts 24.1.3(a), 24.1.3(b) TPP.
[91] Art 24.1.4 TPP. [92] Art 15.21.2 TPP.
[93] Art 15.21.3(a) TPP. On definitions of SMEs, see also the Annex of this volume.
[94] See, for example, Arts 26.3(b), 26.4.2(a) TPP. [95] Art 2.12.8 TPP.
[96] See, for example, Art 2.28.2 TPP. [97] Art 13.18.2(a) TPP.
[98] Art 11.13.9 TPP. [99] Art 16.2 TPP.
[100] Art 15.14.1 TPP (sufficient time for suppliers to get tender documents and submit a responsive tender).
[101] Art 19.8.3 TPP. [102] Art 18.23 TPP. [103] Annex 26-A, Art 3 TPP.
[104] Art 15.15.1 TPP.

remedy proceedings,[105] trade facilitation,[106] and investment.[107] These provisions usually require the explanation of reasons for negative decisions for applicants (eg the denial of an import licence application,[108]and the denial of a licence for public telecommunication services[109]), the opportunity to contest the initial refusal to register a trademark, the independence of the judicial and administrative tribunals, and the required time frame for decision-making. Some of these requirements are quite detailed. For instance, the rules on competition law enforcement provide for a reasonable opportunity to be represented by counsel,[110] a reasonable opportunity to consult with competition authorities regarding significant legal, factual, or procedural issues,[111] written procedures for national competition law investigations,[112] rules of procedure and evidence for enforcement proceedings,[113] and the opportunity to seek review of the sanction or remedy.[114]

For SMEs, these general and sector-specific requirements of procedural fairness improve the predictability and fairness of regulatory decisions, and thereby reduce regulatory risks as well as the volatility of the regulatory environment.

### 3. *Regulatory coherence*

Regulatory coherence requirements cover a very wide range of areas and extend to the whole process of regulatory measures, starting from planning, designing, and issuing to implementation and review.[115] By conducting regulatory impact assessments (RIAs), the TPP parties should evaluate the need for regulatory proposals, investigate feasible regulatory alternatives, explain the reasons for the chosen alternative, and utilize best reasonably available information.[116] Leaning in favour of light-handed regulation,[117] regulatory coherence could promote consistency among different regulations, in particular through mutual learning and conciseness of rules. In planning new regulatory measures, regulatory agencies are encouraged to consider regulatory measures in other TPP parties and the development in multilateral and regional fora.[118] New covered regulatory measures need to be 'plainly written … clear, concise, well organised and easy to understand'.[119] Regulatory measures may later be streamlined or repealed following review.[120]

105 The TPP is expected to yield due process through recognition of best practices. Office of the US Trade Representative, 'Summary of the Trans-Pacific Partnership Agreement' (October 2015) <https://ustr.gov/about-us/policy-offices/press-office/press-releases/2015/october/summary-trans-pacific-partnership> accessed 20 January 2017.

106 Art 5.5 TPP.

107 Art 9.6.2(a) TPP (compliance with due process regarding adjudicatory proceedings in minimum standard of treatment).

108 Art 2.12.8 TPP. 109 Art 13.18.2(a) TPP. 110 Art 16.2.1(b) TPP.

111 Art 16.2.9 TPP. 112 Art 16.2.2 TPP. 113 Art 16.2.3 TPP.

114 Art 16.2.4 TPP. 115 Art 25.2.1 TPP. 116 Art 25.5.2 TPP.

117 Eugenio Briales Gómez-Tarragona and Daniela Gómez-Altamirano, 'The TPP: How to Facilitate Business through Legislative and Regulatory Reform?' (2015) 21 ILSA Journal of International and Comparative Law 369, 375.

118 Art 25.5.8 TPP. 119 Art 25.5.4 TPP. 120 Art 25.5.6 TPP.

Two SME-specific provisions exist in the chapter on regulatory coherence. In the process of RIA, the potential impact of the proposed regulation on SMEs may be taken into account.[121] In discharging their duty to cooperate in order to facilitate regulatory coherence, the TPP parties may interact with SMEs of other TPP members through information exchange, dialogues, or meetings.[122]

SMEs may thus benefit from regulatory coherence by having their concerns heard in the process of rule formation. Regulations might, therefore, be streamlined and more comprehensible for SMEs.

### 4. *Other requirements*

Other requirements in the TPP help to reduce the NTBs. For instance, enhanced people mobility provisions would expedite the service provision by SMEs in export markets, such as installation and after-sale services. Among them, one TPP provision on government procurement is particularly designed to benefit SMEs. A special article is incorporated to facilitate the participation by SMEs in government procurement. 'Best endeavours' clauses under this provision call for the free provision of tender documentation, the conduction of procurement through electronic means or other new technologies, and the consideration of the design of the procurement, including the possible subcontracting by SMEs.[123]

Several additional governance requirements are analysed below, which benefit businesses at large, but are particularly relevant to small businesses. These requirements are either commonly encountered by SMEs (trade facilitation and rules of origin), or exist across several areas (standards harmonization and equivalence of foreign regulations).

#### (a) Standards harmonization and equivalence of foreign regulations

As the TPP highlights for the TBT area, both the harmonization of standards and the acceptance of regulations of other TPP parties as equivalent help to pursue greater regulatory alignment.[124] SMEs in particular would benefit from such regulatory alignment since it is more difficult for small firms to bear the costs of complying with different standards and regulations.

Standards harmonization is closely connected to the alignment of national standards with international standards. The importance of international standards for global compatibility is explicitly highlighted in relation to telecommunications.[125] The TPP also calls for greater alignment of national standards with international standards in TBT areas,[126] the facilitation of greater use of international standards as the basis for TBT measures,[127] and the use of international standards regarding the procedures dealing with the release of goods.[128] Similarly, in government

[121] Art 25.5.3 TPP. [122] Art 25.7.1(b) TPP. [123] Art 15.21.3 TPP.
[124] Art 8.9.2 TPP. [125] Art 13.25 TPP. [126] Art 8.9.2(b) TPP.
[127] Art 8.9.2(c) TPP. [128] Art 5.6.1(a) TPP.

procurement, technical specifications need to be based on international standards if appropriate.[129]

The TPP also encourages the acceptance of technical regulations[130] and SPS measures[131] of other TPP members as equivalent, as well as the recognition of professional qualifications, licensing, registration, or prudential measures in services and financial services.[132]

### (b) Trade facilitation

Customs administration and trade facilitation rules would enable the faster delivery of goods by businesses, large or small, and easier interaction with customs.[133] In order to expedite trade, trade facilitation streamlines and simplifies trade procedure, in particular through the efficient release of goods,[134] expedited customs procedures for express shipments,[135] advance rulings,[136] and automation.[137] It helps to address red tape and unreasonable delay in trade. Small firms are among the biggest winners from trade facilitation as they face the greatest difficulties in navigating these trade rules,[138] and are vulnerable to the financial and administrative burden of customs formalities.

### (c) Rules of origin

TPP rules of origin may enable SMEs within the free-trade area to gain better access to markets, such as the US–Dominican Republic–Central America Free Trade Agreement (DR-CAFTA). The DR-CAFTA contains 'yarn forward' rules of origin under which the essential component for the import of most textiles and apparel are to be made from inputs produced in the FTA usually from the yarn stage forward,[139] and without which many American SME textile businesses facing low-cost Asian counterparts would not be able to survive.[140] Having similar effects, TPP 'yarn forward' rules of origin could benefit textile SMEs within the region, since the products need to have inputs from TPP parties in order to enjoy the TPP benefits.[141] Moreover, accumulation is provided so that inputs from one TPP member will be regarded as a good from other TPP members when certain conditions are met.[142] Notably, the certification of origin can also be waived for imports of low value,[143] which may be useful for SMEs in view of their generally low-value trade.

129 Art 15.12.2(b) TPP. 130 Art 8.9.2(d) TPP. 131 Art 7.8 TPP.

132 Arts 10.9, 11.12, Annex 10-A, para 1 TPP.

133 On trade facilitation, see also Arancha González, Chapter 2 of this volume.

134 Art 5.10.1 TPP (simplified customs procedure for the efficient release of goods).

135 Art 5.7 TPP. 136 Art 5.3 TPP. 137 Art 5.6 TPP.

138 Sangsuvan (n 2) 394. 139 US International Trade Commission (n 1) 5–8 and n 28.

140 ibid.

141 Under the 'short supply list' mechanism, certain non-originating materials may be treated as originating for five years after the TPP comes into force. Art 4.2.9 TPP.

142 Art 3.10 TPP. 143 Art 3.23 TPP.

## IV. Conclusion

First, cooperation to support SMEs, tariff elimination or reduction, and the reduction of NTBs are the major opportunities which the TPP holds for SMEs. These opportunities should bring enhanced market opening and predictability. Covering tariffs and non-tariff issues, the support for SMEs will help them better to utilize the TPP. Tariffs and NTBs 'across substantially all trade' will be eliminated or reduced.[144] Tariff and NTB reductions cover a wide range of areas, involving border measures and behind-the-border measures. The absolute levels of tariffs and NTBs are crucial for SMEs as they are usually neither able nor fully prepared to invest overseas in order to manufacture in foreign markets.

However, these opportunities may have limited effect in improving the market position of certain SMEs. The opportunities arising for SMEs are often also available to larger businesses, and there are concerns that the TPP in fact favours the big corporates.[145] Moreover, the opportunities may be limited in certain circumstances, such as tariff benefits for SMEs from TPP members other than the United States with regard to exports to the United States. This is due to the fact that the average applied tariff in the United States is currently as low as 1.4 per cent, and nearly 70 per cent of imports entering the United States are not subject to any tariffs.[146]

Second, the reduction of NTBs, if properly implemented, is likely to benefit SMEs most. The adoption of good practices (eg enhanced transparency) is encouraged, which would help to put small businesses on an equal footing. SMEs are particularly vulnerable to regulatory measures and their implementation, including procedures hedged about with red tape, and inconsistencies in trade policy and regulations. Regulatory convergence or at least regulatory compatibility is pursued in the TPP and this will lead to market consistency and enhance cost-effectiveness. The reduction of NTBs may also benefit those SMEs outside the free trade area to which they apply.

Last but not least, SMEs are subject to increased special attention and support than before. The level of support should not, however, be exaggerated. The new stand-alone SME chapter and other chapters (in particular, regulatory coherence, government procurement, development, trade facilitation) provide support for SMEs. They also establish institutional arrangements for joint efforts by TPP parties and require TPP members to consider the possible impact on SMEs or provide support for them. However, provisions directly benefitting SMEs remain limited. The SME chapter, for instance, contains three articles with limited commitments

[144] Office of the US Trade Representative (n 105).

[145] The TPP is criticized for lacking concrete benefits and increasing inequality through 'enshrining power among big corporates'. See, for example, Zoe Daniel, 'Malcolm Turnbull and Barack Obama Hold White House Talks; PM Urges Powerbrokers to Back TPP' *ABC News* (New York, 20 January 2016) <http://www.abc.net.au/news/2016-01-20/turnbull-and-obama-hold-white-house-talks/7099808> accessed 20 January 2017.

[146] Office of the US Trade Representative, 'Leveling the Playing Field' (2016) <https://ustr.gov/sites/default/files/USTR-Tariff-Information-by-Sector-6115.pdf> accessed 20 January 2017.

from TPP members, including one on non-application of dispute settlement that may limit the enforcement of the SME chapter.

This conclusion provokes a number of questions. Why does the TPP in fact favour big corporates? Is it likely that the TPP is going to be properly implemented? Why do the provisions benefitting SMEs remain limited? These questions will be addressed in the following section.

## C. Challenges

In trade and investment, SMEs face both internal challenges (eg limited expertise, fewer personnel and financial resources) and external challenges (eg tariffs, NTBs including market access restrictions, and obstacles to investment). With regard to the former, the TPP contains provisions aimed at supporting SMEs through capacity building and other assistance. With regard to the latter, the TPP may lead to more favourable conditions for SMEs particularly through tariff reduction and the improvement and harmonization of relevant regulation, all of which should help to provide a more predictable business environment. Meanwhile, there are still a number of thorny questions to be addressed.

### I. Insufficient opportunities for SMEs

Although FTAs can open up opportunities for SMEs, the latter are often unable to incorporate them into their export practice.[147] Usage rate remains low for many FTAs,[148] and SMEs are usually less ready to utilize FTAs compared with larger businesses. SMEs may not be fully capable of exercising rights under and extracting benefits from the TPP due to their capacity constraints. As indicated in the preamble of the TPP, the development of SMEs will be supported through the enhancement of their capacity for 'participating in and benefitting from' the opportunities under the FTA. However, there remain real questions about whether the TPP rules will be sufficient to enable small businesses fully to engage in trade. Rules closely related to SMEs face enforcement difficulties as they are often 'without teeth'. The four chapters on capacity building, competitiveness and business facilitation, development, and SMEs are all relatively short, general and vague in content, and not subject to the TPP dispute settlement system.[149] The chapter on regulatory coherence contains more specific provisions, but is not subject to the dispute settlement mechanism either.[150] Many of these provisions are largely 'soft' or best endeavours clauses and their effect is yet to be seen.

[147] Battisti and Martin (n 43) 284.

[148] For instance, the average usage rate of the more than fifty FTAs surveyed is 26 per cent. See the Economist Intelligence Unit, 'FTAs: Fantastic, Fine or Futile? Business Views on Trade Agreements in Asia' (2014) 4 <https://globalconnections.hsbc.com/downloads/ftas_fantastic_fine_or_futile.pdf> accessed 20 January 2017.

[149] Arts 21.6, 22.5, 23.9, 24.3 TPP.

[150] Art 25.11 TPP.

First, the special support under the SME chapter may not meet the needs of SMEs. SME issues are among the 'devilishly' difficult ones in FTAs, and the TPP has not proved very innovative regarding its SME chapter.[151] This chapter provides support mainly through information sharing via websites and the activities of the SMEs Committee. The information provided on the websites may not be sufficient to explain regulatory requirements fully, especially with regard to local government regulations. More detailed information on export processes, comprehensive trade databases in all TPP countries including frequently updated information on tariff and export control, and other aspects (eg detailed guidance on how to trade with and in other countries) would be very useful for SMEs. Financial barriers are another example. The volatility of currencies, the insufficient bank support for SMEs, and the taxation of overseas income constitute financial barriers for SMEs, although they may not be directly related to FTAs.[152] Along with tariffs, financial barriers are deemed one of the main reasons why SMEs do not utilize the FTAs.[153] The shortage of working capital to finance export has been identified as one of the top two barriers to SMEs accessing international markets in a study of the Organisation for Economic Co-operation and Development[154] and remains a key challenge, particularly for start-up SMEs. These funding, currency, and taxation issues are largely outside the coverage of the TPP.[155] Even those funding issues that do seem to be covered by the TPP are not adequately addressed. The SMEs Committee will exchange experience and best practices in areas such as trade finance.[156] The support provided by the SMEs Committee is, however, far from enough to ensure SMEs' easy access to trade finance.

The assistance provided by the SMEs Committee is laid down in general and soft language rather than being binding and detailed. Consequently, such assistance may not be sufficient to achieve its proclaimed goals. Furthermore, the assistance provided does not cover all relevant areas. The SMEs Committee is designed to assist SMEs in capitalizing on business opportunities,[157] to exchange and examine best practices in supporting SME exporters in relevant aspects (eg training programmes, trade finance, finding business partners, and establishing business credentials),[158] and to develop seminars and other activities to inform SMEs of the TPP benefits.[159] Other relevant activities of the SMEs Committee include exploring capacity-building opportunities to help TPP members provide

[151] Elms (n 6) 391 (the SME chapter has 'basically become a website to help smaller firms take advantage of TPP rules').

[152] Battisti and Martin (n 43) 281.

[153] Battisti and Martin (n 43) 280.

[154] OECD, *Removing Barriers to SME Access to International Markets* (OECD 2008) <http://www.oecd-ilibrary.org/industry-and-services/removing-barriers-to-sme-access-to-international-markets_9789264045866-en> accessed 20 January 2017.

[155] The side deal on currency policy reached among TPP members on 5 November 2015 does not require signing and will take the form of a 'Joint Declaration of the Macroeconomic Policy Authorities of Trans-Pacific Partnership Countries'. This side deal is not covered by any form of dispute settlement. 'Legal Scrub of TPP Side Letters Still Underway: Currency Deal Won't Be Signed' (2016) Inside US Trade 34.

[156] Art 24.2(b) TPP.

[157] Art 24.2.2(a) TPP.

[158] Art 24.2.2(b) TPP.

[159] Art 24.2.2(c) TPP.

better SME export counselling and assistance,[160] recommending information for the TPP members to share with the public,[161] and facilitating the development of programmes to assist SMEs in engaging in supply chains.[162] The TPP has not further clarified the information and programmes that are referred to here. Moreover, some concerns of SMEs are not fully addressed in the TPP, including the possibility of support for SMEs negatively affected by trade liberalization regarding laid-off workers.

Second, special support provided to SMEs under other chapters may also prove to be insufficient. Outside the SME chapter, special provisions on SMEs exist in areas including government procurement,[163] considerations relating to express shipment,[164] and small-scale fisheries.[165] It remains doubtful whether these provisions will have any tangible effect on small businesses. Several examples can be given here. As the first example, TPP members seek to help SMEs overcome obstacles in using electronic commerce.[166] Compared with larger businesses, SMEs still face substantial difficulties in conducting electronic commerce under the TPP rules. Besides the difficulties of operating e-marketplaces, SMEs from developing countries are less visible online and benefit very little from international e-commerce.[167] USAID, for instance, tried to establish business-to-business (B2B) e-marketplaces to engage SMEs online but encountered sustainability issues.[168] The TPP may not be able fully to solve the problem of lack of resources faced by SMEs. Financial barriers discussed above are largely outside the scope of the TPP and are thus left to the members. Further, in relation to financial barriers covered by the agreement, the TPP rules are inadequate. To promote the economic development, TPP members are encouraged to introduce policies 'related to the promotion of market-based approaches aimed at improving trading conditions and access to finance for … SMEs'.[169] It is a soft obligation. Thus, these problems are not completely solved, and could still pose major impediments for SMEs in their attempts to utilize the TPP.

Third, in relation to opportunities common to SMEs and larger businesses, SMEs may still find it difficult to engage in trade and investment. With regard to trade in goods, trade in many 'sensitive' products is not liberalized or is liberalized only slightly.[170] These sensitive products include dairy and sugar.[171] Certain reductions

[160] Art 24.2.2(d) TPP. [161] Art 24.2.2(e) TPP. [162] Art 24.2.2(g) TPP.
[163] Art 15.21 TPP. [164] Art 5.7.1(f) TPP. [165] Art 20.16.1 TPP.
[166] Art 14.15(a) TPP.
[167] Martin Labbé, 'Harnessing Information and Communication Technologies for Development: The Trade-Related Technical Assistance Perspective' in Mira Burri and Cottier Thomas (eds), *Trade Governance in the Digital Age* (Cambridge University Press 2012) 430.
[168] ibid. [169] Art 23.3.4 TPP.
[170] Simon Lester, 'The TPP's Contribution to Public International Law' *ASIL Insights* (2 December 2015) <https://www.asil.org/insights/volume/19/issue/26/tpps-contribution-public-international-law> accessed 20 January 2017.
[171] Anna Vidot, 'TPP to Cut Agricultural Tariffs Across the Board, But US Sugar Protections Remain' *ABC News* (New York, 7 October 2015) <http://www.abc.net.au/news/2015-10-06/agriculture-tariffs-to-fall-under-tpp/6830138> accessed 20 January 2017.

of NTBs seem mainly to benefit larger businesses such as motor manufacturers.[172] The TPP calls for an agreement in the WTO on 'agricultural export state trading enterprises' in order to eliminate trade-distorting restrictions on agricultural export authorization and special financing, and enhance transparency.[173] Given the stalemate in WTO negotiations, it is not likely that such an agreement will be reached in the near future. Moreover, few new disciplines are imposed regarding antidumping and countervailing duties and these areas fall outside the scope of the TPP dispute settlement system.[174] With regard to services, the subsidies and grants by the TPP members (eg loans supported by the government, insurance, and guarantees) for services and financial services are not subject to the disciplines on cross-border services trade.[175] In relation to investment, few Articles deal with special support for SMEs. Regarding competition, under-resourced SMEs may encounter difficulties in exercising the private right of action under the TPP involving domestic competition law,[176] which could be costly and complicated. In the area of government procurement, national authorities shall be established to review violations of TPP rules, but the compensation for loss can be limited to the costs incurred in preparing the tender and/or the complaint.[177] With regard to public participation, the establishment of opportunities for stakeholders to comment on proposed measures and to receive responses to these comments is often not explicitly required[178] or only stipulated as a best endeavour obligation for TPP parties.[179] The effect of these provisions remains to be seen, especially as SMEs may lack the resources (eg funding, time, and expertise) to effectively participate in such comment processes involving proposed SPS or TBT measures and financial regulations. In dispute settlement, the TPP does not grant the right of action under domestic law against TPP-inconsistent measures.[180] There seems to be no explicit support for SMEs with regard to these problems in the TPP.

## II. Complexity of rules

While the TPP takes SMEs into account in some provisions, it also contributes to the overall proliferation of FTAs. The co-existence of the TPP with FTAs that are already in place will not necessarily result in an overall simplification of trade and investment rules.[181] The lengthy TPP is unprecedented in terms of its scope and complexity.[182] Apart from the TPP agreement itself, approximately 120 side letters exist to clarify trade issues between two TPP parties and these could significantly

[172] 'US–Japan Letter Exchange on Certain Auto Non-Tariff Measures' (4 February 2016) <https://ustr.gov/sites/default/files/TPP-Final-Text-US-JP-Letter-Exchange-on-Certain-Auto-NTMs.pdf> accessed 20 January 2017.

[173] Art 2.23 TPP.

[174] Art 6.8.3 TPP.

[175] Arts 10.2.3(d), 11.2.5 TPP.

[176] Art 16.3 TPP.

[177] Art 15.19.4 TPP.

[178] Art 7.13.5 TPP.

[179] Art 11.13.3(b), 11.13.4 TPP.

[180] Art 28.22 TPP.

[181] Patrick B Fazzone, 'The Trans-Pacific Partnership: Towards a Free Trade Agreement of Asia-Pacific?' (2012) 43 Georgetown Journal of International Law 695, 740.

[182] Donald Robertson, 'Impact of Trans-Pacific Partnership on the Energy Sector' (Herbert Smith Freehills, 2 November 2015) (on file with the author).

affect bilateral trade.[183] SMEs thus face the difficulty of ascertaining and understanding a very complex set of rules, covering a wide range of subjects. This is, for instance, the case with origin rules (including product-specific rules of origin) and origin procedures,[184] especially when businesses change from one market to another under an FTA.[185] As seen in other FTAs, SMEs may encounter impediments emerging from the rules of origin.[186] This is an example of an area with especially complex regulations. The TPP has endeavoured to establish a uniform set of origin rules, and it remains to be seen how these will work in practice. In addition, becoming familiar with the relevant domestic law of different TPP members is equally complicated, although efforts are made to encourage TPP members to ensure new domestic regulatory measures are 'plainly written and are clear, concise, well organised and easy to understand'.[187] As discussed below, the complexity of rules may also lead to difficulties in enforcement.

## III. Difficulties in interpretation and implementation

The implementation of the TPP may prove challenging, especially for smaller and developing TPP members. In comparison with bilateral FTAs, the higher legal and regulatory requirements of the TPP demand more expertise and experience. Moreover, it is not easy to interpret the often vague TPP rules, and some TPP rules are subject to domestic law that could differ greatly among TPP members. Certain obligations are expressed in soft language (eg 'should encourage'[188] and 'endeavour to'[189]) and need to be consistent with domestic law (eg the consideration of regulatory measures of other TPP parties in planning regulatory measures,[190] the annual public notice of new regulatory measures[191]). Similarly, other rules may be subject to domestic law, such as the requirement regarding the publicity of new regulatory measures covered by the TPP.[192] A number of terms (eg a 'reasonable opportunity' to be represented by counsel,[193] a 'reasonable opportunity' to consult with competition authorities,[194] and 'the opportunity' to seek review of the sanction or remedy[195]) may be subject to different interpretations. Certain mechanisms, such as the imposition of transitional safeguard measures,[196] including the interpretation of their conditions, also deserve attention. At the very least, the implementation and interpretation of the TPP could benefit from more clarity.

The coordination within and among different agencies is crucial for SMEs in order to reduce regulatory compliance costs and obtain support. Divergent regulatory frameworks can make an enormous impact on the trade costs for businesses and in particular SMEs.[197] The costs of regulatory compliance may even exceed

[183] 'Legal Scrub of TPP' (n 155). [184] Chapter 3 TPP.
[185] Viviane De Beaufort, 'The European Union and the New Face(s) of International Trade' (2015) 1 International Business Law Journal 39.
[186] Fazzone (n 181) 718–19. [187] Art 25.5.4 TPP. [188] Art 25.5.8 TPP.
[189] For instance, Art 5.6.1(a) TPP. [190] Art 25.5.8 TPP. [191] Art 25.5.7 TPP.
[192] Art 25.5.5 TPP. [193] Art 16.2.1(b) TPP. [194] Art 16.2.9 TPP.
[195] Art 16.2.4 TPP. [196] Art 6.3 TPP.
[197] Gómez-Tarragona and Gómez-Altamirano (n 117) 372.

the profits of export by SMEs. Even within the same regulatory entity, it is not rare to find SMEs facing a regulatory process that is interpreted inconsistently.[198] Thus, coordination within a given agency is of great significance. TPP rules relating to SMEs may also involve the joint efforts of a huge range of governments, businesses, trade associations, international organizations, and other actors. The government agencies in twelve countries include trade ministries, customs authorities, the administration for small businesses, and other agencies responsible for finance and standards (eg licensing and inspection), as well as intellectual property, to name but a few. The TPP contains certain requirements regarding increased domestic interagency consultation and coordination.[199] TPP obligations (eg equivalence of SPS measures[200]) may also require efficient coordination between countries of different development levels, which can be more challenging. It remains to be seen what TPP member countries need to do within and beyond the border to fulfil their regulatory improvement commitments (eg through legislative amendments) and how regulatory developments will unfold in reality.

Such challenges may co-exist with regard to the same TPP obligation. Taking the obligation to share information under the SME chapter as an example, the first issue is whether this obligation needs to be implemented through certain domestic procedures. The second issue is determining the scope of information useful for private actors, bearing in mind that information sharing is a self-judging provision.[201] In other words, the TPP members will have discretion regarding the scope of the information that is shared with the public. The third issue is the language in which the information is to be shared, since TPP parties must only endeavour and are thus not required to provide the information to SMEs in English.[202] Other issues such as inter-agency coordination are also encountered, since the websites and their links could potentially involve a large number of government agencies and other entities as a result of the wide coverage of the TPP.

## IV. Other challenges

Other challenges include, inter alia, negative effects of trade liberalization on SMEs and the reduced impact of SMEs on trade policy-making compared with larger firms. After the implementation of the TPP (if the TPP is approved), the impact of the resulting market opening on SMEs of importing countries or on SMEs that currently export to related markets could be severe. Market opening and increased investment must be expected to increase competition for these SMEs. It could be challenging for SMEs in certain sectors that have not previously been liberalized, including the Mexican energy sector with regard to foreign participation[203] and government procurement in Malaysia.[204] In the same vein, for instance, there are

[198] ibid 373. [199] Art 25.4 TPP. [200] Art 7.8 TPP. [201] Art 24.1.2(b) TPP.
[202] Art 24.1.3 TPP. [203] Robertson (n 182).
[204] The TPP is the first of the FTAs concluded by Malaysia that addresses government procurement. SME Corporation Malaysia, 'TPPA: Its Benefits and Challenges' (2015) (on file with the author).

concerns that global e-commerce giants may cause 'problems for local brick and mortar retailers' under the TPP.[205] Two challenges deserve attention here.

### 1. *Remaining regulatory differences*

Regulatory improvements under the TPP will reduce, but can hardly eliminate all regulatory differences. The regulatory coherence chapter is among the most relevant of the TPP rules, but it does not affect the parties' right to regulate in the areas of public health, security, safety, and other public interest considerations.[206] The regulatory coherence chapter is also subject to other chapters in the case of conflict.[207] Thus, regulatory differences will often exist at the intersections between trade and legitimate regulatory objectives (eg health, environment, and safety), with the latter concerning the protection level that a TPP member deems appropriate. For instance, there may be differences in positions taken by SMEs, such as those between pharmaceutical SMEs in one country and generic medicines SMEs in other countries.[208] TPP members would need to address these differences, which may not always lead to the same approach. As another example, SPS and TBT requirements of TPP countries could be different, although regulatory convergence is to be pursued. The compliance costs resulting from different sets of rules could jeopardize small-scale exports for SMEs. The TPP rules seem to be insufficient to address these regulatory differences. Some writers have proposed that small-scale trade could be excluded from regulations that would otherwise constitute insurmountable barriers and that administrative processes be developed to assist access for frequent small volume exports vulnerable to excessive compliance costs related to regulations.[209]

### 2. *Disadvantaged positions of SMEs from developing TPP members*

SMEs from developing TPP countries may encounter additional challenges. First, such SMEs could be less capable of utilizing TPP rules. They could encounter difficulties in reaping benefits due to limited resources (eg expertise and experience). The disadvantaged position of SMEs from developing countries seems to exist under the North American Free Trade Agreement (NAFTA), which bears certain similarities with the TPP such as with regard to tariff reductions.[210] Under NAFTA, exports by US SMEs to Canada and Mexico have risen significantly.[211] In contrast, Mexican SMEs have encountered difficulties in reaping benefits

[205] Ramli and Lynch (n 10).
[206] Office of the US Trade Representative (n 105).
[207] Art 25.10 TPP.
[208] For an analysis of different positions of Amercian SMEs and Australian generic medicines SMEs, see Thomas A Faunce and Ruth Townsend, 'The Trans-Pacific Partnership Agreement: Challenges for Australian Health and Medicine Policies' (2011) 194 Medical Journal of Australia 83, 83–85.
[209] Battisti and Martin (n 43) 284.
[210] Bill Curry, 'The ABCs of TPP' *The Globe and Mail* (Toronto, 5 November 2015).
[211] US International Trade Commission (n 1) E-8, n 35.

from the NAFTA due to lack of financial resources, planning, management, and obsolete techniques.[212] It is possible that a similar situation would develop under the TPP. For instance, SMEs from developing countries may also be in a disadvantaged position in the area of e-commerce due to the lack of infrastructure (eg e-marketplaces), funding, and expertise. In certain areas such as financial services, in which substantial progress has been made under the TPP, SMEs in developing countries are also less likely to utilize these complicated rules. Another example is provided by the fact that trade associations may help SMEs to efficiently utilize TPP provisions, providing support for SMEs. However, trade associations in developing countries may be less organized and less effective than those in developed countries.

Second, developing TPP countries may not be able to provide sufficient assistance to their SMEs to benefit from the TPP to the same extent as developed TPP countries. To provide effective support and assistance, countries need to ascertain, inter alia, how many SMEs are exporting and investing overseas, the barriers they encounter in FTA partners, and their competitiveness. This will not be easy given the large number of SMEs and the range of market sections and regulatory regimes involved. The TPP SME chapter, however, does not provide for special treatment for developing countries.

In a broader sense, developing countries could also support SMEs through broad-based economic growth, sustainable development, and the reduction of poverty,[213] all of which are recognized by the TPP to be related to SME issues. However, as one writer observes, the TPP's role in generating economic growth and poverty reduction is 'not at all certain'.[214]

## V. Conclusion

First, the major challenges resulting from or not overcome by the TPP include the insufficiency of opportunities provided for SMEs, the complexity of rules, difficulties in rule interpretation and implementation, remaining regulatory differences, the disadvantaged position of SMEs from developing TPP countries, and the impact on SMEs negatively affected by trade liberalization. Some of these challenges (eg the complexity of rules and difficulties in interpretation and implementation) are common to large and small businesses, but SMEs may be disproportionately affected by them. As a key issue, one might argue that the TPP does not create sufficient opportunities, including concrete binding requirements, to provide assistance to SMEs. This is particularly the case for SMEs in developing countries and for micro-sized enterprises.[215] The support for SMEs often appears

[212] Francisco J Reyes Avila and Amy Preiss, 'Strategic Management: A Survival Need for Mexican SMEs' (2015) 6 Business Management and Strategy 65, 67.

[213] Art 23.3.4 TPP.

[214] Raj Bhala, 'Trans-Pacific Partnership or Trampling Poor Partners? A Tentative Critical Review' (2014) 11 Manchester Journal of International Economic Law 2, 3.

[215] Art 1.3 TPP (SMEs include micro-sized enterprises).

to be largely confined to hortatory pronouncements and relatively feeble measures, and larger businesses may be in a position to better take advantage of commercial opportunities. This insufficiency may also stem from a lack of capacity within the TPP nations, particularly developing TPP countries.

Second, the challenges of the TPP to SMEs are not the same as those of older FTAs. On the one hand, the TPP is much more complicated, making it more difficult for SMEs to understand and utilize. On the other hand, the TPP may provide more assistance to SMEs than previous FTAs that do not have an SME chapter, helping SMEs through learning by doing. Moreover, the economic impacts of the TPP should not be underestimated. From an economic point of view, a larger number of businesses and stakeholders are likely to get involved in TPP practice compared to a typical bilateral FTA with smaller trade benefits and fewer participants. The large number of private and public participants of the TPP could help SMEs to gain experience at higher speed as presumably more resources (eg webpages and workshops) will be available regarding the utilization of the TPP. Given that the TPP is a mega FTA with potentially greater economic benefits resulting from the larger number of FTA partner countries, more SMEs may become aware of the TPP due to its economic impact and the increased publicity surrounding it (eg information sharing under the TPP SME chapter). SMEs also have more incentive to learn and utilize the TPP. It will therefore be interesting to observe whether the usage rate of the TPP by SMEs will be higher than that of other FTAs if the TPP is approved.

Last but not least, looking beyond the TPP, there will be more challenges for SMEs from non-parties than those from TPP members. The TPP aims to level the playing field between the parties, but it would come with the inherent flaw of placing SMEs inside and outside the TPP on an unequal footing. For instance, the TPP will eliminate over 18,000 tariffs on US exports, benefitting sectors like manufacturing, the automotive industry, and agriculture, as well as information and computer technology.[216] These benefits are largely confined to SMEs of TPP countries. The TPP also strengthens regional value chains and encourages businesses to source inputs within the region. The TPP yarn forward provision would negatively affect Chinese businesses in textiles and apparel.[217] TPP TRQs rules only apply to TRQs listed on the TPP schedules of the contracting parties rather than those set out in their WTO schedules.[218] According to a recent World Bank report, in the post-TPP era exports by non-TPP members may fall in contrast to an increase in exports among TPP members.[219]

[216] Keating (n 9).

[217] Chris Devonshire-Ellis, 'The U.S. TPP "Yarn Forward" Program and Implications for China & Vietnam' *China Briefing* (4 November 2015) <http://www.china-briefing.com/news/2015/11/04/the-u-s-tpp-yarn-forward-program-and-implications-for-china-vietnam.html> accessed 20 January 2017.

[218] Art 2.28.1, n 16 TPP.

[219] After the entry into force of TPP, the exports of Thailand are expected to fall by 2 per cent in contrast with a 30 per cent increase in exports from Vietnam. Peter Martin, 'TransPacific Partnership Will Barely Benefit Australia, Says World Bank Report' *The Sydney Morning Herald* (12 January 2016).

## D. Conclusion

First, the key benefits the TPP can be expected to bring for SMEs are enhanced market liberalization and a more predictable regulatory environment. These benefits stem from the opportunities of support for SMEs, and the reduction of tariffs and unwarranted NTBs. Compared with previous FTAs, the TPP starts to pay more attention to the special constraints encountered by SMEs in trade and investment. SMEs will benefit specifically from a small number of special provisions tailored for SMEs, including the new stand-alone SME chapter and rules explicitly related to SMEs in a number of other chapters. Good governance rules are ubiquitous in the TPP and will lead to regulatory improvements that should reduce compliance costs of small businesses. In particular, transparency and regulatory compatibility are to play a vital role.

Second, the TPP poses serious challenges for SMEs, but different types of SMEs will face very different problems. Most of the benefits for SMEs are also available to larger businesses, while the challenges could be more difficult for SMEs to overcome. Since the assistance provided by the TPP may be insufficient, SMEs still face difficulties due to their capacity limitation (eg expertise and funding). Within the TPP parties, SMEs from countries with better assistance capacity are likely to be in a better position than those from other TPP countries. Some TPP countries already provide a certain degree of support to SMEs and have highlighted SME issues in the TPP negotiations. They may increase their assistance under the TPP. For instance, the United States has provided an online Free Trade Agreement Tariff Tool, including a searchable database,[220] which helps American SMEs better to understand tariff rates in FTA partner countries. The United States also proclaimed support for American SMEs as one of its core goals in the TPP negotiations.[221] Moreover, SMEs from non-TPP parties are likely to encounter much more serious challenges and would not directly benefit from the TPP. The TPP may provide a level playing field in certain respects for SMEs of TPP countries, and this could result in a competitive advantage over their counterparts in non-TPP countries.

Third, the TPP, if properly managed, should bring more opportunities than challenges to SMEs. Interestingly, the opportunities and challenges could be linked to each other. For example, the review of the customs-duties-exempt threshold regarding express shipments may take into account the impact on SMEs,[222] and the RIA may consider the proposed regulation's potential impact on SMEs.[223] Both provisions bring opportunities. However, the TPP neither requires such impact on SMEs to be evaluated nor prescribes how it is to be considered. Thus, it is also a challenge for SMEs to have their needs catered for. Similarly, many SME-related TPP provisions are vague or not subject to the dispute settlement system

[220] Office of the US Trade Representative, 'Small Business' (2016) <https://ustr.gov/issue-areas/small-business> 12 May 2016.

[221] Office of the US Trade Representative (n 7).

[222] Art 5.7.1(f) TPP.

[223] Art 25.5.3 TPP.

(eg the regulatory coherence provisions related to SMEs). Therefore, while the TPP could help to internationalize SMEs, the extent of this support will depend on the interpretation and implementation of the TPP and further efforts will be needed (eg trade finance and capacity building in developing countries).

Finally, opportunities and challenges to SMEs under the TPP may not always be the same as those under bilateral FTAs given the unique nature of this mega FTA. As an example, the TPP may bring more opportunities for SMEs to access much larger markets, but may also involve much more complicated rules and a wider range of actors. While SME-related issues get attention in the TPP, they remain a difficult topic (eg the support to SMEs, and the implementation of SME-related provisions). The TPP parties seem to hesitate in making concrete commitments in this area. It will therefore be interesting to observe closely the impact the TPP will ultimately have on SMEs.

## References

Battisti, M and Martin, P, 'Creating Opportunity for Small-Firm Exporters through Regional Free Trade Agreements: A Strategic Perspective from New Zealand' (2008) 14 Australasian Journal of Regional Studies 275

Bhala, R, 'Trans-Pacific Partnership or Trampling Poor Partners? A Tentative Critical Review' (2014) 11 Manchester Journal of International Economic Law 2

Curry, B, 'The ABCs of TPP' *The Globe and Mail* (Toronto, 5 November 2015)

Daniel, Z, 'Malcolm Turnbull and Barack Obama Hold White House Talks; PM Urges Powerbrokers to Back TPP' *ABC News* (New York, 20 January 2016) <http://www.abc.net.au/news/2016-01-20/turnbull-and-obama-hold-white-house-talks/7099808> accessed 20 January 2017

De Beaufort, V, 'The European Union and the New Face(s) of International Trade' (2015) 1 International Business Law Journal 39

Devonshire-Ellis, C, 'The U.S. TPP "Yarn Forward" Program and Implications for China & Vietnam' *China Briefing* (4 November 2015) <http://www.china-briefing.com/news/2015/11/04/the-u-s-tpp-yarn-forward-program-and-implications-for-china-vietnam.html> accessed 20 January 2017

Elms, DK, 'The Trans-Pacific Partnership Trade Negotiations: Some Outstanding Issues for the Final Stretch' (2013) 8 Asian Journal of WTO & International Health Law and Policy 379

European Commission Directorate General for Trade, 'EU, U.S. Trade: Negotiators Explore Ways to Help SMEs Take Advantage of TTIP, as Fourth Round of Talks Ends in Brussels' (1 May 2014) <http://trade.ec.europa.eu/doclib/press/index.cfm?id=1041> accessed 20 January 2017

Faunce, TA and Townsend, R, 'The Trans-Pacific Partnership Agreement: Challenges for Australian Health and Medicine Policies' (2011) 194 The Medical Journal of Australia 83

Fazzone, PB, 'The Trans-Pacific Partnership: Towards a Free Trade Agreement of Asia-Pacific?' (2012) 43 Georgetown Journal of International Law 695

Gómez-Tarragona, EB and Gómez-Altamirano, D, 'The TPP: How to Facilitate Business through Legislative and Regulatory Reform?' (2015) 21 ILSA Journal of International and Comparative Law 369

Keating, RJ, 'What the Trans-Pacific Partnership (TPP) Means for U.S. Economic Growth and Small Business' (6 October 2015) <http://www.sbecouncil.org/2015/10/06/what-the-trans-pacific-partnership-tpp-means-for-the-u-s-economy-and-small-business/> accessed 20 January 2017

Labbé, M, 'Harnessing Information and Communication Technologies for Development: The Trade-Related Technical Assistance Perspective' in Mira Burri and Cottier Thomas (eds), *Trade Governance in the Digital Age* (Cambridge University Press 2012)

Lavender, T, 'Not Too Late to Mitigate TPP Effects, Minister of International Trade Chrystia Freeland Told' *University of Toronto News* (Toronto, 19 January 2016) <http://news.utoronto.ca/not-too-late-mitigate-tpp-effects-minister-international-trade-chrystia-freeland-told> accessed 20 January 2017

'Legal Scrub of TPP Side Letters Still Underway: Currency Deal Won't Be Signed', (2016) Inside US Trade 34

Lester, S, 'The TPP's Contribution to Public International Law' *ASIL Insights* (2 December 2015) <https://www.asil.org/insights/volume/19/issue/26/tpps-contribution-public-international-law> accessed 20 January 2017

Martin, P, 'TransPacific Partnership Will Barely Benefit Australia, Says World Bank Report' *The Sydney Morning Herald* (Sydney, 12 January 2016)

Miner, S, 'Commitments on State-Owned Enterprises' in Jeffrey J Schott and Cathleen Cimino-Isaacs (eds), *Assessing the Trans-Pacific Partnership*, Vol 2: *Innovations in Trading Rules* (Peterson Institute for International Economics 2016)

Ministry of Trade and Industry of Singapore, 'Trans Pacific Partnership Free Trade Agreement (TPP): 7 Things You Should Know' (2016) <https://www.mti.gov.sg/MTIInsights/SiteAssets/Pages/TPP/Seven%20things%20you%20should%20know%20about%20the%20TPP%20(Final).pdf> accessed 20 January 2017

OECD, *Removing Barriers to SME Access to International Markets* (OECD 2008) <http://www.oecd-ilibrary.org/industry-and-services/removing-barriers-to-sme-access-to-international-markets_9789264045866-en> accessed 20 January 2017

Office of the US Trade Representative, 'Summary of the Trans-Pacific Partnership Agreement' (October 2015) <https://ustr.gov/about-us/policy-offices/press-office/press-releases/2015/october/summary-trans-pacific-partnership> accessed 20 January 2017

Office of the US Trade Representative, 'Transatlantic Trade & Investment Partnership: Opportunities for Small and Medium-Sized Enterprises' (2015) <https://ustr.gov/sites/default/files/TTIP%20Brochure%20v3%20%284-16-15%29FINAL.pdf> accessed 20 January 2017

Office of the US Trade Representative, 'Leveling the Playing Field' (2016) <https://ustr.gov/sites/default/files/USTR-Tariff-Information-by-Sector-6115.pdf> accessed 20 January 2017

Office of the US Trade Representative, 'Outlines of TPP' (2016) <https://ustr.gov/tpp/outlines-of-TPP> accessed 20 January 2017

Office of the US Trade Representative, 'Small Business' (2016) <https://ustr.gov/issue-areas/small-business> 20 January 2017

Office of the US Trade Representative, 'The Trans-Pacific Parnership: Leveling the Playing Field for American Workers & American Businesses' (2016) Chapter 24 <https://ustr.gov/tpp/> accessed 20 January 2017

Persin, D, 'Market Access for Small versus Large Service Enterprises: The Preferential and Multilateral Trade Liberalization Tracks Compared' (2011) 45 Journal of World Trade 785

Ramli, D and Lynch, J, 'TPP: What It Means for Australian Business' *The Sydney Morning Herald* (Sydney, 6 October 2015)

Reyes Avila, FJ and Preiss, A, 'Strategic Management: A Survival Need for Mexican SMEs' (2015) 6 Business Management and Strategy 65

Robertson, D, 'Impact of Trans-Pacific Partnership on the Energy Sector' (Herbert Smith Freehills, 2 November 2015) (on file with the author)

Sangsuvan, K, 'Small Businesses in the WTO: Small Fish in a Big Pond or Globalization 3.0' (2015) 23 Michigan State International Law Review 372

SME Corporation Malaysia, 'TPPA: Its Benefits and Challenges' (2015) (on file with the author)

'TPP SME Chapter Includes Commitments to Set Up Websites, Committee' (2013) Inside US Trade 31

US Department of Commerce, International Trade Administration, 'Opportunities for the U.S. Textiles and Apparel Sector' (November 2015) <http://trade.gov/fta/tpp/industries/pdfs/textile.pdf> accessed 20 January 2017

US International Trade Commission, 'Small and Medium-Sized Enterprises: U.S. and EU Export Activities, and Barriers and Opportunities Experienced by U.S. Firms' (Investigation No 332-509, USITC Publication 4169, July 2010), <http://www.usitc.gov/publications/332/pub4169.pdf> accessed 20 January 2017

'US–Japan Letter Exchange on Certain Auto Non-Tariff Measures' (4 February 2016) <https://ustr.gov/sites/default/files/TPP-Final-Text-US-JP-Letter-Exchange-on-Certain-Auto-NTMs.pdf> accessed 20 January 2017

Vidot, A, 'TPP to Cut Agricultural Tariffs across the Board, But US Sugar Protections Remain' *ABC News* (New York, 7 October 2015) <http://www.abc.net.au/news/2015-10-06/agriculture-tariffs-to-fall-under-tpp/6830138> accessed 20 January 2017

# 8

# Support of Small and Medium-Sized Enterprises under European State Aid Law

*Ilan Sherr, Katrien Miclotte, and Rebecca Fawcett-Feuillette*

## A. Introduction

EU State aid rules are designed to create a level playing field to allow businesses to compete effectively and fairly. State aid rules prohibit Member States from providing advantages to competitors from State resources. However, the European Commission (Commission) has identified that small and medium-sized enterprises (SMEs) find it harder to access finance and obtain information.[1] As a result, SMEs have a favoured status under the State aid rules to allow Member States to provide grants to offset and rebalance the disadvantages that SMEs are subject to.

This chapter sets out the relevant State aid legal framework, and provides details of the special rules that are aimed at supporting SMEs within the State aid framework.

### I. Relevant State aid rules

EU law prohibits Member States from granting any form of financial assistance or advantage that is selective and favours certain economic undertakings (or products or services) where it has the effect of distorting competition and effecting inter-State trade within the European Union. Nevertheless, certain financial or other aids granted by Member States can assist in the Union's economic development. As such, the Treaty on the Functioning of the European Union (TFEU) permits certain categories of 'State aid' because they promote an open market in a proportionate manner. 'State aid' is not specifically defined in the TFEU, and is interpreted broadly (the relevant legislation refers to aid 'in any form whatsoever'[2]) to encompass any advantage. Typically, aid will take the form of a direct subsidy, but

[1] European Commission, Commission Regulation (EU) No 651/2014 of 17 June 2014 declaring certain categories of aid compatible with the internal market in application of Articles 107 and 108 of the Treaty [2014] OJ L187/1 (the 'General Block Exemption Regulation' or 'GBER'), para 40 of the Preamble.

[2] Art 107(1) TFEU.

may include preferential interest rates, guarantees, tax exemptions,[3] reductions in contributions ordinarily payable, or other advantages.

## II. Notification of State aid

Member States must notify any aid scheme in advance of implementation to the Commission, usually to the Directorate-General for Competition (DG COMP), and aid should not be distributed until the Commission's approval is granted. Any State aid that is granted unlawfully can result in the imposition of a range of sanctions, including the requirement for the aid-granting Member State to recover all unlawfully granted aid with interest. Only in certain circumstances can recipients of unlawful aid recover damages from the state, and such actions can be lengthy and costly. It is, therefore, prudent for all businesses to consider the legality of any form of financial or other aid that they receive from the government or other public bodies.

The Commission has also published a number of block exemption regulations[4] whereby aid will be automatically allowed without the need for pre-notification and approval. However, the aid must fit within the strict parameters set out in the block exemption, and some form of notice may still need to be given to disclose to the Commission that aid has been provided.

## III. The role of SMEs

SMEs play a crucial role in the European Union's economic development strategy. SMEs were highlighted as important for the Union's strategy for growth and jobs and critical in supporting the Europe 2020 initiative.[5] However, the Commission has highlighted that, while SMEs are important for job creation and economic development, they have problems accessing finance and information.[6] As a result, to address certain market failures which impact SMEs most significantly, a special regime was put in place, encouraging Member States to provide assistance to SMEs without being in breach of State aid rules.[7] The most recent changes come as part

[3] ECJ, Case C-387/92 *Banco de Credito Industrial SA (Banco Exterior de Espana SA) v Ayuntamiento de Valencia* [1994] ECR I-877; ECJ, Cases C-182 and 217/03 *Belgium and Forum 187 ASBL v Commission* [2006] ECR I-5479.

[4] Now consolidated in the GBER: see Section IV.

[5] Europe 2020 summit, February 2012.

[6] GBER, para 40 of the Preamble.

[7] The Commission published its first guidelines setting out criteria for the approval of aid to SMEs in 1992. European Commission, Community Guidelines on State aid for small and medium-sized enterprises (SMEs) [1992] OJ C213/2. A revised version was published in 1996 before the Commission developed a block exemption for SMEs in 2001. European Commission, Commission Regulation (EC) No 70/2001 of 12 January 2001 on the application of Articles 87 and 88 of the EC Treaty to State aid to small and medium-sized enterprises [2001] OJ L10/33, as amended in 2004 and 2006, extending the scope of the block exemption to cover, among others, aid to SMEs for R&D activities and the processing and marketing of agricultural products. The general block exemption regulation came into force on 20 August 2008 and was replaced by the new general block exemption regulation that came into force on 1 July 2014 (n 1).

of the European Commission's major reform package (State aid modernization or 'SAM'), which began in 2012 and which aims to foster sustainable growth in the European economy.[8] Among the stated aims of the SAM package are: tangible cuts in 'red tape'; the promotion of the more efficient use of limited public resources; and an increased use of aid to encourage growth.[9] As part of the SAM package, the Commission has adopted ten guidelines based on common principles, and five regulations to render existing State aid control instruments and procedures more efficient. As a result, SMEs are generally awarded higher levels of aid intensity for allowable aid and are also able to access certain types of aid exclusively for SMEs.

## IV. The new GBER

The favoured status of SMEs is highlighted in the new revised general block exemption regulation (GBER), which came into force on 1 July 2014.[10] The GBER exempts categories of State aid where the Commission considers that the benefit to society outweighs the possible distortions of competition in the single market, resulting in faster access for businesses to aid and a reduction in the administrative burden associated with satisfying the conditions for an exemption. The enhanced measures of the new GBER, one of the cornerstones of the SAM reforms, seek to better target the application of State aid for the benefit of the economy as a whole and provide even greater opportunities for SMEs to access State aid. In particular, the recently revised legislation recognizes the two major barriers for SMEs in the present economic climate: access to risk capital and access to information.[11] The revised GBER seeks to address these barriers by facilitating access to funding for SMEs, in terms of both the scope and the level of notification exemptions.

## V. 'Think Small First'

The GBER aims, among other things, to introduce measures in favour of SMEs and investment in them, consistent with the Small Business Act published in 2008.[12] The application of the 'Think Small First Principle' of the Small Business Act has led to simplified State aid procedures, meaning decreased costs and increased ease in access to State aid for SMEs, as well as higher levels of aid intensity available

[8] See European Commission, Communication from the Commission to the European Parliament, the Council, the European Economic and Social Committee and the Committee of the Regions: EU State Aid Modernisation (SAM) (8 May 2012) COM/2012/209 final.

[9] See European Commission, 'State Aid Modernisation: A Major Revamp of EU State Aid Control' (Policy Brief, November 2014) <http://ec.europa.eu/competition/publications/cpb/2014/011_en.pdf> accessed 20 January 2017.

[10] cf GBER (n 1).

[11] See, for example, comments in ECJ, Case XS-29/2001 *Regional aid scheme for SMEs* [2002] OJ C58/19.

[12] European Commission, '"Think Small First": A "Small Business Act" for Europe' (Communication, 25 June 2008) COM(2008) 394 final; see also Company Law Newsletter, 'European Commission Proposes Small Business Act' (Company Law Newsletter 236, 2008) 1–3.

for micro, small, and medium-sized enterprises.[13] The requirements for qualification for State aid have been simplified; for example, SMEs benefit from the more straightforward approach to assessing the incentive effect[14] and the qualification as 'undertakings in difficulty'.[15] All twenty-six categories of aid provided for in the GBER are available to SMEs, and many of these are specific SME exemptions, based on the particular difficulties faced by SMEs in the market. In addition, where exemptions are also available to larger enterprises, SMEs benefit from increased aid intensity and notification ceilings.

## B. State Aid and SMEs

### I. General framework

State aid (ie assistance granted by the State or through State resources) is generally contrary to the TFEU where it has not been subject to prior notification, and approval from the European Commission, and it does not obtain the benefit of an exemption from such requirements.

### II. Article 107 TFEU

The general prohibition against State aid is contained in Article 107(1) of the TFEU:

> Save as otherwise provided in this Treaty, any aid granted by a Member State or through State resources in any form whatsoever which distorts or threatens to distort competition by favouring certain undertakings or the production of certain goods shall, in so far as it affects trade between Member States, be incompatible with the common market.

[13] In the Small Business Act, the 'Think Small First' principle is explained as follows: 'As a key contribution to achieving an SME-friendly environment, the perception of the role of entrepreneurs and risk-taking in the EU will therefore have to change: entrepreneurship and the associated willingness to take risks should be applauded by political leaders and the media, and supported by administrations. Being SME-friendly should become mainstream policy, based on the conviction that rules must respect the majority of those who will use them: the "Think Small First" principle.'

[14] Article 6(1) of the GBER requires for the aid to have incentive effect in order to qualify for the exemption under the GBER. According to recital 18, aid has insufficient incentive effect where the beneficiary would already engage under market conditions alone in activities or projects. For measures under the GBER, the aid is deemed to have an incentive effect if the beneficiary has submitted a written application for the aid to the Member State concerned before work on the project or activity starts. Furthermore, the obligatory elements of the aid application are listed in Art 6(2), which among others requires the description of the type of aid (grant, loan, guarantee, repayable advance, equity injection, or other) and denomination of the amount of public funding needed for the project.

[15] Article 2(18)(c) of the GBER refers to national insolvency proceedings. Thus, it is for national law in each Member State to define the conditions under which an undertaking is to be regarded as insolvent. Whenever an undertaking, under this national definition, is (i) subject to collective insolvency proceedings or (ii) fulfils the criteria for being placed under such proceedings at the request of its creditors, it shall be regarded as an 'undertaking in difficulty'.

## III. Exceptions

Paragraphs 2 and 3 of Article 107 identify three categories of aid that are always permitted, and five categories of aid which may be permitted if approved by the Commission.

Furthermore, Article 109 TFEU provides for the existence of block exemptions which exempt certain categories of aid from the general prohibition; currently, two block exemptions exist—the de minimis regulation,[16] which deals with aid of minor value, and the GBER. The GBER simplifies aid-granting procedures by authorizing a wide variety of measures which fulfil objectives of horizontal common interest.

## IV. Definition of State aid

The TFEU does not provide a definition of State aid. However, the Commission has published draft guidance to assist national authorities in identifying notifiable State aid measures.[17] It is important to note that State aid has been interpreted by both the Commission and the European courts very widely to include all forms of economic advantage provided by the State or through State resources (even if administered by a private body).

## V. Assessing aid to SMEs

When assessing aid provided by a State to SMEs, consider the following:

### 1. *Does the aid constitute State aid?*

#### (a) Interpreting Article 107(1) TFEU

To constitute 'aid', a measure will reflect the following features: the measure amounts to an intervention by the State or through State resources; the intervention gives the recipient undertaking an advantage on a selective basis over other undertakings; the intervention has distorted or may distort competition; and the intervention is likely to affect trade between Member States.[18]

An intervention by the 'State or through State resources' is assistance granted by any public or private body controlled by the State. The prohibition of State aid extends not only to Member State governments, but also to local authorities and other public sector or publicly funded bodies, including nationalized industries

[16] European Commission, Commission Regulation (EU) No 1407/2013 of 18 December 2013 on the application of Articles 107 and 108 of the Treaty on the Functioning of the European Union to de minimis aid [2013] OJ L352/1.

[17] European Commission, Commission Notice on the notion of State aid as referred to in Article 107(1) of the Treaty on the Functioning of the European Union [2016] OJ C262/1.

[18] See Art 107(1) TFEU.

and State-owned universities. 'Through state resources' would also encompass payments made by private sector bodies from State-derived funds.[19]

While the aid may be actual payments of cash, such as grants, it also includes a State body forgoing revenue to which it is entitled. This may be in the form of tax reliefs, favourable interest rates or loans, and guarantees. Other examples of an intervention through State resources include government holdings of all or part of a company, or a public body or publicly controlled body providing goods and services on preferential terms.

However, if the State receives a value equivalent to the cost of the resources used in the assistance it provides, and the aid recipient has not received favourable treatment, then that would not amount to State aid under the Market Economy Operator Principle.[20]

The advantage to which the intervention gives rise must be selective. Such an advantage could be to specific companies, industry sectors, or regions. However, measures that apply to all undertakings in a relevant Member State will not constitute State aid. This may include measures such as tax breaks or subsidies which are available to all businesses and all businesses have the ability to take advantage of such measures, should they choose to do so.[21]

In order for an 'advantage' to be conferred, the recipient must receive an economic benefit greater than the one it could have obtained on the market. The 'undertaking' must be engaged in an economic activity (ie they operate in a market with potential for competition), though it is important to note that it does not necessarily need to make a profit. This can include operators and middlemen if they benefit from the funding.

The potential to distort competition does not need to be substantial or significant, and in practice, if State aid is found to have been granted, it will usually be found to at least threaten to distort competition.

The interpretation of the condition that intervention is likely to affect trade between Member States must be broadly interpreted. For example, it would be sufficient that a product or service is tradeable between Member States—the recipient itself does not need to export to other EU markets.[22]

[19] ECJ, Case 78/76 *Firma Steinike und Weinlig v Bundesamt für Ernährung und Forstwirtschaft* [1977] ECR 595; ECJ, Case 290/83 *Re Grants to Poor Farmers; Commission v France* [1985] ECR 439; ECJ, Case 57/86 *Commission v Greece* [1988] ECR 2855; ECJ, Case T-358/94 *Compagnie Nationale Air France v Commission* [1996] ECR II-2109.

[20] cf José Antonio Rodriguez-Miguez, 'EDF, A Leading Case Revisited: The Application of the Market Economy Operator Test to Fiscal Measures and the Energy Sector' (International Conference State Aids, Taxation and the Energy Sector: Looking for a Better Coordination and Efficiency, CEU San Pablo University, Madrid, 13–14 June 2016) <http://ssrn.com/abstract=2790801> accessed 20 January 2017.

[21] ECJ, Case C-308/01 *GIL Insurance Ltd v Commissioners of Customs and Excise* [2004] ECR I-4777.

[22] ECJ, Case 730/79 *Philip Morris Holland BV v Commission* [1980] ECR 2671; ECJ, Cases T-81, 82, and 83/07, *Maas v Commission* [2009] ECR II-2411; ECJ, Case T-369/06 *Holland Malt BV v Commission* [2009] ECR II-03313.

**(b) When is aid to an SME unlikely to be State aid?**

Some SME support measures may not constitute State aid if they do not meet all of the criteria laid out in Article 107(1) TFEU. For example, access to finance will not meet the criteria for State aid if it has been provided at market rates, such that there is no economic advantage.[23] In addition, a measure is unlikely to be State aid if it is provided through a regulated public procurement or auction, or the State is investing in an undertaking on ordinary market terms. Most notably for SMEs, the requirement of an effect on inter-State trade may not be satisfied.[24]

**(c) De minimis and State guarantees**

In addition, the existence of the de minimis regulation and the ability of the State to provide guarantees are particularly important tools that the State can use to support the development of SMEs and increase their access to finance without falling within the scope of regulated State aid (see Sections C and D below).

## 2. *Does the State aid fall under an exemption?*

**(a) GBER**

If all of the criteria for State aid are met, any aid falling within the categories and meeting the conditions laid out in the GBER may be granted without prior notification and approval.

The GBER contains both specific block exemptions for SMEs and more general horizontal and regional aid provisions which tend to permit favourable aid intensity exemptions to SMEs. For each category of aid, the GBER specifies the eligible beneficiaries, expenses, and the maximum proportion of the eligible costs that can benefit from State aid.[25]

**(b) Article 107(2) exemptions**

There are also a number of expressly limited exemptions laid out in Article 107(2) TFEU:

(a) aid having a social character, granted to individual consumers, provided that such aid is granted without discrimination related to the origin of the products concerned;
(b) aid to make good the damage caused by natural disasters or exceptional occurrences;
(c) aid granted to the economy of certain areas of the Federal Republic of Germany affected by the division of Germany, in so far as such aid is required in order to compensate for the economic disadvantages caused by that division. Five years after the entry into force of the Treaty of Lisbon, the Council, acting on a proposal from the Commission, may adopt a decision repealing this point.

[23] For example, European Commission Decision of 24 May 2011, State aid, 31792—Germany, SME scheme of the Land Saxony for support after insolvency, C(2011)3457 final, where the relevant loans were in line with the Commission's reference and discount costs, and covered ex ante costs.

[24] cf the general principles in relation to state aid: Services of General Economic Interest (SGEI), Market Economy Principle, Art 107 TFEU.

[25] For details, see Section E.

#### (c) Services of general economic interest

Finally, certain 'services of general economic interest' are permitted under the State aid rules, services provided by public bodies. These are services of public benefit which are not provided to the public by the market, and in the past have included aids for education, medical services, social housing, and the provision of certain utilities and transport services.[26]

### 3. *Can approval be obtained?*

#### (a) Article 107(3) TFEU

SME aid measures not exempted under the GBER may still be individually approved by the Commission under Article 107(3) TFEU. Many SME aids will be covered by the specific horizontal and/or regional guidelines. In the remaining cases, it is necessary to refer simply to the general principles governing Article 107(3) TFEU.

#### (b) General

Where there is a genuine failure in the market, State aid may be justified, necessary and proportionate, and compatible with the EU rules. The Commission has provided detailed policy guidelines applying its assessment of aid to three broad categories:

- *Sectoral aid.* There are special rules for specific industries, including broadcasting, audio-visual production, textiles, motor vehicles, shipbuilding, coal and steel, fisheries, agriculture and transport, and the rapid deployment of broadband networks (all of which are outside the scope of this chapter).[27]
- *Regional aid* granted to regions of a Member State that are economically underdeveloped. The guidelines for regional State aid for 2014 to 2020 entered into operation on 1 July 2014.[28]
- *Horizontal aid*—for example, for research and development exports, employment, environment protection, training, and SMEs. The range of horizontal rules is considered in greater detail below.[29] It is worth noting that significant

[26] See, therefore: ECJ, Case C-280/00 *Altmark Trans GmbH and Regierungspräsidium Magdeburg v Nahverkehrsgesellschaft Altmark GmbH and Oberbundesanwalt beim Bundesverwaltungsericht* [2003] ECR I-07747; European Commission, Communication on the application of the European Union State aid rules to compensation granted for the provision of services of general economic interest [2012] OJ C8/4.

[27] European Commission, Communication on the application of State aid rules to public service broadcasting [2009] OJ C257/1; European Commission, Communication on State aid for films and other audiovisual works [2013] OJ C332/1; European Commission, Framework on State aid for shipbuilding [2011] OJ C364/9; European Commission, Communication on the modification of the Multisectoral Framework on regional aid for large investment projects (2002) with regard to the establishment of a list of sectors facing structural problems and on a proposal of appropriate measures pursuant to Article 88 paragraph 1 of the EC Treaty, concerning the motor vehicle sector and the synthetic fibres sector [2003] OJ C263/3; European Commission, EU Guidelines for the application of State aid rules in relation to the rapid deployment of broadband networks [2013] OJ C25/1.

[28] See Section J below; European Commission, Guidelines on regional State aid for 2014–2020 [2013] OJ C209/1.

[29] cf Sections F, G, and H.

changes have been made regarding a number of horizontal rules in 2014. The revised frameworks on research and development and innovation (which includes aid to early-stage innovative enterprises) as well as environmental protection and energy entered into operation on 1 July 2014.[30] New guidelines on State aid for rescuing and restructuring non-financial undertakings in difficulty entered into force on 1 August 2014.[31]

Article 107(3)(c) TFEU is an important provision under which State aid for SMEs is likely to be approved.[32] This paragraph covers aid which is granted to facilitate the development of regions or industries and is the most frequently used basis for authorizing State aid. Furthermore, some forms of aid to SMEs may fall under the derogation in Article 107(3)(d) TFEU relating to aid for the promotion of culture and heritage conservation.

As with other aids falling outside the GBER, the Commission is still likely to assess the aid in accordance with the guiding principles of the GBER.[33] Aid that does not meet all of the criteria of the GBER should therefore be constructed in a way that is, otherwise, as similar to the GBER as possible.

## C. De Minimis Regulation

### I. De minimis and SMEs

The de minimis regulation provides an exemption for aid which falls below a specific threshold.[34] The existence of the de minimis regulation is particularly relevant to SMEs, to whom small amounts of State aid will likely make a greater impact to their overall available capital. State aid falling within the de minimis threshold can be granted by Member States to undertakings, particularly SMEs, very rapidly, without notification to the Commission or any administrative procedure.

### II. De minimis thresholds

The de minimis regulation applies as follows:

[30] European Commission, Framework for State aid for research and development and innovation [2014] OJ C198/1.

[31] European Commission, Guidelines on State aid for rescuing and restructuring non-financial undertakings in difficulty [2014] OJ C249/1; European Commission, Guidelines on State aid for environmental protection and energy 2014–2020 [2014] OJ C200/1.

[32] See, for example, European Commission Decision of 13 July 2009, State aid, NN 32/2009—United Kingdom: Enterprise Management Incentives (EMI), C(2009)5082 final. See, for example, European Commission Decision of 15 October 2014, State aid, SA.36061 (204/N)—United Kingdom, The British Business Bank, C(2014)7366 final.

[33] See GBER (n 1) para 91, where the Commission compared the aid ceiling under the scheme and the comparable ceiling under the old GBER.

[34] European Commission, Commission Regulation (EU) No 1407/2013 of 18 December 2013 on the application of Articles 107 and 108 of the Treaty on the Functioning of the European Union to de minimis aid [2013] OJ L352/1.

- the ceiling for the aid covered by the de minimis regulation is up to €200,000 (gross cash grant equivalent)[35] over a three-fiscal-year period;[36]
- the ceiling applies to the total value of all public assistance that is de minimis aid of all kinds, irrespective of its form (except for export aid). The €200,000 total is cumulative, but the accumulation is only with other de minimis aid and the recipient may still obtain other State aid without prejudice to the cumulation rule;[37] and
- the regulation only applies to 'transparent' forms of aid.[38] The excepted industry sectors noted above do not benefit from the regulation,[39] and there is a lower €100,000 ceiling for the road freight transport sector.[40]

SMEs are required to keep complete records of aid granted pursuant to the de minimis regulation.

Given the financial difficulties regularly experienced by SMEs during the first few years of their existence, the fact that the new de minimis rules adopted in January 2014 no longer exclude undertakings in difficulty was aimed at increasing the number of SMEs able to benefit from the application of de minimis aid.[41]

## D. State Guarantees

State guarantees are also considered aid, as they confer an advantage provided by the State. State guarantees are a crucial tool that can be used by the state to support SMEs because they expand the number of private loans available to SMEs without requiring immediate contribution by the State (the payment of the guarantee is only needed in the case of default by the SME).

## E. General Block Exemption Regulation

### I. General structure of the GBER

The GBER contains a set of shared conditions and procedural provisions applicable to all types of aid, provided it is transparent aid (ie aid for which it is possible to calculate precisely the amount of aid ex ante and without the need to undertake a risk assessment).

### II. SMEs overview

Importantly, the GBER specifically addresses the situation of SMEs. SMEs benefit from cumulation rules which allow them to receive awards for different types of aid

[35] ibid Art 3(6). [36] ibid Art 3(2). [37] ibid Art 5. [38] ibid Art 4(1).
[39] ibid Art 1(1). [40] ibid Art 3(3).
[41] European Commission, Answer given by Mr Tajani on behalf of the Commission (Parliamentary question of 4 February 2014) [2014] OJ C237/64.

measures without having to go through the notification procedure if they concern different activities.

## III. Sectoral exemptions

The GBER applies to most sectors of the economy. However, a limited number of sectoral exceptions apply to State aid. Notably, the primary agricultural production, aquaculture, and fisheries sectors are excluded from the full application of the GBER. Furthermore, State aid for 'export-related activities' is not allowed (except insofar as it relates to support for attendance at trade fairs), and operating aid (aid to cover costs which a company would be expected to pay in the normal course of business, such as rent and utilities) is not allowed except under the de minimis regulation.

## IV. Definition of SME

An enterprise is defined as 'any entity engaged in an economic activity, irrespective of its legal form'.[42] This includes self-employed persons and family businesses, as well as partnerships or associations regularly engaged in economic activity. Article 2 of Annex 1 to the GBER defines micro, small, and medium-sized enterprises.[43] These categorizations are important for determining the levels of aid that can be authorized pursuant to the various provisions of the GBER. In general, the levels of aid available to smaller enterprises is greater. For newly established enterprises, whose accounts have not yet been approved, the enterprise may use a bona fide estimate made in the course of the financial year.[44]

## V. Block exempted State aid

1. *Investment aid* can be granted to SMEs,[45] up to €7.5 million (per undertaking, per project).[46] The GBER allows for aid provided for up to 20 per cent for small enterprises and 10 per cent for medium enterprises for: (i) the costs of investments in tangible and intangible assets; and (ii) the estimated wage costs of employment directly caused by the investment

[42] Art 1, Annex I GBER.

[43] This information is set out in the Annex in tabular form. See the Annex of this volume, Table. For a recent discussion of the calculation of annual work units (AWU) in the context of seasonal employment, see the ECJ's judgment in ECJ, Case 415/07 *Lodato Gennaro & C SpA v Istituto nazionale della previdenza sociale (INPS), SCCI* [2009] ECR I-02599. Under Art 5, Annex I GBER, national labour rules apply to determine which categories of staff should be taken into account.

[44] See Art 4(3), Annex 1 GBER.

[45] Art 17 GBER.

[46] Art 17 GBER.

over two years (ie employment concerning the activity to which the investment relates).[47]

2. *Aid for consultancy in favour of SMEs*[48] is exempted up to €2 million (per undertaking, per project). Aid can be provided for up to 50 per cent of the costs of consultancy services provided by external consultants.[49]
3. *Aid to SMEs for participation in fairs*[50] is exempted up to €2 million (per undertaking, per year). Fairs provide opportunities to access information that may be useful for SMEs, as well as providing a platform for SMEs to display the goods or services they are able to offer. Aid for SME participation is therefore exempted up to a maximum of 50 per cent of the costs incurred in renting, setting-up, and running a stand for the first participation in any fair or exhibition. Consistent with the Commission's previous practice, aid for subsequent participation in any particular fair or exhibition will not be covered.[51]
4. *Aid for cooperation costs incurred by SMEs in European Territorial Cooperation projects*[52] is exempted up to €2 million (per undertaking, per project). Aid can be provided for up to 50 per cent of the costs for: (i) organizational cooperation (including the cost of staff and offices to the extent that it is linked to the cooperation project); and (ii) costs of advisory and support services linked to cooperation and delivered by external consultants and service providers.
5. *Risk finance aid.*[53] SMEs can now qualify for risk finance aid of up to €15 million in total per undertaking. The scope of the aid encompasses a range of financial instruments, including equity, quasi-equity, loans and guarantees, and facilitating access to finance.

If the SME has not been operating in any market, 10 per cent of the risk finance provided must be private investment. If the SME has been operating in any market for less than seven years following their first commercial sale, 40 per cent of the risk finance provided must be private investment. If the SME requires an initial risk finance investment, based on a business plan prepared in view of entering a new product or geographical market, then 60 per cent of the risk finance provided must be private investment.

[47] For an example under the old SME block exemption, see European Commission Decision of 14 June 2001, State aid, N 606/2000—United Kingdom, Highlands and Islands aid scheme, SG (2001) 289173.

[48] Art 18 GBER.

[49] See, for example, under the old SME block exemption, Information communicated by Member States regarding State aid granted under Commission Regulation (EC) No 70/2001 on the application of Articles 87 and 88 of the EC Treaty to State aid to small and medium-sized enterprises, Aid no XS 182/2006 Consultancy aid for software development [2007] OJ C174/21.

[50] Art 19 GBER.

[51] See, for example, European Commission Decision 2003/226/EC of 24 September 2002 on an aid scheme which the Federal Republic of Germany is planning to implement—'Guidelines on assistance for SMEs—Improving business efficiency in Saxony' [2003] OJ L91/13.

[52] Art 20 GBER. [53] Art 21 GBER.

In certain circumstances, undertakings may be eligible after the first seven years following their first commercial sale (see below). In such circumstances, 60 per cent of the risk finance provided must be private investment.

(6) *Aid for start-ups.*[54] Eligible undertakings are unlisted small enterprises, for a period of up to five years following their registration (or, if not subject to registration, from when it starts its economic activity or is liable for tax for its economic activity), which have not yet distributed profits and have not been formed through a merger. The aid may take the form of loans with interest rates that are better than prevailing market conditions, guarantees with premiums which do not conform with market conditions, and grants. Certain conditions and aid limits for each category are laid out in Article 22 GBER, with the aid limits doubled for small and innovative undertakings.

(7) *Aid for alternative trading platforms specialized in SMEs.*[55] Where the platform is a small enterprise, it may be awarded start-up aid (see above, point 6) or tax incentives to natural persons investing in the platform in the form of risk finance aid (see above, point 5).

(8) *Innovation aid for SMEs* is exempted up to €5 million (per undertaking, per project). Aid can be provided for up to 50 per cent of the costs for: (i) obtaining, validating, and defending patents and other intangible assets;[56] and (ii) secondment of highly qualified personnel working on research, development, and innovation activities in a newly created function and not replacing other personnel; and up to 100 per cent of the costs for innovation advisory and support services provided that the total amount does not exceed €200,000 in a three-year period.

## VI. Favourable aid intensity for SMEs

In addition to the exemptions specifically aimed at SMEs, SMEs benefit from more favourable terms than larger enterprises in many of the other exemptions specified by the GBER.

Aid intensity can be increased by ten percentage points if the aid is granted to medium-sized companies and twenty percentage points if the aid is granted to small-sized companies for the following:

- training aid[57] (up to €2 million per training project);
- aid for environmental protection[58] (up to €7.5 million per undertaking, per project);
- investment aid for energy efficiency measures[59] (up to €10 million);

[54] Art 22 GBER. [55] Art 23 GBER.

[56] See, for example, European Commission Decision of 23 August 2007, State aid, N 278/2007—Germany, Promotion of patent protection for small enterprises, Sachsen-Anhalt, C/245/2007.

[57] Art 31 GBER. [58] Art 36 GBER. [59] Art 38 GBER.

- investment for high-efficiency cogeneration[60] (up to €10 million);
- investment aid for the promotion of energy from renewable sources[61] (up to €15 million per undertaking, per project);
- investment aid for energy efficient district heating and cooling[62] (up to €20 million per undertaking, per project); and
- investment aid for waste recycling and re-utilization[63] (up to €15 million per undertaking, per project).

Aid for environmental studies can be exempted up to €15 million (per undertaking, per project).[64] Aid intensity can be increased by five percentage points if the aid is granted to medium-sized companies and ten percentage points if the aid is granted to small-sized companies for investment aid for early adaption to future Union standards.[65]

Furthermore, regional investment aid might be exempted under the GBER.[66] SMEs generally benefit from increased aid intensity and shorter time requirements. For example, aid granted to SMEs in assisted areas may be for any form of initial investment, whilst aid to large enterprises may only be granted for an initial investment for a new economic activity in the area concerned. In addition, for aid granted for investment costs in tangible and intangible assets, in the case of SMEs the assets need not be new assets. Furthermore, there are special provisions that in the outermost regions an investment made by an SME can receive aid above the maximum aid intensity of 75 per cent.

Aid for process and organizational innovation can be exempted up to €7.5 million (per undertaking, per project).[67] SMEs must incur at least 30 per cent of the eligible costs in the aided collaborative activity. SMEs can receive up to 50 per cent of the costs, and larger organizations can receive up to 15 per cent of the costs of: (1) personnel; (2) instruments, equipment, buildings, and land to the extent and for the period used for the project; (3) contractual research, knowledge, and patents bought or licensed from outside sources at arm's length conditions; and (4) additional overheads and other operational costs directly resulting from the activity.

Also, aid for research and development projects might be exempted under the GBER. The level of support available is set out in the framework for State aid for research and development and innovation,[68] and depends on the type of research or development being carried out (see Table 8.1).[69]

[60] Art 40 GBER. [61] Art 41 GBER. [62] Art 46 GBER. [63] Art 47 GBER.
[64] Art 49 GBER. [65] Art 37 GBER. [66] Art 14 GBER. [67] Art 29 GBER.
[68] cf n 30.
[69] United Kingdom, Department for Business Innovation & Skills, 'State Aid: General Block Exemption Guidance' (July 2014) 17 <https://www.gov.uk/government/uploads/system/uploads/attachment_data/file/325465/bis-14-943-state-aid-general-block-exemption-guidance.pdf> accessed 20 January 2017.

**Table 8.1** Research and development aid intensity for small, medium, and large enterprises[i]

| Category of research and development projects | Notification threshold (€) | Small enterprise (%) | Medium enterprise (%) | Large enterprise (%) |
|---|---|---|---|---|
| Fundamental research | 40 million | 100 | 100 | 100 |
| Industrial research | 20 million | 70 | 60 | 50 |
| Fundamental research | 40 million | 100 | 100 | 100 |
| Industrial research projects involving collaborations[ii] or where the results will be disseminated | 20 million | 80 | 75 | 65 |
| Experimental development | 15 million | 45 | 35 | 25 |
| Experimental development projects involving collaborations[ii] | 15 million | 60 | 50 | 40 |
| Feasibility studies | 7.5 million | 70 | 60 | 50 |

Notes:
[i] United Kingdom, Table from Department for Business Innovation & Skills, 'State Aid: General Block Exemption Guidance' (July 2014) 17 <https://www.gov.uk/government/uploads/system/uploads/attachment_data/file/325465/bis-14-943-state-aid-general-block-exemption-guidance.pdf> accessed 20 January 2017.
[ii] Collaborations between businesses and research organizations where the research organization bears at least 10 per cent of the costs and has the right to publish their own research, or business-to-business collaborations which involve more than one Member State of the EU/EEA or involve at least one SME, provided that no one business partner carries more than 70 per cent of the project costs.

## F. Research, Development, and Innovation (R&D&I) Aid

### I. When could State aid apply?

Aid granted by a Member State generally to promote fundamental research and development will not fall within Article 107(1) TFEU where there is no selective advantage to a particular firm. However, if aid has been granted for R&D&I on a selective basis, then State aid may be involved, and such aid must therefore be notified for approval by the Commission. In practice, the closer the research is to the marketing stage, the less likely the Commission will approve aid in that field.

### II. 2014 Framework

The Commission adopted a revised framework for R&D&I aid (the R&D&I Framework) at the same time as the new GBER.[70] The new GBER was extended to

[70] cf n 65.

cover a greater range of R&D&I aid, and as such the R&D&I Framework covers only the R&D&I aid not covered by the GBER (either because the category is not covered in the GBER or because the GBER thresholds were exceeded). Note, however, that it does not cover aid for R&D&I for firms in difficulty.

## III. Qualifying State aid

Under the R&D&I Framework and in accordance with the common assessment principles, State aid for R&D&I may be compatible with the internal market where it leads to increased R&D&I activities without adversely affecting trading conditions in the European Union. The Commission has identified a range of R&D&I measures which may, in certain conditions, qualify as allowable State aid under Article 107(3)(b) or 107(3)(c) TFEU.

These are the following measures:

- aid for R&D projects where the aided part of the research project falls within the categories of fundamental research and applied research (industrial research and experimental development);
- aid for feasibility studies related to R&D projects;
- aid for the construction and upgrade of research infrastructures; and
- aid for innovation activities (including innovation aid for SMEs and aid for process and organizational innovation).

## IV. Application in practice

The Commission will still assess each grant of aid according to its common assessment criteria; all of the criteria must be met. The Commission will balance the positive effects of the aid against possible distortions on competition. A key criterion is that the State aid measure must still provide material improvement where the market is unable to do so—in the sphere of R&D&I, market failures are often on account of inefficiency or failure of cohesion or knowledge-sharing. The State aid measure must also still be appropriate and proportionate (ie limited to the minimum level of grant necessary to achieve the aim, despite the maximum limits set out in the R&D&I Framework), generate the least possible distortions in competition in trade between Member States, and provide an incentive effect and be for the common interest.

Under the R&D&I Framework, any aid schemes that aim to implement EU schemes are assumed to be appropriate. Furthermore, aid to assist a comprehensive national programme to stimulate R&D&I activities, aid directly or indirectly financed by the European Union, or aid that increases R&D&I activities more broadly in the sector concerned or the European Union will be favourably viewed as 'for the common interest'.

### V. Aid intensities and SMEs

SMEs in particular are likely to meet huge funding barriers in research and development fields. Such activities can involve regular economic input for long periods of time before any economic output is received. Most SMEs simply will not have the funds to support this level of investment. The R&D&I Framework reflects the difficulties faced by SMEs—Annex II of the R&D&I Framework lists out the maximum aid intensities permitted for each type of R&D&I activity, splitting up small, medium, and large enterprises with differing maximums for each.[71]

### VI. Information and SMEs

In addition, SMEs often disproportionately suffer from lack of access to technology platforms and lack of information-sharing within industries with strong commercial players; the ability of SMEs to receive State aid to address these market failures is crucial in technology and other markets. Innovation clusters play key roles in connecting market players, encouraging innovation, and supporting the growth of SMEs.

### VII. Innovation aid

Most notable, however, is the specific innovation aid for SMEs. SMEs may be awarded aid for obtaining, validating, and defending patents and other intangible assets, for the secondment of highly qualified personnel, and for acquiring innovation advisory and support services. This addresses many key issues for SMEs, most notably the lack of access to intellectual property rights at a reasonable cost for SMEs and their inability to attract or fund the same quality of employees and advisers as larger companies.

## G. Restructuring Aid, Rescue, and Temporary Restructuring Support

### I. Rescue and restructuring aid

Rescue aid is urgent and temporary assistance to an undertaking facing a serious deterioration of its financial situation in order to provide it with time to develop an appropriate action plan. Restructuring aid is more permanent assistance to restore the long-term financial health of a company based on a coherent restructuring plan. Temporary restructuring support is liquidity assistance to SMEs in certain situations. None of these forms of aid is intended to artificially preserve ailing companies, and therefore strict criteria must be met for each of them to be granted.

[71] cf n 30.

## II. 2014 Guidelines and SMEs

On 1 August 2014, new Commission guidelines on State aid for rescuing and restructuring non-financial undertakings in difficulty came into force.[72] For each aid to be granted, the Member State must demonstrate on objective grounds that the undertaking concerned is in difficulty, that is to say that without intervention by the state, it will almost certainly be condemned to insolvency in the short or medium term. A newly created undertaking (one in its first three years of operation) is not eligible for aid under these guidelines, regardless of its financial position.

## III. Temporary restructuring support

Of particular relevance to SMEs is the introduction of temporary restructuring support, through which loans and guarantees can be granted to SMEs on simplified terms for up to eighteen months. This is in contrast to non-SMEs, to whom aid can only be provided for six months without Commission approval. The aim of the new measure is to allow Member States to better assist SMEs in addressing liquidity problems, which became particularly important following the 2008 economic downturn. On this basis, as well as assisting SMEs in difficulty, temporary restructuring support can also be granted to undertakings that are not in difficulty, but are facing acute liquidity issues due to exceptional and unforeseen circumstances.

## IV. Simplified compatibility criteria

In addition, the compatibility criteria used to assess rescue and restructuring aid for larger organizations (which mirror that in the R&D&I Framework[73]) are simplified for SMEs.

In order to demonstrate that the failure of the beneficiary is likely to involve social hardship or a market failure, it is sufficient to show:

- for innovative SMEs, SMEs with high growth potential, or SMEs with extensive links to other local or regional undertakings (particularly other SMEs), their exit from the market would have potential negative consequences;
- the failure or adverse incentives of credit markets would push an otherwise viable undertaking into bankruptcy; or
- similar situations of hardship would arise.

Own contribution costs of the beneficiary to restructuring aid is reduced from 50 to 40 per cent of the restructuring costs in the case of medium-sized enterprises or 25 per cent in the case of small enterprises.

[72] cf n 31. [73] See Section F.

### V. Limits

It is important to note that limits still remain with regard to the provision of rescue aid, restructuring aid, and temporary restructuring support to SMEs. The Commission has made it clear that such aid should normally be granted under schemes with predetermined maximum amounts of aid that can be awarded to a single undertaking. Further, the maximum total amount of aid available under all schemes or other sources that can be received by an SME is €10 million. In addition, the 'one time, last time' condition means that no further aid may be granted within ten years of any aid approved under this category unless there are exceptional and unforeseeable circumstances for which the beneficiary is not responsible.[74]

## H. Other Guidelines

### I. Risk capital aid

#### *1. 2014 Guidelines*

From 1 July 2014, new guidelines on State aid to promote risk finance investments came into force (Risk Finance Guidelines), which set out the conditions under which State aid can be granted to SMEs (and other small and innovative companies with medium capitalization) to facilitate their access to finance.[75] The Risk Finance Guidelines set out how the Commission will assess risk finance State aid which does not fall within the scope of the GBER and must therefore be notified to the Commission for approval.

#### *2. Scope*

The Risk Finance Guidelines only apply to risk finance schemes (not ad hoc measures to individual undertakings) deployed through financial intermediaries or alternative trade platforms to SMEs (up to 250 employees), small midcaps (up to 499 employees), and/or innovative midcaps (up to 1,500 employees and with R&D and innovation costs representing 10 per cent of total operating costs).

The aid can be paid through a wide range of financial instruments (recently widened by the new guidelines), including equity, quasi-equity, loans, and guarantees. The recent widening of companies and financial instruments to which the Risk Capital Guidelines apply (including to SMEs beyond their initial start-up period to

[74] European Commission, Guidelines on State aid [2014] OJ C249/1 (n 31) para 3.6.1. See, for example, the decision of the Commission of 5 November 2015 not to raise objections in relation to two schemes planned by France with the aim of facilitating investment in innovative SMEs. European Commission, 'State Aid: Commission Approves Two Schemes Aimed at Encouraging Investment in Innovative SMEs' (Press Release, 5 November 2015) <http://europa.eu/rapid/press-release_IP-15-6001_en.pdf> accessed 20 January 2017.

[75] European Commission, Guidelines on State aid to promote risk finance intervention [2014] OJ C19/04.

later stages in their development) is a realistic reaction to the 2008 economic downturn and, like the GBER, recognizes the difficulties such entities meet in accessing adequate financing.

### *3. Application*

The Risk Finance Guidelines apply the market economy operator test to determine whether there is State aid involved in risk finance measures. As with R&D&I aid, the Commission will consider aid to be compatible with the TFEU only if it satisfies the common assessment criteria. The Risk Finance Guidelines set out three main categories of notifiable risk finance measures which are likely to be found compatible with Article 107(3)(c) TFEU:

- those which target undertakings that do not fulfil the risk finance requirements under the GBER;
- those whose design parameters differ from those set out in the GBER, but target the same defined eligible undertakings; and
- large schemes which do not fall within the GBER on account of their large budget (€100 million).

Nonetheless, the inclusion of the common compatibility assessment in the Risk Finance Guidelines, replacing the previously 'softer' version in the previous guidelines, encourages Member States all the more to ensure that aid measures fall within the GBER as much as possible.

### *4. Private participation ratio*

Unlike the previous risk capital guidelines, there is no longer a flat private participation rate; instead, the private capital participation ratio is tailored in relation to the inherent riskiness of the investee, which works in favour of SMEs. For example, for investments in SMEs before their first commercial sale, the private capital participation requirement can be as low as 10 per cent, in order to take into account the reluctance of private investors to fund such entities. However, as the target companies become more established, the required rate of private investment increases up to 60 per cent.

## II. Environmental aid

### *1. Environmental guidelines*

The new guidelines on State aid for environmental protection and energy 2014 to 2020 identify a number of types of environmental and energy aid which, if they meet certain conditions, may be permitted under Article 107(3)(c) TFEU.[76] The

[76] European Commission, Guidelines on State aid for environmental protection and energy 2014–2020 [2014] OJ C200/1 (Environmental Guidelines).

Environmental Guidelines extend the previous guidelines to cover, among other things, aid to energy infrastructure projects, generation adequacy measures, and support for energy-intensive users (electricity costs at least 20 per cent of gross value), as well as setting out a framework for aid to energy (especially electricity) from renewable sources.

### 2. *Regulation or State aid?*

Member States can use national regulation to overcome market failure. However, they may also be justified in using State aid to meet higher levels of environmental protection than those required under EU law. In principle, State aid cannot be used to support investments necessary to comply with EU law; only those surplus costs associated with the extra protection are eligible for State aid funding.

### 3. *Application of the Environmental Guidelines*

If certain notification thresholds laid out in the guidelines are met, individual aid granted on the basis of an aid scheme must be notified to the Commission. The common principles (outlined above) will be used by the Commission to assess aid covered by the Environmental Guidelines. However, the Environmental Guidelines also set out particular conditions in relation to certain types of aid, in particular aid to energy from renewable sources, waste management, and environmental tax reductions.

### 4. *Environmental Guidelines and SMEs*

The Environmental Guidelines lay out maximum aid intensities for the aid they cover, the aid intensities are progressively higher for medium-sized enterprises and small enterprises have the highest level of allowable aid intensity. The details of the Environmental Guidelines are beyond the scope of this chapter. However, any SME involved in activities relating to environmental protection and energy should carefully consider the newly expanded categories of State aid available to them in this area.

## III. Projects of common European interest

From 1 July 2014, and as part of its SAM programme, new guidelines on how Member States can support transnational projects which are strategically important for the European Union came into effect (the IPCEI Guidelines).[77] The IPCEI Guidelines set out the criteria that the Commission will use to assess

[77] European Commission, Criteria for the analysis of the compatibility with the internal market of State aid to promote the execution of important projects of common European Interest [2014] OJ C188/4.

whether a particular project is eligible under Article 107(3)(b) TFEU and how the Commission will assess the compatibility of State aid for such projects. Namely, it will consider the necessity and proportionality of the aid, prevention of undue distortions of competition, and transparency.

# I. Regional Aid

## I. Compatibility with Article 107 TFEU

Regional aid is designed to assist the development of the most disadvantaged areas by supporting investment and job creation in a sustainable context. Article 107(3)(a) TFEU permits certain aid to promote the economic development of areas where the standard of living is abnormally low or where there is serious underemployment, by development of new establishments. Article 107(3)(c) TFEU permits aid to facilitate the development of certain economic activities or of certain economic areas, where such aid does not adversely affect trading conditions contrary to the common interest.

## II. 2014 Regional Aid Guidelines

The new guidelines on regional State aid for 2014 to 2020 (RAG) apply to both regional aid schemes and individual aid, and the aid can take the form of either operating aid or investment aid.[78] Under RAG, the areas that fulfil the Article 107(3)(a) and (c) TFEU conditions must be identified on a regional aid map notified to the Commission for approval before regional aid can be awarded to any economic entity in the area. The maps must also specify the maximum aid intensities applicable in these areas. As with R&D&I aid above, a compatibility assessment of each grant of aid will be made by the Commission along with the criteria described above. Once again, all of the criteria must be met and the Commission will balance the positive effects of the aid against possible distortions on competition. The RAG do not apply to certain sectors with sector-specific rules, and regional aid cannot be awarded to economic entities in financial difficulty.

## III. Limitations

Under RAG, a beneficiary making an investment in an approved region must provide a financial contribution of at least 25 per cent of the eligible costs (either through its own resources or by external financing, but neither may consist of any form of public financial support). Furthermore, to ensure that any investment makes a real and sustained contribution to the region's development, the

[78] European Commission (n 28).

investment made (or job made available) must be available for at least five years, or three years for SMEs, after its completion.

## IV. SMEs and RAG

Any SME whose activities are based in, or relate to, investments in regions which may fulfil the Article 107(3)(a) and (c) TFEU conditions should carefully consider the newly expanded categories of State aid available to them in this area. In addition, if the activities of economic entities are so connected to such regions, it is always important to consider the interaction of RAG with other horizontal guidelines. For example, under the GBER and the Environmental Guidelines, higher aid intensities may be allowed if the investment takes place in an assisted region.

## References

Company Law Newsletter, 'European Commission Proposes Small Business Act' (Company Law Newsletter 236, 2008)

European Commission, 'State Aid Modernisation: A Major Revamp of EU State Aid Control' (Policy Brief, November 2014) <http://ec.europa.eu/competition/publications/cpb/2014/011_en.pdf> accessed 20 January 2017

European Commission, 'State Aid: Commission Approves Two Schemes Aimed at Encouraging Investment in Innovative SMEs' (Press Release, 5 November 2015) <http://europa.eu/rapid/press-release_IP-15-6001_en.pdf> accessed 20 January 2017

United Kingdom, Department for Business Innovation & Skills, 'State Aid: General Block Exemption Guidance' (July 2014) <https://www.gov.uk/government/uploads/system/uploads/attachment_data/file/325465/bis-14-943-state-aid-general-block-exemption-guidance.pdf> accessed 20 January 2017

Rodriguez-Miguez, JA, 'EDF, A Leading Case Revisited: The Application of the Market Economy Operator Test to Fiscal Measures and the Energy Sector' (International Conference State Aids, Taxation and the Energy Sector: Looking for a Better Coordination and Efficiency, CEU San Pablo University, Madrid, 13–14 June 2016) <http://ssrn.com/abstract=2790801> accessed 20 January 2017

# PART III

# INTERNATIONAL INVESTMENT LAW

# 9

# The Treatment of Small and Medium-Sized Enterprises in International Investment Law

*Joachim Karl**

## A. The Economic Importance of SMEs and Its Reflection in Domestic Investment Policies

Small and medium-sized enterprises (SMEs) are the backbone of almost all economies.[1] In most countries, they constitute more than 90 per cent of all companies, they employ the great majority of the workforce, and they make the biggest contribution to GDP (Box 9.1).

Although at a much lower scale, SMEs are also involved in international economic relations, thereby generating export revenues or creating new jobs. Trade (import and export), as one would expect, is by far predominant, but a non-negligible part consists in foreign direct investment (FDI) or non-equity forms of investment, in particular subcontracting (Figure 9.1).

Looking more specifically at foreign investment by German SMEs, FDI stock abroad amounted to approximately €42.1 billion by the end of 2011.[2] This amount originated from 1,288 SMEs, holding assets in 2,793 companies abroad.[3] Overall, German FDI stock at the end of 2011 stood at €1.14 trillion, involving 6,598 investor companies and 33,556 subsidiaries abroad. This means that the share of

* The views expressed by the author do not necessarily reflect those of UNCTAD.

[1] There is no internationally recognized definition of an 'SME'. Differences in the definition can be substantial. According to EU rules, for instance, the category of micro, small, and medium-sized enterprises is made up of enterprises which employ fewer than 250 persons and which have an annual turnover not exceeding €50 million and/or an annual balance sheet total not exceeding €43 million. See European Commission, Commission Recommendation 2003/361/EC of 6 May 2003 concerning the definition of micro, small and medium-sized enterprises [2003] OJ L124/36, Annex, Art 2. By contrast, the German 'Institut für Mittelstandsforschung' considers as 'SMEs' those companies that employ fewer than 500 employees and have an annual turnover not exceeding €50 million. See Institut für Mittelstandsforschung Bonn, 'KMU-Definition des IfM Bonn' <http://www.ifm-bonn.org/definitionen/kmu-definition-des-ifm-bonn/> accessed 20 January 2017. See also Rudolf Adlung and Marta Soprana, Annex of this volume.

[2] Data based on information from the German Federal Bank.

[3] These figures only include German SMEs with fewer than 250 employees. Excluded are investments of less than €3 million, since they do not fall under the reporting requirements of the Bundesbank.

**Box 9.1 Economic importance of SMEs in Germany (2013)**

- Approx 3.62 million companies were SMEs, constituting 99.6 per cent of all companies.
- German SMEs achieved a turnover of approx €2.16 trillion—35.5 per cent of the turnover of all German companies.
- German SMEs employed approx 16.14 million people (ie 59.2 per cent of all employees in Germany paying social contributions).
- 82.2 per cent of all apprentices were employed in companies with fewer than 500 employees.
- Export turnover generated by German SMEs amounted to approx €198.6 billion (ie 18 per cent of all exports of German companies).
- German SMEs contributed approx 55.5 per cent to total GDP generated by German companies.
- SMEs with fewer than 500 employees had a share of 13.2 per cent (€9 billion) in all R&D expenses by German companies.

Source: Institut für Mittelstandsforschung Bonn, 'Mittelstand im Überblick' <http://www.ifm-bonn.org/statistiken/mittelstand-im-ueberblick/#accordion=0&tab=0> accessed 20 January 2017.

SMEs in the overall FDI stock amounted to 4 per cent. The share of SMEs among all investors was 20 per cent, and the share of subsidiaries 8 per cent.

The importance of SMEs as outward investors is also documented in the number, share, and amount of investment guarantees granted to these enterprises. Between 2008 and 2012, the share of German SMEs among all German recipients of investment guarantees stood at an average of 20 per cent. The annual number of SMEs benefiting from a new guarantee averaged twenty-four companies. The annual average volume of the guarantees granted to SMEs was €112 million (Table 9.1).

Looking at the sectoral distribution of foreign investment activities of European SMEs, research and transport are predominant, but many other industries also play a significant role (Figure 9.2).

Domestic policies play an important role in supporting SMEs in their internationalization strategies. Entrepreneurship policies, support for business start-ups, and R&D promotion are crucial for making SMEs 'fit' for cooperation with transnational corporations (TNCs), for deriving maximum benefit out of this collaboration and minimizing associated risks, as well as for preparing SMEs for becoming foreign investors in their own right.[4] Export promotion, for instance through export guarantees, assistance in the establishment of business contacts, and the provision of information about foreign markets help SMEs when making their 'first steps' into foreign markets. Investment guarantees, preferential public loans, and

[4] See also Fiorina Mugione and Fulvia Farinelli, Chapter 13 of this volume.

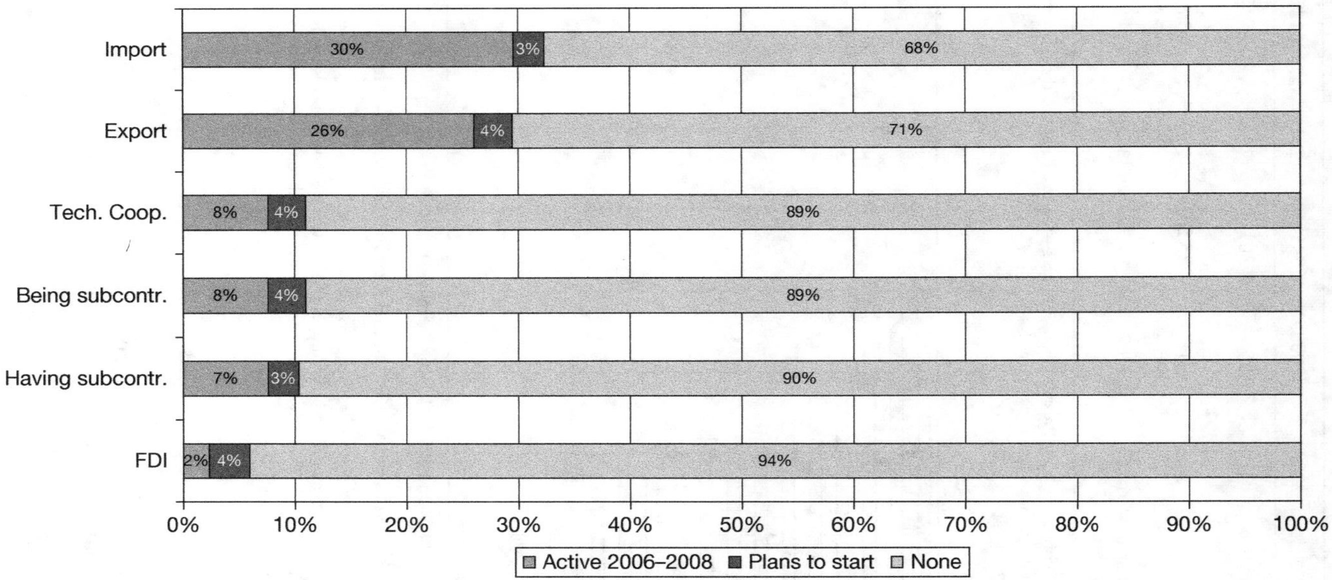


**Figure 9.1** Percentage of European SMEs involved in international business activities

Source: European Commission, 'Internationalisation of European SMEs' (Final Report, Brussels 2010) 15 <http://ec.europa.eu/DocsRoom/documents/10008/attachments/1/translations/en/renditions/native> accessed 20 January 2017.

**Table 9.1** Share of German SMEs in the granting of investment guarantees

| | 2008 | 2009 | 2010 | 2011 | 2012 |
|---|---|---|---|---|---|
| Number of new guarantees for SMEs | 25 | 25 | 30 | 24 | 17 |
| Share among all new guarantees | 22.94% | 21.74% | 23.26% | 18.32% | 13.82% |
| Volume of new guarantees of SMEs (million €) | 162.6 | 48.9 | 94.7 | 39.1 | 214.9 |

Note: Data based on information from PricewaterhouseCoopers—the mandatary of the German Government for the granting of investment guarantees.

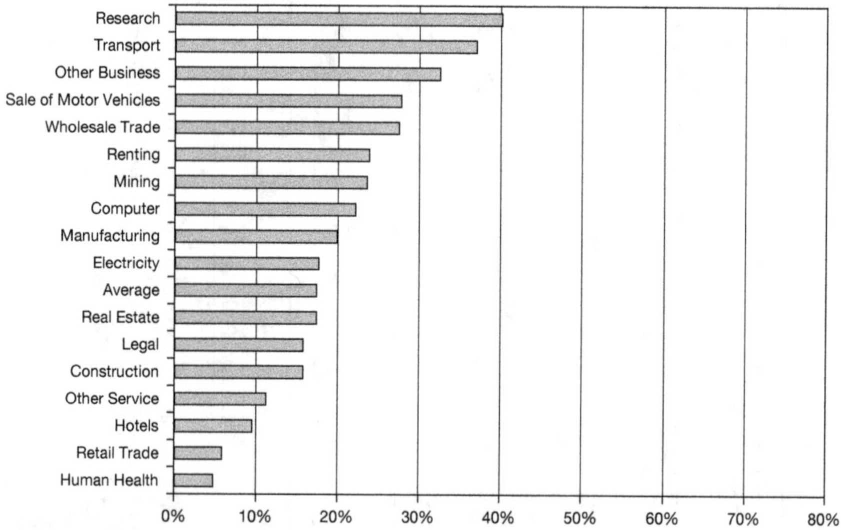


**Figure 9.2** Percentage of SMEs with FDI, technical cooperation, and/or foreign subcontractor relationships (2006–2008, by sector)

Source: European Commission, 'Internationalisation of European SMEs' (Final Report, Brussels 2010) 27 <http://ec.europa.eu/DocsRoom/documents/10008/attachments/1/translations/en/renditions/native> accessed 20 January 2017.

information services about foreign business opportunities support SMEs once they have reached the stage where they are able to invest abroad.

This chapter focuses on an additional policy instrument to assist SMEs, namely the role of international investment law. To what extent do international investment policies cover investments by SMEs? Do they contain any specific rules or support for them? Is the current situation satisfactory from an SME perspective and where would there be room for improving the situation of SMEs in international investment law?

## B. SMEs in International Investment Law

### I. The specific situation of SMEs as international investors

SMEs often find themselves in a particular situation compared to larger companies with respect to foreign investment (Table 9.2).

As investors, SMEs may be confronted with particular challenges when planning, implementing, and operating an investment abroad. First, they may face financial and managerial constraints, as well as a lack of knowledge of and experience with foreign markets, together with language problems. Second, unfamiliarity with foreign legal systems and limited knowledge of protection afforded under international investment agreements may make it more difficult for them to invest compared to larger investors.[5] Third, SMEs usually have a weaker bargaining power than multinationals, putting them in an inferior position when negotiating with host country authorities. They may therefore not be able to secure the best possible conditions for their investment, both with regard to the establishment in the host country and the subsequent operational phase, including the settlement of disputes with the host country. Fourth, SMEs might suffer from potential disadvantages with regard to the granting of investment incentives as countries may be biased in favour of some mega projects. Fifth, SMEs may not have the financial means to pursue international arbitration in case of an investor-state dispute.[6]

However, many SMEs, in particular in developing countries, do not wish or are not able to establish business relations abroad. For them, the issue is therefore not so much what kind of obstacles they would face as foreign investors, but how they could become *suppliers of TNCs* in industries where they have comparative advantages (eg agriculture, agro-processing, tourism, small-scale manufacturing, and services).[7] Domestic SMEs may have difficulties in connecting with foreign TNCs and their subsidiaries, because they fail to make themselves known or because of language and other cultural barriers. Moreover, SMEs may have problems complying with quality and other standards (corporate social responsibility standards) imposed on them by their foreign business partners.

In addition, domestic SMEs may perceive the presence of larger foreign investors in their home market as a threat to their existence. TNCs may—intentionally or unintentionally—crowd out smaller competitors.[8]

[5] Laza Kekic and Karl P Sauvant (eds), *World Investment Prospects to 2011: Foreign Direct Investment and the Challenge of Political Risk* (Economist Intelligence Unit 2007) 96; Jason Webb Yackee, 'How Much Do U.S. Corporations Know (and Care) About Bilateral Investment Treaties? Some Hints from New Survey Evidence' (Vale Columbia Center on Sustainable International Investment, Columbia FDI Perspectives No 31, 23 November 2010) 2.

[6] See also Alexander Gebert, Chapter 11 of this volume; and Perry S Bechky, Chapter 10 of this volume.

[7] UNCTAD, 'Integrating Developing Countries' SMEs into Global Value Chains' (United Nations 2010) <http://unctad.org/en/Docs/diaeed20095_en.pdf> accessed 20 January 2017.

[8] See Tilman Michael Dralle, Chapter 4 of this volume.

**Table 9.2** Major obstacles for SMEs in their internationalization strategies

| Export | FDI |
|---|---|
| • Foreign legal jurisdiction | • Foreign legal jurisdiction |
| • Administrative procedures for export business | • Lack of suitable business partners |
| • Customer payment practice | • Problems regarding bureaucracy |
| • Export financing | • Export financing |
| | • Language barrier |
| | • Lack of international experience |

Source: Kreditanstalt für Wiederaufbau (KfW), 'Internationalisation in Germany's SME Sector—Step by Step to Global Presence' (Frankfurt am Main 2012) paras 14–19 <https://www.kfw.de/Download-Center/Konzernthemen/Research/Research-englisch/PDF-Dateien-Paper-and-Proceedings/Internationalisation-in-Germanys-SME-sector.pdf> accessed 20 January 2017.

On the other hand, being small can also have some advantages. SMEs investing abroad may be less on the 'radar screen' of host country authorities, for instance in respect of national security concerns or with regard to potential 'crowding out' concerns of local enterprises. SMEs may therefore face less political opposition in host countries. SMEs may also be more flexible than TNCs in their business operations. This may allow them to react to regulatory or political changes in the host country more quickly, including through a possible divestment if the investment climate deteriorates substantially. In addition, domestic SMEs may actually benefit from host country policies with regard to FDI. For instance, in 2012, the Indian Government opened multi-brand retailing to foreign investors only under the condition that they source a certain minimum of food and services from local firms.[9]

## II. Regional promotion of internationalization strategies of SMEs

Numerous regional economic integration schemes include support programmes for SMEs. This reflects the fact that—as explained above—SMEs wishing to invest abroad may have considerable logistical, managerial, and other difficulties due to their lack of knowledge of and experience with the host country. In addition, domestic SMEs in the host country might face considerable difficulties in connecting with incoming foreign investors.

Adopted in June 2008, the European Union's 'Small Business Act for Europe'[10] reflects the Commission's political will to recognize the central role of SMEs in the EU economy and for the first time puts into place a comprehensive SME policy

[9] Government of India, Ministry of Commerce and Industry, 'Press Note No 5' (2012 Series, 20 September 2012) <http://dipp.nic.in/english/acts_rules/Press_Notes/pn5_2012.pdf> accessed 20 January 2017. See also Tilman Michael Dralle, Chapter 4 of this volume.

[10] European Commission, '"Think Small First": A "Small Business Act" for Europe' (Communication, 25 June 2008) COM(2008) 394 final.

framework for the European Union and its Member States. It aims to improve the overall approach to entrepreneurship, permanently anchor the 'Think Small First' principle in policymaking from regulation to public service, and to promote SMEs' growth by helping them tackle the remaining problems which hamper their development.

Accordingly, the European Commission has developed a programme for SME support, called 'Small Business, Big World: A New Partnership to Help SMEs Seize Global Opportunities'.[11] It aims to expand their business outside the European Union through six fields of action: strengthening and mapping the existing supply of support services; creating a single virtual gateway to information for SMEs; making support schemes at the EU level more consistent; promoting clusters and networks for SME internationalization; rationalizing new activities in priority markets; and leveraging existing EU external policies.

NAFTA established an SME Task Force to propose several action items that would help SMEs reap the benefits of NAFTA integration and the development of regional supply chains. The NAFTA Commission instructed officials to identify additional means, including the production of informational materials and existing platforms to allow SMEs to take more advantage of export opportunities.

One of the main challenges faced by SMEs is access to information. To address this issue, the publication 'NAFTA Certificate of Origin: Frequently Asked Questions' has been designed to answer basic questions about completing the NAFTA Certificate of Origin form and made available on the web.[12] Furthermore, 'Small Business Development Centers' (SBDCs) in the United States and Mexico are linking SMEs for trade opportunities through an interactive platform, called 'SBDCGlobal.com'. Canada is exploring the potential to join this network.[13]

In APEC, a 'Small and Medium Enterprises Working Group (SMEWG)' encourages the development of SMEs and helps to build their capacity to engage in international trade. The SMEWG works towards the achievement of the so-called APEC 'Bogor Goals' by fostering enabling business environments for SMEs to grow and develop into export-ready (internationalized) firms, through the sharing of information on best practice initiatives and conducting capacity-building activities. In August 2012, the ministers, at their Nineteenth Meeting in Saint Petersburg, endorsed the SMEWG Strategic Plan for 2013 to 2016, which provides a roadmap to address critical issues and concerns pertaining to the growth of SMEs and micro-enterprises in the APEC region. Priority areas for action include: (i) building

[11] European Commission, 'Small Business, Big World: A New Partnership to Help SMEs Seize Global Opportunities' (Communication, 9 November 2011) COM(2011) 702 final.

[12] Michael Froman, Ildefonso Guajardo Villarreal, and Edward Fast, 'The NAFTA Certificate of Origin: Frequently Asked Questions' <http://www.economia.gob.mx/files/nafta_certificate_of_origin_2014.pdf> accessed 20 January 2017.

[13] NAFTA Free Trade Commission, '2012 NAFTA Commission Meeting, Joint Statement' (3 April 2012) <http://www.international.gc.ca/trade-agreements-accords-commerciaux/agr-acc/nafta-alena/js-washington-dc.aspx?lang=eng> accessed 20 January 2017.

management capability, entrepreneurship, and innovation; (ii) financing; and (iii) business environment, market access, and internationalization.[14]

In 2015, 'fostering SMEs' participation in the regional and global markets' was chosen as one of the four priorities to promote inclusive growth. The discussions on micro, small, and medium enterprises (MSMEs) have been guided by a collective desire to provide MSMEs with opportunities to contribute to the region's growth. The APEC ministers responsible for trade (MRT) endorsed in May 2015 the 'Boracay Action Agenda to Globalize MSMEs'.[15] The APEC finance ministers agreed to the 'Cebu Action Plan', which aims, among other things, to improve policy frameworks that enable MSMEs to use their transaction records and a broader range of collateral to access loans, and expand trade and supply chain finance.[16] Furthermore, the APEC ministers responsible for SMEs adopted in September 2015 the 'Iloilo Initiative', which sets priorities on: (i) providing a bigger voice and better opportunities for MSMEs; and (ii) advancing policy frameworks to promote MSME participation in global value chains (GVCs) and international trade through the APEC MSME marketplace.[17]

ASEAN developed a Strategic Action Plan for SME development, the goals of which are: (i) enhancing internationalization of SMEs and SME marketing capabilities; (ii) improving SME access to finance; (iii) strengthening SME human resource development and capacity building; (iv) incubator and local SME development; (v) establishing an SME service centre/ASEAN SME service desk; and (vi) setting up an ASEAN SME regional development fund.

Programmes and policies to achieve these six goals include, for example: (1) SME entrepreneurship and human resource development; (2) SME capacity building in management, marketing, networking and supply chain formation, technology, and financing; (3) level policy playing field for SMEs, including information dissemination on and inter-agency coordination to enable SMEs to take advantage of the various ASEAN Trade and Investment Agreements; and (4) public-private sector partnership for SME development and networking.[18]

[14] APEC, 'Small and Medium Enterprises Working Group' (2016) <http://www.apec.org/Groups/SOM-Steering-Committee-on-Economic-and-Technical-Cooperation/Working-Groups/Small-and-Medium-Enterprises.aspx> accessed 20 January 2017.

[15] APEC, 'Boracay Action Agenda to Globalize MSMEs' (24 May 2015) <http://www.apec.org/Meeting-Papers/Sectoral-Ministerial-Meetings/Trade/2015_trade/2015_mrt_standalone.aspx> accessed 20 January 2017.

[16] APEC, 'APEC Finance Ministers Launch Cebu Action Plan' (11 September 2015) <http://www.apec.org/Press/News-Releases/2015/0911_FM.aspx> accessed 20 January 2017.

[17] APEC, 'The APEC Iloilo Initiative: Growing Global MSMEs for Inclusive Development' (25 September 2015) <http://www.apec.org/Meeting-Papers/Sectoral-Ministerial-Meetings/Small-and-Medium-Enterprise/2015_sme/Annex%20A.aspx> accessed 20 January 2017.

[18] ASEAN, 'ASEAN Strategic Action Plan for SME Development (2010–2015)' <http://www.asean.org/storage/images/archive/SME/SPOA-SME.pdf> accessed 20 January 2017; ASEAN, 'ASEAN Strategic Action Plan for SME Development 2016–2025' <http://www.asean.org/?static_post=asean-strategic-action-plan-for-sme-development-2016-2025-2> accessed 20 January 2017.

In Africa, the Treaty establishing the COMESA,[19] inter alia, identifies target areas for technical cooperation, including with regard to SME development.[20]

Likewise, the treaty establishing the ECOWAS explicitly mentions the promotion of SMEs through the creation of an enabling environment (Article 3(2)(g)) as a means of economic development.[21]

Furthermore, the African Development Bank (AfDB) runs the 'Africa Small and Medium Enterprises (SME) Program', a four-year, US$125 million funding programme combined with a US$3.98 million technical assistance package granted by the Fund for African Private Sector Assistance (FAPA), aiming at supporting micro, small, and medium enterprises in Africa. The programme provides standardized lines of credit and technical assistance to targeted financial institutions, predominantly in low-income countries spread over all five African regions.[22]

In South America, MERCOSUR developed a 'Policy Support for Micro, Small and Medium Enterprises'. It includes the creation of regional lenders to support these enterprises, tax harmonization, and the implementation of training programmes to sustain competitiveness, among others.[23] The Andean Community established a Committee for Micro, Small and Medium Enterprises in 2011. It is tasked with formulating regional strategies to strengthen SMEs through technological innovation, partnerships, and internationalization.[24]

## III. The treatment of SMEs in international investment agreements

### 1. *The importance of IIAs from an SME perspective*

The most important international policy instruments relating to foreign investment are international investment agreements (IIAs). Their main objective is to

[19] Treaty establishing the Common Market for Eastern & South Africa (signed 5 November 1994, entered into force 8 December 1994) (1994) 33 International Legal Materials 1067 (COMESA Treaty) <http://www.comesa.int/summit2016/wp-content/uploads/2016/09/160920_Latest_Comesa_Treaty.pdf> accessed 20 January 2017.

[20] COMESA Treaty, Arts 62, 100, 146, 151, 155.

[21] Revised Treaty of the Economic Community of West African States (ECOWAS) (signed 24 July 1993) (1996) 35 International Legal Materials 660 <http://www.ecowas.int/wp-content/uploads/2015/01/Revised-treaty.pdf> accessed 20 January 2017.

[22] African Development Bank Group, 'The AfDB SME Program Approval: Boosting Inclusive Growth in Africa' (22 July 2013) <http://www.afdb.org/en/news-and-events/article/the-afdb-sme-program-approval-boosting-inclusive-growth-in-africa-12135> accessed 20 January 2017.

[23] MERCOSUR, 'Políticas de Apoyo a las Micro, Pequeñas y Medianas Empresas del MERCOSUR—Etapa II' (MERCOSUR/GMC/RES No 59/98) <http://www.saij.gob.ar/convert-html-to-pdf?url=/59-internacional-politicas-apoyo-micro-pequenas-medianas-empresas-mercosur-etapa-ii-rmr1998000059-1998-12-08/123456789-0abc-de9-5000-08991rserced&name=politicas-de-apoyo-a-las-micro.pdf> accessed 20 January 2017.

[24] Comunidad Andina, 'Creación del Comité Andino de la Micro, Pequeña y Mediana Empresa' (Decisión 748) <http://www.sice.oas.org/trade/junac/Decisiones/DEC748s.pdf> accessed 20 January 2017.

promote and protect foreign investors in the host country. To this purpose, IIAs shield investors against certain political risks, in particular the risk of discrimination, expropriation, and capital transfer restrictions. Most IIAs also allow foreign investors to start international arbitration against the host country in case of an alleged violation of treaty obligations.

Over more than fifty years, the IIA universe has expanded dynamically, consisting of a myriad of more than 3,200 bilateral, regional, sectoral, and plurilateral agreements (Figure 9.3). In parallel, the number of investment disputes has risen substantially, from almost zero some twenty years ago to more than 600 at the end of 2014.

One important development is the recent move towards regional and mega-regional IIAs.[25] Furthermore, recent years have witnessed a number of innovative features in IIAs, such as giving more weight to governments' rights to regulate FDI in the public interest, a clarification of the meaning of certain treaty articles, more provisions on investment promotion, and a reform of the investor-state dispute settlement system. Some of these revisions are particularly interesting from an SME perspective.

Depending on whether a country is predominantly a source or a recipient of FDI, it may have different strategies when negotiating an IIA. Industrialized countries, being net capital exporters and having strong domestic companies, including SMEs, are likely to focus on the role of SMEs as outward investors and how IIAs could further improve their position abroad. They will thus seek strong investment promotion and protection provisions. Many developing countries, by contrast, will tend to concentrate on the role of domestic SMEs as potential suppliers or competitors of TNCs. These countries are likely to focus on investment promotion—in particular, 'matchmaking' services to bring TNCs and local SMEs together. Furthermore, they may wish to take a defensive stance as far as establishment rights of foreign investors are at stake, if they see the entry of foreign TNCs as a potential threat for their domestic SMEs.

## 2. *The general treatment of SMEs in IIAs*

The core IIA provisions (the principle of non-discrimination, fair and equitable treatment, protection against expropriation or nationalization, capital transfer rights, dispute settlement) protect foreign investors independent of their size. It could hardly be argued that SMEs would need more protection than other categories of investors, since they do not face higher political risk in host countries than bigger companies.

[25] UNCTAD, *World Investment Report 2013: Global Value Chains: Investment and Trade for Development* (United Nations 2013) 103 <http://unctad.org/en/publicationslibrary/wir2013_en.pdf> accessed 20 January 2017; UNCTAD, *World Investment Report 2014: Investing in the SDGs: An Action Plan* (United Nations 2014) 114 <http://unctad.org/en/publicationslibrary/wir2014_en.pdf> accessed 20 January 2017.

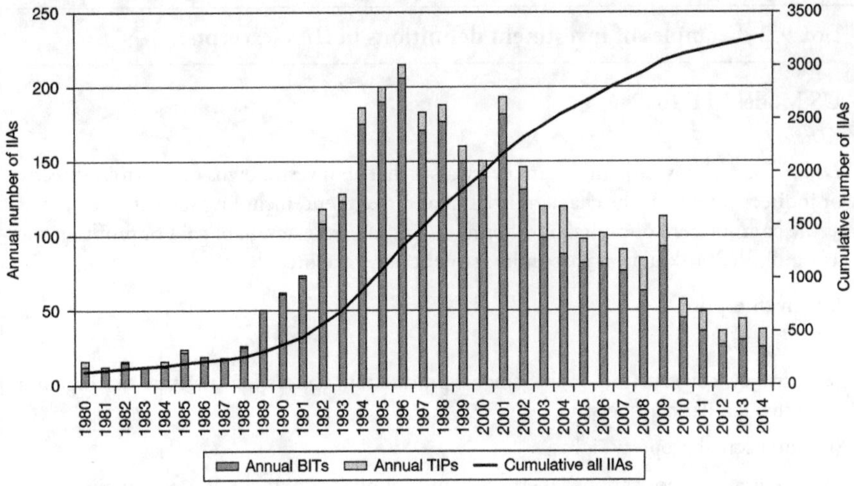


**Figure 9.3** Trends in IIAs, 1980–2014

Source: UNCTAD, 'World Investment Report 2015: Reforming International Investment Governance' (UN Publication, New York and Geneva 2015) 106 <http://unctad.org/en/PublicationsLibrary/wir2015_en.pdf> accessed 20 January 2017.

However, this legal equality of investors under IIAs would not impede contracting parties to reflect specific SME needs in generally applicable IIA provisions.

### (a) Acknowledging the special situation of SMEs in the preamble

IIA preambles spell out the overall policy objectives associated with the conclusion of a treaty. Typically, IIAs mention the strengthening of economic cooperation between the treaty partners as a main objective. Negotiating parties wishing to enhance the position of SMEs could do so by adding preamble language for this purpose. While not legally binding, such text could nevertheless send a political signal about the importance the contracting parties attach to SMEs in the context of foreign investment, including the spillover and multiplier effect that FDI can have on domestic SMEs.

### (b) Definition of 'investment'

Most IIAs cover as 'investment' any kind of asset of an investor in the host country. However, a considerable number of IIAs follow an alternative approach and use an enterprise-based definition, thereby mainly limiting 'investment' to the establishment of a subsidiary or branch in the host country. Box 9.2 provides examples for both approaches.

As mentioned above, SMEs may neither have the financial means nor be interested in setting up an affiliate in a foreign country. Rather, they may prefer to cooperate with foreign business partners in the host country through licensing agreements, in the form of contract manufacturing or contract farming. From an SME perspective, it is therefore important whether such non-equity forms of

**Box 9.2 Examples of investment definitions in IIAs (excerpts)**

**US Model BIT 2012**

*Article 1*

*Definitions* … 'investment' means every asset that an investor owns or controls, directly or indirectly, that has the characteristics of an investment, including such characteristics as the commitment of capital or other resources, the expectation of gain or profit, or the assumption of risk. Forms that an investment may take include:

(a) an enterprise;

(b)–(d) …

(e) turnkey, construction, management, production, concession, revenue-sharing, and other similar contracts;

(f) intellectual property rights;

(g) licenses, authorizations, permits, and similar rights conferred pursuant to domestic law …

**German Model BIT 2009**

*Article 1*

*Definitions* Within the meaning of this Treaty, 1. the term 'investments' comprises every kind of asset which is directly or indirectly invested by investors of one Contracting State in the territory of the other Contracting State. The investments include in particular:

(a) movable and immovable property …

(b) …

(c) claims to money which has been used to create an economic value or claims to any performance having an economic value;

(d) intellectual property rights, in particular copyrights and related rights, patents, utility-model patents, industrial designs, trademarks, plant variety rights;

(e) trade-names, trade and business secrets, technical processes, know-how, and good-will;

(f) …

Note: Text is available at the UNCTAD investment policy hub website: <http://investmentpolicyhub.unctad.org> accessed 20 January 2017.

investment are covered by the IIA. An asset-based definition of 'investment' would usually be broad enough to capture these forms of economic cooperation.[26] To erase remaining doubts, IIA negotiating parties have the possibility of including an illustrative list of possible forms of investment covered by the treaty.

[26] As to this issue, see also Perry S Bechky, Chapter 10 of this volume.

**Box 9.3 The development of international model contracts**

Some international efforts have been undertaken to establish model contracts for non-equity forms of investment (NEMs).

For example, the Model International Franchising Contract, issued by the International Chamber of Commerce (ICC), provides franchisors and franchisees with drafting suggestions.[i] The 1998 International Institute for the Unification of Private Law (UNIDROIT) Guide to International Master Franchising Arrangements (in its 2007 revision) comprehensively examines and explains master franchise arrangements.[ii] Some of these international initiatives also aim at addressing potential negative effects of NEMs. For instance, in terms of strengthening the bargaining power of domestic NEM partners, the 2002 Model Franchise Disclosure Law[iii] developed by UNIDROIT addresses pre-contractual disclosure on the part of the franchisor, and the ICC Model Contract explicitly aims at striking a balance between the interests of the franchisor and franchisee.[iv]

It could be beneficial for SMEs if such model contracts could also be developed for other types of NEMs, such as contract manufacturing, contract farming, and licensing.

Notes:

[i] International Chamber of Commerce (ICC), *ICC Model International Franchising Contract* (2nd edn, Paris 2011) <http://store.iccwbo.org/content/uploaded/pdf/ICC-Model-International-Franchising-Contract.pdf> accessed 20 January 2017.

[ii] International Institute for the Unification of Private Law (UNIDROIT), *Guide to International Master Franchising Arrangements* (2nd edn, Rome 2007) <http://www.unidroit.org/english/guides/2007franchising/franchising2007-guide-2nd-e.pdf> accessed 20 January 2017.

[iii] International Institute for the Unification of Private Law (UNIDROIT), *Model Franchise Disclosure Law* (Rome 2002) <http://www.unidroit.org/english/modellaws/2002franchise/2002modellaw-e.pdf> accessed 20 January 2017.

[iv] UNCTAD, 'World Investment Report 2011, Non-Equity Modes of International Production and Development' (UN Publication 2011) 171 <http://unctad.org/en/docs/wir2011_embargoed_en.pdf> accessed 20 January 2017.

In addition—and outside the scope of IIAs—it can help SMEs to develop model contracts for specific forms of non-equity modes of investment (Box 9.3).

### (c) Investment promotion and facilitation

A small minority of IIAs include provisions on investment promotion and facilitation. These provisions are not SME-specific, but apply to foreign investors independent of their size (Box 9.4).

From an SME perspective, it could be useful to supplement these general investment promotion provisions by concrete examples on what such promotion should look like. Some IIAs mention, for instance, matchmaking services of national investment promotion agencies or the organization of industrial fairs. It could also be helpful to recognize in IIAs the specific needs of SMEs in respect of investment facilitation, for example, through a designation of a particular host country agency, dealing with investment applications from SMEs.

**Box 9.4 IIA and investment promotion**

**1. Technical assistance and capacity building**

1993 Cooperation Agreement between the EU and India on Partnership and Development

*Article 4*

*Economic cooperation*

...

2. The Contracting Parties agree that economic cooperation will involve three broad fields of action:

...

(b) facilitating contacts between economic operators and other measures designed to promote commercial exchanges and investment

...

4. The Contracting Parties shall consider in particular the following means to achieve these aims:

- exchange of information and ideas,
- preparation of studies,
- provision of technical assistance,
- training programmes,
- establishment of links between research and training centres, specialized agencies and business organizations,
- promotion of investment and joint ventures.

**2. Host country incentives**

*Czech Republic—UAE BIT*

*Article 2*

Promotion and Protection of Investments

...

(4)(i) Each Contracting State shall endeavour to take the necessary measures in accordance with its legislation for granting of appropriate facilities, incentives and other forms of encouragement for investments

...

**3. Investment guarantees**

*Partnership Agreement between the ACP States and the EU*

*Article 77*

1. Investment guarantees are an increasingly important tool for development finance as they contribute to reducing project risks and inducing private capital

flows. Cooperation shall therefore ensure the increasing availability and use of risk insurance as a risk-mitigating mechanism in order to boost investor confidence in the ACP States.

2. Cooperation shall offer guarantees and assist with guarantees funds covering risks for qualified investment....

Source: UNCTAD, 'Investment Promotion Provisions in International Investment Agreements' (New York and Geneva 2008) 30–38, 43–48 <http://unctad.org/en/docs/iteiit20077_en.pdf> accessed 20 January 2017.

### 3. *SME-specific IIA provisions*

SME-specific IIA provisions can only be found in a small minority of agreements (Box 9.5). They focus on cooperation between the contracting parties as regards the promotion of SME development.

### 4. *IIA provisions with potential negative side effects on SMEs*

Some IIA provisions might have some negative effects on domestic SMEs in their role as suppliers or competitors of TNCs. Careful drafting of these IIA clauses and investment-related policies at the domestic level can avoid that such effects materialize.

#### (a) Establishment rights for foreign investors

Although still a minority, numerous IIAs include an entry right for foreign investors, usually meaning that foreign investors shall not be discriminated against vis-à-vis domestic investors in respect of their establishment in the host country.[27] Such IIA provisions can be a mixed blessing for SMEs. While they would benefit from such a right when investing abroad, it could hurt them at home insofar as their foreign competitors receive an establishment right in the SMEs' domestic market. This could increase the risk of being crowded out by larger and more efficient TNCs.

A crucial issue is whether foreign TNCs, once established in the host country, would rather become business partners or competitors for domestic SMEs. The latter scenario may materialize in industries so far dominated by SMEs, such as local retailing or farming. Caution is needed in particular if the IIA were to open an industry to foreigners for the first time rather than 'only' confirming an already existing openness. Even in the latter case, establishment rights in IIAs may have important implications, because once a country has confirmed its openness to foreign investors in an international treaty, this policy would be difficult to reverse.

To reduce the risk of crowding out domestic SMEs, host countries need an effective competition policy to monitor potential abuses of a dominant market position

[27] This is the case, for example, for bilateral investment treaties of the United States and Canada, or for free trade agreements of the European Union that include investment provisions.

**Box 9.5 Examples of SME promotion provisions in bilateral IIAs**

**EC–Egypt IIA**

*Article 46*

Co-operation shall aim at increasing the flow of capital, expertise and technology to Egypt through, inter alia:

- …
- examining the creation of joint ventures, especially for SMEs and, when appropriate, the conclusion of agreements between the Member States and Egypt;
- …

**EC–Montenegro IIA**

*Article 95*

*Small and medium-sized enterprises* Cooperation between the Parties shall be aimed at developing and strengthening private sector small and medium-sized enterprises (SMEs), the establishment of new undertakings in areas offering potential for growth and cooperation between SMEs in the Community and in Montenegro. Cooperation shall take due account of priority areas related to the Community acquis in the field of SMEs, as well as the ten guidelines enshrined in the European Charter for Small Enterprises.

**Japan–Philippines EPA (Implementing Agreement)**

*Chapter 11*

*Cooperation in the Field of Small and Medium Enterprises*
*Article 45*

*General Principles* Pursuant to Chapter 14 of the Basic Agreement, the Parties, recognizing the fundamental role of small and medium enterprises (hereinafter referred to in this Chapter as 'SMEs') in maintaining the dynamism and enhancing the competitiveness of the national economies of their respective Countries, shall cooperate in promoting the development of SMEs of the Countries.

**Tunisia and Turkey FTA**

*Article 37*

*Co-operation Between Small and Medium-Sized Enterprises*

1. With the view to further enhance trade and economic activities, the Parties shall give priority to promoting business and investment opportunities as well as joint ventures between small and medium sized enterprises (SMEs) of the two countries. Within this context, the Parties will:
   (a) exchange expertise on entrepreneurship, management, research and management centers, quality and production standards;
   (b) provide market information to create investment opportunities;
   (c) furnish published documents concerning SMEs.

Source: UNCTAD, 'Investment Promotion Provisions in International Investment Agreements' (New York and Geneva 2008) 26–28 <http://unctad.org/en/docs/iteiit20077_en.pdf> accessed 20 January 2017.

of foreign investors and to control cartels. Some IIAs underline the importance of competition policies through specific provisions on this subject. For instance, in recent years, a trend has arisen in free trade agreements requiring parties to restrict anticompetitive practices that may impact on cross-border trade between the contracting parties. Such provisions feature, for instance, in EU Association and other free trade agreements of the European Union.[28]

**(b) Access to land**

In many countries, land rights for foreigners are a politically sensitive issue. In particular, there have been allegations of illegal 'land grabbing' by foreigners in recent years, displacing local communities and smallholders. SMEs, for instance in the form of farmer associations or agricultural cooperatives, might become victims of such land grabbing in developing countries.

Whether foreigners can acquire land is predominantly an issue for the domestic law of the host country. However, there are also international efforts to strengthen the position of small domestic landowners. The best-known example up to now is the case of the joint FAO/UNCTAD/World Bank/IFAD Principles for Responsible Agricultural Investment, which respect rights, livelihoods, and resources.[29] They are intended to provide a framework for national regulations, international investment agreements, global corporate social responsibility initiatives, and individual investor contracts. More international support for these principles could indirectly help SMEs to defend their claims to land.

**(c) State support for SMEs and the issue of non-discrimination**

Many countries maintain special support programmes for SMEs, providing them with financial or other assistance, such as improved access to finance, R&D-related subsidies, or training of SME employees. From the perspective of domestic SMEs, it is important to ensure that IIAs do not unduly reduce policy space of host countries in the design and implementation of these programmes. One IIA provision that has the potential of negatively affecting the freedom of host countries to provide assistance to domestic SMEs is the non-discrimination principle. The standard of national treatment obliges IIA contracting parties to treat foreign investors no less favourably than domestic investors, including with regard to the granting of subsidies.

Host countries face the risk that foreign investors—independent of their size—use the national treatment principle for claiming subsidies exclusively designed for SMEs. Such a scenario could indirectly have negative consequences for SMEs, since

[28] UNCTAD, 'Competition, Competitiveness and Development: Lessons from Developing Countries' (United Nations 2004) 34 <http://unctad.org/en/Docs/ditcclp20041_en.pdf> accessed 20 January 2017.

[29] UNCTAD and others, 'The Principles for Responsible Agricultural Investment (PRAI)' (25 January 2010) <http://unctad.org/en/Pages/DIAE/G-20/PRAI.aspx> accessed 20 January 2017.

the host country—rather than extending the subsidies to all companies—may feel compelled to stop the SME subsidy programme altogether ('freezing effect').

Numerous investment treaties seek to reduce the risk of IIAs interfering with national subsidy programmes by explicitly stating that the principle of national treatment only applies to investors 'in like circumstances'. This can clarify that subsidies reserved for SMEs do not have to be extended to bigger companies. Some countries have gone even one step further by including an explicit carve-out of subsidies for domestic SMEs from the scope of application of the national treatment principle in their IIAs. This means that even those foreign investors that are SMEs cannot claim subsidies that the host country grants its domestic SMEs.

For example, Protocol 2 of the bilateral investment treaty (BIT) between Indonesia and Switzerland allows derogating from national treatment of Swiss investors 'in view of the present stage of development of the Indonesian national economy'.[30] However, Indonesia would grant 'identical or compensating facilities to investments and nationals of the Swiss Confederation in similar economic activities'.[31] Germany has accepted certain exceptions to national treatment provided that these are undertaken for development purposes only, for example the development of small-scale industries, and that the measures do not substantially impair investments from a German investor.[32] The BIT between Italy and Morocco provides:

> Investors of the two Contracting Parties shall not be entitled to national treatment in terms of benefiting from aid, grants, loans, insurance and guarantees accorded by the Government of one of the Contracting Parties exclusively to its own nationals or enterprises within the framework of activities carried out under national development programs.[33]

Several FTAs derogate from the treaty obligations on national treatment, most favoured nation treatment and performance requirements in favour of domestic SMEs. For instance, in the India–Japan Economic Partnership Agreement (EPA), India excludes SMEs in sectors such as wood and wood products, leather, and tobacco from the prohibition to impose certain performance requirements. It also excludes SMEs in all industries from the obligation to grant national treatment and most favoured nation (MFN) treatment.[34]

One can also think of general industry-specific exceptions to the principle of non-discrimination. If a host country wishes to favour its domestic SMEs, and such SMEs are predominantly active in certain industries, a carve-out from the national treatment principle of subsidies provided to this industry would indirectly have a similar effect as a direct carve-out for SMEs.

[30] UNCTAD, 'Bilateral Investment Treaties in the Mid-1990s' (UN Publications No E.98.II.D.8, 1998) 64.

[31] ibid. [32] ibid.

[33] UNCTAD, 'National Treatment' (UN Publications No E.99.II.D.16, 1999) 49–50.

[34] Comprehensive Economic Partnership Agreement between Japan and the Republic of India (16 February 2011) <http://www.mofa.go.jp/region/asia-paci/india/epa201102/pdfs/ijcepa_ba_e.pdf> accessed 20 January 2017.

### (d) Prohibition of performance requirements

From a host country point of view, it is a key challenge to help domestic SMEs to link to foreign TNCs, and to generate spillover and multiplier effects for the local economy. This may be achieved through incentivizing foreign investors to establish such linkages, but also through mandatory performance requirements imposed upon foreign investors to cooperate with domestic SMEs.[35] An intermediary policy approach is to condition the granting of subsidies or other advantages to the fulfilment of certain performance requirements, such as an obligation to source locally, to transfer technology or know-how, to employ or to train domestic personnel.

Most IIAs are silent on the issue of performance requirements, thus leaving it to the discretion of the host countries as to whether to impose them or not, provided that they are not discriminatory in nature. More recent IIAs, however, show a certain trend towards limiting the use of performance requirements. The most prominent example is the WTO Agreement on Trade Related Investment Measures (TRIMS) prohibiting certain export-related performance requirements that are in violation of the national treatment principle of the General Agreement on Tariffs and Trade (GATT) or the imposition of quantitative restrictions. Some IIAs have gone even further by extending the prohibitions to service-related performance requirements and others (Box 9.6).

By losing the right to impose certain performance requirements, host countries may give up a policy tool to help domestic SMEs integrate into the network of TNCs. On the other hand, it is questionable as to what extent mandatory performance requirements could actually achieve their objective, since TNCs may be reluctant to invest in a country where their contractual freedom is severely curtailed.

## IV. Corporate social responsibility and SMEs

In recent years, the issue of corporate social responsibility (CSR) has gained considerable importance as a significant tool to promote sustainable development and inclusive growth. In the context of SMEs, the issue of CSR is being discussed almost exclusively from a compliance angle (ie how policymakers can assist their domestic SMEs in complying with CSR standards of their foreign business partners).[36]

[35] Regarding performance requirements for the pre-establishment phase, see Tilman Michael Dralle, Chapter 4 of this volume.

[36] UNCTAD, *World Investment Report 2012: Towards a New Generation of Investment Policies* (United Nations 2012) 93–95 <http://unctad.org/en/PublicationsLibrary/wir2012_embargoed_en.pdf> accessed 20 January 2017; UNCTAD, 'Corporate Social Responsibility in Global Value Chains: Evaluation and Monitoring Challenges for Small and Medium Sized Suppliers in Developing Countries' (United Nations 2012) <http://unctad.org/en/PublicationsLibrary/diaeed2012d3_en.pdf> accessed 20 January 2017. See also Michael Addo, Chapter 12 of this volume.

**Box 9.6 Example of IIA provisions extending to non-trade-related performance requirements**

Examples of this approach can be found in BITs of Japan, such as the agreement with Viet Nam (2003).

**BIT Japan–Viet Nam (2003)**
*Article 4*

1. Neither Contracting Party shall impose or enforce, as a condition for investment activities in its Area of an investor of the other Contracting Party, any of the following requirements:
   (a) to export a given level or percentage of goods or services;
   (b) to achieve a given level or percentage of domestic content;
   (c) to purchase, use or accord a preference to goods produced or services provided in its Area, or to purchase goods or services from natural or legal persons or any other entity in its Area;
   (d) to relate the volume or value of imports to the volume or value of exports or to the amount of foreign exchange inflows associated with investments of that investor;
   (e) to restrict sales of goods or services in its Area that investments of that investor produces or provides by relating such sales to the volume or value of its exports or foreign exchange earnings;
   (f) to appoint, as executives, managers or members of boards of directors, individuals of any particular nationality;
   (g) to transfer technology, a production process or other proprietary knowledge to a natural or legal person or any other entity in its Area, except when the requirement (i) is imposed or enforced by a court, administrative tribunal or competition authority to remedy an alleged violation of competition laws; or (ii) concerns the transfer of intellectual property rights which is undertaken in a manner not inconsistent with the Agreement on Trade-Related Aspects of Intellectual Property Rights, Annex 1C of the Marrakesh Agreement Establishing the World Trade Organization;
   (h) to locate the headquarters of that investor for a specific region or the world market in its Area;
   (i) to achieve a given level or value of research and development in its Area; or
   (j) to supply one or more of the goods that the investor produces or the services that the investor provides to a specific region or the world market, exclusively from the Area of the former Contracting Party.
2. The provisions of paragraph 1 above do not preclude either Contracting Party from conditioning the receipt or continued receipt of an advantage, in connection with investment activities in its Area of an investor of the other Contracting Party, on compliance with any of the requirements set forth in paragraph 1 (f) through (j) above.

Source: UNCTAD, 'Bilateral Investment Treaties 1995–2006: Trends in Investment Rulemaking' (UN Publications No E.98.II.D.8, New York and Geneva 2007) 67–68 <http://unctad.org/en/docs/iteiia20065_en.pdf> accessed 20 January 2017.

A stronger internationalization of SMEs would call for an approach where these companies not only react to CSR standards as suppliers of foreign investors, but develop their own CSR codes for going abroad. One initiative in this respect was taken by the European Commission, which developed a guidebook on 'improving the quality and quantity of CSR advice available to European SMEs'.[37] In the Asia-Pacific region, APEC is developing business ethics for SMEs, particularly in the health and in engineering and construction sectors.[38]

## V. International investment disputes

SMEs may face particular problems in case of an investment dispute with the host country. The settlement of such disputes is not only expensive and time-consuming; it also requires special legal expertise.[39] In fact, the number of SMEs that resorted to international dispute settlement mechanisms constituted approximately 15 per cent of all disputes from 2008 to 2013 (Figure 9.4).

Most IIAs focus on legally binding international arbitration as the preferred means for settling a dispute between a foreign investor and the host country. However, in light of the above considerations, alternative means of dispute resolution (ADR), such as conciliation and mediation, may be of particular

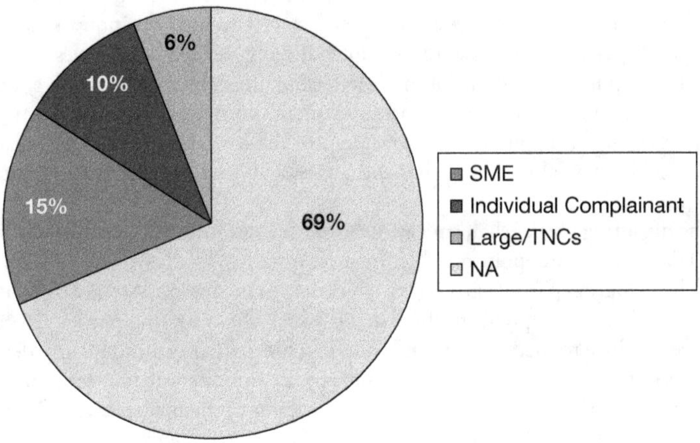


**Figure 9.4** SMEs and international investor-state arbitration, 2008–2013
Source: Based on preliminary UNCTAD research.

[37] European Commission, *Tips and Tricks for Advisors: Corporate Social Responsibility for Small and Medium-Sized Enterprises* (European Union 2013) <http://ec.europa.eu/DocsRoom/documents/10368/attachments/1/translations/en/renditions/pdf> accessed 20 January 2017.

[38] APEC, 'The 20th APEC Small and Medium Enterprises Ministerial Meeting: Joint Ministerial Statement' (7 September 2013) <http://mddb.apec.org/Documents/2013/MM/SMEMM/13_smemm_jms.pdf> accessed 20 January 2017.

[39] See Alexander Gebert, Chapter 11 of this volume.

interest for SMEs. They may have the advantage of being less expensive, less formal, faster, and allowing for a less legalistic approach to find an amicable solution.

Although still a small minority, ADR provisions can be found in an increasing number of IIAs (Box 9.7). To make full use of these mechanisms requires, however, that SMEs become more familiar with them. It is not enough to include ADR in investment agreements; it is equally important that experts and business associations inform and educate about these innovative means to solve an investment dispute.

**Box 9.7 Examples of ADR provisions in IIAs**

An example can be found in the investment chapter of the Comprehensive and Economic Trade Agreement (CETA) between the European Union and Canada of 2014 (not yet in force). This agreement contains specific provisions on mediation to encourage an amicable solution.

**Article 8.20**

*Mediation*

1. The disputing parties may at any time agree to have recourse to mediation.
2. Recourse to mediation is without prejudice to the legal position or rights of either disputing party under this Chapter and is governed by the rules agreed to by the disputing parties including, if available, the rules for mediation adopted by the Committee on Services and Investment pursuant to Article 8.44.3(c).
3. The mediator is appointed by agreement of the disputing parties. The disputing parties may also request that the Secretary-General of ICSID appoint the mediator.
4. The disputing parties shall endeavour to reach a resolution of the dispute within 60 days from the appointment of the mediator.
5. If the disputing parties agree to have recourse to mediation, Articles 8.19.6 and 8.19.8 shall not apply from the date on which the disputing parties agreed to have recourse to mediation to the date on which either disputing party decides to terminate the mediation. A decision by a disputing party to terminate the mediation shall be transmitted by way of a letter to the mediator and the other disputing party.

CETA also introduces some provisions specifically addressing SMEs.

**Article 8.19**

*Consultations*

3. The disputing parties may hold the consultations through videoconference or other means where appropriate, such as in the case where the investor is a small or medium-sized enterprise.

**Article 8.23**

*Submission of a claim to the Tribunal*

5. The investor may, when submitting its claim, propose that a sole Member of the Tribunal should hear the claim. The respondent shall give sympathetic consideration to that request, in particular if the investor is a small or medium-sized enterprise or the compensation or damages claimed are relatively low.

**Article 8.27**

*Constitution of the Tribunal*

9. Notwithstanding paragraph 6, the disputing parties may agree that a case be heard by a sole Member of the Tribunal to be appointed at random from the third country nationals. The respondent shall give sympathetic consideration to a request from the claimant to have the case heard by a sole Member of the Tribunal, in particular where the claimant is a small or medium-sized enterprise or the compensation or damages claimed are relatively low. Such a request shall be made before the constitution of the division of the Tribunal.

**Article 8.39**

*Final award*

6. The CETA Joint Committee shall consider supplemental rules aimed at reducing the financial burden on claimants who are natural persons or small and medium-sized enterprises. Such supplemental rules may, in particular, take into account the financial resources of such claimants and the amount of compensation sought.

Source: UNCTAD, 'Investor–State Disputes: Prevention and Alternatives to Arbitration' (New York and Geneva 2010) 45 <http://unctad.org/en/docs/diaeia200911_en.pdf> accessed 20 January 2017.

## C. Conclusions

International investment policies reflect the special situation of SMEs through a number of specific investment promotion and facilitation programmes. This, however, does not mean that the treatment of SMEs in international investment law could not be further improved.

One policy instrument for such improvement is IIAs. SMEs could benefit from treaty coverage that extends to non-equity modes of investment and from giving more prominence to mediation and conciliation as alternative forms of dispute resolution. It is also important that IIAs do not unduly limit policy space of host countries in respect of domestic SME support programmes.

SMEs could further benefit from the current move towards more regional integration, given the fact that SMEs often prefer regional instead of global cooperation in view of their limited capacities. Examples are the regional harmonization of rules and standards, cross-border infrastructure development, and easier market access through geographical proximity or similarities in customer preferences, languages, and business processes.[40]

Finally, SMEs could draw advantages from the increasing conclusion of joint trade and investment agreements.[41] Often, FDI is only made after export connections have successfully been established with the host country.[42] Especially SMEs are likely to make an investment abroad only as a second step and in a form that includes both trade and investment components (such as contract manufacturing or licensing arrangements). The simultaneous coverage of trade and investment in one agreement thus gives SMEs the best assurance that, whatever type of business form chosen, they are protected by the treaty.

## References

African Development Bank Group, 'The AfDB SME Program Approval: Boosting Inclusive Growth in Africa' (22 July 2013) <http://www.afdb.org/en/news-and-events/article/the-afdb-sme-program-approval-boosting-inclusive-growth-in-africa-12135> accessed 20 January 2017

APEC, 'The 20th APEC Small and Medium Enterprises Ministerial Meeting: Joint Ministerial Statement' (7 September 2013) <http://mddb.apec.org/Documents/2013/MM/SMEMM/13_smemm_jms.pdf> accessed 20 January 2017

APEC, 'Boracay Action Agenda to Globalize MSMEs' (24 May 2015) <http://www.apec.org/Meeting-Papers/Sectoral-Ministerial-Meetings/Trade/2015_trade/2015_mrt_standalone.aspx> accessed 20 January 2017

APEC, 'APEC Finance Ministers Launch Cebu Action Plan' (11 September 2015) <http://www.apec.org/Press/News-Releases/2015/0911_FM.aspx> accessed 20 January 2017

APEC, 'The APEC Iloilo Initiative: Growing Global MSMEs for Inclusive Development' (25 September 2015) <http://www.apec.org/Meeting-Papers/Sectoral-Ministerial-Meetings/Small-and-Medium-Enterprise/2015_sme/Annex%20A.aspx> accessed 20 January 2017

APEC, 'Small and Medium Enterprises Working Group' (2016) <http://www.apec.org/Groups/SOM-Steering-Committee-on-Economic-and-Technical-Cooperation/Working-Groups/Small-and-Medium-Enterprises.aspx> accessed 20 January 2017

ASEAN, 'ASEAN Strategic Action Plan for SME Development (2010–2015)' <http://www.asean.org/storage/images/archive/SME/SPOA-SME.pdf> accessed 20 January 2017

ASEAN, 'ASEAN Strategic Action Plan for SME Development 2016–2025' <http://www.asean.org/?static_post=asean-strategic-action-plan-for-sme-development-2016-2025-2> accessed 20 January 2017

European Commission, '"Think Small First": A "Small Business Act" for Europe' (Communication, 25 June 2008) COM(2008) 394 final

[40] Kreditanstalt für Wiederaufbau (KfW), 'Internationalisation in Germany's SME Sector: Step by Step to Global Presence' (2012) para 6 <https://www.kfw.de/Download-Center/Konzernthemen/Research/Research-englisch/PDF-Dateien-Paper-and-Proceedings/Internationalisation-in-Germanys-SME-sector.pdf> accessed 20 January 2017.

[41] See Martina Lodrant and Lucian Cernat, Chapter 6 of this volume; Heng Wang, Chapter 7 of this volume.

[42] KfW (n 40) para 8.

European Commission, 'Small Business, Big World: A New Partnership to Help SMEs Seize Global Opportunities' (Communication, 9 November 2011) COM(2011) 702 final

European Commission, 'Tips and Tricks for Advisors: Corporate Social Responsibility for Small and Medium-Sized Enterprises' (European Union 2013) <http://ec.europa.eu/DocsRoom/documents/10368/attachments/1/translations/en/renditions/pdf> accessed 20 January 2017

Froman, M, Villarreal, IG, and Fast, E, 'The NAFTA Certificate of Origin: Frequently Asked Questions' <http://www.economia.gob.mx/files/nafta_certificate_of_origin_2014.pdf> accessed 20 January 2017

Government of India, Ministry of Commerce and Industry, 'Press Note No 5' (2012 Series, 20 September 2012) <http://dipp.nic.in/english/acts_rules/Press_Notes/pn5_2012.pdf> accessed 20 January 2017

Institut für Mittelstandsforschung Bonn, 'KMU-Definition des IfM Bonn' <http://www.ifm-bonn.org/definitionen/kmu-definition-des-ifm-bonn/> accessed 20 January 2017

Kekic, L and Sauvant, KP (eds), *World Investment Prospects to 2011: Foreign Direct Investment and the Challenge of Political Risk* (Economist Intelligence Unit 2007)

Kreditanstalt für Wiederaufbau (KfW), 'Internationalisation in Germany's SME Sector: Step by Step to Global Presence' (2012) <https://www.kfw.de/Download-Center/Konzernthemen/Research/Research-englisch/PDF-Dateien-Paper-and-Proceedings/Internationalisation-in-Germanys-SME-sector.pdf> accessed 20 January 2017

MERCOSUR, 'Políticas de Apoyo a las Micro, Pequeñas y Medianas Empresas del MERCOSUR—Etapa II' (MERCOSUR/GMC/RES No 59/98) <http://www.saij.gob.ar/convert-html-to-pdf?url=/59-internacional-politicas-apoyo-micro-pequenas-medianas-empresas-mercosur-etapa-ii-rmr1998000059-1998-12-08/123456789-0abc-de9-5000-08991rserced&name=politicas-de-apoyo-a-las-micro.pdf> accessed 20 January 2017

NAFTA Free Trade Commission, '2012 NAFTA Commission Meeting, Joint Statement' (3 April 2012) <http://www.international.gc.ca/trade-agreements-accords-commerciaux/agr-acc/nafta-alena/js-washington-dc.aspx?lang=eng> accessed 20 January 2017

UNCTAD, 'Bilateral Investment Treaties in the Mid-1990s' (UN Publications No E.98.II.D.8, 1998)

UNCTAD, 'National Treatment' (UN Publications No E.99.II.D.16, 1999) <http://unctad.org/en/Docs/psiteiitd11v4.en.pdf> accessed 20 January 2017

UNCTAD, 'Competition, Competitiveness and Development: Lessons from Developing Countries' (United Nations 2004) <http://unctad.org/en/Docs/ditcclp20041_en.pdf> accessed 20 January 2017

UNCTAD, 'Integrating Developing Countries' SMEs into Global Value Chains' (United Nations 2010) <http://unctad.org/en/Docs/diaeed20095_en.pdf> accessed 20 January 2017

UNCTAD, 'Corporate Social Responsibility in Global Value Chains: Evaluation and Monitoring Challenges for Small and Medium Sized Suppliers in Developing Countries' (United Nations 2012) <http://unctad.org/en/PublicationsLibrary/diaeed2012d3_en.pdf> accessed 20 January 2017

UNCTAD, *World Investment Report 2012. Towards a New Generation of Investment Policies* (United Nations 2012) <http://unctad.org/en/PublicationsLibrary/wir2012_embargoed_en.pdf> accessed 20 January 2017

UNCTAD, *World Investment Report 2013: Global Value Chains: Investment and Trade for Development* (United Nations 2013) <http://unctad.org/en/publicationslibrary/wir2013_en.pdf> accessed 20 January 2017

UNCTAD, *World Investment Report 2014: Investing in the SDGs: An Action Plan* (United Nations 2014) <http://unctad.org/en/publicationslibrary/wir2014_en.pdf> accessed 20 January 2017

UNCTAD, FAO, IFAD, and World Bank, 'The Principles for Responsible Agricultural Investment (PRAI)' (25 January 2010) <http://unctad.org/en/Pages/DIAE/G-20/PRAI.aspx> accessed 20 January 2017

Yackee, JW, 'How Much Do U.S. Corporations Know (and Care) About Bilateral Investment Treaties? Some Hints from New Survey Evidence' (Vale Columbia Center on Sustainable International Investment, Columbia FDI Perspectives No 31, 23 November 2010)

# 10

# Microinvestment Disputes

*Perry S Bechky**

Dr Seuss once posited that '[a] person's a person, no matter how small'.[1] This chapter examines whether an investment's an investment, no matter how small. In the context of international investment disputes, this question matters because the jurisdiction of the International Centre for Settlement of Investment Disputes (ICSID or the Centre) hinges on the meaning of *investment*.[2]

Nothing in the text of the ICSID Convention excludes small investments (or small claims) from the Centre's jurisdiction or otherwise discriminates against small investments.[3] Indeed, the negotiating history reveals the conscious rejection of proposals excluding small disputes and small investments from the Centre's reach.[4]

Article 25(1) of the ICSID Convention gives ICSID jurisdiction over '*any legal dispute arising directly out of an investment*, between a Contracting State ... and a national of another Contracting State, which the parties to the dispute consent in writing to submit to the Centre'.[5] Yet the Convention omits any definition of *investment*.

In 2001, in *Salini v Morocco*, an ICSID tribunal held that the 'investment requirement' of Article 25(1) has objective content limiting ICSID jurisdiction.[6] The tribunal added:

> The doctrine generally considers that investment infers: [i] contributions, [ii] a certain duration of performance of the contract and [iii] a participation in the risks of the transaction ...

* A longer version of this chapter was published originally in the Vanderbilt Journal of Transnational Law. See Perry S Bechky, 'Microinvestment Disputes' (2012) 45 Vanderbilt Journal of Transnational Law 1043. I previously worked as Counsel at Shearman & Sterling LLP, which represented parties in several of the cases discussed in this chapter, although I did not personally work on any of them.

[1] Dr Seuss, *Horton Hears a Who!* (Random House 1954).

[2] This chapter italicizes a word when talking about the word instead of using the word in the ordinary way. For example: Smith made an investment; the tribunal construed *investment*. Here, *investment* is shorthand for 'the word "investment"'.

[3] See Convention on the Settlement of Investment Disputes between States and Nationals of Other States (opened for signature 18 March 1965) 575 UNTS 159 (ICSID Convention).

[4] See discussion accompanying nn 31–38.

[5] ICSID Convention (n 3) Art 25(1) (emphasis added).

[6] *Salini Costruttori SpA v Kingdom of Morocco*, ICSID Case No ARB/00/4, Decision on Jurisdiction (23 July 2001), translated in (2003) 42 ILM 609, para 52.

In reading the Convention's preamble, one may add [iv] the contribution to the economic development of the host State of the investment as an additional condition.[7]

*Salini* went on to note, 'In reality, these various elements may be interdependent' and they 'should be assessed globally even if, for the sake of reasoning, the Tribunal considers them individually here'.[8] The tribunal then determined that the claimant satisfied each of the four elements and '[c]onsequently … consider[ed]' that the claimant had made an investment within the meaning of Article 25.[9] Notwithstanding *Salini*'s call for sensitivity in examining the elements 'globally', later tribunals have generally attributed to *Salini* the creation of a four-part 'test'.[10] Some tribunals have followed 'the *Salini* test',[11] other tribunals have rejected it,[12] while still others have suggested modifying it into three-,[13] five-,[14] and six-part tests.[15] Some tribunals have changed one or more of the *Salini* criteria, insisting, for example, that the investor must contribute 'substantial' assets or must make a 'significant' contribution to the development of the host state.[16] The *Salini* test thus birthed a lively debate between objectivists and subjectivists, and among the former. This debate is crucial to shaping ICSID's docket and, more, its character.

This chapter problematizes *Salini*'s fourth prong, which requires an investment to 'contribut[e] to the economic development of the host State' as a condition of access to ICSID arbitration. It does this by focusing on *Salini*'s impact on micro-investment disputes, a concept introduced by the present author. Criticism of the development prong is not new—indeed, Christoph Schreuer has called this 'the most controversial' part of *Salini*.[17] Yet the microinvestment lens reveals new problems with the development prong: it imposes a backdoor size requirement that inhibits access to ICSID by micro-investors who may have the greatest need

[7] ibid. [8] ibid. [9] ibid paras 53–58.

[10] See, for example, *Phoenix Action, Ltd v Czech Republic*, ICSID Case No ARB/06/5, Award (15 April 2009) paras 39 n 18, 81–83 (describing *Salini* as 'seminal').

[11] See, for example, *Bayindir Insaat Turizm Ticaret Ve Sanayi AS v Islamic Republic of Pakistan*, ICSID Case No ARB/03/29, Decision on Jurisdiction (14 November 2005) paras 130–38 (applying a four-part '*Salini* test').

[12] See, for example, *Abaclat v Argentine Republic*, ICSID Case No ARB/07/5, Decision on Jurisdiction and Admissibility (4 August 2011) para 364: '[T]he Tribunal does not see any merit in following and copying the *Salini* criteria.'

[13] See, for example, *Fakes v Republic of Turkey*, ICSID Case No ARB/07/20, Award (14 July 2010) paras 110–14 (accepting the first three *Salini* criteria, while reviewing and rejecting other candidates).

[14] See, for example, *Joy Mining Machinery Ltd v Arab Republic of Egypt*, ICSID Case No ARB/03/11, Award on Jurisdiction (6 August 2004) para 53 (adding to the *Salini* criteria a requirement of 'regularity of profit and return').

[15] See, for example, *Phoenix Action* (n 10) Award (15 April 2009) para 114 (adding to the *Salini* criteria requirements that assets must be invested bona fide (ie in good faith) and in conformity with the domestic laws of the host state).

[16] See, for example, *Helnan International Hotels A/S v Arab Republic of Egypt*, ICSID Case No ARB/05/19, Decision on Objection to Jurisdiction (17 October 2006) para 77: '[T]o be characterized as an investment, a project must show … [inter alia] a substantial commitment and a significant contribution to the host State's development' (internal punctuation omitted).

[17] Christoph H Schreuer and others, *The ICSID Convention: A Commentary* (2nd edn, Cambridge University Press 2009) 131.

for such access, thereby harming ICSID's ability to fulfil its objectives, including development promotion. This chapter thus critiques *Salini*'s fourth prong from the perspectives of text, negotiating history, teleology, and such fundamental policies as access to justice and contribution to development itself.

In keeping with Article 25, a *microinvestment dispute* is a legal dispute arising directly out of a microinvestment, between a state and a foreign investor. A *micro investment*, in turn, is an investment worth less than US$5 million[18] made by an individual, a micro-enterprise, or a small or medium enterprise (SME).[19] This definition focuses on claims arising from microinvestments, not on small claims per se, which may arise from investments of any size. The point is to identify cases that are, despite their small size, genuinely important to the business concerned. The importance of a dispute about an investment—and hence the investor's need for access to ICSID—is a function of the size of the claim relative to the value of the investment. Simply put, a large company is better able than a small company to bear a loss of the same amount.[20] While a loss of US$5 million would give rise to 'bet the company' litigation for many companies, the same loss only gives rise to an 'ordinary business dispute' for larger companies. Where a smaller company may have urgent need in a US$5 million case for the effectiveness and neutrality promised by international arbitration, a larger company may be willing to litigate it in a domestic court or even write off the loss altogether in the pursuit of other, larger business dealings with the country concerned. This is why the definition of *microinvestment dispute* excludes claims by large businesses. In principle, then, the definition is tied to the size of

[18] According to Susan Franck's data set of awards in investment treaty arbitrations rendered (and made available publicly) before 1 June 2006, forty-four awards quantified the damages claimed, with the amounts sought varying from approximately US$155,314 to US$9.4 billion. Susan D Franck, 'Empirically Evaluating Claims about Investment Treaty Arbitration' (2007) 86 North Carolina Law Review 1, 16–17, 57. The mode and median claims were US$50 million and approximately US$59 million, respectively, while the mean was significantly higher at approximately US$343 million. ibid 58 and n 254. The US$5 million threshold for *microinvestment* is much smaller than the average claim, clearly low enough that investors with qualifying disputes can be expected to experience difficulties related to the small size of the investment in dispute (see Section C). At the same time, this threshold is also high enough to identify a meaningful number of qualifying cases.

[19] According to the OECD:

> SMEs are generally considered to be non-subsidiary, independent firms which employ fewer than a given number of employees. This number varies across countries. The most frequent upper limit designating an SME is 250 employees, as in the European Union. However, some countries set the limit at 200, while the United States considers SMEs to include firms with fewer than 500 employees. Small firms are mostly considered to be firms with fewer than 50 employees while micro-enterprises have at most ten, or in some cases, five employees.

OECD, *SME and Entrepreneurship Outlook 2005* (OECD 2005) (OECD Outlook) 17; see also Tom Gibson and HJ van der Vaart, 'Defining SMEs: A Less Imperfect Way of Defining Small and Medium Enterprises in Developing Countries' (Brookings Global Economy and Development, September 2008) 4–8 <https://www.brookings.edu/research/defining-smes-a-less-imperfect-way-of-defining-small-and-medium-enterprises-in-developing-countries/> accessed 20 January 2017 (surveying definitions of *SME*).

[20] The materiality concept from US securities law makes a helpful analogy, as a loss of US$5 million might be material to a small company, but not to a larger company; see Louis Loss, Joel Seligman, and Troy Paredes, *Securities Regulation* (4th edn, Kluwer Law & Business 2009) 613–60 and n 436.

both the investment and the investor, not to the amount in controversy. In practice, however, data about the size of the investment and the investor is often unavailable and the amount in controversy serves as a proxy for the (claimed) value of the investment, because most cases allege the taking or (nearly) complete destruction of the investment.[21] Ultimately, the aim of this chapter is more to introduce the concept of a *microinvestment dispute* than to fix its exact definition—that is, to establish that a real class of these disputes exists and, regardless of its precise parameters, it matters how ICSID treats them.

It matters, of course, to injured micro-investors whether they have access to an effective mechanism for dispute settlement. It matters systemically as well, for micro-investors' collective economic power is awesome, they may have the greatest need for access to ICSID, and their investment may be chilled the most by lack of that access, and their political support may prove crucial to preserve and improve the investment arbitration system.[22]

Section A of this chapter describes ICSID's purposes, particularly the aim to promote development, and argues that those purposes do not justify *Salini*'s development prong. Section B examines *Salini*'s impact on two recent microinvestment disputes: *Mitchell v DR Congo* and *Malaysian Historical Salvors v Malaysia*. Section C critiques *Salini*'s development prong from the microinvestment perspective. The chapter then concludes in Section D.

In offering this microinvestment critique of *Salini*'s development prong, this chapter does not contend that this jurisdictional hurdle is the chief impediment to the successful prosecution of microinvestment claims. The economics of these claims are inherently challenging—they invoke expensive procedures in pursuit of (by definition) small recoveries—and are worsened by the risk that a tribunal may subject an unsuccessful micro-investor to the 'loser pays' rule. A full treatment of the economics of microinvestment disputes is beyond the scope of this chapter. The contention here is that *Salini*'s development prong unnecessarily and inappropriately adds to the inherent burdens on micro-investors' access to ICSID.

## A. ICSID, Development, and *Salini*'s Development Prong

ICSID was created by multilateral treaty in 1966. It is an 'autonomous international institution',[23] but it is closely related to the World Bank: the Bank conceived

[21] This proxy is imperfect. To determine whether a particular case genuinely qualifies as a microinvestment dispute as defined here, it may be necessary to drill into data beyond what is included in an award. For example, in *Petrobart*, the claimant sought about US$4 million, but it is a natural gas distribution company and so may well be too large to qualify as an SME. *Petrobart Ltd v Kyrgyz Republic*, Arbitration No 126/2003, Award (Arbitration Institute of the Stockholm Chamber of Commerce, 29 March 2005) 4, 78.

[22] See discussion under Section C.

[23] International Bank for Reconstruction and Development, 'Report of the Executive Directors on the Convention on the Settlement of Investment Disputes between States and Nationals of Other States' (18 March 1965) (Executive Directors' Report) para 15.

of ICSID and sponsored the talks leading to its creation, the Bank houses ICSID at its headquarters, and the Bank's president serves ex officio as chairman of ICSID's Administrative Council and is responsible for nominating ICSID's Secretary-General (a position occupied until 2009 by the Bank's general counsel).[24]

ICSID's primary purpose is to facilitate the resolution of disputes between international investors and Member States, mainly by arbitration. Access to international adjudication traditionally had been reserved to states, as remains the case today at the International Court of Justice.[25] A private business injured by a foreign state in violation of international standards had to persuade its home state to 'espouse' the claim, which international law then regarded as the home state's claim to control and dispose of.[26] ICSID represented a profound step from this traditional conception of *inter*national law towards transnational law with meaningful participation by non-state actors.[27]

ICSID arbitration, like other forms of arbitration, is a creature of consent. The state's consent may be expressed in several ways, but ICSID's docket has come to be dominated by cases where the state unilaterally pre-consented in a treaty, mainly in a bilateral investment treaty (BIT). In a BIT, each party grants substantive rights to investors from the other party, typically including fair and equitable treatment, national treatment, and a promise to pay compensation for any expropriation.[28] The parties also typically consent to international arbitration at ICSID or other fora (or both) over any dispute submitted by an investor from the other party alleging a violation of the BIT.[29] The state's pre-consent by treaty empowers qualifying investors to initiate arbitration at one of the specified fora by consenting themselves just before filing a claim. Treaty-based cases transformed ICSID's docket, now vastly larger than in the recent past.[30]

[24] See ICSID Convention (n 3) Arts 2, 5, 10(1) (establishing ICSID with numerous connections to the World Bank); Executive Directors' Report (n 23) paras 1–8, 15–18 (describing the role the World Bank had in the creation of ICSID).

[25] See Statute of the International Court of Justice (opened for signature 26 June 1945) 3 Bevans 1179, 59 Stat 1031, Art 34(1) ('Only states may be parties in cases before the Court').

[26] See, for example, *Mavrommatis Palestine Concessions (Greece v Great Britain)* PCIJ Series A No 2 (30 August 1924) 12:

> By taking up the case of one of its subjects ... a State is in reality asserting its own rights—its right to ensure, in the person of its subjects, respect for the rules of international law ... Once a State has taken up a case on behalf of one of its subjects before an international tribunal, in the eyes of the latter the State is sole claimant.

[27] See Aron Broches, 'The Convention on the Settlement of Investment Disputes between States and Nationals of Other States' (1972) 136 Recueil des Cours 331: '[T]he most striking feature of the Convention is that it firmly establishes the capacity of a private individual or a corporation to proceed directly against a State in an international forum, thus contributing to the growing recognition of the individual as a subject of international law'.

[28] See generally Rudolf Dolzer and Margrete Stevens, *Bilateral Investment Treaties* (Martinus Nijhoff 1995) 58–65, 108–14.

[29] ibid 129–30.

[30] See ICSID, *The ICSID Caseload—Statistics* (ICSID 2016) 7, 10 <https://icsid.worldbank.org/apps/ICSIDWEB/resources/Documents/ICSID%20Web%20Stats%202016-2%20(English)%20Sept%2020%20-%20corrected.pdf> accessed 20 January 2017 (showing that 88 per cent of ICSID cases have been registered since 2000 and 74 per cent are treaty-based).

As mentioned, ICSID has jurisdiction over legal disputes 'arising directly from an investment', but the ICSID Convention does not define the crucial term *investment*. The negotiating history reveals ample discussion of the issue.[31] Of particular relevance to microinvestments, the negotiators debated whether to exclude small investments or small disputes from ICSID jurisdiction. 'In fact, [an early text] provided that … the Centre would not exercise jurisdiction in respect of disputes involving claims of less than US$100,000.'[32] Other 'delegates felt that the total value of the investment and not the claim under dispute should be determinative'.[33] Still others favoured procedural mechanisms, such as screening by the Secretary-General or the investor's home state 'to shield the Centre from insignificant claims'.[34] None of these proposals prevailed, however. Unable to agree to a definition of *investment*, the negotiators agreed instead to omit one.[35]

Throughout the negotiations, Aron Broches opposed the efforts to define *investment*, arguing that a definition was 'danger[ous]', because

> recourse to the services of the Center might in a given situation be precluded because the dispute in question did not precisely qualify under the definition … There was the further danger that a definition might provide a reluctant party with an opportunity to frustrate or delay the proceedings by questioning whether the dispute was encompassed by the definition.[36]

Broches thus objected to the wrangling that would follow from defining *investment*, deeming jurisdictional details best left to each Member State to decide which cases to submit to ICSID.[37] Broches made this point repeatedly—and specifically in opposition to a minimum dollar value requirement.[38]

[31] The first draft of the Convention included a definition of *investment* as 'any contribution of money or other assets of economic value for an indefinite period or, if the period be defined, for not less than five years' (Schreuer and others (n 17) 115). The Secretariat later revised the definition to read:

> the acquisition of (i) property rights or contractual rights (including rights under a concession) for the establishment or in the conduct of an industrial, commercial, agricultural, financial or service enterprise; (ii) participations or shares in any such enterprise; or (iii) financial obligations of a public or private entity other than obligations arising out of short-term banking or credit facilities.

ibid 115.

[32] ibid.

[33] ibid 116. Julian Mortenson added:

> The first draft of the Convention imposed a minimum US$100,000 amount in dispute as a jurisdictional prerequisite. The dollar minimum was withdrawn in the next draft, and despite occasional expressions of concern that it might leave ICSID open to 'small or frivolous' disputes, it was never reinstated … *The same held true for all efforts to impose a substantiality requirement on the investment itself.*

Julian Mortenson, 'The Meaning of "Investment": ICSID's *Travaux* and the Domain of International Investment Law' (2010) 51 Harvard International Law Journal 257, 297–98 (emphasis added).

[34] Schreuer and others (n 17) 116.

[35] ibid 115.

[36] ICSID, *History of the ICSID Convention*, vol II: *Documents Concerning the Origin and the Formulation of the Convention on the Settlement of Investment Disputes between States and Nationals of Other States* (ICSID 1968) 54. In a similar vein, the staff comment to the October 1963 draft convention expressed concern that defining investment would 'open the door to frequent disagreements' about jurisdiction. Mortenson (n 33) 282–83.

[37] See Schreuer and others (n 17) 114–16 (discussing Broches's views).

[38] ibid 115–16. Mortenson added:

## I. Development as ICSID's object and purpose

Andreas Lowenfeld briefly captured the '[w]ave of [e]xpropriations' that swept much of the globe in the first decades after the Second World War:

> [E]xpropriations and nationalizations of all kinds took place, in Eastern Europe, in former colonies, and in newly invigorated countries of Latin America. All the countries that had come under Communist rule ... nationalized land and private industrial property, including the property of aliens. Utilities, mines, and other major enterprises were subject to state takings in Bolivia, Brazil, Argentina, Peru, and Guatemala, among other states of Latin America ... The most widely known instances of state take-overs were the expropriation of Dutch properties in Indonesia (1958–59), the nationalization of the Anglo-Iranian Oil Company's properties in Iran (1951), and Egypt's nationalization of the Suez Canal Company (1956).[39]

In a series of debates through the 1960s into the 1970s, the UN General Assembly struggled over the state of customary international law on the property rights of aliens.[40] In 1964, in a case emerging out of Cuba's nationalization of American-owned properties, the US Supreme Court observed: 'There are few if any issues in international law today on which opinion seems to be so divided as the limitations on a state's power to expropriate the property of aliens.'[41]

The World Bank would have known these events and controversies, of course. Indeed, a member of the World Bank team that helped to negotiate compensation for Egypt's nationalization of the Suez Canal became President of the Bank in 1963.[42]

The purposes of the World Bank include 'promot[ing] private foreign investment'.[43] It can certainly be said that the World Bank conceived ICSID and sponsored the talks to create it for the purpose of promoting investment. The Bank's executive directors asserted, for example, that 'the primary purpose of the [ICSID] Convention' was to 'stimulate a larger flow of private international investment'.[44]

> As the Bank drafters explained in their elimination of 'lower limit[s]' from the draft circulated to the Consultative Meetings of Legal Experts, 'the parties would in practice be best qualified to decide whether, having regard to pertinent facts and circumstances including the value of the subject-matter, a dispute is one which ought to be submitted to the Center.'

Mortenson (n 33) 298.

[39] Andreas F Lowenfeld, *International Economic Law* (2nd edn, Oxford University Press 2008) 483–84.

[40] See, for example, ibid 486–94 (describing the UN debates).

[41] *Banco Nacional de Cuba v Sabbatino* (1964) 376 US 398, 428–30.

[42] Lowenfeld (n 39) 484, 537 n 2.

[43] Articles of Agreement of the International Bank for Reconstruction and Development (opened for signature 22 July 1944) 2 UNTS 134, Art I(ii). The clause continues 'by means of guarantees or participations in loans and other investments made by private investors', although ICSID is an example of the Bank not limiting itself to these means unless the arbitral process is seen as a form of 'guarantee'. Broches described ICSID as being within the Bank's 'institutional ambit', though outside its 'professional experience and competence', and characterized it as a 'semi-extra-curricular exercise'. Broches (n 27) 345, 347.

[44] Executive Directors' Report (n 23) para 12.

This account, however, is incomplete. Investment promotion is only ICSID's 'intermediary purpose', not its 'ultimate purpose'.[45] Ultimately, the Bank initiated ICSID 'to further [the Bank's own] overall purpose of promoting economic development in the world's poor countries'.[46] The Bank's mission is even captured in its name: the International Bank for Reconstruction and *Development*. Its statement of purposes makes clear that 'facilitating the investment of capital for productive purposes' is itself meant to serve the end of 'assist[ing] in the ... development' of Member States.[47] Ibrahim Shihata, a general counsel of the World Bank and Secretary-General of ICSID, thus wrote: 'ICSID must be regarded as an instrument of international policy for the promotion of investments and of economic development.'[48] Support for this view of ICSID as an instrument of development can be found in the Preamble to the ICSID Convention, which is predicated on 'the need for international cooperation for economic development, and the role of private international investment therein'.[49]

Investment promotion should thus be viewed as a means to the end of economic development. Indeed, fifty years after ICSID's founding, one might venture that economic development is not ICSID's ultimate purpose either. Rather, economic development serves to improve human welfare, a true end.

## II. *Salini*'s development prong

Schreuer has identified five 'typical characteristics' of investments.[50] He included 'significance for the host state's development' in this list, for purposes of the ICSID Convention, while acknowledging that '[t]his is not necessarily characteristic of investments in general'.[51]

[45] cf Anne van Aaken and Tobias A Lehmann, 'Sustainable Development and International Investment Law: A Harmonious View from Economics' in Roberto Echandi and Pierre Sauvé (eds), *Prospects in International Investment Law and Policy* (Cambridge University Press 2013) 317, 332.

[46] Lowenfeld (n 39) 537.

[47] Articles of Agreement (n 43) Art I(i); see also Broches (n 27) 342 ('[A]s a development institution ... the Bank was and is vitally concerned with capital flows from the developed to the developing countries').

[48] Ibrahim Shihata, 'Towards a Greater Depoliticization of Investment Disputes: The Roles of ICSID and MIGA' in Franziska Tschofen and Antonio R Parra (eds), *The World Bank in a Changing World* (1st edn, Martinus Nijhoff 1991) 314; see also Executive Directors' Report (n 23) para 9 ('[T]he Executive Directors are prompted by the desire to strengthen the partnership between countries in the cause of economic development'). Sornarajah has stressed that: 'The very essence of the system of investment protection ... is economic development ... Subjection to ... the ICSID system is achieved at the cost of a surrender of sovereignty, and this is justified by the belief that economic development will take place as a result.' M Sornarajah, *The International Law on Foreign Investment* (3rd edn, Cambridge University Press 2010) 313.

[49] ICSID Convention (n 3) Preamble.

[50] See Schreuer and others (n 17) 128. Four of Schreuer's characteristics were adopted by *Salini*, while the last, expectation of profit, sometimes finds support among *Salini*'s progeny. See, for example, *Joy Mining* (n 14) Award on Jurisdiction (6 August 2004) para 53.

[51] Schreuer and others (n 17) 128 (emphasis omitted).

The first two cases to apply ICSID's development objective to the construction of *investment* both approached the question in a liberal spirit, treating contribution-to-development as a factor easing access to ICSID arbitration.[52] This began to change with *Salini*, particularly in its more rigid manifestations as a 'fixed and inflexible'[53] checklist of mandatory criteria. With this, the development language of the Preamble transformed from a door-opening aid into a door-closing obstacle for otherwise eligible claimants.

The liberal approach is preferable. It respects Member States' autonomy,[54] maximizing their freedom to use ICSID as they deem best. A fixed *Salini* test with a mandatory development prong sets Article 25's 'outer limits' of ICSID jurisdiction more restrictively than does the 'ordinary meaning' of *investment*.[55]

The drafters of the ICSID Convention were free to define *investment* as they wished, whether more or less expansively than, or otherwise akilter from, its ordinary meaning. They did not do so. Tribunals do not enjoy the drafters' freedom. Drafters are the masters of language; tribunals are not. Tribunals are bound to construe undefined terms in accordance with their ordinary meaning and the customary rules of treaty interpretation. In the context of ICSID jurisdiction, absent clear limitations in Article 25, tribunals should acknowledge that states are the masters of jurisdiction—that the Convention empowers states with broad discretion to determine in good faith which matters to submit to ICSID arbitration. Tribunals should, accordingly, abandon *Salini*'s development prong as an unwarranted restriction on state discretion even if they otherwise persist with *Salini*'s objective approach.[56]

Furthermore, if *investment* is to have an objective meaning in Article 25, whatever that meaning might be, it must be the same meaning for all ICSID members. If an investor must demonstrate that its investment made a (substantial) contribution to development in the host state as a condition of ICSID jurisdiction, as the *Salini* line would have it, this condition must apply wherever the investment is made. But what does it mean to make a substantial contribution to development in the United States or Japan? Is it even possible to contribute to development in a country that is already 'developed'? At the very least, it is much more difficult for an investor to prove that it made a substantial contribution to development in a developed country than in a developing country. The development prong therefore

[52] See *Fedax NV v Republic of Venezuela*, ICSID Case No ARB/96/3, Decision on Jurisdiction (11 July 1997) para 43; *Ceskoslovenska Obchodni Banka, AS v Slovak Republic (CSOB)*, ICSID Case No ARB/97/4, Decision on Jurisdiction (24 May 1999), (1999) 14 ICSID Review 250, 276–77, para 76.

[53] *Biwater Gauff (Tanz) Ltd v United Republic of Tanzania*, ICSID Case No ARB/05/22, Award (24 July 2008) para 314.

[54] cf Louis Henkin, *International Law: Politics and Values* (Brill 1995) 101: 'Commitment to state autonomy has been shaken since the Second World War, but it is still a basic, perhaps *the* basic, value of the system.'

[55] See Vienna Convention on the Law of Treaties (opened for signature 23 May 1969) 1155 UNTS 331, Art 31(1) (requiring that a treaty be interpreted 'in accordance with [its] ordinary meaning').

[56] I have omitted here for reasons of space my broader argument that *Salini*'s objectivist approach should be replaced by 'bounded deference'. See Perry S Bechky, 'Microinvestment Disputes' (2012) 45 Vanderbilt Journal of Transnational Law 1043, 1053–63.

creates an imbalance of obligations among ICSID members. Consider: If a German investor builds a factory in Panama and a Panamanian investor builds a factory in Germany—with identical contributions, durations, and assumptions of risk—it is possible that *Salini* would lead ICSID tribunals to find that only the former made a contribution to development, effectively allowing Germany a jurisdictional out not available to Panama.

Other critiques of the mandatory development prong abound. For example, although some proponents of the *Salini* test attribute credit to Schreuer's 'typical features' of investment, he has denied paternity.[57] He has called 'unfortunate' the trend towards calcification of his 'typical features' into a 'rigid list of criteria', arguing that it will neither 'facilitate the task of tribunals' nor 'make decisions more predictable'.[58] He has warned that a test insisting on a showing of contribution to development needs 'particular care'.[59] He has favoured a liberal spirit in which an investor who contributes to development 'enjoys the presumption of being an investment', but without automatically 'exclud[ing] from the Convention's protection' 'an activity that does not obviously contribute to economic development'.[60] And he has supported an expansive view of development, which embraces 'development of human potential, political and social development and the protection of the local and the global environment'.[61]

Some tribunals have rejected *Salini*'s development prong. One held that contribution to development is 'implicitly covered' by any investment, rendering a separate prong unnecessary.[62] Another rejected the contention that the ICSID Convention's Preamble requires a development prong, holding that 'economic development ... is an expected consequence, not a separate requirement, of the investment projects carried out by a number of investors in the aggregate'.[63]

A third tribunal found it 'impossible to ascertain' whether an investment contributes to development, 'the more so as there are highly diverging views on what constitutes "development"'.[64] It proposed focusing on contribution to the economy, rather than to development, and adopting the rebuttable presumption that investments so contribute.[65] This approach is superior to *Salini*, helpfully moving from the vague and value-laden question of whether an investment aimed to 'contribute to development' to the more readily ascertainable question of whether it aimed to 'contribute to the economy'. It would be better still, however, to eliminate the development prong than to recast it in a way that continues to limit Member State autonomy with an even weaker textual basis, while collapsing the complexity of development into a single criterion.

[57] See Schreuer and others (n 17) 133: 'The First Edition of this Commentary cannot serve as authority for this development.'

[58] ibid. [59] ibid 134. [60] ibid. [61] ibid.

[62] *Fakes* (n 13) Award (14 July 2010) para 102 and n 65 (quoting *Consozio Groupement LESI-Dipenta v People's Republic of Algeria*, ICSID Case No ARB/03/08, Award (10 January 2005) para II.13(iv)).

[63] ibid para 111. [64] *Phoenix Action* (n 10) Award (15 April 2009) para 85.

[65] ibid paras 85–86.

## B. Application of *Salini*'s Development Prong to Microinvestment Disputes

This section describes *Salini*'s impact on two microinvestment disputes: *Mitchell v DR Congo* and *Malaysian Historical Salvors v Malaysia*. This is not meant to be a comprehensive survey of all (arguable) microinvestment disputes, as it omits cases decided before *Salini*, when the size of the investment did not figure prominently in the jurisdictional analysis,[66] microinvestment disputes brought to investor-state arbitration outside ICSID,[67] and a 'mass claims' case that joined the claims of many micro-investors.[68]

### I. *Mitchell v Democratic Republic of Congo*

Patrick Mitchell owned Mitchell & Associates, a small law firm in the Democratic Republic of Congo (hereinafter Congo). On 5 March 1999, Congolese authorities sealed the firm's premises, seized documents and other items, and detained two attorneys. The premises remained sealed and the attorneys remained imprisoned for more than eight months.[69] With these actions, Congo effectively put Mitchell & Associates out of business.[70]

Mitchell, a US citizen, brought an ICSID claim under the BIT between the United States and Congo. The ICSID tribunal ruled that 'Mitchell has been the victim of an expropriation' in violation of the BIT. It awarded him US$750,000 plus interest. The tribunal also ordered Congo to pay US$95,000 as a contribution to Mitchell's share of the tribunal's fees and costs.[71]

Congo had objected to the tribunal's jurisdiction, arguing, inter alia, that Mitchell had not made an investment within the meaning of Article 25. The tribunal 'received ample information' to determine whether Mitchell's activities in Congo qualified as an investment.[72] The tribunal concluded that Mitchell

[66] See, for example, *Maffezini v Kingdom of Spain*, ICSID Case No ARB/97/7, Decision on Jurisdiction (25 January 2000), (2002) 5 ICSID Report 296 paras 65–70.

[67] See, for example, *Bogdanov v Moldova*, Award (Arbitration Institute of the Stockholm Chamber of Commerce, 22 September 2005) paras 5.1(ii), 5.2.

[68] *Abaclat* (n 12) paras 294–98.

[69] *Mitchell v Democratic Republic of Congo*, ICSID Case No ARB/99/7, Award (9 February 2004) para 62.

Luke Peterson has reported some further details about Mitchell's dispute with Congo. Apparently, Mitchell & Associates represented a Canadian mining company, Banro, in its own expropriation dispute with Congo. The Congolese authorities claimed that Mitchell's firm was cooperating with rebels and charged the two detained attorneys with treason. Among the items seized was 'a large sum of cash'. Luke Eric Peterson, 'Research Note: Emerging Bilateral Investment Treaty Arbitration and Sustainable Development' (IISD 2003) <http://www.iisd.org/pdf/2003/investment_investsd_note_2003.pdf> accessed 20 January 2017; Luke Eric Peterson, 'ICSID Award against Democratic Republic of Congo Annulled' (Investment Treaty News, 24 November 2006) <http://www.iisd.org/pdf/2006/itn_nov24_2006.pdf> accessed 20 January 2017.

[70] See *Mitchell* (n 69) paras 64–65. [71] ibid para 102. [72] ibid para 47.

transferred into Congo money and other assets which constituted the foundations for his professional activities … Together with the returns on the initial investments, which also qualify as investments … these activities and the economic value associated therewith qualify as an investment within the meaning of the BIT and the ICSID Convention.[73]

The tribunal further considered that Mitchell's 'movable property', his 'right to "know-how" and "goodwill" ', and his 'right to exercise [his] activities' in Congo all qualified as investment.[74] The tribunal thus laid emphasis on the bits and pieces of Mitchell & Associates without adequate attention to the whole as a going concern.[75]

Congo had also argued that Mitchell's activities were not 'a long-term operation', did not involve a 'significant contribution of resources', and were 'not of such importance for the State's economy that it distinguishes itself from an ordinary commercial transaction'.[76] The tribunal rejected these contentions, finding that, while many investments possess these attributes, they are not necessary to qualify as an investment. The tribunal declared that the ICSID Convention 'equally include[s] … "smaller investments" of shorter duration and with more limited benefit to the host State's economy …'.[77]

Congo requested that an ad hoc committee annul the tribunal award, contending that the tribunal manifestly exceeded its powers and failed to provide reasons for its decision. Congo argued, inter alia, that the tribunal lacked jurisdiction over the matter because Mitchell had not made an investment within the meaning of Article 25. Congo won. The ad hoc committee negated Mitchell's award and ordered him to pay US$100,000 as a contribution to Congo's share of the committee's fees and costs.[78]

The committee relied on the *Salini* test for its analysis. To avoid the possibility that Member States might sign an investment treaty that 'arbitrarily' defined business activities as investments, the committee stressed that 'the [ICSID] Convention has supremacy over … a BIT'.[79] The committee staked out this position even though it conceded that the relevant language in the US–Congo BIT was 'altogether usual and in no way exorbitant'.[80] It held that Article 25 limits jurisdiction to investments with four interdependent characteristics, including 'contribution to the economic development of the host country'.[81] It regarded the development prong as 'fundamental', 'essential', and 'unquestionable'—deeming it 'doubtless covered' implicitly by ICSID decisions where it 'had not been mentioned expressly'.[82]

[73] ibid para 55. [74] ibid para 48.

[75] It appears to be this weakness in the tribunal's jurisdictional analysis that drew a dissent from one arbitrator, even though the dissenter accepted (contra the DRC's position) that 'the activity as an attorney or legal counsel may serve as a framework for an investment justifying the jurisdiction of the Tribunal'. *Mitchell v Democratic Republic of Congo*, ICSID Case No ARB/99/7, Dissenting Opinion of Yawovi Agboyibo (23 January 2004) para 10. The dissent also agreed with the tribunal on the merits that 'the measures applied to [Mitchell's] firm are tantamount to expropriation'. ibid paras 4–5.

[76] *Mitchell* (n 69) Award (9 February 2004) para 56. [77] ibid.

[78] *Mitchell v Democratic Republic of Congo*, ICSID Case No ARB/99/7, Decision on Annulment (1 November 2006) para 67.

[79] ibid para 31. [80] ibid para 32. [81] ibid para 27. [82] ibid paras 30, 33.

The committee stated that the mandatory contribution to economic development need not be 'sizable or successful … It suffices for the operation to contribute in one way or another to the economic development of the host State, and this concept of economic development is, in any event, extremely broad but also variable depending on the case'.[83] Nevertheless, the committee was unable to accept that Mitchell's small law firm made the kind of contribution to development it deemed necessary. It declared that the firm was not 'readily recognizable' as an investment and was instead 'a somewhat uncommon operation from the standpoint of the concept of investment',[84] noting this was the first ICSID case about a law firm.[85] It considered irrelevant the 'minimal' funds contributed by Mitchell to start and operate his firm.[86] Thus, while the committee disclaimed any desire to discriminate against 'smaller' investments, its whole analysis began from the premise that the law firm was not 'readily recognizable' as an investment and that Mitchell's financial contribution was 'minimal'.

The committee also excluded the firm's movable property, know-how, and goodwill from its analysis, deciding these only mattered if 'the *services* of the "Mitchell & Associates" firm … constitute [an] investment within the meaning of the Convention and the [BIT]'.[87] The committee thus considered that the firm's services had to make a contribution to development.[88] The committee added that this requirement could only be satisfied if the firm 'had concretely assisted [Congo], for example by providing it with legal services in a regular manner or by specifically bringing investors'.[89]

The committee concluded that the tribunal had made a 'particularly grave' error in failing to establish a link between the firm's services and Congo's development, because the absence of such a link 'boils down to granting the qualification as investor to any … law firm established in a foreign country'.[90] But the committee failed to explain why every law firm should not qualify as an investment. Contrary to the committee's view, law firms do indeed share the characteristics typical of investment: they contribute assets for an indefinite duration and bear risk in the expectation of profit. They also hire and train employees, buy goods and services, pay taxes and fees, and otherwise generate economic activity. What they lack is physicality: the physical footprint is small, the equipment needed is limited, bricks and mortar are largely absent. Most of the value of a law firm is invisible, lying in know-how and goodwill. This invisibility probably explains why the committee deemed that Mitchell's law firm was not 'readily recognizable' as an investment. An investment in a small law firm, to be sure, does not look like an investment in a factory or power plant, but it is still an investment. The committee seems to have been deceived by appearances.

[83] ibid para 33. [84] ibid paras 34, 39 (quoting Broches (n 27)). [85] ibid para 34.
[86] ibid para 38. [87] ibid (emphasis added). [88] ibid para 39.
[89] ibid. The committee conceded here that both parties had presented evidence showing that 'some US investors had indeed consulted the "Mitchell & Associates" firm', but it disregarded this evidence because the tribunal had not mentioned it (at least not with sufficient specificity). ibid.
[90] ibid para 40.

Size also played an explicit role in the committee's reasoning, as when it dismissed Mitchell's financial contribution as 'minimal'. This was a mistake. The committee should have recognized that law is not a capital-intensive industry. Small law firms may be started by 'hanging a shingle' on leased office space with some furniture and basic office equipment. Even large law firms do not require very much capital, especially when compared with services such as telecommunications and transportation. This makes law firms small investments, but still investments. While the committee worried about drawing lines to avoid a rule allowing all law firms access to ICSID, it neglected to consider the costs of a rule excluding many law firms—and, apparently, also many accountants, architects, consultants, doctors, engineers, and other knowledge-intensive professional services. The committee's line-drawing led it to examine the recipients of the services provided by Mitchell & Associates. The committee should not have embarked on this path: a law firm's status as an investment does not change depending on whether the firm counsels the government or private clients, domestic or foreign clients, few or many clients, investors or other clients. Nor should the committee have assumed that providing services to a government necessarily makes a greater contribution than does providing services to private persons. In the end, it is difficult to conceive that a larger investment—whether more physically visible or more capitally intense, which often go together, of course—would be subjected to the same misguided analysis about the nature of its customers.

The committee's analysis, moreover, discounted the value of legal know-how, disregarded the contributions that law firms make to economic growth (eg by drafting contracts and obtaining permits),[91] and ignored the possibility that law firms contribute to the development of the rule of law, which both contributes to economic growth[92] and ought to count inherently as a contribution to development properly understood.[93] This failure is particularly notable here, as it has been reported that Congo moved against Mitchell & Associates in retaliation for the firm's representation of a foreign investor in a separate dispute with the government; if true, this charge evidences the progress needed in Congo to develop the rule of law for the benefit of investors, the Congolese economy, and indeed Congolese society as a whole.[94] Due to its cramped view of what contributes to development, the committee missed an opportunity to hold Congo accountable to the values of the international community.

[91] See Peter Egger and Hannes Winner, 'Does Contract Risk Impede Foreign Direct Investment?' (2003) 139 Swiss Journal of Economics and Statistics 155, 156, 164 (arguing that the viability of contracts correlates with FDI inflows, even when accounting for other measures of the quality of legal institutions).

[92] See, for example, Kenneth W Dam, *The Law-Growth Nexus: The Rule of Law and Economic Development 93–94* (Brookings Institution Press 2006) (discussing studies on the correlation between confidence in the judiciary and economic growth).

[93] Contributing to the rule of law fits comfortably within Schreuer's conception of *development*, which encompasses 'development of human potential' and 'political and social development'. See Schreuer and others (n 17) 134.

[94] See Peterson, 'ICSID Award' (n 69).

## II. *Malaysian Historical Salvors v Malaysia*

In 1991, the Malaysian Government contracted with a marine salvage company, Malaysian Historical Salvors (Salvors), to find and salvage the cargo of a British ship that sank in the Strait of Malacca in 1817.[95] The contract (as described by the tribunal, a sole arbitrator) required Salvors 'to utilize its expertise, labour and equipment to carry out the salvage operation, and to invest and expend its own financial and other resources, and assume all risks of the salvage operation'.[96] Salvors 'finance[d] the salvage operation in its entirety'.[97] Salvors acted on a 'no finds–no pay' basis, under which it bore 'all the costs' and 'attendant risks' of the operation. It would 'recover its expenditure and make a profit only if' it successfully salvaged and auctioned the ship's cargo.[98]

Salvors worked on this project for 'almost four years', recovering 24,000 items.[99] Malaysia placed in its national museum some of the salvaged goods.[100] The rest were auctioned in 1995, earning almost US$3 million. The contract provided for Malaysia to pay Salvors 70 per cent of both the auction proceeds and 'the best attainable value' for the items Malaysia kept, which Salvors valued at over US$400,000.[101] Salvors claimed that Malaysia paid it only US$1.2 million, leaving about US$1.2 million more in controversy.[102]

In 2004, after some proceedings in other fora, Salvors filed an ICSID case under the Malaysia–UK BIT.[103] Malaysia objected to jurisdiction on several grounds, including that the contract in dispute was merely a 'service contract', not an 'investment contract'.[104] *Salini*'s development prong came to be the decisive issue in the case.[105] And Salvors' small size figured prominently in the analysis.

First, the tribunal distinguished one case that had held that a capital contribution is an investment on the ground that the contribution in that case involved 'substantial amounts' of capital, when 'the Tribunal is not satisfied that the amount invested by [Salvors] could be described as "substantial amounts" …'.[106]

Second, although Malaysia conceded that Salvors 'made contributions in money, in kind and in industry', the tribunal nevertheless deemed it noteworthy that 'the size of the contributions were in no way comparable to those found in *Salini*' and other cases.[107] It repeatedly noted that Salvors' contribution was smaller than the bank guarantee found not to be an investment in *Joy Mining v Egypt*.[108]

95 *Malaysian Historical Salvors, Sdn, Bhd v Malaysia*, ICSID Case No ARB/05/10, Award on Jurisdiction (17 May 2007) para 7.

96 ibid para 8. 97 ibid para 9. 98 ibid para 10. 99 ibid para 13.

100 *Salvors* (n 95) Decision on Annulment (16 April 2009) paras 4–5.

101 *Salvors* (n 95) Award on Jurisdiction (17 May 2007) paras 11–14.

102 ibid paras 13–14. 103 ibid paras 15–18.

104 ibid para 41.3; *Salvors* (n 95) Respondent's Memorial on Objections to Jurisdiction (11 March 2006) para 108(c).

105 *Salvors* (n 95) Award on Jurisdiction (17 May 2007) paras 66–68.

106 ibid para 63 (distinguishing *Alcoa Minerals of Jamaica, Inc v Jamaica*, ICSID Case No ARB/74/2).

107 ibid para 109. 108 ibid paras 109, 123, 134 n 19, 143 n 21.

Third, concern for size manifested itself again in the tribunal's analysis of the development prong, which had 'considerable, even decisive, importance'.[109] The tribunal held that a contribution to development does not suffice unless the contribution is 'significant'.[110] '[T]he requirement of significance' is needed, the tribunal warned, lest any contribution, 'however small', qualify.[111] Following *Mitchell*, the tribunal commented that the salvage contract 'is not a "readily recognizable" "investment"'.[112] It accepted that Salvors provided 'gainful employment' to Malaysians, 'cultural and historical benefits' for Malaysia, and 'direct financial benefits' to the treasury through the auction proceeds—but it found these benefits were not 'material', were not of sufficient 'quality or quantity', and were ordinary benefits of a kind resulting from 'any normal service contract'.[113] In the end, the tribunal appears to have concluded that a 'significant contribution' is only made where the investor produced a 'lasting' economic benefit for the host state, typically in the form of 'infrastructure'.[114]

Finally, the tribunal exported its development conclusion into its analysis of the duration of Salvors' activities in Malaysia. It noted that *Salini* had discussed a minimum time of two to five years, which Salvors' four-year effort satisfied 'in a quantitative sense', but only because of the 'fortuity' that Salvors was unable to find and salvage the wreck in eighteen months as originally contemplated.[115] Then, it held that duration also has a 'qualitative sense', which is tied to contribution to development, so a claimant failing the development prong fails the duration prong as well.[116]

Despite all this emphasis on size, the tribunal disclaimed that size was determinative: 'It should not be thought that investments of relatively small cash sums can never amount to an "investment".'[117] However, the next sentence suggested that all this means is that some large investments take forms other than cash (eg intellectual property).[118] It is difficult to conceive of any small investment capable of satisfying the tribunal's test of a lasting, significant contribution to infrastructure.

The tribunal accordingly dismissed the case for lack of jurisdiction. This decision rested solely on the meaning of *investment* in Article 25, as the tribunal declined to decide any other issue, including whether Salvors had made an investment under the definition in the BIT.[119]

Salvors requested annulment of the award. It won. The ad hoc committee, split two-to-one, annulled the award on the ground that the tribunal had manifestly exceeded its powers by failing to exercise its properly invoked jurisdiction.[120] The committee faulted the tribunal for 'exclud[ing] small contributions' from ICSID's

[109] ibid para 123; see also ibid paras 112, 130 (explaining the importance of contribution to development for its analysis).

[110] ibid para 123. [111] ibid. [112] ibid paras 126–30.

[113] ibid paras 131–32, 144.

[114] See ibid paras 143–44 ('The benefit [of Salvors' project] was not lasting, in the sense envisaged in the public infrastructure or banking infrastructure projects').

[115] ibid para 110. [116] ibid paras 110–11. [117] ibid para 139. [118] ibid.

[119] ibid paras 146–49.

[120] *Salvors* (n 95) Decision on Annulment (16 April 2009) para 80.

ambit and adopting a construction at odds with 'the decision[] of the drafters of the ICSID Convention to reject a monetary floor in the amount of an investment'.[121] Evidencing its commitment to ICSID access for small claims, the committee ordered Malaysia to bear the full costs of the annulment procedure (but not Salvors' attorney fees), declaring:

> [I]t was not the intent of the drafters of the ICSID Convention to exclude claimants advancing claims of minor financial dimension. If such claimants are left to pay not only the costs of their legal representation but half of the ICSID costs as well, the practical result could be to discourage if not debar small claims.[122]

The committee considered that the ordinary meaning of *investment* is 'the commitment of money or other assets for the purpose of providing a return' and found no reason to deviate from that meaning in Article 25.[123] The committee emphasized the definition in the BIT, apparently accepting the view that Member States have unbridled freedom to define *investment* as they wish when consenting to ICSID jurisdiction.[124] Given the importance of the BIT to the committee's analysis, it found that the tribunal had committed a 'gross error' by failing to consider and apply the BIT's definition of *investment*.[125] Finally, where the tribunal (like *Mitchell Annulment*) seems to have been driven by a quest for line-drawing to limit access to ICSID, the committee tilted the other way: it favoured access to ICSID for all investments, however defined in the BIT, regardless of size, and particularly where ICSID is the only forum specified in the BIT.[126]

The dissent made an impassioned case for requiring a significant contribution to development as a jurisdictional condition, contending this requirement is what 'separate[s] an ICSID investment from any other kind of investment' and 'ICSID arbitration ... from any other kind of arbitration'.[127] Without this requirement, the dissent warned, ICSID would protect even 'an entity which is systematically earning its wealth at the expense of the development of the host State'.[128] Accordingly, the dissent proclaimed, 'ICSID would seem to have lost its way: it is time to call back the organization to its original mission'.[129]

## C. A Microinvestment Critique

As illustrated by the opinions in *Mitchell Annulment* and *Salvors Award*, one risk posed by *Salini*'s contribution to development test—especially in its 'substantial

121 ibid para 80(b)–(c). 122 ibid para 82. 123 ibid para 57.
124 ibid paras 62, 73. 125 ibid para 74.
126 See, for example, ibid paras 62, 82 (expressing concern for assuring 'international recourse' for small investors and reducing Salvors' share of the costs to facilitate such recourse).
127 *Salvors* (n 95) Dissenting Opinion of Judge Mohamed Shahabuddeen (19 February 2009) paras 30–36. The dissent used the phrase 'an ICSID investment' twenty-eight times, apparently to emphasize the point that *investment* in Art 25 can and does mean something narrower than the ordinary meaning of the word in other contexts.
128 ibid para 22. 129 ibid.

contribution' variant—is that it may devolve into a backdoor mechanism for screening out microinvestments. The Convention does not impose a minimum size requirement and tribunals ought not to invent one. As the *Fakes* tribunal stated, 'small investments are covered by the ICSID Convention in the same way as large investments. An investment can be large or small …'.[130]

In a worst-case scenario, a ruling that a microinvestment is not an investment under Article 25 can deprive the claimant of any international forum to hear the claim. For example, had the *Salvors* Award not been annulled, the claimant would have been left without another forum because the Malaysia–UK BIT makes ICSID the sole forum for dispute settlement,[131] as do a number of other BITs.[132] Even with the annulment in *Salvors*, it should be seen that the development prong imposed costs, risks, and delay on the claimant. These burdens are much plainer, of course, in *Mitchell*, where the ad hoc committee annulled the claimant's award and went so far as to order him to pay Congo US$100,000.[133] Burdens like this may dissuade micro-investors from filing meritorious claims,[134] because they are inherently challenged to afford investment arbitration and each incremental cost further tilts the field against them.[135] These burdens also pressure micro-investors

[130] *Fakes* (n 13) Award (14 July 2010) para 112 n 73.

[131] See Agreement for the Promotion and Protection of Investments (Malaysia–UK) (signed 21 May 1981, entered into force 21 October 1988) UKTS No 16 (1989), Art 7. By contrast, the BIT at issue in *Mitchell* afforded an alternative known as the ICSID Additional Facility. See Treaty Concerning the Reciprocal Encouragement and Protection of Investment (US–Democratic Republic of Congo) (signed 3 August 1984, entered into force 28 July 1989) Art VII(2)(b). However, access to the Additional Facility is conditioned on receiving the Secretary-General's approval, which she can give 'only if [s]he is satisfied … that the underlying transaction has features which distinguish it from an ordinary commercial transaction'. ICSID, 'Additional Facility Rules' (ICSID/11, April 2006) Art 4(3)(b). Also, Additional Facility arbitration is not governed by the ICSID Convention, including its special provisions on enforceability of awards. ibid Art 3; see also Schreuer and others (n 17) 27, 141–43, 1120–23.

[132] See, for example, *SGS Société Générale de Surveillance SA v Islamic Republic of Pakistan*, ICSID Case No ARB/01/13, Decision on Jurisdiction (6 August 2003), (2003) 18 ICSID Review 307 para 151 ('Article 9(2) of the [Swiss–Pakistan] BIT provides only one recourse to an investor, that is, recourse to a tribunal constituted under the ICSID Convention').

[133] *Mitchell* (n 69) Decision on Annulment (1 November 2006) para 67.

[134] Even in a NAFTA case where a majority of the tribunal ordered the unsuccessful claimant to pay 75 per cent of both tribunal costs and Mexico's attorney fees, the tribunal acknowledged that its 'loser pays' approach ought not apply 'in the case of an investor with limited financial resources where considerations of access to justice may play a role'. *International Thunderbird Gaming Corp v United Mexican States*, Arbitral Award (UNCITRAL 2006) paras 214, 220–21. Thomas Wälde dissented from the order of costs, stressing that it 'makes recourse to independent justice for smaller companies prohibitive'. ibid, Separate Opinion of Thomas Wälde, para 142. In this regard, Stephan Schill has argued that tribunals in investment arbitration generally should (and generally do) engage in one-way cost-shifting in favour of successful claimants, but not against unsuccessful claimants, in order to adequately incentivize the prosecution of claims. Stephan W Schill, 'Arbitration Risk and Effective Compliance' (2006) 7 Journal of World Investment and Trade 653, 655. Micro-investors present a compelling instance for Schill's thesis: having lost their business, they are especially vulnerable to the additional risk of adverse cost-shifting and they may need the prospect of favourable cost-shifting to afford to pursue a winning claim.

[135] Literature about the high cost of investment arbitration for small businesses includes Susan D Franck, 'Rationalizing Costs in Investment Treaty Arbitration' (2011) 88 Washington University Law Review 769, 811–13; and Lee M Caplan, 'Making Investor-State Arbitration More Accessible to

to settle on unfavourable terms. The development prong presses a finger on the scale against access to the ICSID system and it weighs particularly heavily against claims by micro-investors—indeed, it may not carry any force at all in cases regarding larger investments,[136] given the conclusory assertions and weak analyses often found in such cases.[137]

The development prong may hinder access to ICSID arbitration in another way as well. While trends in investor-state arbitration appear to favour contingency-fee arrangements or third-party funding,[138] these arrangements may be inhibited by the increased risk of jurisdictional defeat[139] and the greater costs that must be incurred to minimize that risk.[140] This concern ought not to be overstated, however, as micro-investor claimants inherently face significant obstacles to obtaining financial support because their expected recovery is limited.

*Salini*'s development prong may push some microinvestment claims outside ICSID into other arbitral fora, depriving micro-investors of a choice available to larger claimants. From a claimant's perspective, alternative tribunals may be inferior to ICSID, especially when it comes to the enforceability of awards[141]—and a

Small and Medium-Sized Enterprises' in Catherine A Rogers and Roger P Alford (eds), *The Future of Investment Arbitration* (Oxford University Press 2009) 297, 298, 304.

136 cf *Salvors* (n 95) Award on Jurisdiction (17 May 2007) paras 119–21 ('In this Tribunal's view, the main reason why the *PSEG* tribunal did not discuss the *Salini* criteria was because the investment in question was a "readily recognizable investment" ', where the claimant had a US$800 million contract to build a power plant).

137 For example, a tribunal examining whether improvements to a hotel constituted an investment had only this to say: 'As for the contribution to the development of the EGYPT's development [sic], the importance of the tourism industry in the Egyptian economy makes it obvious.' *Helnan International Hotels* (n 16) Decision on Objection to Jurisdiction, para 77. Apparently, the tribunal deemed worthy any contribution to the tourism sector, because of Egypt's existing success in that sector. Does this imply that contributions to less successful or even non-existent sectors are unworthy? Surely not, for development often entails starting or radically improving industries to meet unmet needs. The reason given thus amounts to no reason at all.

138 See, for example, Mark Kantor, 'Third-Party Funding in International Arbitration: An Essay about New Developments' (2009) 24 ICSID Review 65, 76.

139 By way of comparison, Arthur Miller has predicted that recent decisions heightening the standards to commence litigation in US federal courts will cause lawyers to take fewer cases on a contingency fee basis, making it harder for plaintiffs to find representation and thus leaving more meritorious claims uncompensated. Arthur R Miller, 'From *Conley* to *Twombly* to *Iqbal*: A Double Play on the Federal Rules of Civil Procedure' (2010) 60 Duke Law Journal 1, 66–68.

140 Continuing with the analogy to US pleadings standards, one survey of approximately 200 employment lawyers who had filed a federal complaint since the standards began to change in 2007, found that 94 per cent alleged more facts in their complaints and 75 per cent had to respond to motions to dismiss more often. Emery G Lee III and Thomas E Willging, 'Attorney Satisfaction with the Federal Rules of Civil Procedure: Report to the Judicial Conference Advisory Committee on Civil Rules' (Federal Judicial Center, March 2010) 5, 11–12 <http://www.fjc.gov/public/pdf.nsf/lookup/costciv2.pdf/$file/costciv2.pdf> accessed 20 January 2017.

141 Compare Convention on the Recognition and Enforcement of Foreign Arbitral Awards (opened for signature 10 June 1958) 330 UNTS 3 (New York Convention) Art V (listing grounds for refusing enforcement of an award in international commercial arbitration), with ICSID Convention (n 3) Art 54(1) ('Each Contracting State shall recognize an award rendered pursuant to this Convention as binding and enforce the pecuniary obligations imposed by that award within its territories as if it were a final judgment of a court in that State'). Nevertheless, it is possible that the greater automaticity of ICSID awards, which a textual comparison of the two Conventions suggests, may prove less meaningful in actual practice. See Edward Baldwin, Mark Kantor, and Michael Nolan, 'Limits to Enforcement of

*Salini*-like analysis may close access to other tribunals as well.[142] Moreover, from a public perspective, proceedings before alternative tribunals are generally less transparent than ICSID and less open to public participation as amici.[143]

Inhibiting micro-investors' access to ICSID is particularly unfortunate because they may have the most need for treaty-based protection.[144] While large businesses sometimes enjoy sufficient leverage to secure contractual commitments to international arbitration,[145] small businesses are typically less able to protect themselves politically in the host state or to secure diplomatic protection from their home state.[146] And small businesses are more affected by weaknesses in legal systems,[147] especially in countries with comparatively weak legal systems.[148] ICSID ought not to adopt a jurisdictional requirement that impedes access by the very claimants most in need of effective, neutral dispute settlement. Such impediments effectively hang an 'unwelcome' sign on ICSID's door, which may in turn diminish

ICSID Awards' (2006) 23 Journal of International Arbitration 1 (arguing that enforcement of ICSID awards is less automatic than often believed); and Gaëtan Verhoosel, 'Annulment and Enforcement Review of Treaty Awards: To ICSID or Not to ICSID' (2008) 23 ICSID Review 119, 146–47 (concluding that enforcement of ICSID awards is 'undeniably pretty good', while enforcement of non-ICSID awards is 'not so bad at all').

142 In *Romak SA v Republic of Uzbekistan*, Case No AA280, Award (Permanent Court of Arbitration 2009) paras 192–95, 207–08, the tribunal reasoned that the broad definition of *investment* in the Swiss–Uzbek BIT should be limited by the first three prongs of *Salini*, regardless of whether the claimant chose ICSID or UNCITRAL arbitration. See also *Nova Scotia Power Inc Ltd v Venezuela*, ICSID Case No ARB(AF)/11/1, Award (30 April 2014) (excerpts available at <http://icsid.worldbank.org>); cf *White Industries Australia Ltd v India*, Final Award (UNCITRAL 2011), paras 7.4.9–10 (finding that *Salini* does not apply outside ICSID, then showing that the claimant met the *Salini* test anyway). This trend may be ratified as more states refer to objective characteristics in their new investment treaties.

143 See ICSID, 'Rules of Procedure for the Institution of Conciliation and Arbitration Proceedings' in 'ICSID Convention, Regulations and Rules' (ICSID/15, April 2006) 32(2), 37(2), 48(4); and Schreuer and others (n 17) 697–707 (discussing confidentiality and transparency). NAFTA cases outside ICSID have been a notable exception, as the NAFTA parties have been important proponents of transparency in investment arbitration. See NAFTA Free Trade Commission, 'Statement of Interpretation' (31 July 2001) pt A; NAFTA Free Trade Commission, 'Statement on Non-Disputing Party Participation' (2005) 44 ILM 796.

144 See UNCTAD, *The Role of International Investment Agreements in Attracting Foreign Direct Investment to Developing Countries* (UNCTAD 2009) 34 ('BITs may matter as a special protection for small and medium-sized enterprises ...'); ibid 52 ('There is anecdotal evidence from a number of home countries that SMEs are particularly interested in BITs').

145 See Broches (n 27) 344.

146 As Caplan wrote:

> While larger enterprises sometimes pursue arbitration, they may feel, as a general matter, that it is less necessary or even desirous to do so. Their stronger economic and political influence may bring host state governments to the negotiating table more readily and with better settlement terms ... Because larger enterprises are typically more financially resilient than SMEs, they are likely to be in a better position to pursue a broader dispute settlement strategy that is less reliant on investor-state arbitration.

Caplan (n 135) 302.

147 An economic analysis of 'over 4,000 firms in 54 countries' concluded that 'large firms are able to adjust to the inefficiencies of the legal system. However, the same does not seem to be the case for small and medium enterprises, which end up paying for the legal systems' shortcomings in terms of slower growth'. Thorsten Beck, Asli Demirgüç-Kunt, and Vojislav Maksimovic, 'Financial and Legal Constraints to Growth: Does Firm Size Matter?' (2005) 60 Journal of Finance 137, 137, 161.

148 ibid 162–66.

support for investment arbitration among small enterprises, an essential business constituency.[149]

Depriving microinvestments of adequate access is also inconsistent with ICSID's foundational syllogism: the availability of effective, neutral tribunals promotes investment flows and, therefore, promotes development.[150] While the costs of losing any one microinvestment are small (by definition), what is vital from the developmental perspective is the cumulative impact of many microinvestments.[151] Collectively, the economic power of smaller enterprises is awesome.[152] It has also been shown that smaller businesses transfer more technology to developing countries than do larger businesses.[153]

Governments can sometimes entice large investments individually by negotiating one-off deals, but this cannot be done for microinvestments. To encourage microinvestments, governments must instead craft good rules and institutions to attract them en masse. SMEs brim with untapped potential for more foreign direct investment (FDI).[154]

Thus, in the name of promoting development, the *Salini* test may actually hamper that goal. To be sure, the word 'may' in the previous sentence (and elsewhere in this section) indicates an important limit on the claim made in this critique. The argument is essentially theoretical, relying on the theories underpinning ICSID's foundational syllogism and the idea that raising costs and risks for micro-investors will affect their actions on the margins.[155] Lee Caplan has called for 'a comprehensive survey of SME attitudes toward the settlement of investment disputes', including 'their perceptions about the importance of investor-state arbitration in resolving investment disputes, and whether they can effectively afford and utilize

[149] I thank Luke Nottage for this observation.

[150] cf *International Thunderbird* (n 134) Separate Opinion of Thomas Wälde, para 142 (dissenting from order of costs against an unsuccessful claimant on the ground that raising barriers to arbitration for smaller companies 'undermines the very purpose of [investment] treaties' by 'leaving out entrepreneurs with initiative, willingness to take … risk'); see also ibid paras 5, 86, 140 (stressing the importance of making investment arbitration accessible to smaller, entrepreneurial investors).

[151] See Caplan (n 135) 298: 'Though SMEs typically make small investments on an individual basis, their collective efforts can be sizeable, with substantial benefits for international development and cross-border prosperity.'

[152] See, for example, Meghana Ayyagari, Asli Demirgüç-Kunt, and Vojislav Maksimovic, 'Who Creates Jobs in Developing Countries?' (2014) 43 Small Business Economics 75, 95 (concluding that, on average, small businesses (five to twenty employees) accounted for 'just over 20 per cent' of total full-time employment and 45.34 per cent of new jobs in developing countries). This study did not address micro-enterprises (under five employees). ibid 77.

[153] Caplan (n 135) 298.

[154] See OECD Outlook (n 19) 16 ('SMEs [including microenterprises] constitute the dominant form of business organisation in all countries world-wide, accounting for over 95 per cent and up to 99% of the business population depending on the country'); ibid 42 ('Up to two-thirds of micro-enterprises (<10 employees) are not internationalized, compared to one third of medium-sized enterprises … Foreign direct investment (FDI) is a vehicle for SME internationalization, although for most countries, only a fraction (1–4% of European-19 SMEs) have established subsidiaries abroad').

[155] I might add that ICSID's own premise is essentially theoretical. The empirical jury is still out. See generally Karl P Sauvant and Lisa E Sachs (eds), *The Effect of Treaties on Foreign Direct Investment: Bilateral Investment Treaties, Double Taxation Treaties, and Investment Flows* (Oxford University Press 2009).

investor-state arbitration', because at present '[t]he scope of the problem is unfortunately unknown'.[156] Without a better empirical understanding, one cannot know how many micro-investors are dissuaded from bringing claims to ICSID—and why—and, even worse, how many are dissuaded from investing in developing countries. The ICSID decisions only reveal those microinvestment disputes that have been brought to date, obscuring those not brought. Anecdotal evidence (and common sense) suggest there are other microinvestment disputes never submitted to ICSID.[157] One can only presume, for now, that *Salini*'s burdens contribute to the dissuasion.

## D. Conclusion

Like Dr Seuss, ICSID tribunals should conclude that investments are investments, no matter how small. They should discard *Salini*'s objective approach, or at least its development prong, thereby honouring the Hippocratic injunction to 'do no harm' to micro-investors and the goal of development. The ICSID Convention sets no minimum size requirement and none is warranted by ICSID's history or objectives. To the contrary, assuring that the doors to ICSID remain open to microinvestment disputes serves ICSID's values of depoliticization and development promotion.

More fundamentally, ICSID exists to help move the reality of the international community towards community values.[158] Rejecting *Salini*'s development prong serves such core community values as equal access to justice, fairness, *pacta sunt servanda*, peaceful settlement of disputes, and the rule of law. It also helps to move international society towards transnational society with a meaningful ability by private persons—no matter how small—to protect their own rights and interests.

## References

Ayyagari, M, Demirgüç-Kunt, A, and Maksimovic, V, 'Who Creates Jobs in Developing Countries?' (2014) 43 Small Business Economics 75

Baldwin, E, Kantor, M, and Nolan, M, 'Limits to Enforcement of ICSID Awards' (2006) 23 Journal of International Arbitration 1

156 See Caplan (n 135) 307, 311. Absent adequate empirical evidence, Caplan also tempered his factual assertions. For example: 'SMEs may not be as successful in resolving disputes through non-legal means, such as negotiation. Thus, when investment disputes arise, SMEs may place more stock in investor-state arbitration than larger enterprises.' ibid 302.

157 Caplan (n 135) 303: 'The author's own experiences in the field—which include investment disputes involving SMEs that ICSID would not necessarily know about—confirm the existence of these two kinds of barriers [expense of arbitration and access to expert counsel] for at least some SMEs.'

158 cf Owen M Fiss, 'Against Settlement' (1984) 93 Yale Law Journal 1073, 1089: 'Civil litigation is an institutional arrangement for using state power to bring a recalcitrant reality closer to our chosen ideals.'

Bechky, PS, 'Microinvestment Disputes' (2012) 45 Vanderbilt Journal of Transnational Law 1043

Beck, T, Demirgüç-Kunt, A, and Maksimovic, V, 'Financial and Legal Constraints to Growth: Does Firm Size Matter?' (2005) 60 Journal of Finance 137

Broches, A, 'The Convention on the Settlement of Investment Disputes between States and Nationals of Other States' (1972) 136 Recueil des Cours 331

Caplan, LM, 'Making Investor-State Arbitration More Accessible to Small and Medium-Sized Enterprises' in Catherine A Rogers and Roger P Alford (eds), *The Future of Investment Arbitration* (Oxford University Press 2009)

Dam, KW, *The Law-Growth Nexus: The Rule of Law and Economic Development* (Brookings Institution Press 2006)

Dolzer, R and Stevens, M, *Bilateral Investment Treaties* (Martinus Nijhoff 1995)

Dr Seuss, *Horton Hears a Who!* (Random House 1954)

Egger, P and Winner, H, 'Does Contract Risk Impede Foreign Direct Investment?' (2003) 139 Swiss Journal of Economics and Statistics 155

Fiss, OM, 'Against Settlement' (1984) 93 Yale Law Journal 1073

Franck, SD, 'Empirically Evaluating Claims about Investment Treaty Arbitration' (2007) 86 North Carolina Law Review 1

Franck, SD, 'Rationalizing Costs in Investment Treaty Arbitration' (2011) 88 Washington University Law Review 769

Gibson, T and van der Vaart, HJ, 'Defining SMEs: A Less Imperfect Way of Defining Small and Medium Enterprises in Developing Countries' (Brookings Global Economy and Development, September 2008) <https://www.brookings.edu/research/defining-smes-a-less-imperfect-way-of-defining-small-and-medium-enterprises-in-developing-countries/> accessed 20 January 2017

Henkin, L, *International Law: Politics and Values* (Brill 1995)

International Bank for Reconstruction and Development, 'Report of the Executive Directors on the Convention on the Settlement of Investment Disputes between States and Nationals of Other States' (18 March 1965)

ICSID, *History of the ICSID Convention*, vol II: *Documents Concerning the Origin and the Formulation of the Convention on the Settlement of Investment Disputes between States and Nationals of Other States* (ICSID 1968)

ICSID, *The ICSID Caseload—Statistics* (ICSID 2016) <https://icsid.worldbank.org/apps/ICSIDWEB/resources/Documents/ICSID%20Web%20Stats%202016-2%20(English)%20Sept%2020%20-%20corrected.pdf> accessed 20 January 2017

Kantor, M, 'Third-Party Funding in International Arbitration: An Essay about New Developments' (2009) 24 ICSID Review 65

Lee, EG III and Willging, TE, 'Attorney Satisfaction with the Federal Rules of Civil Procedure: Report to the Judicial Conference Advisory Committee on Civil Rules' (Federal Judicial Center, March 2010) <http://www.fjc.gov/public/pdf.nsf/lookup/costciv2.pdf/$file/costciv2.pdf> accessed 20 January 2017

Loss, L, Seligman, J, and Paredes, T, *Securities Regulation* (4th edn, Kluwer Law & Business 2009)

Lowenfeld, AF, *International Economic Law* (2nd edn, Oxford University Press 2008)

Miller, AR, 'From Conley to Twombly to Iqbal: A Double Play on the Federal Rules of Civil Procedure' (2010) 60 Duke Law Journal 1

Mortenson, J, 'The Meaning of "Investment": ICSID's *Travaux* and the Domain of International Investment Law' (2010) 51 Harvard International Law Journal 257

OECD, *SME and Entrepreneurship Outlook 2005* (OECD 2005)

Peterson, LE, 'Research Note: Emerging Bilateral Investment Treaty Arbitration and Sustainable Development' (IISD 2003) <http://www.iisd.org/pdf/2003/investment_investsd_note_2003.pdf> accessed 20 January 2017

Peterson, LE, 'ICSID Award against Democratic Republic of Congo Annulled' (Investment Treaty News, 24 November 2006) <http://www.iisd.org/pdf/2006/itn_nov24_2006.pdf> accessed 20 January 2017

Sauvant, KP and Sachs, LE (eds), *The Effect of Treaties on Foreign Direct Investment: Bilateral Investment Treaties, Double Taxation Treaties, and Investment Flows* (Oxford University Press 2009)

Schill, SW, 'Arbitration Risk and Effective Compliance' (2006) 7 Journal of World Investment and Trade 653

Schreuer, CH, Malintoppi, L, Reinisch, A, and Sinclair, A, *The ICSID Convention: A Commentary* (2nd edn, Cambridge University Press 2009)

Shihata, I, 'Towards a Greater Depoliticization of Investment Disputes: The Roles of ICSID and MIGA' in Franziska Tschofen and Antonio R Parra (eds), *The World Bank in a Changing World* (1st edn, Martinus Nijhoff 1991)

Sornarajah, M, *The International Law on Foreign Investment* (3rd edn, Cambridge University Press 2010)

UNCTAD, *The Role of International Investment Agreements in Attracting Foreign Direct Investment to Developing Countries* (UNCTAD 2009)

van Aaken, A and Lehmann, TA, 'Sustainable Development and International Investment Law: A Harmonious View from Economics' in Roberto Echandi and Pierre Sauvé (eds), *Prospects in International Investment Law and Policy* (Cambridge University Press 2013)

Verhoosel, G, 'Annulment and Enforcement Review of Treaty Awards: To ICSID or Not to ICSID' (2008) 23 ICSID Review 119

# 11

# Legal Protection for Small and Medium-Sized Enterprises through Investor-State Dispute Settlement

## Status Quo, Impediments, and Potential Solutions

*Alexander Gebert*

Small and medium-sized enterprises (SMEs) are the backbone of many domestic economies. But as globalization of businesses and markets continues, SMEs are also increasingly engaging and investing in foreign countries.[1]

Aside from the ordinary risks associated with commercial investments, investing in foreign countries can pose additional risks of state interference, in particular—but not only—in states with an unstable economic and political environment. To balance these risks, attract investments by foreign investors, and protect businesses investing abroad, over 180 states have entered into bilateral or multilateral investment treaties.[2] To date, more than 3,300 investment treaties have been concluded, of which more than 2,600 are in force.[3]

Investment treaties typically contain reciprocal substantive protections against expropriation and equivalent interferences, as well as obligations for states to provide protection and security for investments by investors from the other signatory state(s), and to treat investors fairly and equally well as domestic investors and investors from third countries. In addition, states regularly agree to investor-state dispute settlement (ISDS) mechanisms, allowing foreign investors to commence arbitration proceedings before international tribunals against the state and claim damages for violations of the substantive protections of the treaties.

[1] UNCTAD, 'Smaller Firms Have Major Potential as Foreign Investors' (Press Release, 28 May 1998) <http://unctad.org/en/pages/PressReleaseArchive.aspx?ReferenceDocId=3245> accessed 5 June 2016.

[2] UNCTAD, 'International Investment Agreements Navigator: IIAs by Economy' (2016) <http://investmentpolicyhub.unctad.org/IIA/IiasByCountry#iiaInnerMenu> accessed 20 March 2016.

[3] UNCTAD, 'International Investment Agreements Navigator' (2016) <http://investmentpolicyhub.unctad.org/IIA> accessed 20 March 2016.

Investor-state dispute settlement offers foreign investors direct access to dispute resolution procedures against a host state in a neutral and de-politicized forum. Due to the possible lack of impartial and independent domestic courts in some jurisdictions and the substantive protections granted in investment treaties, foreign investors often prefer to resolve disputes before arbitral tribunals instead of domestic state courts,[4] as evidenced by a steadily increasing number of ISDS proceedings over the past two decades.[5]

ISDS is often perceived and criticized as a dispute settlement mechanism solely for large multinational corporations with the resources to take on states in large-scale and costly arbitration proceedings.[6] Contrary to this perception, the claimants in ISDS proceedings are to a significant extent SMEs and individuals. It is true, however, that high costs and the long duration of ISDS proceedings are obstacles particularly for SMEs with limited financial resources that could potentially deter them from claiming remedies through ISDS.

On the other hand, arbitration proceedings are very flexible and provide sufficient opportunities to limit and control costs while allowing the parties to determine the procedure that best fits their needs.[7] Even in cases where the costs of the proceeding exceed the financial resources an SME has available or is willing to invest to seek a remedy, there are possibilities to finance such proceedings through multi-party arbitrations or specialized arbitration funders.

This chapter will examine the current involvement of SMEs in the ISDS system and the obstacles that potentially keep them from playing an even greater role. Potential solutions will then be discussed that would enable SMEs to benefit to a greater extent from ISDS.

## A. The Current Role of SMEs in ISDS

Despite the long and contentious debate about the perceived limited accessibility of ISDS for smaller enterprises, there has been little empirical research on the subject.[8] However, the available studies and recent data show that, in contrast to the widespread notion of ISDS as a dispute resolution method benefitting only large multinational enterprises, small investors represent a significant share of claimants in ISDS proceedings.[9]

[4] Lee M Caplan, 'Making Investor-State Arbitration More Accessible to Small and Medium-Sized Enterprises' in Catherine A Rogers and Roger P Alford (eds), *The Future of Investment Arbitration* (Oxford University Press 2009) 297, 300.

[5] UNCTAD, 'Investor-State Dispute Settlement (ISDS): Review of Developments in 2014' (IIA Issues Note No 2, 2015) 2 <http://unctad.org/en/PublicationsLibrary/webdiaepcb2015d2_en.pdf> accessed 3 March 2016.

[6] See, for example, 'Investor-State Dispute Settlement: The Arbitration Game' *The Economist* (London, 11 October 2014) <http://www.economist.com/news/finance-and-economics/21623756-governments-are-souring-treaties-protect-foreign-investors-arbitration> accessed 3 March 2016.

[7] David Brown, 'What Steps Should Arbitrators Take to Limit the Cost of Arbitration?' (2014) 31 Journal of International Arbitration 499, 499.

[8] Caplan (n 4) 303.

[9] cf Joachim Karl, Chapter 9 of this volume, Section B.V.

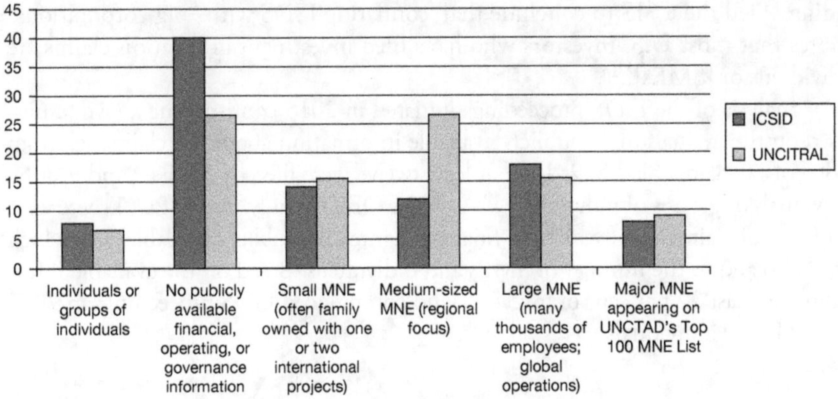


**Figure 11.1** Types of investors as claimants in fifty ICSID and forty-five UNCITRAL cases (percentage of cases)

Source: David Gaukrodger and Kathrin Gordon, 'Investor-State Dispute Settlement: A Scoping Paper for the Investment Policy Community' (OECD Working Paper on International Investment 2012/03) 18 <http://www.oecd.org/investment/investment-policy/WP-2012_3.pdf> accessed 3 September 2014.

In a study on international investment, the Organisation for Economic Co-operation and Development (OECD) ascertained that in the 95 ISDS proceedings examined, less than half of the claimants were large multinational enterprises. At the other end of the spectrum, 22 per cent of claimants were individuals or small corporations. The OECD also discovered that no or only little public information was available for a significant number of claimants and suggested that some of these were also small investors without reporting obligations (Figure 11.1).[10]

The OECD study suggests that by the end of 2011, as many as 30 per cent of the claimants in ISDS proceedings were SMEs (or individuals). The study concludes that

> a wide range of investor types avail themselves of the ISDS system. If there is a problem of investor access to justice in this system … then it is not the sort of problem that can be revealed by a survey of investor claimants.[11]

A more recent study by the Center for Strategic & International Studies (CSIS) revealed an even larger share of SMEs among claimants in ISDS proceedings. In its analysis of 105 ISDS proceedings initiated by US American investors before the International Centre for Settlement of Investment Disputes (ICSID), the CSIS identified two-thirds of them to be SMEs or individuals.[12] This 'interesting

[10] David Gaukrodger and Kathrin Gordon, 'Investor-State Dispute Settlement: A Scoping Paper for the Investment Policy Community' (OECD Working Paper on International Investment 2012/03) 17–18 <http://www.oecd.org/investment/investment-policy/WP-2012_3.pdf> accessed 3 September 2014.

[11] ibid 19.

[12] Scott Miller and Gregory N Hicks, 'Investor-State Dispute Settlement: A Reality Check' (Center for Strategic and International Studies, A Report of the CSIS Scholl Chair in International Business

finding'[13] led the CSIS to conclude that 'conflating ISDS with "big corporations" ignores that most U.S. investors who have filed investment arbitration claims are individuals or [SMEs]'.[14]

An analysis of the ISDS proceedings initiated in 2015 confirms the above results. Based on the evaluation of publicly available information about the claimants, from a total of 70 claims filed in 2015,[15] at least twelve were filed by SMEs[16] and four by individuals or groups of individuals.[17] As in the OECD study, also in 2015 there were a number of claimants of which no financial figures are publicly available, and which could also add to the number of SMEs and individuals. Based on the available information, at least 22 per cent of investors who commenced ISDS proceedings in 2015 were SMEs or individuals.

## B. Impediments for SMEs to Engage in ISDS

Irrespective of the significant current involvement of SMEs in ISDS, there are, indeed, conditions that may inhibit SMEs from bringing actions before arbitral tribunals under investment treaties.[18]

### I. Costs and duration of ISDS proceedings

First, the expected costs could be significant. In recent cases, the average overall costs of ISDS proceedings were approximately US$8 million, and in some exceptional cases more than US$30 million.[19] In addition to having to bear its own costs, a claimant also bears the risk of paying the costs of the entire proceedings if the investor's claim is dismissed and the arbitral tribunal orders the investor to reimburse the state for its costs and expenses.

According to the definition by the European Commission, SMEs are enterprises employing fewer than 250 people and with an annual turnover not exceeding €50 million and/or an annual balance sheet total not exceeding €43 million.[20] For

2015) 18 <http://csis.org/files/publication/150116_Miller_investorStateDispute_web.pdf> accessed 3 March 2016.

[13] ibid 18. [14] ibid V–VI.

[15] UNCTAD, 'Investment Dispute Settlement Navigator' (2016) <http://investmentpolicyhub.unctad.org/ISDS/FilterByYear> accessed 19 March 2016.

[16] According to the definition of SME by the European Commission, see below Section B.I.

[17] Individual claimants not including persons appearing to be oligarchs or billionaires.

[18] Caplan (n 4) 303.

[19] Gaukrodger and Gordon (n 10) 19; see, for example, *Spyridon Roussalis v Romania*, ICSID Case No ARB/06/1, Award (7 December 2011). The claimant had to pay 60 per cent of Romania's legal fees in the amount of €6,053,443.78.

[20] European Commission, Commission Recommendation 2003/361/EC of 6 May 2003 Concerning the Definition of Micro, Small and Medium-Sized Enterprises [2003] OJ L124/36, Annex, Art 2; see also the Annex of this volume, Table.

a company of that size, the costs of initiating ISDS proceedings and the associated cost risk are a daunting if not prohibitive financial burden.[21]

One reason for the cost development in arbitral proceedings is their duration: 'the longer the proceedings, the more expensive they will be'.[22] ISDS proceedings regularly take four to five years until the arbitral tribunal renders an award. Especially in the case of SMEs with limited financial resources, a lengthy and cost-intensive arbitration may strain the SME's capability to withstand the financial pressure for such a long period of time.

### II. Asymmetry of financial resources

Second, many SMEs may hesitate to initiate ISDS proceedings because of the asymmetry of financial resources. Their opponent will be a state with larger financial resources determined to defend itself against an allegation of having unlawfully interfered with the business of a foreign investor. Over the last few years in particular, following the global financial crisis, the increasing demand for funding of ISDS proceedings (so-called 'third-party funding') revealed the financial constraints and the disparity between investors and states.[23]

## C. Possibilities of Cost Reduction

In order to contain the problem of high procedural costs as well as the long duration of arbitral proceedings, there are specific options for the parties to reduce costs and techniques for conducting cost- and time-efficient ISDS proceedings.

Approximately 20 per cent of the total costs arise from arbitrator fees and institutional costs,[24] whereas approximately 80 per cent accrue for legal counsel and expert fees. In particular, the latter largely depend on the duration and complexity of the case.[25]

[21] Caplan (n 4) 304.

[22] International Chamber of Commerce (ICC), *Techniques for Controlling Time and Costs in Arbitration* (ICC 2012) 6. As to the expenses and the length of arbitral proceedings as the two most commonly mentioned disadvantages of international arbitration, cf Andreas Respondek, 'Five Proposals to Further Increase the Efficiency of International Arbitration Proceedings' (2014) 31 Journal of International Arbitration 507, 507.

[23] Leo Szolnoki, 'ICCA and Queen Mary Examine Third-Party Funding' (Global Arbitration Review, 11 October 2013) <http://globalarbitrationreview.com/news/article/31962> accessed 3 September 2014; see also Perry S Bechky, Chapter 10 of this volume, Section C.

[24] The average tribunal costs in UNCITRAL proceedings are at US$853,000 and in ICSID proceedings at US$769,000: see Matthew Hodgson, 'Counting the Costs of Investment Treaty Arbitration' (2014) 9(2) Global Arbitration Review <http://globalarbitrationreview.com/news/article/32513> accessed 12 September 2014.

[25] Inna Uchkunova, 'ICSID: Curious Facts' *Kluwer Arbitration Blog* (25 October 2012) <http://kluwerarbitrationblog.com/blog/2012/10/25/icsid-curious-facts/comment-page-1> accessed 3 September 2014.

## I. Concepts for cost allocation

Arbitrators generally have significant discretionary power over how the costs of proceedings are allocated between the parties. Due to the absence of mandatory rules, there is a degree of uncertainty for investors considering ISDS proceedings as to how the arbitral tribunal will allocate the costs of the proceedings. This uncertainty has the potential of precluding effective access to justice for SMEs, especially for smaller enterprises with smaller claims.[26]

In arbitral practice, two principles of cost allocation are frequently applied.

### *1. 'Pay your own way'*

Under the traditional 'pay your own way' approach, each party covers its own costs for legal counsel and witnesses, while arbitrators' and institutional costs are equally shared.[27] This rule was applied in about 60 per cent of the publicly available awards through 2009.[28]

Although this approach burdens both parties regardless of the outcome of the proceedings, it also limits the financial risk because each party only has to bear the costs for which it is responsible and, with regard to costs of legal counsel and experts, it can influence.[29]

### *2. 'Costs follow the event'/'The loser pays'*

In recent years, arbitral tribunals increasingly seem to favour the 'costs follow the event' (or 'loser pays') rule. Under this rule, the costs of the proceedings and legal costs of both parties are proportionally allocated to the extent the parties prevail or lose the arbitration, and the tribunal awards reimbursement for costs accordingly.[30]

If, for example, a tribunal determines that a claim is entirely justified, it orders the respondent to bear the entire costs of the proceedings and the claimant's legal costs. If the tribunal awards only 75 per cent of the claimant's claim, the tribunal orders the respondent to reimburse the claimant for 75 per cent of the costs of the proceeding and its legal costs. On the other hand, the tribunal orders the claimant

[26] Gaukrodger and Gordon (n 10) 23; Caplan (n 4) 305.

[27] James Nicholson and John Gaffney, 'Cost Allocation in Investment Arbitration: Forward toward Incentivisation' (Columbia FDI Perspectives No 123, 2014) 1 <http://ccsi.columbia.edu/files/2013/10/No-123-Nicholson-and-Gaffney-FINAL.pdf> accessed 3 September 2014; Matthew Weiniger and Matthew Page, 'Treaty Arbitration and Investment Disputes: Adding up the Costs' (2006) 1(3) Global Arbitration Review <http://globalarbitrationreview.com/journal/article/16512/treaty-arbitration-investment-disputes-adding-costs> accessed 3 September 2014.

[28] Gaukrodger and Gordon (n 10) 22.

[29] Baiju S Vasani and Anastasiya Ugale, 'Cost Allocation in Investment Arbitration: Back toward Diversification' (Columbia FDI Perspectives No 100, 2013) 2 <http://ccsi.columbia.edu/files/2014/01/FDI_100.pdf> accessed 3 September 2014.

[30] ibid 1.

to reimburse the respondent for its share of the costs of the proceedings and its legal costs if the claim is dismissed.[31]

From the investor's perspective, the risk of having to bear the entire costs of the proceedings and the opposing state's legal costs without being able to predetermine the amount of those costs may have a significant deterring effect. However, this should not necessarily discourage investors from considering ISDS proceedings. Rather, it should urge investors to conduct an early case assessment and only bring claims with a reasonable probability of success (ie cases where taking the risk of paying all costs is justified by sound business judgment).[32] Arbitral tribunals have applied the 'costs follow the event' rule to the detriment of claimants particularly in cases where the claims were viewed as frivolous.[33]

## II. Guidelines on cost allocation in arbitration rules

As illustrated above, there is no clear consensus or generally accepted principle regulating how to allocate arbitral costs. The award on costs is ultimately a case-by-case-decision, and the arbitral tribunal will usually apply discretion when fixing and allocating the costs.[34]

For investors considering ISDS proceedings, the choice of forum and applicable arbitration rules could provide some guidance with regard to the allocation of costs in the award. Under most investment treaties, investors can choose between institutional arbitration under the auspices of the International Centre for Settlement of Investment Disputes and its convention and arbitration rules, or ad-hoc arbitration under the rules of the UN Commission on International Trade Law (UNCITRAL).

In ICSID proceedings, there is no provision as to how to allocate costs.[35] Article 61(2) of the ICSID Convention merely states that:

> In the case of arbitration proceedings the Tribunal shall, except as the parties otherwise agree, assess the expenses incurred by the parties in connection with the proceedings, and shall decide how and by who those expenses, the fees and expenses of the members of the Tribunal and the charges for the use of the facilities of the Centre shall be paid.

Under ICSID rules, the tribunal's decision on costs is entirely within its discretion. Consequently, a claimant cannot be certain which cost allocation principle the tribunal will apply and that it will not have to bear some costs even if it has fully prevailed in the proceedings.

The UNCITRAL arbitration rules, as revised in 2010, favour the 'costs follow the event' approach as the basic principle for the arbitral tribunal's decision on

[31] An award to reimburse one party for the costs of its legal counsel is generally subject to the determination of the arbitral tribunal that the incurred costs are reasonable.

[32] Nicholson and Gaffney (n 27) 1.

[33] Weiniger and Page (n 27).

[34] Brown (n 7) 500.

[35] Gaukrodger and Gordon (n 10) 22.

costs, while leaving the tribunal discretion to depart from this rule. Under Article 42(1) of the UNCITRAL arbitration rules:

The costs of arbitration shall in principle be borne by the unsuccessful party or parties. However, the arbitral tribunal may apportion each of such costs between the parties if it determines that the apportionment is reasonable, taking into account the circumstances of the case.

## III. Benefits of each approach dependent on the strength of the case

There is no clear evidence whether either of the above approaches is more favourable to investors or states in ISDS proceedings.[36] In essence, the advantages and disadvantages of each approach depend on the strength of the case: If the investor believes it has a strong case, the 'costs follow the event' approach under the UNCITRAL arbitration rules would seem more favourable. If the case appears weaker, or if the investor prefers to limit its financial risk, the 'pay your own way' approach could be preferable.

## IV. Cost- and time-efficient proceedings

In order to prevent costs from getting out of hand, it is essential to shape and conduct an arbitration efficiently by streamlining the proceedings for each individual case. There are a number of considerations to be taken into account prior to and during an arbitration which facilitate time- and cost-efficiency. It must be noted, however, that establishing cost-saving proceedings is not solely within the control of the investor. Generally, both parties must agree on the procedural schedule and commit to conducting the proceedings professionally and without delay or unnecessary cost-intensive procedural steps.

The International Chamber of Commerce (ICC) has published general recommendations for effective case management,[37] providing 'a practical toolkit for making decisions on how to conduct an arbitration in a time- and cost-effective manner'.[38] Although these recommendations were developed under the ICC arbitration rules, they can be used for 'any arbitration' and for large or small cases.[39] They are therefore equally valuable for claimants in ISDS proceedings under ICSID or UNICTRAL rules.

### 1. *Early case assessment—Cost-benefit analysis*

An early and diligent case assessment considering all potential issues of the case, including a cost-benefit analysis, is essential for any investor before commencing

[36] Gaukrodger and Gordon (n 10) 23.

[37] ICC, *Effective Management of Arbitration: A Guide for In-House Counsel and Other Party Representatives* (ICC 2014); and ICC (n 22).

[38] ICC (n 37) 1. [39] ibid 1.

ISDS proceedings and also during the arbitration. Arbitrating cases where the chances of success are low or not worth the time and financial effort should be avoided,[40] particularly considering the potential cost risk.[41]

### 2. *Choice of arbitrators and representatives*

A critical decision to be made by the parties at the very beginning of arbitral proceedings concerns the question of how many and which arbitrators should be appointed to the tribunal. Based on the parties' case assessment, it must be determined whether, in light of the amount in dispute and the complexity of the case, a one- or three-member tribunal is appropriate to hear the case.

Evidently, the fees for one arbitrator will be lower than for three arbitrators. Moreover, a sole arbitrator need not discuss its schedule and decisions with other arbitrators, allowing the proceeding to move forward faster.[42] In particular, in cases involving smaller claims, a three-member tribunal may be oversized and a sole arbitrator sufficient and more suitable.

Aside from the number of arbitrators, it is just as important to carefully consider who to select as arbitrators. Although the parties have broad autonomy to shape the proceedings, the arbitrators are equally responsible for effective case management. Conducting arbitral proceedings requires a degree of judgment, expertise, and experience, particularly in complex cases. Therefore, the parties need to carefully select an arbitrator or arbitrators with the necessary knowledge on the relevant issues, as well as the time, experience, and judgment to manage the case effectively and issue the award in a timely manner.[43]

The same considerations as to experience and judgment also apply to the selection of legal counsel. Experienced legal counsel with the necessary knowledge on the issues of fact and law as well as the sensitivity to the time and costs of the proceedings are more likely to shape and manage the proceedings effectively.[44] Moreover, legal counsel in the United States or in Great Britain at times charge higher fees than, for instance, in continental Europe, but are not necessarily more experienced or better suited for handling the case. Therefore, when comparing offers of legal counsel, a look at the cost structure of the team handling the case is always worthwhile.

### 3. *Effective case management: Developing a strategy for the specific case and setting up a tight but realistic schedule for the proceedings*

An early case assessment also should enable the investor to shape an efficient strategy to present its claim, depending on the pertinent issues and the complexity of the case.

[40] ibid 5. [41] Caplan (n 4) 306. [42] ICC (n 22) 7.
[43] ibid 8. [44] ibid 7.

When developing the case strategy, the following considerations should be taken into account:

- The concentration of issues in separate procedural stages, for example, in case the jurisdiction of the arbitral tribunal is disputed and/or the determination of the amount of damages is a distinct and contentious issue (so-called bifurcation of the proceedings into two stages or trifurcation into three stages).[45] Separating the issues may allow for an early termination or settlement of the case and relieve the parties from the burden of having to argue issues in detail that are not material for the tribunal's holding;[46]
- limiting the rounds of written submissions and discovery to the extent necessary for the particular case;
- conducting procedural conferences by telephone or video conference instead of personal meetings;
- being efficient with the involvement of witnesses and experts in the proceedings and hearings—for example, limiting the testimony of fact witnesses to written statements and limiting the scope of cross-examination of witnesses and experts during the hearings;
- limiting the number and duration of oral hearings, including witness examination, and selecting the venue for the hearing; and
- considering the necessity and number of post-hearing submissions.

For each stage of the arbitration, the parties must determine whether it is useful to resolve the dispute and, if so, how it can be conducted in a cost-efficient manner. Particularly the degree of discovery or document production and the manner in which it is executed may have a significant impact on time and costs.[47] Each party should, therefore, analyse if and to what extent document production is useful and weigh the additional time and costs against the probability that the document production will assist in making its case.

Apart from the general concepts of cost allocation discussed above,[48] the cost decision in an arbitration award may also be influenced by considerations such as whether the parties have presented their case in an 'efficient and professional manner'.[49] A party may try to delay or to increase costs in the proceeding by making knowingly inconsistent allegations of fact or futile procedural motions.[50] Such tactics may influence the cost decision by the arbitral tribunal, and the tribunal

[45] See rule 41(3) and (4) ICSID arbitration rules and Art 21(4) UNCITRAL arbitration rules.

[46] *Mesa Power Group, LLC v Canada*, PCA Case No 2012-17, Procedural Order No 2 (18 January 2013), 5: 'Indeed, it is good practice to let the parties "know where they stand" ... at an early stage and not to impose the burden of full fledged proceedings on a party that disputes being subject to arbitration'.

[47] ICC (n 37) 33. [48] See above, Section C.I.

[49] See, for example, *Thunderbird v Mexico*, UNCITRAL, Award (26 January 2006) paras 217–18; *Azinian v Mexico*, ICSID Case No ARB(AF)/97/2, Award (1 November 1999) para 126.

[50] Jeff Waincymer, *Procedure and Evidence in International Arbitration* (Kluwer Law International 2012) 1227.

may order that unnecessary costs must be borne by the party that caused them by engaging in bad faith or inefficient tactics.[51]

### 4. *Consideration of amicable settlement at any time during the proceedings*

As part of the continuing reassessment of the case throughout the arbitration, each party should always consider the possibility of a settlement as an alternative to litigating the case. A settlement can be reached at any time before or during the proceedings.[52]

Newly discovered facts, partial awards on decisive issues (eg jurisdiction or liability), or other relevant developments during the arbitration may lead to a changed perspective on the case and the risk assessment, and ultimately to the conclusion that an amicable settlement would be preferable to continuing with the proceedings.[53]

Moreover, a rejected settlement offer may have positive effects, since it can be taken into account by the arbitral tribunal in its cost decision. If the arbitral award contains provisions similar to an earlier settlement offer by one party, the tribunal may order the party that rejected the offer to bear the costs that could have been avoided had it accepted the offer.[54] Therefore, a fair and serious settlement offer may be an instrument to influence the cost decision and reduce the cost risk.

## D. Finance Options

SMEs with limited financial capacities or who are reluctant to take significant cost risks in ISDS proceedings may wish to consider options for financing such proceedings, for example by joining forces with other equally affected investors and initiating a multi-party arbitration, or by acquiring the necessary funds for the proceedings from an external funder.

### I. Multi-party arbitration

In cases where several investors are affected and their investment impaired by the same state measures (eg measures in a specific industry amounting to an indirect expropriation), it may make sense for those investors to form an alliance and jointly initiate ISDS proceedings to challenge these measures.

A joint approach by several investors may lead to a significant increase in efficiency and a reduction of costs, in particular if they choose to be represented by the same legal counsel and experts. Moreover, although the fees for multi-party

[51] See, for example, *Plama Consortium v Bulgaria*, ICSID Case No ARB/03/24, Award (27 August 2008) paras 321–23; *Europe Cement Investment v Turkey*, ICSID Case No ARB(AF)/07/2, Award (13 August 2009) paras 182–86.

[52] ICC (n 37) 6. [53] ibid 6, 9, 11. [54] Waincymer (n 50) 1225.

proceedings may be higher compared to proceedings between one investor and a state, they will likely be lower compared to the aggregate fees if each investor initiated proceedings individually. By the same token, the investors share the cost risk if their claim is not successful, as each investor will only have to bear its per capita share of the costs.

In several cases over the last few years, unrelated investors, for example individuals or companies that are not affiliated, have launched collective claims in ISDS proceedings concerning measures imposed on them by a particular state. In August 2011, the majority of an ICSID tribunal in *Abaclat and Others v Argentine Republic* issued a groundbreaking decision, acknowledging the admissibility and its jurisdiction over a mass claim brought by 60,000 Italian holders of Argentinian bonds challenging measures taken by Argentina after the financial crisis in 2001 to restructure its sovereign debt.[55]

Although neither the ICSID Convention nor the ICSID arbitration rules explicitly deal with multi-party proceedings,[56] the tribunal found that it had jurisdiction over individual claims under the applicable investment treaty, and that 'it is difficult to conceive why and how the Tribunal could lose such jurisdiction where the number of Claimants outgrows a certain threshold'.[57] As a prerequisite for consolidating the claims in one collective arbitration, it considered that the claims need to be 'identical or at least sufficiently homogenous' by being raised against the same respondent state under the same investment treaty and based on the same breach of obligation or other culpable behaviour.[58] Since these requirements were met in the *Abaclat* case, the arbitral tribunal dealt with the multitude of claimants as a question of procedure, and relied on Article 44 of the ICSID Convention stipulating that any question of procedure not covered by the ICSID Convention, the arbitration rules, or other rules agreed by the parties can be decided by the tribunal.[59] Other ICSID tribunals have followed this approach.[60]

In ISDS proceedings under UNCITRAL arbitration rules, the admissibility of collective claims by unrelated claimants has not been recognized by tribunals in publicly available decisions. For example, the Permanent Court of Arbitration in August 2013 did not allow a collective claim of ten claimants to proceed because they were neither affiliates nor had invested in the same operation, forcing the claimants to continue with their claims in six separate proceedings.[61] However,

[55] *Abaclat and Others v Argentine Republic*, ICSID Case No ARB/07/5, Decision on Jurisdiction and Admissibility (4 August 2011); Jessica Beess und Chrostin, 'Sovereign Debt Restructuring and Mass Claims Arbitration before ICSID, the *Abaclat* Case' (2012) 53(2) Harvard International Law Journal 505.

[56] Beess und Chrostin (n 55) 514.

[57] *Abaclat and Others v Argentine Republic*, para 490.

[58] ibid para 540; Beess and Chrostin (n 55) 515.

[59] *Abaclat and Others v Argentine Republic*, para 521.

[60] *Ambiente Ufficio SpA and Others v Argentine Republic*, ICSID Case No ARB/08/9, Decision on Jurisdiction and Admissibility (8 February 2013); *Giovanni Alemanni and Others v Argentine Republic*, ICSID Case No ARB/07/8, Decision on Jurisdiction and Admissibility (17 November 2014).

[61] *Antaris Solar GmbH and Others v Czech Republic*, PCA Case No 2014/01, Notice of Arbitration (8 May 2013) only available as IA Reporter Story by Luke Eric Peterson, 'Solar Investors File Arbitration against Czech Republic: Intra-EU BITs and Energy Charter Treaty at Center of Dispute' *Investment*

the decisions by arbitral tribunals in other multi-party proceedings are still pending.[62]

In cases where a large number of foreign investors are affected by the same state measures, a mass claim in single ISDS proceedings may be the most appropriate solution, avoiding unsatisfactory results with higher overall costs and possibly inconsistent decisions.[63] In particular for SMEs or individuals, mass claims appear to be an appropriate and effective way for cost-sensitive access to justice. In the aftermath of the *Abaclat* decision, collective claims by groups of claimants will presumably increase in the future.[64] It has to be noted, however, that the tribunal's jurisdiction and admissibility of each collective claim is dependent on the circumstances of the particular case.[65]

## II. Third-party funding

A completely different approach for claimants to make ISDS proceedings financially affordable, apart from reducing or sharing costs, is to obtain financing from an external funder to conduct the proceeding, so-called 'third-party funding' (TPF). In cases where investors such as SMEs or individuals are not able to bear the costs of the proceedings or seek to relieve their balance sheets of these costs, TPF is an opportunity to outsource these costs and the associated financial risk.[66] It is, therefore, an option to balance the asymmetry of financial resources between small investors and states.[67]

Over the past few years, ISDS proceedings, but also high-value commercial arbitration and litigation, has become an appealing field of investment for financial investors, particularly since the beginning of the global financial crisis.[68]

### *1. The concept behind third-party funding*

Third-party funders do not participate as claimants in ISDS proceedings. They are usually insurance companies, banks, or specialized funding companies unrelated

*Arbitration Reporter* (18 June 2013) <http://www.iareporter.com/articles/20130515_1> accessed 3 September 2014; Sebastian Perry and Kyriaki Karadelis, 'Sun Rises on Czech Energy Claims' Global Arbitration Review (19 February 2014) <http://globalarbitrationreview.com/news/article/32436/sun-rises-czech-energy-claims> accessed 3 September 2014.

62 IA Reporter, 'Spain Round-Up: Twin Energy Charter Claims Moving at Different Speeds; Arbitrator in Third Case Agrees to Hear Jurisdictional Objections First' *Investment Arbitration Reporter* (18 June 2013) <http://www.iareporter.com/articles/20130617_1> accessed 3 September 2014. The decision of bifurcation from March 2013 was not published.

63 Brian King and Alexander Yanos, 'Mass Claims in International Investment Arbitration' *The Deal Pipeline* (18 January 2012) <http://www.thedeal.com/content/restructuring/mass-claims-in-international-investment-arbitration.php> accessed 3 September 2014.

64 Beess und Chrostin (n 55) 505, 517.

65 King and Yanos (n 63).

66 Roula Harfouche and James Searby, 'Third-Party Funding: Incentives and Outcomes' Global Arbitration Review (31 October 2013) <http://globalarbitrationreview.com/reviews/50/sections/172/chapters/1926/third-party-funding-incentives-outcomes> accessed 3 September 2014; Lisa Bench Nieuwveld and Victoria Shannon, *Third-Party Funding in International Arbitration* (Kluwer Law International 2012) 11.

67 See above, Section B.II.

68 Bench Nieuwveld and Shannon (n 66) 10–11; Szolnoki (n 23).

to the legal dispute between the investor and the state, viewing such disputes as investments.[69]

Depending on the scope and amount of funding agreed between the claimant and the funder, the funder covers all or some of the claimant's legal fees, the costs for the arbitral tribunal, and potentially also a cost award against the claimant if the claim is dismissed, in return for a success fee (eg a multiple of the provided funds) and/or an agreed percentage of the award's amount if the claim is successful.[70] If the claim is dismissed, however, the funder loses its investment and is not entitled to compensation. Accordingly, TPF shifts the financial risk of the proceedings largely to the funder. The above-mentioned *Abaclat* arbitration, for example, was funded by banks.[71]

In order to make a decision whether to fund a certain dispute or not, the funder will analyse the strengths and weaknesses of the case and the potential for recovery from the opponent if the claim is successful.[72]

Since funders are often experienced in the field of investor-state arbitration, their advice can also be considered by still undecided investors. SMEs might also benefit from the funders' network within the ISDS community. Given their market experience, they can, for instance, support the investor in its selection of counsel and arbitrators. Depending on the content of the funding contract, the funder may not be allowed to seek influence on the strategic control or conduct of the arbitral proceedings,[73] or it may allow the funder to have regular involvement in the proceedings.[74]

### 2. *Recent developments: Cost security by third-party-funded claimants*

A discussion has recently arisen as to whether a third-party-funded claimant would have to provide a guarantee or security covering the costs of the proceedings in the event that the claim is dismissed.[75]

In the ICSID case *RSM Production Corporation v St Lucia*, the tribunal granted the state's request and ordered RSM to post security for costs of the proceedings.[76] The particular circumstances of this case prompted the tribunal to require security for costs from the claimant in order to protect the state's potential claim for reimbursement of its costs were it to prevail in the dispute.[77] First, the tribunal was concerned that the claimant would not comply with a possible cost award since the claimant had a history of not paying cost advances or complying with awards for

[69] Bench Nieuwveld and Shannon (n 66) 4. [70] ibid 2, 4.

[71] See above, Section D.I. [72] Bench Nieuwveld and Shannon (n 66) 3.

[73] Harfouche and Searby (n 66). [74] Bench Nieuwveld and Shannon (n 66) 7.

[75] Kyriaki Karadelis, 'Should Funded Claimants Have to Pay Security?' Global Arbitration Review (1 September 2014) <http://globalarbitrationreview.com/news/article/32932> accessed 4 September 2014.

[76] *RSM Production Corp v Saint Lucia*, ICSID Case No ARB/12/10, Decision on Saint Lucia's for Security for Costs (13 August 2014) para 90.

[77] ibid para 63.

reimbursement of costs in previous proceedings,[78] and St Lucia presented evidence that RSM did not have sufficient financial resources.[79] Second, RSM had admitted that a third-party funder was funding the proceedings,[80] which supported the tribunal in its view that the claimant might not honour a cost award rendered against it, and that it was doubtful whether the third-party funder would cover such award.[81]

The tribunal in *RSM Production* considered the use of third-party funding in connection with the claimant's admitted lack of financial resources and its history of non-payments as an indication that RSM would be unable to reimburse St Lucia for its costs of the proceeding. The decision has been much debated and it is so far a particular and isolated case. Therefore, SMEs should not generally fear security orders or similar injunctions if they consider initiating ISDS proceedings funded by third parties.

## E. Supplement to ISDS: Investment Guarantees

As a supplement (or alternative) to ISDS proceedings, SMEs may consider to protect foreign investments through investment guarantees or insurances. As opposed to the finance options illustrated above, guarantees or insurances need to be concluded prior to making the investment. They provide protection against non-commercial risks, especially in developing countries.[82] Investment guarantees are also referred to as political risk insurance. Depending on the specific insurance agreement, an SME may insure its investment particularly against expropriation, currency transfer risk, restrictions on capital movement, breach of contract in certain limited circumstances, and political violence (eg losses due to war, revolution, insurrection, or terrorist acts).[83]

Public and government-subsidized insurers like the Multilateral Insurance Guarantee Agency (MIGA) established under the auspices of the World Bank are prompted by the recognition 'that the flow of foreign investment to developing countries would be facilitated and further encouraged by alleviating concerns related to non-commercial risks'.[84]

Moreover, national governments provide guarantees, for example, the Federal Republic of Germany for foreign investments of German enterprises. Such a guarantee requires a bilateral investment agreement between Germany and the country where the investment will be made (§ 2(1) of the General Requirements

[78] ibid paras 77 ff. [79] ibid para 82. [80] ibid para 33. [81] ibid para 83.

[82] R Doak Bishop, James Crawford, and W Michael Reisman, *Foreign Investment Dispute: Cases, Materials and Commentary* (Kluwer Law International 2005) 491–92.

[83] Rudolf Dolzer and Christoph Schreuer, *Principles of International Investment Law* (2nd edn, Oxford University Press 2012) 228; Bishop and others (n 82) 491–92.

[84] Preamble of the Convention Establishing the Multilateral Investment Guarantee Agency, published in UNCTAD, International Investment Instruments: A Compendium, Vol 1 Multilateral Instruments, UNCTAD/DTCI/30(Vol.I) (United Nations 1996) 213.

of Investment Guarantees). But before enforcing the guarantee, Germany may demand the investor seek legal remedies to protect its investment through ISDS proceedings or other means (§ 20(1) of the General Requirements of Investment Guarantees). The guarantee, however, does not cover the costs of such proceedings.

Private insurance companies have also entered the investment insurance market[85] with individually tailored insurance contracts for investors.[86] Nevertheless, private insurers will always exclude extremely high risks[87] since they accept or reject risks on the basis of commercial considerations.[88]

## F. Conclusion

ISDS offers legal remedies for SMEs to protect their investments abroad. Already today, SMEs frequently take advantage of the opportunity to enforce their rights against states under investment treaties before arbitral tribunals in ISDS proceedings. However, the procedural costs for ISDS proceedings may exceed the financial resources an SME is able to afford or willing to dedicate to such proceedings and, thereby, may limit access to justice for SMEs.

In order to overcome this impediment, initiating and conducting an arbitration with continuing case assessment and management may effectively limit the costs for ISDS proceedings. To further reduce the procedural costs for an investor, several similar claims of unaffiliated investors may be joined in one arbitration, allowing the claimants to share the costs of the proceedings and limit their risk in case the claim is not successful. Furthermore, an investor with a strong case and good prospects of success may be able to obtain financial support by an external funder covering its costs and also potentially the opponent's costs in case of an adverse cost award. These approaches to limiting or reducing procedural costs for ISDS proceedings could eventually enable more SMEs to benefit from the protections granted under investment treaties.

Finally, a rather forward-looking means for an investor to protect its foreign investment against potential future state interference is to obtain an investment guarantee from its government or a private insurance company.

## References

Beess und Chrostin, J, 'Sovereign Debt Restructuring and Mass Claims Arbitration before ICSID, the *Abaclat* Case' (2012) 53(2) Harvard International Law Journal 505

Bench Nieuwveld, L and Shannon, V, *Third-Party Funding in International Arbitration* (Kluwer Law International 2012)

Bishop, RD, Crawford, J, and Reisman, WM, *Foreign Investment Dispute: Cases, Materials and Commentary* (Kluwer Law International 2005)

[85] Dolzer and Schreuer (n 83) 288; Bishop and others (n 82) 616.
[86] Bishop and others (n 82) 622. [87] ibid. [88] Dolzer and Schreuer (n 83) 229.

Brown, D, 'What Steps Should Arbitrators Take to Limit the Cost of Arbitration?' (2014) 31 Journal of International Arbitration 499

Caplan, LM, 'Making Investor-State Arbitration More Accessible to Small and Medium-Sized Enterprises' in Catherine A Rogers and Roger P Alford (eds), *The Future of Investment Arbitration* (Oxford University Press 2009) 297

Dolzer, R and Schreuer, C, *Principles of International Investment Law* (2nd edn, Oxford University Press 2012)

Gaukrodger, D and Gordon, K, 'Investor-State Dispute Settlement: A Scoping Paper for the Investment Policy Community' (OECD Working Paper on International Investment 2012/03) <http://www.oecd.org/investment/investment-policy/WP-2012_3.pdf> accessed 3 September 2014

Harfouche, R and Searby, J, 'Third-Party Funding: Incentives and Outcomes' Global Arbitration Review (31 October 2013) <http://globalarbitrationreview.com/reviews/50/sections/172/chapters/1926/third-party-funding-incentives-outcomes> accessed 3 September 2014

Hodgson, M, 'Counting the Costs of Investment Treaty Arbitration' (2014) 9(2) Global Arbitration Review <http://globalarbitrationreview.com/news/article/32513> accessed 12 September 2014

IA Reporter, 'Spain Round-Up: Twin Energy Charter Claims Moving at Different Speeds; Arbitrator in Third Case Agrees to Hear Jurisdictional Objections First' *Investment Arbitration Reporter* (18 June 2013) <http://www.iareporter.com/articles/20130617_1> accessed 3 September 2014

ICC, *Techniques for Controlling Time and Costs in Arbitration* (ICC 2012)

ICC, *Effective Management of Arbitration: A Guide for In-House Counsel and Other Party Representatives* (ICC 2014)

'Investor-State Dispute Settlement: The Arbitration Game' *The Economist* (London, 11 October 2014) <http://www.economist.com/news/finance-and-economics/21623756-governments-are-souring-treaties-protect-foreign-investors-arbitration> accessed 3 March 2016

Karadelis, K, 'Should Funded Claimants Have to Pay Security?' Global Arbitration Review (1 September 2014) <http://globalarbitrationreview.com/news/article/32932> accessed 4 September 2014

King, B and Yanos, A, 'Mass Claims in International Investment Arbitration' *The Deal Pipeline* (18 January 2012) <http://www.thedeal.com/content/restructuring/mass-claims-in-international-investment-arbitration.php> accessed 3 September 2014

Miller, S and Hicks, GN, 'Investor-State Dispute Settlement: A Reality Check' (Center for Strategic and International Studies, A Report of the CSIS Scholl Chair in International Business 2015) <http://csis.org/files/publication/150116_Miller_investorStateDispute_web.pdf> accessed 3 March 2016

Nicholson, J and Gaffney, J, 'Cost Allocation in Investment Arbitration: Forward toward Incentivisation' (Columbia FDI Perspectives No 123, 2014) <http://ccsi.columbia.edu/files/2013/10/No-123-Nicholson-and-Gaffney-FINAL.pdf> accessed 3 September 2014

Perry, S and Karadelis, K, 'Sun Rises on Czech Energy Claims' Global Arbitration Review (19 February 2014) <http://globalarbitrationreview.com/news/article/32436/sun-rises-czech-energy-claims> accessed 3 September 2014

Peterson, LE, 'Solar Investors File Arbitration against Czech Republic: Intra-EU BITs and Energy Charter Treaty at Center of Dispute' *Investment Arbitration Reporter* (18 June 2013) <http://www.iareporter.com/articles/20130515_1> accessed 3 September 2014

Respondek, A, 'Five Proposals to Further Increase the Efficiency of International Arbitration Proceedings' (2014) 31 Journal of International Arbitration 507

Szolnoki, L, 'ICCA and Queen Mary Examine Third-Party Funding' Global Arbitration Review (11 October 2013) <http://globalarbitrationreview.com/news/article/31962> accessed 3 September 2014

Uchkunova, I, 'ICSID: Curious Facts' *Kluwer Arbitration Blog* (25 October 2012) <http://kluwerarbitrationblog.com/blog/2012/10/25/icsid-curious-facts/comment-page-1> accessed 3 September 2014

UNCTAD, 'Smaller Firms Have Major Potential as Foreign Investors, Says UNCTAD' (Press Release, 28 May 1998) <http://unctad.org/en/pages/PressReleaseArchive.aspx?ReferenceDocId=3245> accessed 5 June 2016

UNCTAD, 'Investor-State Dispute Settlement (ISDS): Review of Developments in 2014' (IIA Issues Note No 2, May 2015) <http://unctad.org/en/PublicationsLibrary/webdiaepcb2015d2_en.pdf> accessed 3 March 2016

UNCTAD, 'International Investment Agreements Navigator' (2016) <http://investmentpolicyhub.unctad.org/IIA> accessed 20 March 2016

UNCTAD, 'International Investment Agreements Navigator: IIAs by Economy' (2016) <http://investmentpolicyhub.unctad.org/IIA/IiasByCountry#iiaInnerMenu> accessed 20 March 2016

UNCTAD, 'Investment Dispute Settlement Navigator' (2016) <http://investmentpolicyhub.unctad.org/ISDS/FilterByYear> accessed 19 March 2016

Vasani, BS and Ugale, A, 'Cost Allocation in Investment Arbitration: Back toward Diversification' (Columbia FDI Perspectives No 100, 2013) <http://ccsi.columbia.edu/files/2014/01/FDI_100.pdf> accessed 3 September 2014

Waincymer, J, *Procedure and Evidence in International Arbitration* (Kluwer Law International 2012)

Weiniger, M and Page, M, 'Treaty Arbitration and Investment Disputes: Adding up the Costs' (2006) 1(3) Global Arbitration Review <http://globalarbitrationreview.com/journal/article/16512/treaty-arbitration-investment-disputes-adding-costs> accessed 3 September 2014

# PART IV

# HUMAN RIGHTS, DEVELOPMENT, AND ENTREPRENEURSHIP

# 12

# Business and Human Rights and the Challenges for Small and Medium-Sized Enterprises

*Michael K Addo**

## A. Introduction

The subject of human rights that is slowly assuming a central importance in the conduct of business is not, in the wider scheme of responsible business conduct, an entirely new phenomenon.[1] Recent initiatives such as the UN Guiding Principles on Business and Human Rights (Guiding Principles, or UNGPs)[2] have elevated the profile of business and human rights considerably. This profile has been reinforced by similarly useful developments such as the UN Global Compact,[3] the 2011 update of the OECD Guidelines for Multinational Enterprises,[4] the International Finance Corporation Performance Standards on Environmental and Social Sustainability,[5] the Voluntary Principles on Security and Human Rights,[6] and the Equator Principles.[7]

* School of Law, University of Exeter. I am grateful to Christy Rush for his invaluable research assistance in the preparation of this chapter. The views expressed here are those of the author personally and do not represent those of the UN Working Group on Business and Human Rights.

[1] See Michael Addo and Jena Martin, 'The Evolving Business and Society Landscape: Can Human Rights Make a Difference?' in Jena Martin and Karen Bravo (eds), *The Business and Human Rights Landscape: Moving Forward, Looking Back* (Cambridge University Press 2015) 348.

[2] See UN Human Rights Council (UNHRC), 'Guiding Principles on Business and Human Rights: Implementing the United Nations "Protect, Respect and Remedy" Framework, Report of the Special Representative of the Secretary-General on the Issue of Human Rights and Transnational Corporations and Other Business Enterprises, John Ruggie' (21 March 2011) UN Doc A/HRC/17/31 (UNGPs). For an initial review of the UNGPs, see Radu Mares (ed), *The UN Guiding Principles on Business and Human Rights* (Martinus Nijhoff 2011). See also Wesley Cragg, 'Corporate Responsibility to Respect Human Rights: A Critical Look at the Justificatory Foundations of the UN Framework' (2012) 22 Corporate Ethics Quarterly 9.

[3] See the official website at <https://www.unglobalcompact.org> accessed 20 January 2017.

[4] See Organisation for Economic Co-operation and Development (OECD), *OECD Guidelines for Multinational Enterprises* (OECD 2011) <http://dx.doi.org/10.1787/9789264115415-en> accessed 20 January 2017.

[5] See International Finance Corporation (IFC), 'IFC Performance Standards on Environmental and Social Sustainability' (1 January 2012) <http://www.ifc.org/wps/wcm/connect/c8f524004a73daeca09afdf998895a12/IFC_Performance_Standards.pdf?MOD=AJPERES> accessed 20 January 2017.

[6] See <http://www.voluntaryprinciples.org> accessed 20 January 2017; text available at <http://www.voluntaryprinciples.org/files/voluntary_principles_english.pdf> accessed 20 January 2017.

[7] See The Equator Principles (June 2013) <http://www.equator-principles.com/resources/equator_principles_III.pdf> accessed 20 January 2017.

Unanimously endorsed by the UN Human Rights Council in 2011,[8] after six years of multi-stakeholder consultations by the former Special Representative of the Secretary-General, John Ruggie, the UN Guiding Principles have come to be seen as the most authoritative standard for preventing and remedying adverse corporate human rights impacts. In addition to the support that the UNGPs enjoy from states, the business community, and civil society alike, they have provided inspiration and steer for other initiatives.

The consensus concerning the applicable standard in this matter represents a sharp contrast to the potential challenges that face stakeholders, including government officials responsible for the implementation of the Guiding Principles, business practitioners, academic scholars, and civil society activists in their efforts to find common understandings between previously separated discourses.

The challenges of implementation of the UNGPs are multifaceted, multidimensional, and multi-layered and this is as true of the emerging issues as it is of the varied perspectives of the many stakeholders. In the latter instance, for example, it is not simply that the challenges confronting government officials are remarkably different from those in the business community as with other stakeholders, but also that within individual stakeholder communities there are different layers and dimensions of challenges. Typically, different government ministries and departments will perceive the issues of business and human rights differently and this may also be true of different levels of government such as federal, state, and municipal entities.

Intergovernmental institutions also reflect similar layers, facets, and dimensions. There is not a single perspective to the implementation of business and human rights in the wider UN family. The perspective of the World Bank will differ from that of UNICEF and so also that of the World Trade Organization (WTO), to mention only a few of the many agencies, funds, and programmes.[9] The same analysis may be applied to other organizations, including regional intergovernmental organizations such as the African Union, the Association of South East Asian Nations (ASEAN), the Organization of American States (OAS), etc.

The different dimensions, facets, and layers of challenges concerning implementation of the UNGPs may similarly be appreciated from the diversity of actors among business enterprises. The UNGPs already recognize this kaleidoscopic effect when they propose that:

> The responsibility of business enterprises to respect human rights applies to all enterprises regardless of size, sector, operational context, ownership and structure. Nevertheless, the scale and complexity of the means through which enterprises meet that responsibility may vary according to these factors and with the severity of the enterprise's adverse human rights impacts.[10]

[8] See UNHRC Res 17/4 (6 July 2011) UN Doc A/HRC/RES/17/4.

[9] On this see UNHRC, 'Report of the Secretary-General on the Challenges, Strategies and Developments with Regard to the Implementation of the Resolution 21/5 by the United Nations System, including Programmes, Funds and Agencies' (1 April 2014) UN Doc A/HR/26/20.

[10] UNHRC (n 2) Principle 14.

Seen in isolation, the above text exposes some broad aspects of the reality of the complexities of the challenges that the implementation of the UNGPs by business enterprises can pose. The truism from the text suggests, as a minimum, that the implementation of the UNGPs by business entities will require different strategies for different enterprises, including parent transnational enterprises, their subsidiaries, their subcontractors, franchises, partnerships, and sole traders. It may also be significant whether they are part of the formal or informal economy.

This is what makes the lessons concerning the challenges that confront small, medium-sized, and micro enterprises (SMEs) especially interesting. Considering the novelty of the UNGPs and yet taking account of the similarity of the ideals that they share with the wider corporate social responsibility (CSR) discourse, this chapter will draw on the lessons from business, but especially SME engagement with the CSR regime.[11] Some of the lessons are transferable from the general and structural aspects of the modern business environment and yet some other lessons arise from the very specific nature of SMEs concerning their size, their management, and their relationships with other stakeholders, including governmental entities, workers' organizations, social partners such as advocacy groups, affected communities, and peer group associations.

## B. The (In)visibility of SMEs in Business and Human Rights

Despite their significance in the global economy,[12] SMEs have not been a central feature or driving force in the crafting of the business and human rights strategy. In fact, SMEs have either been overlooked or not recognized, while the primary attention of business and human rights is focused on transnational enterprises. This oversight of a dedicated place for SMEs may be traced back through the history of the subject. The early attempts at the international level to define the human rights responsibilities of business was through the UN Commission on Transnational Corporations in its effort to propose a code of conduct.[13] As the title and indeed the content of the draft code[14] suggest, the focus of attention for that exercise was transnational corporations, especially for their operations abroad. This was no surprise as the motivation behind the entire exercise was to seek to counter the economic and political excesses of TNCs abroad.[15] Similar initiatives[16] around the same time, including the OECD Guidelines for Multinational Enterprises[17] and

[11] See also Joachim Karl, Chapter 9 of this volume, Section B.IV.

[12] See Section III.

[13] See Karl P Sauvant, 'The Negotiations of the United Nations Code of Conduct on Transnational Corporations' (2015) 16 Journal of World Investment and Trade 11; see also Theodore H Moran, 'The United Nations and Transnational Corporations: A Review and a Perspective' (2009) 18(2) Transnational Corporations 91 <http://unctad.org/en/Docs/diaeiia200910a4_en.pdf> accessed 20 January 2017; Norbert Horn, 'International Rules for Multinational Enterprises: The ICC, OECD and ILO Initiatives' (1980–81) 30 American University Law Review 923.

[14] Draft United Nations Code of Conduct on Transnational Corporation (1984) 23 International Legal Materials 626.

[15] Moran (n 13).

[16] Horn (n 13).

[17] OECD (n 4).

the International Labour Organization (ILO) Tripartite Declaration of Principles Concerning Multinational Enterprises and Social Policy,[18] had a similar international focus. To the extent that most SMEs are relatively small and have most of their activities at home, they were not within the purview of these initiatives.

While the title of subsequent initiatives such as the UN Norms on the Responsibilities of Transnational Corporations and Other Business Enterprises with Regard to Human Rights[19] suggest a change of focus to include more than the TNCs, it remains uncertain the extent to which SMEs can be said to have become visible in the emerging discourse. Other initiatives such as the Global Compact that are normally open to all business enterprises have, in practice, been unattractive to SMEs primarily because of the challenging requirements that membership of the Global Compact imposes on them.[20] This gap in terms of the invisibility of SMEs in the business and human rights discussions continues today as reflected in the recent UN Human Rights Council resolution[21] establishing an Open-ended Intergovernmental Working Group on Transnational Corporations and Other Business Enterprises with Respect to Human Rights (IGWG).[22] The mandate of this new body is listed as 'to elaborate an international legally binding instrument to regulate, in international human rights law, the activities of transnational corporations and other business enterprises'.[23] The phrase 'other business enterprises' that may be assumed to capture enterprises other than TNCs and conceivably therefore SMEs is elaborated in a footnote to denote 'all business enterprises that have a transnational character in their operational activities, and does not apply to local businesses registered in terms of relevant domestic law'.[24] This footnote removes any possible association that one may reasonably have between the work of the IGWG and its work with SMEs.

The invisibility of SMEs in the business and human rights conversation is, however, not entirely due to the policies at the international level. National policies may also have contributed to this unfortunate outlook. In certain jurisdictions, SMEs are official instruments of economic growth, in terms of redressing

[18] See International Labour Organization (ILO), *Tripartite Declaration of Principles Concerning Multinational Enterprises and Social Policy* (4th edn, International Labour Office 2006) <http://www.ilo.org/wcmsp5/groups/public/---ed_emp/---emp_ent/---multi/documents/publication/wcms_094386.pdf> accessed 20 January 2017.

[19] UN Economic and Social Council, 'Norms on the Responsibilities of Transnational Corporations and Other Business Enterprises with Regard to Human Rights' (26 August 2003) UN Doc E/CN.4/Sub.2/2003/12/Rev.2. See also David Weissbrodt and Muria Kruger, 'UN Norms on the Responsibilities of Transnational Corporations and Other Business Enterprises with Regard to Human Rights' (2003) 97 American Journal of International Law 901.

[20] See Jette Steen Knudsen, 'Which Companies Benefit Most from UN Global Compact Membership?' *European Business Review* (24 November 2011) <http://www.europeanbusinessreview.com/?p=3167> accessed 20 January 2017.

[21] See UNHRC Res 26/9 (14 July 2014) UN Doc A/HRC/RES/26/9.

[22] See <http://www.ohchr.org/EN/HRBodies/HRC/WGTransCorp/Pages/IGWGOnTNC.aspx> accessed 20 January 2017.

[23] See UNHRC Res 26/9 (n 21) para 1.

[24] See ibid.

unemployment in particular political constituencies or seeking to harness its comparative advantage in the wider global economy.[25] Viewed as instruments of local policy, they are not exposed to external conversations. In fact, they tend to be protected by legislation that offers exemptions, subsidies, and exclusive access to government advice through specifically established supervisory departments and agencies for which issues of human rights are not especially relevant. When governments employ SMEs as instruments of economic policy, it is unlikely to be founded upon principles of social responsibility and more likely to be for reasons of protectionism. Even where there may be interest in competitive advantage, this often lies in undermining social indicators such as labour (cheap or forced, poor working conditions), discrimination (race and gender), health, and education. This character of SMEs places them in a framework outside of conversations about human rights.

In addition to parochial governments' visions concerning SMEs, there are characteristics of SMEs that make them difficult to engage with in a coherent manner. The SME domain is rather large and diverse.[26] While we may draw together some definitional indicators,[27] the reality is that there is a lot more that divides SMEs than unites them, including size, geography, sector, contexts of operation, levels of development, governance, etc. It is therefore difficult to identify a 'typical' SME and for that matter to ascertain a 'typical' human rights footprint with which to link interactions concerning business and human rights. The situation can often be compounded by the rather high levels of informality among SMEs. According to the ILO, only 9 per cent of the total number of estimated SMEs are formally registered.[28] For the ILO, even in the absence of detailed data on informal enterprises alongside the variations of informality,

> it is clear that the number of informal enterprises is high and that they account for a large share of all SMEs. In some developing countries, informal SMEs far outnumber formal enterprises of the same size. India, one of the few countries with reliable data on informal enterprises, reported 17 unregistered SMEs for every registered SME in 2007.[29]

This is, however, not to say that the ideals of business and human rights are of no relevance to SMEs. There have been numerous efforts to promote SME engagement with the CSR agenda.

[25] A good example is the Small and Medium Business Administration set up by the Korean Government as part of the Ministry of Trade, Industry, and Energy, with a mandate to: create jobs by promoting growth of the startup and venture industry; strengthen the technological competitiveness of SMEs to create new growth engines; provide support for business management, including financial and market development; invigorate the base of the economy to promote shared growth; and create a policy environment friendly to SMEs.

[26] The ILO estimates that there are between 420 and 510 million SMEs worldwide. See ILO, *Small and Medium-Sized Enterprises and Decent and Productive Employment Creation* (International Labour Office 2015) 5.

[27] See Section C. [28] ILO (n 26). [29] ibid.

## C. Small and Medium-Sized Enterprises and the Challenges of Identity

SMEs are important commercial actors. They make up a significant proportion of the number of the world's total businesses—between 85 and 99.9 per cent—both in developed and developing nations. According to approximations by one source, globally, SMEs account for 52 per cent of private sector value added and 67 per cent of private sector employment.[30]

The potentially significant human rights footprint of SMEs—particularly when viewed collectively—has led to discussions regarding their engagement with issues of corporate responsibility and respect for human rights. The UK Environment Agency, for example, has estimated that SMEs are the largest contributors to pollution, carbon dioxide emissions, and commercial waste.[31] Even before the publication of the UN Guiding Principles on Business and Human Rights in 2011, efforts to promote SME engagement with the CSR agenda were common.[32] It seems reasonable to assume that a large proportion of SMEs have always been involved in CSR activities,[33] with half of European SMEs currently involved in external socially responsible activities.[34] While the challenges associated with encouraging SMEs to act responsibly can be significant, their importance to the global economy means that they are seen as key drivers of economic development and important partners in the fight against poverty globally.[35]

To the extent that it is arguable that CSR can accommodate human rights and vice versa,[36] it will still be necessary to review and adjust how SMEs

[30] Association of Chartered Certified Accountants (ACCA), 'Small Business: A Global Agenda' (2010) 8 <http://www.accaglobal.com/content/dam/acca/global/PDF-technical/small-business/pol-afb-sbaga.pdf> accessed 20 January 2017.

[31] NetRegs, 'SME-nvironment' (2003) 1 <http://www.netregs.org.uk/media/1080/sme_2003_uk_1409449.pdf> accessed 20 January 2017.

[32] Heledd Jenkins, 'Small Business Champions for Corporate Social Responsibility' (2006) 67 Journal of Business Ethics 241, 241; UK Department of Trade and Industry, 'Engaging SMEs in Community and Social Issues' (2002) 3.

[33] European Commission, 'Opportunity and Responsibility: How to Help More Small Businesses to Integrate Social and Environmental Issues into What They Do' (2007) 8 <http://ec.europa.eu/DocsRoom/documents/10373/attachments/1/translations/en/renditions/native> accessed 20 January 2017.

[34] European Commission, *European SMEs and Social and Environmental Responsibility* (Observatory of European SMEs, No 1, 2002) 7 <http://ec.europa.eu/DocsRoom/documents/3157/attachments/1/translations/en/renditions/pdf> accessed 20 January 2017.

[35] ACCA (n 30) 9; see also Perumal Koshy and VN Prasad, 'Small and Micro Enterprises: A Tool in the Fight Against Poverty' (Munich Personal RePEc Archive, September 2007) <https://mpra.ub.uni-muenchen.de/22827/1/MPRA_paper_22827.pdf> accessed 20 January 2017. However, it has been pointed out that some of the positive claims made by policymakers and advocacy groups are not readily supported by the available evidence. See Thorsten Beck, Asli Demirguc-Kunt, and Ross Levine, 'SMEs, Growth, and Poverty: Cross-Country Evidence' (2005) 10 Journal of Economic Growth 199.

[36] UN Office of the High Commissioner for Human Rights (OHCHR), 'Frequently Asked Questions About the Guiding Principles on Business and Human Rights' (United Nations 2014) 10 <http://www.ohchr.org/Documents/Publications/FAQ_PrinciplesBussinessHR.pdf> accessed 20 January 2017.

currently engage with the broader CSR agenda in order to take account of human rights. Drawing on literature on SMEs and CSR, this chapter looks at some common characteristics of SMEs and how these may be reviewed and adjusted in order to fulfil the expectations of their corporate responsibility to respect human rights.

If SMEs are to be brought into the business and human rights fold generally and to implement the UNGPs specifically, then, they need to be located and identified. This poses some initial challenges, as, although national definitions have moved from being vague and qualitative to more objective thresholds that can be unambiguously verified,[37] the definition of an SME can vary throughout the world.[38] The boundaries between small, medium, and large are much more fluid and unstable and differ between nations.[39] There are not even consistent naming conventions: some countries separate small from medium, some introduce the concept of a 'micro' enterprise, while some further still do both or neither of these things. There have even been calls for the recognition of a 'nano' enterprise.[40] However, a small group of key variables (size, independence and legal status, sector, employment, turnover, capital investment, and balance sheet totals) are considered in most government definitions.[41]

One of the most widely accepted definitions is from the European Commission,[42] which uses staff headcount and either turnover or balance sheet total to determine whether an enterprise is an SME.[43]

There are tensions within the quantitative indicators approach with the possibility of companies with small staff headcount, but with enormous turnover or balance sheet totals. The company could be an independent or stand-alone business or inextricably part of a large group such as an international subcontracting network.[44] The European Commission has acknowledged the significance of these aspects of detail in its extensive user guidance regarding the definition.[45] The matter is complicated further by the fact that nothing prevents each EU Member State from setting separate definitions for SMEs for domestic purposes. Finally, regardless or perhaps because of indicators, some SMEs may have to apply for their recognition as SMEs to certain EU agencies

[37] ibid.

[38] Vrassidas Leopoulos, 'Editorial' (2006) 17 Production Planning & Control 225.

[39] ibid.

[40] Professional Contractors Group (PCG), 'Consultation on the Future "EU 2020 Strategy": PCG Response' (January 2010) <http://ec.europa.eu/dgs/secretariat_general/eu2020/docs/pcg_en.pdf> accessed 20 January 2017.

[41] ACCA (n 30) 6.

[42] ibid.

[43] European Commission, 'What is an SME?' (2016) <http://ec.europa.eu/growth/smes/business-friendly-environment/sme-definition/index_en.htm> accessed 20 January 2017. The cut-off points are shown in the table in the Annex of this volume.

[44] Charles Harvie and Boon-Chye Lee (eds), *The Role of SMEs in National Economies in East Asia* (Edward Elgar 2002).

[45] European Commission, *User Guide to the SME Definition* (European Union 2015) <http://ec.europa.eu/DocsRoom/documents/10109/attachments/1/translations/en/renditions/native> accessed 20 January 2017.

if they wish to benefit from incentives available to them,[46] for example under the SME Regulation.[47]

The complexities of SME identities can be worsened when looked at from different multilateral institutions and international organizations. Some of the main definitions are as shown in Table 12.1.

The variations between these definitions are not entirely logical except to acknowledge the significance of contextual and regional aspirations and expectations based on local practice, alongside the availability and reliability of relevant data.

The wide variation in the definition and identification of SMEs may be attributed to the adoption of definitions for purposes that are entirely different from the respect of human rights. Governments may employ these quantitative definitions for the collection of statistics or to administer subsidies to SMEs or to calibrate tax schedules. Such narrow objectives may not allow for easy adaptation for 'other' purposes such as preventing and redressing adverse human rights impacts.

The task of locating SMEs is not helped by the fact that an estimated 91 per cent worldwide operate in the informal economy.[48] There is, generally, a correlation between the informal economy and adverse human rights impacts because it is in this environment that employees tend to find themselves without rights such as a stable income and social protection. Even in instances where enterprises are part of a formal structure, employees can be without the most basic of protections and so it is arguable that enterprises in the informal economy are less likely to dedicate resources to preventing and addressing adverse human rights impacts. Indeed, the environmental record of businesses in the informal sector is in many cases worse than those of their formal counterparts.[49] As informal businesses are often diffused and unorganized, it is more difficult and more expensive for authorities to work with these businesses to help implement standards and then to track and enforce implementation. There are initiatives in some countries as well as by intergovernmental organizations such as the ILO to support the formalization of SMEs.[50] Unfortunately, this is often done for reasons other than social responsibility or human rights responsibility of these enterprises. It is not entirely clear whether and if so how formalization will enhance the human rights responsibility of SMEs.[51]

If the current nomenclature of the identity of SMEs is to be adaptable for the business and human rights agenda, then it may have to engineer a credible balance between its traditional quantitative indicators and the emerging qualitative ones

[46] For example, through the European Medicines Agency; for more information, see European Medicines Agency, 'Applying for SME Status' <http://www.ema.europa.eu/ema/index.jsp?curl=pages/regulation/general/general_content_000061.jsp> accessed 20 January 2017.

[47] European Commission, Commission Regulation 2049/2005/EC of 15 December 2005 laying down, pursuant to Regulation (EC) No 726/2004 of the European Parliament and of the Council, rules regarding the payment of fees to, and the receipt of administrative assistance from, the European Medicines Agency by micro, small and medium-sized enterprises [2005] OJ L329/4.

[48] ILO (n 26) 5.

[49] Emily Benson, 'Informal and Green? The Forgotten Voice in the Transition to a Green Economy' (IIED 2014) 14 <http://pubs.iied.org/pdfs/16566IIED.pdf> accessed 20 January 2017.

[50] See ILO (n 26) 44. [51] ibid 46.

**Table 12.1** Definitions of 'SMEs' by international organizations

| Institution | Maximum number of employees | Maximum revenues or turnover (US$) | Maximum assets (US$) |
|---|---|---|---|
| **World Bank** | 300 | 15 million | 15 million |
| **Multilateral Investment Fund, Inter-American Development Bank** | 100 | 3 million | — |
| **African Development Bank** | 50 | — | — |
| **Asian Development Bank** | No official definition. Uses only definitions of individual national governments. | | |
| **UN Development Programme** | 200 | — | — |

Source: T Gibson and HJ van der Vaart, 'Defining SMEs: A Less Imperfect Way of Defining Small and Medium Enterprises in Developing Countries' (Brookings Global Economy and Development 2008) 5 <http://seaf.com/wp-content/uploads/2014/10/Defining-SMEs-September-20081.pdf> accessed 20 January 2017.

such as the impact on human rights, the relationships with other enterprises, and the geographical and cultural contexts of its operations, as well as the relationships with government institutions. In these circumstances, it is useful to explore the management structures and governance of SMEs, and their existing commitments to CSR and other social responsibility initiatives such as environmental policies, security, and human rights issues.

## D. Organization, Size, and the Double-Edged Effect

The smaller size, both in terms of employees and turnover of SMEs, leads to specific challenges. The relatively fewer number of employees supports an organizational structure that tends to be more organic compared to a more bureaucratic structure in large firms. This can have a double-edged effect, for, whilst on the one hand, this can lead to an absence of standardization and the prevalence of loose and informal working relationships where staff development is limited,[52] on the other hand this can make the adaptation to new processes and programmes such as the UNGPs relatively smoother.

A particularly salient feature of the organization of SMEs is the dominance of a single personality—the owner-manager—who tends to be an entrepreneur.[53] The other employees of the SMEs who tend to be quite close to this central figure

[52] Abby Ghobadian and David N Gallear, 'Total Quality Management in SMEs' (1996) 24 Omega 83, 87.

[53] On SMEs and entrepreneurship, see also Fiorina Mugione and Fulvia Farinelli, Chapter 13 of this volume.

will have an informal relationship with him or her, leading to a ready influence of these employees by the owner-manager.[54] The dominance of this central figure also results in the likelihood of success or failure of an SME being directly tied to the skills, drive, and vision of him or her,[55] in significant contrast to larger organizations where their size means that the influence of any one person, even the Chief Executive Officer or Managing Director, is significantly weaker.

Furthermore, as entrepreneurs, these figures tend to be of a certain character: they are creative and show initiative as well as being energetic and committed, and they may be relatively more willing to take moderate risks. However, such a character may also come with flaws: including difficulty in delegating and consulting.

The advantage of a smaller structure with one central figure is that there is one easily identifiable person who will be aware of all of the business's operations. This could be a useful tool for the implementation of the UNGPs by the business, as the owner-manager would be easy to identify and thanks to his or her reach and power within the business would be an ideal implementer. This is in contrast to larger organizations, where there may not be a single person with sufficient insight into a sufficiently broad range of areas of the firm, meaning that a cross-departmental committee may have to be established to oversee the firm's compliance with human rights. The owner-manager structure also means that SMEs do not have to answer to shareholders,[56] removing a potential barrier to the adaptation of existing mechanisms so as to respect human rights.

Studies have concluded that it is the personal views and ethical considerations of SME owners and employees that lead to undertaking CSR activities.[57] This strong personal commitment to the respect for human rights often results in a genuine engagement beyond 'box-ticking' exercises. Convincing the entrepreneur to commit to new social responsibility initiatives such as the UNGPs and the responsibility to respect human rights represents in this context the primary challenge, especially as they may not even be aware of these initiatives or where they may be aware of them have rather limited understanding of their implications. This means they will be unable to share the necessary vision for change.

The prognosis for change is not especially healthy as research on SMEs' engagement with CSR has revealed that such companies often see little relevance, if at all, of social engagement and believe that they have 'no social responsibilities outside the narrow confines of their business'.[58] Other researchers have confirmed the lack

[54] ibid.

[55] Robert C MacGregor, Deborah Bunker, and Mira Kartiwi, 'The Perception of Barriers to E-Commerce Adoption by SMEs: A Comparison of Three Countries' in Pratush Bharati, In Lee, and Abhijit Chaudhury, *Global Perspectives on Small and Medium Enterprises and Strategic Information Systems: International Approaches* (IGI Global 2010) 155.

[56] Denise A Baden, Ian A Harwood, and David G Woodward, 'The Effects of Procurement Policies on "Downstream" Corporate Social Responsibility Activity: Content-Analytic Insights into the Views and Actions of SME Owner-Managers' (2011) 29 International Small Business Journal 259, 261.

[57] ibid; Federation of Small Businesses, *Social and Environmental Responsibility and the Small Business Owner* (2008) <http://www.fsb.org.uk/LegacySitePath/policy/assets/CSR%20Dec%202008.pdf> accessed 20 January 2017; European Commission (n 34).

[58] UK Department of Trade and Industry (n 32) 9.

of awareness of CSR among half of Indian SMEs.[59] In the matter of social responsibility, many SMEs are thought of as being 'vulnerably compliant', that is to say they are not aware of the rules to which they are supposed to adhere, but comply out of 'good luck'.[60] If there is low awareness among SMEs of corporate social responsibility—where the clues for action are fairly evident in the name—then it is fair to assume that there will be increased difficulty in raising awareness of the relevance of human rights—a term that, in popular parlance, is often associated with the relationship between the state and the individual. Even where awareness exists, SMEs tend to prioritize 'internal' human rights issues[61] such as the right to work, collective bargaining, and non-discrimination, while neglecting 'external' human rights concerns such as community consultation, free, prior informed consent, etc.

In the few circumstances where an entrepreneur is motivated for a particular reason, even if only for ideological reasons, to champion human rights, they may nevertheless face some practical challenges relating to financial pressure that may prove too much to bear. The owner-manager of an SME would normally have invested significant personal wealth in the business with the understandable expectation that she will be able to recover this initial investment and also make some profitable return on it. This is not unreasonable in the normal conduct of any business. However, the consequences of an overemphasis on economic returns, especially in the constraining environment in which SMEs operate, is that if they considered that a commitment to human rights may undermine the return on their investment, they may well pull back on their enthusiasm.

Furthermore, a 'willing' entrepreneur may be daunted by the technicalities of business and human rights agenda as has been observed in relation to CSR. The technical nature of the CSR agenda has been described as 'incomprehensible and unrealistic' for SMEs,[62] with language that is unfamiliar.[63] There is nothing to suggest that the business and human rights agenda will be received differently with the risks of confusion about its terminology concerning due diligence, remediation, and grievance mechanisms. The valuable concept of 'smart mix' of mechanisms and processes that underlies the UNGPs may prove to be a source of confusion for listing private responsibilities alongside public duties.

Related is the notion that strong entrepreneurial personalities may see the external imposition of norms and standards as a direct threat to their autonomy and thus

[59] Abhishek Tripathi and Anupama Bains, 'An Investigation into SMEs' Awareness of Corporate Social Responsibility Practices in Punjab, India' (18 February 2016) <http://papers.ssrn.com/sol3/papers.cfm?abstract_id=2764348> accessed 20 January 2017.

[60] Francesco Ciliberti, Pierpaolo Pontrandolfo, and Barbara Scozzi, 'Investigating Corporate Social Responsibility in Supply Chains: A SME Perspective' (2008) 16 Journal of Cleaner Production 1579, 1580; European Commission (n 34) 7; Judith Petts and others, 'The Climate and Culture of Environmental Compliance within SMEs' (1999) 8 Business Strategy and the Environment 14.

[61] Baden and others (n 56); UK Department of Trade and Industry (n 32).

[62] Pavel Castka and others, 'How Can SMEs Effectively Implement the CSR Agenda? A UK Case Study Perspective' (2004) 11 Corporate Social Responsibility and Environmental Management 140, 141.

[63] European Commission (n 33); Federation of Small Businesses (n 57).

potentially rebel against them.[64] The psychology of rewards and motivation has also been employed to conclude that both regulation and incentives may weaken the strength of any intrinsic motivation of SME owner-managers.[65] A caveat of this personal desire to 'do the right thing' is that the owners and staff of SMEs may be ignorant of the relevant norms. In the voluntary arena of CSR, opportunistic and ad hoc implementation of standards may not raise particular problems. With business and human rights, however, and especially with the UNGPs, a deliberate strategy is essential[66] and so awareness of the UN Guiding Principles and the scope of the corporate responsibility to respect human rights is crucial.

In this respect, the UNGPs are not so typical of what has come to be understood as CSR. They are set out broadly under three pillars—the so-called Protect, Respect, and Remedy pillars. Under the first of these, the state duty to protect against human rights abuse by third parties, the Guiding Principles emphasize the importance of the steps to be taken by states in terms of effective policies, legislation, and regulations to prevent, investigate, punish, and redress human rights abuses.[67] The UNGPs provide an excellent opportunity for states to set out their expectation of all business enterprises within their jurisdiction to respect human rights in their operations.[68] Other important operational indicators of the state duty to protect human rights include the need for policy coherence[69] (both horizontal and vertical) and the need for extra vigilance in the regulation of business in conflict-affected areas[70] or when there is a state–business nexus.[71]

Under Pillar II, the corporate responsibility to respect human rights, the Guiding Principles not only emphasize the need to avoid infringing on the human rights of others,[72] but business enterprises must know that they do this and demonstrate how they do this. The 'knowing and showing' principle is operationalized through the conduct of a human rights due diligence[73] by business enterprises and the communication of outcomes of the due diligence policies.[74] The corporate responsibility to respect human rights covers both direct and indirect impacts, that is to say, impacts that are linked to the enterprise's operations, products, and services, or through their business relationships even if they have not contributed directly to those impacts.[75]

[64] Baden and others (n 56) 433. [65] ibid 431.

[66] According to Guiding Principle 16 (Policy Commitment):

> As the basis for embedding their responsibility to respect human rights, business enterprises should express their commitment to meet this responsibility through a statement of policy that:
>
> a. Is approved at the most senior level of the business enterprise;
> b. Is informed by relevant internal and/or external expertise;
> c. Stipulates the enterprise's human rights expectations of personnel, business partners and other parties directly linked to its operations, products or services;
> d. Is publicly available and communicated internally and externally to all personnel, business partners and other relevant parties;
> e. Is reflected in operational policies and procedures necessary to embed it throughout the business enterprise.

[67] See UNHRC (n 2) Principle 1. [68] ibid Principle 2. [69] ibid Principle 8.
[70] ibid Principle 7. [71] ibid Principle 4. [72] ibid Principle 11.
[73] ibid Principles 15–20. [74] ibid Principle 21. [75] ibid Principle 13.

Finally, the Guiding Principles under Pillar III—access to remedy—emphasize the need for an integrated application of different redress mechanisms, including formal judicial, administrative, and non-judicial processes[76] alongside corporate grievance mechanisms.[77] The Guiding Principles set out important criteria by which to determine the effectiveness of non-judicial grievance mechanisms. These include legitimacy, accessibility, predictability, transparency, and human rights compatibility.[78] In addition, for operational level grievance mechanisms, the Guiding Principles recommend the engagement and dialogue with stakeholder groups[79] as especially necessary.

Some of the challenges associated with the size of SMEs may be alleviated by the development of specific guidelines to help SMEs understand the nature and scope of business and human rights generally and UNGPs in particular. The Global Reporting Initiative (GRI) guidelines on sustainability reporting for SMEs aim to help SMEs 'to identify their most significant issues to focus on and from there improve productivity and make cost savings'.[80] It has been suggested that small businesses respond best to case studies, because 'if SMEs can see specific practices that impact profitability and business improvement, they tend to be more likely to become involved'.[81] The Guidance prepared by the EU Commission for SMEs on the implementation of the UNGPs takes the time to break down different components of the corporate responsibility to respect human rights, giving examples of the different rights that may be affected as well as quotes from business owners and links to further case studies.[82] If there are too many guidelines, however, their value may start to diminish as SMEs fear 'bombardment' and 'too many organizations overlapping in advice'.[83]

## E. Resource Poverty

Another significant feature of SMEs, arising principally from their smaller size, is what Welsh and White have termed their 'resource poverty'.[84] Indeed, governments started defining SMEs and providing specific support to them in order to level out the playing field arising from such disadvantages.[85] This poverty is not only that

[76] ibid Principles 25–27. [77] ibid Principles 28–30. [78] ibid Principle 31.

[79] ibid Principle 31(h).

[80] Global Reporting Initiative, 'Ready to Report? Introducing Sustainability Reporting for SMEs' (2014) 3 <https://www.globalreporting.org/resourcelibrary/Ready-to-Report-SME-booklet-online.pdf> accessed 20 January 2017.

[81] Castka and others (n 62) 141.

[82] European Commission, 'My Business and Human Rights: A Guide to Human Rights for Small and Medium-Sized Enterprises' (2012) <http://ec.europa.eu/DocsRoom/documents/10375/attachments/1/translations/en/renditions/native> accessed 20 January 2017.

[83] UK Department of Trade and Industry (n 32) 18.

[84] John A Welsh and Jerry F White, 'A Small Business Is Not a Little Big Business' (1981) 59 Harvard Business Review 18 <https://hbr.org/1981/07/a-small-business-is-not-a-little-big-business> accessed 20 January 2017.

[85] ACCA (n 30) 6.

of financial resources, but also affects other areas such as knowledge, expertise, and staff who are sufficiently trained and qualified.

Millions of SMEs lack access to financial services: between 45 and 55 per cent of formally registered SMEs do not have access to formal institutional loans or overdrafts despite a need for these facilities and despite contributing to 45 per cent of total employment in the developing world.[86] Access to finance has been restricted further due to the 2008 financial crisis and its aftermath.[87] This financial poverty means that many SMEs will have entered the market with only a single product without the finance to diversify their offerings even if this were considered to be strategically desirable.[88] Furthermore, the salary of an owner-manager will represent a much larger fraction of revenues than in a larger company. This will mean that there may be insufficient resources remaining to pay for additional professional managers with a mandate to oversee social responsibility issues such as the respect for human rights. Finally, they may not be able to afford to pay for the kind of professional services, including accounting and reporting, that new initiatives may require.[89]

Lack of resources means that SMEs turn more to brain power, and indeed the depth of human capital is a fundamental element to the success of an SME.[90] However, in spite of this need, SMEs often experience poor staff planning, multi-functional management, high employee turnover rate, low productivity, difficulties in recruiting quality staff,[91] and an inability to adequately test and train employees in advance.[92] In particular, red tape and regulation remain a huge burden for SMEs, in both developed[93] and developing countries,[94] while cost and expense reduction represented the top business opportunity for SMEs in 2015.[95] The limited resources of SMEs and the entrepreneur's values as the driver for ethical conduct have led SME owners and some academics to claim that CSR regulation would be counterproductive,[96] in particular through the amount of red tape added that

[86] Global Partnership for Financial Inclusion, 'Report to the Leaders' (G20 Leaders Summit, Cannes, 5 November 2011) 4 <https://www.oecd.org/g20/summits/cannes/Global%20Partnership%20for%20Financial%20Inclusion%20Report%20to%20Leaders.pdf> accessed 20 January 2017.

[87] Edinburgh Group, 'Growing the Global Economy through SMEs' (2013) 13 <http://www.edinburgh-group.org/media/2776/edinburgh_group_research_-_growing_the_global_economy_through_smes.pdf> accessed 20 January 2017.

[88] David John Storey, *Entrepreneurship and the New Firm* (Taylor & Francis 1982).

[89] Welsh and White (n 84).

[90] Christian M Rogerson, 'Growing the SMME Manufacturing Economy of South Africa: Evidence from Gauteng Province' (2001) 19 Journal of Contemporary African Studies 267 <http://www.tandfonline.com/doi/abs/10.1080/02589000120066498> accessed 20 January 2017.

[91] Christian M Rogerson, 'The Impact of the South African Government's SMME Programmes: A Ten-Year Review (1994–2003)' (2004) 21 Development Southern Africa 765, 768.

[92] Welsh and White (n 84).

[93] Castka and others (n 62) 144.

[94] Economist Intelligence Unit, *Emerging Markets SMEs Capture Growth in Expanding Markets* (2012) 4.

[95] Zurich, 'Biggest Opportunities for Small and Medium Enterprises (SMEs) in 2015: Global Survey Report' (October 2015) <https://www.zurich.com/_/media/dbe/corporate/docs/whitepapers/biggest-opportunities-for-sme-2015-survey-report.pdf?la=en> accessed 20 January 2017.

[96] Denise A Baden, Ina A Harwood, and David G Woodward, 'The Effect of Buyer Pressure on Suppliers in SMEs to Demonstrate CSR Practices: An Added Incentive or Counter Productive?' (2009)

would divert resources from actually improving behaviour.[97] However, there is evidence to the contrary in the case of SMEs' environmental behaviour where it has been demonstrated that regulation is more effective than voluntary initiatives[98] and, in this instance, while time and cost are the main barriers to further engagement in responsible activities cited by SMEs, this is not the experience of the majority of SMEs who are actually engaged.[99]

The risk and therefore challenges posed by increased red tape, both internally and externally, to the company are real, especially as there is little doubt that an effective implementation of the UNGPs will generate additional red tape and paperwork for most companies. Additional paperwork will be necessary to secure the requirements of due diligence as set out in the UNGPs,[100] especially in seeking to reflect the UNGPs' principle of 'knowing and showing', under which enterprises will be expected to identify their direct human rights impacts, as well as those of their business relationships.[101] Furthermore, enterprises must track and measure their progress,[102] as well as communicate and report on these developments.[103] Where there is evidence of adverse impact, enterprises must provide remediation,[104] often using internal, industry, or multi-stakeholder grievance mechanisms.[105] Designing a grievance mechanism or responding to an externally managed one that is in alignment with Guiding Principle 31[106] demands the adaptation to new guidelines, multi-stakeholder consultations, rules, and enquiries.

The Federation of Small Businesses has suggested that the stress and concerns about red tape may be countered by highlighting the 'business case' for improving human rights as an effective way of encouraging SMEs to act responsibly[107] in order to fulfil their responsibility to respect human rights. The European Commission concurs with this approach when in their Guidance to SMEs on implementing the UNGPs, they take time to explain how effective implementation of the UNGPs may lead to increased revenue for business.[108] However, the idea of the 'business case' may not be without its shortcomings. First, it has not been demonstrated that a sufficiently robust business case exists for the implementation of the UNGPs by SMEs. The evidence from the business case for CSR[109] may not support the claim made in favour of the UNGPs. In addition, enhancing business performance is not necessarily a demonstrated motivator for SMEs engaging in responsible behaviour.

27 European Management Journal 429; Baden and others (n 56); Yves Fassin, 'SMEs and the Fallacy of Formalising CSR' (2008) 17 Business Ethics: A European Review 364.

[97] European Commission (n 33) 4.

[98] Laura J Spence, 'Does Size Matter? The State of the Art in Small Business Ethics' (1999) 8 Business Ethics: A European Review 163.

[99] UK Department of Trade and Industry (n 32).

[100] UNGPs Principles 17–21.

[101] ibid Principle 18.

[102] ibid Principle 20.

[103] ibid Principle 21.

[104] ibid Principle 22.

[105] ibid Principles 28–31.

[106] According to Principle 31, for a grievance mechanism to be credible it has to be legitimate, accessible, predictable, equitable, transparent, rights-compatible, a source of continuous learning, and based on engagement and dialogue.

[107] Federation of Small Businesses (n 57).

[108] European Commission (n 82).

[109] Castka and others (n 62) 142.

The evidence from the traditional CSR field suggests that the extent of engagement will always be influenced by commercial factors, with advantages and disadvantages analysed in the same way as any other commercial decision.[110]

## F. Flexibility

The flexibility of SMEs as compared to their larger counterparts has long been acknowledged.[111] Their strategic advantage is based on reaction and adaptation to the social environment[112] and thus they are able to respond better to changes and disturbances in the social environment. Complementing this flexibility is the short-term outlook of most SMEs: their strategies are often intuitive and opportunistic. These traits can be both a strength and a weakness. Grouped in local systems of production, SMEs can often be more flexible and responsive to customer needs than large firms. They can pool resources and share the costs of training, research, and marketing with other firms of a similar size and industry.[113] Their products tend to reflect local technology and are arguably more likely to satisfy the needs of poor people than the products of large enterprises and foreign technology,[114] and they can also nimbly adapt new technologies to gain an edge over larger corporations.[115] All of these could be strengths that may be used to adapt to the challenges posed by the implementation of the UNGPs. SMEs are potentially 'quicker on and off their feet', which allows them to be 'better placed than major corporate entities to take advantage of the fact that society and the media revere qualities such as honesty, integrity, and the ability to say sorry'.[116]

However, their approach also results in having a limited strategy, especially for the long term,[117] and their limited share of the market means that they are heavily reliant on just a few customers—in some cases on just one customer.[118] Indeed, this

[110] Castka and others (n 62) 143–44.

[111] ibid.

[112] Marc Desaulniers and Yvon Bigras, 'Transformed SME: Value Chain Management and New Forms of Organization: A Synthesis Report', presented to Canada Economic Development as part of the Globalization, Knowledge Economy and Competitiveness Project, a synthesis of trends and strategic issues for the Québec SME (Globalization and Innovative SMEs) (Canada Economic Development, 2000).

[113] OECD, 'Small and Medium-Sized Enterprises: Local Strength, Global Reach' (Policy Brief, June 2000) <http://www.oecd.org/cfe/leed/1918307.pdf> accessed 20 January 2017.

[114] Henry Rwigema and Peter Karungu, 'SMME Development in Johannesburg's Southern Metropolitan Local Council: An Assessment' (1999) 16 Development Southern Africa 107, 111 <http://www.tandfonline.com/doi/abs/10.1080/03768359908440064> accessed 20 January 2017.

[115] Economist Intelligence Unit (n 94) 2.

[116] Nigel Sarbutts, 'Can SMEs "do" CSR? A Practitioner's View of the Ways Small- and Medium-Sized Enterprises Are Able to Manage Reputation through Corporate Social Responsibility' (2003) 7 Journal of Communication Management 340, 346 <http://www.emeraldinsight.com/doi/abs/10.1108/13632540310807476> accessed 20 January 2017.

[117] Lawrence P Ettkin, Farhas ME Raiszadeh, and Harold R Hunt, 'Just-In-Time: A Timely Opportunity for Small Manufacturers' (1990) 32 Industrial Management 16.

[118] Vitesse Media, 'SMEs Dangerously Reliant on One Customer' (3 June 2009) <http://smallbusiness.co.uk/smes-dangerously-reliant-on-one-customer-1049717/> accessed 20 January 2017.

'dynamic' aspect of SMEs also results in their constant creation and destruction: in 2002, it was estimated that 460 million adults around the world were involved in entrepreneurial activity, which might result in the creation of 100 million new businesses.[119] However, in the Philippines, for every ten people currently starting or running a new business, there are seven who have discontinued one in the past year.[120] Half of European businesses started in 2001 had ceased operation by 2006.[121]

Despite the fact that SMEs are of vital importance for the promotion of economic growth, job creation, and the mitigation of poverty, particularly in less developed countries,[122] the increased risk associated with their operation means that on average, in Africa at least, there are more SME closures than expansion and only 1 per cent of micro-enterprises grow from five employees or fewer to ten or more.[123] Such occurrences in themselves generate the sort of adverse human rights impacts which the human rights due diligence under the UNGPs can help avoid or where these are unavoidable require remediation.

This means that any guidance on business and human rights targeted at SMEs must take into account the increased risks of SMEs failing in terms of the content of the guidance and the directions it gives, and also be aware that the target audience of the guidance will be in constant flux and that owner-managers who understand the importance of business and human rights will be constantly replaced by new entrepreneurs with new businesses but with little or no awareness of human rights.

## G. Position in Supply Chains

While there are numerous challenges in conveying the importance of business and human rights and encouraging the implementation of the Guiding Principles by SMEs, it must be remembered that these businesses do not operate in a vacuum. Many of them will maintain relationships with large businesses, who may be in a position to assist small companies with the business and human rights responsibilities.

The UK survey on SMEs provides some helpful information on how SMEs are connected to large businesses in developed economies. There may be connections

[119] Paul D Reynolds and others, 'Global Entrepreneurship Monitor: 2002 Executive Report' (Babson College/Ewing Marion Kauffman Foundation/London Business School 2002) <http://www.esbri.se/gemglobalreport_2002.pdf> accessed 20 January 2017.

[120] Donna J Kelley, Slavica Singer, and Mike Herrington, 'Global Entrepreneurship Monitor: 2015/16 Global Report' (Entrepreneurship Research Association 2016) <http://www.gemslovenia.org/scripts/download.php?file=/data/upload/gem_d007_complete_final_1454681517(1).pdf> accessed 20 January 2017.

[121] Hartmut Schrör, 'Business Demography: Employment and Survival' (Eurostat, Statistics in Focus 70/2009) 4 <http://edz.bib.uni-mannheim.de/www-edz/pdf/statinf/09/KS-SF-09-070-EN.pdf> accessed 20 January 2017.

[122] Rogerson (n 90) 267.

[123] Donald C Mead and Carl Liedholm, 'The Dynamics of Micro and Small Enterprises in Developing Countries' (1998) 26 World Development 61, 67.

through formal supply chain relationships, as well as more informal or general links with larger companies. A large proportion of SMEs (77 per cent) who responded to a recent UK survey considered that they were part of a supply chain, with the largest supply relationship contributing between a quarter and a half of the SME's total turnover in 30 per cent of cases.[124] The SMEs' role in the supply chain tended to be utilizing their ability to provide a niche product or service that larger businesses are unable to provide themselves or cannot provide as cheaply. Of the businesses who considered that they were part of a supply chain, two-thirds provided a standardized product or service, half provided a bespoke product service, and one in five provided some form of research and development (R&D).

In terms of non-supply chain relationships, almost half of the SMEs networked with larger companies, primarily in order to become more established in their marketplace and with the hope of gaining additional business. This networking was crucial for SMEs in sectors dominated by large businesses in particular. Larger businesses can spur on SMEs in the supply chain to improve technological and human capital:[125] in the UK survey, one-quarter[126] of SMEs were involved in R&D partnerships with larger companies, while 15 per cent[127] were in more formal joint ventures with large enterprises. Fifteen per cent of SMEs received some mentoring from a larger business as the latter sought to enhance productivity through their supply chain. SMEs' links with larger businesses may provide opportunities for alleviating some of the problems that SMEs' resource poverty may cause for the business and human rights agenda. With existing supply-chain relationships already in place, and a culture of mentoring and advice-giving, it is possible to see how important business and human rights concepts such as human rights due diligence can be implemented through a partnership between smaller and larger businesses and how the latter can set standards which dictate conditions to the former.[128]

Business and human rights can enter the supply chain in a number of ways. Human rights criteria may be a precondition for tendering to supply or a factor taken into consideration when the supplier is chosen. This seems to work in practice, at least in some instances: a British study found that SMEs risked exclusion from supply chains through not engaging in CSR[129] and it has been claimed that 'supply chain pressures are proving to be a more powerful force for social and environmental change than local regulation'.[130] Similarly encouraging conclusions have

[124] Dougal Jamieson and others, 'Large Businesses and SMEs: Exploring How SMEs Interact with Large Businesses' (ORC International 2012) <https://www.gov.uk/government/uploads/system/uploads/attachment_data/file/34639/12-1196-exploring-how-smes-interact-with-large-businesses.pdf> accessed 20 January 2017.

[125] ACCA (n 30) 22. [126] Jamieson and others (n 124) 5. [127] ibid 6.

[128] Laura J Spence, 'CSR and Small Business in a European Policy Context: The Five "C"s of CSR and Small Business Research Agenda 2007' (2007) 112 Business and Society Review 533.

[129] Sarah Roberts, Rob Lawson, and Jeremy Nicholls, 'Generating Regional-Scale Improvements in SME Corporate Responsibility Performance: Lessons from Responsibility Northwest' (2006) 67 Journal of Business Ethics 275.

[130] George Starcher, 'Responsible Entrepreneurship: Engaging Small and Medium-Sized Enterprises in Socially and Environmentally Responsible Partners' (European Bahá'í Business Forum 2005) 23.

been reported in other areas of the world.[131] Bearing in mind the earlier conclusions regarding the limited resources of SMEs, such pressures should be more than a box-ticking exercise in order to reduce administrative burden and encourage true ethical behaviour.[132]

An example of this relationship being put to use in business and human rights is the United Kingdom's Modern Slavery Act 2015.[133] While the core obligations—to monitor and control operations and ensure the absence of human trafficking and slavery—only apply to businesses with an annual turnover of more than £36 million, these businesses also have reporting obligations with regard to their supply chains. This means that SMEs are likely to see contractual requirements in dealings with large businesses, requiring the former to report how they operate in respect of the Act.[134] As a result, SMEs will have in practice similar reporting obligations to the large businesses they contract with, and along with the rest of the supply chain will contribute to efforts to eliminate slavery and human trafficking.

Joining with other firms in non-supply chain relationships could also lead to greater SME respect for human rights: SMEs who are members of more business networks and associations perceive their social and environmental responsibilities as more important.[135] Networks can also help to engage SMEs holistically, with approaches tailored for specific sectors.[136]

In practice, it may not be the easiest way to secure the corporate responsibility to respect human rights using the contractual form because of the challenges and handicaps that this approach may engender. What form will the contract take? A distinct social responsibility contract or a clause in a main contract? For a clause in the contract, will it be a specific condition or a generic clause or indeed a clause by reference to another document such as a code of conduct? Will it matter that the reference document, in this case the code of conduct, is normally not binding? Furthermore, a normal business contract involving immediate parties may not be able to take account of actors down a long supply chain. This explains why even the willing companies tend to secure social responsibilities with one tier of the supply chain and at best encouraging them to ensure that actors down the supply chain will observe their social responsibilities such as respect for human rights. This tier-by-tier approach is not sufficiently in line with the UNGPs that call for avoiding or mitigating impacts in the operations of business relationships.[137] Under the UNGPs, although each business entity is responsible for its own human rights footprint, it must also take responsibility for impacts linked to their operations.[138] This 'impacts' approach contrasts with the tier-by-tier approach in expecting enterprises to look beyond immediate tiers to as far down the chain as can be said to be directly linked to their operations.

131 See the literature review in Baden and others (n 56). 132 ibid.

133 Modern Slavery Act 2015 (UK) <http://www.legislation.gov.uk/ukpga/2015/30/contents/enacted> accessed 20 January 2017.

134 Devant, 'The Modern Slavery Act 2015: A Guide for SMEs' (2015) <http://devant.co.uk/the-modern-slavery-act-2015-a-guide-for-smes> accessed 20 January 2017.

135 UK Department of Trade and Industry (n 32). 136 ibid.

137 UNGPs Principle 13. 138 ibid.

Admittedly, by adjusting the contractual form to require the first-tier party to ensure that parties down the chain respect human rights, it may be possible to follow human rights impacts linked to a corporation's operations. This may, however, not be the easiest task to monitor, as it will rely on parties to provide information up the chain to be assessed by the main contractor. Alternatively, the main contractor may retain the services of an independent third party to undertake the monitoring on its behalf. This is time-consuming, expensive, and not necessarily effective.[139]

The lessons on the ground suggest that there is not much evidence that larger transnational corporations support and share lessons of social responsibility with the SMEs in their supply chain. If anything, it is more likely that the tight terms of contracts with SME subcontractors can generate adverse human rights practices and even in certain circumstances, larger corporations knowingly outsource human rights risks to SMEs.[140]

Using the contractual form may also raise some difficult issues of extra-territorial application of contractual terms, especially if the law of the jurisdiction of the contract does not require social responsibility or human rights clauses. It is unclear how the dispute settlement institutions will respond to such clauses leaving the whole process open to uncertainty.

## H. Looking Forward

So far, this chapter has identified some of the challenges of engaging SMEs with the corporate responsibility to respect human rights and has sought to suggest solutions through the help of, among others, governments and companies in the supply chain. But in order to effectively engage with SMEs on human rights issues, it is essential to explore the subject from within the institution that is the SME by recognizing the opportunities provided by the enterprise as it is currently constructed, taking account of its size, management, and governance, as well as its relationships with the different stakeholders. It is useful, in the circumstances, for example, to note that the small size and informal structure of SMEs may lead to positive human rights outcomes.

SMEs are more labour-intensive than large corporations and have shown remarkable capacity to absorb labour (albeit largely unskilled),[141] which can help to lift families and communities out of poverty. The difficulty for SMEs in recruiting and retaining employees makes it less likely that they discriminate routinely on account of age, race, or disability.[142] Small businesses are usually locally owned and

[139] On this, see Richard A Locke, Fei Qin, and Alberto Brause, 'Does Monitoring Improve Labour Standards? Lessons from Nike' (2007) 61 Industrial and Labour Relations Review 3.

[140] Mark Anner, Jennifer Bair, and Jeremy Blasi, 'Toward Joint Liability in Global Supply Chains: Addressing the Root Causes of Labor Violations in International Subcontracting Networks' (2013–14) 35 Comparative Labor Law & Policy Journal 1. See also Richard Locke, *The Promise and Limits of Private Power: Promoting Labor Standards in a Global Economy* (Cambridge University Press 2013) 126 ff.

[141] Rwigema and Karungu (n 114) 111.

[142] Federation of Small Businesses (n 57) 11.

controlled, and can therefore strengthen the extended family as well as other social systems and cultural traditions. Indeed, family-owned companies in particular often exhibit strong ethical and philanthropic approaches,[143] which may provide a strong platform for a wider strategy to respect human rights. Some studies have found size to have a positive relationship with responsible engagement,[144] with other studies contradicting this,[145] and a further paper claiming a 'U-shape' relationship between size and engagement.[146]

There are aspects of SMEs that may lead to outcomes that are beneficial to human rights. For example, small firms play an important economic and social role in general, and the development and growth of small firms can go some way to redressing social and economic exclusion. Being 'civil society builders'[147] deeply embedded in the community context,[148] SMEs may have a greater understanding of local cultural and political contexts and more links with civil society,[149] which may in turn increase their socially responsible practices.[150] In particular, SMEs are often at the forefront of the struggle against disadvantage[151] and offer an opportunity to enter the workforce to those who have been traditionally excluded from employment in large businesses in some states (eg women[152] and ethnic minorities).[153] These groups have used self-employment and ownership of small businesses 'as a vehicle to draw upon their differences and diversity, enabling them to engage in economic life'.[154] In South Africa, SMEs provided critical first attempts for non-whites to own businesses, after having been historically discouraged from doing so.[155]

SMEs are generally perceived as being at the bottom of the supply and value chain. The reality is, however, more nuanced. For example, a significant proportion of SMEs engage in exporting and importing (particularly in more developed countries), with a minority engaging in foreign direct investment.[156] They have links at

[143] UN Industrial Development Organization, 'Corporate Social Responsibility: Implications for Small and Medium Enterprises in Developing Countries' (UNIDO 2002) ix <http://www.unido.org/fileadmin/import/userfiles/puffk/corporatesocialresponsibility.pdf> accessed 20 January 2017.

[144] European Commission (n 34). [145] Baden and others (n 56).

[146] Krishna Udayasankar, 'Corporate Social Responsibility and Firm Size' (2008) 83 Journal of Business Ethics 167. For further discussion, see Jan Lepoutre and Aimé Heene, 'Investigating the Impact of Firm Size on Small Business Social Responsibility: A Critical Review' (2006) 67 Journal of Business Ethics 257; and Spence (n 98).

[147] European Parliament, European Parliament Resolution 2005/2207(INI) on small and medium-sized enterprises in the developing countries [2006] OJ C298E/171.

[148] Bengt Johannisson, 'Globalisation as a Generic Entrepreneurial Activity' in Anders Lundström (ed), *The Role of SMEs and Entrepreneurship in a Globalised Economy* (The Globalisation Council 2009).

[149] Baden and others (n 56) 261. [150] ACCA (n 30) 9.

[151] ACCA, 'Beyond the Equality Bill: Embedding Equality and Diversity in SMEs' (Policy Paper, 2010) <http://www.accaglobal.com/content/dam/acca/global/PDF-technical/small-business/tech-tp-beb.pdf> accessed 20 January 2017.

[152] Rwigema and Karungu (n 114) 112. On the role of women in entrepreneurship, see also Fiorina Mugione and Fulvia Farinelli, Chapter 13 of this volume, Section F.II.

[153] Rowena Barrett and John Burgess, 'Small Firms and the Challenge of Equality, Diversity and Difference' (2008) 27 Equal Opportunities International 213, 213.

[154] ibid. [155] Rwigema and Karungu (n 114) 111.

[156] Edinburgh Group (n 87) 19.

the top, the middle, and the bottom of the business chain. They are, in effect, the nerves that bind the business fabric together. A conscious strategy to embed the UNGPs in SMEs is an effective way, therefore, of reaching out to the entire system and, here, the role of other stakeholders, including governments and social partners such as peer group associations, is crucial.

Governments are already in close contact with SMEs through the subsidies, grants, and training they provide. They can provide a systematic plan for lifting SMEs from the informal to the formal economy and so provide opportunities for engaging directly with the UNGPs. However, this will have to overcome the traditional psychological hurdle of perceiving SMEs as local economic growth institutions with little or no focus on social responsibility. This is not too difficult, especially with the UNGPs that attach importance to the shared responsibility between governments and business entities in preventing and redressing adverse human rights impacts. The indivisibility of the three Pillars of the UNGPs means that the government's duty to protect human rights of all[157] can be complemented by the corporate responsibility to respect human rights[158] as part of a common policy strategy. SMEs are well situated to be employed to achieve this complementarity. Similarly, governments have been invited to develop National Action Plans (NAPs) for business and human rights,[159] as part of which they are urged to involve all stakeholders. The large transnational corporations will, no doubt, have a place in this exercise, but the SMEs may easily be overlooked. This will be an unfortunate error in the process considering the potential reach of SMEs.[160]

Business and peer group associations can play an important role in harnessing the potential of SMEs to develop their capacity to respect human rights. Business associations such as the International Organization of Employers (IOE),[161] which boasts of member organizations representing a range of businesses, including SMEs in 150 countries, have breadth and depth of knowledge of the UNGPs. In providing support in terms of training, advice, resources such as benchmarking, and communication standards and indicators, business associations provide SMEs with opportunities to understand the requirements of the UNGPs, as well as bring together enterprises of similar size, focus, and within the same geographical region to share lessons on good practices concerning the UNGPs.

## I. Conclusions

The starting point in assessing the challenges concerning the implementation of the UNGPs by SMEs is not an especially promising one, as they seem to have been

[157] See UNGPs Principles 1–10.

[158] ibid Principles 11–24.

[159] See UNHRC Res 26/9 (n 21).

[160] See UN Working Group on Business and Human Rights, 'Guidance on National Action Plans on Business and Human Rights' (2014) <http://www.ohchr.org/Documents/Issues/Business/UNWG_%20NAPGuidance.pdf> accessed 20 January 2017.

[161] See IOE website <http://www.ioe-emp.org> accessed 20 January 2017.

overlooked or not to have had a distinct voice in the consultations that led to the development and construction of the UNGPs. Not only does this risk missing the unique pressure points of human rights within the unique environment of SMEs, but it also places them rather low on the awareness spectrum of the emerging standards for preventing and addressing adverse human rights impacts. To redress this gap in knowledge requires an adjustment of communications with key interlocutors, such as government departments responsible for the supervision and regulation of SMEs, as well as other corporate enterprises that form part of the supply and value chains of which the SMEs are a part. Unfortunately, the level of awareness of the UNGPs in government departments, especially those whose focus is economic growth, can be rather limited. In any case, these governmental institutions tend to see their role as supporting SMEs to deliver economic outcomes with rather little interest in social responsibility. For the companies, including the larger transnational corporations in the supply chain, with which SMEs may share knowledge and lessons concerning the implementation of the UNGP, the challenges of awareness and implementation cannot be said to have been wholly overcome for themselves. While the opportunities for sharing knowledge concerning the UNGPs with SMEs clearly exist, the necessary action for taking advantage of these opportunities still remains to be taken.

In essence, there is an urgent need for strategic leadership both from governmental institutions and agencies and from within the business community if the business and human rights agenda is to take off within SMEs.

It is important to note that SMEs are, after all, not just a scaled-down version of a large firm.[162] It might be tempting to view them as mirrors of big businesses but with lower sales, smaller assets, and fewer employees, but in fact they are completely different entities. They don't just face smaller versions of the same issues faced by larger companies, but rather they tend to have unique identity characteristics and face different sorts of challenges, and therefore opportunities may not so easily be recognized as typical. In trying to make the UNGPs relevant to SMEs, it is helpful to recognize these nuances about SMEs and to remember that they have different motivations, constraints, and uncertainties compared to larger firms.[163] An effective strategy has to take account of their handicaps, including their resource poverty, limited market share, predominantly informal economy, and relationships with other entities. Concerning the matter of relationships, that SMEs have often been employed by governments as instruments of economic policy such as employment creation may have a double-edged effect, including the effective implementation of the responsibility to respect human rights alongside the government's duty to protect the rights of all. The development of NAPs by governments offers an excellent window through which to recompose the role of SMEs on the national

[162] Welsh and White (n 84).

[163] Paul Westhead and David Storey, 'Management Training and Small Firm Performance: Why Is the Link So Weak?' (1996) 14 International Small Business Journal 13.

economic landscape, as part of which the social responsibility of SMEs and especially the implementation of the UNGPs can form a central part.

The implementation of the UNGPs cannot be done in isolated business groups and so the strategy for SMEs, while recognizing their unique situation, should be part of an integrated strategy that pulls together the roles of all business communities, government agencies, and other stakeholders.

Effective implementation of the UNGPs will entail a transformation of the ethos of SME business conduct—the so-called SME business culture—and for some SMEs this may involve the movement from the informal to the formal economy, alongside the commitment of the entrepreneurs who drive them to engage fully with the challenges of human rights. An easily accessible and user-friendly information exchange will be a good starting point for the essential awareness of the evolving business landscape in which human rights form a core part rather than merely as an incidental appendage. This should be complemented by continuing learning opportunities including training workshops—peer learning programmes that apply the 'how to' approach. Specific programmes on the nature and expectations of modern CSR instruments, especially the UNGPs, can help to transform the current business culture that privileges economic returns by demonstrating the virtues of non-financial values.

For their unique characteristics, SMEs present valuable opportunities and windows for the implementation of the UNGPs. Their flexibility and adaptability, alongside their closeness to all stakeholder groups (upstream and downstream), makes them sensitive to their social needs, including their human rights. Changing mindsets and the way in which business is undertaken can be a long and slow process and may not always be rewarding in the conventional commercial sense in the short term. It is a marathon and not a sprint, for which SMEs will need support from internal and external stakeholders, including workers' organizations, business associations, government departments, and international agencies.

## References

ACCA, 'Beyond the Equality Bill: Embedding Equality and Diversity in SMEs' (Policy Paper 2010) <http://www.accaglobal.com/content/dam/acca/global/PDF-technical/small-business/tech-tp-beb.pdf> accessed 20 January 2017

ACCA, 'Small Business: A Global Agenda' (2010) <http://www.accaglobal.com/content/dam/acca/global/PDF-technical/small-business/pol-afb-sbaga.pdf> accessed 20 January 2017

Addo, M and Martin, J, 'The Evolving Business and Society Landscape: Can Human Rights Make a Difference?' in Jena Martin and Karen Bravo (eds), *The Business and Human Rights Landscape: Moving Forward, Looking Back* (Cambridge University Press 2015)

Anner, M, Bair, J, and Blasi, J, 'Toward Joint Liability in Global Supply Chains: Addressing the Root Causes of Labor Violations in International Subcontracting Networks' (2013–14) 35 Comparative Labor Law & Policy Journal 1

Baden, DA, Harwood, IA, and Woodward, DG, 'The Effect of Buyer Pressure on Suppliers in SMEs to Demonstrate CSR Practices: An Added Incentive or Counter Productive?' (2009) European Management Journal 429

Baden, DA, Harwood, IA, and Woodward, DG, 'The Effects of Procurement Policies on "Downstream" Corporate Social Responsibility Activity: Content-Analytic Insights into the Views and Actions of SME Owner-Managers' (2011) 29 International Small Business Journal 259

Barrett, R and Burgess, J, 'Small Firms and the Challenge of Equality, Diversity and Difference' (2008) 27 Equal Opportunities International 213

Beck, T, Demirguc-Kunt, A, and Levine, R, 'SMEs Growth and Poverty: Cross-Country Evidence' (2005) 10 Journal of Economic Growth 199

Benson, E, 'Informal and Green? The Forgotten Voice in the Transition to a Green Economy' (IIED 2014) <http://pubs.iied.org/pdfs/16566IIED.pdf> accessed 20 January 2017

Castka, P, Balzarova, MA, Bamber, CJ, and Sharp, JM, 'How Can SMEs Effectively Implement the CSR Agenda? A UK Case Study Perspective' (2004) 11 Corporate Social Responsibility and Environmental Management 140

Ciliberti, F, Pontrandolfo, P, and Scozzi, B, 'Investigating Corporate Social Responsibility in Supply Chains: A SME Perspective' (2008) 16 Journal of Cleaner Production 1579

Cragg, W, 'Corporate Responsibility to Respect Human Rights: A Critical Look at the Justificatory Foundations of the UN Framework' (2012) 22 Corporate Ethics Quarterly 9

Desaulniers, M and Bigras, Y, 'Transformed SME: Value Chain Management and New Forms of Organization: A Synthesis Report', presented to Canada Economic Development as part of the Globalization, Knowledge Economy and Competitiveness Project, a synthesis of trends and strategic issues for the Québec SME (Globalization and Innovative SMEs) (Canada Economic Development 2000)

Devant, 'The Modern Slavery Act 2015: A Guide for SMEs' (2015) <http://devant.co.uk/the-modern-slavery-act-2015-a-guide-for-smes> accessed 20 January 2017

Economist Intelligence Unit, 'Emerging Markets SMEs Capture Growth in Expanding Markets', *The Economist* (2012)

Edinburgh Group, 'Growing the Global Economy through SMEs' (2013) <http://www.edinburgh-group.org/media/2776/edinburgh_group_research_-_growing_the_global_economy_through_smes.pdf> accessed 20 January 2017

Ettkin, LP, Raiszadeh, FME, and Hunt, HR, 'Just-In-Time: A Timely Opportunity for Small Manufacturers' (1990) 32 Industrial Management 16

European Commission, *European SMEs and Social and Environmental Responsibility* (Observatory of European SMEs, No 1, 2002) <http://ec.europa.eu/DocsRoom/documents/3157/attachments/1/translations/en/renditions/pdf> accessed 20 January 2017

European Commission, 'Opportunity and Responsibility: How to Help More Small Businesses to Integrate Social and Environmental Issues into What They Do' (2007) <http://ec.europa.eu/DocsRoom/documents/10373/attachments/1/translations/en/renditions/native> accessed 20 January 2017

European Commission, 'My Business and Human Rights: A Guide to Human Rights for Small and Medium-Sized Enterprises' (2012) <http://ec.europa.eu/DocsRoom/documents/10375/attachments/1/translations/en/renditions/native> accessed 20 January 2017

European Commission, 'User Guide to the SME Definition' (European Union 2015) <http://ec.europa.eu/DocsRoom/documents/10109/attachments/1/translations/en/renditions/native> accessed 20 January 2017

European Commission, 'What is an SME?' (2016) <http://ec.europa.eu/growth/smes/business-friendly-environment/sme-definition/index_en.htm> accessed 20 January 2017

European Medicines Agency, 'Applying for SME Status' <http://www.ema.europa.eu/ema/index.jsp?curl=pages/regulation/general/general_content_000061.jsp> accessed 20 January 2017

Fassin, Y, 'SMEs and the Fallacy of Formalising CSR' (2008) 17 Business Ethics: A European Review 364

Federation of Small Businesses, *Social and Environmental Responsibility and the Small Business Owner* (2008) <http://www.fsb.org.uk/LegacySitePath/policy/assets/CSR%20Dec%202008.pdf> accessed 20 January 2017

Ghobadian, A and Gallear, DN, 'Total Quality Management in SMEs' (1996) 24 Omega 83

Global Partnership for Financial Inclusion, 'Report to the Leaders' (G20 Summit, Cannes, 5 November 2011) 4 <https://www.oecd.org/g20/summits/cannes/Global%20Partnership%20for%20Financial%20Inclusion%20Report%20to%20Leaders.pdf> accessed 20 January 2017

Global Reporting Initiative, 'Ready to Report? Introducing Sustainability Reporting for SMEs' (2014) <https://www.globalreporting.org/resourcelibrary/Ready-to-Report-SME-booklet-online.pdf> accessed 20 January 2017

Harvie, C and Lee, BC (eds), *The Role of SMEs in National Economies in East Asia* (Edward Elgar 2002)

Horn, N, 'International Rules for Multinational Enterprises: The ICC, OECD and ILO Initiatives' (1980–81) 30 American University Law Review 923

IFC, 'IFC Performance Standards on Environmental and Social Sustainability' (1 January 2012) <http://www.ifc.org/wps/wcm/connect/c8f524004a73daeca09afdf998895a12/IFC_Performance_Standards.pdf?MOD=AJPERES> accessed 20 January 2017

ILO, 'Tripartite Declaration of Principles Concerning Multinational Enterprises and Social Policy' (4th edn, International Labour Office 2006) <http://www.ilo.org/wcmsp5/groups/public/---ed_emp/---emp_ent/---multi/documents/publication/wcms_094386.pdf> accessed 20 January 2017

ILO, *Small and Medium-Sized Enterprises and Decent and Productive Employment Creation* (International Labour Office 2015)

Jamieson, D, Fettiplace, S, York, C, Lambourne, E, Braidford, P, and Stone, I, 'Large Businesses and SMEs: Exploring How SMEs Interact with Large Businesses' (ORC International 2012) <https://www.gov.uk/government/uploads/system/uploads/attachment_data/file/34639/12-1196-exploring-how-smes-interact-with-large-businesses.pdf> accessed 20 January 2017

Jenkins, H, 'Small Business Champions for Corporate Social Responsibility' (2006) 67 Journal of Business Ethics 241

Johannisson, B, 'Globalisation as a Generic Entrepreneurial Activity' in Anders Lundström (ed), *The Role of SMEs and Entrepreneurship in a Globalised Economy* (The Globalisation Council 2009)

Kelley, DJ, Singer, S, and Herrington, M, 'Global Entrepreneurship Monitor: 2015/16 Global Report' (Entrepreneurship Research Association 2016) <http://www.gemslovenia.org/scripts/download.php?file=/data/upload/gem_d007_complete_final_1454681517(1).pdf> accessed 20 January 2017

Knudsen, JS, 'Which Companies Benefit Most from UN Global Compact Membership?' *European Business Review* (24 November 2011) <http://www.europeanbusinessreview.com/?p=3167> accessed 20 January 2017

Koshy, P and Prasad, VN, 'Small and Micro Enterprises: A Tool in the Fight against Poverty' (Munich Personal RePEc Archive, September 2007) <https://mpra.ub.uni-muenchen.de/22827/1/MPRA_paper_22827.pdf> accessed 20 January 2017

Leopoulos, V, 'Editorial' (2006) 17 Production Planning & Control 225

Lepoutre, J and Heene, A, 'Investigating the Impact of Firm Size on Small Business Social Responsibility: A Critical Review' (2006) 67 Journal of Business Ethics 257

Locke, RA, *The Promise and Limits of Private Power: Promoting Labor Standards in a Global Economy* (Cambridge University Press 2013)

Locke, RA, Qin, F, and Brause, A, 'Does Monitoring Improve Labour Standards? Lessons from Nike' (2007) 61 Industrial and Labour Relations Review 3

Mares, R (ed), *The UN Guiding Principles on Business and Human Rights* (Martinus Nijhoff 2011)

MacGregor, RC, Bunker, D, and Kartiwi, M, 'The Perception of Barriers to E-Commerce Adoption by SMEs: A Comparison of Three Countries' in Pratush Bharati, In Lee, and Abhijit Chaudhury (eds), *Global Perspectives on Small and Medium Enterprises and Strategic Information Systems: International Approaches* (IGI Global 2010)

Mead, DC and Liedholm, C, 'The Dynamics of Micro and Small Enterprises in Developing Countries' (1998) 26 World Development 61

Moran, TH, 'The United Nations and Transnational Corporations: A Review and a Perspective' (2009) 18(2) Transnational Corporations 91 <http://unctad.org/en/Docs/diaeiia200910a4_en.pdf> accessed 20 January 2017

NetRegs, 'SME-nvironment' (2003) <http://www.netregs.org.uk/media/1080/sme_2003_uk_1409449.pdf> accessed 20 January 2017

OECD, 'Small and Medium-Sized Enterprises: Local Strength, Global Reach' (Policy Brief, June 2000) <http://www.oecd.org/cfe/leed/1918307.pdf> accessed 20 January 2017

OECD, *OECD Guidelines for Multinational Enterprises* (OECD 2011) <http://dx.doi.org/10.1787/9789264115415-en> accessed 20 January 2017

OHCHR, 'Frequently Asked Questions about the Guiding Principles on Business and Human Rights' (United Nations 2014) <http://www.ohchr.org/Documents/Publications/FAQ_PrinciplesBussinessHR.pdf> accessed 20 January 2017

Petts, J, Herd, A, Gerrard, S, and Horne, C, 'The Climate and Culture of Environmental Compliance within SMEs' (1999) 8 Business Strategy & the Environment 14

PCG, 'Consultation on the Future "EU 2020 Strategy": PCG Response' (January 2010) <http://ec.europa.eu/dgs/secretariat_general/eu2020/docs/pcg_en.pdf> accessed 20 January 2017

Reynolds, PD, Bygrave, WD, Autio, E, and Hay, M, 'Global Entrepreneurship Monitor: 2002 Executive Report' (Babson College/Ewing Marion Kauffman Foundation/London Business School 2002) <http://www.esbri.se/gemglobalreport_2002.pdf> accessed 20 January 2017

Roberts, S, Lawson, R, and Nicholls, J, 'Generating Regional-Scale Improvements in SME Corporate Responsibility Performance: Lessons from Responsibility Northwest' (2006) 67 Journal of Business Ethics 275

Rogerson, CM, 'Growing the SMME Manufacturing Economy of South Africa: Evidence from Gauteng Province' (2001) 19 Journal of Contemporary African Studies 267 <http://www.tandfonline.com/doi/abs/10.1080/02589000120066498> accessed 20 January 2017

Rogerson, CM, 'The Impact of the South African Government's SMME Programmes: A Ten-Year Review (1994–2003)' (2004) 21 Development Southern Africa 765

Rwigema, H and Karungu, P, 'SMME Development in Johannesburg's Southern Metropolitan Local Council: An Assessment' (1999) 16 Development Southern Africa 107 <http://www.tandfonline.com/doi/abs/10.1080/03768359908440064> accessed 20 January 2017

Sarbutts, N, 'Can SMEs "Do" CSR? A Practitioner's View of the Ways Small- and Medium-Sized Enterprises Are Able to Manage Reputation through Corporate Social Responsibility' (2003) 7 Journal of Communication Management 340

Sauvant, KP, 'The Negotiations of the United Nations Code of Conduct on Transnational Corporations' (2015) 16 Journal of World Investment and Trade 11

Schrör, H, 'Business Demography: Employment and Survival' (Eurostat, Statistics in Focus 70/2009) <http://edz.bib.uni-mannheim.de/www-edz/pdf/statinf/09/KS-SF-09-070-EN.pdf> accessed 20 January 2017

Spence, LJ, 'Does Size Matter? The State of the Art in Small Business Ethics' (1999) 8 Business Ethics: A European Review 163

Spence, LJ, 'CSR and Small Business in a European Policy Context: The Five "C"s of CSR and Small Business Research Agenda 2007' (2007) 112 Business and Society Review 533

Starcher, G, 'Responsible Entrepreneurship: Engaging Small and Medium-Sized Enterprises in Socially and Environmentally Responsible Partners' (European Bahá'í Business Forum, Paris 2005)

Storey, DJ, *Entrepreneurship and the New Firm* (Taylor & Francis 1982)

Tripathi, A and Bains, A, 'An Investigation into SMEs' Awareness of Corporate Social Responsibility Practices in Punjab, India' (18 February 2016) <http://papers.ssrn.com/sol3/papers.cfm?abstract_id=2764348> accessed 20 January 2017

Udayasankar, K, 'Corporate Social Responsibility and Firm Size' (2006) 83 Journal of Business Ethics 167

UK Department of Trade and Industry, 'Engaging SMEs in Community and Social Issues' (2002)

UN Industrial Development Organization, 'Corporate Social Responsibility: Implications for Small and Medium Enterprises in Developing Countries' (UNIDO, 2002) <http://www.unido.org/fileadmin/import/userfiles/puffk/corporatesocialresponsibility.pdf> accessed 20 January 2017

UN Working Group on Business and Human Rights, 'Guidance on National Action Plans on Business and Human Rights' (2014) <http://www.ohchr.org/Documents/Issues/Business/UNWG_%20NAPGuidance.pdf> accessed 20 January 2017

Vitesse Media, 'SMEs Dangerously Reliant on One Customer' (2009) <http://small-business.co.uk/smes-dangerously-reliant-on-one-customer-1049717> accessed 20 January 2017

Weissbrodt, D and Kruger, M, 'UN Norms on the Responsibilities of Transnational Corporations and Other Business Enterprises with Regard to Human Rights' (2003) 97 American Journal of International Law 901

Welsh, JA and White, JF, 'A Small Business Is Not a Little Big Business' (1981) 59 Harvard Business Review 18 <https://hbr.org/1981/07/a-small-business-is-not-a-little-big-business> accessed 20 January 2017

Westhead, P and Storey, D, 'Management Training and Small Firm Performance: Why Is the Link So Weak?' (1996) 14 International Small Business Journal 13

Zurich, 'Biggest Opportunities for Small and Medium Enterprises (SMEs) in 2015: Global Survey Report' (October 2015) <https://www.zurich.com/_/media/dbe/corporate/docs/whitepapers/biggest-opportunities-for-sme-2015-survey-report.pdf?la=en> accessed 20 January 2017

# 13

# Promoting Entrepreneurship for Development

*Fiorina Mugione and Fulvia Farinelli**

## A. Introduction

Entrepreneurship—the act of being an entrepreneur—implies the capacity and willingness to undertake the conception, organization, and management of a productive new venture, accepting all attendant risks and seeking profit as a reward. Entrepreneurship policies focus on policies aimed at the promotion of new entrepreneurs and facilitating new business start-ups. Entrepreneurship is vital for economic growth and development. The creation of new business entities generates added value, fiscal revenues, employment, and innovation, and it is an essential ingredient for the development of a vibrant small and medium-sized enterprise (SME) sector.[1] Compared with large corporations, growth-oriented SMEs are more flexible and dynamic. They are an important vehicle for diversification and industrialization, and can contribute to structural transformation by building new industries, including eco-friendly economic activities.[2] In this sense, SMEs can help combat climate change, foster sustainable consumption and production patterns, and promote sustainable cities, thereby contributing towards the sustainable use of water, energy, land, forests, marine, and other resources.

Entrepreneurship development is at the core of SME development interventions and, even more broadly, of efforts aimed at supporting the private sector and its contribution to sustainable development objectives. As such, entrepreneurship has the potential to contribute to the implementation of the Sustainable Development Goals (SDGs) recently adopted by the UN General Assembly, and can have a positive impact on the achievement of multiple targets, such as the employment of young people or disadvantaged groups, the improvement of living conditions in

* UNCTAD. The chapter relies on the analytical and technical assistance work carried out by UNCTAD on entrepreneurship development. However, the views expressed in this chapter are those of the authors and may not always coincide with those of their organization or member countries.

[1] UNCTAD, 'Accra Accord' (2008) <http://unctad.org/en/docs/iaos20082_en.pdf> accessed 20 January 2017. See also Joachim Karl, Chapter 9 of this volume. Concerning the various definitions of SMEs, see Rudolf Adlung and Marta Soprana in the Annex of this volume.

[2] UNCTAD, 'Integrating Developing Countries' SMEs into Global Value Chains' (United Nations 2010) <http://unctad.org/en/docs/diaeed20095_en.pdf> accessed 20 January 2017.

post-conflict zones, gender empowerment and equality, poverty eradication, and food security.[3] This chapter identifies the critical elements to develop and implement entrepreneurship policies that are conducive to inclusive growth and embedded in long-term development objectives. It will address the following questions: What are the priorities for entrepreneurship development in the 2030 development agenda? Which are the best practices in entrepreneurship policy formulation? How can the national regulatory environment for start-ups be improved?

## B. Entrepreneurship and the Sustainable Development Goals

In the last decade, the UN General Assembly has repeatedly recognized the role of entrepreneurship in development. At its sixty-seventh session in December 2012, the General Assembly adopted its first resolution on 'Entrepreneurship for Development',[4] which identified entrepreneurship as a means to address sustainable development challenges—notably, unemployment and poverty—and to expand opportunities for all, including socially disadvantaged groups, in particular women and youth. In 2014, the Department of Economic and Social Affairs requested the UN Conference on Trade and Development (UNCTAD) to prepare a report to the General Assembly on the implementation of this resolution, recognizing the work carried out by UNCTAD on entrepreneurship-related issues for more than two decades.[5] The report served as a background document for a second resolution on 'Entrepreneurship for Development'.[6] This resolution reinforced the centrality of entrepreneurship in the achievement of sustainable development and stressed the need for evaluating the success of entrepreneurship promotion policies and impact measurement tools and indicators.

The 2030 Agenda for Sustainable Development, adopted by UN Member States in September 2015,[7] emphasized the role of entrepreneurship in sustainable development, particularly in Goals 4 (ensure inclusive and equitable quality education and promote lifelong learning opportunities for all) and 8 (promote sustained, inclusive, and sustainable economic growth, full and productive employment, and decent work for all). More specifically, target 4.4 calls for increasing the number of youth and adults who have relevant skills, including technical and vocational skills

[3] UNCTAD, 'Multi-Year Expert Meeting on Investment, Innovation and Entrepreneurship for Productive Capacity-Building and Sustainable Development, Third Session' (Conference, 30–31 March 2015) <http://unctad.org/en/pages/MeetingDetails.aspx?meetingid=645> accessed 20 January 2017.

[4] UN General Assembly (UNGA) Resolution 67/202 (21 December 2012) UN Doc A/RES/67/202.

[5] UNGA Resolution 69/210 (10 December 2014) UN Doc A/RES/69/210.

[6] UNGA Resolution C.2/69/L.14 (20 October 2014) UN Doc A/C.2/69/L.14; cf UNGA Resolution C.2/69/L.14/Rev.1 (11 November 2014) UN Doc A/C.2/69/L.14/Rev.1.

[7] United Nations, 'Transforming our World: The 2030 Agenda for Sustainable Development' (United Nations 2015) <https://sustainabledevelopment.un.org/post2015/transformingourworld/publication> accessed 20 January 2017; cf UNGA Resolution 70/1 (25 September 2015) UN Doc A/RES/70/1.

for employment, decent jobs, and entrepreneurship. Target 8.3 calls for the promotion of development-oriented policies that support productive capacities, decent job creation, entrepreneurship, creativity, and innovation, and encourage the formalization and growth of SMEs, including through access to financial services.[8]

Indeed, the 2030 Development Agenda builds a new scenario in which entrepreneurs and all economic actors shall operate. At the international level, there is a clear sense that a deep change is needed in the way business is usually done. In order to achieve the global goals for sustainable development, multi-stakeholder partnerships are needed in all areas and at all levels, including the private sector. The new focus should be on the promotion of innovative, more inclusive business models, creating economic opportunities for all, providing necessary safeguards to protect vulnerable groups, and fostering social inclusion through poverty alleviation. In this framework, the contribution of SMEs is key to generate urgent transformative changes and alternative forms of the economy, and to achieve sustainable development in a balanced and equitable manner.[9]

## C. UNCTAD's Entrepreneurship Policy Framework and Implementation Guidance

Recognizing that policymakers in developing countries need support in promoting entrepreneurship, UNCTAD developed the Entrepreneurship Policy Framework (EPF) in 2012, with the support of experts from more than 100 countries who have attended the series of Multi-Year Expert Meetings on Enterprise Development and Capacity Building on Science, Technology and Innovation, held in Geneva from 2009 to 2012. While cautioning that one size does not fit all, the EPF suggests policy options and recommended actions in six priority policy areas that have a direct impact on entrepreneurial activity: formulating national entrepreneurship strategies; optimizing the regulatory environment; enhancing entrepreneurship education and skills development; facilitating technology exchanges and innovation; improving access to finance; and promoting awareness and networking.[10]

For each area, the framework identifies policy objectives and options in the form of recommended actions. It proposes checklists, case studies, and good practices, and contains a set of indicators to measure progress. It also includes a user guide, a step-by-step approach to developing entrepreneurship policy based on the country's overall development objectives, particularly with regard to sustainable development. An interactive online inventory of good practices in entrepreneurship development[11] complements the EPF and provides an opportunity for all stakeholders to contribute cases, examples, comments, and suggestions.

[8] ibid, United Nations, 'Transforming our World'. [9] UNCTAD (n 3).

[10] UNCTAD, 'Entrepreneurship Policy Framework and Implementation Guidance' (2012) <http://unctad.org/en/PublicationsLibrary/diaeed2012d1_en.pdf> accessed 20 January 2017.

[11] ibid.

The inventory includes selected policies and programmes from developing countries, aimed at inspiring policy options that can be adopted and adapted to specific circumstances and goals, keeping in mind the need for holistic policy design and implementation.

Negative socio-cultural perceptions about entrepreneurship, for example, can act as significant barriers to enterprise creation and can undermine the impact of policy intervention in support of entrepreneurship. The impact of regulatory reforms in support of start-ups or to facilitate access to finance for entrepreneurs will be less than optimal if large sections of the population do not consider entrepreneurship as a viable and rewarding option (ie if they would only consider entrepreneurship if forced, or out of necessity).[12] Fostering an entrepreneurial culture that positively values entrepreneurs and entrepreneurship is a key determinant of the success of an entrepreneurship policy framework and it is also a crucial factor to overcome the culture of dependency—either from governments or aid donors. Through its Entrepreneurship Policies and Capacity Building Programme, UNCTAD is actively pursuing this objective.

In this undertaking, UNCTAD is not alone. A number of well-known policy guides exist to analyse and compare the business climate of countries and to inform policymakers about reform needs and options. These include the World Bank's 'Doing Business' Report and Governance Indicators, the World Competitiveness Report, the Index of Economic Freedom, and the Bertelsmann Transformation Index, among others. The Global Entrepreneurship Monitor provides more specific guidelines for entrepreneurship policies, and the Donor Committee for Enterprise Development has published guidelines for development agencies that support business environment reforms. UNCTAD's specific role is to support developing countries' policymakers in the design of initiatives, measures, and institutions to promote entrepreneurship tailored to each country's specific conditions and needs, based on a systemic and holistic approach. Entrepreneurship is in fact multifaceted, and a bottleneck in one area may become a bottleneck for all other areas.

## D. Good Practices and Lessons Learned from EPF Implementation

Following the launch of the EPF in 2012, several countries, including Brazil, Cameroun, Dominican Republic, Ecuador, Gambia, Ghana, Nigeria, Panama, Tanzania, and Zimbabwe, implemented the framework, with some variation across countries. In most cases, national governments initiated a consultation on entrepreneurship through national forums, regional seminars, benchmarking exercises, and review mechanisms engaging stakeholders. At the very inception, the participatory

[12] Donna J Kelley, Niels Bosma, and José Ernest Amorós, 'Global Entrepreneurship Monitor: 2010 Global Report' (2010) <http://www.av-asesores.com/upload/479.PDF> accessed 20 January 2017.

dialogue between public and private sector stakeholders provided a solid base to build trust and define common goals. Such initial phase was critical and provided guidelines to set a mechanism to gauge the current state of entrepreneurship in the country and to identify priorities and targets. In all the countries mentioned above, UNCTAD has collaborated with policymakers through the network of established Empretec centres, facilitating the dialogue between public and private sector. Based on this experience, the following good practices can be recommended:

## I. Creating a lead entity to guide the development of the national entrepreneurship policy

An entity within or outside of government is needed to initiate the agenda, define the process, and engage stakeholders in the development of the policy. In Ecuador, the Alliance for Entrepreneurship and Innovation (AEI), a public-private alliance partially funded by Ecuadorian entrepreneurs convened key stakeholders and facilitated the policy development process. The EPF's implementation in Ecuador focused on the identification of gaps and the prioritization of entrepreneurship objectives. A mapping of all stakeholders in the ecosystem was carried out in two main regions, and the country's entrepreneurship strategy was carefully laid out. To trigger implementation, each group identified a first pilot action that can produce results in the short term, facilitating feedback and learning by doing. Objectives to address the gaps identified and policy initiatives to be undertaken were clearly prioritized through a bottom-up approach, but the leadership of AEI remained crucial in all aspects related to the coordination, pilot implementation, monitoring, and evaluation of new initiatives.

## II. Establishing a structured policy development process

A structured approach that clearly defines and engages stakeholders in a national consultation for the purpose of defining objectives and national priorities on entrepreneurship is integral to the development of a national entrepreneurship policy. In Panama, 2012 was a landmark year for entrepreneurship. Important events included the inauguration of an Entrepreneurship Centre by the Ministry of Micro, Small and Medium-sized Enterprises (AMPYME), which initiated a Master Plan on the development of an entrepreneurship ecosystem, and the organization of the First National Entrepreneurship Forum, engaging UNCTAD together with AMPYME, the Development Bank of Latin America (CAF), the City of Knowledge Foundation, and Empretec Panama. The forum gathered more than 300 participants from the entrepreneurial ecosystem of Panama, including representatives from public and private sector, NGOs, and academia. Three working groups used UNCTAD's EPF methodology as a guideline for identifying relevant policy options and recommended actions. These recommendations were presented to the President of Panama on the occasion of the inauguration of AMPYME's new Entrepreneurship Centre in Panama City.

## III. Engaging in a participatory approach

A participatory multi-stakeholder process that engages key stakeholders from different sectors and policy areas at the local, regional, and national levels is critical in ensuring that the process is inclusive. In Brazil, the Minister of Development, Industry and Foreign Trade (MDIC) convened an International Seminar of the Entrepreneurship National Policy in June 2012. The Federal Government, with the support of Endeavor Brazil and the Brazilian Micro-Enterprise and Small Business Support Service (SEBRAE), conducted six workshops with stakeholders around the country to come to a full understanding of the specific challenges facing entrepreneurial development. Stakeholders identified specific objectives to pursue through the promotion of entrepreneurship using the World Café methodology to stimulate brainstorming and interaction. Based on UNCTAD's database on good practices, the seminar provided insights of what worked best in the region. The initiative culminated in 2013 with a consultative process aimed at reviewing a draft national public policy on entrepreneurship proposed by the Government of Brazil.

## IV. Building on and strengthening existing frameworks and initiatives

Beyond the identification of new actions and measures to promote entrepreneurship, the development of the national strategy on entrepreneurship should also articulate existing areas that need further support. Following UNCTAD's EPF methodology, experts gathered in Ghana in 2013 at a workshop organized in collaboration with the Ghanaian Panel on Economic Development, under the auspices of the Friedrich Ebert Foundation and ISSER-University[13] of Ghana. Experts agreed that Ghana's Second National Medium Term Private Sector Development Strategy (PSDS II) 2010–2015 was an ambitious and well-crafted strategy, addressing most of the constraints of the private sector. In particular, the 'SME Growth Initiative' and the 'Business Innovation and Linkages Challenge Fund' rightly put SME development within the broader national competitiveness agenda. However, based on the adaptation of UNCTAD's EPF checklists to the case of Ghana, experts realized that entrepreneurship policy had not fully been engrained in this strategy. As an outcome of the workshop, representatives from the Ministry of Trade and Industry noted the need for greater coordination among initiatives and expressed their interest in raising the awareness of the importance of entrepreneurship among public officials.

## V. Building concrete Actions Plans

A matrix of proposed recommendations and initiatives to simplify procedures and remove roadblocks should be developed by area, indicating implementing agencies,

[13] Institute of Statistical, Social and Economic Research.

resource requirements, and deadlines. In the Dominican Republic, a national workshop aimed at validating the National Entrepreneurship Strategy and drafting an Action Plan was held in Santo Domingo, in March 2016, in collaboration with the Ministry of Industry, Commerce and SMEs (MIC). The workshop was highly successful and was attended by more than forty members of the National Entrepreneurship Network (Red Nacional de Emprendimiento), from government, private sector, academia, and NGOs. As an outcome of the workshop, five different working groups were created, with identified coordinators, which continued meeting to finalize the Action Plan and to initiate advocacy to trigger necessary reforms. Among the main issues that were identified as priority actions were: the creation of a public–private sector alliance; the design of a communication campaign to promote the initiatives being implemented; the creation of a commission for proposing amendments to the National Entrepreneurship Act under discussion in the Parliament; the preparation of a study to integrate entrepreneurship and SME issues into the existing Labour Law; the generation of financial mechanisms to reduce the risks of co-investment; the provision of entrepreneurship training to school teachers and university professors; and the utilization of open source tools for SMEs.

## E. Reforming the Regulatory Environment

Governments can play a key role in creating an enabling regulatory environment that will unleash the potential of entrepreneurship by adopting regulatory and policy measures that will promote dynamic and inclusive businesses. An enabling regulatory environment encouraging entrepreneurs to engage in new ventures is essential. Entry barriers can pose challenges to new firms seeking to enter emerging sustainable entrepreneurship sectors. In the green sector, for example, regulatory barriers can hinder new firms' ability to take advantage of new technological or business opportunities or challenge the business model of existing firms.[14] Reducing business entry costs such as business registration and start-up costs such as legal fees for start-ups, for example, can enhance the regulatory environment for entrepreneurship, and help to stimulate the development of new businesses in emerging sectors.

From a regulatory perspective, the EPF focuses on a specific set of key issues, illustrated in detail below,[15] which have the greatest immediate relevance for start-up activities. The underlying assumption is that the regulatory environment should encourage entrepreneurs to set up their own business, to try new business ideas, and to take on calculated risks, keeping administrative burdens to the minimum

[14] OECD, 'Interim Report of the Green Growth Strategy: Implementing Our Commitment for a Sustainable Future' (2010) <https://www.oecd.org/greengrowth/45312720.pdf> accessed 20 January 2017.

[15] This section summarizes the policy objectives and recommended actions included in the Entrepreneurship Policy Framework. cf UNCTAD (n 10).

required to support public policy and sustainable development objectives. Countries that impose more onerous administrative requirements on firms and where the cost of registration is higher typically show much lower rates of entrepreneurial activity. In developing countries, the negative consequences of excessive administrative requirements and higher registration costs are often even more significant, as they weigh heavier on the capacity and resources of local entrepreneurs.

## I. Examining regulatory requirements for start-ups

The first step in establishing a regulatory environment conducive to business is to understand the extent to which existing rules and procedures may hold back entrepreneurial activity. This implies distinguishing between: regulations that are essential for the functioning of businesses; those that are essential, but can be simplified or otherwise managed in a more efficient way; and those that produce more costs than benefits and should be abolished. Making this distinction can best be achieved in three steps. The first step is benchmarking the national business climate against other countries. Countries can draw on numerous systems of indicators that are published on an annual basis by international organizations, such as the World Bank's 'Ease of Doing Business'. It should be noted that these indicators make different underlying assumptions about what a 'good' business climate is, and therefore arrive at different rankings; also, they should be interpreted with caution as reported figures may be based on the perceptions of a limited number of business people and may not be representative of the views of the whole business community. It is also important to set up regular national surveys, introducing benchmarking among regions.

The second step is to look at specific sectors and regions and assess whether or not specific licensing or administrative requirements are justified. Again, benchmarking such requirements against international experiences, or between regions or sectors, may provide valuable information. Rankings alone, however, tell little about optimal levels of regulation, because country conditions vary considerably and societies and governments have different preferences with regard to regulations. Benchmarking exercises need to be complemented with a third step: the organization of a public–private dialogue on the costs and benefits of regulations. Such a dialogue is important to convey the business communities' concerns about excessive regulations and increase the regulators' awareness about the costs of regulation; conversely, the public sector may convince the business community that certain regulations are needed. This way, public–private commissions can incrementally develop a shared understanding and step by step weed out unnecessary regulations and improve the remaining ones.

## II. Minimizing regulatory hurdles for business start-ups

Many developing countries continue to work to reduce or eliminate obstacles to business, including bureaucratic procedures and transparency issues such as lack of accurate information, or costly and time-consuming customs procedures. Still, institutional inefficiency and overlapping institutional involvement in administrative procedures coupled with deficient interdepartmental coordination often result in delays and unnecessary financial requirements in obtaining business licences. In many developing countries, it takes up to six public institutions involved in the process four months to legalize economic activities. These obstacles impose tremendous costs on entrepreneurs and prejudice the environment for doing business in a country.

It is internationally recognized that burdensome regulation also encourages corruption.[16] Faced with requirements of going through various procedures in different offices, entrepreneurs may end up using illicit methods to accelerate the process. In developing countries, the costs of 'smoothing the process' to start a business or to get a licence for an investment project are often much higher than the official registration fee. Small-scale entrepreneurs often suffer most from a heavy regulatory burden and its derivative—corruption.

In many developing countries, a significant part of the economy remains in the informal sector, the size of which is crucially determined by the quality of the legal framework, more precisely company entry costs and regulatory burden, including corruption and financial constraints. Breaking down these hurdles thus promotes and facilitates formal entrepreneurship. Often, procedures for start-ups can be abolished without any negative side effects. Three measures have shown to be particularly successful in this regard: (i) systematic procedures to review and cut business start-up requirements in terms of number of licences, procedures, and administrative fees; (ii) the introduction of fast-track mechanisms and one-stop-shops to bundle procedures; and (iii) the introduction of information and communications technology-based procedures for businesses' registration and reporting. For example, online registration procedures—where feasible—are one of the most effective ways to speed up a company registration. Electronic systems are also a good way to share information among agencies, offering an integrated and cost-effective service to the users. Online, entrepreneurs can easily access documents and obtain certificates if appropriate regulations are in place for the use and acceptance of electronic signatures.

## III. Building entrepreneurs' confidence in the regulatory environment

A sound regulatory framework is one that operates based on predictability and transparency, as well as proper enforcement mechanisms. It is important to emphasize the significance of the quality of regulatory enforcement, which remains a challenge for a number of national regulators.

[16] See, among others, World Bank, 'Governance: The World Bank's Experience' (World Bank 1994) <http://www-wds.worldbank.org/external/default/WDSContentServer/WDSP/IB/1994/05/01/000009265_3970716142854/Rendered/PDF/multi0page.pdf> accessed 20 January 2017.

There are several aspects that affect the efficiency of regulation enforcement and compliance: the first is related to the regulator's power to enforce rules. Differences in market and regulatory maturity, as well as legal and judicial practices, influence the enforcement practices and procedures of individual countries. Compliance can be improved by training government officers both at the national and local levels, especially those who deal directly with starting entrepreneurs, accompanied by a sufficiently strong and transparent system to carry out enforcement activities, and by dealing with complaints of non-compliance and conducting investigations on suspected violations. The second main element is related to entrepreneurs' awareness. Working closely with business associations to update regulatory information, educate entrepreneurs, and guide them on how to comply with laws and regulations is essential to improve compliance. It is important to ensure the display of information on regulations and administrative procedures on the relevant agencies' websites. Another useful measure is to introduce the Customers' Charter, a short statement describing the level of service a customer can expect from a governmental agency. It will not only improve information dissemination, but also increase compliance. As an example, South Africa drafted a service charter for the delivery of administrative services.[17]

Property rights (including intellectual property rights) are fundamental for doing business and require appropriate protection. However, protection comes through formalization or registration. In many developing countries, registration of property remains time-consuming or prohibitively expensive. This represents a major impediment to doing business as it eliminates an important form of security for the business owner or investor. Policies that guarantee property rights and improve the enforceability of contracts are essential to create investor confidence and can make a country an attractive location for investment. Confidence in entrepreneurship can also be strengthened by reducing the bankruptcy stigma and facilitating re-starts. In many societies, entrepreneurs who have failed once are unlikely to get credit again. However, societies that understand the experimental character of entrepreneurship and the risks involved, and that support second and third chances, tend to fare better in terms of enterprise development. Companies need insolvency procedures which recognize that viable businesses can suffer from temporary problems (eg due to an economy-wide recession). A key objective of bankruptcy laws should be to help viable companies survive while safeguarding the interests of creditors.

## IV. Guiding entrepreneurs through the start-up administrative process

The complexity of many aspects of business regulation makes it important to put in place effective mechanisms to help entrepreneurs through administrative procedures

[17] For the Service Charter of the Republic of South Africa, see Resolution 1 of 2013, <http://www.dpsa.gov.za/documents/PUBLIC%20SERVICE%20CHARTER%202013.pdf> accessed 20 January 2017.

for starting their business. This may be particularly important for certain groups of entrepreneurs, and it is generally important for start-ups, because new entrepreneurs are unfamiliar with common processes and often have to go through many initial administrative procedures for registering their business, obtaining licences and authorizations, exactly at the time when they are struggling to build their new business. One of the initiatives that has proven very successful in developing countries is the systemization and display of information on regulations and administrative procedures for starting a business on a relevant government entity's website or at the business registration agency. Permanent and efficient help desks at competent entities, ready to answer questions and counsel on any administrative requirements to start up a business, can be of great help. In addition, it is important that the business community sees the advantages of regulations and receives benefits from them.

To this purpose, UNCTAD has launched in 2007 the e-regulations system, a web-based e-government system[18] to help developing countries and countries in transition work towards business facilitation through transparency, simplification, and automation of rules and procedures relating to enterprise creation and operation. It allows governments to present procedures online in a detailed and precise way and to make administrative procedures transparent, swift, and efficient. Procedures (eg for business start-ups) are detailed step by step from the user's perspective. For each step, the system shows what is expected at the end of the step, who are the civil servants in charge, what are the forms and other documents required, the costs involved (if any), processing time, legal justification of the step, and ways to file complaints or recourse in case of disagreement. Since its inception, the programme has helped prepare such step-by-step guides in twelve countries and one city: Benin, Burkina Faso, Cape Verde, Cameroon, Colombia, Comoros, Costa Rica, Guatemala, Mali, Nicaragua, Vietnam, Rwanda, and Moscow. The information is certified by the entities in charge of each step.

UNCTAD has also partnered with the Kauffman Foundation's Global Entrepreneurship Network (GEN) and the US Department of State (DOS), and in 2014 put in place a platform called Global Enterprise Registration (GER.co), aimed at inspiring all governments to put their business registration processes online by 2019, and to make it as clear and as simple as possible. GER.co[19] aims to be every entrepreneur's first stop to register a business anywhere in the world. The site shows whether a country's online registration process is clear and complete. The Global Enterprise Registration (GER) green dot rating system indicates which websites provide these basics, so entrepreneurs can process their applications online ('single windows') or at least know what to do, why to do it, and how to do it ('information portals'). Presenting links to all the world's online business registration sites in one location helps governments identify best practices and simplify procedures; this benefits entrepreneurs and investors everywhere. Governments,

[18] UNCTAD, 'Business Facilitation Program' (2016) <http://www.businessfacilitation.org> accessed 20 January 2017.

[19] Global Enterprise Registration (GER) <http://ger.co> accessed 20 January 2017.

for example, can improve their GER green dot rating by improving their website, adding more simultaneous online services, and monitor improvements through an online self-assessment form, which lets a government see its website from the user's point of view.

## F. Reforming the Regulatory Environment to Address the Needs of Specific Target Groups

For aspiring entrepreneurs from socially disadvantaged groups who tend to have lower levels of entrepreneurship skills as well as greater difficulty in navigating the business and regulatory environment, governments need to tailor policy measures to help them manage and grow their businesses. For emerging areas such as social entrepreneurship, legal frameworks that recognize social enterprises can play an important role in promoting entrepreneurship for sustainable development. Policymakers can also ensure that the public sector plays a role in promoting inclusive and sustainable outcomes through public procurement and devising provisions that support investments in underserved areas, thereby promoting equitable outcomes for all.

Responding to the increasing need to foster entrepreneurship for development, UNCTAD has developed additional policy guidance targeting specific target groups, in particular women and youth, as well as social entrepreneurs.

### I. Youth entrepreneurship

Youth entrepreneurship has become a priority for the development agenda of many countries that are faced with the challenge of a youth bulge and unemployment. According to the Global Entrepreneurship Monitor (GEM) 2013 report, young people are more likely to have fresh ideas, to be 'born-digital', and in some societies to have received more education than their parents. They are also less likely to have responsibilities like mortgages and families, factors that generally make individuals risk averse. To tap into this potential, in recent years several countries have introduced policies and programmes to foster young entrepreneurs. African countries, for example, have spearheaded the introduction of entrepreneurship curriculum in the secondary school systems.

To respond to a growing focus on youth entrepreneurship, UNCTAD, in collaboration with the Commonwealth Secretariat, has developed a new document entitled 'Policy Guide on Youth Entrepreneurship', aimed to support policymakers design policies that will unleash the potential of youth entrepreneurship.[20] Among its main recommendations are the following:

[20] UNCTAD, 'Policy Guide on Youth Entrepreneurship' (2015) <http://unctad.org/en/PublicationsLibrary/webdiaeed2015d1_en.pdf> accessed 20 January 2017.

- Orienting business development services to provide services to young entrepreneurs is essential in ensuring that they obtain adequate support. Policymakers can enhance the regulatory environment by addressing regulatory barriers that hinder young entrepreneurs from starting up, introducing online registration and simplified regulations, minimizing stigma around business failure, and facilitating re-starts. The public and private sectors as well as other relevant partners can come together to improve education and skills development, and better align the skills acquired by young people with the labour market's demands. Building the capacity of teachers to inculcate entrepreneurship skills among students is critical. In addition, there is need for strengthening the capacity of vocational training and apprenticeship.
- Policymakers can take a leadership role in supporting technology and innovation by providing incentives that will encourage private sector investment. They can also promote the establishment of favourable regulatory frameworks and crafting innovation policies, investing in higher education and training, and research and development. Investments need to be made in technological infrastructure to create the foundation for a thriving digital economy and to provide the impetus for the spread of innovation, as well as to ensure that young people have access to, knowledge of, and the competencies and skills to exploit technology and create commercial products and services.
- Promoting financial inclusion through financial reforms, with the support of entities in the financial sector as well as non-governmental organizations (NGOs), is key. Collateral requirements, high banking fees, and lack of financial literacy are key bottlenecks for young people. Proposed measures include the establishment of guarantees, financing supported by capacity building, and special mobile money schemes. Furthermore, young people need to be partners and collaborators in youth entrepreneurship. To assume this role, a concerted effort on the part of government, NGOs, and the private sector is required to develop platforms to engage young people, as well as to promote the development of youth entrepreneurship networks and associations that advocate on behalf of young entrepreneurs.

## II. Women entrepreneurship

Globally, women lag behind in earnings and productivity when compared with men, in part due to unequal access to economic opportunities for women. Women entrepreneurs, for example, are more likely to operate smaller firms in less profitable sectors, and are therefore less productive and earn less than their male counterparts.[21] In addition, in urban areas in some countries in Eastern Europe and Central

[21] World Bank, *World Development Report 2012: Gender Equality and Development* (World Bank 2012) <https://siteresources.worldbank.org/INTWDR2012/Resources/7778105-1299699968583/7786210-1315936222006/Complete-Report.pdf> accessed 20 January 2017.

Asia, Latin America, and Sub-Saharan Africa, the value added per worker is lower in female-headed businesses when compared with male-headed businesses, as are differences in profitability between female-headed and male-headed businesses in rural Bangladesh, Ethiopia, Indonesia, and Sri Lanka, which is attributed to gender differences in time use, access to credit and assets, and treatment by markets and formal institutions, which constrain women's economic opportunities. To address these issues, UNCTAD's EPF recommends the following:

- Policymakers should reduce the barriers that women entrepreneurs continue to face. Large and significant gender disparities in access to inputs, including land, credit, and asset ownership, are at the root of the gender productivity gap, with lack of access to inputs further compounded by the availability of 'market time', which can make the same investment less productive for women than men, resulting in women entrepreneurs being engaged in activities that are less profitable and less likely to expand. This has detrimental effects on women entrepreneurs as they not only work in an uneven playing field, but also have unequal access to inputs, with significant costs to women's welfare and economic empowerment.
- Legal barriers preventing many women from engaging in business should be addressed as a priority.[22] In some countries, laws permit a husband to formally object to his wife engaging in a business or a profession. Lack of transparency, corruption, and complex regulations in some countries, compounded by institutional discrimination against women, make the business environment particularly difficult for women entrepreneurs to operate in. Also, relatively lower levels of education and skills among women in developing countries are barriers that constrain women's entrepreneurship and the growth potential of women-led SMEs, limiting women's economic empowerment and, ultimately, gender equality. Policies need to reflect the multi-faceted approach to women growing a business.
- Other barriers faced by women entrepreneurs include lack of access to financing. Lack of collateral, which if further exacerbated in countries where women lack access to property rights, is a barrier for women seeking financing from financial institutions. Policies that focus on access to capital need to ensure that sources of financing align to the needs of women entrepreneurs and access to innovative sources of funding for start-ups. Micro-financing institutions that lend to women empower them to become micro-entrepreneurs. Also, engaging women in value chains as distributors or employees can contribute to their economic empowerment. There is growing recognition that with the appropriate incentives and support systems targeted to women entrepreneurs, the levels of female entrepreneurship are likely to grow.[23]

[22] See World Bank, 'Women, Business and the Law' (database) <http://wbl.worldbank.org> accessed 20 January 2017.

[23] UNCTAD, 'Empretec Women in Business Award 2012' (2011) <http://unctad.org/en/docs/webdiaeed2011d10_en.pdf> accessed 20 January 2017.

## III. Social entrepreneurship

For emerging areas such as social entrepreneurship, legal frameworks that recognize social enterprises can play an important role.[24] In North America and in most European countries, laws recognizing social enterprises have helped to institutionalize these entities and catalyse the social economy sector's growth. Out of twenty-eight states in the European Union, twenty have a national definition of social enterprises. Finland, Lithuania, Poland, Slovakia, and Sweden clearly articulate social enterprises in their national laws and/or in policy documents. In the United Kingdom, the Community Investment Tax Relief which is available to social enterprises has encouraged these entities to invest in poor communities. Similarly, Thailand's newly drafted law on social enterprises—the Social Enterprise Promotion Act—has a provision on a favourable taxation structure for these entities. Belgium has implemented measures for a social economy, including a reduced value added tax (VAT) rate for some social economy initiatives and a reduced tax exemption for integration enterprises.[25] Based on the above, UNCTAD recommends the following:

- *Recognizing social enterprises as legal entities offers new opportunities for sustainable development.* This can allow these entities to register and start their businesses and to access funding and other business support that is essential for their operations. Conversely, where social entrepreneurship is in its infancy, lack of laws recognizing social enterprises as legal entities has not only constrained the development of the sector by making it difficult for social enterprises to register and obtain licences to operate as businesses, but has also restricted their access to funding, as well as public business support that could be available to these entities.
- *Reviewing incentives and tax regimes to support the development of social entrepreneurship.* Recognizing their importance in sustainable development, governments can review incentives aimed at encouraging the development and uptake of social enterprises. Tax incentives may be used to stimulate investment in underserved areas, thereby creating the conditions that will spur economic and social development. It is important to note that favourable taxation structures that take into account social enterprises' dual mission and provide appropriate fiscal relief that does not penalize these entities for pursuing social goals can enhance the development and ensure the long-term sustainability of social enterprises.
- *Removing regulatory barriers will facilitate the transition from inefficient and ineffective sectors to those that are more efficient and effective.* Despite the growing recognition that green processes, products, and services can contribute to efficiency while enhancing sustainability, many countries lack frameworks that can

[24] This section summarizes the recommendations included in a forthcoming UNCTAD publication on Entrepreneurship for Development.

[25] OECD and European Union, *Policy Brief on Social Entrepreneurship: Entrepreneurial Activities in Europe* (OECD and European Union 2013) <http://ec.europa.eu/social/main.jsp?catId=738&langId=en&pubId=7552> accessed 20 January 2017.

encourage the use of efficient products and services such as clean technology and renewable energies which can help to spur the development of the green sector. The adoption of regulatory frameworks that support the transition to efficient green processes and practices, as well as products and services that contribute to environmental sustainability can also catalyse the green sector's development.

## G. Conclusions

Entrepreneurship can contribute to sustainable development and the achievement of social development goals adopted by the UN General Assembly, and it has the potential to address development challenges, in particular poverty reduction and economic inclusion, as well as social and environmental concerns. For entrepreneurship to effectively contribute to the achievement of sustainable development, policymakers can create an enabling entrepreneurial environment by developing entrepreneurship policies that integrate and align SDGs into an overarching national entrepreneurship strategy.

Adopting holistic policies according to the areas identified by the UNCTAD's EPF, policymakers can create an enabling entrepreneurial environment which also takes into account inclusive and sustainable business models. UNCTAD has advocated the convening of a 'Global Forum on Entrepreneurship for SDGs' to provide guidelines on how to incorporate entrepreneurship in the sustainable development process and propose measures for implementation. To leverage existing national and regional policy networks in order to scale up and transfer their experiences and encourage the adoption of common impact indicators, this global forum could be supported by regional preparatory consultations. Global and regional partners could participate in organizing preparatory meetings and the forum itself.

UNCTAD also promotes the development of national, regional, and global networks of entrepreneurship and enterprise educators. Engaging trainers, local communities, and social organizations to join networks at sub-national, national, and global levels is crucial in order to establish sharing of experiences and knowledge among entrepreneurial schools, colleges, universities, and communities. The inclusion of disadvantaged social groups such as minorities, migrants, and disabled people requires dedicated attention. Encouraging their integration into entrepreneurial networks and bringing together community-based and social organizations to support these efforts may offer significant value in leveraging an untapped human resource into productive sectors.

## References

Global Enterprise Registration (GER) <http://ger.co> accessed 20 January 2017

Kelley, DJ, Bosma, N, and Amorós, JE, 'Global Entrepreneurship Monitor: 2010 Global Report' (2010) <http://www.av-asesores.com/upload/479.PDF> accessed 20 January 2017

OECD, 'Interim Report of the Green Growth Strategy: Implementing Our Commitment for a Sustainable Future' (2010) <https://www.oecd.org/greengrowth/45312720.pdf> accessed 20 January 2017

OECD and European Union, *Policy Brief on Social Entrepreneurship: Entrepreneurial Activities in Europe* (OECD and European Union 2013) <http://ec.europa.eu/social/main.jsp?catId=738&langId=en&pubId=7552> accessed 20 January 2017

UNCTAD, 'Integrating Developing Countries' SMEs into Global Value Chains' (United Nations 2010) <http://unctad.org/en/docs/diaeed20095_en.pdf> accessed 20 January 2017

UNCTAD, 'Empretec Women in Business Award 2012' (2011) <http://unctad.org/en/docs/webdiaeed2011d10_en.pdf> accessed 20 January 2017

UNCTAD, 'Entrepreneurship Policy Framework and Implementation Guidance' (2012) <http://unctad.org/en/PublicationsLibrary/diaeed2012d1_en.pdf> accessed 20 January 2017

UNCTAD, 'Multi-Year Expert Meeting on Investment, Innovation and Entrepreneurship for Productive Capacity-Building and Sustainable Development, Third Session' (Conference, 30–31 March 2015) <http://unctad.org/en/pages/MeetingDetails.aspx?meetingid=645> accessed 20 January 2017

UNCTAD, 'Policy Guide on Youth Entrepreneurship' (2015) <http://unctad.org/en/PublicationsLibrary/webdiaeed2015d1_en.pdf> accessed 20 January 2017

UNCTAD, 'Business Facilitation Program' (2016) <http://www.businessfacilitation.org> accessed 20 January 2017

United Nations, 'Transforming Our World: The 2030 Agenda for Sustainable Development' (United Nations 2015) <https://sustainabledevelopment.un.org/post2015/transformingourworld/publication> accessed 20 January 2017

World Bank, *World Development Report 2012: Gender Equality and Development* (World Bank 2012) <https://siteresources.worldbank.org/INTWDR2012/Resources/7778105-1299699968583/7786210-1315936222006/Complete-Report.pdf> accessed 20 January 2017

World Bank, 'Governance: The World Bank's Experience' (World Bank 1994) <http://www-wds.worldbank.org/external/default/WDSContentServer/WDSP/IB/1994/05/01/000009265_3970716142854/Rendered/PDF/multi0page.pdf> accessed 20 January 2017

World Bank, 'Women, Business and the Law' (database) <http://wbl.worldbank.org> accessed 20 January 2017

# Annex

## How Small Are Small and Medium-Sized Enterprises?

*Rudolf Adlung and Marta Soprana*

The definitions of SMEs that are used at national and international level may vary widely, building on criteria such as number of employees, annual turnover, and, occasionally, sales, asset values, market shares, or investment. According to a delimitation frequently, though not exclusively, applied within the World Bank Group, small enterprises have more than ten and fewer than 300 employees and assets and annual sales of between US$100,000 and US$15 million.[1] Of course, it is obvious that the use of such a uniform benchmark across countries of varying size, levels of economic development, etc, while facilitating international comparisons, might be of limited relevance for national policy analysis and decision-making. It is not surprising, therefore, to find a broad range of definitions and concepts at country level.[2]

An EU recommendation defines micro enterprises as having fewer than ten employees and total annual turnover or balance sheet below €2 million, followed by small enterprises with up to forty-nine employees and annual turnover or balance sheet below €10 million, and medium enterprises with fewer than 250 employees and annual turnover or balance sheet of up to €50 million or €43 million, respectively (table).[3]

[1] Independent Evaluation Group, 'The Big Business of Small Enterprises: Evaluation of the World Bank Group Experience with Targeted Support to Small and Medium-Size Enterprises, 2006–12' (March 2014) <http://ieg.worldbank.org/Data/reports/sme_eval1_0.pdf> accessed 20 January 2017. As noted in the study, apparently for the sake of consistency, this definition is used by the International Finance Corporation (IFC) and Multilateral Investment Guarantee Agency (MIGA) without variation across all countries and sectors.

[2] See the discussion in Tom Gibson and Hubertus Jan van der Vaart, 'Defining SMEs: A Less Imperfect Way of Defining Small and Medium Enterprises in Developing Countries' (September 2008) <https://www.brookings.edu/wp-content/uploads/2016/06/09_development_gibson.pdf> accessed 20 January 2017. As a common reference point, the two authors suggest defining an SME as 'a formal enterprise with annual turnover, in U.S. dollar terms, of between 10 and 1000 times the mean per capita gross national income, at purchasing power parity, of the country in which it operates'. Ibid 18. Certainly not an easily workable solution …

[3] European Commission, Commission Recommendation of 6 May 2003 concerning the definition of micro, small and medium-sized enterprises [2003] OJ L124/36.

**Table** Definition of micro, small, and medium-sized enterprises according to the European Commission

| Category of enterprise | Number of employees[i] | Annual turnover (€) | Annual balance sheet total (€) |
|---|---|---|---|
| Micro | < 10 | ≤ 2 million | ≤ 2 million |
| Small | < 50 | ≤ 10 million | ≤ 10 million |
| Medium-sized | < 250 | ≤ 50 million | ≤ 43 million |

Notes:
[i] European Commission, 'What is an SME?' (2016) <http://ec.europa.eu/growth/smes/business-friendly-environment/sme-definition/index_en.htm> accessed 20 January 2017. The data have been calculated on the basis of the number of AWUs (Annual Work Units), namely, the number of persons who worked full time within the enterprise or on its behalf during the entire reference year under consideration: GBER, Annex I, Article 5.

In contrast, in a comparatively small country such as Barbados, small firms are defined, in the respective Business Development Act, to meet any two of the following criteria: fewer than twenty-five employees, no more than BB$1 million (approximately US$500,000 in January 2016) as stated or paid-up capital, and/or BB$2 million in annual sales.[4] In New Zealand, enterprises with fewer than five employees are classified as micro businesses, followed by small businesses with fewer than twenty employees, and SMEs or small to medium-sized enterprises with fewer than fifty employees.[5] The Australian Bureau of Statistics reportedly uses the same size limits, five and twenty employees, respectively, to define micro and small businesses.[6]

Sectoral specificities may be taken into account as well. For example, in India, under a law of 2006, manufacturing firms are classified as micro, small, or medium if their investment in equipment does not exceed Rs 25 lakh (approximately US$36,900 in January 2016), Rs 5 crore (US$737,000) and Rs 10 crore (US$1,475,000), respectively. The limits for services firms are Rs 10 lakh, Rs 2 crore, and Rs 5 crore.[7] In Japan, enterprises in the manufacturing sector qualify as SMEs if they employ fewer than 300 persons and their capital is inferior to 300 million

[4] Government of Barbados, Small Business Development Act, CAP 318C(3)(1)(b) <http://www.investbarbados.org/docs/Small%20Business%20Development%20Act%20-%20Cap.%20318C.pdf> accessed 20 January 2017.

[5] New Zealand Ministry of Business, Innovation & Employment, 'The Small Business Sector Report 2014' <http://www.mbie.govt.nz/info-services/business/business-growth-agenda/pdf-and-image-library/2014/The%20Small%20Business%20Sector%20Report%202014%20-PDF%208.8%20MB-1.pdf> accessed 20 January 2017.

[6] Department of Industry, Innovation, Science, Research and Tertiary Education, *Australian Small Businesses—Key Statistics and Analysis* (Department of Industry, Innovation, Science, Research and Tertiary Education, Canberra 2012).

[7] According to press reports, the relevant legislation was up for review in 2014/15. See Mahim Pratap Singh, 'Centre Open to Revising MSME Investment Limits' *The Hindu* (New Delhi, 30 October 2014) <http://www.thehindu.com/business/Industry/centre-open-to-revising-msme-investment-limits/article6545358.ece> accessed 20 January 2017.

yen. In contrast, SMEs operating in retail trade have fewer than fifty employees (wholesale trade and other services: 100 employees) and their capital remains below 50 million yen (wholesale trade: 100 million yen; other services: 50 million yen).[8] In China, a construction firm with up to 600 employees, 30 million renminbi in total sales, and 40 million renminbi in total assets is considered to be small, while its medium-sized equivalent has up to 3,000 employees and total sales and total assets of up to 300 and 400 million renminbi, respectively. In wholesale trade, small firms have fewer than 100 employees and total sales inferior to 30 million renminbi, and medium-sized firms have up to 200 employees and no more than 300 million renminbi in total sales.[9]

Similarly, various size brackets are used by the US Small Business Administration (SBA). In manufacturing and mining industries, the upper size limit for SMEs is set at between 500 and 1,500 employees, depending on the sector; in wholesale trade, it varies between 100 and 250 employees. In most of telecommunications and air transport, SMEs may count up to 1,500 employees. In a variety of other industries, the definition focuses on average annual receipts. This includes most retail sectors (convenience stores: US$29.5 million), broadcasting (radio stations: US$38.5 million), truck transportation (US$27.5 million), legal services (US$11 million), and accounting services (US$20.5 million).[10] In turn, USITC classifies enterprises as micro, small, or medium if they employ, respectively, up to nineteen, ninety-nine, and 499 staff.[11]

In Germany, small and medium-sized enterprises are commonly defined in line with the European Union's approach.[12] However, the government also refers to a definition used by a specialized research institute, IfM Bonn.[13] Accordingly, micro firms have fewer than ten employees and an annual turnover of up to €2 million, followed by small enterprises with up to forty-nine employees and turnover of €10 million, and medium enterprises with up to 499 employees and turnover of €50 million.

Although various GATS schedules contain explicit references to small businesses and similar concepts, the underlying definitions are not normally spelled out. However, two of the reviewed RTAs do contain relevant information for at least some signatories. Dominica's schedule under the EC-CARIFORUM EPA

[8] Economist Intelligence Unit, 'SMEs in Japan: A New Growth Driver?' (EIU 2010) 7.

[9] Asia-Pacific Economic Cooperation, *SME Market Access and Internationalization: Medium-Term KPIs for the SMEWG Strategic Plan* (APEC Policy Support Unit 2010) 35 f.

[10] These standards have been effective since 26 February 2016. See US Small Business Administration, 'Table of Small Business Size Standards Matched to North American Industry Classification System Codes' <https://www.sba.gov/sites/default/files/files/Size_Standards_Table.pdf> accessed 20 January 2017.

[11] US International Trade Commission (USITC), 'Trade Barriers that U.S. Small and Medium-Sized Enterprises Perceive as Affecting Exports to the European Union' (Investigation No 332-541, USITC Publication 4455, March 2014) <http://www.usitc.gov/publications/332/pub4455.pdf> accessed 20 January 2017.

[12] See n 3.

[13] IfM, the Institute for Small Business Research, is funded out of the federal budget and the budget of the State of North Rhine-Westphalia. See <http://www.ifm-bonn.org> accessed 20 January 2017.

uses one or more of the following criteria to define small business investments: an initial investment of below ECD 2.7 million[14] (US$1 million); up to fifty initial employees; and projected annual sales of less than ECD 2.7 million (US$1 million) in the first year. The above criteria are to be reviewed from time to time. In turn, the schedules of Honduras and El Salvador under the Central America–Dominican Republic–US Free Trade Agreement provide that a 'small-scale enterprise' is an enterprise with a capitalization not greater than US$200,000 (El Salvador) and that 'small-scale industry and trade' means an enterprise with capital of less than 150,000 Lempiras, excluding land, buildings, and vehicles (Honduras).

## References

Asia-Pacific Economic Cooperation, *SME Market Access and Internationalization: Medium-Term KPIs for the SMEWG Strategic Plan* (APEC Policy Support Unit 2010)

Department of Industry, Innovation, Science, Research and Tertiary Education, *Australian Small Businesses—Key Statistics and Analysis* (Department of Industry, Innovation, Science, Research and Tertiary Education, Canberra 2012)

Economist Intelligence Unit, 'SMEs in Japan: A New Growth Driver?' (EIU 2010) 7

Gibson, T and van der Vaart, HJ, 'Defining SMEs: A Less Imperfect Way of Defining Small and Medium Enterprises in Developing Countries' (September 2008) <https://www.brookings.edu/wp-content/uploads/2016/06/09_development_gibson.pdf> accessed 20 January 2017

Independent Evaluation Group, 'The Big Business of Small Enterprises: Evaluation of the World Bank Group Experience with Targeted Support to Small and Medium-Size Enterprises, 2006–12' (March 2014) <http://ieg.worldbank.org/Data/reports/sme_eval1_0.pdf> accessed 20 January 2017

New Zealand Ministry of Business, Innovation & Employment, 'The Small Business Sector Report 2014' <http://www.mbie.govt.nz/info-services/business/business-growth-agenda/pdf-and-image-library/2014/The%20Small%20Business%20Sector%20Report%202014%20-PDF%208.8%20MB-1.pdf> accessed 20 January 2017

Singh, MP, 'Centre Open to Revising MSME Investment Limits' *The Hindu* (New Delhi, 30 October 2014) <http://www.thehindu.com/business/Industry/centre-open-to-revising-msme-investment-limits/article6545358.ece> accessed 20 January 2017

USITC, 'Trade Barriers that U.S. Small and Medium-Sized Enterprises Perceive as Affecting Exports to the European Union' (Investigation No 332-541, USITC Publication 4455, March 2014) <http://www.usitc.gov/publications/332/pub4455.pdf> accessed 20 January 2017

US Small Business Administration, 'Table of Small Business Size Standards Matched to North American Industry Classification System Codes' <http://www.sba.gov/sites/default/files/files/Size_Standards_Table.pdf> accessed 20 January 2017

[14] ECD means Eastern Caribbean Dollars.

# Index